C000319858

PLA
FOO
ANNUAL 2012-2013

EDITED BY
GLENDA ROLLIN AND JACK ROLLIN

headline

Cataloguing in Publication Data is available from the British Library

ISBN 978 0 7553 6358 2

Typeset by Wearset Ltd, Boldon, Tyne and Wear

Printed and bound in the UK by Clays Ltd, St Ives plc

Headline's policy is to use papers that are natural, renewable and recyclable products and made from wood grown in sustainable forests. The logging and manufacturing processes are expected to conform to the environmental regulations of the country of origin.

HEADLINE PUBLISHING GROUP
An Hachette UK Company
338 Euston Road
London NW1 3BH

www.headline.co.uk
www.hachette.co.uk

CONTENTS

Other Football

Information and Records

EDITORIAL

Euro 2012 produced a defining, cultured performance from Spain. Despite criticism of a formation that scorned the use of any striking force, the preferred option was to keep control for as long as possible before squeezing out the most clear-cut of chances in front of goal. They still won the title in some style to be admired. Yet many claimed the football they played in the early stages to be just boring. The rest of the world needs be as tiresome.

With back-to-back Euro trophies and a World Cup sandwiched in between, Spain now had the rest of the leading nations scratching their heads to find an answer to their dominance. As to the Euro 2012 competition as a whole, the overall standard of performance was surprisingly better than expected and with less than a handful of players being sent off.

England were given little chance by the critics before the tournament began, but as is often the case, once the first match loomed it changed. When this was followed by what proved to be the best display of the four matches involved, drawing with the much fancied French team on the back of its run of 21 unbeaten games, expectations grew.

Though England had beaten Sweden earlier in the season in a friendly, the statistic that the Scandinavians had never lost a competitive match between the two, suggested there was more of a balance when forecasting the outcome. Ahead, then going behind, England had to come back before edging the match by the odd goal in five. Thence to face Ukraine and a point was required to reach the last eight. Wayne Rooney, back after suspension, scored with a close header to ensure progress.

Italy, unconvincing during the early stages, held the territorial advantage for most of the quarter-final but were prevented from inflicting damage by England's defence, the most impressive department of the formation. The midfield lacked cohesion and the attack rarely appeared threatening. However, as long as the score remained as a stalemate, there was always the chance from the inevitable shoot-out, though this had been England's Achilles heel in the past. And so it proved again.

Amazingly in the aftermath of the finals, FIFA announced the top four countries in the world and England found themselves fourth! Spain, unsurprisingly were top, Germany second and Uruguay, who had won the Copa America, third. Even then second place for the Germans was questionable in view of the disappointing display against Italy in the quarter-final after a strong showing in the group matches.

Of course, these lists from FIFA are meaningless but are snapped up by the media and given too much prominence. The best method of dealing with such a trivial pursuit is to ignore it, but it will not happen. Again FIFA are promising goal-line technology. For once England even benefited from failing human eyes behind the goal against the Ukraine as surely the use of goal judges has proved inadequate.

The spectre of racism remains a problem, off the field and on it, too. Alas, the punishment does in no way fit the crime. There were incidents in Euro 2012 and at home the beautiful game has shown its ugly side in this manner.

Awaiting England now is the World Cup 2014 in Brazil and the qualifying schedule at least on paper is not too daunting to expect England to fail in their attempt to reach it. Roy Hodgson, now settled in as the squad's manager, emerged from the Euro 2012 commitment with some credit given the short time he had had taking over from Fabio Capello. The experience of a high profile competition will have increased his confidence.

Under these two managers, England fielded thirty-five different players during 2011–12, only eight of whom had not been capped at full international level before. The Under-21s blooded eighteen among the thirty-one called upon. It will be interesting to see comparative figures in a year's time.

Yet returning to Spain, whereas one might imagine its current dominance to be but a passing phase, there are other indications that perhaps the system which has produced players of such a high standard is one that should be closely examined by others. Moreover it is a further sobering thought that the Spanish Under-19s have won two European titles at this level within a year.

Failure for England in winning major tournaments usually brings the critics to blame too many foreign players in the Premier League, taking places that should be occupied by native born talent. Another favourite is the introduction of a winter break, forgetting that vagaries of the British climate make it almost impossible to predict the best time for such an interruption. Rest for the better players can only be achieved by fewer matches, not a rearrangement of the calendar. There are no simple answers.

It could be said that we possess more top-class domestic players than any other country, but fewer at international level where it is needed to achieve major tournament successes. We have had our successes in European club competitions, yet often with teams possessing more than a sprinkling of overseas players. Therein is the dilemma.

But trying to find a team from these shores in the past to have won a European club trophy without one or two players ineligible to play for England is almost impossible. Of course this has meant those from Scotland, Wales and Northern Ireland as well as further afield.

CLUB AND OTHER RECORDS 2011–2012

Aldershot Town – Club record 6 consecutive wins January to March.

Bolton Wanderers – Most capped player, Ricardo Gardner, 63 (109), Jamaica.

Bournemouth – Most League appearances, Steve Fletcher, 617.

Burton Albion – Most capped player, Jacques Maghoma, with 3 caps for DR Congo.
Most League appearances, John McGrath, 117.

Charlton Athletic – Record League points, 101.

Chelsea – Most capped player, Frank Lampard, 88 (90), England.
First London club to win the Champions League.

Cheltenham Town – Equal most League goals, 66, FL 2.

Dagenham & Redbridge – Most capped player, Jon Nurse, with 6 caps for Barbados.
Most League appearances, Jon Nurse, 179.

Derby County – Youngest League player, Mason Bennett, 15 years 99 days.

Huddersfield Town – Set new Football League record 43 unbeaten matches January to November.
Jordan Rhodes equals record number of League goals in a season at 35.

Liverpool – Most capped player, Steven Gerrard, 96, England.

Manchester City – Record transfer fee paid, £38,000,000 to Atletico Madrid for Sergio Aguero.

Manchester United – Ryan Giggs takes his number of League appearances to 638, and is a goalscorer for the 20th Premier League season. He also reaches 900 first class matches for the club.

Milton Keynes Dons – Most League goals, 84, FL 1.
Most League appearances, Dean Lewington, 347.
Youngest League player, Brendon Galloway, 16 years 42 days.

Morecambe – Record League victory, 6-0 v Crawley T, FL 2, 10 September 2011.
Most League goals, Stuart Drummond 32, and most League appearances, 184.

Sheffield Wednesday – Most League points, 93, FL 1.

Shrewsbury Town – Most League points, 88, FL 2.

Southampton – Club record sequence of League wins, 10, April to August.

Stevenage – Reached fifth round of the FA Cup.
Most League points, 73, FL 1.
Most League goals, 69, FL 1.

Stoke City – Record transfer fee paid, £10,000,000 to Tottenham H for Peter Crouch.

Swindon Town – Club record sequence of League wins, 10, December to February.

Wycombe Wanderers – Youngest League player, Jordon Ibe, 15 years 311 days.

FA Cup – George Williams (MK Dons) becomes youngest goalscorer at 16 years 2 months and 5 days; Brendon Galloway (MK Dons) the youngest player in the FA Cup proper at 15 years 7 months and 26 days.

England – Register 2,000th goal in a full international, 15 November v Sweden.

Scotland – Airdrie United club record 11 goals v Gala Fairydean, William Hill Scottish Cup.
Stranraer equal club record score beating Wigtown & Bladnoch 9-0 in William Hill Scottish Cup.

Play-Off – Record number of penalties, Huddersfield Town beating Sheffield United 8-7 (22 kicks taken).

Premier League – Record number of goals scored, 1,066.

LEAGUE REVIEW AND CLUB SECTION

In arguably the most dramatic finish to a championship ever recorded, the last seconds of the 2011–12 Premier League season saw Manchester City win in overtime but the difference between their figures and runners-up Manchester United was on goals scored as otherwise they had identical records.

Certainly it was more than likely during the campaign that the title was likely to stay in Manchester. The question was on which side the destination. City started fourteen unbeaten. United went eight before the incredible 6-1 defeat at Old Trafford to their neighbours. Sir Alex Ferguson's teams invariably respond positively to adversity and went another nine games undefeated.

Home and away defeats respectively against Blackburn Rovers and Newcastle United at the turn of the year was United's most worrying snap, while Roberto Mancini's team found March even more of a concern having dropped their first two points at home as the gap went from five points to eight with United ahead. Yet City recovered and won its last six including the return with United who lost twice in the same period.

As their exploits in Europe, neither City nor United did as well as anticipated. Both had to be shovelled from the Champions League into the Europa League after failing to make the cut and again disappointed there. Manchester United lost home and away to Athletic Bilbao, while City lost out on the away goals rule to Sporting Lisbon.

Manchester City used 24 different players in their Premier League commitments, three of them with just one substitute appearance each. Only goalkeeper Joe Hart was ever present. David Silva made the most of the outfield players missing two games and coming on three times from the bench. Gareth Barry and Sergio Aguero also made three substitute appearances each in missing just four times. Aguero the title winner on the last day was top scorer with 23 four behind Wayne Rooney at United, though the leading marksman was Robin Van Persie at Arsenal with 30 goals.

The 20th Premier League season also produced a record 1,066 goals. The average per game at 2.81 was the best in the top flight for 35 years. Manchester United's 89 points was the highest by a runner-up in the Premier.

Sixth placed Chelsea after a change at the helm with Roberto Di Matteo replacing Andre Villas-Boas won the cup double taking the FA Cup and adding the Champions League trophy. Liverpool beat Cardiff City in the Carling Cup, a consolation after a disappointing season at Anfield.

One of the reverses at the start for third-placed Arsenal was against Tottenham Hotspur. But one win in nine to mid-April did nothing to increase confidence, though the Gunners had their moments in Europe. Their highlight was a battling performance against the odds with AC Milan which only just failed. Even so only a point separated them from Spurs, who failed less well in the Europa League. Newcastle United might have improved on fifth place after an excellent undefeated beginning of eleven matches.

Seventh was the highest for Everton all season and came after the last nine unbeaten matches and enabled them to finish above Liverpool. Fulham struggled for its first win. It came in the seventh match. West Bromwich Albion held Manchester City to a goalless draw at The Hawthorns on Boxing Day to take ninth place; it proved their highest all season.

Swansea City would have been generally satisfied. Fourteen clean sheets and several times squeezing into the top ten. Norwich City, too, was eighth in October and again in February Sunderland had a new manager during the term with Martin O'Neill taking command. But they slipped away towards the end.

Stoke City gave a good account of itself in Europe but then not a victory in the last six of the season. Yet escape artists personified were Wigan Athletic. They won seven of their last nine and accounted for Manchester United and Arsenal in successive matches!

Aston Villa with 17 draws, a record from 38 Premier games, scored only 37 goals, one more than Stoke. Queens Park Rangers managed the feat of alternate wins and defeats in the last eleven matches, but survived. Not so Bolton Wanderers, Blackburn Rovers and Wolverhampton Wanderers, the first time three Football League founders had foundered together.

Heading back in the Premier League after four years, Reading timed its gallop to perfection beating both of its chief rivals Southampton and West Ham United in a run of six successive wins to mid-April. Southampton joined them having lost its way at one stage. The Hammers made it through the play-offs after looking automatic candidates at one time, overcoming Birmingham City who had reached the group stage of the Europa League.

Portsmouth with ten points deducted, Coventry City and Doncaster Rovers were relegated, their places in the Championship taken by Charlton Athletic, Sheffield Wednesday and Huddersfield Town via a marathon penalty play-off final with Sheffield United.

Swindon Town, Shrewsbury Town and Crawley Town were automatic promotion successes from League Two, while seventh finishing Crewe Alexandra made it from the play-offs. Wycombe Wanderers, Chesterfield, Exeter City and Rochdale went down to make way. Into the Blue Square Premier went Hereford United and Macclesfield Town to be replaced by newcomers Fleetwood Town and the former Football League club York City.

BARCLAYS PREMIER LEAGUE 2011–2012

(P) *Promoted into division at end of 2010–11 season.*
(R) *Relegated into division at end of 2010–11 season.*

		Total					Home					Away					
	P	W	D	L	F	A	W	D	L	F	A	W	D	L	F	A	GD	Pts
1 Manchester C	38	28	5	5	93	29	18	1	0	55	12	10	4	5	38	17	64	89
2 Manchester U	38	28	5	5	89	33	15	2	2	52	19	13	3	3	37	14	56	89
3 Arsenal	38	21	7	10	74	49	12	4	3	39	17	9	3	7	35	32	25	70
4 Tottenham H	38	20	9	9	66	41	13	3	3	39	17	7	6	6	27	24	25	69
5 Newcastle U	38	19	8	11	56	51	11	5	3	29	17	8	3	8	27	34	5	65
6 Chelsea	38	18	10	10	65	46	12	3	4	41	24	6	7	6	24	22	19	64
7 Everton	38	15	11	12	50	40	10	3	6	28	15	5	8	6	22	25	10	56
8 Liverpool	38	14	10	14	47	40	6	9	4	24	16	8	1	10	23	24	7	52
9 Fulham	38	14	10	14	48	51	10	5	4	36	26	4	5	10	12	25	–3	52
10 WBA	38	13	8	17	45	52	6	3	10	21	22	7	5	7	24	30	–7	47
11 Swansea C (P)	38	12	11	15	44	51	8	7	4	27	18	4	4	11	17	33	–7	47
12 Norwich C (P)	38	12	11	15	52	66	7	6	6	28	30	5	5	9	24	36	–14	47
13 Sunderland	38	11	12	15	45	46	7	7	5	26	17	4	5	10	19	29	–1	45
14 Stoke C	38	11	12	15	36	53	7	8	4	25	20	4	4	11	11	33	–17	45
15 Wigan Ath	38	11	10	17	42	62	5	7	7	22	27	6	3	10	20	35	–20	43
16 Aston Villa	38	7	17	14	37	53	4	7	8	20	25	3	10	6	17	28	–16	38
17 QPR (P)	38	10	7	21	43	66	7	5	7	24	25	3	2	14	19	41	–23	37
18 Bolton W	38	10	6	22	46	77	4	4	11	23	39	6	2	11	23	38	–31	36
19 Blackburn R	38	8	7	23	48	78	6	1	12	26	33	2	6	11	22	45	–30	31
20 Wolverhampton W	38	5	10	23	40	82	3	3	13	19	43	2	7	10	21	39	–42	25

LEADING GOALSCORERS 2011–2012

BARCLAYS PREMIER LEAGUE

	League	Carling Cup	FA Cup	Other	Total
Only goals scored in the same division are included.					
Robin Van Persie (*Arsenal*)	30	0	2	5	37
Wayne Rooney (*Manchester U*)	27	0	2	5	34
Sergio Aguero (*Manchester C*)	23	1	1	5	30
Clint Dempsey (*Fulham*)	17	0	3	3	23
Emmanuel Adebayor (*Tottenham H*)	17	0	1	0	18
(*On loan from Manchester C*).					
Aiyegbeni Yakubu (*Blackburn R*)	17	1	0	0	18
Demba Ba (*Newcastle U*)	16	0	0	0	16
Grant Holt (*Norwich C*)	15	0	2	0	17
Edin Dzeko (*Manchester C*)	14	3	0	2	19
Mario Balotelli (*Manchester C*)	13	1	0	3	17
Papiss Cisse (*Newcastle U*)	13	0	0	0	13
Danny Graham (*Swansea C*)	12	0	2	0	14
Steven Fletcher (*Wolverhampton W*)	12	0	0	0	12
Highest overall total of players with 11 League games:					
Jermain Defoe (*Tottenham H*)	11	0	3	3	17

Other matches consist of European games, J Paint Trophy, Community Shield and Football League play-offs. Players listed in order of League goals total.

NPOWER CHAMPIONSHIP 2011–2012

			Total					Home					Away						
		P	W	D	L	F	A	W	D	L	F	A	W	D	L	F	A	GD	Pts
1	Reading	46	27	8	11	69	41	14	5	4	36	18	13	3	7	33	23	28	89
2	Southampton (P)	46	26	10	10	85	46	16	4	3	49	18	10	6	7	36	28	39	88
3	West Ham U¶ (R)	46	24	14	8	81	48	11	8	4	41	26	13	6	4	40	22	33	86
4	Birmingham C (R)	46	20	16	10	78	51	13	9	1	37	14	7	7	9	41	37	27	76
5	Blackpool (R)	46	20	15	11	79	59	13	7	3	42	21	7	8	8	37	38	20	75
6	Cardiff C	46	19	18	9	66	53	11	7	5	37	29	8	11	4	29	24	13	75
7	Middlesbrough	46	18	16	12	52	51	8	10	5	22	21	10	6	7	30	30	1	70
8	Hull C	46	19	11	16	47	44	12	4	7	28	22	7	7	9	19	22	3	68
9	Leicester C	46	18	12	16	66	55	11	6	6	36	22	7	6	10	30	33	11	66
10	Brighton & HA (P)	46	17	15	14	52	52	11	8	4	36	21	6	7	10	16	31	0	66
11	Watford	46	16	16	14	56	64	10	6	7	32	33	6	10	7	24	31	−8	64
12	Derby Co	46	18	10	18	50	58	11	4	8	28	23	7	6	10	22	35	−8	64
13	Burnley	46	17	11	18	61	58	7	9	7	33	27	10	2	11	28	31	3	62
14	Leeds U	46	17	10	19	65	68	9	3	11	34	41	8	7	8	31	27	−3	61
15	Ipswich T	46	17	10	19	69	77	11	3	9	39	32	6	7	10	30	45	−8	61
16	Millwall	46	15	12	19	55	57	7	7	9	27	30	8	5	10	28	27	−2	57
17	Crystal Palace	46	13	17	16	46	51	7	11	5	22	19	6	6	11	24	32	−5	56
18	Peterborough U (P)	46	13	11	22	67	77	10	3	10	41	38	3	8	12	26	39	−10	50
19	Nottingham F	46	14	8	24	48	63	6	5	12	21	32	8	3	12	27	31	−15	50
20	Bristol C	46	12	13	21	44	68	7	6	10	26	32	5	7	11	18	36	−24	49
21	Barnsley	46	13	9	24	49	74	9	4	10	31	37	4	5	14	18	37	−25	48
22	Portsmouth*	46	13	11	22	50	59	10	5	8	30	24	3	6	14	20	35	−9	40
23	Coventry C	46	9	13	24	41	65	8	7	8	28	26	1	6	16	13	39	−24	40
24	Doncaster R	46	8	12	26	43	80	4	8	11	22	35	4	4	15	21	45	−37	36

*Portsmouth deducted 10 points. ¶West Ham U promoted via play-offs.

NPOWER CHAMPIONSHIP

	League	Carling Cup	FA Cup	Other	Total
Rickie Lambert *(Southampton)*	27	2	2	0	31
Ricardo Vaz Te *(West Ham U)*	20	0	2	0	22
(Includes 10 League and 2 FA Cup goals for Barnsley).					
Ross McCormack *(Leeds U)*	18	1	0	0	19
Marlon King *(Birmingham C)*	16	0	0	2	18
Charlie Austin *(Burnley)*	16	1	0	0	17
Kevin Phillips *(Blackpool)*	16	0	1	0	17
Matt Fryatt *(Hull C)*	16	0	0	0	16
Jay Rodriguez *(Burnley)*	15	5	1	0	21
Darius Henderson *(Millwall)*	15	0	4	0	19
David Nugent *(Leicester C)*	15	0	1	0	16
Marvin Emnes *(Middlesbrough)*	14	3	1	0	18
Carlton Cole *(West Ham U)*	14	1	0	0	15
Michael Chopra *(Ipswich T)*	14	0	0	0	14
Robert Snodgrass *(Leeds U)*	13	0	0	0	13

NPOWER LEAGUE 1 2011–2012

			Total				Home					Away						
	P	W	D	L	F	A	W	D	L	F	A	W	D	L	F	A	GD	Pts
1 Charlton Ath	46	30	11	5	82	36	15	6	2	46	20	15	5	3	36	16	46	101
2 Sheffield W	46	28	9	9	81	48	17	4	2	48	19	11	5	7	33	29	33	93
3 Sheffield U (R)	46	27	9	10	92	51	16	4	3	54	27	11	5	7	38	24	41	90
4 Huddersfield T¶	46	21	18	7	79	47	14	6	3	35	19	7	12	4	44	28	32	81
5 Milton Keynes D	46	22	14	10	84	47	12	6	5	45	22	10	8	5	39	25	37	80
6 Stevenage	46	18	19	9	69	44	10	10	3	36	23	8	9	6	33	21	25	73
7 Notts Co	46	21	10	15	75	63	13	5	5	42	29	8	5	10	33	34	12	73
8 Carlisle U	46	18	15	13	65	66	12	7	4	41	30	6	8	9	24	36	−1	69
9 Brentford	46	18	13	15	63	52	10	6	7	36	24	8	7	8	27	28	11	67
10 Colchester U	46	13	20	13	61	66	8	11	4	38	33	5	9	9	23	33	−5	59
11 Bournemouth	46	15	13	18	48	52	9	5	9	23	23	6	8	9	25	29	−4	58
12 Tranmere R	46	14	14	18	49	53	9	11	3	27	16	5	3	15	22	37	−4	56
13 Hartlepool U	46	14	14	18	50	55	6	6	11	21	22	8	8	7	29	33	−5	56
14 Bury (P)	46	15	11	20	60	79	8	8	7	31	32	7	3	13	29	47	−19	56
15 Preston NE (R)	46	13	15	18	54	68	7	9	7	30	35	6	6	11	24	33	−14	54
16 Oldham Ath	46	14	12	20	50	66	9	5	9	26	26	5	7	11	24	40	−16	54
17 Yeovil T	46	14	12	20	59	80	10	3	10	34	41	4	9	10	25	39	−21	54
18 Scunthorpe U (R)	46	10	22	14	55	59	5	10	8	28	33	5	12	6	27	26	−4	52
19 Walsall	46	10	20	16	51	57	7	9	7	27	27	3	11	9	24	30	−6	50
20 Leyton O	46	13	11	22	48	75	6	6	11	23	34	7	5	11	25	41	−27	50
21 Wycombe W (P)	46	11	10	25	65	88	7	6	10	37	38	4	4	15	28	50	−23	43
22 Chesterfield (P)	46	10	12	24	56	81	7	6	10	26	33	3	6	14	30	48	−25	42
23 Exeter C	46	10	12	24	46	75	8	8	7	31	29	2	4	17	15	46	−29	42
24 Rochdale	46	8	14	24	47	81	6	8	9	30	39	2	6	15	17	42	−34	38

¶Huddersfield T promoted via play-offs.

LEADING GOALSCORERS 2011–2012
NPOWER LEAGUE 1

	League	Carling Cup	FA Cup	Other	Total
Jordan Rhodes (Huddersfield T)	35	2	0	2	39
Ched Evans (Sheffield U)	29	0	5	1	35
Bradley Wright-Phillips (Charlton Ath)	22	0	0	0	22
Stuart Beavon (Wycombe W)	21	1	0	3	25
Gary Madine (Sheffield W)	18	0	0	0	18
Andy Williams (Yeovil T)	16	0	1	0	17
Lee Miller (Carlisle U)	14	0	1	0	15
Jeff Hughes (Notts Co)	13	0	4	0	17
Lee Novak (Huddersfield T)	13	2	1	1	17
Francois Zoko (Carlisle U)	13	0	0	1	14
Lee Williamson (Sheffield U)	13	0	0	0	13
Anthony Wordsworth (Colchester U)	13	0	0	0	13

NPOWER LEAGUE 2 2011–2012

				Total					Home					Away				
	P	W	D	L	F	A	W	D	L	F	A	W	D	L	F	A	GD	Pts
1 Swindon T (R)	46	29	6	11	75	32	19	3	1	49	8	10	3	10	26	24	43	93
2 Shrewsbury T	46	26	10	10	66	41	18	5	0	37	12	8	5	10	29	29	25	88
3 Crawley T (P)	46	23	15	8	76	54	14	5	4	47	25	9	10	4	29	29	22	84
4 Southend U	46	25	8	13	77	48	12	6	5	36	18	13	2	8	41	30	29	83
5 Torquay U	46	23	12	11	63	50	12	8	3	36	23	11	4	8	27	27	13	81
6 Cheltenham T	46	23	8	15	66	50	13	5	5	32	16	10	3	10	34	34	16	77
7 Crewe Alex¶	46	20	12	14	67	59	11	6	6	38	28	9	6	8	29	31	8	72
8 Gillingham	46	20	10	16	79	62	13	4	6	44	27	7	6	10	35	35	17	70
9 Oxford U	46	17	17	12	59	48	10	9	4	36	24	7	8	8	23	24	11	68
10 Rotherham U	46	18	13	15	67	63	12	4	7	31	22	6	9	8	36	41	4	67
11 Aldershot T	46	19	9	18	54	52	11	5	7	26	19	8	4	11	28	33	2	66
12 Port Vale*	46	20	9	17	68	60	12	3	8	38	26	8	6	9	30	34	8	59
13 Bristol R (R)	46	15	12	19	60	70	10	6	7	37	29	5	6	12	23	41	-10	57
14 Accrington S	46	14	15	17	54	66	11	4	8	34	33	3	11	9	20	33	-12	57
15 Morecambe	46	14	14	18	63	57	6	6	11	31	29	8	8	7	32	28	6	56
16 AFC Wimbledon (P)	46	15	9	22	62	78	9	4	10	39	40	6	5	12	23	38	-16	54
17 Burton Alb	46	14	12	20	54	81	8	7	8	24	32	6	5	12	30	49	-27	54
18 Bradford C	46	12	14	20	54	59	8	9	6	34	27	4	5	14	20	32	-5	50
19 Dagenham & R (R)	46	14	8	24	50	72	9	3	11	31	35	5	5	13	19	37	-22	50
20 Northampton T	46	12	12	22	56	79	6	6	11	30	43	6	6	11	26	36	-23	48
21 Plymouth Arg (R)	46	10	16	20	47	64	6	9	8	23	26	4	7	12	24	38	-17	46
22 Barnet	46	12	10	24	52	79	6	6	11	29	39	6	4	13	23	40	-27	46
23 Hereford U	46	10	14	22	50	70	5	5	13	23	41	5	9	9	27	29	-20	44
24 Macclesfield T	46	8	13	25	39	64	5	11	7	25	26	3	2	18	14	38	-25	37

*Port Vale deducted 10 points. ¶Crewe Alex promoted via play-offs.

NPOWER LEAGUE 2

	League	Carling Cup	FA Cup	Other	Total
Izale McLeod *(Barnet)*	18	0	1	3	22
Lewis Grabban *(Rotherham U)*	18	0	3	0	21
Jack Midson *(AFC Wimbledon)*	18	1	1	0	20
Adebayo Akinfenwa *(Northampton T)*	18	0	0	0	18
Marc Richards *(Port Vale)*	17	0	0	0	17
Matt Harrold *(Bristol R)*	16	1	0	1	18
Kevin Ellison *(Morecambe)*	15	1	0	1	17
James Collins *(Shrewsbury T)*	14	2	0	0	16
Danny Hylton *(Aldershot T)*	13	2	0	1	16
Nick Powell *(Crewe Alex)*	14	0	0	1	15
Tyrone Barnett *(Crawley T)*	14	0	1	0	15
James Hanson *(Bradford C)*	13	0	1	0	14
Bilel Mohsni *(Southend U)*	13	0	0	0	13

BARCLAYS PREMIER LEAGUE

HOME TEAM	Arsenal	Aston Villa	Blackburn R	Bolton W	Chelsea	Everton	Fulham	Liverpool	Manchester C	Manchester U
Arsenal	—	3-0	7-1	3-0	0-0	1-0	1-1	0-2	1-0	1-2
Aston Villa	1-2	—	3-1	1-2	2-4	1-1	1-0	0-2	0-1	0-1
Blackburn R	4-3	1-1	—	1-2	0-1	0-1	3-1	2-3	0-4	0-2
Bolton W	0-0	1-2	2-1	—	1-5	0-2	0-3	3-1	2-3	0-5
Chelsea	3-5	1-3	2-1	3-0	—	3-1	1-1	1-2	2-1	3-3
Everton	0-1	2-2	1-1	1-2	2-0	—	4-0	0-2	1-0	0-1
Fulham	2-1	0-0	1-1	2-0	1-1	1-3	—	1-0	2-2	0-5
Liverpool	1-2	1-1	1-1	3-1	4-1	3-0	0-1	—	1-1	1-1
Manchester C	1-0	4-1	3-0	2-0	2-1	2-0	3-0	3-0	—	1-0
Manchester U	8-2	4-0	2-3	3-0	3-1	4-4	1-0	2-1	1-6	—
Newcastle U	0-0	2-1	3-1	2-0	0-3	2-1	2-1	2-0	0-2	3-0
Norwich C	1-2	2-0	3-3	2-0	0-0	2-2	1-1	0-3	1-6	1-2
QPR	2-1	1-1	1-1	0-4	1-0	1-1	0-1	3-2	2-3	0-2
Stoke C	1-1	0-0	3-1	2-2	0-0	1-1	2-0	1-0	1-1	1-1
Sunderland	1-2	2-2	2-1	2-2	1-2	1-1	0-0	1-0	1-0	0-1
Swansea C	3-2	0-0	3-0	3-1	1-1	0-2	2-0	1-0	1-0	0-1
Tottenham H	2-1	2-0	2-0	3-0	1-1	2-0	2-0	4-0	1-5	1-3
WBA	2-3	0-0	3-0	2-1	1-0	0-1	0-0	0-2	0-0	1-2
Wigan Ath	0-4	0-0	3-3	1-3	1-1	1-1	0-2	0-0	0-1	1-0
Wolverhampton W	0-3	2-3	0-2	2-3	1-2	0-0	2-0	0-3	0-2	0-5

2011–2012 RESULTS

Newcastle U	Norwich C	QPR	Stoke C	Sunderland	Swansea C	Tottenham H	WBA	Wigan Ath	Wolverhampton W
2-1	3-3	1-0	3-1	2-1	1-0	5-2	3-0	1-2	1-1
1-1	3-2	2-2	1-1	0-0	0-2	1-1	1-2	2-0	0-0
0-2	2-0	3-2	1-2	2-0	4-2	1-2	1-2	0-1	1-2
0-2	1-2	2-1	5-0	0-2	1-1	1-4	2-2	1-2	1-1
0-2	3-1	6-1	1-0	1-0	4-1	0-0	2-1	2-1	3-0
3-1	1-1	0-1	0-1	4-0	1-0	1-0	2-0	3-1	2-1
5-2	2-1	6-0	2-1	2-1	0-3	1-3	1-1	2-1	5-0
3-1	1-1	1-0	0-0	1-1	0-0	0-0	0-1	1-2	2-1
3-1	5-1	3-2	3-0	3-3	4-0	3-2	4-0	3-0	3-1
1-1	2-0	2-0	2-0	1-0	2-0	3-0	2-0	5-0	4-1
—	1-0	1-0	3-0	1-1	0-0	2-2	2-3	1-0	2-2
4-2	—	2-1	1-1	2-1	3-1	0-2	0-1	1-1	2-1
0-0	1-2	—	1-0	2-3	3-0	1-0	1-1	3-1	1-2
1-3	1-0	2-3	—	0-1	2-0	2-1	1-2	2-2	2-1
0-1	3-0	3-1	4-0	—	2-0	0-0	2-2	1-2	0-0
0-2	2-3	1-1	2-0	0-0	—	1-1	3-0	0-0	4-4
5-0	1-2	3-1	1-1	1-0	3-1	—	1-0	3-1	1-1
1-3	1-2	1-0	0-1	4-0	1-2	1-3	—	1-2	2-0
4-0	1-1	2-0	2-0	1-4	0-2	1-2	1-1	—	3-2
1-2	2-2	0-3	1-2	2-1	2-2	0-2	1-5	3-1	—

NPOWER CHAMPIONSHIP

HOME TEAM	Barnsley	Birmingham C	Blackpool	Brighton & HA	Bristol C	Burnley	Cardiff C	Coventry C	Crystal Palace	Derby C
Barnsley	—	1-3	1-3	0-0	1-2	2-0	0-1	2-0	2-1	3-2
Birmingham C	1-1	—	3-0	0-0	2-2	2-1	1-1	1-0	3-1	2-2
Blackpool	1-1	2-2	—	3-1	5-0	4-0	1-1	2-1	2-1	0-1
Brighton & HA	2-0	1-1	2-2	—	2-0	0-1	2-2	2-1	1-3	2-0
Bristol C	2-0	0-2	1-3	0-1	—	3-1	1-2	3-1	2-2	1-1
Burnley	2-0	1-3	3-1	1-0	1-1	—	1-1	1-1	1-1	0-0
Cardiff C	5-3	1-0	1-3	1-3	3-1	0-0	—	2-2	2-0	2-0
Coventry C	1-0	1-1	2-2	2-0	1-0	1-2	1-1	—	1-1	2-0
Crystal Palace	1-0	1-0	1-1	1-1	1-0	2-0	1-2	2-1	—	1-1
Derby C	1-1	2-1	2-1	0-1	2-1	1-2	0-3	1-0	3-2	—
Doncaster R	2-0	1-3	1-3	1-1	1-1	1-2	0-0	1-1	1-0	1-2
Hull C	3-1	2-1	0-1	0-0	3-0	2-3	2-1	0-2	0-1	0-1
Ipswich T	1-0	1-1	2-2	3-1	3-0	1-0	3-0	3-0	0-1	1-0
Leeds U	1-2	1-4	0-5	1-2	2-1	2-1	1-1	1-1	3-2	0-2
Leicester C	1-2	3-1	2-0	1-0	1-2	0-0	2-1	2-0	3-0	4-0
Middlesbrough	2-0	3-1	2-2	1-0	1-1	0-2	0-2	1-1	0-0	2-0
Millwall	0-0	0-6	2-2	1-1	1-2	0-1	0-0	3-0	0-1	0-0
Nottingham F	0-0	1-3	0-0	1-1	0-1	0-2	0-1	2-0	0-1	1-2
Peterborough U	3-4	1-1	3-1	1-2	3-0	2-1	4-3	1-0	2-1	3-2
Portsmouth	2-0	4-1	1-0	0-1	0-0	1-5	1-1	2-1	2-1	1-2
Reading	1-2	1-0	3-1	3-0	1-0	1-0	1-2	2-0	2-2	2-2
Southampton	2-0	4-1	2-2	3-0	0-1	2-0	1-1	4-0	2-0	4-0
Watford	2-1	2-2	0-2	1-0	2-2	3-2	1-1	0-0	0-2	0-1
West Ham U	1-0	3-3	4-0	6-0	0-0	1-2	0-1	1-0	0-0	3-1

Doncaster R	Hull C	Ipswich T	Leeds U	Leicester C	Middlesbrough	Millwall	Nottingham F	Peterborough U	Portsmouth	Reading	Southampton	Watford	West Ham U
2-0	2-1	3-5	4-1	1-1	1-3	1-3	1-1	1-0	2-0	0-4	0-1	1-1	0-4
2-1	0-0	2-1	1-0	2-0	3-0	3-0	1-2	1-1	1-0	2-0	0-0	3-0	1-1
2-1	1-1	2-0	1-0	3-3	3-0	1-0	1-2	2-1	1-1	1-0	3-0	0-0	1-4
2-1	0-0	3-0	3-3	1-0	1-1	2-2	1-0	2-0	2-0	0-1	3-0	2-2	0-1
2-1	1-1	0-3	0-3	3-2	0-1	1-0	0-0	1-2	0-0	2-3	2-0	0-2	1-1
3-0	1-0	4-0	1-2	1-3	0-2	1-3	5-1	1-1	0-1	0-1	1-1	2-2	2-2
2-0	0-3	2-2	1-1	0-0	2-3	0-0	1-0	3-1	3-2	3-1	2-1	1-1	0-2
0-2	0-1	2-3	2-1	0-1	3-1	0-1	1-0	2-2	2-0	1-1	2-4	0-0	1-2
1-1	0-0	1-1	1-1	1-2	0-1	0-0	0-3	1-0	0-0	0-0	0-2	4-0	2-2
3-0	0-2	0-0	1-0	0-1	0-1	3-0	1-0	1-1	3-1	0-1	1-1	1-2	2-1
—	1-1	2-3	0-3	2-1	1-3	0-3	0-1	1-1	3-4	1-1	1-0	0-0	0-1
0-0	—	2-2	0-0	2-1	2-1	2-0	2-1	1-0	1-0	1-0	0-2	3-2	0-2
2-3	0-1	—	2-1	1-2	1-1	0-3	1-3	3-2	1-0	2-3	2-5	1-2	5-1
3-2	4-1	3-1	—	1-2	0-1	2-0	3-7	4-1	1-0	0-1	0-1	0-2	1-1
4-0	2-1	1-1	0-1	—	2-2	0-3	0-0	1-1	1-1	0-2	3-2	2-0	1-2
0-0	1-0	0-0	0-2	0-0	—	1-1	2-1	1-1	2-2	0-2	2-1	1-0	0-2
3-2	2-0	4-1	0-1	2-1	1-3	—	2-0	2-2	1-0	1-2	2-3	0-2	0-0
1-2	0-1	3-2	0-4	2-2	2-0	3-1	—	0-1	2-0	1-0	0-3	1-1	1-4
1-2	0-1	7-1	2-3	1-0	1-1	0-3	0-1	—	0-3	3-1	1-3	2-2	0-2
3-1	2-0	0-1	0-0	1-1	1-3	0-1	3-0	2-3	—	1-0	1-1	2-0	0-1
2-0	0-1	1-0	2-0	3-1	0-0	2-2	1-0	3-2	1-0	—	1-1	0-2	3-0
2-0	2-1	1-1	3-1	0-2	3-0	1-0	3-2	2-1	2-2	1-3	—	4-0	1-0
4-1	1-1	2-1	1-1	3-2	2-1	2-1	0-1	3-2	2-0	1-2	0-3	—	0-4
1-1	2-1	0-1	2-2	3-2	1-1	2-1	2-1	1-0	4-3	2-4	1-1	1-1	—

NPOWER LEAGUE 1

HOME TEAM	Bournemouth	Brentford	Bury	Carlisle U	Charlton Ath	Chesterfield	Colchester U	Exeter C	Hartlepool U	Huddersfield T
Bournemouth	—	1-0	1-2	1-1	0-1	0-3	1-1	2-0	1-2	2-0
Brentford	1-1	—	3-0	4-0	0-1	2-1	1-1	2-0	2-1	0-4
Bury	1-0	1-1	—	0-2	1-2	1-1	4-1	2-0	1-2	3-3
Carlisle U	2-1	2-2	4-1	—	0-1	2-1	1-0	4-1	1-2	2-1
Charlton Ath	3-0	2-0	1-1	4-0	—	3-1	0-2	2-0	3-2	2-0
Chesterfield	1-0	2-3	1-0	4-1	0-4	—	0-1	0-2	2-3	0-2
Colchester U	1-1	2-1	4-1	1-1	0-2	1-2	—	2-0	1-1	1-1
Exeter C	0-2	1-2	3-2	0-0	0-1	2-1	1-1	—	0-0	0-4
Hartlepool U	0-0	0-0	3-0	4-0	0-4	1-2	0-1	2-0	—	0-0
Huddersfield T	0-1	3-2	1-1	1-1	1-0	1-0	3-2	2-0	1-0	—
Leyton Orient	1-3	2-0	1-0	1-2	1-0	1-1	0-1	3-0	1-1	1-3
Milton Keynes D	2-2	1-2	2-1	1-2	1-1	6-2	1-0	3-0	2-2	1-1
Notts Co	3-1	1-1	2-4	2-0	1-2	1-0	4-1	2-1	3-0	2-2
Oldham Ath	1-0	0-2	0-2	2-1	0-1	5-2	1-1	0-0	0-1	1-1
Preston NE	1-3	1-3	1-1	3-3	2-2	0-0	2-4	1-0	1-0	1-0
Rochdale	1-0	1-2	3-0	0-0	2-3	1-1	2-2	3-2	1-3	2-2
Scunthorpe U	1-1	0-0	1-3	1-2	1-1	2-2	1-1	1-0	0-2	2-2
Sheffield U	2-1	2-0	4-0	1-0	0-2	4-1	3-0	4-4	3-1	0-3
Sheffield W	3-0	0-0	4-1	2-1	0-1	3-1	2-0	3-0	2-2	4-4
Stevenage	2-2	2-1	3-0	1-0	1-0	2-2	0-0	0-0	2-2	2-2
Tranmere R	0-0	2-2	2-0	1-2	1-1	1-0	0-0	2-0	1-1	1-1
Walsall	2-2	0-1	2-4	1-1	1-1	3-2	3-1	1-2	0-0	1-1
Wycombe W	0-1	0-1	0-2	1-1	1-2	3-2	0-0	3-1	5-0	0-6
Yeovil T	1-3	2-1	1-3	0-3	2-3	3-2	3-2	2-2	0-1	0-1

2011–2012 RESULTS

Leyton Orient	Milton Keynes D	Notts Co	Oldham Ath	Preston NE	Rochdale	Scunthorpe U	Sheffield U	Sheffield W	Stevenage	Tranmere R	Walsall	Wycombe W	Yeovil T
1-2	0-1	2-1	0-0	1-0	1-1	2-0	0-2	2-0	1-3	2-1	0-2	2-0	0-0
5-0	3-3	0-0	2-0	1-3	2-0	0-0	0-2	1-2	0-1	0-2	0-0	5-2	2-0
1-1	0-0	2-2	0-0	1-0	2-4	0-0	0-3	2-1	1-2	2-0	2-1	1-4	3-2
4-1	1-3	0-3	3-3	0-0	2-1	0-0	3-2	3-2	1-0	0-0	1-1	2-2	3-2
2-0	2-1	2-4	1-1	5-2	1-1	2-2	1-0	1-1	2-0	1-1	1-0	2-1	3-0
0-0	1-1	1-3	1-1	0-2	2-1	1-4	0-1	1-0	1-1	1-0	1-1	4-0	2-2
1-1	1-5	4-2	4-1	3-0	0-0	1-1	1-1	1-1	1-6	4-2	1-0	1-1	2-2
3-0	0-2	1-1	2-0	1-2	3-1	0-0	2-2	2-1	1-1	3-0	4-2	1-3	1-1
2-1	1-1	3-0	0-1	0-1	2-0	1-2	0-1	0-1	0-0	0-2	1-1	1-3	0-1
2-2	1-1	2-1	1-0	3-1	2-2	1-0	0-1	0-2	2-1	2-0	1-1	3-0	2-0
—	0-3	0-3	1-3	2-1	2-1	1-3	1-1	0-1	0-0	0-1	1-1	1-3	2-2
4-1	—	3-0	5-0	0-1	3-1	0-0	1-0	1-1	1-0	3-0	0-1	4-3	0-1
1-2	1-1	—	1-0	0-0	2-0	3-2	2-5	1-2	1-0	3-2	2-1	1-1	3-1
0-1	2-1	3-2	—	1-1	2-0	1-2	0-2	0-2	1-1	1-0	2-1	2-0	1-2
0-2	1-1	2-0	3-3	—	0-1	0-0	2-4	0-2	0-0	2-1	0-0	3-2	4-3
0-2	1-2	0-1	3-2	1-1	—	1-0	2-5	0-0	1-5	0-2	3-3	2-1	0-0
2-3	0-3	0-0	1-2	1-1	1-0	—	1-1	1-3	1-1	4-2	0-1	4-1	2-1
3-1	2-1	2-1	2-3	2-1	3-0	2-1	—	2-2	2-2	1-1	3-2	3-0	4-0
1-0	3-1	2-1	3-0	2-0	2-0	3-2	1-0	—	0-1	2-1	2-2	2-0	2-1
0-1	4-2	0-2	1-0	1-1	4-2	1-2	2-1	5-1	—	2-1	0-0	1-1	0-0
2-0	0-2	1-1	1-0	2-1	0-0	1-1	1-1	1-2	3-0	—	2-1	2-0	0-0
1-0	0-2	0-1	0-1	1-0	0-0	2-2	3-2	2-1	1-1	0-1	—	2-0	1-1
4-2	1-1	3-4	2-2	3-4	3-0	1-1	1-0	1-2	0-1	2-1	1-1	—	2-3
2-2	0-1	1-0	3-1	2-1	3-1	2-2	0-1	2-3	0-6	2-1	2-1	1-0	—

HOME TEAM	Accrington S	AFC Wimbledon	Aldershot T	Barnet	Bradford C	Bristol R	Burton Alb	Cheltenham T	Crawley T	Crewe Alex
Accrington S	—	2-1	3-2	0-3	1-0	2-1	2-1	0-1	0-1	0-2
AFC Wimbledon	0-2	—	1-2	1-1	3-1	2-3	4-0	4-1	2-5	1-3
Aldershot T	0-0	1-1	—	4-1	1-0	1-0	2-0	1-0	0-1	3-1
Barnet	0-0	4-0	2-1	—	0-4	2-0	3-6	2-2	1-2	2-0
Bradford C	1-1	1-2	1-2	4-2	—	2-2	1-1	0-1	1-2	3-0
Bristol R	5-1	1-0	0-1	0-2	2-1	—	7-1	1-3	0-0	2-5
Burton Alb	0-2	3-2	0-4	1-2	2-2	2-1	—	0-2	0-0	1-0
Cheltenham T	4-1	0-0	2-0	2-0	3-1	0-2	2-0	—	3-1	0-1
Crawley T	1-1	1-1	2-2	1-0	3-1	4-1	3-0	4-2	—	1-1
Crewe Alex	2-0	3-3	2-2	3-1	1-0	3-0	3-2	1-0	1-1	—
Dagenham & R	2-1	0-2	2-5	3-0	1-0	4-0	1-1	0-5	1-1	2-1
Gillingham	1-1	3-4	1-0	3-1	0-0	4-1	3-1	1-0	0-1	3-4
Hereford U	1-1	2-1	0-2	1-0	2-0	1-2	2-3	1-1	1-1	0-1
Macclesfield T	1-1	4-0	0-1	0-0	1-0	0-0	0-2	1-3	2-2	2-2
Morecambe	1-2	1-2	2-0	0-1	1-1	2-3	2-2	3-1	6-0	1-2
Northampton T	0-0	1-0	3-1	1-2	1-3	3-2	2-3	2-3	0-1	1-1
Oxford U	1-1	1-0	1-1	2-1	1-1	3-0	2-2	1-3	1-1	0-1
Plymouth Arg	2-2	0-2	1-0	0-0	1-0	1-1	2-1	1-2	1-1	0-1
Port Vale	4-1	1-2	4-0	1-2	3-2	1-0	3-0	1-2	2-2	1-1
Rotherham U	1-0	1-0	2-0	2-2	3-0	0-1	0-1	1-0	1-2	1-1
Shrewsbury T	1-0	0-0	1-1	3-2	1-0	1-0	1-0	2-0	2-1	2-0
Southend U	2-2	2-0	0-1	3-0	0-1	1-1	0-1	4-0	0-0	1-0
Swindon T	2-0	2-0	2-0	4-0	0-0	0-0	2-0	1-0	3-0	3-0
Torquay U	1-0	4-0	1-0	1-0	1-2	2-2	2-2	2-2	1-3	1-1

2011–2012 RESULTS

Dagenham & R	Gillingham	Hereford U	Macclesfield T	Morecambe	Northampton T	Oxford U	Plymouth Arg	Port Vale	Rotherham U	Shrewsbury T	Southend U	Swindon T	Torquay U
3-0	4-3	2-1	4-0	1-1	2-1	0-2	0-4	2-2	1-1	1-1	1-2	0-2	3-1
2-1	3-1	1-1	2-1	1-1	0-3	0-2	1-2	3-2	1-2	3-1	1-4	1-1	2-0
1-1	1-2	1-0	1-2	1-0	0-1	0-3	0-0	1-2	2-2	1-0	2-0	2-1	0-1
2-2	2-2	1-1	2-1	0-2	1-2	0-2	2-0	1-3	1-1	1-2	0-3	0-2	0-1
0-1	2-2	1-1	1-0	2-2	2-1	2-1	1-1	1-1	2-3	3-1	2-0	0-0	1-0
2-0	2-2	0-0	0-0	2-1	2-1	0-0	2-3	0-3	5-2	1-0	1-0	1-1	1-2
1-1	1-0	0-2	1-0	3-2	0-1	1-1	2-1	1-1	1-1	1-1	0-2	2-0	1-4
2-1	0-3	0-0	2-0	1-2	2-2	0-0	2-1	2-0	1-0	0-0	3-0	1-0	0-1
3-1	1-2	0-3	2-0	1-1	3-1	4-1	2-0	3-2	3-0	2-1	3-0	0-3	0-1
4-1	1-2	1-0	0-1	0-1	1-1	3-1	3-2	1-1	1-2	1-1	1-3	2-0	0-3
—	2-1	0-1	2-0	1-2	0-1	0-1	2-3	1-2	3-2	0-2	2-3	1-0	1-1
1-2	—	5-4	2-0	2-0	4-3	1-0	3-0	1-1	0-0	0-1	1-2	3-1	2-0
1-0	1-6	—	0-4	0-3	0-0	0-1	1-1	1-2	2-3	0-2	2-3	1-2	3-2
0-1	0-0	2-2	—	1-1	3-1	1-1	1-1	2-1	0-0	1-3	0-2	2-0	1-2
1-2	2-1	0-1	1-0	—	1-2	0-0	2-2	0-0	3-3	0-1	1-0	0-1	1-2
2-1	1-1	1-3	3-2	0-2	—	2-1	0-0	1-2	1-1	2-7	2-5	1-2	0-0
2-1	0-0	2-2	1-1	1-2	2-0	—	5-1	2-1	2-1	2-0	0-2	2-0	2-2
0-0	0-1	1-1	2-0	1-1	4-1	1-1	—	0-2	1-4	1-0	2-2	0-1	1-2
0-1	2-1	1-0	1-0	0-4	3-0	3-0	1-0	—	2-0	2-3	2-3	0-2	0-0
3-1	3-0	1-0	4-2	3-2	1-1	1-0	1-0	0-1	—	1-1	0-4	1-2	0-1
1-0	2-0	3-1	1-0	2-0	1-1	2-2	1-1	1-0	3-1	—	2-1	2-1	2-0
1-1	1-0	1-0	2-0	1-1	2-2	2-1	2-0	3-0	0-2	3-0	—	1-4	4-1
4-0	2-0	3-3	1-0	3-0	1-0	1-2	1-0	5-0	3-2	2-1	2-0	—	2-0
1-0	2-5	2-0	3-0	1-1	1-0	0-0	3-1	2-1	3-3	1-0	0-0	1-0	—

ACCRINGTON STANLEY   FL CHAMPIONSHIP 2

Player	Ht	Wt	Birthplace	D.O.B.	Source
Barnett Charlie (M)	5 7	11 07	Liverpool	19/9/88	Tranmere R
Dunbavin Ian (G)	6 1	12 11	Knowsley	27/5/80	Shrewsbury T
Hatfield Will (M)	5 8	10 00	Liversedge	10/10/91	Leeds U
Joyce Luke (M)	5 11	12 03	Bolton	9/7/87	Carlisle U
Lindfield Craig (F)	6 0	10 05	Greasby	7/9/88	Macclesfield T
Murphy Peter (D)	6 0	11 10	Liverpool	13/2/90	Scholar
Richardson Leam (D)	5 7	11 04	Leeds	19/11/79	Blackpool
Winnard Dean (D)	5 9	10 04	Wigan	20/8/89	Blackburn R

League Appearances: Amond, P. 37(5); Barnett, C. 27(15); Bender, T. (2); Burton, A. (1); Carver, M. 1(1); Coid, D. 16(5); Craney, I. 7(15); Devitt, J. 15(1); Dobie, L. (4); Dunbavin, I. 25; Evans, M. 14(9); Fletcher, W. 10; Grant, R. 8; Guthrie, K. 6(7); Hatfield, W. 4(13); Hessey, S. 17; Hopper, R. 1(3); Hughes, B. 15(6); Joyce, L. 43; Kiernan, R. 3; Liddle, M. 12; Lindfield, C. 29(10); Long, K. 24; McIntyre, K. 44(1); Miller, K. 2; Moult, L. 1(3); Murdoch, S. 12(1); Murphy, P. 36(2); Nicholls, L. 9; Nsiala, A. 19; Procter, A. 25; Richardson, L. (1); Smith, M. 4(2); Spray, J. 3; Stockley, J. 5(4); Taylor, N. 1(1); Willis, L. 1(1); Winnard, D. 30.
Goals – League (54): Amond 7, Lindfield 4, Long 4, Murphy 4, Evans 3, Grant 3, Hatfield 3, Hughes 3, Smith 3, Stockley 3, Devitt 2, Fletcher 2, Hessey 2, Joyce 2, McIntyre 2, Procter 2, Barnett 1, Coid 1, Craney 1, Winnard 1, own goal 1.
Carling Cup (0).
FA Cup (1): Joyce 1.
J Paint Trophy (3): Dunbavin 1, Lindfield 1, Procter 1.
Ground: The Fraser Eagle Stadium, Livingstone Road, Accrington, Lancashire BB5 5BX. Telephone: (0871) 434 1968.
Capacity: 5,057.
Record Attendance: 13,181 v Hull C, Division 3 (N), 28 September 1948 (at Peel Park); 4,368 v Colchester U, FA Cup 1st rd, 3 January 2004 (at Fraser Eagle Stadium – Crown Inn).
Manager: Paul Cook.
Most League Goals: 96, Division 3 (N), 1954–55.
Highest League Scorer in Season: George Stewart, 35, Division 3 (N), 1955–56; George Hudson, 35, Division 4, 1960–61.
Most League Goals in Total Aggregate: George Stewart, 136, 1954–58.
Most Capped Player: Romuald Boco, 19 (42), Benin.
Most League Appearances: Jim Armstrong, 260, 1927–34.
Colours: All red.
Honours: None.

AFC WIMBLEDON   FL CHAMPIONSHIP 2

Harrison Byron (F)	6 3	13 01	Wandsworth	15/6/87	Stevenage
Johnson Huw (F)			Hammersmith	22/6/93	Youth
Jolley Christian (F)	6 0	10 00	Fleet	12/5/88	Kingstonian
Kiernan Brendan (M)	5 9	11 11	Lambeth	10/11/92	Youth
McNaughton Callum (D)	6 2	13 05	Harlow	25/10/91	West Ham U
Midson Jack (F)	5 8	11 07	Stevenage	21/7/83	Oxford U
Mitchel-King Mat (D)	6 4	13 00	Reading	12/9/83	Crewe Alex
Moore Luke (M)	5 11	11 07	Gravesend	27/4/88	Ebbsfleet U
Moore Sammy (M)	5 8	9 00	Dover	7/9/87	Ipswich T
Prior Jason (F)	6 1	11 11	Portsmouth	20/12/88	Bognor Regis T
Yussuff Rashid (M)	6 1	10 07	Poplar	23/9/89	Gillingham

League Appearances: Ademeno, C. 5(10); Balkestein, P. 6; Brown, S. 44; Bush, C. 16(6); Djilali, K. 4(8); Euell, J. 8(1); Franks, F. 3(1); Gwillim, G. 27; Harrison, B. 11(8); Hatton, S. 41(3); Hoyte, G. 2(1); Jackson, R. 3(4); Johnson, B. 14(4); Johnson, H. (1); Jolley, C. 23(14); Jones, R. 1; Kiernan, B. 1(8); Knott, B. 14(6); McNaughton, C. 18; Midson, J. 43(3); Minshull, L. 13(5); Mitchel-King, M. 24; Moncur, G. 20; Moore, L. 29(8); Moore, S. 40(1); Mulley, J. 3(7); Porter, M. 11(4); Prior, J. 2(1); Stuart, J. 33(1); Turner, J. 2; Wellard, R. 16(6); Yussuff, R. 29(11).

Goals – League (62): Midson 18 (3 pens), Moore, L. 9 (1 pen), Jolley 7, Moore, S. 6, Yussuff 4, Knott 3, Harrison 2, Moncur 2, Ademeno 1, Djilali 1, Gwillim 1, Hatton 1, Porter 1, Stuart 1, Wellard 1, own goals 4.

Carling Cup (2): Midson 1, Moore, L. 1.

FA Cup (2): Midson 1, Moore, L. 1.

J Paint Trophy (3): Yussuff 2, Hatton 1 (pen).

Ground: The Cherry Red Records Fans' Stadium, Kingsmeadow, Jack Goodchild Way, 422a Kingston Road, Kingston-upon-Thames, Surrey KT1 3PB. Telephone: (0208) 547 3528.

Capacity: 5,194 (1,265 seated).

Record Attendance: 4,722 v St Albans C, Blue Square Premier, 25 April 2009.

Manager: Terry Brown.

Most League Goals: 62, FL 2, 2011–12.

Highest League Scorer in Season: Jack Midson, 18, 2011–12.

Most League Goals in Total Aggregate: Kevin Cooper, 107, 2002–04.

Most League Appearances: Jack Midson, 46, 2011–12.

Colours: All blue with yellow trim.

Honours: None.

ALDERSHOT TOWN   FL CHAMPIONSHIP 2

Bergqvist Doug (D)	6 0	13 07	Stockholm	29/3/93	Scholar
Breimyr Henrik (D)	6 1	12 02	Stavanger	20/7/93	Scholar
Bubb Bradley (F)	5 7	11 00	Brent	30/5/88	Farnborough T
Connolly Reece (F)	6 0	11 09	Frimley	22/1/92	Scholar
Herd Ben (D)	5 9	10 13	Welwyn	21/6/85	Shrewsbury T
Hylton Danny (F)	6 0	11 13	Camden	25/2/89	Youth
Madjo Guy (F)	6 0	13 05	Cameroon	1/6/84	Bylis Ballsh
Mekki Adam (M)	5 9	11 00	Chester	24/12/91	Scholar
Morris Aaron (D)	6 1	12 05	Cardiff	30/12/89	Cardiff C
Payne Josh (M)	6 0	11 09	Basingstoke	25/11/90	Doncaster R
Rankine Michael (F)	6 1	14 12	Doncaster	15/1/85	Scunthorpe U
Roberts Jordan (M)	5 11	12 13	Watford	5/1/94	Scholar
Rodman Alex (F)	6 2	12 08	Sutton Coldfield	15/2/87	Tamworth
Straker Anthony (D)	5 9	11 11	Ealing	23/9/88	Crystal Palace Scholar
Vincenti Peter (F)	6 2	11 13	St Peter	7/7/86	Stevenage
Worner Ross (G)	6 1	12 05	Hindhead	3/10/89	Charlton Ath
Young Jamie (G)	5 11	13 00	Brisbane	25/8/85	Wycombe W

League Appearances: Andrade, B. (1); Bergqvist, D. (2); Bradley, S. 13(1); Brown, A. 6(5); Brown, J. 2(1); Brown, T. 14(3); Bubb, B. 1(8); Collins, C. (1); Collins, J. 21(4); Connolly, R. 1(6); Davies, S. 3(5); Doig, C. 2; Doughty, M. 2(3); Guttridge, L. 24(1); Henry, C. 3(4); Herd, B. 45; Hylton, D. 43(1); Jones, D. 42; Madjo, G. 15(5); McGlashan, J. 18(5); Mekki, A. 16(9); Molesley, M. 2(6); Morris, A. 36(3); Murphy, D. 2(1); Panther, M. (1); Payne, J. 14(3); Payne, S. (1); Pearson, G. 1(4); Pulis, A. 1(4); Rankine, M. 21(1); Risser, N. 8(8); Roberts, J. 1(3); Rodman, A. 15(3); Sinclair, R. 1(3); Smith, A. 7(5); Smith, B. 3(5); Straker, A. 44; Taylor, J. (3); Vincenti, P. 33(9); Worner, R. 22; Young, J. 24(1).

Goals – League (54): Hylton 13, Madjo 8, Vincenti 6, Guttridge 4, McGlashan 4, Risser 3, Brown, T. 2, Morris 2, Payne, J. 2 (2 pens), Rankine 2 (1 pen), Straker 2, Davies 1, Mekki 1, Molesley 1, Rodman 1, own goals 2.
Carling Cup (6): Hylton 2, Rankine 2, Guttridge 1, own goal 1.
FA Cup (3): Guttridge 1, Rankine 1, Rodman 1.
J Paint Trophy (1): Hylton 1.
Ground: The EBB Stadium at the Recreation Ground, High Street, Aldershot GU11 1TW. Telephone: (01252) 320211.
Capacity: 7,100.
Record Attendance: 19,138 v Carlisle U, FA Cup 4th rd (replay), 28 January 1970.
Manager: Dean Holdsworth.
Most League Goals: 83, Division 4, 1963–64.
Highest League Scorer in Season: John Dungworth, 26, Division 4, 1978–79.
Most League Goals in Total Aggregate: Jack Howarth, 171, 1965–71 and 1972–77.
Most Capped Player: Anthony Straker, 5, Grenada.
Most League Appearances: Murray Brodie, 461, 1970–83.
Colours: All red shirts with blue sleeves, red shorts with blue and white trim, red stockings with blue and white trim.
Honours – Blue Square Premier League: Champions 2007–08. **Setanta Shield:** Winners 2008.

ARSENAL

FA PREMIERSHIP

Afobe Benik (F)	5 10	11 00	Leyton	12/2/93	Scholar
Andre Santos Clarindo (D)	5 10	11 13	Sao Paulo	8/3/83	Fenerbahce
Aneke Chuks (M)	6 3	13 01	Newham	3/7/93	Scholar
Angha Martin (D)	6 2	12 10	Switzerland	22/1/94	Zurich
Ansah Zak (F)	5 10	11 00	Sidcup	4/5/94	Scholar
Arshavin Andrei (F)	5 8	9 11	St Petersburg	29/5/81	Zenit
Arteta Mikel (M)	5 9	10 08	San Sebastian	26/3/82	Everton
Bartley Kyle (D)	5 11	11 00	Stockport	22/5/91	Scholar
Bendtner Nicklas (F)	6 2	13 00	Copenhagen	16/1/88	Scholar
Boateng Daniel (D)	6 0	12 04	Enfield	2/9/92	Scholar
Bothelo Pedro (D)	6 2	13 00	Salvador	14/12/89	Salamanca
Campbell Joel (F)	5 10	12 00	Costa Rica	26/6/92	Saprissa
Chamakh Marouane (F)	6 1	11 00	Tonnens	10/1/84	Bordeaux
Coquelin Francis (M)	5 10	11 08	Laval	13/5/91	Laval
Denilson (M)	5 10	10 10	Sao Paulo	16/2/88	Sao Paulo
Diaby Abou (M)	6 2	12 04	Paris	11/5/86	Auxerre
Djourou Johan (D)	6 2	13 00	Ivory Coast	18/1/87	Scholar
Eastmond Craig (D)	6 0	11 11	Wandsworth	9/12/90	Scholar
Ebecilio Kyle (M)	5 11	12 02	Rotterdam	17/2/94	Feyenoord
Eisfeld Thomas (M)			Finsterwalde	18/1/93	Bor Dortmund
Fabianski Lukasz (G)	6 3	13 01	Costrzyn nad Odra	18/4/85	Legia
Frimpong Emmanuel (M)	5 11	10 07	Ghana	10/1/92	Scholar
Galindo Samuel (M)	6 3	12 00	Bolivia	18/4/92	Real America
Gervinho (F)	5 10	10 10	Anyama	27/5/87	Lille
Gibbs Kieran (M)	5 10	10 02	Lambeth	26/9/89	Scholar
Hajrovic Sead (D)	6 0	12 08	Brugg	4/6/93	Scholar
Hayden Isaac (D)			Chelmsford	22/3/95	Scholar
Henderson Conor (M)	6 1	11 13	Sidcup	8/9/91	Scholar
Jenkinson Carl (D)	6 1	12 02	Harlow	8/2/92	Charlton Ath
Koscielny Laurent (D)	6 1	11 11	Tulle	10/9/85	Lorient
Lansbury Henri (M)	6 0	13 06	Enfield	12/10/90	Scholar
Mannone Vito (G)	6 0	11 08	Milan	2/3/88	Atalanta
Martinez Damian (G)	6 3	13 05	Mar del Plata	2/9/92	Independiente
Meade Jernade (M)	5 8	11 09	Luton	25/10/92	Scholar

Name	Height	Weight	Birthplace	D.O.B.	Previous Club
Mertesacker Per (D)	6 6	14-02	Hannover	29/9/84	Werder Bremen
Miquel Ignasi (D)	6 4	13 05	Barcelona	28/9/92	Scholar
Miyaichi Ryo (F)	6 0	11 02	Okazaki	14/12/92	Chukyodai
Monteiro Elton (D)	6 3	13 05	Sion	22/2/94	Scholar
Neita Nigel (F)	5 11	11 11	Southwark	23/12/93	Scholar
Oxlade-Chamberlain Alex (M)	5 11	11 01	Portsmouth	15/8/93	Southampton
Ozyakup Oguzhan (M)	5 10	11 00	Zaandam	23/9/92	Scholar
Park Chu-Young (F)	6 0	11 11	Daegu	10/7/85	Monaco
Ramsey Aaron (M)	5 9	10 07	Caerphilly	26/12/90	Cardiff C
Rees Josh (M)	5 9	11 00	Hemel Hempstead	4/10/93	Scholar
Rosicky Tomas (M)	5 10	10 10	Prague	4/10/80	Borussia Dortmund
Sagna Bakari (D)	5 10	11 05	Sens	14/2/83	Auxerre
Shea James (G)	5 11	12 00	Islington	16/6/91	Scholar
Silva Wellington (M)	5 6	10 00	Rio de Janeiro	6/1/93	Fluminense
Song Billong Alexandre (M)	5 11	12 04	Douala	9/9/87	Bastia
Squillaci Sebastien (D)	6 0	11 13	Toulon	11/8/80	Sevilla
Szczesny Wojciech (G)	5 10	11 11	Warsaw	18/4/90	Scholar
Toral Harper Jon-Miquel (M)	6 3	13 00	Reus	5/2/95	Scholar
Van Persie Robin (F)	6 0	11 00	Rotterdam	6/8/83	Feyenoord
Vela Carlos (F)	5 9	10 05	Cancun	1/3/89	Osasuna
Vermaelen Thomas (D)	6 0	11 11	Antwerp	14/11/85	Ajax
Walcott Theo (F)	5 9	11 01	Stanmore	16/3/89	Southampton
Watt Sanchez (M)	5 11	12 00	Hackney	14/2/91	Scholar
Wilshere Jack (M)	5 7	11 03	Stevenage	1/1/92	Scholar
Yennaris Nico (D)	5 7	10 03	Leytonstone	23/5/93	Scholar

League Appearances: Andre Santos, C. 10(5); Arshavin, A. 8(11); Arteta, M. 29; Benayoun, Y. 10(9); Bendtner, N. (1); Chamakh, M. 1(10); Coquelin, F. 6(4); Diaby, A. (4); Djourou, J. 14(4); Frimpong, E. 3(3); Gervinho, 19(9); Gibbs, K. 15(1); Henry, T. (4); Jenkinson, C. 5(4); Koscielny, L. 33; Lansbury, H. (2); Mertesacker, P. 21; Miquel, I. 1(3); Nasri, S. 1; Oxlade-Chamberlain, A. 6(10); Park, C. (1); Ramsey, A. 27(7); Rosicky, T. 19(9); Sagna, B. 20(1); Song Billong, A. 34; Squillaci, S. (1); Szczesny, W. 38; Traore, A. 1; Van Persie, R. 37(1); Vermaelen, T. 28(1); Walcott, T. 32(3); Yennaris, N. (1).

Goals – League (74): Van Persie 30 (2 pens), Walcott 8, Arteta 6, Vermaelen 6, Benayoun 4, Gervinho 4, Andre Santos 2, Koscielny 2, Oxlade-Chamberlain 2, Ramsey 2, Arshavin 1, Chamakh 1, Gibbs 1, Henry 1, Rosicky 1, Sagna 1, Song Billong 1, own goal 1.

Carling Cup (5): Arshavin 1, Benyoun 1, Gibbs 1, Park 1, Oxlade-Chamberlain 1.

FA Cup (4): Van Persie 2 (2 pens), Henry 1, Walcott 1.

Champions League (13): Van Persie 5 (1 pen), Walcott 2, Andre Santos 1, Benayoun 1, Koscielny 1, Oxlade-Chamberlain 1, Ramsey 1, Rosicky 1.

Ground: Emirates Stadium, Highbury House, 75 Drayton Park, Islington, London N5 1BU. Telephone: (020) 7619 5003.

Capacity: 60,361.

Record Attendance: 73,295 v Sunderland, Div 1, 9 March 1935 (at Highbury); 73,707 v RC Lens, UEFA Champions League, 25 November 1998 (at Wembley); 60,162 v Manchester U, FA Premier League, 3 November 2007 (at Emirates).

Manager: Arsène Wenger.

Most League Goals: 127, Division 1, 1930–31.

Highest League Scorer in Season: Ted Drake, 42, 1934–35.

Most League Goals in Total Aggregate: Thierry Henry, 174, 1999–2007.

Most Capped Player: Thierry Henry, 81 (123), France.

Most League Appearances: David O'Leary, 558, 1975–93.

Colours: Red shirts with white trim, white shorts, white stockings with red tops.

Honours – FA Premier League: Champions – 1997–98, 2001–02, 2003–04. **Football League:** Division 1 Champions – 1930–31, 1932–33, 1933–34, 1934–35, 1937–38, 1947–48, 1952–53, 1970–71, 1988–89, 1990–91. **FA Cup:** Winners – 1929–30, 1935–36,

1949–50, 1970–71, 1978–79, 1992–93, 1997–98, 2001–02, 2002–03, 2004–05. **Football League Cup:** Winners – 1986–87, 1992–93. **European Competitions: European Cup-Winners' Cup:** Winners – 1993–94. **Fairs Cup:** Winners – 1969–70.

ASTON VILLA   FA PREMIERSHIP

Agbonlahor Gabriel (F)	5 11	12 05	Birmingham	13/10/86	Scholar
Albrighton Marc (M)	6 2	12 06	Tamworth	18/11/89	Scholar
Baker Nathan (D)	6 2	11 11	Worcester	23/4/91	Scholar
Bannan Barry (D)	5 10	10 08	Glasgow	1/12/89	Scholar
Bent Darren (F)	5 11	12 07	Wandsworth	6/2/84	Sunderland
Burke Graham (F)	5 11	11 11	Dublin	21/9/93	Scholar
Cameron Courtney (D)			Northampton	22/1/93	Scholar
Carruthers Samir (F)	5 8	11 00	Islington	4/4/93	Scholar
Clark Ciaran (D)	6 2	12 00	Harrow	26/9/89	Scholar
Collins James M (D)	6 2	14 03	Newport	23/8/83	West Ham U
Delfouneso Nathan (F)	6 1	12 04	Birmingham	2/2/91	Scholar
Delph Fabian (D)	5 8	11 00	Bradford	21/11/89	Leeds U
Devine Danny (M)			Dublin	8/5/93	Scholar
Drennan Michael (F)			Kilkenny	2/2/94	Scholar
Dunne Richard (D)	6 2	15 10	Dublin	21/9/79	Manchester C
Gardner Gary (M)	6 2	12 13	Solihull	29/6/92	Scholar
Given Shay (G)	6 0	13 03	Lifford	20/4/76	Manchester C
Graham Jordan (M)			Coventry	5/3/95	Scholar
Guzan Brad (G)	6 4	14 11	Chicago	9/9/84	Chivas USA
Herd Chris (M)	5 9	11 04	Perth	4/4/89	Scholar
Hutton Alan (D)	6 1	11 05	Glasgow	30/11/84	Tottenham H
Ireland Stephen (F)	5 8	10 07	Cork	22/8/86	Manchester C
Johnson Daniel (M)	5 8	10 07	Kingston, Jam	8/10/92	Scholar
Lichaj Eric (D)	5 11	12 05	Chicago	17/11/88	Chicago M
Makoun Jean II (M)	5 8	10 12	Yaounde	29/5/83	Lyon
Marshall Andy (G)	6 3	14 08	Bury St Edmunds	14/4/75	Coventry C
N'Zogbia Charles (M)	5 9	11 00	Le Havre	28/5/86	Wigan Ath
Petrov Stilian (M)	5 11	11 09	Sofia	5/7/79	Celtic
Serrano Juan Jose (M)			Lleida	30/11/93	Scholar
Siegrist Benjamin (G)	6 4	13 05	Basle	31/1/92	Scholar
Stevens Enda (D)	6 0	12 04	Dublin	9/7/90	Shamrock R
Stieber Andras (M)			Zarvar	8/10/91	
Warnock Stephen (D)	5 7	11 09	Ormskirk	12/12/81	Blackburn R
Weimann Andreas (F)	5 9	11 09	Vienna	5/8/91	Scholar
Williams Derrick (D)	5 11	11 11	Waterford	17/1/93	Scholar

League Appearances: Agbonlahor, G. 32(1); Albrighton, M. 15(11); Baker, N. 6(2); Bannan, B. 10(18); Bent, D. 21(1); Carruthers, S. (3); Clark, C. 13(2); Collins, J. 31(1); Cuellar, C. 17(1); Delfouneso, N. 1(5); Delph, F. 10(1); Dunne, R. 28; Gardner, G. 5(9); Given, S. 32; Guzan, B. 6(1); Herd, C. 19; Heskey, E. 18(10); Hutton, A. 29(2); Ireland, S. 19(5); Jenas, J. 1(2); Keane, R. 5(1); Lichaj, E. 9(1); N'Zogbia, C. 24(6); Petrov, S. 26(1); Warnock, S. 34(1); Weimann, A. 5(9); Young, L. 2.
Goals – League (37): Bent 9 (2 pens), Agbonlahor 5, Petrov 4, Keane 3, Albrighton 2, N'Zogbia 2, Warnock 2, Weimann 2, Bannan 1 (1 pen), Clark 1, Collins 1, Dunne 1, Herd 1, Heskey 1, Ireland 1, Lichaj 1.
Carling Cup (2): Delfouneso 1, Lichaj 1.
FA Cup (5): Agbonlahor 1, Albrighton 1, Bent 1, Clark 1, Dunne 1.
Ground: Villa Park, Birmingham B6 6HE. Telephone: (0121) 327 2299.
Capacity: 42,582.
Record Attendance: 76,588 v Derby Co, FA Cup 6th rd, 2 March 1946.
Manager: Paul Lambert.

Most League Goals: 128, Division 1, 1930–31.
Highest League Scorer in Season: 'Pongo' Waring, 49, Division 1, 1930–31.
Most League Goals in Total Aggregate: Harry Hampton, 215, 1904–15.
Most Capped Player: Steve Staunton 64 (102), Republic of Ireland.
Most League Appearances: Charlie Aitken, 561, 1961–76.
Colours: Claret body, blue sleeve shirts, white shorts, sky blue stockings.
Honours – Football League: Division 1 Champions – 1893–94, 1895–96, 1896–97, 1898–99, 1899–1900, 1909–10, 1980–81. Division 2 Champions – 1937–38, 1959–60. Division 3 Champions – 1971–72. **FA Cup:** Winners – 1887, 1895, 1897, 1905, 1913, 1920, 1957. **Football League Cup:** Winners – 1961, 1975, 1977, 1994, 1996. **European Competitions: European Cup:** Winners – 1981–82. **European Super Cup:** Winners – 1982–83. **Intertoto Cup:** Winners – 2001, 2008.

BARNET   FL CHAMPIONSHIP 2

Byrne Mark (M)	5 9	11 00	Dublin	9/11/88	Nottingham F
Holmes Ricky (M)	6 2	11 11	Southend	19/6/87	Chelmsford C
Kabba Steven (F)	5 10	11 04	Lambeth	7/3/81	Brentford
Kamdjo Clovis (D)	5 11	12 02	Cameroon	15/12/90	Reading Youth
O'Brien Liam (G)	6 1	12 06	Ruislip	30/11/91	Portsmouth
Saville Jack (D)	6 3	12 00	Camberley	2/4/91	Southampton
Vilhete Mauro (M)	5 8	11 09	Sintra	10/5/93	Scholar
Yiadom Andy (M)	5 11	11 11	Holloway	2/12/91	Braintree T

League Appearances: Baseya, C. (2); Borrowdale, G. 11; Brill, D. 36; Byrne, M. 38(5); Deering, S. 39(5); Dennehy, D. 18(1); Downing, P. 25(1); Fraser, T. 2(3); Gambin, L. (1); Geohaghon, E. (2); Hajrovic, S. 7(3); Hector, M. 26(1); Holmes, R. 33(8); Hughes, M. 44(1); Kabba, S. 5(4); Kamdjo, C. 41; Leach, D. 9(1); Marshall, M. 24(1); May, B. 9(2); McCallum, G. (2); McGleish, S. 5(4); McLeod, I. 43(1); Mustoe, J. 15(3); N'Diaye, A. 2(4); O'Brien, L. 10; Obita, J. 3(2); Owusu, L. (5); Parkes, J. 11; Price, J. 5; Saville, J. 14(3); Senda, D. 19; Taylor, C. 2(16); Uddin, A. 9; Vilhete, M. (3); Yiadom, A. 1(6).
Goals – League (52): McLeod 18 (5 pens), Holmes 8, Byrne 5, May 4, Deering 3, Hughes 3, Kamdjo 3, Hector 2, Kabba 1 (1 pen), Leach 1, Marshall 1, Price 1, Taylor 1, Yiadom 1.
Carling Cup (3): Holmes 1, Hughes 1, Kabba 1.
FA Cup (3): Kamdjo 1, McLeod 1, Taylor 1.
J Paint Trophy (9): McLeod 3 (2 pens), Marshall 2, Holmes 1, Hughes 1, Kabba 1, Taylor 1.
Ground: Underhill Stadium, Barnet Lane, Barnet, Herts EN5 2DN. Telephone: (020) 8441 6932.
Capacity: 5,345.
Record Attendance: 11,026 v Wycombe Wanderers, FA Amateur Cup 4th rd, 1951–52.
Head Coach: Mark Robson.
Most League Goals: 81, Division 4, 1991–92.
Highest League Scorer in Season: Dougie Freedman, 24, Division 3, 1994–95.
Most League Goals in Total Aggregate: Sean Devine, 47, 1995–99.
Most Capped Player: Ken Charlery, 4, St Lucia.
Most League Appearances: Lee Harrison, 270, 1996–2002, 2006–09.
Colours: All black with amber trim.
Honours – Football League: GMVC: Winners – 1990–91. **Football Conference:** Winners – 2004–05. **FA Amateur Cup:** Winners 1945–46.

BARNSLEY   FL CHAMPIONSHIP

Butterfield Jacob (D)	5 10	11 00	Bradford	10/6/90	Scholar
Clark Jordan (F)	6 0	11 07	Barnsley	22/9/93	Scholar

Collins Lee (D)	6 1	11 10	Telford	23/9/83	Wolverhampton W
Dagnall Chris (F)	5 8	12 03	Liverpool	15/4/86	Scunthorpe U
Davies Craig (F)	6 2	13 05	Burton-on-Trent	9/1/86	Chesterfield
Dawson Stephen (M)	5 9	11 09	Dublin	4/12/85	Leyton Orient
Digby Paul (M)	5 9	10 00	Sheffield	2/2/95	Scholar
Done Matt (M)	5 10	10 02	Oswestry	22/6/88	Rochdale
Edwards Rob (D)	6 1	11 10	Telford	25/12/82	Blackpool
Foster Stephen (D)	6 0	11 05	Warrington	10/9/80	Burnley
Golbourne Scott (M)	5 8	11 08	Bristol	29/2/88	Exeter C
Hassell Bobby (D)	5 10	12 00	Derby	4/6/80	Mansfield T
McNulty Jim (D)	6 1	12 00	Runcorn	13/2/85	Brighton & HA
Noble-Lazarus Reuben (F)	5 11	13 07	Huddersfield	16/8/93	Youth
O'Brien Jim (F)	6 0	11 11	Alexandria	28/9/87	Motherwell
Perkins David (D)	5 6	11 06	Heysham	21/6/82	Colchester U
Rose Danny (F)	5 8	9 02	Barnsley	10/12/93	Scholar
Steele Luke (G)	6 2	12 00	Peterborough	24/9/84	WBA
Stones John (D)	6 2	11 00	Barnsley	28/5/94	Scholar
Wiseman Scott (D)	6 0	11 06	Hull	9/10/85	Rochdale

League Appearances: Addison, M. 9(2); Butterfield, J. 24; Button, D. 9; Clark, J. 1(1); Collins, L. 4(3); Cotterill, D. 6(5); Dagnall, C. 4(5); Davies, C. 33(7); Dawson, S. 9(3); Digby, P. 2(2); Done, M. 22(9); Doyle, N. 16(5); Drinkwater, D. 16(1); Edwards, R. 17; Foster, S. 41; Golbourne, S. 10(2); Gray, A. 25(7); Hassell, B. 17(2); Haynes, D. 4(8); Higginbotham, K. 2(3); McEveley, J. 25(4); McNulty, J. 43(1); Noble-Lazarus, R. 2(6); Nouble, F. 5(1); O'Brien, J. 23(8); Park, C. 1(2); Perkins, D. 31(2); Preece, D. 1; Ranger, N. 3(2); Rose, D. 2(2); Smith, K. 10(2); Steele, L. 36; Stones, J. (2); Taylor, A. (1); Tonge, M. 7(3); Vaz Te, R. 12(10); Wiseman, S. 34(9).

Goals – League (49): Davies 11 (1 pen), Vaz Te 10, Gray 8 (2 pens), Butterfield 5, Done 4, McNulty 2, O'Brien 2, Cotterill 1, Drinkwater 1, Foster 1, Golbourne 1, Perkins 1, Wiseman 1, own goal 1.

Carling Cup (0).

FA Cup (2): Vaz Te 2.

Ground: Oakwell Stadium, Grove Street, Barnsley, South Yorkshire S71 1ET. Telephone: (01226) 211 211.

Capacity: 23,186.

Record Attendance: 40,255 v Stoke C, FA Cup 5th rd, 15 February 1936.

Manager: Keith Hill.

Most League Goals: 118, Division 3 (N), 1933–34.

Highest League Scorer in Season: Cecil McCormack, 33, Division 2, 1950–51.

Most League Goals in Total Aggregate: Ernest Hine, 123, 1921–26 and 1934–38.

Most Capped Player: Gerry Taggart, 35 (50), Northern Ireland.

Most League Appearances: Barry Murphy, 514, 1962–78.

Colours: Red shirts with white trim, white shorts, red stockings.

Honours – Football League: Division 3 (N) Champions – 1933–34, 1938–39, 1954–55.

FA Cup: Winners – 1912.

BIRMINGHAM CITY   FL CHAMPIONSHIP

Asante Akwasi (F)	5 7	10 00	Amsterdam	22/9/92	Scholar
Burke Chris (M)	5 9	10 10	Glasgow	2/12/83	Cardiff C
Butland Jack (G)	6 4	12 00	Clevedon	10/3/93	Scholar
Caldwell Steven (D)	6 2	13 12	Stirling	12/9/80	Wigan Ath
Davies Curtis (D)	6 2	11 13	Waltham Forest	15/3/85	Aston Villa
Deaman Jack (D)			Camden	18/5/93	Wrexham Scholar
Doyle Colin (G)	6 5	14 05	Cork	12/8/85	
Elliott Wade (M)	5 10	10 03	Eastleigh	14/12/78	Burnley
Fahey Keith (M)	5 10	12 07	Dublin	15/1/83	St Patrick's Ath

Foster Ben (G)	6 2	12 08	Leamington Spa	3/4/83	Manchester U
Gnahore Eddy (M)			Paris	14/11/93	Scholar
Gomis Morgaro (M)	5 9	11 00	Le Blanc-Mesnil	14/7/85	Dundee U
Jervis Jake (F)	6 3	12 13	Birmingham	17/9/91	Scholar
Kerr Fraser (D)	6 3	13 03	Motherwell	17/1/93	Scholar
King Marlon (F)	5 10	12 10	Dulwich	26/4/80	Coventry C
Murphy David (D)	6 1	12 03	Hartlepool	1/3/84	Hibernian
Mutch Jordon (M)	5 9	10 03	Derby	2/12/91	Scholar
Ntambwe Brice (M)			Brussels	29/4/93	Scholar
Pablo (D)	6 3	13 07	Madrigueras	3/8/81	WBA
Packwood Will (M)			Concord	21/5/93	Scholar
Redmond Nathan (M)	5 8	11 11	Birmingham	6/3/94	Scholar
Rooney Adam (F)	5 10	12 02	Dublin	21/4/87	Inverness CT
Spector Jonathan (D)	6 0	12 08	Chicago	1/3/86	West Ham U
Zigic Nikola (F)	6 8	14 02	Backa Topola	25/9/80	Valencia

League Appearances: Beausejour, J. 22; Burke, C. 45(1); Caldwell, S. 43; Carr, S. 20; Davies, C. 42; Doyle, C. 4(1); Elliott, W. 15(14); Fahey, K. 34(1); Gomis, M. 13(3); Huseklepp, E. 4(7); Jerome, C. (1); King, M. 37(3); Murphy, D. 30(3); Mutch, J. 18(3); Myhill, B. 42; N'Daw, G. 17(2); Pablo, 7(6); Ramage, P. 14; Redmond, N. 5(19); Ridgewell, L. 13(1); Rooney, A. 6(12); Spector, J. 31; Townsend, A. 11(4); Wood, C. 13(10); Zigic, N. 20(15).
Goals – League (78): King 16 (2 pens), Burke 12, Zigic 11, Wood 9, Davies 5, Redmond 5, Fahey 4, Murphy 4, Rooney 4 (1 pen), Elliott 2 (2 pens), Huseklepp 2, Mutch 2, Beausejour 1, own goal 1.
Carling Cup (0).
FA Cup (6): Elliott 2, Rooney 2, Murphy 1, Redmond 1.
Europa League (11): King 2 (1 pen), Murphy 2, Wood 2, Beausejour 1, Burke 1, Elliott 1, Redmond 1, Rooney 1.
Play-Offs (2): Davies 1, Zigic 1.
Ground: St Andrews Stadium, Birmingham B9 4RL. Telephone: (0844) 557 1875.
Capacity: 30,079.
Record Attendance: 66,844 v Everton, FA Cup 5th rd, 11 February 1939.
Manager: Lee Clark.
Most League Goals: 103, Division 2, 1893–94 (only 28 games).
Highest League Scorer in Season: Joe Bradford, 29, Division 1, 1927–28.
Most League Goals in Total Aggregate: Joe Bradford, 249, 1920–35.
Most Capped Player: Maik Taylor, 50 (88), Northern Ireland.
Most League Appearances: Frank Womack, 491, 1908–28.
Colours: Blue shirts with white trim, white shorts, blue stockings.
Honours – Football League: Division 2 Champions – 1892–93, 1920–21, 1947–48, 1954–55, 1994–95. **Football League Cup:** Winners – 1963, 2011. **Leyland Daf Cup:** Winners – 1991. **Auto Windscreens Shield:** Winners – 1995.

BLACKBURN ROVERS   FL CHAMPIONSHIP

Anderson Myles (D)			Westminster	9/1/90	Aberdeen
Blackman Nick (F)	6 2	11 08	Whitefield	11/11/89	Macclesfield T
Bunn Mark (G)	6 0	12 02	Southgate	16/11/84	Northampton T
Cotton Robert (M)			Rotherham	15/9/94	Scholar
Dann Scott (D)	6 2	12 00	Liverpool	14/2/87	Birmingham C
Dilo Christopher (G)			Paris	5/1/94	Scholar
Dunn David (M)	5 10	12 03	Gt Harwood	27/12/79	Birmingham C
Edwards Ryan (D)			Liverpool	7/10/93	Scholar
Evans Micah (F)			Manchester	3/3/93	Portogruaro
Formica Mauro (M)	5 9	10 01	Rosario	4/4/88	Newell's Old Boys
Givet Gael (D)	5 11	11 11	Arles	9/10/81	Marseille

Goodwillie David (F)	5 9	11 02	Stirling	28/3/89	Dundee U
Hands Reece (M)			Rotherham	6/10/93	Scholar
Hanley Grant (D)	6 2	12 00	Dumfries	20/11/91	Scholar
Hanley Raheem (D)	5 8	11 00	Blackburn	24/3/94	Manchester U Scholar
Henley Adam (D)	5 10	12 02	Knoxville	14/6/94	Scholar
Hoilett Junior (M)	5 8	11 00	Ottowa	5/6/90	Scholar
Kean Jake (G)	6 4	11 13	Derby	4/2/91	Derby Co Scholar
Lenihan Darragh (M)			Dublin	16/3/94	Belvedere
Linganzi Amine (M)	6 1	10 00	Algiers	16/11/89	St Etienne
Lowe Jason (M)	6 0	12 08	Wigan	2/9/91	Scholar
Molina Hugo (D)			Spain	30/11/93	Scholar
Morris Josh (M)	5 9	10 00	Preston	30/9/91	Scholar
N'Zonzi Steven (M)	6 3	11 11	Paris	15/12/88	Amiens
O'Connor Anthony (D)			Cork	25/10/92	Scholar
O'Sullivan John (M)			Birmingham	18/9/93	Scholar
Olsson Marcus (M)	5 11	10 10	Gavle	17/5/88	Halmstad
Olsson Martin (D)	5 7	12 12	Gavle	17/5/88	Hogaborg
Orr Bradley (D)	6 0	11 11	Liverpool	1/11/82	QPR
Payne Tim (F)			New Zealand	10/1/94	Waitakere U
Pedersen Morten (F)	5 11	11 00	Vadso	8/9/81	Tromso
Petrovic Radosav (M)	6 4	13 01	Ub	8/3/89	Partizan Belgrade
Pivkovski Filip (M)			Sweden	31/1/94	Scholar
Robinson Paul (G)	6 1	14 07	Beverley	15/10/79	Tottenham H
Rochina Ruben (F)	5 11	11 00	Sagunto	23/3/91	Barcelona B
Slew Jordan (F)	6 3	12 10	Sheffield	7/9/92	Sheffield U
Usai Sebastian (G)			Brisbane	28/2/90	Brisbane Strikers
Vukcevic Simon (M)	5 10	12 02	Podgorica	29/1/86	Sporting Lisbon
Yakubu Ayegbeni (F)	6 0	14 07	Benin City	22/11/82	Everton

League Appearances: Blackman, N. (1); Bunn, M. 3; Dann, S. 27; Dunn, D. 21(5); Emerton, B. 2; Formica, M. 25(9); Givet, G. 21(1); Goodwillie, D. 4(16); Grella, V. (1); Hanley, G. 19(4); Henley, A. 4(3); Hoilett, D. 34; Kean, J. 1; Lowe, J. 30(2); Modeste, A. 3(6); Morris, J. (2); N'Zonzi, S. 31(1); Nelsen, R. 1; Olsson, Marcus 10(2); Olsson, Martin 23(4); Orr, B. 10(2); Pedersen, M. 33; Petrovic, R. 10(9); Roberts, J. 5(5); Robinson, P. 34; Rochina, R. 9(9); Salgado, M. 9; Samba, C. 16; Slew, J. (1); Vukcevic, S. 4(3); Yakubu, A. 29(1).

Goals – League (48): Yakubu 17 (4 pens), Hoilett 7, Formica 4, Pedersen 3, Dunn 2, Goodwillie 2, N'Zonzi 2, Rochina 2, Samba 2, Dann 1, Hanley 1, Vukcevic 1, own goals 4.

Carling Cup (10): Rochina 4, Givet 1, Goodwillie 1, Pedersen 1, Roberts 1 (pen), Vukcevic 1, Yakubu 1 (pen).

FA Cup (1): Goodwillie 1.

Ground: Ewood Park, Blackburn, Lancs BB2 4JF. Telephone: (0871) 702 1875.

Capacity: 31,367.

Record Attendance: 62,522 v Bolton W, FA Cup 6th rd, 2 March 1929.

Manager: Steve Kean.

Most League Goals: 114, Division 2, 1954–55.

Highest League Scorer in Season: Ted Harper, 43, Division 1, 1925–26.

Most League Goals in Total Aggregate: Simon Garner, 168, 1978–92.

Most Capped Player: Henning Berg, 58 (100), Norway.

Most League Appearances: Derek Fazackerley, 596, 1970–86.

Colours: Blue and white halved shirts, white shorts, blue stockings.

Honours – FA Premier League: Champions – 1994–95. **Football League:** Division 1 Champions – 1911–12, 1913–14. Division 2 Champions – 1938–39. Division 3 Champions – 1974–75. **FA Cup:** Winners – 1884, 1885, 1886, 1890, 1891, 1928. **Football League Cup:** Winners – 2002. **Full Members' Cup:** Winners – 1986–87.

Addai Alex (M)			Stepney		Scholar
Almond Louis (F)	5 11	12 00	Blackburn	5/1/92	Scholar
Angel (M)	5 9	11 13	Girona	31/1/86	Girona
Barkhuizen Tom (F)	5 9	11 00	Blackpool	4/7/93	Scholar
Basham Chris (M)	5 11	12 08	Hebburn	20/7/88	Bolton W
Bignot Paul (D)	6 1	12 03	Birmingham	14/2/86	Crewe Alex
Bruna Gerardo (M)	5 8	10 02	Mendoza	29/1/91	Liverpool
Cathcart Craig (D)	6 2	11 06	Belfast	6/2/89	Manchester U
Crainey Stephen (D)	5 9	9 11	Glasgow	22/6/81	Leeds U
Dodd Adam (D)			Kirkham	25/6/93	Scholar
Eardley Neal (M)	5 11	11 10	Llandudno	6/11/88	Oldham Ath
Eastham Ashley (D)	6 3	12 05	Preston	22/3/91	Scholar
Evatt Ian (D)	6 3	13 12	Coventry	19/11/81	QPR
Ferguson Barry (M)	5 7	9 10	Hamilton	2/2/78	Birmingham C
Fleck John (M)	5 9	11 05	Glasgow	24/8/91	Rangers
Gilks Matthew (G)	6 3	13 12	Rochdale	4/6/82	Norwich C
Grandin Elliot (F)	5 10	10 07	Caen	17/10/87	CSKA Sofia
Halstead Mark (G)	6 3	14 00	Blackpool	1/9/90	Scholar
Harris Robert (D)	5 8	10 00	Glasgow	28/8/87	Queen of the S
Ince Thomas (F)	5 10	10 05	Liverpool	30/1/92	Liverpool
John-Baptiste Alex (D)	6 0	11 11	Sutton-in-Ashfield	31/1/86	Mansfield T
Kettings Chris (G)	6 2	12 04	Bolton	25/10/92	Stuttgart
Lua-Lua Lomano (F)	5 8	12 02	Kinshasa	28/12/80	Omonia
Phillips Kevin (F)	5 7	11 02	Hitchin	25/7/73	Birmingham C
Phillips Matthew (M)	6 0	12 10	Aylesbury	13/3/91	Wycombe W
Southern Keith (M)	5 10	12 06	Gateshead	24/4/81	Everton
Sutherland Craig (F)	6 0	11 11	Edinburgh	17/12/88	N Carolina Univ
Sylvestre Ludovic (M)	6 0	11 09	Le Blanc-Mesnil	5/2/84	Mlada Boleslav
Taylor-Fletcher Gary (F)	6 0	11 00	Widnes	4/6/81	Huddersfield T
Tomsett Liam (M)			Ulverston	1/11/92	Scholar

League Appearances: Angel, 10(5); Basham, C. 8(9); Bednar, R. 3(6); Bogdanovic, D. 1(7); Bruna, G. (1); Cathcart, C. 27; Clarke, B. 4(5); Crainey, S. 40(2); Dicko, N. 4(6); Dobbie, S. 5(2); Eardley, N. 22(4); Evatt, I. 37(2); Ferguson, B. 40(2); Fleck, J. 4(3); Gilks, M. 42; Grandin, E. 4(3); Harris, R. 4(1); Hill, M. 4; Howard, M. 4; Hurst, J. (2); Ince, T. 22(11); John-Baptiste, A. 43; Lua-Lua, L. 18(11); McManaman, C. 9(5); Ormerod, B. 10(7); Phillips, K. 20(18); Phillips, M. 25(8); Shelvey, J. 10; Southern, K. 24(1); Sutherland, C. 2(5); Sylvestre, L. 20(8); Taylor-Fletcher, G. 34(3); Wilson, D. 6.

Goals – League (79): Phillips, K. 16, Taylor-Fletcher 8, Phillips, M. 7 (1 pen), Ince 6, Shelvey 6 (1 pen), Dobbie 5 (2 pens), Dicko 4, Lua-Lua 4, Crainey 3, Evatt 3, Basham 2, Bogdanovic 2, Grandin 2, McManaman 2, Angel 1, Bednar 1, Eardley 1, Ferguson 1, John-Baptiste 1, Ormerod 1, Southern 1, Sylvestre 1, own goal 1.

Carling Cup (0).

FA Cup (9): Phillips, M. 4, LuaLua 2, Ince 1, Phillips, K. 1 (pen), Sylvestre 1.

Play-Offs (4): Dobbie 1, Ince 1, Phillips, M. 1, own goal 1.

Ground: Bloomfield Road, Seasiders Way, Blackpool FY1 6JJ. Telephone: (0871) 6221 953.

Capacity: 9,491.

Record Attendance: 38,098 v Wolverhampton W, Division 1, 17 September 1955.

Manager: Ian Holloway.

Most League Goals: 98, Division 2, 1929–30.

Highest League Scorer in Season: Jimmy Hampson, 45, Division 2, 1929–30.

Most League Goals in Total Aggregate: Jimmy Hampson, 248, 1927–38.

Most Capped Player: Jimmy Armfield, 43, England.

Most League Appearances: Jimmy Armfield, 568, 1952–71.

Colours: Tangerine shirts with white trim, white shorts, tangerine stockings with white tops.
Honours – Football League: Division 2 Champions – 1929–30. **FA Cup:** Winners – 1953.
Anglo-Italian Cup: Winners – 1971. **LDV Vans Trophy:** Winners – 2002, 2004.

BOLTON WANDERERS   FL CHAMPIONSHIP

Alonso Marcus (D)	6 2	13 05	Madrid	28/12/90	RM Castilla
Blakeman Adam (D)			Widnes	3/12/91	Scholar
Bogdan Adam (G)	6 4	14 02	Budapest	27/9/87	Vasas
Davies Kevin (F)	6 0	12 10	Sheffield	26/3/77	Southampton
Davies Mark (M)	5 11	11 06	Willenhall	18/2/88	Wolverhampton W
Eagles Chris (M)	5 10	11 07	Hemel Hempstead	19/11/85	Burnley
Eaves Tom (M)	6 3	13 07	Liverpool	14/1/92	Oldham Ath
Holden Stuart (M)	5 10	11 07	Aberdeen	1/8/85	Houston Dynamo
Lainton Robert (G)	6 2	12 06	Ashton-under-Lyne	12/10/89	Scholar
Lee Chung Yong (M)	5 11	10 09	Seoul	2/7/88	FC Seoul
Mears Tyrone (D)	5 11	11 10	Stockport	18/2/83	Burnley
Muamba Fabrice (M)	6 1	11 10	DR Congo	6/4/88	Birmingham C
N'Gog David (F)	6 3	12 04	Paris	1/4/89	Liverpool
O'Halloran Michael (F)	6 2	12 06	Glasgow	6/1/91	Scholar
Petrov Martin (F)	6 0	12 02	Vzatza	15/1/79	Manchester C
Pratley Darren (M)	6 1	10 12	Barking	22/4/85	Swansea C
Ream Tim (D)	6 1	11 05	St Louis	5/10/87	New York Red Bulls
Reo-Coker Nigel (M)	5 8	12 01	Southwark	14/5/84	Aston Villa
Ricketts Sam (D)	6 1	12 01	Aylesbury	11/10/81	Hull C
Riley Joe (D)	6 0	11 02	Salford	13/10/91	Scholar
Sampson Jack (F)			Wigan	14/4/93	Scholar
Sordell Marvin (F)	5 9	12 06	Pinner	17/2/91	Watford
Vela Joshua (M)	5 11	11 07	Salford	14/12/93	Scholar
Wheater David (D)	6 5	12 12	Redcar	14/2/87	Middlesbrough

League Appearances: Alonso, M. 4(1); Blake, R. (1); Bogdan, A. 20; Boyata, D. 13(1); Cahill, G. 19; Davies, K. 21(10); Davies, M. 29(6); Eagles, C. 26(8); Gardner, R. 2(2); Jaaskelainen, J. 18; Kakuta, G. (4); Klasnic, I. 16(13); Knight, Z. 21(4); Lee, C. (2); Mears, T. 1; Miyaichi, R. 8(4); Muamba, F. 18(2); N'Gog, D. 24(9); Petrov, M. 30(1); Pratley, D. 14(11); Ream, T. 13; Reo-Coker, N. 37; Ricketts, S. 20; Riley, J. 2(1); Robinson, P. 15(2); Sordell, M. (3); Steinsson, G. 20(3); Tuncay, S. 3(13); Vela, J. (3); Wheater, D. 24.
Goals – League (46): Klasnic 8 (1 pen), Davies, K. 6, Davies, M. 4, Eagles 4, Petrov 4 (4 pens), N'Gog 3, Reo-Coker 3, Cahill 2, Wheater 2, Alonso 1, Boyata 1, Muamba 1, Pratley 1, Ricketts 1, Steinsson 1, own goals 4.
Carling Cup (5): Eagles 1, Kakuta 1, Muamba 1, Petrov 1, Tuncay 1.
FA Cup (9): Davies, K. 2, Eagles 1, Klasnic 1, Miyaichi 1, N'Gog 1, Petrov 1, Pratley 1, Wheater 1.
Ground: The Reebok Stadium, Burnden Way, Lostock, Bolton BL6 6JW. Telephone: (0844) 871 2932.
Capacity: 28,101.
Record Attendance: 69,912 v Manchester C, FA Cup 5th rd, 18 February 1933 (at Burnden Park); 28,353 v Leicester C, FA Premier League, 23 December 2003 (at The Reebok Stadium).
Manager: Owen Coyle.
Most League Goals: 100, Division 1, 1996–97.
Highest League Scorer in Season: Joe Smith, 38, Division 1, 1920–21.
Most League Goals in Total Aggregate: Nat Lofthouse, 255, 1946–61.
Most Capped Player: Ricardo Gardner, 63 (109), Jamaica.
Most League Appearances: Eddie Hopkinson, 519, 1956–70.
Colours: White shirts with blue body trim, blue shorts, white stockings.

Honours – Football League: Division 1 Champions – 1996–97. Division 2 Champions – 1908–09, 1977–78. Division 3 Champions – 1972–73. **FA Cup:** Winners – 1923, 1926, 1929, 1958. **Sherpa Van Trophy:** Winners – 1989.

AFC BOURNEMOUTH   FL CHAMPIONSHIP 1

Arter Harry (M)	5 9	11 07	Sidcup	28/12/89	Charlton Ath
Barrett Adam (D)	5 10	12 00	Dagenham	29/11/79	Crystal Palace
Bowles Gary (D)			Yeovil	30/12/88	Dorchester T
Carmichael Josh (M)	6 0	12 06	Poole	27/9/94	Youth
Cook Steve (D)	6 1	12 13	Hastings	19/4/91	Brighton & HA
Cooper Shaun (D)	5 10	10 05	Newport (IW)	5/10/83	Portsmouth
Daniels Charlie (M)	6 1	12 12	Harlow	7/9/86	Tottenham H
Flahavan Darryl (G)	5 11	12 05	Southampton	9/9/77	Crystal Palace
Fletcher Steve (F)	6 2	14 07	Hartlepool	26/7/72	Chesterfield
Fogden Wes (F)	5 8	10 04	Brighton	12/4/88	Brighton & HA
Francis Simon (D)	6 0	12 06	Nottingham	16/2/85	Southend U
Gregory Steven (D)	6 1	12 04	Haddenham	19/3/87	Wycombe W
Jalal Shwan (G)	6 2	14 02	Baghdad	14/8/83	Peterborough U
MacDonald Shaun (M)	6 1	11 04	Swansea	17/6/88	Swansea C
Malone Scott (D)	6 2	11 11	Rowley Regis	25/3/91	Wolverhampton W
McDermott Donal (F)	6 6	12 00	Co. Meath	19/10/89	Huddersfield T
Molesley Mark (M)	6 1	12 07	Hillingdon	11/3/81	Grays
Partington Joe (M)	5 11	11 13	Portsmouth	1/4/90	Scholar
Pugh Marc (M)	5 11	11 04	Bacup	2/4/87	Hereford U
Purches Stephen (D)	5 11	11 13	Ilford	14/1/80	Leyton Orient
Sheringham Charlie (F)	6 1	11 06	Chingford	17/4/88	Crystal Palace
Stockley Jayden (F)	6 2	12 07	Poole	10/10/93	School
Strugnell Dan (D)	6 1	12 08	Christchurch	30/6/92	Youth
Thomas Wesley (F)	5 10	11 00	Barking	23/1/87	Cheltenham T
Tubbs Matt (F)	5 9	11 00	Salisbury	15/7/84	Crawley T
Zubar Stephane (D)			Guadeloupe	9/10/86	Plymouth Arg

League Appearances: Addison, M. 14; Arter, H. 28(6); Barrett, A. 21; Baudry, M. 5(2); Byrne, N. 9; Carmichael, J. (1); Cook, S. 26; Cooper, S. 25(1); Cummings, W. 10(4); Daniels, C. 20(1); Doble, R. 4(3); Feeney, L. 5; Flahavan, D. 44; Fletcher, S. 2(18); Fogden, W. 20(7); Francis, S. 29; Gregory, S. 23(5); Hines, Z. 7(1); Ings, D. 1; Jalal, S. 2(1); Lovell, S. 1(1); MacDonald, S. 22(3); Malone, S. 28(4); McDermott, D. 10(4); Molesley, M. 4(7); Parsons, A. (1); Partington, J. 1(4); Peters, J. 8; Pugh, M. 42; Purches, S. 20(4); Sheringham, C. 2(4); Stockley, J. 1(9); Strugnell, D. (1); Symes, M. 7(8); Taylor, L. 7(11); Thomas, W. 36; Tubbs, M. 5(2); Wakefield, J. (2); Zubar, S. 17(5).
Goals – League (48): Thomas, W. 11, Pugh 8, Arter 5 (2 pens), Malone 5, Fogden 3, Symes 3 (2 pens), Daniels 2 (1 pen), Gregory 2, Addison 1, Barrett 1, Fletcher 1, Hines 1, MacDonald 1, McDermott 1, Sheringham 1, Tubbs 1, own goal 1.
Carling Cup (6): Taylor 2, Cooper 1, Feeney 1, Lovell 1, Pugh 1.
FA Cup (5): Arter 1, Malone 1, Purches 1, Zubar 1, own goal 1.
J Paint Trophy (7): Pugh 3, Stockley 2, MacDonald 1, own goal 1.
Ground: Seward Stadium, Kings Park, Bournemouth, Dorset BH7 7AF. Telephone: (0844) 576 1910.
Capacity: 10,375 (with temporary stand, 9,776 without).
Record Attendance: 28,799 v Manchester U, FA Cup 6th rd, 2 March 1957.
Manager: Paul Groves.
Most League Goals: 88, Division 3 (S), 1956–57.
Highest League Scorer in Season: Ted MacDougall, 42, 1970–71.
Most League Goals in Total Aggregate: Ron Eyre, 202, 1924–33.
Most Capped Player: Gerry Peyton, 7 (33), Republic of Ireland.
Most League Appearances: Steve Fletcher, 617, 1992–2007; 2008–12.

Colours: Red shirts with thin black vertical stripes, black shorts, black stockings.
Honours – Football League: Division 3 Champions – 1986–87. **Associate Members' Cup:** Winners – 1984.

BRADFORD CITY   FL CHAMPIONSHIP 2

Branston Guy (D)	6 1	15 01	Leicester	9/1/79	Torquay U
Burns Andrew (D)			Liverpool	2/7/93	Bolton W Scholar
Duke Matt (G)	6 5	13 03	Sheffield	16/7/77	Hull C
Hannah Ross (F)	5 9	11 11	Sheffield	14/5/86	Matlock T
Hanson James (F)	6 4	12 04	Bradford	9/11/87	Guiseley
Jones Richie (M)	6 0	11 00	Manchester	26/9/86	Oldham Ath
McLaughlin Jon (G)	6 2	13 00	Edinburgh	9/9/87	Harrogate T
Oliver Luke (D)	6 6	14 05	Acton	1/5/84	Wycombe W
Overson Dean (D)			Stoke	16/6/93	Burnley Scholar
Ramsden Simon (D)	6 0	12 06	Bishop Auckland	17/12/81	Rochdale
Ravenhill Ricky (M)	5 10	11 02	Doncaster	16/1/81	Darlington
Reid Kyel (M)	5 10	12 05	Deptford	26/11/87	Charlton Ath
Rowe Dominic (F)	5 6	10 07	Leeds	23/4/93	Scholar
Stephenson Darren (F)			Jamaica	6/3/93	Scholar
Stewart Mark (F)	5 7	10 07	Glasgow	22/6/88	Falkirk
Syers Dave (M)	6 0	11 07	Leeds	30/11/87	Harrogate T
Wells Nahki (F)	5 7	11 00	Bermuda	1/6/90	Carlisle U
Williams Steve (D)	6 4	13 06	Preston	24/4/87	Bamber Bridge

League Appearances: Atkinson, W. 6(6); Baker, A. (1); Branston, G. 15(1); Bryan, M. 5(3); Bullock, L. 14(5); Compton, J. 9(5); Dagnall, C. 5(2); Davies, A. 26; Dean, L. (1); Devitt, J. 5(2); Duke, M. 18; Fagan, C. 29(2); Flynn, M. 27(3); Fry, M. 5(1); Hannah, R. 4(14); Hansen, M. 4; Hanson, J. 36(3); Haworth, A. 2(1); Hunt, L. (1); Jansson, O. 1; Jones, R. 31(1); Kozluk, R. 17; McLaughlin, J. 23; Mitchell, C. 10(1); Moore, L. 16(1); O'Brien, L. 3(6); Oliver, L. 39; Ramsden, S. 16(1); Ravenhill, R. 25(1); Reed, A. 4; Reid, K. 32(5); Rodney, N. (5); Seip, M. 23; Smalley, D. 7(6); Stewart, M. 5(7); Syers, D. 8(10); Taylor, C. 1(2); Threlfall, R. 16(1); Wells, N. 18(15); Williams, S. 1.
Goals – League (54): Hanson 13, Wells 10, Fagan 7 (4 pens), Flynn 4 (4 pens), Reid 4, Davies 2, Hannah 2, Syers 2, Atkinson 1, Branston 1, Dagnall 1, Devitt 1, Jones 1, Mitchell 1, Oliver 1, Ravenhill 1, Seip 1, own goal 1.
Carling Cup (2): Compton 1, Flynn 1.
FA Cup (6): Wells 2, Fagan 1 (pen), Hannah 1, Hanson 1, own goal 1.
J Paint Trophy (3): Flynn 1, Oliver 1, own goal 1.
Ground: Coral Window Stadium, Valley Parade, Bradford, West Yorkshire BD8 7DY. Telephone: (0871) 978 1911.
Capacity: 25,136.
Record Attendance: 39,146 v Burnley, FA Cup 4th rd, 11 March 1911.
Manager: Phil Parkinson.
Most League Goals: 128, Division 3 (N), 1928–29.
Highest League Scorer in Season: David Layne, 34, Division 4, 1961–62.
Most League Goals in Total Aggregate: Bobby Campbell, 121, 1981–84, 1984–86.
Most Capped Player: Jamie Lawrence, 19 (24), Jamaica.
Most League Appearances: Cec Podd, 502, 1970–84.
Colours: Claret and amber striped shirts with claret sleeves, black shorts, black stockings.
Honours – Football League: Division 2 Champions – 1907–08. Division 3 Champions – 1984–85. Division 3 (N) Champions – 1928–29. **FA Cup:** Winners – 1911.

Balkestein Pim (D)	6 3	12 02	Gouda	29/4/87	Ipswich T
Bellamy Liam (M)			Wanstead	16/10/91	Welling U
Diagouraga Toumani (M)	6 2	11 05	Paris	10/6/87	Peterborough U
Donaldson Clayton (F)	6 1	11 07	Bradford	7/2/84	Crewe Alex
Douglas Jonathan (M)	5 11	11 11	Monaghan	22/11/81	Swindon T
Eger Marcel (D)	6 3	13 05	Nuremberg	23/3/83	St Pauli
Forrester Harry (F)	5 9	11 03	Milton Keynes	2/1/91	Aston Villa
German Antonio (F)	5 10	12 03	Wembley	26/12/91	QPR
Gounet Antoine (G)			France	16/10/88	Tours
Griffiths Sam (D)			Bilston	2/11/92	Wolverhampton W Scholar
Kamau Michael (D)			Slough	22/1/93	Fulham Scholar
Lee Richard (G)	6 0	12 06	Oxford	5/10/82	Watford
Legge Leon (D)	6 1	11 02	Bexhill	1/7/85	Tonbridge Angels
McGinn Niall (M)	6 0	13 01	Dungannon	20/7/87	Celtic
Moore Simon (G)	6 3	12 04	Sandown	19/5/90	Farnborough T
O'Connor Kevin (F)	5 11	12 00	Blackburn	24/2/82	Trainee
Pierre Aaron (D)			Southall	17/2/93	Fulham Scholar
Reeves Jake (M)	5 8	11 11	Lewisham	30/6/93	Scholar
Saunders Sam (M)	5 6	11 04	Erith	29/8/83	Dagenham & R
Weston Myles (M)	5 11	12 05	Lewisham	12/3/88	Notts Co
Woodman Craig (D)	5 9	10 11	Tiverton	22/12/82	Wycombe W

League Appearances: Adams, B. 6(1); Alexander, G. 20(4); Balkestein, P. 2(3); Bean, M. 22(10); Bennett, D. 5; Berahino, S. 5(3); Bidwell, J. 24; Clarkson, D. 4; Dean, H. 23(3); Diagouraga, T. 30(5); Donaldson, C. 40(6); Douglas, J. 46; Eger, M. 13(3); Forrester, H. 7(12); Forshaw, A. 6(1); German, A. 2(2); Grella, M. 1(10); Lee, R. 37; Legge, L. 23(5); Llera, M. 10(1); Logan, S. 26(1); MacDonald, C. (3); McGinn, N. 27(10); Moore, S. 9(1); Morrison, C. 4(4); Norris, L. (1); O'Connor, K. 9(5); Osborne, K. 22(3); Oyeleke, E. 1; Reeves, J. 7(1); Saunders, S. 29(8); Spillane, M. (1); Thompson, A. 16(4); Weston, M. 11(15); Wood, S. 3(2); Woodman, C. 18.
Goals – League (63): Alexander 12 (5 pens), Donaldson 11 (2 pens), Saunders 10, McGinn 5, Berahino 4, Diagouraga 4, Legge 4, Logan 3, Bean 2, Douglas 2, Bennett 1, Clarkson 1, Dean 1, O'Connor 1 (1 pen), Weston 1, own goal 1.
Carling Cup (0).
FA Cup (1): Saunders 1.
J Paint Trophy (12): Grella 4, Alexander 2, Adams 1, Diagouraga 1, Logan 1, O'Connor 1 (pen), Saunders 1, Thompson 1.
Ground: Griffin Park, Braemar Road, Brentford, Middlesex TW8 0NT. Telephone: (0845) 3456 442.
Capacity: 12,400.
Record Attendance: 38,678 v Leicester C, FA Cup 6th rd, 26 February 1949.
Manager: Uwe Rosler.
Most League Goals: 98, Division 4, 1962–63.
Highest League Scorer in Season: Jack Holliday, 38, Division 3 (S), 1932–33.
Most League Goals in Total Aggregate: Jim Towers, 153, 1954–61.
Most Capped Player: John Buttigieg, 22 (98), Malta.
Most League Appearances: Ken Coote, 514, 1949–64.
Colours: White shirts with red sleeves and black trim underneath, four separated red vertical stripes on body, black shorts, black stockings.

Honours – Football League: Championship 2 Winners – 2008–09. Division 2 Champions – 1934–35. Division 3 Champions – 1991–92, 1998–99. Division 3 (S) Champions – 1932–33. Division 4 Champions – 1962–63.

BRIGHTON & HOVE ALBION   FL CHAMPIONSHIP

Agdestein Torbjorn (F)	6 0	12 10	Norway	18/9/91	Stord
Ankergren Casper (G)	6 3	14 07	Koge	9/11/79	Leeds U
Barker George (F)	5 8	11 02	Portsmouth	26/9/91	Scholar
Barnes Ashley (F)	6 0	12 00	Bath	30/10/89	Plymouth Arg
Bergkamp Rowland (F)	6 4	13 03	Amstelveen	3/4/91	Excelsior
Brezovan Peter (G)	6 6	14 13	Bratislava	9/12/79	Swindon T
Bridcutt Liam (M)	5 9	11 07	Reading	8/5/89	Chelsea
Buckley Will (F)	6 0	13 02	Oldham	12/8/88	Watford
Calderon Inigo (D)	5 10	12 02	Vitoria	4/1/82	Alaves
Dickenson Ben (F)			Ferndown	9/8/93	Dorchester T
Dicker Gary (M)	6 0	12 00	Dublin	31/7/86	Stockport Co
Dunk Lewis (D)	6 3	12 02	Brighton	1/12/91	Scholar
East Daniel (G)			Northwich	18/3/93	Wolverhampton Scholar
El-Abd Adam (D)	5 10	13 05	Brighton	11/9/84	Scholar
Elphick Tommy (M)	5 11	11 07	Brighton	7/9/87	Scholar
Forster-Caskey Jake (M)	5 10	10 00	Southend	25/4/94	Scholar
Greer Gordon (D)	6 2	12 05	Glasgow	14/12/80	Swindon T
Hall Grant (D)	5 9	11 02	Brighton	29/10/91	Lewes
Harley Ryan (M)	5 11	11 00	Bristol	22/1/85	Swansea C
Hoskins Will (F)	5 11	11 02	Nottingham	6/5/86	Bristol R
Kasim Yaser (M)	5 11	11 07	Bagdad	10/5/91	Tottenham H Scholar
LuaLua Kazenga (F)	5 11	12 00	Kinshasa	10/12/90	Newcastle U
Mackail-Smith Craig (F)	6 3	12 04	Watford	25/2/84	Peterborough U
Noone Craig (M)	6 3	12 07	Kirkby	17/11/87	Plymouth Arg
Painter Marcos (D)	5 11	12 04	Solihull	17/8/86	Swansea C
Rodgers Anton (M)			Reading	26/1/93	Chelsea Scholar
Sampayo Ben (D)			Dagenham	10/12/92	Chelsea Scholar
Sparrow Matt (M)	5 11	10 06	Wembley	3/10/81	Scunthorpe U
Vicente Rodriguez (M)	5 9	11 05	Valencia	16/7/81	Valencia
Vincelot Romain (M)	5 9	11 02	Poitiers	29/10/85	Dagenham & R

League Appearances: Agdestein, T. (4); Ankergren, C. 19; Assulin, G. 2(5); Barnes, A. 36(7); Brezovan, P. 20; Bridcutt, L. 43; Buckley, W. 16(13); Calderon, I. 30(2); Caskey, J. 3(1); Cook, S. 1; Dicker, G. 17(1); Dunk, L. 31; El-Abd, A. 21(2); Gonzalez, D. 2; Greer, G. 42; Hall, G. (1); Harley, R. 13(3); Harper, S. 5; Hoskins, W. 2(5); Jara, G. 4; Jara, G. 10; LuaLua, K. 11(16); Mackail-Smith, C. 40(5); Mattock, J. 14(1); Navarro, A. 24(9); Noone, C. 18(15); Painter, M. 20; Paynter, B. 6(4); Razak, A. 4(2); Sparrow, M. 15(3); Taricco, M. 9(2); Vicente, R. 11(6); Vincelot, R. 10(5); Vokes, S. 7(7).

Goals – League (52): Barnes 11 (3 pens), Mackail-Smith 9, Buckley 8, Calderon 4, Vicente 3, Vokes 3, Harley 2, Noone 2, Sparrow 2, Caskey 1, Greer 1, Hoskins 1, LuaLua 1, Mattock 1, Navarro 1, Vincelot 1, own goal 1.

Carling Cup (3): Barnes 2 (2 pens), Mackail-Smith 1.

FA Cup (4): Barnes 1, Forster-Caskey 1, LuaLua 1, own goal 1.

Ground: American Express Community Stadium, Village Way, Falmer, Brighton BN1 9BL. Telephone: (01273) 878 288.

Capacity: 22,374.

Record Attendance: 36,747 v Fulham, Division 2, 27 December 1958 (at Goldstone Ground); 8,691 v Leeds U, FL 1, 20 October 2007 (at Withdean).

Manager: Gus Poyet.

Most League Goals: 112, Division 3 (S), 1955–56.

Highest League Scorer in Season: Peter Ward, 32, Division 3, 1976–77.
Most League Goals in Total Aggregate: Tommy Cook, 114, 1922–29.
Most Capped Player: Steve Penney, 17, Northern Ireland.
Most League Appearances: 'Tug' Wilson, 509, 1922–36.
Colours: Blue and white striped shirts, white sleeves with blue trim, white shorts, white stockings.
Honours – Football League: FL 1 Champions – 2010–11. Division 2 Champions – 2001–02. Division 3 Champions – 2000–01. Division 3 (S) Champions – 1957–58. Division 4 Champions – 1964–65.

BRISTOL CITY   FL CHAMPIONSHIP

Adomah Albert (F)	6 1	11 08	Lambeth	13/12/87	Barnet
Andrews Zac (D)			Bristol		Scholar
Bolasie Yannick (M)	6 2	13 02	DR Congo	24/5/89	Plymouth Arg
Bryan Joe (D)	5 7	11 05	Bristol	17/9/93	Scholar
Carey Lewis (G)			Tunbridge Wells	2/6/93	Scholar
Carey Louis (D)	5 10	11 00	Bristol	20/1/77	Coventry C
Edwards Joe (D)	5 8	11 07	Gloucester	31/10/90	Scholar
Elliott Marvin (M)	6 0	12 03	Wandsworth	15/9/84	Millwall
Fontaine Liam (D)	5 11	11 09	Beckenham	7/1/86	Fulham
Foster Ricky (D)	5 9	12 00	Aberdeen	31/7/85	Aberdeen
Gerken Dean (G)	6 3	12 08	Southend	22/5/85	Colchester U
Holloway Aaron (M)	6 2	13 01	Cardiff	21/2/93	Scholar
Kilkenny Neil (M)	5 8	10 08	Enfield	19/12/85	Leeds U
Nyatanga Lewin (D)	6 2	12 09	Burton	18/8/88	Derby Co
Pearson Stephen (M)	6 0	11 01	Lanark	2/10/82	Celtic
Pitman Brett (F)	6 0	11 00	Jersey	31/1/88	Bournemouth
Reid Bobby (M)	5 7	10 10	Bristol	1/3/93	Scholar
Skuse Cole (M)	6 1	11 05	Bristol	29/3/86	Scholar
Stead Jon (F)	6 3	13 03	Huddersfield	7/4/83	Ipswich T
Stewart Damion (D)	6 3	13 10	Jamaica	18/8/80	QPR
Taylor Ryan (F)	6 2	10 10	Rotherham	4/5/88	Rotherham U
Wilson James (D)	6 2	11 05	Chepstow	26/2/89	Scholar
Woolford Martyn (M)	6 0	11 09	Castleford	13/10/85	Scunthorpe U

League Appearances: Adomah, A. 39(6); Bikey, A. 7; Bolasie, Y. 7(16); Bryan, J. 1; Campbell-Ryce, J. 12(5); Carey, L. 18(2); Cisse, K. 26(6); Clarkson, D. (4); Davis, S. 2(1); Edwards, J. 1(1); Elliott, M. 28; Ephraim, H. 3(2); Fontaine, L. 26; Foster, R. 20; Gerken, D. 10; James, D. 36; Keinan, D. (1); Kilkenny, N. 32(9); Maynard, N. 26(1); McAllister, J. 11(1); McGivern, R. 26(5); McManus, S. 6; Nyatanga, L. 28(1); Pearson, S. 28; Pitman, B. 12(23); Skuse, C. 36; Spence, J. 9(1); Stead, J. 16(8); Stewart, D. 3; Taylor, R. (7); Wilson, J. 14(7); Wood, C. 12(7); Woolford, M. 11(14).
Goals – League (44): Maynard 8, Pitman 7, Stead 6 (1 pen), Adomah 5, Pearson 3, Wood 3 (1 pen), Cisse 2, Elliott 2, Skuse 2, Bolasie 1, Ephraim 1, Kilkenny 1, Taylor 1, Woolford 1, own goal 1.
Carling Cup (0).
FA Cup (0).
Ground: Ashton Gate Stadium, Bristol BS3 2EJ. Telephone: (0117) 963 0600.
Capacity: 21,804.
Record Attendance: 43,335 v Preston NE, FA Cup 5th rd, 16 February 1935.
Manager: Derek McInnes.
Most League Goals: 104, Division 3 (S), 1926–27.
Highest League Scorer in Season: Don Clark, 36, Division 3 (S), 1946–47.
Most League Goals in Total Aggregate: John Atyeo, 314, 1951–66.
Most Capped Player: Billy Wedlock, 26, England.
Most League Appearances: John Atyeo, 597, 1951–66.

Colours: Red shirts with white trim, white shorts, red stockings.
Honours – Football League: Division 2 Champions – 1905–06. Division 3 (S) Champions – 1922–23, 1926–27, 1954–55. **Welsh Cup:** Winners – 1934. **Anglo-Scottish Cup:** Winners – 1977–78. **Freight Rover Trophy:** Winners – 1985–86. **LDV Vans Trophy:** Winners – 2002–03.

BRISTOL ROVERS   FL CHAMPIONSHIP 2

Anyinsah Joe (M)	5 8	11 00	Bristol	8/10/84	Charlton Ath
Bevan Scott (G)	6 6	15 10	Southampton	16/9/79	Torquay U
Brown Lee (M)	6 0	12 06	Bromley	10/8/90	QPR
Brown Wayne (M)	5 9	12 05	Kingston	6/8/88	Fulham
Carayol Mustapha (F)	5 10	11 12	Gambia	10/6/89	Lincoln C
Clarke Ollie (M)	5 11	11 09	Bristol	29/6/92	
Gill Matthew (M)	5 11	11 10	Cambridge	8/11/80	Norwich C
Harrold Matt (F)	6 1	11 10	Leyton	25/7/84	Shrewsbury T
Paterson Jim (M)	5 11	12 13	Airdrie	25/9/79	Shamrock R
Richards Eliot (M)	5 9	11 09	New Tredegar	1/9/91	Scholar
Sawyer Gary (D)	6 0	11 08	Bideford	5/7/85	Plymouth Arg
Smith Michael (D)	5 11	11 02	Ballyclare	4/9/88	Ballymena U
Stanley Craig (M)	5 8	10 08	Bedworth	3/3/83	Morecambe
Virgo Adam (D)	6 2	13 12	Brighton	25/1/83	Yeovil T
Woodards Danny (D)	5 11	11 01	Forest Gate	7/10/83	Milton Keynes D
Zebroski Chris (F)	6 1	11 08	Swindon	29/10/86	Torquay U

League Appearances: Anthony, B. 14(2); Anyinsah, J. 23(8); Bevan, S. 37; Bolger, C. 38(1); Brown, L. 35(7); Brown, W. 4(8); Campbell, S. 10(1); Carayol, M. 24(6); Cronin, L. (1); Dorman, A. 20(5); Downes, A. 8; Gill, M. 32(1); Gough, C. 1; Harding, M. (1); Harrold, M. 35(5); Lines, C. (1); Lund, M. 9(4); McGleish, S. 14(13); McLaggon, K. (1); Norburn, O. 1(4); Osei-Kuffour, J. 3(2); Parkes, T. 14; Paterson, J. 17; Poke, M. 8; Rendell, S. 4(1); Richards, E. 18(14); Sawyer, G. 23(1); Smith, M. 8(12); Stanley, C. 30(4); Virgo, A. 9; Woodards, D. 39; Zebroski, C. 28(11).
Goals – League (60): Harrold 16 (5 pens), Brown, L. 7 (1 pen), McGleish 7 (2 pens), Richards 7, Anyinsah 4, Carayol 4, Zebroski 3, Bolger 2, Dorman 2, Lund 2, Anthony 1, Osei-Kuffour 1, Paterson 1, Stanley 1, Virgo 1 (1 pen), Woodards 1.
Carling Cup (3): Harrold 1, Richards 1, Zebroski 1.
FA Cup (10): McGleish 2 (1 pen), Richards 2, Carayol 2, Anthony 1, Anyinsah 1, Woodards 1, Zebroski 1.
J Paint Trophy (1): Harrold 1.
Ground: The Memorial Stadium, Filton Avenue, Horfield, Bristol BS7 0BF. Telephone: (0117) 909 6648.
Capacity: 11,626.
Record Attendance: 38,472 v Preston NE, FA Cup 4th rd, 30 January 1960 (at Eastville); 9,464 v Liverpool, FA Cup 4th rd, 8 February 1992 (at Twerton Park); 12,011 v WBA, FA Cup 6th rd, 9 March 2008 (at Memorial Stadium).
Manager: Mark McGhee.
Most League Goals: 92, Division 3 (S), 1952–53.
Highest League Scorer in Season: Geoff Bradford, 33, Division 3 (S), 1952–53.
Most League Goals in Total Aggregate: Geoff Bradford, 242, 1949–64.
Most Capped Player: Vitalijs Astafjevs, 31 (167), Latvia.
Most League Appearances: Stuart Taylor, 546, 1966–80.
Colours: Blue and white quarters, white shorts, white stockings.
Honours – Football League: Division 3 (S) Champions – 1952–53. Division 3 Champions – 1989–90.

Anderson Tom (D)			Burnley	2/9/93	Scholar
Austin Charlie (F)	6 2	13 03	Hungerford	5/7/89	Swindon T
Bartley Marvyn (M)	6 1	12 04	Reading	4/7/86	Bournemouth
Coleman Alex (D)			Bury	17/12/93	Scholar
Conlan Luke (D)			Portaferry	31/10/94	Scholar
Duff Michael (D)	6 1	11 08	Belfast	11/1/78	Cheltenham T
Edgar David (D)	6 2	12 13	Ontario	19/5/87	Newcastle U
Errington Jack (D)			Wallsend	9/12/94	Scholar
Evans Adam (F)			Dublin	3/5/94	Scholar
Fletcher Wes (F)	5 11	12 06	Ormskirk	28/2/91	Scholar
Grant Lee (G)	6 3	13 01	Hemel Hempstead	27/1/83	Sheffield W
Hewitt Steven (M)	5 7	11 00	Manchester	5/12/93	Scholar
Hines Zavon (F)	5 10	10 07	Jamaica	27/12/88	West Ham U
Howieson Cameron (M)	5 9	11 00	Dunedin	22/12/94	Scholar
Ings Danny (F)	5 10	11 07	Winchester	16/3/92	Bournemouth
Jackson Joe (F)	5 11	10 07	Barrow	3/2/93	Scholar
Jensen Brian (G)	6 1	12 04	Copenhagen	8/6/75	WBA
Lafferty Danny (D)	6 0	12 08	Derry	1/4/89	Derry C
Lazaar Mehdi (F)			Liege	9/3/93	Scholar
Long Kevin (D)	6 3	13 01	Cork	18/8/90	Cork City
Love Archie (M)			Manchester	12/1/93	Scholar
MacDonald Alex (F)	5 7	11 03	Warrington	14/4/90	Scholar
Marney Dean (M)	5 10	11 09	Barking	31/1/84	Hull C
McCann Chris (M)	6 1	11 11	Dublin	21/7/87	Scholar
Mee Ben (D)	5 11	11 09	Sale	21/9/89	Manchester C
Paterson Martin (F)	5 9	10 11	Tunstall	13/5/87	Scunthorpe U
Rodriguez Jay (F)	6 0	12 00	Burnley	29/7/89	Stirling Alb
Stanislas Junior (M)	6 0	12 00	Kidbrooke	26/11/89	West Ham U
Stewart Jon (G)	6 2	13 01	Hayes	13/3/89	Portsmouth
Treacy Keith (M)	6 0	13 02	Dublin	13/9/88	Preston NE
Trippier Keiran (D)	5 10	11 00	Bury	19/9/90	Manchester C
Wallace Ross (M)	5 6	9 12	Dundee	23/5/85	Preston NE
Williams Aryn (D)			Perth	28/10/93	Scholar

League Appearances: Austin, C. 30(11); Bartley, M. 25(14); Bikey, A. 9(5); Duff, M. 30(1); Easton, B. 17(4); Edgar, D. 44; Elliott, W. 2(2); Fox, D. 1; Grant, L. 42(1); Hewitt, S. (1); Hines, Z. (13); Howieson, C. (2); Ings, D. 9(6); Jackson, J. (1); Jensen, B. 4; Lafferty, D. 5; MacDonald, A. (5); Marney, D. 29(8); McCann, C. 45(1); McCartan, S. (1); McQuoid, J. 9(8); Mee, B. 29(2); Paterson, M. 9(5); Rodriguez, J. 36(1); Stanislas, J. 25(6); Treacy, K. 16(8); Trippier, K. 46; Vokes, S. 3(6); Wallace, R. 41(3).
Goals – League (61): Austin 16 (1 pen), Rodriguez 15 (3 pens), Wallace 5, McCann 4, Bartley 3, Ings 3, Paterson 3, Trippier 3, Edgar 2, Treacy 2, Vokes 2, McQuoid 1, own goals 2.
Carling Cup (11): Rodriguez 5 (2 pens), Austin 1, Bikey 1, Elliott 1, McCann 1, Trippier 1, Wallace 1.
FA Cup (1): Rodriguez 1.
Ground: Turf Moor, Harry Potts Way, Burnley, Lancashire BB10 4BX. Telephone: (0871) 221 1882.
Capacity: 22,610.
Record Attendance: 54,775 v Huddersfield T, FA Cup 3rd rd, 23 February 1924.
Manager: Eddie Howe.
Most League Goals: 102, Division 1, 1960–61.
Highest League Scorer in Season: George Beel, 35, Division 1, 1927–28.
Most League Goals in Total Aggregate: George Beel, 179, 1923–32.
Most Capped Player: Jimmy McIlroy, 51 (55), Northern Ireland.

Most League Appearances: Jerry Dawson, 522, 1907–28.

Colours: Claret shirts with blue sleeves, white shorts, claret stockings.

Honours – Football League: Division 1 Champions – 1920–21, 1959–60. Division 2 Champions – 1897–98, 1972–73. Division 3 Champions – 1981–82. Division 4 Champions – 1991–92. **FA Cup:** Winners – 1913–14. **Anglo-Scottish Cup:** Winners – 1978–79.

BURTON ALBION   FL CHAMPIONSHIP 2

Name			Birthplace	DOB	Previous club
Ada Patrick (D)	6 0	13 05	Yaounde	14/1/85	Kilmarnock
Corbett Andy (F)	6 0	11 07	Worcester	20/2/82	Kidderminster H
Dyer Jack (M)	5 9	11 00	Sutton Coldfield	11/12/91	Aston Villa Scholar
Kee Billy (F)	5 9	11 04	Loughborough	1/12/90	Torquay U
Maghoma Jacques (M)	5 9	11 07	Lubumbashi	23/10/87	Tottenham H
McGrath John (M)	5 10	10 04	Limerick	27/3/80	Limerick
Palmer Chris (D)	5 7	11 00	Derby	16/10/83	Gillingham
Phillips Jimmy (M)	5 7	10 00	Stoke	20/9/89	Stoke C
Ramsey-Dickson Kristian (D)			Birmingham	23/8/89	Continental Star
Richards Justin (F)	5 11	11 00	Sandwell	16/10/80	Port Vale
Stanton Nathan (D)	5 9	12 06	Nottingham	6/5/81	Rochdale
Taylor Cleveland (M)	5 8	10 07	Leicester	9/9/83	Brentford
Webster Aaron (D)	6 1	12 00	Burton-on-Trent	19/12/80	Youth
Wren James (G)			Birmingham	26/6/93	Walsall Scholar
Zola Calvin (F)	6 3	14 06	Kinshasa	31/12/84	Crewe Alex

League Appearances: Ada, P. 5(4); Ainsworth, L. 4(3); Amankwaah, K. 8; Atkins, R. 45; Austin, R. 34(4); Banton, J. (1); Blanchett, D. 9(5); Bolder, A. 41(3); Clucas, S. 1(1); Corbett, A. 31(2); Driver, C. 8; Dyer, J. 16(1); Gurrieri, A. 6(7); Harriott, M. 3(1); James, T. 29(1); Kee, B. 14(6); Legzdins, A. 1; Lucas, L. 1; Maghoma, J. 32(4); McGrath, J. 28(3); Moore, D. 1(3); Palmer, C. 16(18); Parkes, T. 4; Pearson, G. 6(6); Phillips, J. 21(12); Richards, J. 28(7); Stanton, N. 22; Taylor, C. 23(8); Webster, A. 33(2); Yussuf, A. 2(15); Zola, C. 34(2).

Goals – League (54): Kee 12, Zola 12, Richards 11 (3 pens), Maghoma 4, Bolder 3, Palmer 3, Webster 3, Taylor 2, Driver 1, Dyer 1, Yussuf 1, own goal 1.

Carling Cup (3): Maghoma 1, Taylor 1, Zola 1.

FA Cup (1): Zola 1.

J Paint Trophy (1): Richards 1.

Ground: Pirelli Stadium, Princess Way, Burton-on-Trent, Staffordshire DE13 0AR. Telephone: (01283) 565 938.

Ground Capactiy: 6,350 (2,034 seated).

Record Attendance: 5,806 v Weymouth, Southern League Cup final 2nd leg 1964 (at Eton Park); 6,192 v Oxford U, Blue Square Premier, 17 April 2009 (at Pirelli Stadium).

Manager: Gary Rowett.

Most League Goals: 71, FL 2, 2009–10.

Highest League Scorer in Season: Shaun Harrad, 21, 2009–10.

Most League Goals in Total Aggregate: Shaun Harrad, 31, 2009–11.

Most Capped Player: Jacques Maghoma, 3, DR Congo.

Most League Appearances: John McGrath, 117, 2009–12.

Colours: Yellow shirts with black insert, black shorts, black stockings.

Honours: Conference: Champions – 2008–09. **Southern League Cup:** Winners – 1964, 1997, 2000. **Northern Premier League:** Champions – 2001–02. **Northern Premier League Shield:** 1983. **Challenge Cup:** Winners – 1983. **Birmingham Senior Cup:** Winners – 1954, 1997. **Staffordshire Senior Cup:** Winners – 1956. **Midland Floodlit Cup:** Winners – 1976.

BURY

Belford Cameron (G)	6 1	11 10	Nuneaton	16/10/88	Coventry C Scholar
Bishop Andy (F)	6 0	10 10	Cannock	19/10/82	Walsall
Carrington Mark (M)	6 0	11 00	Warrington	4/5/87	Milton Keynes D
Futcher Ben (D)	6 7	12 05	Manchester	20/2/81	Peterborough U
Grella Mike (F)	5 11	12 04	New York	23/1/87	Brentford
Harrad Shaun (F)	5 10	12 04	Nottingham	11/12/84	Northampton T
Harrop Max (M)	5 8	10 00	Oldham	30/6/93	Scholar
Hughes Mark (D)	6 1	13 03	Liverpool	9/12/86	N Queensland Fury
John-Lewis Lemell (M)	5 10	11 10	Hammersmith	17/5/89	Lincoln C
Jones Andrai (D)	5 11	10 10	Liverpool	1/1/92	Scholar
McCarthy Luke (M)	5 9	10 10	Bolton	7/7/93	Scholar
Picken Phil (D)	5 9	10 07	Droylsden	12/11/85	Chesterfield
Schumacher Steven (M)	5 10	11 00	Liverpool	30/4/84	Crewe Alex
Skarz Joe (D)	5 10	11 04	Huddersfield	13/7/89	Huddersfield T
Sodje Efe (D)	6 1	12 00	Greenwich	5/10/72	Gillingham
Sweeney Peter (M)	6 0	12 11	Glasgow	25/9/84	Grimsby T
Williams Tony (G)	6 2	13 09	Maesteg	20/9/77	Neath
Worrall David (M)	6 0	11 03	Manchester	12/6/90	WBA

League Appearances: Amoo, D. 19(8); Belford, C. 23; Bishop, A. 33(7); Bond, J. 6; Byrne, S. 10(4); Carrington, M. 12(9); Carson, T. 8; Carson, T. 9; Clarke, N. 11; Coke, G. 28(2); Cregg, P. 5(2); Cullen, M. 1(3); Doble, R. 3(2); Eastham, A. 22(3); Elford-Alliyu, L. 4(9); Grella, M. 8(2); Harrad, S. 14(12); Harrop, M. (5); Haworth, A. (6); Hughes, M. 21(4); John-Lewis, L. 8(20); Jones, A. 9(2); Jones, M. 24; Lowe, R. 5; Mozika, D. 3(1); Oyenuga, K. (1); Picken, P. 36(1); Schumacher, S. 29(3); Skarz, J. 45; Sodje, E. 40(1); Sweeney, P. 41; Worrall, D. 29(12).
Goals – League (60): Bishop 8 (1 pen), Coke 6 (1 pen), Schumacher 6 (1 pen), John-Lewis 5, Amoo 4, Grella 4, Lowe 4, Sweeney 4, Jones, M. 3, Worrall 3, Eastham 2, Elford-Alliyu 2, Harrad 2, Sodje 2, Carrington 1, Mozika 1, Skarz 1, own goals 2.
Carling Cup (5): Lowe 3, Bishop 1, Jones, M. 1.
FA Cup (0).
J Paint Trophy (0).
Ground: Gigg Lane, Bury, Lancs BL9 9HR. Telephone: (08445) 790009.
Capacity: 11,669.
Record Attendance: 35,000 v Bolton W, FA Cup 3rd rd, 9 January 1960.
Manager: Richie Barker.
Most League Goals: 108, Division 3, 1960–61.
Highest League Scorer in Season: Craig Madden, 35, Division 4, 1981–82.
Most League Goals in Total Aggregate: Craig Madden, 129, 1978–86.
Most Capped Player: Bill Gorman, 11 (13), Republic of Ireland and (4), Northern Ireland.
Most League Appearances: Norman Bullock, 506, 1920–35.
Colours: Black and blue halved shirts, white shorts, black stockings.
Honours – Football League: Division 2 Champions – 1894–95, 1996–97. Division 3 Champions – 1960–61. **FA Cup:** Winners – 1900, 1903.

CARDIFF CITY

Blake Darcy (M)	5 10	12 05	New Tredegar	13/12/88	Scholar
Conway Craig (M)	5 7	10 07	Irvine	2/5/85	Dundee U
Cowie Don (M)	5 5	8 05	Inverness	15/2/83	Watford
Earnshaw Robert (F)	5 6	10 00	Mulfulira	6/4/81	Nottingham F
Farah Ibrahim (M)			Cardiff	24/1/92	Scholar
Gerrard Anthony (D)	6 2	13 07	Huyton	6/2/86	Walsall

Gestede Rudy (F)	6 4	13 07	Nancy	10/10/88	Metz
Gunnarsson Aron (M)	5 9	11 00	Akureyri	22/9/89	Coventry C
Harris Kedeem (M)	5 9	10 08	Westminster	8/6/93	Wycombe W
Hudson Mark (D)	6 1	12 01	Guildford	30/3/82	Charlton Ath
Jarvis Nathaniel (F)	6 0	12 06	Cardiff	20/10/91	Scholar
Keinan Dekel (D)	6 0	11 09	Rosh Hanikra	15/9/84	Blackpool
Kiss Filip (M)	6 1	11 11	Dunajska	13/10/90	Slovan Bratislava
Marshall David (G)	6 3	13 04	Glasgow	5/3/85	Norwich C
Mason Joe (F)	5 9	11 11	Plymouth	13/5/91	Plymouth Arg
McNaughton Kevin (D)	5 10	10 06	Dundee	28/8/82	Aberdeen
McPhail Stephen (M)	5 8	11 04	Westminster	9/12/79	Barnsley
Miller Kenny (F)	5 10	10 09	Edinburgh	23/12/79	Rangers
Parish Elliot (G)	6 2	13 00	Towcester	20/5/90	Aston Villa
Parkin Jon (F)	6 4	13 07	Barnsley	30/12/81	Preston NE
Ralls Joe (M)	5 10	11 00	Farnborough	13/10/93	Scholar
Taiwo Soloman (M)	6 1	13 02	Lagos	29/4/85	Dagenham & R
Taylor Andrew (D)	5 10	11 04	Hartlepool	1/8/86	Middlesbrough
Turner Ben (D)	6 4	14 04	Birmingham	21/1/88	Coventry C
Whittingham Peter (M)	5 10	9 13	Nuneaton	8/9/84	Aston Villa

League Appearances: Blake, D. 9(11); Conway, C. 24(7); Cowie, D. 43; Earnshaw. R. 8(11); Gerrard, A. 18(2); Gestede, R. 5(20); Gunnarsson, A. 41(1); Heaton, T. 1(1); Hudson, M. 38(1); Keinan, D. (1); Kiss, F. 13(13); Lawrence, L. 12(1); Marshall, D. 45; Mason, J. 23(16); McNaughton, K. 41(1); McPhail, S. 11(8); Miller, K. 41(2); Naylor, L. 2; Quinn, P. (1); Ralls, J. 5(5); Taiwo, S. (1); Taylor, A. 42; Turner, B. 36(1); Vuckic, H. 2(3); Whittingham, P. 46.

Goals – League (66): Whittingham 12 (3 pens), Miller 10, Mason 9, Gunnarsson 5, Hudson 5, Cowie 4, Conway 3, Earnshaw 3, Gestede 2, Turner 2, Gerrard 1, Kiss 1, Lawrence 1, Ralls 1, Taylor 1, Vuckic 1, own goals 5.

Carling Cup (16): Cowie 3, Conway 2, Mason 2, Gerrard 1, Gestede 1, Gyepes 1, Jarvis 1, Miller 1, Parkin 1, Turner 1, Whittingham 1, own goal 1.

FA Cup (2): Earnshaw 1, Mason 1.

Play-Offs (0).

Ground: Cardiff City Stadium, Leckwith Road, Cardiff CF11 8AZ. Telephone: (0845) 365 1115.

Capacity: 26,828.

Record Attendance: 57,893 v Arsenal, Division 1, 22 April 1953 (at Ninian Park); 26,055 v Leicester C, FL C Play-Off semi-final 2nd leg, 12 May 2010 (at Cardiff City Stadium).

Ground Record Attendance: 62,634, Wales v England, 17 October 1959 (at Ninian Park).

Manager: Malky Mackay.

Most League Goals: 95, Division 3, 2000–01.

Highest League Scorer in Season: Robert Earnshaw, 31, Division 2, 2002–03.

Most League Goals in Total Aggregate: Len Davies, 128, 1920–31.

Most Capped Player: Alf Sherwood, 39 (41), Wales.

Most League Appearances: Phil Dwyer, 471, 1972–85.

Colours: Red shirts, black shorts, red stockings.

Honours – Football League: Division 3 (S) Champions – 1946–47; Division 3 Champions – 1992–93. **FA Cup:** Winners – 1926–27 (only occasion the Cup has been won by a club outside England). **Welsh Cup:** Winners – 22 times. **Charity Shield:** Winners 1927.

CARLISLE UNITED   FL CHAMPIONSHIP 1

Berrett James (M)	5 10	10 13	Halifax	13/1/89	Huddersfield T
Chantler Chris (M)	5 8	11 00	Cheadle Hulme	16/12/90	Manchester C

Collin Adam (G)	6 2	12 00	Penrith	9/12/84	Doncaster R
Gillespie Mark (G)	6 3	13 07	Newcastle	27/3/92	Scholar
Livesey Danny (D)	6 3	13 03	Salford	31/12/84	Bolton W
Loy Rory (F)	5 10	10 07	Dumfries	19/3/88	Rangers
Madden Patrick (F)	6 0	11 13	Dublin	4/3/90	Bohemians
McGovern John-Paul (M)	5 10	12 02	Glasgow	3/10/80	Swindon T
Michalik Lubomir (D)	6 4	13 00	Cadca	13/8/83	Leeds U
Miller Lee (F)	6 0	11 07	Lanark	18/5/83	Middlesbrough
Murphy Peter (M)	5 10	12 10	Dublin	27/10/80	Blackburn R
Noble Liam (M)	5 9	10 05	Newcastle	8/5/91	Sunderland
Robson Matty (D)	5 10	11 02	Spennymoor	23/1/85	Hartlepool U
Simek Frankie (D)	6 0	11 06	St Louis	13/10/84	Sheffield W
Taiwo Tom (M)	5 8	10 07	Pudsey	27/2/90	Chelsea
Thirlwell Paul (M)	5 11	12 08	Washington	13/2/79	Derby Co
Welsh Andy (M)	5 8	10 03	Manchester	24/11/83	Yeovil T
Zoko Francois (F)	6 0	11 05	Daloa	13/9/83	Ostend

League Appearances: Beck, M. (2); Berrett, J. 42; Chantler, C. 10(2); Collin, A. 46; Cook, J. 6(8); Curran, C. 2(10); Helan, J. (2); Livesey, D. 26(2); Loy, R. 18(2); Madden, P. 6(12); McGovern, J. 40(5); Michalik, L. 33(3); Miller, L. 33; Murphy, P. 38(2); Noble, L. 32(8); O'Halloran, S. 3; Parker, B. 5; Ribeiro, C. 5; Robson, M. 25(2); Simek, F. 25; Taiwo, T. 32(5); Tavernier, J. 16; Thirlwell, P. 25(1); Welsh, A. 4(17); Zoko, F. 34(11).
Goals – League (65): Miller 14 (3 pens), Zoko 13, Berrett 9 (1 pen), Noble 6, Cook 4 (1 pen), Loy 3 (1 pen), McGovern 3, Taiwo 3, Robson 2, Livesey 1, Madden 1, Murphy 1, Parker 1, Thirlwell 1, own goals 3.
Carling Cup (1): McGovern 1.
FA Cup (4): Berrett 1, Loy 1, Miller 1, Noble 1.
J Paint Trophy (2): McGovern 1, Zoko 1.
Ground: Brunton Park, Warwick Road, Carlisle CA1 1LL. Telephone: (01228) 526 237.
Capacity: 16,981.
Record Attendance: 27,500 v Birmingham C, FA Cup 3rd rd, 5 January 1957 and v Middlesbrough, FA Cup 5th rd, 7 February 1970.
Manager: Greg Abbott.
Most League Goals: 113, Division 4, 1963–64.
Highest League Scorer in Season: Jimmy McConnell, 42, Division 3 (N), 1928–29.
Most League Goals in Total Aggregate: Jimmy McConnell, 126, 1928–32.
Most Capped Player: Eric Welsh, 4, Northern Ireland.
Most League Appearances: Allan Ross, 466, 1963–79.
Colours: Blue shirts with white and red trim, white shorts, white stockings.
Honours – Football League: Division 3 Champions – 1964–65, 1994–95; FL 2 Champions – 2005–06. **Auto Windscreen Shield:** Winners 1997. **Johnstone's Paint Trophy:** Winners – 2010–11.

CHARLTON ATHLETIC   FL CHAMPIONSHIP

Bover Ruben (M)	5 7	10 05	Mallorca	24/6/92	Halesowen T
Clarke Leon (F)	6 2	14 02	Birmingham	10/2/85	Swindon T
Cort Leon (D)	6 3	13 01	Bermondsey	11/9/79	Stoke C
Cousins Jordan (D)			Greenwich	6/3/94	Scholar
Evina Cedric (D)	5 11	12 08	Cameroon	16/11/91	Oldham Ath
Green Danny (M)	5 11	12 00	Harlow	9/7/88	Dagenham & R
Hamer Ben (G)	5 11	12 04	Chard	20/11/87	Reading
Harriott Callum (M)	5 5	10 05	Norbury	4/3/94	Scholar
Hayes Paul (F)	6 0	12 11	Dagenham	20/9/83	Preston NE
Haynes Danny (F)	5 11	12 04	Peckham	19/1/88	Barnsley
Hollands Danny (M)	6 0	11 11	Ashford (Middlesex)	6/11/85	Bournemouth
Hughes Andy (M)	5 11	12 01	Stockport	2/1/78	Scunthorpe U

Jackson Johnnie (M)	6 1	12 00	Camden	15/8/82	Notts Co
Kermorgant Yann (F)	6 0	13 03	Vannes	8/11/81	Leicester C
Mambo Yado (D)	6 3	13 01	Kilburn	22/10/91	Scholar
Morrison Michael (D)	6 0	12 00	Bury St Edmunds	3/3/88	Sheffield W
Osborne Harry (D)			Greenwich	3/3/94	Scholar
Pope Nick (G)	6 3	11 13	Cambridge	19/4/92	Bury T
Pritchard Bradley (M)	6 1	14 02	Zimbabwe	19/12/85	Hayes & Yeading U
Smith Michael (F)	6 4	11 02	Wallsend	17/10/91	Rangers
Solly Chris (D)	5 8	10 07	Rochester	20/1/91	Scholar
Stephens Dale (M)	5 7	11 04	Bolton	12/6/89	Oldham Ath
Sullivan John (G)	5 10	11 04	Brighton	8/3/88	Millwall
Taylor Matthew (D)	6 0	12 04	Chorley	30/1/82	Exeter C
Wagstaff Scott (M)	5 10	10 03	Maidstone	31/3/90	Scholar
Wiggins Rhoys (D)	5 8	11 05	Uxbridge	4/11/87	Bournemouth
Wright-Phillips Bradley (F)	5 10	10 07	Lewisham	12/3/85	Plymouth Arg

League Appearances: Benson, P. (1); Clarke, L. 1(6); Cook, L. 3(1); Cort, L. 10(5); Doherty, G. (3); Elliot, R. 4; Ephraim, H. 4(1); Euell, J. (11); Evina, C. 2(1); Green, D. 25(7); Hamer, B. 41; Hayes, P. 12(7); Haynes, D. 3(11); Hollands, D. 43; Hughes, A. 5(10); Jackson, J. 35(1); Kermorgant, Y. 33(3); Morrison, M. 45; N'Guessan, D. 6(1); Pritchard, B. 10(10); Russell, D. 8(3); Solly, C. 44; Stephens, D. 28(2); Sullivan, J. 1(2); Taylor, M. 38(3); Wagstaff, S. 19(15); Wiggins, R. 45; Wright-Phillips, B. 41(1).

Goals – League (82): Wright-Phillips 22, Jackson 12 (5 pens), Kermorgant 12, Hollands 7, Stephens 5, Morrison 4, N'Guessan 4, Wagstaff 4, Green 3, Hayes 3, Haynes 2, Russell 2, Ephraim 1, Wiggins 1.

Carling Cup (2): Benson 1, Euell 1.

FA Cup (6): Euell 1, Hollands 1, Jackson 1, Morrison 1, Pritchard 1, Taylor 1.

J Paint Trophy (0).

Ground: The Valley, Floyd Road, Charlton, London SE7 8BL. Telephone: (020) 8333 4000.

Capacity: 27,111.

Record Attendance: 75,031 v Aston Villa, FA Cup 5th rd, 12 February 1938 (at The Valley).

Manager: Chris Powell.

Most League Goals: 107, Division 2, 1957–58.

Highest League Scorer in Season: Ralph Allen, 32, Division 3 (S), 1934–35.

Most League Goals in Total Aggregate: Stuart Leary, 153, 1953–62.

Most Capped Player: Jonatan Johansson, 42 (105), Finland.

Most League Appearances: Sam Bartram, 579, 1934–56.

Colours: Red shirts with white trim, white shorts, white stockings with red tops.

Honours – Football League: Division 1 Champions – 1999–2000. Division 3 (S) Champions – 1928–29, 1934–35. FL 1 – Champions 2011–12. **FA Cup:** Winners – 1947.

CHELSEA   FA PREMIERSHIP

Affane Amin (M)			Gothenburg	21/1/94	Scholar
Ashton James (D)			Gravesend	2/10/92	Scholar
Bamford Patrick (F)	6 1	11 02	Newark	5/9/93	Nottingham F
Benayoun Yossi (M)	5 10	11 00	Beer Sheva	6/6/80	Liverpool
Bertrand Ryan (D)	5 10	11 00	Southwark	5/8/89	Scholar
Blackman Jamal (G)			Croydon	27/10/93	Scholar
Bruma Jeffrey (D)	6 1	12 00	Rotterdam	13/11/91	Feyenoord
Cahill Gary (D)	6 2	12 06	Dronfield	19/12/85	Bolton W
Cech Petr (G)	6 5	14 07	Plzen	20/5/82	Rennes
Chalobah Nathaniel (D)	6 1	11 11	Sierra Leone	12/12/94	Scholar
Clifford Billy (M)			Slough	18/10/92	Scholar
Clifford Conor (M)	5 8	10 08	Dublin	1/10/91	Scholar

Name	Height	Weight	Birthplace	Date	Previous Club
Cole Ashley (D)	5 8	10 05	Stepney	20/12/80	Arsenal
Courtois Thibaut (G)			Bree	11/5/92	Genk
Davila Ulises (M)			Guadalajara	13/4/91	Guadalajara
De Bruyne Kevin (M)	5 11	12 00	Ghent	28/6/91	Genk
Deen-Conteh Aziz (D)			Sierra Leone	14/1/93	Scholar
Delac Matej (G)			Bosnia	20/8/92	Inter Zapresic
Essien Michael (M)	5 10	13 06	Accra	3/12/82	Lyon
Gordon Ben (D)	5 11	12 06	Bradford	2/3/91	Scholar
Hilario (G)	6 2	13 05	San Pedro da Cova	21/10/75	Nacional
Hutchinson Sam (M)	6 0	11 07	Windsor	3/8/89	Scholar
Ince Rohan (D)			Whitechapel	8/11/92	Scholar
Ivanovic Branislav (M)	6 0	12 04	Sremska Mitreovica	22/2/84	Lokomotiv Moscow
Kakuta Gael (F)	5 8	10 03	Lille	21/6/91	Lens
Kalas Tomas (D)	6 0	12 00	Olomouc	15/5/93	Sigma Olomouc
Kane Todd (D)			Huntingdon	17/9/93	Scholar
Lalkovic Milan (F)			Kosice	9/12/92	Scholar
Lampard Frank (M)	6 0	14 02	Romford	20/6/78	West Ham U
Luiz David (D)	6 2	13 03	Sao Paulo	22/4/87	Benfica
Lukaku Romelu (F)	6 3	13 00	Antwerp	13/5/93	Anderlecht
Malouda Florent (M)	6 0	11 06	Guyane	13/6/80	Lyon
Mata Juan (M)	5 7	11 00	Ocon de Villafranca	28/4/88	Valencia
McEachran Josh (D)	5 10	10 03	Oxford	1/3/93	Scholar
Mikel John Obi (M)	6 0	13 05	Plateau State	22/4/87	Lyn
Nkumu Archange (M)			Tottenham	5/11/93	Scholar
Omeruo Kenneth (D)	6 1	12 00	Nigeria	17/10/93	Standard Liege
Pappoe Daniel (D)			Accra	30/12/93	Scholar
Paulo Ferreira (D)	6 0	11 13	Cascais	18/1/79	Porto
Phillip Adam (F)	5 10	11 00	Carshalton	19/6/91	Scholar
Piazon Lucas (M)			Curitiba	20/1/94	Scholar
Pirez Jhon (F)			Montevideo	20/2/93	Scholar
Ramires (M)	5 11	10 03	Rio de Janeiro	24/3/87	Benfica
Raul Meireles (M)	5 10	10 12	Oporto	17/3/83	Liverpool
Romeu Oriol (M)	6 0	12 06	Ulldecona	24/9/91	Barcelona B
Saville George (M)			Camberley	1/6/93	Scholar
Sturridge Daniel (F)	6 2	12 02	Birmingham	1/9/89	Manchester C
Terry John (D)	6 1	14 01	Barking	7/12/80	Trainee
Torres Fernando (F)	5 9	12 03	Madrid	20/3/84	Liverpool
Turnbull Ross (G)	6 4	15 00	Bishop Auckland	4/1/85	Middlesbrough
Van Aanholt Patrick (D)	5 9	10 08	Den Bosch	3/7/88	
Walker Sam (G)	6 5	14 00	Gravesend	2/10/91	Scholar

League Appearances: Alex, 3; Anelka, N. 3(6); Benayoun, Y. (1); Bertrand, R. 6(1); Bosingwa, J. 24(3); Cahill, G. 9(1); Cech, P. 34; Cole, A. 31(1); Drogba, D. 16(8); Essien, M. 10(4); Hilario, 2; Hutchinson, S. 1(1); Ivanovic, B. 26(3); Kalou, S. 7(5); Lampard, F. 26(4); Luiz, D. 18(2); Lukaku, R. 1(7); Malouda, F. 11(15); Mata, J. 29(5); McEachran, J. (2); Mikel, J. 15(7); Paulo Ferreira, 3(3); Ramires, 28(2); Raul Meireles, 23(5); Romeu, O. 11(5); Sturridge, D. 28(2); Terry, J. 31; Torres, F. 20(12); Turnbull, R. 2.

Goals – League (65): Lampard 11 (3 pens), Sturridge 11, Mata 6, Terry 6, Torres 6, Drogba 5 (1 pen), Ramires 5, Ivanovic 3, Luiz 2, Malouda 2, Raul Meireles 2, Anelka 1, Bosingwa 1, Cahill 1, Kalou 1, own goals 2.

Carling Cup (2): Kalou 1, Sturridge 1.

FA Cup (20): Mata 4 (1 pen), Ramires 4, Drogba 2, Lampard 2, Raul Meireles 2, Torres 2, Cahill 1, Kalou 1, Malouda 1, Sturridge 1.

Champions League (25): Drogba 6, Lampard 3 (2 pens), Ramires 3, Torres 3, Ivanovic 2, Kalou 2, Mata 2, Raul Meireles 2, David Luiz 1, Terry 1.

Ground: Stamford Bridge, Fulham Road, London SW6 1HS. Telephone: (0871) 984 1955.

Capacity: 41,841.
Record Attendance: 82,905 v Arsenal, Division 1, 12 October 1935.
Manager: Roberto Di Matteo.
Most League Goals: 103, FA Premier League, 2009–10.
Highest League Scorer in Season: Jimmy Greaves, 41, 1960–61.
Most League Goals in Total Aggregate: Bobby Tambling, 164, 1958–70.
Most Capped Player: Frank Lampard, 88 (90), England.
Most League Appearances: Ron Harris, 655, 1962–80.
Colours: Reflex blue shirt, reflex blue shorts, white stockings with blue trim.
Honours – FA Premier League: Champions – 2004–05, 2005–06, 2009–10. **Football League:** Division 1 Champions – 1954–55. Division 2 Champions – 1983–84, 1988–89. **FA Cup:** Winners – 1970, 1997, 2000, 2007, 2009, 2010, 2012. **Football League Cup:** Winners – 1964–65, 1997–98, 2004–05, 2006–07. **Full Members' Cup:** Winners – 1985–86. **Zenith Data Systems Cup:** Winners – 1989–90. **European Champions League** Winners – 2011–12. **European Cup-Winners' Cup:** Winners – 1970–71, 1997–98. **Super Cup:** Winners – 1999.

CHELTENHAM TOWN   FL CHAMPIONSHIP 2

Andrew Danny (D)	5 11	11 06	Holbeach	23/12/90	Peterborough U
Bennett Alan (D)	6 2	12 08	Cork	4/10/81	Wycombe W
Brown Scott P (G)	6 2	13 01	Wolverhampton	26/4/85	Bristol C
Duffy Darryl (F)	5 11	12 01	Glasgow	16/4/84	Bristol R
Elliott Steve (D)	6 1	14 00	Derby	29/10/78	Bristol R
Goulding Jeff (F)	6 2	11 11	Sutton	13/5/84	Bournemouth
Graham Bagasan (M)			Plaistow	6/10/92	QPR Scholar
Hooman Harry (D)	5 11	12 06	Worcester	27/4/91	Shrewsbury T
Jombati Sido (D)	6 0	11 11	Lisbon	20/8/87	Bath C
Lowe Keith (D)	6 2	13 05	Wolverhampton	13/9/85	Hereford U
McGlashan Jermaine (M)	5 7	10 00	Croydon	14/4/88	Aldershot T
Mohammed Kaid (F)	5 11	12 06	Cardiff	23/7/84	Swindon T
Pack Marlon (M)	6 2	11 09	Portsmouth	25/3/91	Portsmouth
Penn Russ (M)	5 11	12 13	Dudley	8/11/85	Burton Alb
Summerfield Luke (M)	6 0	11 00	Ivybridge	6/12/87	Plymouth Arg

League Appearances: Andrew, D. 10; Bennett, A. 44; Brown, S. 22; Burgess, B. 6(1); Butland, J. 24; Duffy, D. 25(16); Elliott, S. 38; Garbutt, L. 34; Goulding, J. 16(19); Graham, B. 1(6); Hooman, H. 1(1); Jackson, M. (1); Jombati, S. 33(3); Lewis, T. 1; Low, J. 26(13); Lowe, K. 24(6); MacLean, S. 3; McGlashan, J. 10(6); Mohammed, K. 39(6); Pack, M. 43; Penn, R. 39(4); Reid, B. (1); Smikle, B. 3(32); Spencer, J. 27(14); Summerfield, L. 37(4).
Goals – League (66): Duffy 11 (5 pens), Mohammed 11, Spencer 10, Goulding 5 (1 pen), Pack 5, Summerfield 4, Low 3, Bennett 2, Burgess 2, Elliott 2, Garbutt 2, Jombati 2, McGlashan 2, Lowe 1, MacLean 1, Penn 1, Smikle 1, own goal 1.
Carling Cup (1): Summerfield 1.
FA Cup (5): Duffy 2 (1 pen), Pack 1, Penn 1, Summerfield 1.
J Paint Trophy (5): Duffy 2, Goulding 1, Smikle 1, Spencer 1.
Play-Offs (4): McGlashan 2, Burgess 1, Pack 1.
Ground: The Abbey Business Stadium, Whaddon Road, Cheltenham, Gloucestershire GL52 5NA. Telephone: (01242) 573 558.
Capacity: 7,136.
Record Attendance: 10,389 v Blackpool, FA Cup 3rd rd, 13 January 1934 (at Cheltenham Athletic Ground); 8,326 v Reading, FA Cup 1st rd, 17 November 1956 (at Whaddon Road).
Manager: Mark Yates.
Most League Goals: 66, Division 3, 2001–02; 66, FL 2, 2011–12.
Highest League Scorer in Season: Julian Alsop, 20, Division 3, 2001–02.

Most League Goals in Total Aggregate: Julian Alsop, 39, 2000–03; 2009–10.
Most Capped Player: Grant McCann, 7 (39), Northern Ireland.
Most League Appearances: David Bird, 288, 2001–11.
Colours: All red with white trim.
Honours – Football Conference: Champions – 1998–99. **FA Trophy:** Winners – 1997–98.

CHESTERFIELD   FL CHAMPIONSHIP 2

Allott Mark (M)	5 11	11 07	Middleton	3/10/77	Oldham Ath
Boden Scott (F)	5 11	11 00	Sheffield	19/12/89	Marlehamn
Bowery Jordan (F)	6 1	12 00	Nottingham	2/7/91	Scholar
Clay Craig (M)	5 11	11 07	Nottingham	5/5/92	Scholar
Darikwa Tendayi (M)	6 2	12 02	Nottingham	13/12/91	Scholar
Lee Tommy (G)	6 2	12 02	Keighley	3/1/86	Macclesfield T
Lester Jack (F)	5 9	12 08	Sheffield	8/10/75	Nottingham F
Randall Mark (M)	6 0	12 12	Milton Keynes	28/9/89	Arsenal
Smith Nathan (D)	5 11	12 00	Enfield	11/1/87	Yeovil T
Talbot Drew (F)	5 10	11 00	Barnsley	19/7/86	Luton T
Thompson Josh (D)	6 4	12 00	Bolton	25/2/91	Rochdale
Trotman Neal (D)	6 3	13 08	Manchester	11/3/87	Preston NE
Westcarr Craig (F)	5 11	11 04	Nottingham	29/1/85	Notts Co
Whitaker Danny (M)	5 10	11 00	Wilmslow	14/11/80	Oldham Ath

League Appearances: Ajose, N. 5(7); Allott, M. 36; Boden, S. 7(19); Bowery, J. 23(17); Clarke, L. 14; Clay, C. (5); Darikwah, T. 2; Davis, D. 9; Downes, A. 8(1); Fleming, G. 9(1); Ford, S. 18; Griffiths, S. 3; Grounds, J. 13; Holden, D. 9(5); Hurst, J. 10; Johnson, L. 11; Juan, J. 6(1); Lee, T. 35; Lester, J. 16(5); Lowry, J. 2(4); Mattis, D. 6(1); Mendy, A. 31(3); Morgan, D. 10(7); Moussa, F. 10; Niven, D. 4(3); Obadeyi, T. 3(2); Randall, M. 10(6); Ridehalgh, L. 20; Robertson, G. 11(1); Smith, N. 22(3); Soderberg, O. 2; Talbot, D. 43; Thompson, J. 20; Trotman, N. 23; Westcarr, C. 32(6); Whitaker, D. 23(7).
Goals – League (56): Clarke 9, Bowery 8, Westcarr 8, Whitaker 5 (2 pens), Boden 4, Moussa 4, Lester 3, Morgan 3 (1 pen), Mendy 2, Talbot 2, Ajose 1, Allott 1, Holden 1, Juan 1, Randall 1, Ridehalgh 1, Thompson 1, Trotman 1.
Carling Cup (2): Whitaker 2 (1 pen).
FA Cup (1): Bowery 1.
J Paint Trophy (13): Bowery 3, Westcarr 3, Boden 1, Lester 1, Mendy 1, Morgan 1, Randall 1, Whitaker 1 (pen), own goal 1.
Ground: b2net Stadium, 1866 Sheffield Road, Whittington Moor, Chesterfield S41 8NZ. Telephone: (01246) 209 765.
Capacity: 8,502.
Record Attendance: 30,968 v Newcastle U, Division 2, 7 April 1939 (at Saltergate).
Manager: John Sheridan.
Most League Goals: 102, Division 3 (N), 1930–31.
Highest League Scorer in Season: Jimmy Cookson, 44, Division 3 (N), 1925–26.
Most League Goals in Total Aggregate: Ernie Moss, 161, 1969–76, 1979–81 and 1984–86.
Most Capped Player: Walter McMillen, 4 (7), Northern Ireland; Mark Williams, 4 (30), Northern Ireland.
Most League Appearances: Dave Blakey, 613, 1948–67.
Colours: Blue shirts with white trim, white shorts, white stockings.
Honours – Football League: FL 2 Champions – 2010–11. Division 3 (N) Champions – 1930–31, 1935–36. Division 4 Champions – 1969–70, 1984–85. **Johnstone's Paint Trophy:** Winners – 2011–12. **Anglo-Scottish Cup:** Winners – 1980–81.

Aldred Tom (D)	6 2	13 02	Bolton	11/9/90	Watford
Bender Tom (M)	6 3	12 00	Harlow	19/1/93	Scholar
Bond Andy (M)	5 10	11 07	Wigan	16/3/86	Barrow
Coker Ben (D)	5 11	11 09	Hatfield	17/6/89	Bury T
Cousins Mark (G)	6 2	12 02	Chelmsford	9/1/87	Scholar
Duguid Karl (M)	5 11	11 06	Letchworth	21/3/78	Plymouth Arg
Eastman Tom (D)	6 3	13 12	Clacton	21/10/91	Ipswich T
Gilbey Alex (M)			Dagenham		Scholar
Gillespie Steven (F)	5 9	11 02	Liverpool	4/6/84	Cheltenham T
Hamilton Bradley (D)	6 0	10 00	Newham	30/8/92	Scholar
Heath Matt (D)	6 4	13 13	Leicester	1/11/81	Leeds U
Henderson Ian (F)	5 10	11 06	Thetford	25/1/85	Luton T
Izzet Kem (M)	5 7	10 05	Mile End	29/9/80	Charlton Ath
James Lloyd (M)	5 11	11 01	Bristol	16/2/88	Southampton
Ladapo Freddie (F)			Romford	1/2/93	Scholar
Okuonghae Magnus (D)	6 3	13 02	Nigeria	16/2/86	Dagenham & R
Pentney Carl (G)	6 0	12 00	Colchester	3/2/89	Leicester C
Rose Michael (D)	5 11	12 04	Salford	28/7/82	Swindon T
Rowlands Martin (M)	5 9	10 10	Hammersmith	8/2/79	QPR
Sanderson Jordan (M)	6 0	11 02	Chingford	7/8/93	Scholar
White John (D)	6 0	12 01	Maldon	26/7/86	Scholar
Williams Ben (G)	6 0	13 01	Manchester	27/8/82	Carlisle U
Wilson Brian (D)	5 10	11 00	Manchester	9/5/83	Bristol C
Wordsworth Anthony (M)	6 1	12 00	Camden	3/1/89	Scholar

League Appearances: Antonio, M. 14(1); Baldwin, P. 4(1); Bond, A. 28(12); Coker, B. 15(5); Cousins, M. 10; Duguid, K. 16(9); Eastman, T. 24(1); Gillespie, S. 19(14); Hamilton, B. (1); Heath, M. 22(4); Henderson, I. 45(1); Izzet, K. 29(5); James, L. 17(6); Massey, G. 2(1); Massey, G. 2(3); O'Toole, J. 8(7); Odejayi, K. 33(10); Okuonghae, M. 42; Rose, M. 12(2); Rowlands, M. 7(2); Sears, F. 5(6); Thomas, C. (2); Vincent, A. 5(4); White, J. 21(5); Williams, B. 36; Wilson, B. 46; Wordsworth, A. 44.

Goals – League (61): Wordsworth 13 (2 pens), Gillespie 11 (2 pens), Henderson 9, Antonio 4, Odejayi 4, Bond 3, Duguid 3, Eastman 3, Heath 2, Rowlands 2, Sears 2 (1 pen), James 1, Vincent 1, own goals 3.

Carling Cup (3): Gillespie 1 (pen), Henderson 1, Odejayi 1.

FA Cup (4): James 2, Bond 1, Coker 1.

J Paint Trophy (1): Baldwin 1.

Ground: Weston Homes Community Stadium, United Way, Colchester, Essex CO4 5UP. Telephone: (01206) 755 100.

Capacity: 10,000.

Record Attendance: 19,072 v Reading, FA Cup 1st rd, 27 November 1948 (at Layer Road); 10,064 v Norwich C, FL 1, 16 January 2010 (at Community Stadium).

Manager: John Ward.

Most League Goals: 104, Division 4, 1961–62.

Highest League Scorer in Season: Bobby Hunt, 38, Division 4, 1961–62.

Most League Goals in Total Aggregate: Martyn King, 130, 1956–64.

Most Capped Player: Bela Balogh, 2 (9), Hungary.

Most League Appearances: Micky Cook, 613, 1969–84.

Colours: Royal blue and white striped shirts with white sleeves, royal blue shorts, white stockings.

Honours – GM Vauxhall Conference: Winners – 1991–92. **FA Trophy:** Winners: 1991–92.

COVENTRY CITY

Baker Carl (M)	6 2	12 06	Prescot	26/12/82	Stockport Co
Bell David (M)	5 10	11 05	Wellingborough	21/4/84	Norwich C
Bigirimana Gael (M)	5 9	11 09	Burundi	22/10/93	Scholar
Burge Lee (G)			Hereford	9/1/93	Scholar
Cameron Nathan (D)	6 2	12 04	Birmingham	21/11/91	Scholar
Christie Cyrus (D)	6 2	12 02	Coventry	30/9/92	Scholar
Clarke Jordan (D)	6 0	11 02	Coventry	19/11/91	Scholar
Cranie Martin (D)	6 1	12 09	Yeovil	23/9/86	Portsmouth
Deegan Gary (M)	5 9	11 11	Dublin	28/9/87	Bohemians
Dunn Chris (G)	6 5	13 11	Brentwood	23/10/87	Northampton T
Hussey Chris (D)	5 10	10 03	Hammersmith	2/1/89	AFC Wimbledon
Jeffers Shaun (F)	6 1	11 03	Bedford	14/4/92	Scholar
Keogh Richard (D)	6 0	11 02	Harlow	11/8/86	Carlisle U
McDonald Cody (F)	5 10	11 01	Witham	30/5/86	Norwich C
McPake James (D)	6 2	12 08	Airdrie	2/6/84	Livingston
McSheffrey Gary (F)	5 8	10 06	Coventry	13/8/82	Birmingham C
Murphy Joe (G)	6 2	13 06	Dublin	21/8/81	Scunthorpe U
O'Donovan Roy (F)	5 10	11 07	Cork	10/8/85	Sunderland
Platt Clive (F)	6 4	12 07	Wolverhampton	27/10/77	Colchester U
Thomas Conor (M)	6 1	11 05	Coventry	29/10/93	Scholar
Wilson Callum (M)	5 11	10 06	Coventry	27/2/92	Scholar
Wood Richard (D)	6 3	12 13	Ossett	5/7/85	Sheffield W

League Appearances: Baker, C. 20(6); Bell, D. 19(9); Bigirimana, G. 16(10); Cameron, N. 11(3); Christie, C. 27(10); Clarke, J. 17(2); Clingan, S. 34(2); Cranie, M. 38; Deegan, G. 19(5); Dunn, C. (2); Eastwood, F. (4); Gardner, G. 4; Henderson, J. (1); Hreidarsson, H. 2; Hussey, C. 28(1); Jeffers, S. (3); Jutkiewicz, L. 25; Keogh, R. 45; McDonald, C. 16(7); McPake, J. 3(2); McSheffrey, G. 37(2); Murphy, J. 46; Nimely-Tchuimeni, A. 16(1); Norwood, O. 17(1); O'Donovan, R. 6(5); Platt, C. 23(10); Roberts, W. (1); Ruffels, J. (1); Thomas, C. 24(3); Willis, J. (2); Wood, R. 12(5).

Goals – League (41): Jutkiewicz 9 (1 pen), McSheffrey 8 (3 pens), McDonald 4, Platt 4, Deegan 3, Clingan 2 (1 pen), Norwood 2, Baker 1, Clarke 1, Gardner 1, Nimely-Tchuimeni 1, Thomas 1, Wood 1, own goals 3.

Carling Cup (1): O'Donovan 1.

FA Cup (1): McSheffrey 1.

Ground: The Ricoh Arena, Phoenix Way, Foleshill, Coventry CV6 6GE. Telephone: (0844) 873 1883.

Capacity: 32,609.

Record Attendance: 51,455 v Wolverhampton W, Division 2, 29 April 1967 (at Highfield Road); 31,407 v Chelsea, FA Cup 6th rd, 7 March 2009 (at Ricoh Arena).

Manager: Andy Thorn.

Most League Goals: 108, Division 3 (S), 1931–32.

Highest League Scorer in Season: Clarrie Bourton, 49, Division 3 (S), 1931–32.

Most League Goals in Total Aggregate: Clarrie Bourton, 171, 1931–37.

Most Capped Player: Magnus Hedman, 44 (58), Sweden.

Most League Appearances: Steve Ogrizovic, 507, 1984–2000.

Colours: Sky blue shirts with grey horizontal stripes, white shorts, sky blue stockings.

Honours – Football League: Division 2 Champions – 1966–67. Division 3 Champions – 1963–64. Division 3 (S) Champions 1935–36. **FA Cup:** Winners – 1986–1987.

CRAWLEY TOWN

Akinde John (F)	6 2	10 01	Camberwell	8/7/89	Bristol C
Akpan Hope (M)	6 0	10 08	Liverpool	14/8/91	Everton

Brodie Richard (F)	6 2	13 00	Gateshead	8/7/87	York C
Bulman Dannie (M)	5 9	11 12	Ashford	24/1/79	Oxford U
Clarke Billy (F)	5 7	10 01	Cork	13/12/87	Blackpool
Davies Scott (M)	5 11	12 00	Aylesbury	10/3/88	Reading
Davis Claude (D)	6 3	14 04	Kingston, Jam	6/3/79	Crystal Palace
Evans Daniel (F)			Peterborough	24/11/93	Peterborough U Scholar
Hunt David (M)	5 11	11 09	Dulwich	10/9/82	Brentford
Kuipers Michels (G)	6 2	14 03	Amsterdam	26/6/74	Brighton & HA
McFadzean Kyle (D)	6 1	13 04	Sheffield	20/2/87	Sheffield U
Neilson Scott (M)	6 0	12 10	Enfield	15/5/87	Bradford C
Shearer Scott (G)	6 3	11 10	Glasgow	15/2/81	Wycombe W
Simpson Josh (M)	5 10	12 02	Cambridge	6/3/87	Peterborough U
Torres Sergio (M)	6 2	12 04	Mar del Plata	8/11/83	Peterborough U
Wassmer Charlie (D)	5 9	11 00	Hammersmith	21/3/91	Hayes & Yeading U
Wickham Aaron (M)			Camden	11/12/93	Peterborough U Scholar

League Appearances: Akinde, J. 7(18); Akpan, H. 17(9); Alexander, G. 14; Barnett, T. 25(1); Batt, S. 2(2); Batt, S. (1); Bulman, D. 41; Clarke, B. 16(1); Clarke, L. 4; Cummings, W. 6(3); Davies, S. 17(3); Davis, C. 27(2); Dempster, J. 6(1); Doughty, M. 2(14); Drury, A. 13; Eastman, T. 6; Gilmartin, R. 6; Griffiths, S. 6; Hawley, K. 1(3); Howell, D. 36(1); Hunt, D. 26(1); James, L. 6; Kuipers, M. 15; McFadzean, K. 36(1); Mills, P. 19(2); Neilson, S. 11(19); Pittman, J. (4); Shearer, S. 25; Simpson, J. 31(9); Smith, B. 3(2); Thomas, W. 2(4); Torres, S. 37(1); Tubbs, M. 23(1); Wassmer, C. 12(1); Watt, S. 6(8); Wilson, G. 2(2).
Goals – League (76): Barnett 14, Tubbs 12 (5 pens), Alexander 7 (3 pens), Bulman 3, Clarke, B. 3, Davis 3, Drury 3, Howell 3, Neilson 3, Torres 3, Davies 2, McFadzean 2, Mills 2, Simpson 2, Wassmer 2, Watt 2, Akinde 1, Akpan 1, Clarke, L. 1, Dempster 1, Pittman 1, Smith 1, Thomas 1, own goals 3.
Carling Cup (3): Akpan 1, Torres 1, Tubbs 1.
FA Cup (9): Tubbs 5 (2 pens), Barnett 1, Doughty 1, Drury 1, McFadzean 1.
J Paint Trophy (0).
Ground: Broadfield Stadium, Winfield Way, Crawley, Sussex RH11 9RX. Telephone: (01293) 410 000.
Capacity: 4,996 (1,150 seated).
Record Attendance: 4,522 v Weymouth, Doc Martens Premier League, 6 March 2004.
Manager: Sean O'Driscoll.
Most League Goals: 76, FL 2, 2011–12.
Highest League Scorer in Season: Tyrone Barnett, 14, 2011–12.
Most League Appearances: Dannie Bulman, 41, 2011–12.
Colours: All red.
Honours: Blue Square Premier – Champions: 2010–11.

CREWE ALEXANDRA   FL CHAMPIONSHIP 1

Clayton Harry (F)			Crewe	15/2/93	Scholar
Clayton Max (F)	5 9	11 00	Crewe	9/8/94	Scholar
Daniels Brendon (M)			Stoke	24/9/93	Scholar
Davis Harry (D)	6 2	12 04	Burnley	24/9/91	Scholar
Dugdale Adam (D)	6 3	12 07	Liverpool	12/9/87	Scholar
Garratt Ben (G)			Market Drayton	25/4/94	Scholar
Leitch-Smith AJ (F)	5 11	12 04	Crewe	6/3/90	Scholar
Mellor Kelvin (D)	5 10	11 09	Copenhagen	25/1/91	Nantwich T
Miller Shaun (F)	5 10	11 08	Alsager	25/9/87	Scholar
Moore Byron (M)	6 0	10 06	Stoke	24/8/88	Scholar
Murphy Luke (M)	6 1	11 05	Alsager	21/10/89	Scholar
Powell Nick (F)	6 0	10 07	Crewe	23/3/94	Scholar

Ray George (D)			Warrington	13/10/93	Scholar
Tootle Matt (D)	5 9	11 00	Widnes	11/10/90	Scholar
Turton Oliver (D)	5 11	11 11	Manchester	6/12/92	Scholar
Westwood Ashley (M)	5 10	11 00	Nantwich	1/4/90	Scholar
White Andrew (D)			Chester	8/10/92	Scholar

League Appearances: Artell, D. 31(1); Bell, L. 22(8); Bodin, B. 8; Brown, J. 2(5); Clayton, M. 1(23); Davis, H. 39(2); Dugdale, A. 43; Fletcher, W. 3(3); Hughes, C. (4); Leitch-Smith, A. 31(7); Lowry, J. 9(1); Martin, C. 26(3); Mellor, K. 6(6); Miller, S. 26(7); Moore, B. 42; Murphy, L. 39(3); Pearson, G. 8(1); Phillips, S. 46; Powell, N. 34(4); Sarcevic, A. 1(5); Shelley, D. 12(14); Tootle, M. 36(1); Tunnicliffe, J. 2; Turton, O. (2); Westwood, A. 39(2).

Goals – League (67): Powell 14, Leitch-Smith 8, Moore 8, Murphy 8, Davis 5 (4 pens), Miller 5, Clayton 3, Dugdale 3, Pearson 3, Westwood 3 (1 pen), Artell 2, Fletcher 1, Mellor 1, Shelley 1, own goals 2.

Carling Cup (2): Artell 1, Miller 1.

FA Cup (1): Moore 1.

J Paint Trophy (2): Clayton 1, Powell 1.

Play-Offs (5): Clayton 1, Dugdale 1, Leitch-Smith 1, Moore 1, Powell 1.

Ground: The Alexandra Stadium, Gresty Road, Crewe, Cheshire CW2 6EB. Telephone: (01270) 213 014.

Capacity: 10,107.

Record Attendance: 20,000 v Tottenham H, FA Cup 4th rd, 30 January 1960.

Manager: Steve Davis.

Most League Goals: 95, Division 3 (N), 1931–32.

Highest League Scorer in Season: Terry Harkin, 35, Division 4, 1964–65.

Most League Goals in Total Aggregate: Bert Swindells, 126, 1928–37.

Most Capped Player: Clayton Ince, 38 (79), Trinidad & Tobago.

Most League Appearances: Tommy Lowry, 436, 1966–78.

Colours: Red shirts with white trim, white shorts, red stockings.

CRYSTAL PALACE   FL CHAMPIONSHIP

Ambrose Darren (M)	6 0	11 00	Harlow	29/2/84	Charlton Ath
Appiah Kwesi (F)	5 11	12 08	Thamesmead	12/8/90	Peterborough U
Cadogan Kieron (M)	6 4	12 07	Tooting	3/8/90	Scholar
Clyne Nathaniel (D)	5 9	10 06	Stockwell	5/4/91	Scholar
De Silva Kyle (F)	5 10	11 05	Croydon	29/11/93	Scholar
Dikgacoi Kagisho (M)	5 11	12 10	Brandfort	24/11/84	Fulham
Dorman Andy (M)	6 0	10 10	Chester	1/5/82	St Mirren
Easter Jermaine (F)	5 9	12 02	Cardiff	15/1/82	Milton Keynes D
Gardner Anthony (D)	6 3	14 00	Stone	19/9/80	Hull C
Garvan Owen (M)	6 0	10 07	Dublin	29/1/88	Ipswich T
Holland Jack (D)	6 3	12 02	West Wickham	1/3/92	Scholar
Jedinak Mile (M)	6 2	13 12	Sydney	3/8/84	Genclerbirligi
King Tom (G)			Plymouth	9/3/95	Scholar
Marrow Alex (M)	6 1	13 00	Tyldesley	21/1/90	Blackburn R
McCarthy Patrick (D)	6 2	13 07	Dublin	31/5/83	Charlton Ath
Moxey Dean (D)	6 2	11 00	Exeter	14/1/86	Derby Co
Murray Glenn (F)	6 1	12 12	Maryport	25/9/83	Brighton & HA
O'Keefe Stuart (M)	5 8	10 00	Eye	4/3/91	Southend U
Parr Jonathan (M)	6 0	11 11	Oslo	21/10/88	Aalesund
Parsons Matthew (D)	5 10	11 09	Catford	23/12/91	Scholar
Pedroza Antonio (F)	5 7	10 07	Chester	20/2/91	Jaguares
Price Lewis (G)	6 3	13 05	Bournemouth	19/7/84	Derby Co
Scannell Sean (F)	5 9	11 07	Croydon	19/9/90	Scholar
Sekajja Ibra (F)	5 11	11 00	Uganda	31/10/92	Scholar

Speroni Julian (G)	6 0	11 00	Buenos Aires	18/5/79	Dundee
Taylor Quade (M)			Tooting	11/12/93	Dulwich Hamlet
Williams Jon (M)	5 6	10 00	Tunbridge Wells	9/10/93	Scholar
Wright David (D)	5 11	11 00	Warrington	1/5/80	Ipswich T
Wynter Alex (M)	6 0	13 04	Camberwell	15/9/93	Scholar
Zaha Wilfred (F)	5 11	10 05	Ivory Coast	10/11/92	Scholar

League Appearances: Ambrose, D. 26(10); Andrew, C. 2(4); Appiah, K. (4); Cadogan, K. 1; Clyne, N. 28; Davies, A. 1; De Silva, K. 2(4); Dikgacoi, K. 24(3); Dorman, A. (1); Dumbuya, M. 2; Easter, J. 18(15); Egan, J. 1; Gardner, A. 25(3); Garvan, O. 13(9); Iversen, S. (3); Jedinak, M. 29(2); Keinan, D. 3; Marrow, A. (1); Martin, C. 20(6); McCarthy, P. 42(1); McGivern, R. 5; McShane, P. 9(2); Moxey, D. 20(4); Murray, G. 25(13); O'Keefe, S. 13; Parr, J. 35(4); Parsons, M. 3(1); Pedroza, A. 1(3); Price, L. 4(1); Ramage, P. 14(3); Scannell, S. 27(10); Sekajja, I. 1; Speroni, J. 42; Tunchev, A. 9; Williams, J. 5(9); Wright, D. 22; Zaha, W. 34(7).
Goals – League (46): Ambrose 7 (4 pens), Martin 7 (1 pen), Murray 6 (1 pen), Zaha 6, Easter 5, Scannell 4, Garvan 3 (2 pens), Dikgacoi 2, McCarthy 2, Parr 2, Jedinak 1, own goal 1.
Carling Cup (11): Ambrose 3, Zaha 3, Andrew 1, Easter 1 (pen), Gardner 1, Murray 1, Williams 1.
FA Cup (0).
Ground: Selhurst Park Stadium, Whitehorse Lane, London SE25 6PU. Telephone: (020) 8768 6000.
Capacity: 26,225.
Record Attendance: 51,482 v Burnley, Division 2, 11 May 1979 (at Selhurst Park).
Manager: Dougie Freedman.
Most League Goals: 110, Division 4, 1960–61.
Highest League Scorer in Season: Peter Simpson, 46, Division 3 (S), 1930–31.
Most League Goals in Total Aggregate: Peter Simpson, 153, 1930–36.
Most Capped Player: Aleksandrs Kolinko, 23 (86), Latvia.
Most League Appearances: Jim Cannon, 571, 1973–88.
Colours: Red and blue striped shirts, blue shorts, blue stockings.
Honours – Football League: Division 1 – Champions 1993–94. Division 2 Champions – 1978–79. Division 3 (S) 1920–21. **Zenith Data Systems Cup:** Winners – 1991.

DAGENHAM & REDBRIDGE   FL CHAMPIONSHIP 2

Bingham Billy (D)	5 11	11 02	London	15/7/90	Crystal Palace
Cunnington Adam (F)			Leighton Buzzard	7/10/87	Kettering T
Dennis Louis (F)			Hendon		Youth
Doe Scott (D)	6 0	11 06	Reading	6/11/88	Weymouth
Edmans Rob (F)	6 5	12 08	Greenwich	25/1/87	Chelmsford C
Elito Medy (M)	6 2	13 00	Kinshasa	20/3/90	Colchester U
Gayle Dwight (F)			Walthamstow	20/10/89	Stansted
Gayle Ian (D)			Welling	23/10/92	Youth
Green Danny J (M)	6 0	12 06	Harlow	4/8/90	Billericay T
Green Dominic (F)	5 6	11 03	Newham	5/7/89	Peterborough U
Howell Luke (D)	5 10	10 05	Heathfield	5/1/87	Lincoln C
Ilesanmi Femi (D)	6 1	11 13	Southwark	18/4/91	Ashford T
Lewington Chris (G)	6 1	12 00	Sidcup	23/8/88	Leatherhead
Maher Kevin (M)	6 0	12 13	Ilford	17/10/76	Gillingham
Ogogo Abu (D)	5 8	10 02	Epsom	3/11/89	Arsenal
Osborn Alex (F)			Walthamstow	29/7/93	Grays Ath
Reed Jake (F)	5 9	11 07	Great Yarmouth	13/5/91	Great Yarmouth T
Reynolds Duran-Rhys (D)			Skegness	27/9/91	Southend U Scholar
Rose Richard (D)	6 0	12 04	Tonbridge	8/9/82	Hereford U
Saunders Matthew (M)	5 11	11 05	Chertsey	12/9/89	Fulham

Scott Josh (F)	6 1	12 00	Camden	10/5/85	Hayes & Yeading U
Spillane Michael (M)	5 9	11 10	Jersey	23/3/89	Norwich C
Tomlin Gavin (F)	6 0	12 02	Gillingham	13/1/83	Yeovil T
Wilkinson Luke (D)	6 2	11 09	Wells	2/12/92	Portsmouth
Williams Sam (F)	5 11	10 08	Greenwich	9/6/87	Yeovil T
Woodall Brian (F)	5 10	11 09	Bielefeld	28/12/87	Gresley

League Appearances: Abdullah, A. 4(1); Akinde, J. 4(1); Arber, M. 32(1); Baudry, M. 11; Bingham, B. 17(10); Bond, J. 5; Cunnington, A. 2(7); Doe, S. 41; Edmans, R. (3); Elito, M. 20(4); Gain, P. 16(4); Geohaghon, E. 1(1); Green, Danny J 4(4); Green, Dominic 8(8); Hewitt, T. 3(3); Hogan, D. (1); Howell, L. 10; Ilesanmi, F. 17; Lee, O. 15(1); Lewington, C. 41; Maher, K. 8; McCrory, D. 32(1); Montano, C. 10; Nurse, J. 36(3); Ogogo, A. 40; Parker, J. 6(2); Reed, J. 1(6); Reeves, B. 5; Rose, R. 9(1); Saunders, M. 5; Scannell, D. 7(7); Scott, J. 12(8); Shea, J. (1); Spillane, M. 29; Tomlin, G. 15(2); Walsh, P. 4(4); Wassmer, C. (1); Wearen, E. (2); Williams, S. 10; Woodall, B. 26(13).
Goals – League (50): Woodall 11, Doe 6, Nurse 5, Elito 4, Spillane 4, Lee 3, Montano 3, Arber 2 (1 pen), Bingham 2, Williams 2, Green, Dominic 1, Green, Danny, J. 1, McCrory 1, Ogogo 1, Rose 1, Saunders 1, Scott 1, own goal 1.
Carling Cup (0).
FA Cup (5): Nurse 3, Woodall 2.
J Paint Trophy (2): McCrory 1, Williams 1.
Ground: The London Borough of Barking and Dagenham Stadium, Victoria Road, Dagenham, Essex RM10 7XL. Telephone: (020) 8592 1549.
Capacity: 6,007.
Record Attendance: 4,791 v Shrewsbury T, FL 2, 2 May 2009.
Manager: John L. Still.
Most League Goals: 77, FL 2, 2008–09.
Highest League Scorer in Season: Paul Benson, 28, Conference, 2006–07.
Most League Goals in Total Aggregate: 40, Paul Benson, 2007–.
Most Capped Player: Jon Nurse, 6, Barbados.
Most League Appearances: Jon Nurse, 179, 2007–12.
Colours: Red shirts with blue sleeves and red trim, blue shorts, blue stockings.
Honours – Conference: Champions – 2006–07. **Isthmian League (Premier):** Champions 1999–2000.

DERBY COUNTY   FL CHAMPIONSHIP

Addison Miles (D)	6 2	13 03	Newham	7/1/89	Scholar
Atkins Ross (G)	6 0	13 00	Derby	3/11/89	Scholar
Bailey James (M)	6 0	12 05	Bollington	18/9/88	Crewe Alex
Ball Callum (F)	6 1	10 03	Leicester	8/10/92	Scholar
Barker Shaun (D)	6 2	12 07	Nottingham	19/9/82	Blackpool
Brayford John (D)	5 8	11 02	Stoke	29/12/87	Crewe Alex
Bryson Craig (M)	5 7	10 00	Rutherglen	6/11/86	Kilmarnock
Buxton Jake (D)	6 1	13 05	Sutton-in-Ashfield	4/3/85	Mansfield T
Croft Lee (F)	5 11	13 00	Wigan	21/6/85	Norwich C
Davies Ben (M)	5 7	12 00	Birmingham	27/5/81	Notts Co
Davies Steve (F)	6 0	12 00	Liverpool	29/12/87	Tranmere R
Deeney Saul (G)	6 0	12 13	Londonderry	12/3/83	Notts Co
Doyle Conor (F)	6 2	12 04	Mckinney	13/10/91	Creighton Univ
Fielding Frank (G)	5 11	12 00	Blackburn	4/4/88	Blackburn R
Hendrick Jeff (M)	6 1	11 11	Dublin	31/1/92	Scholar
Legzdins Adam (G)	6 1	14 02	Penkridge	28/11/86	Burton Alb
Maguire Chris (F)	5 7	10 05	Bellshill	16/1/89	Aberdeen
Naylor Tom (D)	5 11	11 05	Sutton-in-Ashfield	28/6/91	Mansfield T
O'Brien Mark (D)	5 11	12 02	Dublin	20/11/92	Cherry Orchard
Roberts Gareth (D)	5 8	11 12	Wrexham	6/2/78	Doncaster R

Robinson Theo (F)	5 9	10 03	Birmingham	22/1/89	Millwall
Shackell Jason (D)	6 4	13 06	Stevenage	27/9/83	Barnsley
Tyson Nathan (F)	5 10	10 02	Reading	4/5/82	Nottingham F
Ward Jamie (M)	5 5	9 04	Birmingham	12/5/86	Sheffield U
Witham Alex (M)			Harrow	14/9/92	Scholar

League Appearances: Anderson, R. 5(3); Bailey, J. 17(5); Ball, C. 11(12); Barker, S. 19(1); Bennett, M. 2(7); Brayford, J. 22(1); Bryson, C. 44; Buxton, J. 12(9); Carroll, T. 8(4); Croft, L. 4(4); Cywka, T. 3(5); Davies, B. 30(5); Davies, S. 20(6); Doyle, C. 1(5); Fielding, F. 44; Green, P. 26(1); Hendrick, J. 38(4); Hughes, W. 1(2); Kilbane, K. 7(2); Legzdins, A. 2(2); Maguire, C. 2(5); Naylor, T. 8; Noble, R. 1(1); O'Brien, M. 15(5); Priskin, T. 4(1); Roberts, G. 39(2); Robinson, T. 27(12); Shackell, J. 46; Tyson, N. 13(10); Ward, J. 35(2).

Goals – League (50): Davies, S. 11 (2 pens), Robinson 10 (1 pen), Bryson 6, Ward 4, Ball 3, Hendrick 3, Buxton 2, Davies, B. 2, Carroll 1, Cywka 1, Green 1, Kilbane 1, Maguire 1, Priskin 1, Roberts 1, Shackell 1, own goal 1.

Carling Cup (2): Maguire 1, Robinson 1.

FA Cup (1): Robinson 1.

Ground: Pride Park Stadium, Derby DE24 8XL. Telephone: (0871) 472 1884.

Capacity: 33,597.

Record Attendance: 41,826 v Tottenham H, Division 1, 20 September 1969 (at Baseball Ground); 33,597, England v Mexico, 25 May 2001 (at Pride Park).

Manager: Nigel Clough.

Most League Goals: 111, Division 3 (N), 1956–57.

Highest League Scorer in Season: Jack Bowers, 37, Division 1, 1930–31; Ray Straw, 37 Division 3 (N), 1956–57.

Most League Goals in Total Aggregate: Steve Bloomer, 292, 1892–1906 and 1910–14.

Most Capped Player: Deon Burton, 42 (59), Jamaica.

Most League Appearances: Kevin Hector, 486, 1966–78 and 1980–82.

Colours: White shirts with black trim, black shorts with white trim, white stockings with black trim.

Honours – Football League: Division 1 Champions – 1971–72, 1974–75. Division 2 Champions – 1911–12, 1914–15, 1968–69, 1986–87. Division 3 (N) Champions – 1956–57. **FA Cup:** Winners – 1945–46. **Texaco Cup:** Winners 1972.

DONCASTER ROVERS   FL CHAMPIONSHIP 1

Bagayoko Mamadou (F)	6 3	12 06	Paris	21/5/79	PAS Giannina
Bamogo Habib (F)	5 9	11 05	Paris	8/5/82	Panaitolikos
Bennett Kyle (F)	5 5	9 08	Telford	9/9/90	Bury
Beye Habib (D)	6 0	12 06	Paris	19/10/77	Newcastle U
Brown Chris (F)	6 3	13 01	Doncaster	11/12/84	Preston NE
Chimbonda Pascal (D)	5 10	11 05	Les Abymes	21/2/79	QPR
Coppinger James (F)	5 7	10 03	Middlesbrough	10/1/81	Exeter C
Diouf El Hadji (F)	5 11	11 11	Dakar	15/1/81	Blackburn R
Friend George (D)	6 2	13 01	Barnstaple	19/10/87	Wolverhampton W
Husband James (D)	5 10	10 00	Leeds	3/1/94	Scholar
Martis Shelton (D)	6 0	11 11	Willemstad	29/11/82	WBA
O'Connor James (D)	5 10	12 04	Birmingham	20/11/84	Bournemouth
Spurr Tommy (D)	6 1	11 05	Leeds	13/9/87	Sheffield W
Stock Brian (M)	5 11	11 02	Winchester	24/12/81	Preston NE
Sullivan Neil (G)	6 2	12 00	Sutton	24/2/70	Leeds U
Woods Gary (G)	6 1	11 00	Kettering	1/10/90	Manchester U Scholar
Woods Martin (M)	5 11	11 13	Airdrie	1/1/86	Rotherham U

League Appearances: Bagayoko, M. 2(3); Bamogo, H. 4; Barnes, G. 24(9); Baxendale, J. (2); Bennett, K. 15(21); Beye, H. 22; Brown, C. 7(4); Brown, R. 1(2); Button, D. 7;

Chimbonda, P. 16; Coppinger, J. 31(7); Diouf, E. 22; Dumbuya, M. 6(4); Fortune, M. 5; Friend, G. 24(3); Gillett, S. 43(3); Goulon, H. 5(1); Hayter, J. 18(13); Hird, S. 23(8); Husband, J. 2(1); Ikeme, C. 15; Ilunga, H. 19; Keegan, P. 1(1); Kirkland, C. 1; Lalkovic, M. 1(5); Lockwood, A. 11(3); Martis, S. 14(1); Mason, R. 2(2); Naylor, R. 13; O'Connor, J. 24(4); Oster, J. 23(7); Parkin, J. 4(1); Piquionne, F. 8; Robert, F. 7(6); Sharp, B. 18(2); Spurr, T. 19; Stock, B. 24(2); Sullivan, N. 9; Wilson, M. (3); Woods, G. 14; Woods, M. 2(2).
Goals – League (43): Sharp 10 (1 pen), Diouf 6 (2 pens), Bennett 4, Hayter 4 (1 pen), Gillett 3, Bagayoko 2, Beye 2, Brown, C. 2, Coppinger 2, Piquionne 2, Robert 2, Barnes 1, Fortune 1, Oster 1, Stock 1.
Carling Cup (4): Bennett 1, Brown, C. 1 (pen), Hayter 1, Mason 1.
FA Cup (0).
Ground: Keepmoat Stadium, Stadium Way, Lakeside, Doncaster, South Yorkshire DN4 5JW. Telephone: (01302) 764 664.
Capacity: 15,231.
Record Attendance: 37,149 v Hull C, Division 3 (N), 2 October 1948 (at Belle Vue); 15,001 v Leeds U, FL 1, 1 April 2008 (at Keepmoat Stadium).
Manager: Dean Saunders.
Most League Goals: 123, Division 3 (N), 1946–47.
Highest League Scorer in Season: Clarrie Jordan, 42, Division 3 (N), 1946–47.
Most League Goals in Total Aggregate: Tom Keetley, 180, 1923–29.
Most Capped Player: Len Graham, 14, Northern Ireland.
Most League Appearances: Fred Emery, 417, 1925–36.
Colours: Red and white hooped shirts, red sleeves with black trim, black shorts with red trim, black stockings with red tops.
Honours – Football League: Division 3 Champions – 2003–04. Division 3 (N) Champions – 1934–35, 1946–47, 1949–50. Division 4 Champions – 1965–66, 1968–69.
J Paint Trophy: Winners – 2006–07. **Football Conference:** Champions – 2002–03.

EVERTON   FA PREMIERSHIP

Anichebe Victor (F)	6 1	13 00	Nigeria	23/4/88	Scholar
Baines Leighton (D)	5 8	11 00	Liverpool	11/12/84	Wigan Ath
Barkley Ross (M)	6 2	12 00	Liverpool	5/12/93	Scholar
Baxter Jose (F)	5 10	11 07	Bootle	7/2/92	Academy
Bidwell Jake (D)	6 0	11 00	Southport	21/3/93	Scholar
Browning Tyias (D)			Liverpool	27/5/94	Scholar
Cahill Tim (M)	5 10	10 12	Sydney	6/12/79	Millwall
Coleman Seamus (D)	6 4	10 07	Donegal	11/10/88	Sligo R
Distin Sylvain (D)	6 3	14 05	Bagnolet	16/12/77	Portsmouth
Duffy Shane (D)	6 4	12 00	Derry	1/1/92	Scholar
Fellaini Marouane (M)	6 4	13 05	Brussels	22/11/87	Standard Liege
Forrester Anton (F)			Liverpool	11/2/94	Scholar
Forshaw Adam (M)	6 1	11 02	Liverpool	8/10/91	Scholar
Garbutt Luke (D)	5 10	11 07	Harrogate	21/5/93	Scholar
Gibson Darron (M)	6 0	12 04	Derry	25/10/87	Manchester U
Gueye Magaye (F)	5 10	11 07	Paris	6/7/90	Strasbourg
Hammar Johan (D)			Malmo	22/2/94	Scholar
Heitinga Johnny (D)	5 11	11 05	Alphen aan den Rijn	15/11/83	Atletico Madrid
Hibbert Tony (D)	5 9	11 05	Liverpool	20/2/81	Trainee
Hope Hallam (F)			Manchester	17/3/94	Scholar
Howard Tim (G)	6 3	14 12	North Brunswick	6/3/79	Manchester U
Jagielka Phil (D)	6 0	13 01	Manchester	17/8/82	Sheffield U
Jelavic Nikica (F)	6 2	13 12	Capljina	27/8/85	Rangers
Kelly Sam (M)			Huntingdon	21/10/93	Norwich C Scholar
Lundstram John (M)			Liverpool	18/2/94	Scholar
McAleny Conor (F)	5 10	12 05	Liverpool	12/8/92	Scholar
Mucha Jan (G)	6 2	12 00	Bela nad Cirochou	5/12/82	Legia

Neville Phil (M)	5 11	12 00	Bury	21/1/77	Manchester U
Osman Leon (F)	5 8	10 09	Billinge	17/5/81	Trainee
Rodwell Jack (D)	6 2	12 07	Southport	11/3/91	Scholar
Santos Francisco (M)			Guinea-Bissau	18/1/92	Benfica Youth
Silva Joao (F)	6 2	12 08	Vila das Aves	21/5/90	Aves
Springthorpe Mason (D)			Shrewsbury	1/11/94	Scholar
Taudul Mateusz (G)			Bialystok	12/11/94	Scholar
Vellios Apostolos (F)	6 3	12 06	Salonika	8/1/92	Iraklis
Wallace James (M)	5 11	12 08	Fazackerly	19/12/91	Scholar
Yobo Joseph (D)	6 1	13 00	Kano	6/9/80	Marseille

League Appearances: Anichebe, V. 5(7); Arteta, M. 1(1); Baines, L. 33; Barkley, R. 2(4); Baxter, J. (1); Beckford, J. 1(1); Bilyaletdinov, D. 7(3); Cahill, T. 27(8); Coleman, S. 14(4); Distin, S. 24(3); Donovan, L. 7; Drenthe, R. 10(11); Duffy, S. 2(2); Fellaini, M. 31(3); Gibson, D. 11; Gueye, M. 3(14); Heitinga, J. 29(1); Hibbert, T. 31(1); Howard, T. 38; Jagielka, P. 29(1); Jelavic, N. 10(3); McAleny, C. (2); McFadden, J. 2(5); Neville, P. 24(3); Osman, L. 28(2); Pienaar, S. 14; Rodwell, J. 11(3); Saha, L. 15(3); Stracqualursi, D. 7(14); Vellios, A. 2(11).

Goals – League (50): Jelavic 9 (1 pen), Osman 5, Anichebe 4, Baines 4 (3 pens), Pienaar 4, Drenthe 3, Fellaini 3, Vellios 3, Cahill 2, Jagielka 2, Rodwell 2, Arteta 1 (1 pen), Gibson 1, Gueye 1, Heitinga 1, Howard 1, Saha 1, Stracqualursi 1, own goals 2.

Carling Cup (6): Anichebe 1, Arteta 1, Fellaini 1, Neville 1, Saha 1, own goal 1.

FA Cup (10): Jelavic 2, Stracqualursi 2, Baines 1 (pen), Cahill 1, Drenthe 1, Fellaini 1, Heitinga 1, own goal 1.

Ground: Goodison Park, Goodison Road, Liverpool L4 4EL. Telephone: (0871) 663 1878.

Capacity: 40,158.

Record Attendance: 78,299 v Liverpool, Division 1, 18 September 1948.

Manager: David Moyes.

Most League Goals: 121, Division 2, 1930–31.

Highest League Scorer in Season: William Ralph 'Dixie' Dean, 60, Division 1, 1927–28 (All-time League record).

Most League Goals in Total Aggregate: William Ralph 'Dixie' Dean, 349, 1925–37.

Most Capped Player: Neville Southall, 92, Wales.

Most League Appearances: Neville Southall, 578, 1981–98.

Colours: Blue shirts with white trim, white shorts, white stockings.

Honours – Football League: Division 1 Champions – 1890–91, 1914–15, 1927–28, 1931–32, 1938–39, 1962–63, 1969–70, 1984–85, 1986–87. Division 2 Champions – 1930–31. **FA Cup:** Winners – 1906, 1933, 1966, 1984, 1995. **European Competitions:** European Cup-Winners' Cup: Winners – 1984–85.

EXETER CITY   FL CHAMPIONSHIP 2

Archibald-Henville Troy (D)	6 2	13 03	Newham	4/11/88	Tottenham H
Bauza Guillem (F)	5 11	12 01	Palma de Mallorca	25/10/84	Northampton T
Bennett Scott (D)	5 10	12 10	Truro	30/11/90	Scholar
Coles Danny (D)	6 1	11 06	Bristol	31/10/81	Bristol R
Dawson Aaron (M)	5 10	10 10	Exmouth	24/3/92	Scholar
Duffy Richard (D)	5 9	10 03	Swansea	30/8/85	Millwall
Dunne James (M)	5 11	10 12	Bromley	18/9/89	Arsenal
Edwards Rob (D)	6 0	12 02	Kendal	1/4/73	Blackpool
Frear Elliott (F)	5 8	10 01	Exeter	11/9/90	Scholar
Gow Alan (M)	6 0	11 00	Clydebank	9/10/82	East Bengal
Jones Billy (D)	6 1	11 05	Chatham	26/3/83	Crewe Alex
Keohane Jimmy (M)	5 11	11 05	Wexford	22/1/91	Bristol C
Krysiak Artur (G)	6 1	12 00	Lodz	11/8/89	Birmingham C
Nichols Tom (F)	5 10	10 10	Wellington	1/9/93	Scholar

O'Flynn John (F)	5 11	11 11	Cobh	11/7/82	Barnet
Sercombe Liam (M)	5 10	10 10	Exeter	25/4/90	Scholar
Tisdale Paul (M)	5 9	11 13	Valletta	14/1/73	
Tully Steve (D)	5 8	11 02	Paignton	10/2/80	Torquay U

League Appearances: Archibald-Henville, T. 45; Baldwin, P. 9; Bauza, G. 12(15); Bennett, S. 13(2); Bignall, N. 3; Coles, D. 28(3); Cureton, J. 5(2); Dalla Valle, L. 4(1); Dawson, A. 2; Duffy, R. 22(6); Dunne, J. 44(1); Fortune, J. 5; Frear, E. 5(5); Golbourne, S. 26; Gow, A. 6(1); Hackett, C. 5; Jones, B. 16(3); Keohane, J. (4); Krysiak, A. 38; Logan, R. 11(17); McNish, C. 2(3); Nardiello, D. 28(8); Nichols, T. 2(5); Noble, D. 42; O'Brien, L. 2(1); O'Flynn, J. 8(16); Oakley, M. 7; Pidgeley, L. 8(2); Ricketts, R. (1); Sercombe, L. 27(6); Shephard, C. 7(4); Taylor, J. 26(4); Tully, S. 42(2); Vine, R. 4(1); Whichelow, M. 2.
Goals – League (46): Nardiello 9 (3 pens), Sercombe 7, Logan 5, Bennett 3, Gow 3, Taylor 3, Archibald-Henville 2, Bauza 2 (1 pen), Coles 2, Dunne 2, Noble 2, O'Flynn 2 (1 pen), Cureton 1, Jones 1, Nichols 1, own goal 1.
Carling Cup (3): Bauza 1, Nardiello 1 (pen), Shephard 1.
FA Cup (3): Frear 1, Logan 1, Noble 1.
J Paint Trophy (2): Dunne 1, Nardiello 1.
Ground: St James Park, Stadium Way, Exeter EX4 6PX. Telephone: (01392) 411 243.
Capacity: 8,830.
Record Attendance: 20,984 v Sunderland, FA Cup 6th rd (replay), 4 March 1931.
Manager: Paul Tisdale.
Most League Goals: 88, Division 3 (S), 1932–33.
Highest League Scorer in Season: Fred Whitlow, 33, Division 3 (S), 1932–33.
Most League Goals in Total Aggregate: Tony Kellow, 129, 1976–78, 1980–83, 1985–88.
Most Capped Player: Dermot Curtis, 1 (17), Eire.
Most League Appearances: Arnold Mitchell, 495, 1952–66.
Colours: Red and white striped shirts, red sleeves, white shorts, white stockings.
Honours – Football League: Division 4 Champions – 1989–90. **Division 3 (S) Cup:** Winners – 1934.

FLEETWOOD TOWN   FL CHAMPIONSHIP 2

Barry Anthony (M)	5 7	10 01	Liverpool	29/5/86	Chester C
Beeley Shaun (D)	5 10	11 05	Stockport	21/11/88	Southport
Briggs Keith (M)	6 0	11 05	Glossop	11/12/81	Kidderminster H
Brown Junior (M)	5 9	10 10	Crewe	7/5/89	Northwich Vic
Clancy Sean (M)	5 8	9 13	Liverpool	16/9/87	Burscough
Cox Stefan (M)				17/9/91	Tooting & M
Davies Scott (G)	6 0	11 00	Blackpool	27/2/87	Morecambe
Edwards Paul (M)	5 10	12 02	Manchester	1/1/80	Barrow
Goodall Alan (D)	5 9	11 07	Birkenhead	2/12/81	Stockport Co
Linwood Paul (D)	6 2	12 08	Birkenhead	24/10/83	Grimsby T
Mangan Andrew (F)	5 9	11 09	Liverpool	30/8/86	Wrexham
McGuire Jamie (M)	5 7	11 00	Birkenhead	13/11/83	Droylsden
McNulty Steve (D)	6 1	13 12	Liverpool	26/9/83	Barrow
Milligan Jamie (M)	5 7	9 13	Blackpool	3/1/80	AFC Fylde
Pond Nathan (M)				5/1/85	Lancaster C
Seddon Gareth (F)	5 9	12 04	Burnley	23/5/80	Kettering T
St Louis-Hamilton 6 3	12 11	Stevenage		7/5/90	Darlington
Danzelle (G)					
Till Peter (M)	5 11	11 05	Birmingham	7/9/85	York C
Vieira Magno (F)	5 10	11 13	Bahia	13/2/85	Ebbsfleet U

League Appearances: Allen, (2); Atkinson, 15(2); Barry, 2; Beeley, 32(1); Briggs, 8(8); Brodie, 16(18); Brown, J. 18(3); Brown, S. 3(1); Cavanagh, 23; Charnock, 4; Clancy, 7(4); Cox, 3(3); Crowther, (3); Davies, 46; Donnelly, 2(3); Edwards, 7; Flynn, 3; Fowler, 17(2);

Goodall, 29(2); Harvey, 3(2); Holmes, 3; Hughes, 1; Jackson, 4; Linwood, 3; Mangan, 39(2); McGuire, 34(4); McNulty, 39; Milligan, 19(6); Pond, 29(5); Rose, 8(2); Rowe, (2); Seddon, 22(16); Till, 9(9); Vardy, 34(2); Vieira, 16(8); Wassmer, 3; Wilson, 5.

Goals – League (102): Vardy 31, Mangan 19 (5 pens), Brodie 9 (1 pen), Vieira 9 (1 pen), Seddon 8, Milligan 4 (3 pens), Cavanagh 3, Clancy 3, Jackson 2, Rose 2, Atkinson 1, Beeley 1, Briggs 1, Charnock 1, Cox 1, Donnelly 1, McGuire 1, Pond 1, Till 1, own goals 3.

FA Cup (13): Milligan 3 (1 pen), Vardy 3, Mangan 2, Brodie 1, Charnock 1, Clancy 1, McGuire 1, Seddon 1.

Ground: Highbury Stadium, Park Avenue, Fleetwood, Lancs FY7 5TX. Telephone: (01253) 775 080.

Capacity: 5,094.

Record Attendance: (Before 1997) 6,150 v Rochdale, FA Cup 1st Rd, 13 November 1965; (Since 1997) 5,092 v Blackpool, FA Cup 3rd Rd, 7 January 2012.

Manager: Micky Mellon.

Most League Appearances: Percy Ronson, 416, 1949-64.

Colours: Red shirts with white sleeves, white shorts, red stockings.

Honours – Blue Square Premier: Champions – 2011–12.

FULHAM   FA PREMIERSHIP

Name			From	Born	Previous Club
Altman Omri (M)	5 10	11 11	Tel Aviv	23/3/94	Scholar
Arthurworrey Stephen (D)	6 4	13 12	Hackney	15/10/94	Scholar
Baird Chris (D)	5 10	11 11	Ballymoney	25/2/82	Southampton
Banya Charlie (M)			Tulse Hill	18/9/93	Scholar
Bettinelli Marcus (G)			London	24/5/92	Scholar
Briggs Matthew (D)	6 1	11 12	Wandsworth	6/3/91	School
Brister Alex (M)			Epsom	19/12/93	Scholar
Burn Dan (D)	6 6	13 00	Blyth	1/5/92	Darlington
Dalla Valle Lauri (F)	5 9	11 03	Joensuu	14/9/91	Liverpool
Davies Simon (M)	5 10	11 05	Haverfordwest	23/10/79	Everton
Della-Verde Lyle (M)			Leeds	9/1/95	Liverpool
Dembele Moussa (F)	5 9	10 01	Wilrijk	17/7/87	AZ
Dempsey Clint (M)	6 1	12 02	Nacogdoches	9/3/83	New England Rev
Diarra Mahamadou (M)	6 0	11 13	Bamako	18/5/81	Real Madrid
Donegan Tom (M)			Huyton	15/9/92	Everton Scholar
Duff Damien (F)	5 9	12 06	Ballyboden	2/3/79	Newcastle U
Etheridge Neil (G)	6 3	14 00	Enfield	7/2/90	Scholar
Etuhu Dickson (M)	6 2	13 04	Kano	8/6/82	Sunderland
Frei Kerim (M)	5 7	10 05	Feldkirch	19/11/93	Scholar
Gameiro Corey (F)			Wollongong	7/2/93	Academy
Gecov Marcel (M)	5 11	11 00	Prague	1/1/88	Slovan Liberec
Grimmer Jack (M)	6 0	12 06	Aberdeen	25/1/94	Aberdeen
Halliche Rafik (D)	6 2	12 02	Algiers	2/9/86	Hussein Dey
Hangeland Brede (D)	6 4	13 05	Houston	20/6/81	FC Copenhagen
Hoesen Danny (F)	6 1	12 00	Kerkrade	15/1/91	Fortuna Sittard
Hughes Aaron (D)	6 0	11 00	Cookstown	8/11/79	Aston Villa
Jorenen Jesse (G)			Helsinki	21/3/93	Scholar
Kacaniklic Alex (M)	5 11	10 05	Helsingborg	13/8/91	Liverpool
Kasami Pajtim (M)	6 2	11 00	Macedonia	2/6/92	Palermo
Kavanagh Sean (D)			Dublin	20/1/94	Scholar
Kelly Stephen (D)	6 0	12 04	Dublin	6/9/83	Birmingham C
Minkwitz Ronny (M)			Duisburg	9/12/93	Scholar
Na Bangna Buomesca (M)			Guinea-Bissau	6/5/93	Chelsea Scholar
O'Reilly Daniel (D)	5 10	11 13	Dublin	11/4/95	Scholar
Oberschmidt Max (G)			Germany	25/1/95	Scholar
Peniket Richard (F)			Stourbridge	4/3/93	Scholar

Pritchard Josh (M)	5 9	11 02	Stockport	23/9/92	Scholar
Riise John Arne (M)	6 1	14 00	Molde	24/9/80	Roma
Ruiz Bryan (M)	6 2	12 04	Alajuela	18/8/85	Twente
Sa Orlando (F)	6 2	13 05	Barcelos	26/5/88	Porto
Schwarzer Mark (G)	6 4	14 07	Sydney	6/10/72	Middlesbrough
Senderos Philippe (D)	6 1	13 10	Geneva	14/2/85	Arsenal
Sidwell Steve (M)	5 10	11 00	Wandsworth	14/12/82	Aston Villa
Smith Alex (D)	5 9	8 09	Clapham	31/10/91	Scholar
Somogyi Csaba (G)	6 3	13 05	Hungary	7/4/85	Rakospalotai
Stockdale David (G)	6 3	13 04	Leeds	20/9/85	Darlington
Tankovic Muamer (F)			Norrkoping	22/2/95	Scholar
Trotta Marcello (F)	6 1	12 12	Caserta	29/9/92	Napoli
Vigen Christensen Lasse (M)	5 10	12 00	Esbjerg	15/8/94	Midtjylland
Williams Ryan (F)	5 11	12 00	Perth	28/10/93	Portsmouth
Woodrow Cauley (F)			Hemel Hempstead	2/12/94	Scholar

League Appearances: Baird, C. 13(6); Briggs, M. 1(1); Davies, S. 3(3); Dembele, M. 33(3); Dempsey, C. 37; Diarra, M. 8(3); Duff, D. 23(5); Etuhu, D. 9(13); Frei, K. 6(10); Gecov, M. (2); Grygera, Z. 5; Hangeland, B. 38; Hughes, A. 18(1); Johnson, A. 13(7); Kacaniklic, A. 2(2); Kasami, P. 3(4); Kelly, S. 21(3); Murphy, D. 33(3); Pogrebnyak, P. 12; Riise, J. 35(1); Ruiz, B. 17(10); Sa, O. 3(4); Schwarzer, M. 30; Senderos, P. 21; Sidwell, S. 12(2); Stockdale, D. 8; Trotta, M. (1); Zamora, B. 14(1).
Goals – League (48): Dempsey 17, Pogrebnyak 6, Zamora 5 (1 pen), Johnson, A. 3, Dembele 2, Duff 2, Murphy 2 (2 pens), Ruiz 2, Diarra 1, Sa 1, Senderos 1, Sidwell 1, own goals 5.
Carling Cup (0).
FA Cup (5): Dempsey 3 (1 pen), Duff 1, Murphy 1 (pen).
Europa League (24): Johnson 8, Dempsey 3, Duff 3, Murphy 3 (3 pens), Sidwell 2, Zamora 2, Briggs 1, Frei 1, Hughes 1.
Ground: Craven Cottage, Stevenage Road, London SW6 6HH. Telephone: (0843) 208 1222.
Capacity: 26,600.
Record Attendance: 49,335 v Millwall, Division 2, 8 October 1938.
Manager: Martin Jol.
Most League Goals: 111, Division 3 (S), 1931–32.
Highest League Scorer in Season: Frank Newton, 43, Division 3 (S), 1931–32.
Most League Goals in Total Aggregate: Gordon Davies, 159, 1978–84, 1986–91.
Most Capped Player: Johnny Haynes, 56, England.
Most League Appearances: Johnny Haynes, 594, 1952–70.
Colours: White shirts with black trim, black shorts, white stockings.
Honours – Football League: Division 1 Champions – 2000–01. Division 2 Champions – 1948–49, 1998–99. Division 3 (S) Champions – 1931–32. **European Competitions: Intertoto Cup:** Winners – 2002.

GILLINGHAM   FL CHAMPIONSHIP 2

Birchall Adam (F)	5 7	10 09	Maidstone	2/12/84	Dover Ath
Brown Alex (M)			S Woodham Ferrers	30/9/92	Scholar
Brunt Thomas (M)			Chatham	5/1/93	Scholar
Carter Joe (D)			Buckhurst Hill	20/11/92	Charlton Ath
Davies Callum (D)	6 1	11 11	Sittingbourne	8/2/93	Scholar
Essam Connor (D)	6 0	12 00	Sheerness	9/7/92	Scholar
Evans Jack (D)	5 10	11 05	Gravesend	19/3/93	Scholar
Fish Matt (D)			Croydon	5/1/89	Dover Ath
Flitney Ross (G)	6 3	12 07	Hitchin	1/6/84	Barnet
Frampton Andrew (D)	5 11	10 10	Wimbledon	3/9/79	Millwall

Fuller Barry (D)	5 10	11 10	Ashford	25/9/84	Charlton Ath
Gazzaniga Paulo (G)	6 5	14 02	Santa Fe	2/1/92	Valencia Youth
Hawkes Darren (G)			Ashford	24/6/93	Scholar
Jackman Danny (D)	5 4	10 01	Worcester	3/1/83	Northampton T
Kedwell Danny (F)	5 11	12 13	Gillingham	3/8/83	AFC Wimbledon
Lee Charlie (M)	5 11	11 07	Whitechapel	5/1/87	Peterborough U
Martin Joe (M)	6 0	12 13	Dagenham	29/11/88	Blackpool
Miller Ashley (F)	5 7	10 03	Dover	8/6/94	Scholar
Montrose Lewis (M)	6 0	12 00	Manchester	17/11/88	Wycombe W
Payne Jack (M)	5 9	9 02	Gravesend	5/12/91	Scholar
Whelpdale Chris (M)	6 0	12 08	Harold Wood	27/1/87	Peterborough U

League Appearances: Brown, A. (1); Davies, C. (2); Essam, C. 17(1); Evans, J. 4(3); Fish, M. 19(4); Flitney, R. 27; Frampton, A. 27(1); Fuller, B. 9; Gazzaniga, P. 19(1); Jackman, D. 36(4); Kedwell, D. 37(3); King, S. 8(1); Lawrence, M. 24(2); Lee, C. 28(5); Lee, O. 5(3); Martin, J. 32(3); Miller, A. 2(3); Montrose, L. 28(9); Nouble, F. 12(1); Obita, J. 5(1); Oli, D. 4(19); Osei-Kuffour, J. 26(4); Payne, J. 29(1); Payne, S. (12); Richards, G. 24; Rooney, L. 11(6); Spiller, D. 6(9); Tomlin, G. 9(1); Vine, R. 3(6); Weston, C. 21(9); Whelpdale, C. 34(5).
Goals – League (79): Kedwell 12 (7 pens), Whelpdale 12 (1 pen), Osei-Kuffour 9 (1 pen), Lee, C. 6, Tomlin 6, Nouble 5 (1 pen), Jackman 4, Montrose 4, Obita 3, Rooney 3 (2 pens), Oli 2, Payne, J. 2, Spiller 2, Fish 1, King 1, Martin 1, Miller 1, Payne, S. 1, Richards 1, Vine 1, own goals 2.
Carling Cup (0).
FA Cup (8): Kedwell 2, Weston 2, Jackman 1, Payne, J. 1, Payne, S. 1, Richards 1.
J Paint Trophy (1): Richards 1.
Ground: MEMS Priestfield Stadium, Redfern Avenue, Gillingham, Kent ME7 4DD. Telephone: (01634) 300 000.
Capacity: 11,440.
Record Attendance: 23,002 v QPR, FA Cup 3rd rd, 10 January 1948.
Manager: Martin Allen.
Most League Goals: 90, Division 4, 1973–74.
Highest League Scorer in Season: Ernie Morgan, 31, Division 3 (S), 1954–55; Brian Yeo, 31, Division 4, 1973–74.
Most League Goals in Total Aggregate: Brian Yeo, 135, 1963–75.
Most Capped Player: Mamady Sidibe, 7 (14), Mali.
Most League Appearances: John Simpson, 571, 1957–72.
Colours: Red shirts with blue sleeves, white shorts, white stockings.
Honours – Football League: Division 4 Champions – 1963–64.

HARTLEPOOL UNITED FL CHAMPIONSHIP 1

Austin Neil (D)	5 10	11 09	Barnsley	26/4/83	Darlington
Baldwin Jack (D)	6 1	11 00	Barking	30/6/93	Faversham T
Collins Sam (D)	6 2	14 01	Pontefract	5/6/77	Hull C
Flinders Scott (G)	6 4	13 00	Rotherham	12/6/86	Crystal Palace
Hartley Peter (D)	6 0	12 06	Hartlepool	3/4/88	Sunderland
Horwood Evan (D)	6 0	10 06	Billingham	10/3/86	Carlisle U
Humphreys Richie (M)	5 11	12 07	Sheffield	30/11/77	Cambridge U
James Luke (M)	6 0	12 08	Amble	4/11/94	Scholar
Johnson Paul (D)	6 0	12 11	Sunderland	5/4/92	Scholar
Luscombe Nathan (M)	5 8	11 07	Gateshead	6/11/89	Sunderland
Monkhouse Andy (M)	6 1	11 06	Leeds	23/10/80	Swindon T
Murray Paul (M)	5 9	10 08	Carlisle	31/8/76	Shrewsbury T
Nish Colin (F)	6 3	11 07	Edinburgh	7/3/81	Hibernian
Poole James (F)	5 11	12 05	Stockport	20/3/90	Manchester C

Rafferty Andy (G)	6 6	13 07	Sidcup	27/5/88	Guisborough T
Richards Jordan (M)	5 9	11 05	Sunderland	25/4/93	Scholar
Sweeney Anthony (M)	6 0	11 07	Stockton	5/9/83	Scholar

League Appearances: Adjei, S. (1); Austin, N. 46; Baldwin, J. 14(3); Boyd, A. 13(20); Brown, J. 10(14); Collins, S. 35(1); Flinders, S. 45; Hartley, P. 44; Haslam, S. 3(7); Hassan, C. (1); Hawkins, L. 1; Holden, D. 2(1); Horwood, E. 38(3); Humphreys, R. 19(10); James, L. 12(7); Larkin, C. 2; Liddle, G. 37(2); Luscombe, N. 3(10); Monkhouse, A. 39(6); Murray, P. 44(1); Nish, C. 12(7); Noble, R. 9; Poole, J. 15(12); Rafferty, A. 1; Richards, J. 1(1); Rowbotham, J. 1; Rutherford, G. (1); Solano, N. 11(3); Sweeney, A. 39; Wright, S. 10.

Goals – League (50): Sweeney 8, Poole 7, Boyd 6 (2 pens), Hartley 4, Liddle 4, Nish 4, James 3, Monkhouse 3, Noble 2, Solano 2, Austin 1 (1 pen), Brown 1, Collins 1, Horwood 1, Humphreys 1, Luscombe 1, Murray 1.

Carling Cup (1): Sweeney 1.
FA Cup (0).
J Paint Trophy (0).
Ground: Victoria Park, Clarence Road, Hartlepool TS24 8BZ. Telephone: (01429) 272 584.
Capacity: 7,630.
Record Attendance: 17,426 v Manchester U, FA Cup 3rd rd, 5 January 1957.
First Team Coach: Neale Cooper.
Most League Goals: 90, Division 3 (N), 1956–57.
Highest League Scorer in Season: William Robinson, 28, Division 3 (N), 1927–28; Joe Allon, 28, Division 4, 1990–91.
Most League Goals in Total Aggregate: Ken Johnson, 98, 1949–64.
Most Capped Player: Ambrose Fogarty, 1 (11), Republic of Ireland.
Most League Appearances: Wattie Moore, 447, 1948–64.
Colours: Broad blue and white striped shirts with blue sleeves, blue shorts, white stockings.
Honours: None.

HEREFORD UNITED   BLUE SQUARE PREMIER

Bartlett Adam (G)	6 0	11 11	Newcastle-upon-Tyne	27/2/86	Kidderminster H
Clist Simon (D)	5 9	11 09	Shaftesbury	13/6/81	Barnet
Clucas Sam (M)	5 10	11 09	Lincoln	20/8/90	Lincoln C
Dalibard Benoit (D)	6 2	12 08	Landemeau	26/3/91	Guingamp
Evans Will (M)	6 2	11 11	Cricklade	19/10/91	Swindon T
Featherstone Nicky (F)	5 6	11 04	Goole	22/9/88	Hull C
Hanford Daniel (G)			Swansea	6/3/91	Glenn Hoddle Acad
Heath Joe (D)	5 11	11 11	Birkenhead	4/10/88	Exeter C
McQuilkin James (F)	5 8	11 10	Tipton	9/1/89	Zlin
Pell Harry (M)	6 4	13 05	Tilbury	21/10/91	Bristol R
Stam Stefan (D)	6 2	13 02	Amersfoort	14/9/79	Yeovil T
Townsend Michael (D)	6 1	13 12	Walsall	17/5/86	Cheltenham T

League Appearances: Anthony, B. 13(2); Arquin, Y. 16(18); Barkhuizen, T. 32(6); Bartlett, A. 18; Baxendale, J. (1); Chambers, J. 7; Clist, S. 27(1); Clucas, S. 3(14); Colbeck, J. 19(9); Connor, D. 1; Cornell, D. 25; Dalibard, B. 9(1); Elder, N. 13(13); Evans, W. 21(4); Facey, D. 32(8); Featherstone, N. 36(2); Fleetwood, S. 4(1); Green, R. 26(2); Heath, J. 15(2); Hoult, R. 2; Leslie, S. 10; Lunt, K. 24(1); McQuilkin, J. 3(4); Pell, H. 22(8); Peniket, R. 4(3); Purdie, R. 34; Purkiss, B. 15; Stam, S. 21(3); Taylor, L. 6(2); Todd, A. 4; Townsend, M. 36(3); Williams, D. 3(2); Winnall, S. 5(3).

Goals – League (50): Barkhuizen 11, Arquin 8 (1 pen), Facey 6, Evans, W. 5, Purdie 4 (2 pens), Elder 3, Pell 3 (1 pen), Leslie 2, Taylor 2, Winnall 2, Anthony 1, Colbeck 1, own goals 2.

Carling Cup (1): Arquin 1.
FA Cup (0).
J Paint Trophy (1): Barkhuizen 1.
Ground: Athletic Ground, Edgar Street, Hereford HR4 9JU. Telephone: (08442) 761 939.
Capacity: 7,149.
Record Attendance: 18,114 v Sheffield W, FA Cup 3rd rd, 4 January 1958.
Manager: Martin Foyle.
Most League Goals: 86, Division 3, 1975–76.
Highest League Scorer in Season: Dixie McNeil, 35, 1975–76.
Most League Goals in Total Aggregate: Stewart Phillips, 93, 1980–88, 1990–91.
Most Capped Player: Trevor Benjamin, 2, Jamaica.
Most League Appearances: Mel Pejic, 412, 1980–92.
Colours: White shirts with black trim, black shorts, white stockings.
Honours – Football League: Division 3 Champions – 1975–76. **Welsh Cup:** Winners – 1990.

HUDDERSFIELD TOWN   FL CHAMPIONSHIP

Allinson Lloyd (G)	6 2	13 00	Rothwell	7/9/93	Scholar
Arfield Scott (M)	5 10	10 01	Livingston	1/11/88	Falkirk
Atkinson Chris (M)	6 1	11 13		13/2/92	Scholar
Bennett Ian (G)	6 0	12 09	Worksop	10/10/71	Sheffield U
Clarke Peter (D)	6 0	12 00	Southport	3/1/82	Southend U
Clarke Tom (D)	6 0	11 02	Sowerby Bridge	21/12/87	Scholar
Colgan Nick (G)	6 1	12 00	Drogheda	19/9/73	Grimsby T
Crooks Matt (M)			Leeds	20/1/94	Scholar
Gobern Oscar (M)	5 11	10 10	Birmingham	26/1/91	Southampton
Higginbotham Kallum (F)	5 11	10 10	Manchester	15/6/89	Falkirk
Hunt Jack (D)	5 9	11 02	Rothwell	6/12/90	Scholar
Kay Antony (D)	5 11	11 08	Barnsley	21/10/82	Tranmere R
Lee Alan (F)	6 2	13 09	Galway	21/8/78	Crystal Palace
McCombe Jamie (D)	6 5	12 05	Scunthorpe	1/1/83	Bristol C
Novak Lee (F)	6 0	12 03	Newcastle	28/9/88	Gateshead
Pearson Greg (D)			Sowerby Bridge	25/12/92	Scholar
Rhodes Jordan (F)	6 1	11 03	Oldham	5/2/90	Ipswich T
Ridehalgh Liam (D)	5 10	11 05	Halifax	20/4/91	Scholar
Robinson Anton (M)	5 9	10 03	Harrow	17/2/86	Bournemouth
Smithies Alex (G)	6 1	10 01	Huddersfield	25/3/90	Scholar
Spencer James (F)	6 1	13 00	Leeds	13/12/91	Scholar
Wallace Murray (D)	6 2	11 07	Glasgow	10/1/93	Falkirk
Ward Danny (M)	5 11	12 05	Bradford	11/12/91	Bolton W
Woods Calum (D)	5 11	11 07	Liverpool	5/2/87	Dunfermline Ath

League Appearances: Arfield, S. 24(11); Arismendi, D. 7(2); Atkinson, C. (1); Bennett, I. 33; Bruce, A. 3; Cadamarteri, D. 6(9); Clarke, P. 31; Clarke, T. 7(7); Cooper, L. 2(2); Gobern, O. 19(2); Gudjonsson, J. 6(2); Higginbotham, K. 3(1); Hunt, J. 43; Johnson, D. 16(2); Kay, A. 25(3); Lee, A. 18(13); McCombe, J. 20; McDermott, D. 6(3); Miller, T. 24(2); Morrison, S. 19; Naysmith, G. 20(2); Novak, L. 29(12); Parkin, J. 2(1); Rhodes, J. 36(4); Roberts, G. 28(11); Robinson, A. 12(13); Smithies, A. 13; Ward, D. 31(8); Woods, C. 23(3).
Goals – League (79): Rhodes 35 (1 pen), Novak 13, Lee 7, Roberts 6, Ward 4, McCombe 3, Arfield 2, Gobern 2, Hunt 1, Kay 1, Miller 1, Morrison 1, Robinson 1, own goals 2.
Carling Cup (7): Novak 2, Rhodes 2, Hunt 1, Roberts 1, Ward 1.
FA Cup (1): Novak 1.
J Paint Trophy (4): Clarke, P. 1, McDermott 1, Miller 1 (pen), Novak 1.

Play-Offs (3): Rhodes 2, Hunt 1.
Ground: The Galpharm Stadium, Stadium Way, Leeds Road, Huddersfield HD1 6PX. Telephone: (0870) 4444 677.
Capacity: 24,554.
Record Attendance: 67,037 v Arsenal, FA Cup 6th rd, 27 February 1932 (at Leeds Road); 23,678 v Liverpool, FA Cup 3rd rd, 12 December 1999 (at Alfred McAlpine Stadium).
Manager: Simon Grayson.
Most League Goals: 101, Division 4, 1979–80.
Highest League Scorer in Season: Sam Taylor, 35, Division 2, 1919–20; George Brown, 35, Division 1, 1925–26; Jordan Rhodes, 35, 2011–12.
Most League Goals in Total Aggregate: George Brown, 142, 1921–29; Jimmy Glazzard, 142, 1946–56.
Most Capped Player: Jimmy Nicholson, 31 (41), Northern Ireland.
Most League Appearances: Billy Smith, 520, 1914–34.
Colours: Blue and white striped shirts, white shorts, blue stockings.
Honours – Football League: Division 1 Champions – 1923–24, 1924–25, 1925–26. Division 2 Champions – 1969–70. Division 4 Champions – 1979–80. **FA Cup:** Winners – 1922.

HULL CITY   FL CHAMPIONSHIP

Bradley Sonny (D)	6 0	11 05	Hedon	14/6/92	Aberdeen
Cairney Tom (M)	6 0	11 05	Nottingham	20/1/91	Scholar
Chester James (D)	5 11	11 04	Warrington	23/1/89	Manchester U
Cooper Liam (D)	6 2	13 07	Hull	30/8/91	Scholar
Cullen Mark (F)	5 9	11 11	Ashington	24/4/92	Scholar
Devitt Jamie (F)	5 10	10 05	Dublin	6/7/90	Scholar
Dillon Kealan (F)			Mullingar	21/2/94	Derby Co
Dudgeon Joe (D)	5 9	11 02	Leeds	26/11/90	Manchester U
East Danny (D)			Hessle	26/12/91	Scholar
Emerton Danny (M)	5 10	11 02	Beverley	27/9/91	Scholar
Evans Corry (M)	5 8	10 12	Belfast	30/7/90	Manchester U
Fryatt Matty (F)	5 10	11 02	Nuneaton	5/3/86	Leicester C
Garcia Richard (F)	5 11	12 01	Perth	4/9/81	Colchester U
Ghilas Kamel (F)	5 10	11 00	Marseille	9/3/84	Celta Vigo
Hobbs Jack (D)	6 3	13 05	Portsmouth	18/8/88	Leicester C
Koren Robert (M)	5 10	11 03	Ljubljana	20/9/80	WBA
Mainwaring Matty (M)	5 11	12 02	Salford	28/3/90	Stockport Co
McKenna Paul (M)	5 7	11 12	Eccleston	20/10/77	Nottingham F
McLean Aaron (F)	5 9	10 10	Hammersmith	25/5/83	Peterborough U
McShane Paul (D)	6 0	11 05	Wicklow	6/1/86	Sunderland
Olofinjana Seyi (M)	6 4	11 10	Lagos	30/6/80	Stoke C
Oxley Mark (G)	5 11	11 05	Aston	2/6/90	Rotherham U Scholar
Peet Robert (G)	6 2	12 01	Melton Mowbray	11/10/92	Grimsby T Scholar
Rosenior Liam (D)	5 10	11 05	Wandsworth	9/7/84	Reading
Simpson Jay (F)	5 11	13 04	Enfield	1/12/88	Arsenal
Stewart Cameron (M)	5 8	11 05	Manchester	8/4/91	Manchester U
Townsend Conor (D)			Hessle	4/3/93	Scholar

League Appearances: Adebola, D. 2(8); Barmby, N. (8); Basso, A. 12(1); Bradley, S. 1(1); Brady, R. 24(15); Cairney, T. 18(9); Chester, J. 44; Cooper, L. 7; Cullen, M. (4); Dawson, A. 31(1); Dudgeon, J. 17(7); Evans, C. 38(5); Fryatt, M. 39(7); Garcia, R. 6(4); Gulacsi, P. 13(2); Harper, J. (1); Hobbs, J. 40; King, J. 8(10); Koren, R. 41; Mannone, V. 21; McKenna, P. 37(4); McLean, A. 28(11); McShane, P. 1; Olofinjana, S. 1(2); Pusic, M. 2; Rosenior, L. 44; Simpson, J. (3); Stewart, C. 26(5); Waghorn, M. 5.
Goals – League (47): Fryatt 16 (2 pens), Koren 10, McLean 5, Brady 3, Chester 2, Evans 2, Barmby 1, Hobbs 1, King 1, Stewart 1, Waghorn 1, own goals 4.

Carling Cup (0).
FA Cup (3): Cairney 1, McLean 1, Stewart 1.
Ground: The Circle, The KC Stadium, Walton Street, Hull, East Yorkshire HU3 6HU. Telephone: (01482) 504 600.
Capacity: 25,404.
Record Attendance: 25,512 v Sunderland, FL C, 28 October 2007 (at KC Stadium); 55,019 v Manchester U, FA Cup 6th rd, 26 February 1949 (at Boothferry Park).
Manager: Steve Bruce.
Most League Goals: 109, Division 3, 1965–66.
Highest League Scorer in Season: Bill McNaughton, 39, Division 3 (N), 1932–33.
Most League Goals in Total Aggregate: Chris Chilton, 193, 1960–71.
Most Capped Player: Theo Whitmore, 28 (105), Jamaica.
Most League Appearances: Andy Davidson, 520, 1952–67.
Colours: Black and amber striped shirts, black shorts, amber stockings with black hoops.
Honours – Football League: Division 3 (N) Champions – 1932–33, 1948–49. Division 3 Champions – 1965–66.

IPSWICH TOWN   FL CHAMPIONSHIP

Ainsley Jack (D)	5 11	11 00	Ipswich	17/9/90	Scholar
Bullard Jimmy (M)	5 10	11 05	Newham	23/10/78	Hull C
Burke Cormac (M)			Derry	11/8/93	Scholar
Carson Josh (M)	5 9	11 00	Ballymena	3/6/93	Scholar
Chopra Michael (F)	5 9	10 08	Newcastle	23/12/83	Cardiff C
Cresswell Aaron (D)	5 7	10 05	Liverpool	15/12/89	Tranmere R
Delaney Damien (D)	6 3	14 00	Cork	20/7/81	QPR
Drury Andy (M)	5 11	12 06	Sittingbourne	28/11/83	Luton T
Edwards Carlos (M)	5 8	11 02	Port of Spain	24/10/78	Sunderland
Ellington Nathan (F)	5 10	13 01	Bradford	2/7/81	Watford
Emmanuel-Thomas Jay (M)	5 9	11 05	Forest Gate	27/12/90	Arsenal
Hyam Luke (M)	5 10	11 05	Ipswich	24/10/91	Scholar
Lee-Barrett Arran (G)	6 2	14 01	Ipswich	28/2/84	Hartlepool U
Martin Lee (M)	5 10	10 03	Taunton	9/2/87	Manchester U
Murphy Daryl (F)	6 2	13 12	Waterford	15/3/83	Sunderland
Murray Ronan (F)	5 7	11 00	Mayo	12/9/91	Scholar
Peters Jaime (M)	5 7	10 12	Ontario	4/5/87	Kaiserslautern
Scotland Jason (F)	5 8	11 10	Morvant	18/2/79	Wigan Ath
Smith Tommy (D)	6 2	12 02	Macclesfield	31/3/90	Scholar
Stevenson Ryan (M)	5 11	12 07	Ayr	24/8/84	Hearts
Whight Joe (D)	5 10	11 00	Ipswich	6/1/94	Scholar

League Appearances: Ainsley, J. 1; Andrews, K. 19(1); Bowyer, L. 24(5); Bullard, J. 12(9); Carson, J. 5(11); Chopra, M. 39(6); Collins, D. 16; Cresswell, A. 44; Delaney, D. 26(3); Drury, A. 20(1); Edwards, C. 45; Ellington, N. 1(14); Emmanuel-Thomas, J. 28(14); Healy, C. 1; Hyam, L. 7(1); Ingimarsson, I. 6(2); Kennedy, M. 6(1); Lawrence, B. 1(1); Leadbitter, G. 32(2); Lee-Barrett, A. 17(1); Martin, L. 28(6); McCarthy, A. 10; Murphy, D. 31(2); Priskin, T. 1(1); Scotland, J. 20(16); Smith, T. 24(2); Sonko, I. 20(2); Stevenson, R. 3(8); Stockdale, D. 18; Wabara, R. 1(5); Wright, R. 1.
Goals – League (69): Chopra 14, Andrews 9, Scotland 8 (1 pen), Emmanuel-Thomas 6, Leadbitter 5 (2 pens), Martin 5 (1 pen), Murphy, D. 4, Collins 3, Smith 3, Bowyer 2, Carson 2, Drury 2, Bullard 1, Cresswell 1, Sonko 1, Stevenson 1, own goals 2.
Carling Cup (1): Emmanuel-Thomas 1.
FA Cup (1): Scotland 1.
Ground: Portman Road, Ipswich, Suffolk IP1 2DA. Telephone: (01473) 400 500.
Capacity: 30,311.

Record Attendance: 38,010 v Leeds U, FA Cup 6th rd, 8 March 1975.
Manager: Paul Jewell.
Most League Goals: 106, Division 3 (S), 1955–56.
Highest League Scorer in Season: Ted Phillips, 41, Division 3 (S), 1956–57.
Most League Goals in Total Aggregate: Ray Crawford, 204, 1958–63 and 1966–69.
Most Capped Player: Allan Hunter, 47 (53), Northern Ireland.
Most League Appearances: Mick Mills, 591, 1966–82.
Colours: Blue shirts with white trim, white shorts, blue stockings.
Honours – Football League: Division 1 Champions – 1961–62. Division 2 Champions – 1960–61, 1967–68, 1991–92. Division 3 (S) Champions – 1953–54, 1956–57. **FA Cup:** Winners – 1977–78. **European Competitions: UEFA Cup:** Winners – 1980–81.

LEEDS UNITED   FL CHAMPIONSHIP

Becchio Luciano (F)	6 2	13 05	Cordoba	28/12/83	Merida
Bromby Leigh (D)	5 11	11 06	Dewsbury	2/6/80	Watford
Cairns Alex (G)	6 0	11 05	Doncaster	4/1/93	Scholar
Clayton Adam (M)	5 9	11 11	Manchester	14/1/89	Manchester C
Connolly Paul (D)	6 0	11 09	Liverpool	29/9/83	Derby Co
Kisnorbo Patrick (D)	6 1	11 11	Melbourne	24/3/81	Leicester C
Lees Tom (D)	6 1	12 02	Warwick	28/11/90	
Lonergan Andrew (G)	6 4	13 02	Preston	19/10/83	Preston NE
McCormack Ross (F)	5 9	11 00	Glasgow	18/8/86	Cardiff C
Nunez Ramon (M)	5 7	10 00	Tegucigalpa	14/11/85	Cruz Azul
O'Brien Andy (D)	6 2	11 13	Harrogate	29/6/79	Bolton W
Payne Sanchez (M)			Leeds	31/1/93	Scholar
Paynter Billy (F)	6 1	14 01	Liverpool	13/7/84	Swindon T
Pearce Jason (D)	5 11	12 00	Hillingdon	6/12/87	Bournemouth
Pugh Danny (M)	6 0	12 10	Cheadle Hulme	19/10/82	Stoke C
Rachubka Paul (G)	6 1	13 05	San Luis Opispo	21/5/81	Blackpool
Rogers Robbie (F)	5 10	12 13	Los Angeles	12/5/87	Columbus Crew
Snodgrass Robert (M)	6 0	12 02	Glasgow	7/9/87	Livingston
Somma Davide (F)	6 1	12 13	Johannesburg	26/3/85	San Jose Eq
Taylor Charlie (D)	5 9	11 00	York	18/9/93	Scholar
Thompson Zac (M)	5 10	11 00	Billinge	5/1/93	Everton Scholar
Turner Lewis (M)			Garforth	3/9/92	Scholar
Turner Nathan (D)			Garforth	3/9/92	Scholar
White Aidan (D)	5 7	10 00	Otley	10/10/91	Scholar

League Appearances: Becchio, L. 25(16); Bromby, L. 7(3); Brown, M. 21(3); Bruce, A. 8; Cairns, A. (1); Clayton, A. 42(1); Connolly, P. 23(5); Delph, F. 5; Forssell, M. 1(14); Gradel, M. 4; Howson, J. 19; Keogh, A. 17(5); Kisnorbo, P. 18(1); Lees, T. 41(1); Lonergan, A. 35; McCarthy, A. 6; McCormack, R. 42(3); Nunez, R. 6(13); O'Brien, A. 2(2); O'Dea, D. 35; Paynter, B. 2(3); Pugh, D. 31(3); Rachubka, P. 5(1); Robinson, P. 9(1); Rogers, R. 1(3); Sam, L. 3(14); Smith, A. 3; Snodgrass, R. 42(1); Taylor, C. 2; Thompson, Z. 7(2); Townsend, A. 5(1); Vayrynen, M. 2(8); Webber, D. 2(11); White, A. 35(1).
Goals – League (65): McCormack 18, Snodgrass 13 (2 pens), Becchio 11, Clayton 6, Keogh 2, Lees 2, O'Dea 2, Paynter 2, Pugh 2, Brown 1, Gradel 1 (1 pen), Howson 1, Nunez 1, Townsend 1, Webber 1, own goal 1.
Carling Cup (5): Nunez 4, McCormack 1.
FA Cup (0).
Ground: Elland Road, Leeds, West Yorkshire LS11 0ES. Telephone: (0871) 334 1919.
Capacity: 39,457.
Record Attendance: 57,892 v Sunderland, FA Cup 5th rd (replay), 15 March 1967.
Manager: Neil Warnock.
Most League Goals: 98, Division 2, 1927–28.

Highest League Scorer in Season: John Charles, 42, Division 2, 1953–54.
Most League Goals in Total Aggregate: Peter Lorimer, 168, 1965–79 and 1983–86.
Most Capped Player: Lucas Radebe, 58 (70), South Africa.
Most League Appearances: Jack Charlton, 629, 1953–73.
Colours: White shirts, white shorts, white stockings with yellow trim.
Honours – Football League: Division 1 Champions – 1968–69, 1973–74, 1991–92. Division 2 Champions – 1923–24, 1963–64, 1989–90. **FA Cup:** Winners – 1972. **Football League Cup:** Winners – 1967–68. **European Competitions: European Fairs Cup:** Winners – 1967–68, 1970–71.

LEICESTER CITY   FL CHAMPIONSHIP

Bamba Souleymane (D)	6 3	14 02	Ivry-sur-Seine	13/1/85	Hibernian
Beckford Jermaine (F)	6 2	13 02	Ealing	9/12/83	Everton
Bolger Cian (D)	6 4	12 05	Co. Kildare	12/3/92	Scholar
Byrne Shane (M)	5 10	12 02	Dublin	25/4/93	Scholar
Danns Neil (M)	5 10	10 12	Liverpool	23/11/82	Crystal Palace
Drinkwater Daniel (M)	5 10	11 00	Manchester	5/3/90	Manchester U
Dyer Lloyd (M)	5 8	10 01	Birmingham	13/9/82	Milton Keynes D
Gallagher Paul (F)	6 1	11 00	Glasgow	9/8/84	Blackburn R
Hopper Tom (F)			Boston	14/12/93	Scholar
Kennedy Tom (D)	5 10	11 01	Bury	24/6/85	Rochdale
King Andy (M)	6 0	11 10	Barnstaple	29/10/88	Scholar
Konchesky Paul (D)	5 10	11 07	Barking	15/5/81	Liverpool
Larrauri Pier (F)	5 9	11 12	Siena	26/3/94	
Logan Conrad (G)	6 2	14 00	Letterkenny	18/4/86	Scholar
Marshall Ben (F)	5 11	11 13	Salford	29/3/91	Stoke C
Mills Matthew (D)	6 3	12 12	Swindon	14/7/86	Reading
Moore Liam (D)	6 1	13 08	Loughborough	31/1/93	Aberdeen
Morgan Wes (D)	6 2	14 00	Nottingham	21/1/84	Nottingham F
Moussa Franck (M)	5 8	10 08	Brussels	24/7/89	Southend U
Nugent Dave (F)	5 11	12 13	Liverpool	2/5/85	Portsmouth
Panayiotou Harry (F)			Leicester	28/10/94	Scholar
Parkes Tom (D)	6 3	12 05	Sutton-in-Ashfield	15/1/92	Scholar
Peltier Lee (D)	5 10	12 00	Liverpool	11/12/86	Huddersfield T
Schlupp Jeffrey (M)	5 8	11 00	Hamburg	23/12/92	Scholar
Schmeichel Kasper (G)	6 1	13 00	Copenhagen	5/11/86	Leeds U
Smith Adam (G)	5 11	11 00	Sunderland	23/11/92	Scholar
St Ledger-Hall Sean (D)	6 0	11 09	Solihull	28/12/84	Preston NE
Taft George (D)	5 9	11 09	Leicester	29/7/93	Scholar
Waghorn Martyn (F)	5 9	13 01	South Shields	23/1/90	Sunderland
Wellens Richard (M)	5 9	11 06	Manchester	26/3/80	Doncaster R

League Appearances: Abe, Y. 13(3); Bamba, S. 32(4); Beckford, J. 33(6); Danns, N. 22(7); Delfouneso, N. (4); Drinkwater, D. 13(6); Dyer, L. 27(9); Gallagher, P. 18(10); Gelson, 10(5); Howard, S. 3(17); Johnson, M. 3(4); Kennedy, T. 4(1); King, A. 24(6); Konchesky, P. 42; Marshall, B. 12(4); Mills, M. 25; Moore, L. 2; Morgan, W. 15(2); Nugent, D. 41(1); Panayiotou, H. (1); Pantsil, J. 4(2); Peltier, L. 39(1); Schlupp, J. 3(18); Schmeichel, K. 46; St Ledger-Hall, S. 23(3); Tunchev, A. 2; Vassell, D. 10(3); Waghorn, M. 1(3); Weale, C. (1); Wellens, R. 39(2).
Goals – League (66): Nugent 15, Beckford 9, Gallagher 8 (3 pens), Danns 5, Dyer 4, King 4, Marshall 3, Drinkwater 2, Konchesky 2, Peltier 2, Schlupp 2, Vassell 2, Abe 1, Bamba 1, Gelson 1, Mills 1, Panayiotou 1, Waghorn 1, Wellens 1, own goal 1.
Carling Cup (10): Schlupp 4, Dyer 2, Gallagher 2, Danns 1, Howard 1.
FA Cup (10): Beckford 6, Marshall 1, Nugent 1, St Ledger-Hall 1, own goal 1.

Ground: King Power Stadium, Filbert Way, Leicester LE2 7FL. Telephone: (0844) 815 6000.
Capacity: 32,500 (all seated).
Record Attendance: 47,298 v Tottenham H, FA Cup 5th rd, 18 February 1928 (at Filbert Street); 32,148 v Manchester U, FA Premier League, 26 December 2003 (at Walkers Stadium).
Manager: Nigel Pearson.
Most League Goals: 109, Division 2, 1956–57.
Highest League Scorer in Season: Arthur Rowley, 44, Division 2, 1956–57.
Most League Goals in Total Aggregate: Arthur Chandler, 259, 1923–35.
Most Capped Player: John O'Neill, 39, Northern Ireland.
Most League Appearances: Adam Black, 528, 1920–35.
Colours: Blue shirts with white trim, white shorts, blue stockings with white trim.
Honours – Football League: FL 1 Champions – 2008–09. Division 2 Champions – 1924–25, 1936–37, 1953–54, 1956–57, 1970–71, 1979–80. **Football League Cup:** Winners – 1964, 1997, 2000.

LEYTON ORIENT   FL CHAMPIONSHIP 1

Butcher Lee (G)	6 1	12 02	Waltham Forest	11/10/88	Tottenham H
Chorley Ben (D)	6 3	13 00	Sidcup	30/9/82	Tranmere R
Cox Dean (M)	5 4	9 08	Cuckfield	12/8/87	Brighton & HA
Cuthbert Scott (D)	6 2	14 00	Alexandria	15/6/87	Swindon T
Jones Jamie (G)	6 2	14 05	Kirkby	18/2/89	Everton
Laird Marc (M)	6 1	10 07	Edinburgh	23/1/86	Millwall
Lisbie Kevin (F)	5 10	11 06	Hackney	17/10/78	Ipswich T
Lovelock Thomas (G)			Harlow	14/5/93	Scholar
McSweeney Leon (F)	5 10	10 11	Cork	19/2/83	Hartlepool U
Mooney David (F)	6 2	12 06	Dublin	30/10/84	Reading
Odubajo Moses (M)	5 9	11 05	Greenwich	28/7/93	Scholar
Porter George (F)	5 10		Sidcup	27/6/92	Cray W
Smith Jimmy (M)	6 0	10 03	Newham	7/1/87	Chelsea

League Appearances: Alnwick, B. 6; Andrew, C. 2(8); Ben Youssef, S. 6(3); Butcher, L. 23; Button, D. 1; Campbell-Ryce, J. 7(1); Cestor, M. 1; Chicksen, A. 3; Chorley, B. 30(2); Clarke, T. 10; Cook, L. 9; Cox, D. 35(3); Craig, T. 4; Cureton, J. 9(10); Cuthbert, S. 33; Daniels, C. 13; Dawson, S. 20; Dickson, R. 9; Forbes, T. 38(1); Jones, J. 6; Laird, M. 11(11); Leacock, D. 15; Lisbie, K. 34(3); Lobjoit, B. (1); McSweeney, L. 28(1); Mooney, D. 28(9); Obafemi, A. (1); Odubajo, M. 1(2); Omozusi, E. 8(2); Porter, G. 9(25); Rachubka, P. 8; Reed, A. 10(1); Revell, A. 4(1); Richardson, M. 1(2); Smith, Jamie (1); Smith, Jimmy 35(3); Spring, M. 41; Stech, M. 2; Taiwo, S. 2(3); Tehoue, J. 4(10).
Goals – League (48): Lisbie 12 (2 pens), Cox 7, Smith, Jimmy 6, Mooney 5 (1 pen), Spring 4, Tehoue 3, Laird 2, Campbell-Ryce 1, Chorley 1, Cook 1, Cureton 1, Cuthbert 1, Dawson 1, Odubajo 1, Porter 1, own goal 1.
Carling Cup (6): Mooney 2, Chorley 1 (pen), Cox 1, Dawson 1, Richardson 1.
FA Cup (3): Porter 1, Smith, Jimmy 1, Spring 1.
J Paint Trophy (1): Mooney 1.
Ground: Matchroom Stadium, Brisbane Road, Leyton, London E10 5NF. Telephone: (0871) 310 1881.
Capacity: 9,300.
Record Attendance: 34,345 v West Ham U, FA Cup 4th rd, 25 January 1964.
Manager: Russell Slade.
Most League Goals: 106, Division 3 (S), 1955–56.
Highest League Scorer in Season: Tom Johnston, 35, Division 2, 1957–58.
Most League Goals in Total Aggregate: Tom Johnston, 121, 1956–58, 1959–61.
Most Capped Players: Tunji Banjo, 7 (7), Nigeria; John Chiedozie, 7 (9), Nigeria; Tony Grealish, 7 (45), Republic of Ireland.

Most League Appearances: Peter Allen, 432, 1965–78.
Colours: Red shirts with white insert and striped sleeves, red shorts, red stockings.
Honours – Football League: Division 3 Champions – 1969–70. Division 3 (S) Champions – 1955–56.

LIVERPOOL   FA PREMIERSHIP

Name			Birthplace	Date	Club
Adam Charlie (M)	6 1	12 00	Dundee	10/12/85	Blackpool
Adorjan Krisztian (F)			Budapest	19/1/93	Scholar
Agger Daniel (D)	6 2	12 06	Hvidovre	12/12/84	Brondby
Aquilani Alberto (M)	6 0	12 03	Rome	7/7/84	Roma
Baio Yalany (D)			Guinea-Bissau	10/10/94	Scholar
Belford Tyrell (G)			Nuneaton	6/5/94	Scholar
Bellamy Craig (F)	5 9	10 12	Cardiff	13/7/79	Manchester C
Bijev Villyan (F)			Fresno	3/1/93	California Odyssey
Carragher Jamie (D)	5 9	12 01	Liverpool	28/1/78	Trainee
Carroll Andy (F)	6 4	11 00	Gateshead	6/1/89	Newcastle U
Coady Conor (D)	6 1	11 05	Liverpool	25/2/93	Scholar
Coates Sebastian (D)	6 5	13 12	Montevideo	7/10/90	Nacional
Cole Joe (M)	5 9	11 09	Camden	8/11/81	Chelsea
Doni (G)	6 4	14 02	Sao Paulo	22/10/79	Roma
Downing Stewart (M)	5 11	10 04	Middlesbrough	22/7/84	Aston Villa
Dunn Jack (M)			Liverpool	19/11/94	Scholar
Eccleston Nathan (F)	5 10	11 10	Manchester	30/12/90	Scholar
Flanagan John (D)	5 11	12 06	Liverpool	1/1/93	Scholar
Gerrard Steven (M)	6 0	12 05	Huyton	30/5/80	Trainee
Gulacsi Peter (G)	6 3	13 01	Budapest	6/5/90	MTK
Henderson Jordan (M)	6 0	10 07	Sunderland	17/6/90	Sunderland
Johnson Glen (D)	6 0	13 04	Greenwich	23/8/84	Portsmouth
Jones Brad (G)	6 3	12 01	Armidale	19/3/82	Middlesbrough
Jose Enrique (D)	6 0	12 00	Valencia	23/1/86	Newcastle U
Kelly Martin (D)	6 3	12 02	Bolton	27/4/90	Scholar
Kuyt Dirk (F)	6 0	12 02	Katwijk	22/7/80	Feyenoord
Lucas (M)	5 10	11 08	Dourados	9/1/87	Gremio
Lussey Jordan (M)			Ormskirk	2/11/94	Scholar
McLaughlin Ryan (D)			Belfast	30/9/94	Scholar
Mersin Yusuf (G)			Greenwich	23/9/94	Scholar
Morgan Adam (F)			Liverpool	21/4/94	Scholar
Nacho (M)			Spain	16/12/93	
Ngoo Michael (F)			Walthamstow	23/10/92	Southend U Scholar
Pacheco Daniel (F)	5 6	10 07	Malaga	5/1/91	
Pelosi Marc (D)			Bad Sackingen	17/6/94	DeAnza Force
Petersson Kristoffer (M)			Gothenburg	28/11/94	Scholar
Reina Jose (G)	6 2	14 06	Madrid	31/8/82	Villarreal
Robinson Jack (D)	5 11	10 08	Warrington	1/9/93	Scholar
Roddan Craig (M)			Kirkby	22/4/93	Scholar
Rodriguez Maxi (M)	5 11	12 06	Rosario	2/1/81	Atletico Madrid
Sama Stephen (D)			Cameroon	5/3/93	Scholar
Shelvey Jonjo (M)	6 1	11 02	Romford	27/2/92	Charlton Ath
Silva Toni (M)	6 0	11 09	Guinea-Bissau	15/9/93	
Skrtel Martin (D)	6 3	12 10	Handlova	15/12/84	Zenit
Smith Bradley (D)			New South Wales	9/4/94	Scholar
Sokolik Jakub (D)	5 6		Ostrava	28/8/93	Scholar
Spearing Jay (M)	5 6	11 01	Wallasey	25/11/88	Scholar
Stephens James (G)			Wotton-under-Edge	24/8/93	Scholar
Sterling Raheem (F)	5 7	10 00	Kingston	8/12/94	Scholar
Suarez Luis (F)	5 11	12 10	Salto	24/1/87	Ajax

Suso (M)	5 8	10 12	Cadiz	19/11/93	Cadiz B
Teixeira Joao Carlos (M)			Braga	18/1/93	Sporting Lisbon Youth
Ward Danny (G)			Wrexham	22/6/93	Wrexham
Wilson Danny (D)	6 2	12 06	Livingston	27/12/91	Rangers
Wisdom Andre (D)	6 1	12 04	Leeds	9/5/93	Scholar

League Appearances: Adam, C. 27(1); Agger, D. 24(3); Bellamy, C. 12(15); Carragher, J. 19(2); Carroll, A. 21(14); Coates, S. 4(3); Doni, 4; Downing, S. 28(8); Fabio Aurelio, 1(1); Flanagan, J. 5; Gerrard, S. 12(6); Henderson, J. 31(6); Johnson, G. 22(1); Jones, B. (1); Jose Enrique, 33(2); Kelly, M. 12; Kuyt, D. 22(12); Lucas, 12; Raul Meireles, (2); Reina, J. 34; Rodriguez, M. 10(2); Shelvey, J. 8(5); Skrtel, M. 33(1); Spearing, J. 15(1); Sterling, R. (3); Suarez, L. 29(2).

Goals – League (47): Suarez 11, Bellamy 6, Gerrard 5, Carroll 4, Rodriguez 4, Adam 2 (1 pen), Henderson 2, Kuyt 2, Skrtel 2, Agger 1, Coates 1, Johnson 1, Shelvey 1, own goals 5.

Carling Cup (14): Suarez 3, Bellamy 2, Gerrard 2 (2 pens), Kuyt 2, Rodriguez 2, Carroll 1, Kelly 1, Skrtel 1.

FA Cup (18): Carroll 4, Suarez 3, Downing 2, Gerrard 2 (1 pen), Agger 1, Bellamy 1, Kuyt 1, Shelvey 1, Skrtel 1, own goals 2.

Ground: Anfield Stadium, Anfield Road, Liverpool L4 0TH. Telephone: (0151) 260 1433.

Capacity: 45,522.

Record Attendance: 61,905 v Wolverhampton W, FA Cup 4th rd, 2 February 1952.

Manager: Brendan Rodgers.

Most League Goals: 106, Division 2, 1895–96.

Highest League Scorer in Season: Roger Hunt, 41, Division 2, 1961–62.

Most League Goals in Total Aggregate: Roger Hunt, 245, 1959–69.

Most Capped Player: Steven Gerrard, 96, England.

Most League Appearances: Ian Callaghan, 640, 1960–78.

Colours: All red with white trim.

Honours – Football League: Division 1 – Champions 1900–01, 1905–06, 1921–22, 1922–23, 1946–47, 1963–64, 1965–66, 1972–73, 1975–76, 1976–77, 1978–79, 1979–80, 1981–82, 1982–83, 1983–84, 1985–86, 1987–88, 1989–90 (Liverpool have a record number of 18 League Championship wins). Division 2 Champions – 1893–94, 1895–96, 1904–05, 1961–62. **FA Cup:** Winners – 1965, 1974, 1986, 1989, 1992, 2001, 2006. **League Cup:** Winners – 1981, 1982, 1983, 1984, 1995, 2001, 2003, 2012. **League Super Cup:** Winners 1985–86. **European Competitions: European Cup:** Winners – 1976–77, 1977–78, 1980–81, 1983–84. **Champions League:** Winners – 2004–05. **UEFA Cup:** Winners – 1972–73, 1975–76, 2001. **Super Cup:** Winners – 1977, 2005.

MACCLESFIELD TOWN   BLUE SQUARE PREMIER

Bolton James (D)			Stone		Scholar
Brown Nat (D)	6 2	12 05	Sheffield	15/6/81	Lincoln C
Collis Steve (G)	6 3	12 05	Harrow	18/3/81	Bristol C
Daniel Colin (M)	5 11	11 05	Eastwood	15/2/88	Crewe Alex
Diagne Tony (D)	6 2	11 11	Mantes-la-Jolie	17/9/90	Nottingham F
Draper Ross (M)	6 3	15 05	Wolverhampton	20/10/88	Heednesford T
Fairhurst Waide (F)	5 10	10 07	Sheffield	7/5/89	Doncaster R
Hewitt Elliott (D)	5 11	11 11	Rhyl	30/5/94	Scholar
Mendy Arnaud (F)	6 3	13 10	Evreux	10/2/90	Derby Co
Mills Ben (F)	6 2	12 00	Stoke	23/3/89	Nantwich T
Tomlinson Ben (F)	5 11	11 11	Dinnington	31/10/89	Worksop T
Tremarco Carl (D)	5 8	11 11	Liverpool	11/10/85	Wrexham
Wedbury Sam (M)	6 0	12 08	Oldbury	26/2/89	Sheffield U

League Appearances: Aley, Z. 1; Bakare, M. (9); Bateson, J. 17(4); Boden, S. 6(1); Brisley, S. 29; Brown, N. 37; Chalmers, L. 17(6); Connolly, M. 7; Daniel, C. 30(6); Diagne, T. 40(1); Donnelly, G. 28; Draper, R. 27(1); Fairhurst, W. 4(14); Fisher, T. (1); Futcher, B. 10; Grant, J. (4); Gray, D. 2; Hamshaw, M. 30(8); Hewitt, E. 17(4); Kay, S. 10(5); Marshall, M. 13(1); Mattis, D. 1; Mendy, A. 23(5); Mills, B. 5(7); Morgan, P. 2(1); Mukendi, V. 4(12); O'Donnell, R. 11; Roberts, A. 1(1); Sinclair, E. 4(1); Smith, M. 6(2); Thomas, M. 2(4); Tomlinson, B. 15(10); Tremarco, C. 35; Veiga, J. 35; Wedgbury, S. 37(2).

Goals – League (39): Donnelly 6, Tomlinson 6, Draper 4, Brisley 3, Chalmers 3 (3 pens), Diagne 3, Daniel 2, Hamshaw 2, Mendy 2, Marshall 1, Mattis 1, Mukendi 1, Sinclair 1, Smith 1, Wedgbury 1, own goals 2.

Carling Cup (3): Sinclair 3.

FA Cup (7): Tremarco 2, Daniel 1, Diagne 1, Donnelly 1, Hamshaw 1, Mendy 1.

J Paint Trophy (0).

Ground: Moss Rose Ground, London Road, Macclesfield, Cheshire SK11 7SP. Telephone: (01625) 264 686.

Capacity: 6,141.

Record Attendance: 9,008 v Winsford U, Cheshire Senior Cup 2nd rd, 4 February 1948.

Manager: Steve King.

Most League Goals: 66, Division 3, 1999–2000.

Highest League Scorer in Season: Jon Parkin, 22, FL 2, 2004–05.

Most League Goals in Total Aggregate: Matt Tipton, 50, 2002–05; 2006–07; 2009–10.

Most Capped Player: George Abbey, 10 (18), Nigeria.

Most League Appearances: Darren Tinson, 263, 1997–2003.

Colours: Blue shirts with white design, white shorts, blue stockings.

Honours: Vauxhall Conference: Champions – 1994–5, 1996–7. **FA Trophy:** Winners – 1969–70, 1995–96.

MANCHESTER CITY   FA PREMIERSHIP

Abu Mohammed (M)			Ghana	14/11/91	SC Accra
Adebayor Emmanuel (F)	6 4	11 08	Lome	26/2/84	Arsenal
Aguero Sergio (F)	5 8	11 09	Buenos Aires	2/6/88	Atletico Madrid
Balotelli Mario (F)	6 2	13 08	Palermo	12/8/90	Internazionale
Barry Gareth (M)	5 11	12 06	Hastings	23/2/81	Aston Villa
Boyata Dedryck (M)	6 2	12 00	Brussels	8/9/90	Scholar
Bridge Wayne (D)	5 10	12 13	Southampton	5/8/80	Chelsea
Bunn Harry (F)	5 9	11 10	Oldham	25/11/92	Scholar
Clichy Gael (D)	5 9	10 04	Toulouse	26/7/85	Arsenal
Cunningham Greg (D)	6 0	11 00	Galway	31/1/91	Scholar
De Jong Nigel (D)	5 8	11 05	Amsterdam	30/11/84	Hamburg
Drury Adam (M)			Grimsby	21/9/93	Scholar
Dzeko Edin (F)	6 3	12 08	Doboj	17/3/86	Wolfsburg
Elabdellaoui Omar (M)			Norway	5/12/91	Scholar
Guidetti John (F)	5 11	12 06	Stockholm	15/4/92	Scholar
Hart Joe (G)	6 3	13 00	Shrewsbury	19/4/87	Shrewsbury T
Helan Jeremy (M)			Paris	9/5/92	Rennes
Henshall Alex (M)			Swindon	15/2/94	Scholar
Huws Emyr (M)			Llanelli	30/9/93	Scholar
Ibrahim Abdisalam (M)	6 0	11 02	Somalia	4/5/91	Scholar
Johansen Eirik (G)	6 4	14 00	Tonsberg	12/7/92	
Johnson Adam (M)	5 8	10 00	Sunderland	14/7/87	Middlesbrough
Johnson Michael (M)	6 1	12 07	Urmston	3/3/88	Scholar
Kennedy Kieran (D)			Urmston	23/9/93	Scholar
Kolarov Aleksandar (D)	6 2	13 05	Belgrade	10/11/85	Lazio
Kompany Vincent (D)	6 3	13 05	Brussels	10/4/86	Hamburg
Lawlor Ian (G)			Dublin	27/10/94	Scholar

Lescott Jolean (D)	6 2	13 01	Birmingham	16/8/82	Everton
McGivern Ryan (D)	5 10	11 07	Newry	8/1/90	Scholar
Meppen-Walters Courtney (D)			Bury	2/8/94	Scholar
Milner James (M)	5 9	11 00	Leeds	4/1/86	Aston Villa
Nasri Samir (M)	5 9	11 11	Marseille	26/6/87	Arsenal
Nimely-Tchuimeni Alex (F)	5 11	11 03	Monrovia	11/5/91	Scholar
Pantilimon Costel (G)	6 5	15 02	Bacau	1/2/87	Timisoara
Plummer Ellis (D)			Denton	2/9/94	Scholar
Razak Abdul (M)	5 10	11 02	Abidjan	11/11/92	Scholar
Rekik Karim (D)	6 0	12 00	Den Haag	2/12/94	Troyes B
Richards Micah (D)	5 11	13 00	Birmingham	24/6/88	Scholar
Roman Olle Joan Angel (F)	5 7	10 10	Barcelona	18/5/93	Espanyol
Rusnak Albert (M)			Kosice	7/7/94	Scholar
Santa Cruz Roque (F)	6 2	13 12	Asuncion	16/8/81	Blackburn R
Savic Stefan (D)	6 1	11 07	Belgrade	8/9/91	BSK Borca
Scapuzzi Luca (F)	6 0	11 11	Milan	15/4/91	Portogruaro
Silva David (F)	5 7	10 07	Arguineguin	8/1/86	Valencia
Suarez Denis (M)			Tui	6/1/94	Celta Vigo Youth
Swan George (D)			Normanton	12/9/94	Scholar
Tevez Carlos (F)	5 8	11 11	Buenos Aires	5/2/84	Manchester U
Toure Kolo (D)	5 10	13 08	Sokuora Bouake	19/3/81	Arsenal
Toure Yaya (M)	6 3	14 02	Sokoura Bouake	13/5/83	Barcelona
Wabara Reece (D)	6 0	12 06	Birmingham	28/12/91	
Weiss Vladimir (M)	5 9	10 10	Bratislava	30/11/89	Scholar
Zabaleta Pablo (D)	5 8	10 12	Buenos Aires	16/1/85	Espanyol

League Appearances: Aguero, S. 31(3); Balotelli, M. 14(9); Barry, G. 31(3); Clichy, G. 28; De Jong, N. 11(10); Dzeko, E. 16(14); Hargreaves, O. (1); Hart, J. 38; Johnson, A. 10(16); Kolarov, A. 9(3); Kompany, V. 31; Lescott, J. 30(1); Milner, J. 17(9); Nasri, S. 26(4); Onuoha, N. (1); Pizarro, D. 1(4); Razak, A. (1); Richards, M. 23(6); Savic, S. 5(6); Silva, D. 33(3); Tevez, C. 7(6); Toure, K. 8(6); Toure, Y. 31(1); Zabaleta, P. 18(3).
Goals – League (93): Aguero 23 (3 pens), Dzeko 14, Balotelli 13 (3 pens), Johnson, A. 6, Silva 6, Toure, Y. 6, Nasri 5, Tevez 4, Kompany 3, Milner 3 (1 pen), Kolarov 2, Lescott 2, Barry 1, Richards 1, Savic 1, Zabaleta 1, own goals 2.
Carling Cup (10): Dzeko 3, Aguero 1, Balotelli 1, De Jong 1, Hargreaves 1, Johnson, A. 1, Nasri 1, own goal 1.
FA Cup (2): Aguero 1, Kolarov 1.
Champions League (9): Toure, Y. 3, Balotelli 2 (1 pen), Aguero 1, Kolarov 1, Silva 1, own goal 1.
Europa League (9): Aguero 4, Balotelli 1 (pen), Dzeko 1, Pizarro 1, Silva 1, own goal 1.
Community Shield (2): Dzeko 1, Lescott 1.
Ground: Etihad Stadium, Etihad Campus, Manchester M11 3FF. Telephone: (0161) 444 1894.
Capacity: 47,726.
Record Attendance: 84,569 v Stoke C, FA Cup 6th rd, 3 March 1934 (at Maine Road; British record for any game outside London or Glasgow); 47,370 v Tottenham H, FA Premier League, 5 May 2010 (at City of Manchester Stadium).
Manager: Roberto Mancini.
Most League Goals: 108, Division 2, 1926–27, 108, Division 1, 2001–02.
Highest League Scorer in Season: Tommy Johnson, 38, Division 1, 1928–29.
Most League Goals in Total Aggregate: Tommy Johnson, 158, 1919–30.
Most Capped Player: Colin Bell, 48, England.
Most League Appearances: Alan Oakes, 565, 1959–76.
Colours: Sky blue shirts with white detail, white shorts with sky blue detail, white stockings with sky blue tops.
Honours – FA Premier League: Champions – 2011–12. **Football League:** Division 1 Champions – 1936–37, 1967–68, 2001–02. Division 2 Champions – 1898–99, 1902–03, 1909–10, 1927–28, 1946–47, 1965–66. **FA Cup:** Winners – 1904, 1934, 1956, 1969, 2011.

Football League Cup: Winners – 1970, 1976. **European Competitions: European Cup-Winners' Cup:** Winners – 1969–70.

MANCHESTER UNITED   FA PREMIERSHIP

Name			Place	Date	Previous
Amos Ben (G)	6 1	13 00	Macclesfield	10/4/90	Scholar
Anderson (M)	5 8	10 07	Porto Alegre	13/4/88	Porto
Bebe (F)	6 3	11 11	Agualva-cacem	12/7/90	Guimaraes
Berbatov Dimitar (F)	6 2	12 06	Blagoevgrad	30/1/81	Tottenham H
Brady Robert (F)	5 9	10 12	Belfast	14/1/92	Scholar
Brown Reece (D)	6 2	13 02	Manchester	1/11/91	
Carrick Michael (M)	6 1	11 10	Wallsend	28/7/81	Tottenham H
Cleverley Tom (M)	5 9	10 07	Basingstoke	12/8/89	Scholar
Cofie John (F)			Aboso	21/1/93	Scholar
Cole Larnell (M)			Manchester	9/3/93	Scholar
Daehli Mats (M)			Oslo	2/3/95	Scholar
De Gea David (G)	6 3	12 13	Madrid	7/11/90	Atletico Madrid
De Laet Ritchie (D)	6 1	12 02	Antwerp	28/11/88	Stoke C
Ekangamene Charni (M)			Antwerp	16/2/94	Scholar
Evans Jonny (D)	6 2	12 01	Belfast	3/1/88	Scholar
Evra Patrice (D)	5 8	11 10	Dakar	15/5/81	Monaco
Fabio (M)	5 8	10 03	Rio de Janeiro	9/7/90	Fluminense
Ferdinand Rio (D)	6 2	13 12	Peckham	7/11/78	Leeds U
Fletcher Darren (M)	6 0	11 09	Edinburgh	1/2/84	Scholar
Fornasier Michele (D)			Vittorio Veneto	22/8/93	Scholar
Fryers Zeki (D)	6 0	12 00	Manchester	9/9/92	Scholar
Giggs Ryan (F)	5 11	11 02	Cardiff	29/11/73	School
Giverin Luke (D)			Salford	4/2/93	Scholar
Hernandez Javier (F)	5 8	9 11	Guadalajara	1/6/88	Guadalajara
James Matthew (M)	6 0	11 12	Bacup	22/7/91	Scholar
Januzaj Adrian (M)			Brussels	5/2/95	Scholar
Johnstone Samuel (G)	6 0	12 10	Preston	25/3/93	Scholar
Jones Phil (D)	5 11	11 02	Preston	21/2/92	Blackburn R
Keane Michael (D)			Stockport	11/1/93	Scholar
Keane Will (F)	6 2	11 05	Stockport	11/1/93	Scholar
King Josh (F)	5 11	11 09	Oslo	15/1/92	Scholar
Lindegaard Anders (G)	6 4	12 08	Odense	13/4/84	Odense
Lingard Jesse (M)			Warrington	15/12/92	Scholar
Macheda Federico (F)	6 0	11 13	Rome	22/8/91	Scholar
McGinty Sean (D)			Maidstone	11/8/93	Scholar
Nani (M)	5 9	10 04	Cape Verde	17/11/86	Sporting Lisbon
Norwood Oliver (M)	5 11	11 13	Burnley	12/4/91	Scholar
Park Ji-Sung (M)	5 9	11 06	Seoul	25/2/81	PSV Eindhoven
Petrucci Davide (M)			Rome	5/10/91	Scholar
Pogba Paul (M)	6 1	12 08	Lagny-sur-Marne	15/3/93	Scholar
Rafael (D)	5 8	10 03	Rio de Janeiro	9/7/90	Fluminense
Rooney Wayne (F)	5 10	12 13	Liverpool	24/10/85	Everton
Scholes Paul (M)	5 7	11 02	Salford	16/11/74	Trainee
Smalling Chris (D)	6 4	14 02	Greenwich	22/11/89	Fulham
Thorpe Tom (D)	6 0	14 00	Manchester	13/1/93	Scholar
Tunnicliffe Ryan (M)	6 0	14 02	Bury	30/12/92	Scholar
Valencia Antonio (M)	5 10	12 04	Lago Agrio	5/8/85	Wigan Ath
Van Velzen Gyliano (F)			Amsterdam	14/4/94	Scholar
Vermijl Marnick (D)	5 11	11 12	Overpelt	13/1/92	
Veseli Frederic (D)	6 0	12 08	Kosovo	20/11/92	Manchester C
Vidic Nemanja (D)	6 1	13 02	Uzice	21/10/81	Spartak Moscow
Welbeck Danny (F)	6 1	11 07	Manchester	26/11/90	Scholar

| Wootton Scott (D) | 6 2 | 13 00 | Birkenhead | 12/9/91 | Scholar |
| Young Ashley (M) | 5 10 | 10 03 | Stevenage | 9/7/85 | Aston Villa |

League Appearances: Amos, B. 1; Anderson, 8(2); Berbatov, D. 5(7); Carrick, M. 27(3); Cleverley, T. 5(5); De Gea, D. 29; Evans, J. 28(1); Evra, P. 37; Fabio, 2(3); Ferdinand, R. 29(1); Fletcher, D. 7(1); Fryers, E. (2); Gibson, D. 1; Giggs, R. 14(11); Hernandez, J. 18(10); Jones, P. 25(4); Keane, W. (1); Lindegaard, A. 8; Macheda, F. (3); Nani, 24(5); Owen, M. (1); Park, J. 10(7); Pogba, P. (3); Rafael, 10(2); Rooney, W. 32(2); Scholes, P. 14(3); Smalling, C. 14(5); Valencia, A. 22(5); Vidic, N. 6; Welbeck, D. 23(7); Young, A. 19(6).
Goals – League (89): Rooney 27 (6 pens), Hernandez 10 (1 pen), Welbeck 9, Nani 8, Berbatov 7 (2 pens), Young 6, Scholes 4, Valencia 4, Anderson 2, Carrick 2, Giggs 2, Park 2, Evans 1, Fletcher 1, Jones 1, Smalling 1, own goals 2.
Carling Cup (7): Owen 3, Berbatov 1, Giggs 1, Macheda 1 (pen), Valencia 1.
FA Cup (4): Rooney 2, Park 1, Welbeck 1.
Champions League (11): Rooney 2 (2 pens), Welbeck 2, Berbatov 1, Fletcher 1, Giggs 1, Jones 1, Valencia 1, Young 1, own goal 1.
Europa League (6): Rooney 3 (1 pen), Hernandez 2, Young 1.
Community Shield (3): Nani 2, Smalling 1.
Ground: Old Trafford, Sir Matt Busby Way, Manchester M16 0RA. Telephone: (0161) 868 8000.
Capacity: 75,769.
Record Attendance: 76,098 v Blackburn R, FA Premier League, 31 March 2007.
Ground Record Attendance: 76,962 Wolverhampton W v Grimsby T, FA Cup semi-final, 25 March 1939.
Manager: Sir Alex Ferguson CBE.
Most League Goals: 103, Division 1, 1956–57 and 1958–59.
Highest League Scorer in Season: Dennis Viollet, 32, 1959–60.
Most League Goals in Total Aggregate: Bobby Charlton, 199, 1956–73.
Most Capped Player: Bobby Charlton, 106, England.
Most League Appearances: Ryan Giggs, 638, 1991–.
Colours: Red shirts with black chevron, white shorts with red side panels, black stockings.
Honours – FA Premier League: Champions – 1993–94, 1995–96, 1996–97, 1998–99, 1999–2000, 2000–01, 2002–03, 2006–07, 2007–08, 2008–09, 2010–11. **Football League:** Division 1 Champions – 1907–8, 1910–11, 1951–52, 1955–56, 1956–57, 1964–65, 1966–67. Division 2 Champions – 1935–36, 1974–75. **FA Cup:** Winners – 1909, 1948, 1963, 1977, 1983, 1985, 1990, 1994, 1996, 1999, 2004. **Football League Cup:** Winners – 1991–92, 2006, 2009, 2010. **European Competitions: European Cup:** Winners – 1967–68. **Champions League:** Winners – 1998–99, 2007–08. **European Cup-Winners' Cup:** Winners – 1990–91. **Super Cup:** Winners – 1991. **Inter-Continental Cup:** Winners – 1999. **FIFA Club World Cup:** Winners – 2008.

MIDDLESBROUGH   FL CHAMPIONSHIP

Arca Julio (M)	5 9	11 13	Quilmes	31/1/81	Sunderland
Atkinson David (D)			Shildon	27/4/93	Scholar
Bailey Nicky (M)	5 10	12 06	Hammersmith	10/6/84	Charlton Ath
Bennett Joe (D)	5 10	10 04	Rochdale	28/3/90	Scholar
Brobbel Ryan (M)			Hartlepool	5/3/93	Scholar
Dolan Matthew (M)			Hartlepool	11/2/93	Scholar
Edwards Curtis (M)			Middlesbrough	12/1/94	Scholar
Emnes Marvin (M)	5 11	10 06	Rotterdam	27/5/88	Sparta Rotterdam
Fowler Jake (M)			Sunderland	22/9/93	Scholar
Gibson Ben (D)	6 1	12 04	Nunthorpe	15/1/93	Scholar
Halliday Andrew (M)	5 8	10 07	Glasgow	11/10/91	Livingston
Haroun Faris (M)	6 2	13 00	Brussels	22/9/85	Beerschot
Hines Seb (D)	6 1	12 02	Wetherby	29/5/88	Scholar

Jackson Adam (D)			Darlington	18/5/94	Scholar
Jutkiewicz Lucas (F)	6 1	12 09	Southampton	20/3/89	Everton
Main Curtis (F)	5 9	12 02	South Shields	20/6/92	Darlington
McDonald Scott (F)	5 7	12 07	Melbourne	21/8/83	Celtic
McManus Stephen (D)	6 2	13 00	Lanark	10/9/82	Celtic
Oliver Kyle (D)			Ashington	18/4/92	Scholar
Park Cameron (M)	5 10	11 02	Marske	6/7/92	Scholar
Pilatos Bruno (D)			Angola	30/3/93	Scholar
Reach Adam (M)	6 1	11 07	Gateshead	3/2/93	Scholar
Ripley Connor (G)	5 11	11 13	Middlesbrough	13/2/93	Scholar
Smallwood Richard (M)	5 11	11 05	Redcar	29/12/90	Scholar
Steele Jason (G)	6 2	12 07	Newton Aycliffe	18/8/90	Scholar
Thomson Kevin (M)	6 2	11 05	Edinburgh	14/10/84	Rangers
Weldon Paul (D)			Sunderland	27/11/91	Scholar
Williams Luke (F)	6 1	11 08	Middlesbrough	11/6/93	Scholar
Williams Rhys (M)	6 2	11 05	Perth	14/7/88	Scholar
Wyke Charlie (F)			Middlesbrough	6/12/92	Scholar
Zemmama Merouane (M)	5 8	10 05	Rabat	7/10/83	Hibernian

League Appearances: Arca, J. 22(8); Bailey, N. 37; Bates, M. 37; Bennett, J. 40(1); Coyne, D. 1; Emnes, M. 37(5); Halliday, A. (1); Hammill, A. 8(2); Haroun, F. 23(9); Hines, S. 20(3); Hoyte, J. 39; Ikeme, C. 10; Jutkiewicz, L. 17(2); Kink, T. (1); Main, C. (12); Martin, M. (15); McDonald, S. 31(2); McMahon, T. 28(6); McManus, S. 21(3); Nimely-Tchuimeni, A. (9); Ogbeche, B. 5(12); Reach, A. (1); Ripley, C. 1; Robson, B. 37; Smallwood, R. 7(6); Steele, J. 34; Thomson, K. 10(12); Williams, R. 34(1); Zemmama, M. 7(8).

Goals – League (52): Emnes 14, McDonald 9, Robson 7 (2 pens), Martin 3, Ogbeche 3, Bailey 2, Bates 2, Haroun 2, Jutkiewicz 2, Main 2, Williams, R. 2, Bennett 1, Hines 1, McMahon 1, Zemmama 1.

Carling Cup (6): Emnes 3 (1 pen), Hines 1, Robson 1, Zemmama 1.

FA Cup (3): Emnes 1, Jutkiewicz 1, Robson 1.

Ground: Riverside Stadium, Middlesbrough TS3 6RS. Telephone: (0844) 499 6789.

Capacity: 35,100.

Record Attendance: 53,536 v Newcastle U, Division 1, 27 December 1949 (at Ayresome Park); 34,814 v Newcastle U, FA Premier League, 5 March 2003 (at Riverside Stadium).

Manager: Tony Mowbray.

Most League Goals: 122, Division 2, 1926–27.

Highest League Scorer in Season: George Camsell, 59, Division 2, 1926–27 (Second Division record).

Most League Goals in Total Aggregate: George Camsell, 325, 1925–39.

Most Capped Player: Wilf Mannion, 26, England.

Most League Appearances: Tim Williamson, 563, 1902–23.

Colours: Red shirts with white design and one white sleeve, white shorts with red trim, white stockings.

Honours – Football League: Division 1 Champions 1994–95. Division 2 Champions 1926–27, 1928–29, 1973–74. **Football League Cup:** Winners – 2004. **Amateur Cup:** Winners – 1895, 1898. **Anglo-Scottish Cup:** Winners – 1975–76.

MILLWALL   FL CHAMPIONSHIP

Abdou Nadjim (M)	5 10	11 02	Martigues	13/7/84	Plymouth Arg
Barron Scott (D)	5 9	9 08	Preston	2/9/85	Ipswich T
Batt Shaun (M)	6 3	12 08	Harlow	22/2/87	Peterborough U
Bouazza Hameur (M)	5 10	12 01	Evry	22/2/85	Arles-Avignon
Craig Tony (D)	6 0	10 03	Greenwich	20/4/85	Crystal Palace
Dunne Alan (D)	5 10	10 13	Dublin	23/8/82	Trainee

Feeney Liam (M)	5 10	12 02	Hammersmith	21/1/87	Bournemouth
Forde David (G)	6 3	13 08	Galway	20/12/79	Cardiff C
Henderson Darius (F)	6 3	14 03	Sutton	7/9/81	Sheffield U
Henry James (M)	6 1	11 11	Reading	10/6/89	Reading
Keogh Andy (F)	6 0	11 00	Dublin	16/5/86	Wolverhampton W
Lowry Shane (D)	6 1	13 01	Perth	12/6/89	Aston Villa
Marquis John (F)	6 1	11 03	Lewisham	16/5/92	Scholar
McQuoid Josh (F)	5 9	10 10	Southampton	15/12/89	Bournemouth
Mildenhall Steve (G)	6 4	14 01	Swindon	13/5/78	Southend U
Mkandawire Tamika (D)	6 1	12 03	Malawi	28/5/83	Leyton Orient
N'Guessan Dany (M)	6 0	12 13	Paris	11/8/87	Lincoln C
O'Brien Aiden (F)			Islington	4/10/93	Scholar
Racon Therry (M)	5 10	10 02	Paris	1/5/84	Guingamp
Robinson Paul (D)	6 1	11 09	Barnet	7/1/82	Scholar
Smith Jack (D)	5 11	11 05	Hemel Hempstead	14/10/83	Swindon T
Trotter Liam (M)	6 2	12 02	Ipswich	24/8/88	Ipswich T
Ward Darren (D)	6 3	11 04	Harrow	13/9/78	Wolverhampton W

League Appearances: Abdou, N. 35(5); Agyemang, P. 1(1); Baker, N. 6; Barron, S. 18(2); Batt, S. (4); Bouazza, H. 19(7); Craig, T. 21(2); Dunne, A. 25(5); Feeney, L. 27(7); Forde, D. 27; Hackett, C. (3); Henderson, D. 25(6); Henry, J. 24(15); Howard, B. 11(1); Kane, H. 19(3); Keogh, A. 17(1); Lowry, S. 22; Marquis, J. 7(10); Mason, R. 3(2); McQuoid, J. 1(4); Mildenhall, S. 9(1); Mkandawire, T. 10(3); Montgomery, N. (2); N'Guessan, D. 6(9); Robinson, P. 41; Simpson, J. 13(3); Smith, J. 30(3); Stewart, J. 3(1); Taylor, M. 10; Trotter, L. 33(2); Ward, D. 27(3); Wright, J. 16(2).
Goals – League (55): Henderson 15 (2 pens), Keogh 10 (2 pens), Kane 7, Trotter 7 (1 pen), Feeney 4, Simpson 4, Bouazza 2, Lowry 1, Marquis 1, N'Guessan 1, Robinson 1, Wright 1, own goal 1.
Carling Cup (3): Bouazza 1, Mkandawire 1, N'Guessan 1.
FA Cup (9): Henderson 4 (1 pen), Kane 2, Feeney 1, N'Guessan 1, Trotter 1.
Ground: The Den, Zampa Road, London SE16 3LN. Telephone: (020) 7232 1222.
Capacity: 19,734.
Record Attendance: 48,672 v Derby Co, FA Cup 5th rd, 20 February 1937 (at The Den, Cold Blow Lane); 20,093 v Arsenal, FA Cup 3rd rd, 10 January 1994 (at The Den, Bermondsey).
Manager: Kenny Jackett.
Most League Goals: 127, Division 3 (S), 1927–28.
Highest League Scorer in Season: Richard Parker, 37, Division 3 (S), 1926–27.
Most League Goals in Total Aggregate: Neil Harris, 124, 1995–2004; 2006–11.
Most Capped Player: Eamonn Dunphy, 22 (23), Republic of Ireland.
Most League Appearances: Barry Kitchener, 523, 1967–82.
Colours: All blue with white detail on shirts.
Honours – Football League: Division 2 Champions – 1987–88, 2000–01. Division 3 (S) Champions – 1927–28, 1937–38. Division 4 Champions – 1961–62. **Football League Trophy:** Winners – 1982–83.

MILTON KEYNES DONS   FL CHAMPIONSHIP 1

Baldock George (M)	5 9	10 07	Buckingham	26/1/93	Youth
Bowditch Dean (F)	5 11	11 05	Bishops Stortford	15/6/86	Yeovil T
Chadwick Luke (M)	5 11	11 08	Cambridge	18/11/80	Norwich C
Chicksen Adam (D)	5 8	11 09	Milton Keynes	27/9/91	Scholar
Collins Charlie (F)	6 0	11 11	Hammersmith	22/11/91	Scholar
Doumbe Stephen (D)	6 1	12 05	Paris	28/10/79	Plymouth Arg
Flanagan Tom (D)	6 2	11 05	Hammersmith	21/10/91	Scholar
Gleeson Stephen (M)	6 2	11 00	Dublin	3/8/88	Wolverhampton W
Ibehre Jabo (F)	6 2	13 13	Islington	28/1/83	Walsall

Lewington Dean (D)	5 11	11 05	Kingston	18/5/84	Wimbledon
MacDonald Charlie (F)	5 8	12 10	Southwark	13/2/81	Brentford
MacKenzie Gary (D)	6 3	13 01	Lanark	15/10/85	Dundee
Martin David E (G)	6 1	13 04	Romford	22/1/86	Liverpool
McLoughlin Ian (G)	6 3	13 08	Dublin	9/8/91	Ipswich T
O'Shea Jay (M)	5 9	12 00	Dun Laoghaire	10/8/88	Birmingham C
Potter Darren (M)	6 0	10 08	Liverpool	21/12/84	Sheffield W
Powell Daniel (F)	5 11	13 03	Luton	12/3/91	Scholar
Slane Paul (M)	5 8	10 01	Glasgow	25/11/91	Celtic
Williams Shaun (M)	5 9	11 11	Dublin	19/10/86	Sporting Fingal

League Appearances: Balanta, A. 10(10); Baldock, S. 4; Beevers, M. 14; Bowditch, D. 33(8); Chadwick, L. 34(8); Chicksen, A. 14(6); Doumbe, S. 19(1); Flanagan, T. 18(3); Galloway, B. 1; Gleeson, S. 39; Guy, L. (1); Hall, R. (2); Ibehre, J. 23(16); Lewington, D. 46; MacDonald, C. 29(6); MacKenzie, G. 26; Martin, D. 46; McLoughlin, I. (1); McNamee, A. (7); Morrison, C. 5(1); O'Shea, J. 12(16); Potter, D. 40; Powell, D. 22(21); Slane, P. (5); Smith, Adam 17; Smith, Alan 14(2); Tavernier, J. 7; Williams, G. (2); Williams, S. 33(6).
Goals – League (84): Bowditch 12 (2 pens), MacDonald 9, Ibehre 8, Williams, S. 8 (5 pens), Powell 6, Gleeson 5, O'Shea 5 (1 pen), Balanta 4, Baldock, S. 4, Doumbe 4, Flanagan 3, Lewington 3, Morrison 3, Chadwick 2, Potter 2, Smith, Adam 2, Beevers 1, MacKenzie 1, Smith, Alan 1, own goal 1.
Carling Cup (9): Baldock, S. 2, Chadwick 2, Powell 2, Balanta 1, Ibehre 1, Lewington 1.
FA Cup (10): Bowditch 3, Powell 2, Doumbe 1, MacDonald 1, O'Shea 1, Potter 1, Williams, G. 1.
J Paint Trophy (3): Chadwick 1, MacDonald 1, own goal 1.
Play-Offs (2): Powell 1, Smith, Alan 1.
Ground: Stadium*mk*, Stadium Way West, Milton Keynes MK1 1ST. Telephone: (01908) 622 922.
Capacity: 21,189.
Record Attendance: 8,306 v Tottenham H, League Cup 3rd rd, 25 October 2006 (at National Hockey Stadium); 17,717 v Leicester C, FL 1, 28 February 2009 (at Stadium*mk*).
Ground Record Attendance: 20,222, England U21 v Bulgaria U21, 16 November 2007.
Manager: Karl Robinson.
Most League Goals: 84, FL 1, 2011–12.
Highest League Scorer in Season: Izale McLeod, 21, 2006–07.
Most League Goals in Total Aggregate: Izale McLeod, 54, 2004–07.
Most Capped Player: Ali Gerba (29), Canada.
Most League Appearances: Dean Lewington, 347, 2004–12.
Colours: White shirts with black sleeves, white shorts, white stockings with black tops.
Honours – Football League: FL 2 Champions – 2007–08. **Johnstone's Paint Trophy:** Winners – 2007–08.

MORECAMBE   FL CHAMPIONSHIP 2

Alessandra Lewis (F)	5 9	11 07	Heywood	8/2/89	Oldham Ath
Bentley Jim (D)	6 1	13 00	Liverpool	11/6/76	Manchester C
Burrow Jordan (F)	6 1	11 13	Sheffield	12/9/92	Chesterfield Scholar
Carlton Danny (F)	5 11	12 04	Leeds	22/12/83	Bury
Drummond Stuart (M)	6 2	13 06	Preston	11/12/75	Shrewsbury T
Ellison Kevin (M)	6 0	12 00	Liverpool	23/2/79	Rotherham U
Fenton Nick (D)	6 0	10 02	Preston	23/11/79	Rotherham U
Fleming Andy (M)	6 1	12 00	Liverpool	18/2/89	Wrexham
Haining Will (D)	6 0	11 02	Glasgow	2/10/82	St Mirren
McCready Chris (D)	6 1	12 05	Ellesmere Port	5/9/81	Northampton T
McDonald Gary (F)	6 0	11 06	Irvine	10/4/82	Hamilton A

McGee Joe (M)	5 11	10 12	Liverpool	6/3/93	Youth
Mwasilie Joe (M)	5 8	10 01	Zambia	7/6/93	Youth
Parkinson Dan (M)	5 11	11 02	Preston	2/11/92	Youth
Parrish Andy (D)	6 0	11 00	Bolton	22/6/88	Bury
Redshaw Jack (F)	5 6	10 00	Salford	20/11/90	Rochdale
Reid Izak (M)	5 5	10 05	Stafford	8/7/87	Macclesfield T
Roche Barry (G)	6 5	14 08	Dublin	6/4/82	Chesterfield

League Appearances: Alessandra, L. 24(18); Burrow, J. 14(5); Carlton, D. 34(10); Charnock, K. (4); Cowperthwaite, N. 1(2); Curran, C. 6(1); Drummond, S. 36(2); Ellison, K. 26(8); Fenton, N. 35; Fleming, A. 11(6); Haining, W. 36(4); Hunter, G. 30(7); Jevons, P. 14(13); Kettings, C. 2; McCready, C. 46; McDonald, G. 39(3); McGee, J. (1); McGinty, S. 4; Mwasile, J. (6); Parkinson, D. (3); Parrish, A. 29(9); Price, J. 12(6); Redshaw, J. 7(4); Reid, I. 26(10); Roche, B. 44; Wilson, L. 30.
Goals – League (63): Ellison 15, Carlton 9, Drummond 5, Wilson 5 (5 pens), Alessandra 4, Burrow 4, Jevons 4, Fenton 3, McDonald 3, Fleming 2, Price 2, Redshaw 2 (1 pen), Reid 2, Curran 1, Hunter 1, own goal 1.
Carling Cup (2): Carlton 1, Ellison 1.
FA Cup (1): Wilson 1 (pen).
J Paint Trophy (2): Ellison 1, Jevons 1.
Ground: Globe Arena, Christie Way, Westgate, Morecambe LA4 4TB. Telephone: (01524) 411 797.
Capacity: 6,402.
Record Attendance: 9,383 v Weymouth, FA Cup 3rd rd, 6 January 1962 (at Christie Park). 5,003 v Burnley, Lge Cup 2nd rd, 24 August 2010 (at Globe Arena).
Player-Manager: Jim Bentley.
Most League Goals: 73, FL 2, 2009–10.
Highest League Scorer in Season: Phil Jevons, 18, 2009–10.
Most League Goals in Total Aggregate: Stuart Drummond, 32, 2007–12.
Most Capped Player: None.
Most League Appearances: Stuart Drummond, 184, 2007–12.
Colours: Red shirts with black trim, white shorts, red stockings.
Honours – Conference: Promoted to Football League (play-offs) 2006–07. **Presidents Cup:** Winners – 1991–92. **FA Trophy:** Winners 1973–74. **Lancs Senior Cup:** Winners 1967–68. **Lancs Combination:** Champions – 1924–25, 1961–62, 1962–63, 1967–68. **Lancs Combination Cup:** Winners – 1926–27, 1945–46, 1964–65, 1966–67, 1967–68. **Lancs Junior Cup:** Winners – 1927, 1928, 1962, 1963, 1969, 1986, 1987, 1994, 1996, 1999, 2004.

NEWCASTLE UNITED   FA PREMIERSHIP

Abeid Mehdi (M)	6 1	12 08	Paris	6/8/92	Lens B
Alnwick Jak (G)			Hexham	17/6/93	Scholar
Ameobi Sam (F)	6 3	10 04	Newcastle	1/5/92	Scholar
Ameobi Shola (F)	6 3	11 13	Zaria	12/10/81	Trainee
Ba Demba (F)	6 2	12 13	Sevres	25/5/85	West Ham U
Ben Arfa Hatem (M)	5 8	10 08	Clamart	7/3/87	Marseille
Best Leon (F)	6 1	13 03	Nottingham	19/9/86	Coventry C
Cabaye Yohan (M)	5 9	11 05	Tourcoing	14/1/86	Lille
Campbell Adam (F)			North Shields	1/1/95	Wallsend BC
Cisse Papiss (F)	6 0	11 07	Dakar	3/6/85	Freiburg
Coloccini Fabricio (D)	6 0	12 04	Cordoba	22/1/82	La Coruna
Dummett Paul (D)	5 10	10 02	Newcastle	26/9/91	Scholar
Elliot Rob (G)	6 3	14 10	Chatham	30/4/86	Charlton Ath
Ferguson Shane (D)	5 9	10 01	Limavady	12/7/91	Scholar
Forster Fraser (G)	6 0	12 00	Hexham	17/3/88	Scholar
Gosling Dan (M)	6 0	11 00	Brixham	2/2/90	Everton
Gutierrez Jonas (M)	6 0	11 07	Buenos Aires	5/7/82	Mallorca

Harper Steve (G)	6 2	13 10	Easington	14/3/75	Seaham Red Star
Inman Bradden (M)	5 9	11 03	Adelaide	10/12/91	Scholar
Krul Tim (G)	6 2	11 08	Den Haag	3/4/88	Academy
Marveaux Sylvain (M)	5 8	10 05	Vannes	15/4/86	Rennes
Miele Brandon (M)			Dublin	28/8/94	Scholar
Moyo Yven (M)			Orleans	15/3/92	Sochaux
Newton Conor (M)	5 11	11 00	Whickham	17/10/91	Scholar
Obertan Gabriel (F)	6 1	12 06	Paris	26/2/89	Manchester U
Perch James (D)	5 11	11 05	Mansfield	29/9/85	Nottingham F
Ranger Nile (F)	6 2	13 03	Wood Green	11/4/91	Southampton Scholar
Richardson Michael (M)			Newcastle	17/3/92	Walker Central
Santon Davide (D)	6 2	13 00	Portomaggiore	2/1/91	Internazionale
Simpson Danny (D)	5 9	11 05	Eccles	4/1/87	Manchester U
Smith Jamie (D)			Liverpool	21/1/94	Scholar
Streete Remie (D)			Boldon	2/11/94	Scholar
Tavernier James (D)	5 9	11 00	Bradford	31/10/91	Scholar
Taylor Ryan (M)	5 8	10 04	Liverpool	19/8/84	Wigan Ath
Taylor Steven (D)	6 2	13 01	Greenwich	23/1/86	Trainee
Tiote Cheik (M)	5 11	12 06	Yamoussoukro	21/6/86	Twente
Vuckic Haris (F)	6 2	12 02	Ljubljana	21/8/92	Domzale
Williamson Mike (D)	6 4	13 03	Stoke	8/11/83	Portsmouth
Xisco (F)	6 0	13 03	Palma	26/6/86	La Coruna

League Appearances: Ameobi, Sam 1(9); Ameobi, Shola 8(19); Ba, D. 32(2); Barton, J. 2; Ben Arfa, H. 16(10); Best, L. 16(2); Cabaye, Y. 34; Cisse, P. 13(1); Coloccini, F. 35; Ferguson, S. (7); Gosling, D. 1(11); Guthrie, D. 13(3); Gutierrez, J. 37; Krul, T. 38; Lovenkrands, P. 2(7); Marveaux, S. 1(6); Obertan, G. 18(5); Perch, J. 13(12); Santon, D. 19(5); Simpson, D. 35; Smith, A. (2); Taylor, R. 23(8); Taylor, S. 14; Tiote, C. 24; Vuckic, H. 2(2); Williamson, M. 21(1).

Goals – League (56): Ba 16 (2 pens), Cisse 13, Ben Arfa 5, Best 4, Cabaye 4, Ameobi, Shola 2, Gutierrez 2, Taylor, R. 2, Gosling 1, Guthrie 1, Obertan 1, own goals 5.

Carling Cup (9): Lovenkrands 3 (2 pens), Ameobi, Sammy 1, Cabaye 1, Coloccini 1, Guthrie 1, Taylor, R. 1, Simpson 1.

FA Cup (2): Ben Arfa 1, Gutierrez 1.

Ground: St James' Park (Sports Direct Arena), Newcastle-upon-Tyne NE1 4ST. Telephone: (0191) 201 8400.

Capacity: 52,387.

Record Attendance: 68,386 v Chelsea, Division 1, 3 September 1930.

Manager: Alan Pardew.

Most League Goals: 98, Division 1, 1951–52.

Highest League Scorer in Season: Hughie Gallacher, 36, Division 1, 1926–27.

Most League Goals in Total Aggregate: Jackie Milburn, 177, 1946–57.

Most Capped Player: Shay Given, 82 (125), Republic of Ireland.

Most League Appearances: Jim Lawrence, 432, 1904–22.

Colours: Black and white striped shirts, black shorts with white trim, black stockings with white trim.

Honours – Football League: Division 1 – Champions 1904–05, 1906–07, 1908–09, 1926–27, 1992–93. Division 2 Champions – 1964–65. FL C – Champions 2009–10. **FA Cup:** Winners – 1910, 1924, 1932, 1951, 1952, 1955. **Texaco Cup:** Winners – 1973–74, 1974–75. **European Competitions: European Fairs Cup:** Winners – 1968–69. **Anglo-Italian Cup:** Winners – 1973. **Intertoto Cup:** Winners – 2006.

NORTHAMPTON TOWN

FL CHAMPIONSHIP 2

Akinfenwa Adebayo (F)	5 11	13 07	Nigeria	10/5/82	Gillingham
Charles Anthony (D)	6 1	12 05	Isleworth	11/3/81	Aldershot T
Davies Arron (M)	5 9	11 00	Cardiff	22/6/84	Peterborough U

Guttridge Luke (M)	5 6	9 07	Barnstaple	27/3/82	Aldershot T
Harding Ben (M)	5 10	11 02	Carshalton	6/9/84	Wycombe W
Higgs Shane (G)	6 3	14 06	Oxford	13/5/77	Leeds U
Jacobs Michael (M)	5 9	11 08	Rothwell	23/3/92	Scholar
Johnson John (D)	6 0	12 00	Middlesbrough	16/9/88	Middlesbrough
Kitson Neal (G)	6 1	12 13	New York	4/1/86	Rochester Rhinos
Langmead Kelvin (D)	6 1	12 00	Coventry	23/3/85	Shrewsbury T
Ofori-Twumasi Nana (D)	5 8	11 09	Accra	15/5/90	Peterborough U
Robinson Jake (F)	5 7	10 10	Brighton	23/10/86	Shrewsbury T
Tozer Ben (D)	6 1	12 11	Plymouth	1/3/90	Newcastle U
Turnbull Paul (M)	6 0	12 07	Handforth	23/1/89	Stockport Co
Webster Byron (D)	6 5	12 07	Sherburn-in-Elmet	31/3/87	Doncaster R
Wilson Lewis (F)	5 10	11 13	Milton Keynes	19/2/93	Newport Pagnell T

League Appearances: Adams, B. 21(1); Akinfenwa, A. 33(6); Arthur, C. 5(2); Asante, A. 3(1); Baldock, G. 4(1); Berahino, S. 14; Carlisle, C. 18; Charles, A. 5(4); Corker, A. 9(7); Crowe, J. 11; Davies, A. 15; Duke, M. 9; Gilligan, R. (2); Guttridge, L. 19; Hall, F. 2(1); Harding, B. 19; Higgs, S. 3; Holt, A. 5(4); Jackson, M. 5(1); Jacobs, M. 45(1); Johnson, J. 43(2); Kaziboni, G. (3); Kitson, N. 8; Langmead, K. 39(2); McKoy, N. 5(4); Niven, D. 4; Ofori-Twumasi, N. 4(1); Robinson, J. 15(17); Salihu, L. (1); Savage, B. 3(5); Silva, T. 12(3); Thornton, K. (2); Tozer, B. 42(3); Turnbull, P. 9(5); Walker, S. 21; Weale, C. 3; Webster, B. 8(5); Wedderburn, N. 1(1); Westwood, A. 14(3); Williams, B. 8(10); Wilson, L. 2(1); Young, L. 20(10).

Goals – League (56): Akinfenwa 18 (2 pens), Berahino 6, Jacobs 6 (2 pens), Davies 4, Langmead 4, Guttridge 3, Tozer 3, Williams 3, Johnson 2, Asante 1, Carlisle 1, Jackson 1, Silva 1, Westwood 1, Wilson 1, own goal 1.

Carling Cup (2): Tozer 1, Turnbull 1.

FA Cup (0).

J Paint Trophy (1): Jacobs 1.

Ground: Sixfields Stadium, Upton Way, Northampton NN5 5QA. Telephone: (01604) 683 700.

Capacity: 7,300.

Record Attendance: 24,523 v Fulham, Division 1, 23 April 1966 (at County Ground); 7,557 v Manchester C, Division 2, 26 September 1998 (at Sixfields Stadium).

Manager: Aidy Boothroyd.

Most League Goals: 109, Division 3, 1962–63 and Division 3 (S), 1952–53.

Highest League Scorer in Season: Cliff Holton, 36, Division 3, 1961–62.

Most League Goals in Total Aggregate: Jack English, 135, 1947–60.

Most Capped Player: Edwin Lloyd Davies, 12 (16), Wales.

Most League Appearances: Tommy Fowler, 521, 1946–61.

Colours: Claret shirts, white shorts, white stockings.

Honours – Football League: Division 3 Champions – 1962–63. Division 4 Champions – 1986–87.

NORWICH CITY   FA PREMIERSHIP

Adeyemi Tom (M)	6 1	12 04	Milton Keynes	24/10/91	Scholar
Ayala Daniel (M)	6 3	13 03	Sevilla	7/11/90	Liverpool
Barnett Leon (D)	6 0	12 04	Stevenage	30/11/85	WBA
Bennett Elliott (M)	5 9	10 11	Telford	18/12/88	Brighton & HA
Bennett Ryan (M)	6 2	11 00	Thurrock	6/3/90	Peterborough U
Crofts Andrew (D)	5 10	12 07	Chatham	29/5/84	Brighton & HA
Drury Adam (D)	5 10	11 09	Cambridge	29/8/78	Peterborough U
Fox David (M)	5 9	11 08	Leek	13/12/83	Colchester U
Francomb George (D)	5 11	11 07	Hackney	8/9/91	Scholar
Holt Grant (F)	6 1	14 02	Carlisle	12/4/81	Shrewsbury T
Hoolahan Wes (M)	5 6	10 03	Dublin	10/8/83	Blackpool

Howson Jonathan (M)	5 11	12 01	Morley	21/5/88	Leeds U
Jackson Simeon (M)	5 10	10 12	Kingston, Jamaica	28/3/87	Gillingham
Johnson Brad (M)	6 0	12 10	Hackney	28/4/87	Leeds U
Lappin Simon (M)	5 11	9 06	Glasgow	25/1/83	St Mirren
Martin Chris (F)	6 2	12 06	Beccles	4/11/88	Scholar
Martin Russell (M)	6 0	11 08	Brighton	4/1/86	Peterborough U
Morison Steven (F)	6 2	13 07	Enfield	29/8/83	Millwall
Pilkington Anthony (M)	5 11	11 13	Blackburn	3/11/87	Huddersfield T
Rudd Declan (G)	6 3	12 06	Diss	16/1/91	Scholar
Ruddy John (G)	6 3	12 07	St Ives	24/10/86	Everton
Smith Korey (M)	5 9	11 01	Hatfield	31/1/91	Scholar
Steer Jed (G)	6 2	14 00	Norwich	23/9/92	Scholar
Surman Andrew (M)	5 10	11 06	Johannesburg	20/8/86	Wolverhampton W
Tierney Marc (D)	5 11	11 04	Prestwich	23/8/85	Colchester U
Vaughan James (F)	5 11	13 00	Birmingham	14/7/88	Everton
Ward Elliot (D)	6 2	13 00	Harrow	19/1/85	Coventry C

League Appearances: Ayala, D. 6(1); Barnett, L. 13(4); Bennett, E. 22(11); Bennett, R. 8; Crofts, A. 13(11); De Laet, R. 6; Drury, A. 12; Fox, D. 23(5); Holt, G. 24(12); Hoolahan, W. 25(8); Howson, J. 11; Jackson, S. 10(12); Johnson, B. 25(3); Lappin, S. 4; Martin, C. 3(1); Martin, R. 30(3); Morison, S. 22(12); Naughton, K. 29(3); Pilkington, A. 23(7); Rudd, D. 1(1); Ruddy, J. 37; Surman, A. 21(4); Tierney, M. 17; Vaughan, J. 1(4); Ward, E. 12; Whitbread, Z. 18; Wilbraham, A. 2(9).
Goals – League (52): Holt 15 (2 pens), Morison 9, Pilkington 8, Hoolahan 4, Surman 4, Jackson 3, Johnson, B. 2, Martin, R. 2, Barnett 1, Bennett, E. 1, De Laet 1, Howson 1, Wilbraham 1.
Carling Cup (0).
FA Cup (7): Holt 2, Jackson 2, Hoolahan 1, Morison 1, Surman 1.
Ground: Carrow Road, Norwich NR1 1JE. Telephone: (01603) 760 760.
Capacity: 26,034.
Record Attendance: 25,037 v Sheffield W, FA Cup 5th rd, 16 February 1935 (at The Nest); 43,984 v Leicester C, FA Cup 6th rd, 30 March 1963 (at Carrow Road).
Manager: Chris Hughton.
Most League Goals: 99, Division 3 (S), 1952–53.
Highest League Scorer in Season: Ralph Hunt, 31, Division 3 (S), 1955–56.
Most League Goals in Total Aggregate: Johnny Gavin, 122, 1945–54, 1955–58.
Most Capped Player: Mark Bowen, 35 (41), Wales.
Most League Appearances: Ron Ashman, 592, 1947–64.
Colours: Yellow shirts with green trim, green shorts, yellow stockings.
Honours – Football League: FL 1 Champions – 2009–10. Division 1 Champions – 2003–04. Division 2 Champions – 1971–72, 1985–86. Division 3 (S) Champions – 1933–34. **Football League Cup:** Winners – 1962, 1985.

NOTTINGHAM FOREST   FL CHAMPIONSHIP

Blackstock Dexter (F)	6 2	13 00	Oxford	20/5/86	QPR
Blake Jack (M)			Scotland	22/9/94	
Camp Lee (G)	5 11	11 11	Derby	22/8/84	QPR
Cohen Chris (M)	5 11	10 11	Norwich	5/3/87	Yeovil T
Darlow Karl (G)	6 1	12 05	Northampton	8/10/90	Scholar
Derbyshire Matt (F)	5 10	11 01	Gt Harwood	14/4/86	Birmingham C
Findley Robbie (F)	5 9	11 11	Phoenix	4/8/85	Real Salt Lake
Freeman Kieron (D)	5 10	12 05	Nottingham	21/3/92	Scholar
Greening Jonathan (M)	5 11	11 00	Scarborough	2/1/79	Fulham
Gunter Chris (D)	5 11	11 02	Newport	21/7/89	Tottenham H
Lascelles Jamaal (D)	6 2	13 01	Derby	11/11/93	Scholar
Lynch Joel (D)	6 1	12 08	Eastbourne	3/10/87	Brighton & HA

Majewski Radoslaw (M)	5 7	10 06	Pruszkow	15/12/86	Polonia Warsaw
McGoldrick David (F)	6 1	11 10	Nottingham	29/11/87	Southampton
McGugan Lewis (M)	5 9	11 06	Long Eaton	25/10/88	Scholar
Miller Ishmael (F)	6 3	14 00	Manchester	5/3/87	WBA
Moloney Brendan (M)	6 1	11 12	Killarney	18/1/89	Scholar
Morgan David (M)			Northern Ireland	4/7/94	Scholar
Moussi Guy (M)	6 1	12 11	Paris	23/1/85	Angers
Osborn Ben (D)			Derby	5/8/94	Scholar
Reid Andy (M)	5 9	12 08	Dublin	29/7/82	Blackpool
Tudgay Marcus (F)	5 10	12 04	Shoreham	3/2/83	Sheffield W

League Appearances: Anderson, P. 10(7); Bamford, P. (2); Blackstock, D. 16(6); Boateng, G. 5; Camp, L. 46; Chambers, L. 43; Cohen, C. 7; Cunningham, G. 25(2); Derbyshire, M. 7(8); Elokobi, G. 8(4); Findley, R. 10(13); Garner, J. 1(1); Greening, J. 24(7); Guedioura, A. 19; Gunter, C. 44(2); Harewood, M. 4; Higginbotham, D. 5(1); Hill, C. 5; Lascelles, J. 1; Lynch, J. 28(7); Majewski, R. 23(5); McCleary, G. 21(1); McGoldrick, D. 3(6); McGugan, L. 27(8); Miller, I. 13(8); Moloney, B. 3(5); Morgan, W. 22; Moussi, G. 33(1); Reid, A. 22(17); Tudgay, M. 24(10); Wootton, S. 7(6).
Goals – League (48): McCleary 9, Blackstock 8, Majewski 6, Tudgay 5, Findley 3, Lynch 3, McGugan 3 (1 pen), Miller 3, Reid 2 (1 pen), Boateng 1, Derbyshire 1, Guedioura 1, Gunter 1, Higginbotham 1, Morgan 1.
Carling Cup (10): Findley 3, McGugan 2 (1 pen), Derbyshire 1, Majewski 1, Miller 1, Morgan 1, Tudgay 1.
FA Cup (0).
Ground: The City Ground, Nottingham NG2 5FJ. Telephone: (0115) 982 4444.
Capacity: 30,576.
Record Attendance: 49,946 v Manchester U, Division 1, 28 October 1967.
Manager: TBC.
Most League Goals: 110, Division 3 (S), 1950–51.
Highest League Scorer in Season: Wally Ardron, 36, Division 3 (S), 1950–51.
Most League Goals in Total Aggregate: Grenville Morris, 199, 1898–1913.
Most Capped Player: Stuart Pearce, 76 (78), England.
Most League Appearances: Bob McKinlay, 614, 1951–70.
Colours: Red shirt with white trim, white shorts, red stockings.
Honours – Football League: Division 1 – Champions 1977–78, 1997–98. Division 2 Champions – 1906–07, 1921–22. Division 3 (S) Champions – 1950–51. **FA Cup:** Winners – 1898, 1959. **Football League Cup:** Winners – 1977–78, 1978–79, 1988–89, 1989–90. **Anglo-Scottish Cup:** Winners – 1976–77. **Simod Cup:** Winners – 1989. **Zenith Data Systems Cup:** Winners – 1991–92. **European Competitions: European Cup:** Winners – 1978–79, 1979–80. **Super Cup:** Winners – 1979.

NOTTS COUNTY   FL CHAMPIONSHIP 1

Bencherif Hamza (D)	5 9	12 03	Paris	9/2/88	Macclesfield T
Bishop Neil (M)	6 1	12 10	Stockton	7/8/81	Barnet
Edwards Mike (D)	6 0	12 10	Hessle	25/4/80	Grimsby T
Hollis Haydn (D)	6 4	13 01	Selston	14/10/92	Scholar
Hughes Jeff (D)	6 1	11 00	Larne	29/5/85	Bristol R
Hughes Lee (F)	5 10	12 00	Smethwick	22/5/76	Oldham Ath
Judge Alan (F)	5 6	11 03	Dublin	11/11/88	Blackburn R
Kelly Julian (D)	5 8	11 04	Enfield	6/9/89	Reading
Mahon Gavin (M)	5 11	13 05	Birmingham	2/1/77	QPR
Mitchell Liam (G)			Nottingham	18/9/92	Scholar
Pearce Krystian (D)	6 1	13 05	Birmingham	5/1/90	Huddersfield T
Sheehan Alan (D)	5 11	11 02	Athlone	14/9/86	Swindon T

| Thompson Curtis (M) | Nottingham | 2/9/93 | Scholar |
| Waite Tyrell (F) | Derby | 1/7/94 | Ilkeston |

League Appearances: Adebola, D. 3(3); Allen, C. 4(5); Bencherif, H. 14(6); Bishop, N. 41; Bogdanovic, D. 8; Burgess, B. 20(8); Chilvers, L. 16(1); Demontagnac, I. 2(15); Edwards, M. 27(3); Forte, J. 6(4); Freeman, K. 18(1); Harley, J. 11(3); Harris, L. 1(1); Hawley, K. 15(11); Hollis, H. 1; Hughes, J. 44(1); Hughes, L. 28(12); Judge, A. 40(3); Kelly, J. 29(3); Mahon, G. 23(8); Montano, C. 4(7); Montano, C. 1(3); Nelson, S. 46; Orenuga, F. (2); Pearce, K. 25(2); Ravenhill, R. 5; Sam, L. 8(2); Sheehan, A. 39; Sodje, S. 7(9); Speiss, F. (1); Spicer,`J. (1); Stewart, D. 16(1); Stirling, J. (8); Westcarr, C. 2(2); Yennaris, N. 2.

Goals – League (75): Hughes, J. 13 (8 pens), Hughes, L. 10, Judge 7, Forte 5, Sam 5, Burgess 4, Montano 4, Kelly 3, Pearce 3, Bencherif 2, Bishop 2, Bogdanovic 2, Hawley 2, Sheehan 2, Sodje 2, Stewart 2, Adebola 1, Edwards 1, Freeman 1, own goals 4.

Carling Cup (3): Edwards 1, Hughes, L. 1, Westcarr 1.

FA Cup (8): Hughes, J. 4 (1 pen), Hawley 2, Judge 1, Sheehan 1.

J Paint Trophy (1): Hawley 1.

Ground: Meadow Lane Stadium, Meadow Lane, Nottingham NG2 3HJ. Telephone: (0115) 952 9000.

Capacity: 20,300.

Record Attendance: 47,310 v York C, FA Cup 6th rd, 12 March 1955.

Manager: Keith Curle.

Most League Goals: 107, Division 4, 1959–60.

Highest League Scorer in Season: Tom Keetley, 39, Division 3 (S), 1930–31.

Most League Goals in Total Aggregate: Les Bradd, 125, 1967–78.

Most Capped Player: Kevin Wilson, 15 (42), Northern Ireland.

Most League Appearances: Albert Iremonger, 564, 1904–26.

Colours: Black and white striped shirts, black shorts, black stockings.

Honours – Football League: Division 2 Champions – 1896–97, 1913–14, 1922–23. Division 3 Champions – 1997–98. Division 3 (S) Champions – 1930–31, 1949–50. Division 4 Champions – 1970–71; FL 2 Champions – 2009–10. **FA Cup:** Winners – 1893–94. **Anglo-Italian Cup:** Winners – 1995.

OLDHAM ATHLETIC   FL CHAMPIONSHIP 1

Belezika Glenn (D)	5 11	13 01	Camden	24/12/94	Stalybridge C
Bouzanis Dean (G)	6 1	13 06	Sydney	2/10/90	Liverpool
Cisak Aleksander (G)	6 3	14 11	Krakow	19/5/89	Accrington S
Furman Dean (M)	6 0	11 07	Cape Town	22/6/88	Rangers
Hughes Connor (M)	5 11	12 10	Bolton	6/5/93	Scholar
M'Changama Youssouf (M)	5 9	11 00	Marseille	29/8/90	Troyes B
M'Voto Jean-Yves (D)	6 4	14 00	Paris	6/9/88	Sunderland
Mellor David (D)	5 9	11 09	Oldham	10/7/93	Scholar
Millar Kirk (M)	5 9	10 07	Belfast	7/7/92	Linfield
Simpson Robbie (F)	6 1	11 11	Poole	15/3/85	Huddersfield T
Smith Matt (F)	6 6	14 00	Birmingham	7/6/89	Solihull Moors
Tarkowski James (D)	6 1	12 10	Manchester	19/11/92	Scholar
Wesolowski James (M)	5 8	11 11	Sydney	25/8/87	Peterborough U
Winchester Carl (D)	5 10	11 08	Belfast	12/4/93	Scholar

League Appearances: Adeyemi, T. 33(3); Belezika, G. (1); Black, P. 13; Bouzanis, D. 8(1); Brown, R. 15; Bunn, H. 8(3); Cisak, A. 38; Clarke, N. 16; Diallo, B. 12(3); Diamond, Z. 21(2); Furman, D. 21(2); Gerrard, P. (1); Hughes, C. (4); Kuqi, S. 39(1); Lee, K. 43; Lund, M. 2(1); M'Changama, Y. 8(2); M'Voto, J. 35(1); Mancine, A. (1); Marsh-Brown, K. 5(6); Mellor, D. 19(2); Millar, K. 2(2); Morais, F. 23(13); Parker, J. 7(6); Reid, R. 17(3); Scapuzzi, L. 8(2); Simpson, R. 26(3); Smith, M. 3(25); Tarkowski, J. 13(3); Taylor, C. 38; Tounkara, O. 3(5); Wesolowski, J. 21; Winchester, C. 9(3).

Goals – League (50): Kuqi 11 (3 pens), Simpson 6 (1 pen), Morais 5, Reid 5 (3 pens), Smith 3, Wesolowski 3, Adeyemi 2, Diamond 2, Lee 2, Taylor 2, Clarke 1, Furman 1, M'Voto 1, Marsh-Brown 1, Mellor 1, Scapuzzi 1, Tarkowski 1, Tounkara 1, own goal 1.
Carling Cup (1): Reid 1 (pen).
FA Cup (6): Simpson 2, Furman 1, Kuqi 1 (pen), Taylor 1, Wesolowski 1.
J Paint Trophy (7): Kuqi 4, Adeyemi 1, Scapuzzi 1, Simpson 1.
Ground: Boundary Park, Furtherwood Road, Oldham OL1 2PA. Telephone: (0161) 624 4972.
Capacity: 13,624.
Record Attendance: 46,471 v Sheffield W, FA Cup 4th rd, 25 January 1930.
Manager: Paul Dickov.
Most League Goals: 95, Division 4, 1962–63.
Highest League Scorer in Season: Tom Davis, 33, Division 3 (N), 1936–37.
Most League Goals in Total Aggregate: Roger Palmer, 141, 1980–94.
Most Capped Player: Gunnar Halle, 24 (64), Norway.
Most League Appearances: Ian Wood, 525, 1966–80.
Colours: Blue shirts with white sleeves, white shorts, white stockings.
Honours – Football League: Division 2 Champions – 1990–91, Division 3 (N) Champions – 1952–53. Division 3 Champions – 1973–74.

OXFORD UNITED   FL CHAMPIONSHIP 2

Batt Damian (D)	5 10	11 06	Hoddesdon	16/9/84	Barnet
Brown Wayne (G)	6 0	13 11	Southampton	14/1/77	Supersport U
Capaldi Tony (D)	6 0	11 08	Porsgrunn	12/8/81	Morecambe
Chapman Adam (M)	5 10	11 00	Doncaster	29/11/89	Sheffield U
Clarke Ryan (G)	6 3	13 00	Bristol	30/4/82	Bristol R
Constable James (F)	6 2	12 11	Malmesbury	4/10/84	Shrewsbury T
Craddock Tom (F)	5 11	11 10	Durham	14/10/86	Luton T
Davis Liam (M)	5 9	11 07	Wandsworth	23/11/86	Northampton T
Duberry Michael (D)	6 1	13 10	Enfield	14/10/75	Wycombe W
Hall Asa (M)	6 2	11 09	Sandwell	29/11/86	Luton T
Heslop Simon (M)	5 11	11 00	York	1/5/87	Barnsley
Johnson Oli (F)	5 11	12 04	Wakefield	6/11/87	Norwich C
Leven Peter (M)	5 11	12 13	Glasgow	27/9/83	Milton Keynes D
Pittman Jon-Paul (F)	5 9	11 00	Oklahoma City	24/10/86	Wycombe W
Potter Alfie (M)	5 7	9 06	Islington	9/1/89	Peterborough U
Smalley Deane (M)	6 0	11 10	Chadderton	5/9/88	Oldham Ath
Whing Andrew (D)	6 0	12 00	Birmingham	20/9/84	Leyton Orient
Wilson Mark (M)	5 10	12 07	Scunthorpe	9/2/79	Doncaster R
Worley Harry (D)	6 3	13 00	Warrington	25/11/88	Leicester C
Wright Jake (D)	5 10	11 07	Keighley	11/3/86	Brighton & HA

League Appearances: Batt, D. 34(6); Brown, W. 2; Capaldi, T. 1; Chapman, A. 10(4); Clarke, R. 42; Constable, J. 32(8); Craddock, T. 6(3); Davis, L. 41(3); Duberry, M. 36; Franks, J. (1); Guy, L. 8; Hall, A. 24(10); Hall, R. 11(2); Haworth, A. 2(2); Heslop, S. 26(3); Holmes, L. 5(2); Johnson, O. 8(9); Kerrouche, M. 1(3); Kinniburgh, S. (1); Leven, P. 36(3); Martinez, D. 1; McLaren, P. 16(2); Montano, C. 6(3); Morgan, D. 10; Payne, J. 2(4); Philliskirk, D. 2(2); Pittman, J. 6(9); Potter, A. 21(4); Rendell, S. 15(3); Ripley, C. 1; Smalley, D. 7(15); Tonkin, A. 6(8); Whing, A. 36(5); Wilson, M. 3(3); Worley, H. 6(4); Wright, J. 43.
Goals – League (59): Constable 11, Hall, A. 7, Leven 6 (1 pen), Hall, R. 5, Duberry 3, Heslop 3, Johnson 3, Pittman 3, Rendell 3, Davis 2, Holmes 2, Montano 2, Potter 2, Batt 1, Chapman 1, Craddock 1, Guy 1, McLaren 1, Morgan 1, Smalley 1.
Carling Cup (1): Clist 1.
FA Cup (0).
J Paint Trophy (2): Hall, R. 1, Smalley 1.

Ground: The Kassam Stadium, Grenoble Road, Oxford OX4 4XP. Telephone: (01865) 337 500.
Capacity: 12,500.
Record Attendance: 22,730 v Preston NE, FA Cup 6th rd, 29 February 1964 (at Manor Ground); 12,243 v Leyton Orient, FL 2, 6 May 2006 (at The Kassam Stadium).
Manager: Chris Wilder.
Most League Goals: 91, Division 3, 1983–84.
Highest League Scorer in Season: John Aldridge, 30, Division 2, 1984–85.
Most League Goals in Total Aggregate: Graham Atkinson, 77, 1962–73.
Most Capped Player: Jim Magilton, 18 (52), Northern Ireland.
Most League Appearances: John Shuker, 478, 1962–77.
Colours: Yellow shirts, blue shorts, blue stockings.
Honours – Football League: Division 2 Champions – 1984–85. Division 3 Champions – 1967–68, 1983–84. **Football League Cup:** Winners – 1985–86.

PETERBOROUGH UNITED   FL CHAMPIONSHIP

Ajose Nicholas (F)	5 8	11 00	Bury	7/10/91	Manchester U
Alcock Craig (D)	5 8	11 00	Cornwall	8/12/87	Yeovil T
Ball David (F)	6 0	11 08	Whitefield	14/2/89	Manchester C
Barnett Tyrone (F)	6 3	13 05	Stevenage	28/10/85	Crawley T
Boyd George (M)	5 10	11 07	Chatham	2/10/85	Stevenage B
Breeze Matthew (M)			Worcester	6/2/93	Scholar
Brisley Shaun (M)	6 2	12 02	Macclesfield	6/5/90	Macclesfield T
Day Joe (G)			Brighton	13/8/90	Rushden & D
Frecklington Lee (M)	5 8	11 00	Lincoln	8/9/85	Lincoln C
Grant Peter (D)			Scotland		Scholar
Griffiths Scott (D)	5 9	11 08	Westminster	27/11/85	Dagenham & R
Hibbert Dave (F)	6 2	12 00	Eccleshall	28/1/86	Shrewsbury T
Kearns Daniel (M)	5 10	12 00	Belfast	26/8/91	Dundalk
Little Mark (D)	6 1	12 10	Worcester	20/8/88	Wolverhampton W
McCann Grant (M)	5 10	11 02	Belfast	14/4/80	Scunthorpe U
Newell Joe (M)	5 11	11 02	Tamworth	15/3/93	Scholar
Ntlhe Kgosietsile (D)	5 9	10 05	Pretoria	21/2/94	Scholar
Rowe Tommy (M)	5 11	12 11	Manchester	1/5/89	Stockport Co
Sinclair Emile (F)	6 0	11 04	Leeds	29/12/87	Macclesfield T
Taylor Paul (F)	5 11	11 02	Liverpool	4/11/87	Anderlecht
Tomlin Lee (F)	5 11	11 09	Leicester	12/1/89	Rushden & D
Zakuani Gaby (D)	6 1	12 13	DR Congo	31/5/86	Fulham

League Appearances: Ajose, N. 1(1); Alcock, C. 40(1); Ball, D. 6(16); Barnett, T. 12(1); Basey, G. 2(1); Bennett, R. 32; Boyd, G. 45; Briggs, M. 5; Brisley, S. 11; Coulson, C. (1); Frecklington, L. 35(2); Gordon, B. (1); Jones, P. 35; Kearns, D. 5(15); Kennedy, T. 8(2); Lewis, J. 11; Little, M. 26(9); McCann, G. 38(3); Newell, J. 8(6); Ntlhe, K. (2); Rowe, T. 40(3); Sinclair, E. 21(14); Taylor, P. 36(8); Tomlin, L. 31(6); Tunnicliffe, R. 10(17); Wootton, S. 7(4); Zakuani, G. 41.
Goals – League (67): Taylor 12, Sinclair 10, McCann 8 (2 pens), Tomlin 8 (1 pen), Boyd 7, Frecklington 5, Ball 4, Barnett 4, Rowe 4, Bennett 1, Little 1, Newell 1, Zakuani 1, own goal 1.
Carling Cup (4): Ball 2, Boyd 1, Tomlin 1 (pen).
FA Cup (0).
Ground: London Road Stadium, London Road, Peterborough PE2 8AL. Telephone: (01733) 563 947.
Capacity: 15,460.
Record Attendance: 30,096 v Swansea T, FA Cup 5th rd, 20 February 1965.
Manager: Darren Ferguson.
Most League Goals: 134, Division 4, 1960–61.

Highest League Scorer in Season: Terry Bly, 52, Division 4, 1960–61.
Most League Goals in Total Aggregate: Jim Hall, 122, 1967–75.
Most Capped Player: Craig Morgan, 19 (23), Wales.
Most League Appearances: Tommy Robson, 482, 1968–81.
Colours: Blue shirts with white design, white shorts, white stockings.
Honours – Football League: Division 4 Champions – 1960–61, 1973–74.

PLYMOUTH ARGYLE   FL CHAMPIONSHIP 2

Berry Durrell (D)	5 11	11 11	Derby	27/5/92	Aston Villa
Bhasera Onismor (D)	5 9	11 13	Mutare	7/12/86	Kaizer Chiefs
Blanchard Maximo (D)	5 11	11 13	Alencon	27/9/86	Tranmere R
Chadwick Nick (F)	6 0	12 08	Market Drayton	26/10/82	Darlington
Chenoweth Ollie (G)	6 1	11 09	Liskeard	17/2/92	Scholar
Cole Jake (G)	6 2	13 00	Hammersmith	11/9/85	Barnet
Feeney Warren (F)	5 8	12 04	Belfast	17/1/81	Oldham Ath
Hourihane Conor (M)	5 11	9 11	Cork	2/2/91	Ipswich T
Lecointe Matt (F)	5 10	10 07	Plymouth	28/10/94	Scholar
Nelson Curtis (D)	6 0	11 07	Newcastle-u-Lyme	21/5/93	Scholar
Purse Darren (D)	6 2	12 08	Stepney	14/2/77	Sheffield W
Richards Jamie (D)			Newton Abbot	24/6/94	Scholar
Soukouna Ladjie (D)	6 3	12 08	Paris	15/12/90	Creteil
Walton Simon (M)	6 1	13 04	Sherburn-in-Elmet	13/9/87	QPR
Williams Robbie (D)	5 10	11 13	Pontefract	2/10/84	Rochdale
Wotton Paul (D)	5 11	12 00	Plymouth	17/8/77	Yeovil T
Young Luke (M)	5 8	11 05	Ivybridge	22/2/93	Scholar

League Appearances: Atkinson, W. 20(2); Berry, D. 33(2); Bhasera, O. 24(3); Bignot, P. 14; Blanchard, M. 28; Chadwick, N. 19(3); Chenoweth, O. 1; Cole, J. 37; Daley, L. 14(4); Feeney, W. 25(3); Fletcher, C. 8(1); Fletcher, S. 2(3); Fletcher, S. (1); Gibson, B. 12(1); Griffiths, J. 4(5); Hemmings, A. 18(5); Hitchcock, T. 3(5); Hourihane, C. 32(6); King, S. 6; Larrieu, R. 8(2); Lecointe, M. 8(11); Lennox, J. 2(6); MacDonald, A. 15(3); Nelson, C. 16(1); Purse, D. 24; Sims, J. 3; Soukouna, L. 15(5); Sutherland, C. 5(4); Tsoumou, J. 4(7); Vassell, I. (6); Walton, S. 36(5); Williams, R. 27; Wotton, P. 18; Young, L. 21(7); Zubar, S. 4.

Goals – League (47): Walton 8 (6 pens), Chadwick 5 (1 pen), Atkinson 4, MacDonald 4, Blanchard 2, Feeney 2, Hemmings 2, Hourihane 2, Lecointe 2, Purse 2, Tsoumou 2, Williams 2, Young 2, Bhasera 1, Daley 1, Fletcher, C. 1, Soukouna 1, Sutherland 1, Wotton 1, own goals 2.
Carling Cup (0).
FA Cup (3): Bhasera 1, Feeney 1, Fletcher, C. 1.
J Paint Trophy (1): Daley 1.
Ground: Home Park, Plymouth, Devon PL2 3DQ. Telephone: (01752) 562 561.
Capacity: 21,118.
Record Attendance: 43,596 v Aston Villa, Division 2, 10 October 1936.
Manager: Carl Fletcher.
Most League Goals: 107, Division 3 (S), 1925–26 and 1951–52.
Highest League Scorer in Season: Jack Cock, 32, Division 3 (S), 1926–27.
Most League Goals in Total Aggregate: Sammy Black, 180, 1924–38.
Most Capped Player: Moses Russell, 20 (23), Wales.
Most League Appearances: Kevin Hodges, 530, 1978–92.
Colours: Dark green shirts with white design, white shorts, white stockings with green design.
Honours – Football League: Division 2 Champions – 2003–04. Division 3 (S) Champions – 1929–30, 1951–52. Division 3 Champions – 1958–59, 2001–02.

Antelmi Patrick (F)			Sydney	15/3/94	Scholar
Ben Haim Tal (D)	5 11	11 08	Rishon Le Zion	31/3/82	Manchester C
Futacs Marko (F)	6 5	14 00	Budapest	22/2/90	Werder Bremen II
Grant Alex (D)			Perth	23/1/94	Scholar
Halford Greg (D)	6 4	12 10	Chelmsford	8/12/84	Wolverhampton W
Henderson Stephen (G)	6 3	11 00	Dublin	2/5/88	Bristol C
Higgins Andrew (M)			Perth	21/9/93	Scholar
Huseklepp Erik (F)	6 2	14 00	Sandvika	5/9/84	Bari
Kanu Nwankwo (F)	6 5	12 08	Owerri	1/8/76	WBA
Kitson Dave (F)	6 3	12 07	Hitchin	21/1/80	Stoke C
Lawrence Liam (M)	5 11	12 06	Retford	14/12/81	Stoke C
Magri Sam (D)			Portsmouth	30/3/94	Scholar
Mokoena Aaron (D)	6 2	14 00	Johannesburg	25/11/80	Blackburn R
Mullins Hayden (D)	5 11	11 10	Reading	27/3/79	West Ham U
Norris David (M)	5 7	11 06	Stamford	22/2/81	Ipswich T
Varney Luke (F)	5 11	11 00	Leicester	28/9/82	Derby Co
Wallace Jed (M)			Reading	15/12/93	Lewes
Ward Joel (D)	6 2	11 13	Emsworth	29/10/89	Scholar
Webster Adam (D)	6 1	11 11	West Wittering	4/1/95	Scholar

League Appearances: Allan, S. 15; Ashdown, J. 21; Ben Haim, T. 33; Dailly, C. (1); Etuhu, K. 9(4); Futacs, M. 12(17); Halford, G. 42; Harris, A. 2(3); Henderson, S. 25; Hreidarsson, H. 2; Huseklepp, E. 21(6); Kanu, N. 3(7); Kitson, D. 22(11); Lawrence, L. 23; Maguire, C. 10(1); Mattock, J. 7; Mokoena, A. 15(3); Mullins, H. 34; Mwaruwari, B. 6(12); Norris, D. 39(1); Pearce, J. 43; Razak, A. 1(2); Rekik, K. 8; Ricardo Rocha, 31(2); Riise, B. 2; Scapuzzi, L. (2); Thorne, G. 4; Thorne, G. 10; Varney, L. 28(2); Ward, J. 38(6); Webster, A. (3); Williams, R. (4).
Goals – League (50): Norris 8, Halford 7 (5 pens), Huseklepp 6, Varney 6, Futacs 5, Kitson 4, Maguire 3, Ward 3, Pearce 2, Allan 1, Etuhu 1, Kanu 1, Mullins 1, Mwaruwari 1, own goal 1.
Carling Cup (0).
FA Cup (0).
Ground: Fratton Park, Frogmore Road, Portsmouth, Hampshire PO4 8RA. Telephone: (02392) 731 204.
Capacity: 20,688.
Record Attendance: 51,385 v Derby Co, FA Cup 6th rd, 26 February 1949.
Manager: Michael Appleton.
Most League Goals: 97, Division 1, 2002–03.
Highest League Scorer in Season: Guy Whittingham, 42, Division 1, 1992–93.
Most League Goals in Total Aggregate: Peter Harris, 194, 1946–60.
Most Capped Player: Jimmy Dickinson, 48, England.
Most League Appearances: Jimmy Dickinson, 764, 1946–65.
Colours: Blue shirts with white trim, white shorts, red stockings.
Honours – Football League: Division 1 Champions – 1948–49, 1949–50, 2002–03. Division 3 (S) Champions – 1923–24. Division 3 Champions – 1961–62, 1982–83.
FA Cup: Winners – 1939, 2008.

Burge Ryan (M)	5 10	10 03	Cheltenham	12/10/88	Barnet
Dodds Louis (M)	5 10	12 04	Sheffield	8/10/86	Leicester C
Griffith Anthony (M)	6 0	12 00	Huddersfield	28/10/86	Doncaster R
Haldane Lewis (F)	6 0	11 03	Trowbridge	13/3/85	Bristol R
James Kingsley (D)	6 1	11 09	Rotherham	17/2/92	Sheffield U

Johnson Sam (G)			Newcastle-under-Lyme	1/12/92	Scholar
Loft Doug (M)	6 0	12 01	Maidstone	25/12/86	Brighton & HA
McCombe John (D)	6 2	13 02	Pontefract	7/5/85	Hereford U
McDonald Clayton (D)	6 6	16 05	Liverpool	26/12/88	Walsall
Morsy Sam (M)	5 9	12 06	Wolverhampton	10/9/91	Scholar
Owen Gareth (D)	6 1	11 07	Cheadle	21/9/82	Stockport Co
Pope Tom (F)	6 3	11 03	Stoke	27/8/85	Rotherham U
Richards Marc (F)	6 2	12 06	Wolverhampton	8/7/82	Barnsley
Rigg Sean (F)	5 9	12 01	Bristol	1/10/88	Bristol R
Shuker Chris (M)	5 5	9 03	Liverpool	9/5/82	Morecambe
Taylor Rob (D)	6 0	12 08	Shrewsbury	16/1/85	Nuneaton B
Tomlinson Stuart (G)	6 1	11 02	Ellesmere Port	10/5/85	Crewe Alex
Williamson Ben (F)	5 11	11 13	Lambeth	25/12/88	Bournemouth
Yates Adam (D)	5 10	10 07	Stoke	28/5/83	Morecambe

League Appearances: Chilvers, L. 12; Collins, L. 15(1); Davis, J. 7(1); Dodds, L. 21(14); Green, M. 4; Griffith, A. 43; Haldane, L. (3); James, K. (5); Kozluk, R. 4(2); Little, A. 2(5); Lloyd, R. (2); Loft, D. 42(2); Madjo, G. 5(1); Marshall, P. 10(5); Martin, C. 8; McCombe, J. 40; McDonald, C. 23(7); Morsy, S. 11(15); Myrie-Williams, J. 6; Owen, G. 21(3); Pope, T. 34(7); Richards, M. 31(5); Rigg, S. 33(9); Roberts, G. 9(2); Roe, P. (2); Shuker, C. 12(4); Taylor, R. 28(3); Tomlinson, S. 38; Williamson, B. 12(23); Yates, A. 35(3).

Goals – League (68): Richards 17 (3 pens), Rigg 10, Dodds 8, Pope 5, Loft 4 (1 pen), Madjo 4, McCombe 4, Roberts 4 (1 pen), Williamson 3, Taylor, R. 2, Yates 2, Griffith 1, Morsy 1, Myrie-Williams 1, Shuker 1, own goal 1.

Carling Cup (2): Loft 1 (pen), Roberts 1.

FA Cup (0).

J Paint Trophy (1): Taylor, R. 1.

Ground: Vale Park, Hamil Road, Burslem, Stoke-on-Trent ST6 1AW. Telephone: (01782) 655 800.

Capacity: 18,982.

Record Attendance: 22,993 v Stoke C, Division 2, 6 March 1920 (at Recreation Ground); 49,768 v Aston Villa, FA Cup 5th rd, 20 February 1960 (at Vale Park).

Manager: Micky Adams.

Most League Goals: 110, Division 4, 1958–59.

Highest League Scorer in Season: Wilf Kirkham 38, Division 2, 1926–27.

Most League Goals in Total Aggregate: Wilf Kirkham, 154, 1923–29, 1931–33.

Most Capped Player: Chris Birchall, 22 (39), Trinidad & Tobago.

Most League Appearances: Roy Sproson, 761, 1950–72.

Colours: White shirts with black trim, black shorts with white trim, white stockings.

Honours – Football League: Division 3 (N) Champions – 1929–30, 1953–54. Division 4 Champions – 1958–59. **Autoglass Trophy:** Winners – 1993. **LDV Vans Trophy:** Winners – 2001.

PRESTON NORTH END   FL CHAMPIONSHIP 1

Barton Adam (M)	5 11	12 01	Clitheroe	7/1/91	Scholar
Coutts Paul (M)	5 9	11 11	Aberdeen	22/7/88	Peterborough U
Cummins Graham (F)	6 2	11 11	Cork	29/12/87	Cork C
Daley Keammar (M)	5 8	10 00	Kingston	18/2/88	Tivoli Gardens
Holroyd Chris (F)	5 11	12 03	Macclesfield	24/10/86	Rotherham U
Hume Iain (F)	5 7	11 03	Ontario	31/10/83	Barnsley
Mayor Danny (M)	6 0	11 12	Leyland	18/10/90	Scholar
McLaughlin Conor (D)	6 0	11 02	Belfast	26/7/91	Scholar
McLean Brian (D)	6 2	13 00	Rutherglen	28/2/85	Falkirk
Morgan Craig (D)	6 0	11 04	Flint	18/6/85	Peterborough U
Nicholson Barry (M)	5 7	9 01	Dumfries	24/8/78	Aberdeen

Procter Andy (M)	6 0	12 04	Blackburn	13/3/83	Accrington S
Proctor Jamie (F)	6 2	12 03	Preston	25/3/92	Scholar
Robertson Chris (D)	6 3	11 08	Dundee	11/10/85	Torquay U
Russell Darel (M)	5 10	11 09	Mile End	22/10/80	Norwich C
Stuckmann Thorsten (G)	6 6	14 11	Gutersloh	17/3/81	Alemannia Aachen
Tsoumou Juvhel (F)	6 1	13 00	Brazzaville	27/12/90	Alemannia Aachen
Wright Bailey (D)	5 9	13 05	Melbourne	28/7/92	Scholar

League Appearances: Alexander, G. 17(1); Aneke, C. 3(4); Arestidou, A. 7; Ashbee, I. 3(4); Barton, A. 12(4); Brown, A. 4; Bunn, H. 1; Carlisle, C. 20; Clark, L. 2; Clucas, S. (1); Coutts, P. 41; Cummins, G. 13(2); Daley, K. (8); Devine, D. 13; Douglas, J. (4); Doyle, N. 5; Ehmer, M. 7(2); Forte, J. 2(1); Gray, D. 18(5); Hayhurst, W. 1(1); Holroyd, C. 14(6); Hume, I. 21(7); Hunt, N. 15(2); Jervis, J. 3(2); Marrow, A. 3(1); Mayor, D. 22(14); McAllister, J. 4; McCombe, J. 6; McLaughlin, C. 10(7); McLean, B. 15(1); Mellor, N. 15(2); Middleton, D. 1; Miller, G. 2(4); Morgan, C. 18(1); Murphy, R. 1(4); Nicholson, B. 22(8); Parry, P. 39(1); Procter, A. 19; Proctor, J. 24(7); Robertson, C. 17(1); Russell, D. 2; Smith, S. 9(4); Stuckmann, T. 28; Tsoumou, J. 5(11); Turner, I. 11; Wright, B. 11(2).
Goals – League (54): Hume 9, Mellor 8, Parry 4 (3 pens), Carlisle 3, Proctor 3, Tsoumou 3, Alexander 2 (1 pen), Coutts 2, Cummins 2, Jervis 2, Mayor 2, Nicholson 2, Aneke 1, Bunn 1, Daley 1, Devine 1, Douglas 1, Holroyd 1, Hunt 1, McLean 1, Morgan 1, Robertson 1, Turner 1, Wright 1.
Carling Cup (6): Barton 1, Hume 1, Mayor 1, Mellor 1, Russell 1, own goal 1.
FA Cup (0).
J Paint Trophy (4): Barton 1, McCombe 1, McLean 1, Tsoumou 1.
Ground: Deepdale Stadium, Sir Tom Finney Way, Deepdale, Preston PR1 6RU. Telephone: (0844) 856 1964.
Capacity: 23,408.
Record Attendance: 42,684 v Arsenal, Division 1, 23 April 1938.
Manager: Graham Westley.
Most League Goals: 100, Division 2, 1927–28 and Division 1, 1957–58.
Highest League Scorer in Season: Ted Harper, 37, Division 2, 1932–33.
Most League Goals in Total Aggregate: Tom Finney, 187, 1946–60.
Most Capped Player: Tom Finney, 76, England.
Most League Appearances: Alan Kelly, 447, 1961–75.
Colours: White shirts, blue shorts, white stockings.
Honours – Football League: Division 1 Champions – 1888–89 (first champions), 1889–90. Division 2 Champions – 1903–04, 1912–13, 1950–51, 1999–2000. Division 3 Champions – 1970–71, 1995–96. **FA Cup:** Winners – 1889, 1938.

QUEENS PARK RANGERS   FA PREMIERSHIP

Andrade Bruno (M)	5 9	11 09	Aveiro	2/10/93	Scholar
Balanta Angelo (F)	5 10	11 11	Colombia	1/7/90	Scholar
Barton Joey (M)	5 11	12 05	Huyton	2/9/82	Newcastle U
Bothroyd Jay (F)	6 3	14 13	Islington	7/5/82	Cardiff C
Campbell Dudley (F)	5 10	11 00	Hammersmith	12/11/81	Blackpool
Champion Fred (M)			Shepherds Bush	18/1/94	Tottenham H Scholar
Cisse Djibril (F)	6 0	13 00	Arles	12/8/81	Lazio
Connolly Matthew (D)	6 1	11 03	Barnet	24/9/87	Arsenal
Derry Shaun (M)	5 10	10 13	Nottingham	6/12/77	Crystal Palace
Doughty Michael (M)	6 1	12 10	Westminster	20/11/92	Scholar
Dyer Kieron (M)	5 8	10 01	Ipswich	29/12/78	West Ham U
Ehmer Max (M)	6 2	11 00	Frankfurt	3/2/92	Scholar
Ephraim Hogan (F)	5 9	10 06	Islington	31/3/88	West Ham U
Faurlin Alejandro (M)	6 1	12 06	Argentina	9/8/86	Instituto
Ferdinand Anton (D)	6 2	11 01	Peckham	18/2/85	Sunderland
Fitzpatrick David (M)			Surbiton	10/2/95	Scholar

Harriman Michael (D)	5 6	11 10	Chichester	23/10/92	Scholar
Helguson Heidar (F)	5 10	12 09	Akureyri	22/8/77	Bolton W
Hewitt Troy (F)	6 0	12 05	Newham	10/2/90	Harrow B
Hitchcock Tom (F)	5 11	12 08	Hemel Hempstead	1/10/92	Blackburn R
Hulse Rob (F)	6 1	12 04	Crewe	25/10/79	Derby Co
Kenny Paddy (G)	6 1	14 01	Halifax	17/5/78	Sheffield U
Lennox Aaron (G)			Sydney	19/2/93	Australia IOS
Mackie Jamie (F)	5 8	11 00	Dorking	22/9/85	Plymouth Arg
Murphy Brian (G)	6 0	13 00	Waterford	7/5/83	Bohemians
Onuoha Nedum (D)	6 2	12 04	Warri	12/11/86	Manchester C
Parmenter Taylor (D)			Bromley	9/9/92	Scholar
Sendles-White Jamie (D)			Kingston		Scholar
Shariff Mo (F)			Newham	5/3/93	Slough T Youth
Smith Tommy (F)	5 8	11 04	Hemel Hempstead	22/5/80	Portsmouth
Sutherland Frankie (M)	5 9	10 00	Hillingdon	6/12/93	Scholar
Taarabt Adel (M)	5 9	11 00	Marseille	24/5/89	Tottenham H
Trani Tommaso (G)			Florence	30/12/93	AC Milan Youth
Traore Armand (D)	6 1	12 12	Paris	8/10/89	Arsenal
Wright-Phillips Shaun (M)	5 5	10 01	Lewisham	25/10/81	Manchester C
Young Luke (D)	6 0	12 04	Harlow	19/7/79	Aston Villa
Zamora Bobby (F)	6 1	11 11	Barking	16/1/81	Fulham

League Appearances: Agyemang, P. 2; Andrade, B. (1); Barton, J. 31; Bothroyd, J. 12(9); Buzsaky, A. 10(8); Campbell, D. 2(9); Cerny, R. 5; Cisse, D. 7(1); Connolly, M. 5(1); Derry, S. 28(1); Diakite, S. 9; Dyer, K. 1; Ephraim, H. (2); Faurlin, A. 20; Ferdinand, A. 31; Gabbidon, D. 15(2); Hall, F. 11(3); Harriman, M. (1); Helguson, H. 13(3); Hill, C. 19(3); Hulse, R. 1(1); Kenny, P. 33; Macheda, F. (3); Mackie, J. 24(7); Onuoha, N. 16; Orr, B. 2(4); Perone, B. 1; Puncheon, J. (2); Smith, T. 4(13); Taarabt, A. 24(3); Taiwo, T. 13(2); Traore, A. 18(5); Wright-Phillips, S. 24(8); Young, L. 23; Zamora, B. 14.
Goals – League (43): Helguson 8 (2 pens), Mackie 7, Cisse 6, Barton 3, Bothroyd 2, Buzsaky 2, Smith 2, Taarabt 2, Young 2, Zamora 2, Campbell 1, Derry 1, Diakite 1, Faurlin 1, Taiwo 1, own goals 2.
Carling Cup (0).
FA Cup (2): Gabbidon 1, Helguson 1.
Ground: Loftus Road Stadium, South Africa Road, Shepherds Bush, London W12 7PJ. Telephone: (020) 8743 0262.
Capacity: 18,682.
Record Attendance: 41,097 v Leeds U, FA Cup 3rd rd, 9 January 1932 (at White City); 35,353 v Leeds U, Division 1, 27 April 1974 (at Loftus Road).
Manager: Mark Hughes.
Most League Goals: 111, Division 3, 1961–62.
Highest League Scorer in Season: George Goddard, 37, Division 3 (S), 1929–30.
Most League Goals in Total Aggregate: George Goddard, 172, 1926–34.
Most Capped Player: Alan McDonald, 52, Northern Ireland.
Most League Appearances: Tony Ingham, 519, 1950–63.
Colours: Blue and white hooped shirts, white shorts, white stockings.
Honours – Football League: FL C Champions – 2010–11. Division 2 Champions – 1982–83. Division 3 (S) Champions – 1947–48. Division 3 Champions – 1966–67.
Football League Cup: Winners – 1966–67.

READING   FA PREMIERSHIP

Andersen Mikkel (G)	6 5	12 08	Copenhagen	17/12/88	AB Copenhagen
Antonio Michael (M)	6 0	11 11	Wandsworth	28/3/90	Tooting & M
Arnold Nick (D)			Tadley	3/7/93	Scholar
Church Simon (F)	6 0	13 04	Amersham	10/12/88	Scholar
Cummings Shaun (D)	6 0	11 10	Hammersmith	25/2/89	Chelsea

Player	Ht	Wt	Birthplace	Date	From
D'Ath Lawson (M)	5 9	12 02	Witney	24/12/92	Scholar
Edwards Cameron (M)	5 11	12 00	Sydney	27/3/92	Perth Glory
Federici Adam (G)	6 2	14 02	Nowra	31/1/85	
Gorkss Kaspars (D)	6 3	13 05	Riga	6/11/81	QPR
Harte Ian (D)	5 11	12 06	Drogheda	31/8/77	Carlisle U
Hector Michael (D)	6 4	12 13	Newham	19/7/92	Scholar
Hunt Noel (F)	5 8	11 05	Waterford	26/12/82	Dundee U
Karacan Jem (M)	5 10	11 13	Lewisham	21/2/89	Scholar
Kebe Jimmy (M)	6 2	11 07	Paris	19/1/84	Lens
Le Fondre Adam (F)	5 9	11 05	Stockport	2/12/86	Rotherham U
Leigertwood Mikele (D)	6 1	11 05	Enfield	12/11/82	QPR
Losasso Charlie (M)			Marlow	11/11/92	Scholar
MacDonald Angus (D)			Winchester	15/10/92	Real Madrid
Manset Mathieu (F)	6 1	13 08	Metz	5/8/89	Hereford U
McAnuff Jobi (M)	5 11	11 05	Edmonton	9/11/81	Watford
McCarthy Alex (G)	6 4	11 12	Guildford	3/12/89	Scholar
McCleary Garath (M)	5 10	12 06	Oxford	15/5/87	Nottingham F
Mills Joseph (D)	5 9	11 00	Swindon	30/10/89	Southampton
Morrison Sean (D)	6 4	14 00	Plymouth	8/1/91	Swindon T
Obita Jordan (M)	5 11	11 08	Oxford	8/12/93	Scholar
Pearce Alex (D)	6 0	11 10	Wallingford	9/11/88	Scholar
Roberts Jason (F)	6 0	14 01	Acton	25/1/78	Blackburn R
Robson-Kanu Hal (F)	5 7	11 08	Acton	21/5/89	
Samuel Dominic (F)			Southwark	1/4/94	Scholar
Sheppard Karl (F)			Shelbourne	14/2/91	Scholar
Tabb Jay (M)	5 7	10 00	Tooting	21/2/84	Coventry C
Tanner Craig (F)			Reading	27/10/94	Scholar
Taylor Jake (M)	5 10	12 01	Ascot	1/12/91	Scholar
Tshibola Aaron (M)			Newham	2/1/95	Scholar
Ugwu Chigozie (F)			Oxford	22/4/93	Scholar
Williams Brett (F)	6 2	12 07	Southampton	1/12/87	Eastleigh

League Appearances: Afobe, B. 1(2); Antonio, M. 2(4); Church, S. 19(12); Connolly, M. 6; Cummings, S. 32(2); Cywka, T. 1(3); Federici, A. 46; Gorkss, K. 42; Griffin, A. 9; Gunnarsson, B. 1(4); Harte, I. 30(2); Howard, B. (1); Hunt, N. 33(8); Karacan, J. 36(1); Kebe, J. 30(3); Khumalo, B. 4; Le Fondre, A. 17(15); Leigertwood, M. 41; Long, S. 1; Manset, M. 4(11); McAnuff, J. 40; Mills, Joseph 13(2); Mullins, H. 6(1); Pearce, A. 46; Roberts, J. 17; Robson-Kanu, H. 19(17); Tabb, J. 10(9).

Goals – League (69): Le Fondre 12, Hunt 8, Church 7, Roberts 6, Leigertwood 5, McAnuff 5, Pearce 5, Harte 4 (1 pen), Robson-Kanu 4 (1 pen), Gorkss 3, Karacan 3, Kebe 3, Manset 3, own goal 1.

Carling Cup (1): Morrison 1.

FA Cup (0).

Ground: Madejski Stadium, Junction 11, M4, Reading, Berkshire RG2 0FL. Telephone: (0118) 968 1100.

Capacity: 24,082.

Record Attendance: 33,042 v Brentford, FA Cup 5th rd, 19 February 1927 (at Elm Park); 24,122 v Aston Villa, FA Premier League, 10 February 2007 (at Madejski Stadium).

Manager: Brian McDermott.

Most League Goals: 112, Division 3 (S), 1951–52.

Highest League Scorer in Season: Ronnie Blackman, 39, Division 3 (S), 1951–52.

Most League Goals in Total Aggregate: Ronnie Blackman, 158, 1947–54.

Most Capped Player: Kevin Doyle, 26 (50), Republic of Ireland.

Most League Appearances: Martin Hicks, 500, 1978–91.

Colours: Blue and white hooped shirts, blue shorts, blue stockings.

Honours – Football League: FL C Champions – 2005–06, 2011–12. Division 2 Champions – 1993–94. Division 3 Champions – 1985–86. Division 3 (S) Champions – 1925–26. Division 4 Champions – 1978–79. **Simod Cup:** Winners – 1987–88.

ROCHDALE   FL CHAMPIONSHIP 2

Abadaki Godwin (F)	5 11	12 04	Kwara	21/10/93	Scholar
Adams Nicky (F)	5 10	11 00	Bolton	16/10/86	Brentford
Akpa Akpro Jean-Louis (F)	6 0	10 12	Toulouse	4/1/85	Grimsby T
Byrne Neil (D)			Dublin	2/2/93	Nottingham F
Donnelly George (F)	6 2	13 03	Liverpool	28/5/88	Plymouth Arg
Edwards Matty (G)	6 2	12 11	Birkenhead	22/8/90	Leeds U
Gray Reece (F)	5 7	8 08	Oldham	1/9/92	Scholar
Grimes Ashley (M)	6 0	11 04	Swinton	9/12/86	Millwall
Holness Marcus (D)	6 0	12 02	Swinton	8/12/88	Oldham Ath
Jones Gary (M)	5 11	12 05	Birkenhead	3/6/77	Barnsley
Jordan Stephen (D)	6 1	13 00	Warrington	6/3/82	Sheffield U
Kennedy Jason (M)	6 1	13 02	Stockton	11/9/86	Darlington
Thompson Joe (M)	6 0	9 07	Rochdale	5/3/89	Scholar
Tutte Andrew (M)	5 9	10 10	Huyton	21/9/90	Manchester C
Twaddle Marc (D)	6 1	13 00	Glasgow	27/8/86	Falkirk

League Appearances: Abadaki, G. (2); Adams, N. 30(11); Akpa Akpro, J. 30(11); Amankwaah, K. 15(1); Balkestein, P. 12(1); Ball, D. 12(2); Barnes-Homer, M. 1(4); Barry-Murphy, B. 17(5); Benali, A. (2); Bergkamp, R. 2(1); Bogdanovic, D. 5; Bunn, H. 5(1); Byrne, N. 2(1); Darby, S. 34(1); Eccleston, N. 3(2); Edwards, M. 5(2); Edwards, P. 1(2); Gray, R. 1(3); Grimes, A. 27(9); Hackney, S. 1(1); Holden, D. 20(1); Holness, M. 23(1); Jones, G. 45; Jordan, S. 17(2); Kean, J. 14; Kennedy, J. 38(6); Kurucz, P. 11; Long, K. 16; Lucas, D. 16; Marshall, P. (1); McConville, S. 2(2); Minihan, S. 1; O'Grady, C. (1); Obadeyi, T. 3(3); Ormerod, B. 4(1); Symes, M. 14(1); Thompson, J. 8(9); Trotman, N. 12; Tutte, A. 28(12); Twaddle, M. 1(1); Widdowson, J. 30(2).
Goals – League (47): Grimes 8, Akpa Akpro 7, Jones 5 (2 pens), Adams 4, Kennedy 4, Symes 4 (2 pens), Ball 3, Holness 3, Barry-Murphy 1, Bogdanovic 1, Eccleston 1, Gray 1, Obadeyi 1, Ormerod 1, Thompson 1, Tutte 1, own goal 1.
Carling Cup (6): Grimes 3, Akpa Akpro 1, Jones 1, own goal 1.
FA Cup (0).
J Paint Trophy (2): Ball 1, Bunn 1.
Ground: Spotland Stadium, Willbutts Lane, Rochdale OL11 5DS. Telephone: (0844) 826 1907.
Capacity: 9,223.
Record Attendance: 24,231 v Notts Co, FA Cup 2nd rd, 10 December 1949.
Manager: John Coleman.
Most League Goals: 105, Division 3 (N), 1926–27.
Highest League Scorer in Season: Albert Whitehurst, 44, Division 3 (N), 1926–27.
Most League Goals in Total Aggregate: Reg Jenkins, 119, 1964–73.
Most Capped Player: Leo Bertos, 6 (39), New Zealand.
Most League Appearances: Gary Jones, 379, 1998–2001; 2003–.
Colours: Black and blue striped shirts, white shorts, blue stockings with black tops.
Honours: None.

ROTHERHAM UNITED   FL CHAMPIONSHIP 2

Annerson Jamie (G)	6 2	13 02	Sheffield	1/11/88	Sheffield U
Bradley Mark (D)	6 0	11 05	Dudley	14/1/88	Walsall
Brown Troy (D)	6 1	12 01	Croydon	17/9/90	Ipswich T
Cresswell Ryan (D)	5 9	10 06	Rotherham	22/12/87	Bury

Evans Gary (F)	6 0	12 08	Stockport	26/4/88	Bradford C
Grabban Lewis (F)	6 0	11 03	Croydon	12/1/88	Brentford
Mullins John (D)	5 11	12 07	Hampstead	6/11/85	Stockport Co
Naylor Richard (D)	6 1	13 07	Leeds	28/2/77	Doncaster R
Pringle Ben (M)	5 8	11 10	Whitley Bay	25/7/88	Derby Co
Raynes Michael (D)	6 4	12 00	Wythenshawe	15/10/87	Scunthorpe U
Revell Alex (F)	6 3	13 00	Cambridge	7/7/83	Leyton Orient
Schofield Danny (M)	5 10	11 02	Doncaster	10/4/80	Millwall
Taylor Jason (M)	6 1	11 03	Ashton-under-Lyne	28/1/87	Stockport Co
Tonge Dale (D)	5 10	10 06	Doncaster	7/5/85	Barnsley
Warrington Andy (G)	6 3	12 13	Sheffield	10/6/76	Bury

League Appearances: Bradley, M. 18(3); Branston, G. 2; Brown, T. 4(2); Cadogan, K. 7(6); Cresswell, R. 13(3); Denton, A. (1); Evans, G. 29(3); Foster, L. 1(4); Grabban, L. 39(4); Griffiths, S. 8; Harley, J. 11(1); Harrad, S. 6(2); Harrison, D. 35(6); Holroyd, C. 5(10); Hoskins, S. 2(6); Le Fondre, A. 4; Logan, C. 19; Marshall, M. 8(7); Mullins, J. 34(1); Naylor, R. 5; Newey, T. 15(5); Pringle, B. 14(7); Raynes, M. 31(2); Revell, A. 40; Schofield, D. 35(2); Taylor, J. 38(1); Taylor, R. 20; Tonge, D. 28(4); Warne, P. (3); Warrington, A. 7; Williams, B. 4(7); Wood, S. 24(2).

Goals – League (67): Grabban 18 (5 pens), Revell 10, Evans 7 (1 pen), Cresswell 4, Le Fondre 4, Pringle 4, Harrad 3 (1 pen), Harrison 2, Hoskins, S. 2, Mullins 2, Taylor, J. 2, Williams 2, Bradley 1, Brown 1, Cadogan 1, Holroyd 1, Marshall 1, Schofield 1, Wood 1.

Carling Cup (1): own goal 1.

FA Cup (3): Grabban 3 (2 pens).

J Paint Trophy (1): Revell 1.

Ground: Don Valley Stadium, Worksop Road, Sheffield, South Yorkshire S9 3TL. *Club moving to new premises* New York Stadium, Rotherham. *Capacity:* 12,021. Telephone: (0844) 4140 737.

Capacity: 25,000.

Record Attendance: 25,170 v Sheffield U, Division 2, 13 December 1952 (at Millmoor); 7,082 v Aldershot T, FL 2 Play-offs semi-final 2nd leg, 19 May 2010 (at Don Valley).

Manager: Steve Evans.

Most League Goals: 114, Division 3 (N), 1946–47.

Highest League Scorer in Season: Wally Ardron, 38, Division 3 (N), 1946–47.

Most League Goals in Total Aggregate: Gladstone Guest, 130, 1946–56.

Most Capped Player: Shaun Goater, 14 (36), Bermuda.

Most League Appearances: Danny Williams, 459, 1946–62.

Colours: Red shirts with white design, white shorts, red stockings.

Honours – Football League: Division 3 Champions – 1980–81. Division 3 (N) Champions – 1950–51. Division 4 Champions – 1988–89. **Auto Windscreens Shield:** Winners – 1996.

SCUNTHORPE UNITED   FL CHAMPIONSHIP 1

Barcham Andy (F)	5 8	11 10	Basildon	16/12/86	Gillingham
Canavan Niall (D)	6 3	12 00	Guiseley	11/4/91	Scholar
Collins Michael (M)	6 0	11 00	Halifax	30/4/86	Huddersfield T
Duffy Mark (M)	5 9	11 05	Liverpool	7/10/85	Morecambe
Gibbons Robbie (M)	5 11	12 00	Dublin	8/10/91	Alki
Godden Matthew (F)	6 1	12 03	Canterbury	29/7/91	Scholar
Grant Robert (M)	5 11	12 02	Liverpool	1/7/90	Accrington S
Jennings Connor (F)	6 0	12 00	Manchester	21/1/91	Stalybridge C
Mozika Damien (M)	6 0	11 13	Corbell-Essonnes	15/4/87	Bury
Reid Paul (D)	6 2	11 08	Carlisle	18/2/82	Colchester U
Ryan James (M)	5 8	11 08	Maghull	6/9/88	Accrington S
Slocombe Sam (G)	6 0	11 11	Scunthorpe	5/6/88	Bottesford T

League Appearances: Ajose, N. 2(5); Barcham, A. 37(4); Byrne, C. 13(1); Canavan, N. 11(1); Collins, M. (1); Dagnall, C. 19(4); Duffy, M. 27(10); Duffy, S. 18; Gibbons, R. 3(1); Godden, M. (1); Grant, R. 19(10); Jennings, C. (4); Johnstone, S. 12; Lillis, J. 6; McAleny, C. 2(1); Mirfin, D. 19; Mozika, D. 17(1); Nelson, M. 8(2); Nolan, E. 29(1); Norwood, O. 14(1); O'Connor, M. 29(4); Palmer, A. (1); Parkin, J. 13(1); Reckord, J. 17; Reid, P. 36; Ribeiro, C. 10; Robertson, J. 12(7); Ryan, J. 20(4); Slocombe, S. 28; Thompson, G. 19(20); Togwell, S. 35(4); Walker, J. 17(1); Wright, A. 14(4).
Goals – League (55): Barcham 9, Grant 7 (1 pen), Thompson 7, Parkin 6 (1 pen), Dagnall 4, Robertson 3, Walker 3, Duffy, M. 2, Duffy, S. 2, Mozika 2, Ryan 2, Canavan 1, Mirfin 1, Nelson 1, Nolan 1, Norwood 1, O'Connor 1, Reid 1, Togwell 1.
Carling Cup (3): Dagnall 2 (1 pen), Barcham 1.
FA Cup (0).
J Paint Trophy (2): Grant 2.
Ground: Glanford Park, Jack Brownsword Way, Scunthorpe DN15 8TD. Telephone: (0871) 221 1899.
Capacity: 9,088.
Record Attendance: 23,935 v Portsmouth, FA Cup 4th rd, 30 January 1954 (at Old Showground); 9,077 v Manchester U, League Cup 3rd rd, 22 September 2010 (at Glanford Park).
Manager: Alan Knill.
Most League Goals: 88, Division 3 (N), 1957–58.
Highest League Scorer in Season: Barrie Thomas, 31, Division 2, 1961–62.
Most League Goals in Total Aggregate: Steve Cammack, 110, 1979–81, 1981–86.
Most Capped Player: Grant McCann, 10 (39), Northern Ireland.
Most League Appearances: Jack Brownsword, 595, 1950–65.
Colours: Claret shirts with light blue sleeves, white shorts, claret stockings.
Honours – Football League: FL 1 Champions – 2006–07; Division 3 (N) Champions – 1957–58.

SHEFFIELD UNITED   FL CHAMPIONSHIP 1

Chapell Jordan (M)	5 10	10 09	Sheffield	8/9/91	
Collins Neill (D)	6 3	12 05	Irvine	2/9/83	Leeds U
Cresswell Richard (F)	6 0	11 08	Bridlington	20/9/77	Stoke C
Doyle Micky (M)	5 10	11 00	Dublin	8/7/81	Coventry C
Flynn Ryan (M)	5 8	10 00	Falkirk	4/9/88	Falkirk
Howard Mark (G)	6 0	11 13	Southwark	21/9/86	Aberdeen
Kennedy Terry (D)	5 10	12 04	Barnsley	14/11/93	Scholar
Lescinel Jean-Francois (M)	6 2	12 04	Guyane	2/10/86	Swindon T
Long George (G)	6 0	12 05	Sheffield	5/11/93	Scholar
Lowton Matt (M)	5 11	12 04	Chesterfield	9/6/89	Scholar
Maguire Harry (D)	6 2	12 06	Mosborough	5/3/93	Scholar
McAllister David (M)	5 10	11 09	Dublin	29/12/88	Shelbourne
McDonald Kevin (M)	6 2	13 03	Carnoustie	4/11/88	Burnley
McFadzean Callum (D)			Sheffield	16/1/94	Scholar
Montgomery Nick (M)	5 9	11 08	Leeds	28/10/81	Scholar
Morgan Chris (D)	6 1	12 03	Barnsley	9/11/77	Barnsley
Philliskirk Daniel (M)	5 10	11 05	Oldham	10/4/91	Chelsea
Porter Chris (F)	6 1	12 09	Wigan	12/12/83	Derby Co
Quinn Stephen (M)	5 6	9 08	Dublin	4/4/86	Trainee
Tonne Erik (M)	5 11	12 02	Trondheim	7/5/91	Strindheim
Williams Marcus (D)	5 8	10 07	Doncaster	8/4/86	Scunthorpe U
Williamson Lee (M)	5 10	10 04	Derby	7/6/82	Watford

League Appearances: Beattie, J. 2(16); Bogdanovic, D. (2); Clarke, B. 5; Collins, N. 42; Cresswell, R. 32(10); Doyle, M. 39(4); Egan, J. 1; Ertl, J. 2(5); Evans, C. 30(6); Flynn, R. 12(14); Hill, M. 11(1); Hoskins, W. 3(6); Hoskins, W. 1(2); Lescinel, J. 22(3); Long, G. 2;

Lowton, M. 44; Maguire, H. 44; McAllister, D. 3(1); McDonald, K. 30(1); Mendez-Laing, N. 4(4); Montgomery, N. 14(6); O'Halloran, M. 1(6); Phillips, M. 5(1); Porter, C. 18(16); Quinn, S. 43(2); Simonsen, S. 44; Slew, J. 3(1); Taylor, A. 4; Tonne, E. (2); Williams, M. 14(5); Williamson, L. 31(9).
Goals – League (92): Evans 29 (2 pens), Williamson 13, Cresswell 9 (1 pen), Lowton 6, Phillips 5, Porter 5, Quinn 4, Doyle 3, McDonald 3, Collins 2, Flynn 2, Hoskins 2, Clarke 1, Maguire 1, Mendez-Laing 1, Montgomery 1, Slew 1, Tonne 1, own goals 3.
Carling Cup (2): Cresswell 1, Quinn 1.
FA Cup (9): Evans 5, Flynn 1, Porter 1, own goals 2.
J Paint Trophy (5): Evans 1, McAllister 1, Phillips 1, Porter 1, Tonne 1.
Play-Offs (1): Porter 1.
Ground: Bramall Lane Ground, Cherry Street, Bramall Lane, Sheffield S2 4SU. Telephone: (0871) 995 1899.
Capacity: 32,500.
Record Attendance: 68,287 v Leeds U, FA Cup 5th rd, 15 February 1936.
Manager: Danny Wilson.
Most League Goals: 102, Division 1, 1925–26.
Highest League Scorer in Season: Jimmy Dunne, 41, Division 1, 1930–31.
Most League Goals in Total Aggregate: Harry Johnson, 205, 1919–30.
Most Capped Player: Billy Gillespie, 25, Northern Ireland.
Most League Appearances: Joe Shaw, 629, 1948–66.
Colours: Red and white striped shirts with red sleeves, black shorts, black stockings.
Honours – Football League: Division 1 Champions – 1897–98. Division 2 Champions – 1952–53. Division 4 Champions – 1981–82. **FA Cup:** Winners – 1899, 1902, 1915, 1925.

SHEFFIELD WEDNESDAY   FL CHAMPIONSHIP

Beevers Mark (D)	6 4	13 00	Barnsley	21/11/89	Scholar
Bennett Julian (D)	6 1	13 00	Nottingham	17/12/84	Nottingham F
Buxton Lewis (D)	6 1	13 11	Newport (IW)	10/12/83	Stoke C
Bywater Steve (G)	6 2	12 10	Manchester	7/6/81	West Ham U
Coke Giles (M)	6 0	11 11	Westminster	3/6/86	Motherwell
Jameson Arron (G)	6 3	13 01	Sheffield	7/11/89	Scholar
Johnson Jermaine (M)	5 11	11 05	Kingston, Jamaica	25/6/80	Bradford C
Johnson Reda (D)	6 2	13 10	Marseille	21/3/88	Plymouth Arg
Jones Daniel (D)	6 2	13 02	Rowley Regis	14/7/86	Wolverhampton W
Jones Mike (M)	5 11	12 04	Birkenhead	15/8/87	Bury
Jones Rob (D)	6 7	12 02	Stockton	30/11/79	Scunthorpe U
Lines Chris (M)	6 2	12 00	Bristol	30/11/88	Bristol R
Llera Miguel (D)	6 3	13 12	Seville	7/8/79	Milton Keynes D
Lowe Ryan (F)	5 10	12 08	Liverpool	18/9/78	Bury
Madine Gary (F)	6 1	12 00	Gateshead	24/8/90	Carlisle U
Nyoni Cecil (M)			Bulawayo	1/9/92	Scholar
O'Grady Chris (F)	6 3	12 04	Nottingham	25/1/86	Rochdale
Palmer Liam (M)	6 2	12 10	Worksop	19/9/91	Scholar
Prutton David (M)	5 10	13 00	Hull	12/9/81	Swindon T
Reynolds Mark (D)	5 11	10 07	Motherwell	7/5/87	Motherwell
Semedo Jose (D)	6 0	12 08	Setubal	11/1/85	Charlton Ath
Weaver Nick (G)	6 4	14 07	Sheffield	2/3/79	Burnley

League Appearances: Antonio, M. 14; Batth, D. 44; Beevers, M. 4(3); Bennett, J. 16(5); Bostock, J. 2(2); Buxton, L. 36(1); Bywater, S. 32; Johnson, J. 12(12); Johnson, R. 22(2); Jones, D. 1(2); Jones, M. 6(4); Jones, R. 32(1); Lines, C. 37(4); Llera, M. 15(5); Lowe, R. 11(15); Madine, G. 36(2); Marshall, B. 22; McGoldrick, D. 3(1); Morrison, C. 7(12); O'Connor, J. 11(7); O'Donnell, R. 6; O'Grady, C. 25(7); Otsemobor, J. 8(3); Palmer, L. 6(8); Prutton, D. 19(6); Ranger, N. 7(1); Reynolds, M. 3; Sedgwick, C. 5(5); Semedo, J. 46; Tavernier, J. 6; Treacy, K. 2(5); Uchechi, D. (1); Watt, S. 2(2); Weaver, N. 8.

Goals – League (81): Madine 18 (1 pen), Lowe 8 (1 pen), Johnson, R. 7, Antonio 5, Marshall 5, O'Grady 5, Johnson, J. 4, Jones, R. 4, Llera 4, Lines 3, Batth 2, Bennett 2, Prutton 2, Ranger 2, Buxton 1, McGoldrick 1, Morrison, C. 1, O'Connor 1, Palmer 1, Sedgwick 1, Semedo 1, Treacy 1, own goals 2.
Carling Cup (1): Morrison, C. 1.
FA Cup (5): O'Grady 2, Lines 1, Lowe 1, Morrison, C. 1.
J Paint Trophy (0).
Ground: Hillsborough, Sheffield S6 1SW. Telephone: (0871) 995 1867.
Capacity: 39,812.
Record Attendance: 72,841 v Manchester C, FA Cup 5th rd, 17 February 1934.
Manager: Dave Jones.
Most League Goals: 106, Division 2, 1958–59.
Highest League Scorer in Season: Derek Dooley, 46, Division 2, 1951–52.
Most League Goals in Total Aggregate: Andrew Wilson, 199, 1900–20.
Most Capped Player: Nigel Worthington, 50 (66), Northern Ireland.
Most League Appearances: Andrew Wilson, 501, 1900–20.
Colours: Blue and white striped shirts, black shorts, blue stockings.
Honours – Football League: Division 1 Champions – 1902–03, 1903–04, 1928–29, 1929–30. Division 2 Champions – 1899–1900, 1925–26, 1951–52, 1955–56, 1958–59.
FA Cup: Winners – 1896, 1907, 1935. **Football League Cup:** Winners – 1990–91.

SHREWSBURY TOWN   FL CHAMPIONSHIP 1

Bradshaw Tom (F)	5 5	11 02	Shrewsbury	27/7/92	Aberystwyth T
Cansdell-Sheriff Shane (D)	5 11	11 08	Sydney	10/11/82	Tranmere R
Collins James S (F)	6 2	13 08	Coventry	1/12/90	Aston Villa
Goldson Connor (D)	6 3	13 05	York	18/12/92	Youth
Gornell Terry (F)	5 11	12 04	Liverpool	16/12/89	Accrington S
Grandison Jermaine (D)	6 4	13 03	Birmingham	15/12/90	Coventry C
Hazell Reuben (D)	5 11	12 05	Birmingham	24/4/79	Oldham Ath
Jacobson Joe (D)	5 11	12 06	Cardiff	17/11/86	Accrington S
Morgan Marvin (F)	6 4	12 08	Manchester	13/4/83	Aldershot T
Neal Chris (G)	6 2	12 04	St Albans	23/10/85	Preston NE
Richards Matt (D)	5 8	11 02	Harlow	26/12/84	Walsall
Sharps Ian (D)	6 3	14 07	Warrington	23/10/80	Rotherham U
Taylor Jon (M)	5 11	12 04	Liverpool	23/12/89	Youth
Wright Mark (M)	5 11	11 00	Wolverhampton	24/2/82	Bristol R
Wroe Nicky (M)	5 11	10 02	Sheffield	28/9/85	Torquay U

League Appearances: Ainsworth, L. 19(2); Bradshaw, T. 5(3); Cansdell-Sheriff, S. 35(2); Collins, J. 32(10); Goldson, C. 2(2); Gornell, T. 28(13); Grandison, J. 36(2); Hazell, R. 5(2); Hurst, J. 7; Jacobson, J. 37(2); McAllister, D. 15; McAllister, S. 14(3); McLaughlin, C. 4; Morgan, M. 26(16); Neal, C. 35; Regan, C. 12(1); Richards, M. 35(7); Sawyers, R. 2(5); Sharps, I. 43; Smith, B. 11; Taylor, J. 15(18); Wallace, J. 1(2); Wildig, A. 10(2); Wright, M. 45(1); Wroe, N. 32(6).
Goals – League (66): Collins 14 (2 pens), Wright 10, Gornell 9, Morgan 8, Richards 5, Cansdell-Sheriff 4, Wroe 4 (2 pens), Ainsworth 2, Grandison 2, Wildig 2, Bradshaw 1, Jacobson 1, McAllister, S. 1, Sharps 1, own goals 2.
Carling Cup (7): Morgan 3, Collins 2, Wright 1, Wroe 1.
FA Cup (3): Gornell 1, Sharps 1, Wroe 1 (pen).
J Paint Trophy (1): own goal 1.
Ground: Greenhous Meadow, Oteley Road, Shrewsbury SY2 6ST. Telephone: (01743) 289 177.
Capacity: 10,000.
Record Attendance: 18,917 v Walsall, Division 3, 26 April 1961 (at Gay Meadow); 8,429 v Bury, FL 2 Play-off semi-final, 7 May 2009 (at ProStar Stadium).
Manager: Graham Turner.

Most League Goals: 101, Division 4, 1958–59.
Highest League Scorer in Season: Arthur Rowley, 38, Division 4, 1958–59.
Most League Goals in Total Aggregate: Arthur Rowley, 152, 1958–65 (thus completing his League record of 434 goals).
Most Capped Player: Jimmy McLaughlin, 5 (12), Northern Ireland; Bernard McNally, 5, Northern Ireland.
Most League Appearances: Mickey Brown, 418, 1986–91; 1992–94; 1996–2001.
Colours: All blue with yellow and red design.
Honours – Football League: Division 3 Champions – 1978–79, 1993–94. **Welsh Cup:** Winners – 1891, 1938, 1977, 1979, 1984, 1985.

SOUTHAMPTON   FA PREMIERSHIP

Player			Birthplace	Date	Previous Club
Barnard Lee (F)	5 10	10 10	Romford	18/7/84	Southend U
Butterfield Danny (D)	5 10	11 06	Boston	21/11/79	Crystal Palace
Chambers Calum (M)			Petersfield	20/1/95	Scholar
Chaplow Richard (M)	5 9	9 03	Accrington	2/2/85	Preston NE
Cork Jack (D)	6 0	10 12	Carshalton	25/6/89	Chelsea
Davis Kelvin (G)	6 1	11 05	Bedford	29/9/76	Sunderland
De Ridder Steve (F)	5 10	11 07	Gent	25/2/87	De Graafschap
Dickson Ryan (M)	5 10	11 05	Saltash	14/12/86	Brentford
Do Prado Guilherme (F)	6 2	12 04	Sao Paulo	31/12/81	Cesena
Fonte Jose (D)	6 2	12 08	Penafiel	22/12/83	Crystal Palace
Forecast Tommy (G)	6 2	11 10	Newham	15/10/86	Tottenham H
Forte Jonathan (M)	6 0	12 01	Sheffield	25/7/86	Scunthorpe U
Fox Danny (D)	5 11	12 06	Winsford	29/5/86	Burnley
Hammond Dean (M)	6 0	11 09	Hastings	7/3/83	Colchester U
Harding Dan (D)	6 0	11 11	Gloucester	23/12/83	Ipswich T
Hooiveld Jos (D)	6 3	11 11	Zeijen	22/4/83	Celtic
Hoskins Sam (F)	5 8	10 07	Dorchester	4/2/93	Troyes B
Isgrove Lloyd (M)			Yeovil	12/1/93	Scholar
Lallana Adam (M)	5 8	11 06	St Albans	10/5/88	Scholar
Lambert Ricky (F)	6 2	14 06	Liverpool	16/2/82	Bristol R
Lee Tadanari (F)	6 0	11 09	Tokyo	19/12/85	Sanfrecce
Martin Aaron (D)	6 3	11 13	Newport (IW)	29/9/89	Eastleigh
McQueen Sam (M)			Southampton	6/2/95	Scholar
Moore Corby (M)			Salisbury	21/11/93	Scholar
Puncheon Jason (M)	5 9	12 05	Croydon	26/6/86	Plymouth Arg
Reeves Ben (D)	5 10	10 07	Verwood	19/11/91	Scholar
Richardson Frazer (D)	5 11	11 12	Rotherham	29/10/82	Charlton Ath
Robinson Andreas (M)			Bournemouth	16/10/92	Scholar
Schneiderlin Morgan (M)	5 11	11 11	Obernai	8/11/89	Strasbourg
Seaborne Danny (D)	6 0	11 10	Barnstaple	5/3/87	Exeter C
Seidi Alberto (F)			Guinea-Bissau	20/11/92	Scholar
Sharp Billy (F)	5 9	11 00	Sheffield	5/2/86	Doncaster R
Stephens Jack (D)			Torpoint	27/1/94	Plymouth Arg
Turnbull Jordan (D)			Swindon	30/10/94	Scholar
Ward-Prowse James (M)			Portsmouth	1/11/94	Scholar

League Appearances: Barnard, L. (6); Bialkowski, B. 1; Butterfield, D. 9(1); Chaplow, R. 17(8); Connolly, D. 17(9); Cork, J. 39(7); Davis, K. 45; De Ridder, S. 5(27); Do Prado, G. 36(6); Falque, I. 1; Fonte, J. 42; Forte, J. (1); Fox, D. 37(4); Hammond, D. 31(12); Harding, D. 12(8); Holmes, L. (6); Hooiveld, J. 39; Lallana, A. 41; Lambert, R. 42; Lee, T. 4(3); Martin, A. 7(3); Puncheon, J. 4(4); Reeves, B. (2); Richardson, F. 33(1); Schneiderlin, M. 29(13); Seaborne, D. 4; Sharp, B. 11(4).

Goals – League (85): Lambert 27 (9 pens), Lallana 11, Do Prado 10, Sharp 9, Hooiveld 7, Connolly 6, Chaplow 3, De Ridder 3, Schneiderlin 2, Fonte 1, Hammond 1, Harding 1, Holmes 1, Lee 1, Martin 1, own goal 1.

Carling Cup (9): Forte 2, Lambert 2, Chaplow 1, De Ridder 1, Do Prado 1, Hooiveld 1, Lallana 1.

FA Cup (5): Lambert 2, Lallana 1, Martin 1, Ward-Prowse 1.

Ground: St Mary's Stadium, Britannia Road, Southampton SO14 5FP. Telephone: (0845) 688 9448.

Capacity: 32,689.

Record Attendance: 31,044 v Manchester U, Division 1, 8 October 1969 (at The Dell); 32,151 v Arsenal, FA Premier League, 29 December 2003 (at St Mary's).

Manager: Nigel Adkins B.Sc (Hons).

Most League Goals: 112, Division 3 (S), 1957–58.

Highest League Scorer in Season: Derek Reeves, 39, Division 3, 1959–60.

Most League Goals in Total Aggregate: Mike Channon, 185, 1966–77, 1979–82.

Most Capped Player: Peter Shilton, 49 (125), England.

Most League Appearances: Terry Paine, 713, 1956–74.

Colours: White shirts with diagonal red stripe, white shorts, black stockings.

Honours – Football League: Division 3 (S) Champions – 1921–22. Division 3 Champions – 1959–60. **FA Cup:** Winners – 1975–76. **Johnstone's Paint Trophy:** Winners – 2009–10.

SOUTHEND UNITED   FL CHAMPIONSHIP 2

Bentley Daniel (G)	6 2	11 05	Wickford	13/7/93	Scholar
Benyon Elliot (F)	5 9	10 01	High Wycombe	29/8/87	Swindon T
Clohessy Sean (D)	5 11	12 07	Croydon	12/12/86	Gillingham
Corr Barry (F)	6 3	12 07	Co Wicklow	2/4/85	Exeter C
Coughlan Graham (D)	6 2	13 07	Dublin	18/11/74	Shrewsbury T
Ferdinand Kane (D)	6 1	13 05	Newham	7/10/92	Scholar
Grant Anthony (M)	5 10	11 01	Lambeth	4/6/87	Chelsea
Hall Ryan (M)	5 10	10 04	Dulwich	4/1/88	Crystal Palace
Harris Neil (F)	5 10	12 08	Thurrock	12/7/77	Millwall
Kalala Jean-Paul (M)	5 10	12 02	Lubumbashi	16/2/82	Bristol R
Leonard Ryan (D)	6 0	11 01	Plympton	24/5/92	Plymouth Arg
Martin David J (M)	5 9	10 10	Erith	3/6/85	Derby Co
Mohsni Bilel (D)	6 3	11 11	Tunisia	21/7/87	Genevieve Sp
Phillips Mark (D)	6 2	11 00	Lambeth	27/1/82	Brentford
Prosser Luke (D)	6 2	12 04	Waltham Cross	28/5/88	Port Vale
Sturrock Blair (F)	5 10	12 09	Dundee	25/8/81	Swindon T
Timlin Michael (M)	5 8	11 08	New Cross	19/3/85	Fulham
Woodyard Alex (M)	5 9	10 00	Gravesend	3/5/93	Scholar

League Appearances: Baldwin, P. 2; Barker, C. 42(1); Belford, C. 13; Bentley, D. (1); Benyon, E. 8(8); Clohessy, S. 45; Coughlan, G. 2(2); Crawford, H. (3); Dailly, C. 3; Daniels, L. 9; Dickinson, L. 28(2); Eastwood, F. 6(1); Ferdinand, K. 28(8); Flood, A. (1); Gilbert, P. 29(2); Grant, A. 25(8); Hall, R. 35(8); Harris, N. 21(12); Hills, L. 5(2); James-Lewis, M. (1); Johnson, J. 1(4); Kalala, J. 23(1); Leonard, R. 13(4); Martin, D. 11(6); Mohsni, B. 23(8); Morris, G. 24; N'Diaye, A. (1); Phillips, M. 38(1); Prosser, L. 18(3); Sampson, J. 5(4); Sawyer, L. 5(5); Sturrock, B. 5(4); Timlin, M. 39.

Goals – League (77): Mohsni 13, Dickinson 10 (4 pens), Hall 10, Harris 8 (1 pen), Ferdinand 7, Phillips 7, Timlin 4, Gilbert 3, Martin 3, Benyon 2, Eastwood 2, Grant 1, Kalala 1, Leonard 1, Prosser 1, own goals 4.

Carling Cup (1): Phillips 1.

FA Cup (2): Dickinson 1, Hall 1.

J Paint Trophy (6): Hall 3, Dickinson 1 (pen), Harris 1, Sturrock 1.

Play-Offs (2): Barker 1, Harris 1.

Ground: Roots Hall Stadium, Victoria Avenue, Southend-on-Sea, Essex SS2 6NQ. Telephone: (01702) 304 050.
Capacity: 12,260.
Record Attendance: 22,862 v Tottenham H, FA Cup 3rd rd replay, 11 January 1936 (at Southend Stadium); 31,090 v Liverpool, FA Cup 3rd rd, 10 January 1979 (at Roots Hall).
Manager: Paul Sturrock.
Most League Goals: 92, Division 3 (S), 1950–51.
Highest League Scorer in Season: Jim Shankly, 31, 1928–29; Sammy McCrory, 1957–58, both in Division 3 (S).
Most League Goals in Total Aggregate: Roy Hollis, 122, 1953–60.
Most Capped Player: George Mackenzie, 9, Eire.
Most League Appearances: Sandy Anderson, 452, 1950–63.
Colours: Navy blue shirts with white collar, navy blue shorts, white stockings.
Honours – Football League: FL 1 Champions – 2005–06. Division 4 Champions – 1980–81.

STEVENAGE   FL CHAMPIONSHIP 1

Ashton Jon (D)	6 2	13 12	Nuneaton	4/10/82	Oxford U
Beardsley Chris (F)	6 0	12 12	Derby	28/2/84	Mansfield T
Bostwick Michael (D)	6 4	14 00	Eltham	17/5/88	Millwall
Byrom Joel (M)	6 0	12 04	Accrington	14/9/86	Accrington S
Charles Darius (M)	6 1	13 05	Ealing	10/12/87	Brentford
Cowan Don (F)	5 10	13 05	New York	16/11/89	Shamrock R
Day Chris (G)	6 2	13 07	Whipps Cross	28/7/75	Millwall
Freeman Luke (F)	6 0	10 00	Dartford	22/3/92	Gillingham
Laird Scott (D)	5 11	11 06	Taunton	15/5/88	Plymouth Arg
Mousinho John (M)	6 1	12 07	Hounslow	30/4/86	Wycombe W
Reid Craig (F)	5 10	11 10	Coventry	17/12/85	Cheltenham T
Roberts Mark (D)	6 1	12 00	Northwich	16/10/83	Accrington S
Shroot Robin (M)	5 9	11 05	Hammersmith	26/3/88	Birmingham C
Sinclair Robert (M)	5 10	11 02	Bedford	29/8/89	Luton T
Thalassitis Michael (F)	6 1	13 00	Enfield	19/1/93	Youth
Wilson Lawrie (D)	5 11	11 06	London	11/9/87	Colchester U

League Appearances: Agyemang, P. 10(3); Aneke, C. 2(4); Ashton, J. 42(1); Beardsley, C. 15(16); Bostwick, M. 43; Byrom, J. 29(3); Charles, D. 23(5); Cowan, D. 2(6); Day, C. 44; Edwards, P. 11(11); Freeman, L. 22(4); Harrison, B. 10(8); Henry, R. 32; Julian, A. 2(1); Laird, S. 46; Lascelles, J. 5(2); Long, S. 18(12); Madjo, G. (1); May, B. 2(5); Mousinho, J. 14(5); Myrie-Williams, J. 3(14); Reid, C. 24(5); Roberts, M. 46; Shroot, R. 11(14); Slew, J. 6(3); Thalassitis, M. (3); Walker, J. (5); Wilson, L. 44(2).
Goals – League (69): Laird 8, Beardsley 7, Bostwick 7, Freeman 7, Reid 6, Roberts 6, Wilson 5, Byrom 4 (1 pen), Charles 4, Mousinho 3 (1 pen), Shroot 3, Harrison 2, Agyemang 1, Ashton 1, Lascelles 1, Long 1, Walker 1, own goals 2.
Carling Cup (3): Beardsley 1, Bostwick 1, Long 1.
FA Cup (7): Beardsley 2, Byrom 1 (pen), Charles 1, Laird 1 (pen), Shroot 1, own goal 1.
J Paint Trophy (2): Roberts 1, Wilson 1.
Play-Offs (0).
Ground: Lamex Stadium, Broadhall Way, Stevenage, Herts SG2 8RH. Telephone: (01438) 223223.
Capacity: 6,546.
Record Attendance: 6,489 v Kidderminster H, Conference, 25 January 1997.
Manager: Gary Smith.
Most League Goals: 69, FL 1, 2011–12.
Highest League Scorer in Season: Byron Harrison, 8, 2010–11; Scott Laird, 8, 2011–12.

Most Goals in Total Aggregate: Scott Laird, 12, 2010–12; Mark Roberts, 12, 2010–12.
Most League Appearances: Chris Day, 90, 2010–12; Scott Laird, 90, 2010–12.
Colours: White shirts, red shorts, red stockings with white tops.
Honours: Blue Square Premier League: Champions – 2009–10.

STOKE CITY FA PREMIERSHIP

Arismendi Diego (M)	6 2	12 13	Montevideo	25/1/88	Nacional
Bachmann Daniel (G)			Vienna	9/7/94	Scholar
Begovic Asmir (G)	6 5	13 01	Trebinje	20/6/87	Portsmouth
Brunt Ryan (F)	6 1	11 11	Birmingham	26/5/93	Sanfrecce
Collins Danny (D)	6 2	11 13	Buckley	6/8/80	Sunderland
Crouch Peter (F)	6 7	13 03	Macclesfield	30/1/81	Tottenham H
Cuvelier Florent (M)	6 0	11 05	Brussels	12/9/92	Portsmouth
Delap Rory (M)	6 3	12 11	Sutton Coldfield	6/7/76	Sunderland
Etherington Matthew (M)	5 10	10 12	Truro	14/8/81	West Ham U
Higginbotham Danny (D)	6 2	13 01	Manchester	29/12/78	Sunderland
Huth Robert (D)	6 3	14 07	Berlin	18/8/84	Middlesbrough
Jerome Cameron (F)	6 1	13 06	Huddersfield	14/8/86	Birmingham C
Jones Kenwyne (F)	6 2	13 06	Trinidad & Tobago	5/10/84	Sunderland
Lund Matthew (M)	6 0	11 13	Manchester	21/11/90	Crewe Alex
Nash Carlo (G)	6 5	14 01	Bolton	13/9/73	Everton
Palacios Wilson (D)	5 10	11 11	La Ceiba	29/7/84	Tottenham H
Pennant Jermaine (M)	5 9	10 06	Nottingham	15/1/83	Zaragoza
Rossi Karim (F)			Zurich	1/5/94	Scholar
Shawcross Ryan (D)	6 3	13 13	Buckley	4/10/87	Manchester U
Shotton Ryan (D)	6 3	13 05	Stoke	30/9/88	Scholar
Sidibe Mamady (F)	6 4	12 02	Bamako	18/12/79	Gillingham
Sorensen Thomas (G)	6 4	13 10	Fredericia	12/6/76	Aston Villa
Tonge Michael (M)	6 0	11 10	Manchester	7/4/83	Sheffield U
Upson Matthew (D)	6 1	11 04	Eye	18/4/79	West Ham U
Walters Jon (F)	6 0	12 06	Birkenhead	20/9/83	Ipswich T
Whelan Glenn (M)	5 11	12 07	Dublin	13/1/84	Sheffield W
Whitehead Dean (M)	5 11	12 06	Abingdon	12/1/82	Sunderland
Wilkinson Andy (D)	5 11	11 00	Stone	6/8/84	Scholar
Wilson Marc (M)	6 2	12 07	Lisburn	17/8/87	Portsmouth
Woodgate Jonathan (D)	6 2	12 06	Middlesbrough	22/1/80	Tottenham H

League Appearances: Begovic, A. 22(1); Crouch, P. 31(1); Delap, R. 18(8); Diao, S. 2(4); Etherington, M. 30; Fuller, R. 3(10); Higginbotham, D. 1(1); Huth, R. 31(3); Jerome, C. 7(16); Jones, K. 10(11); Palacios, W. 9(9); Pennant, J. 18(9); Pugh, D. (3); Shawcross, R. 36; Shotton, R. 14(9); Sorensen, T. 16; Upson, M. 10(4); Walters, J. 38; Whelan, G. 27(3); Whitehead, D. 24(9); Wilkinson, A. 20(5); Wilson, M. 35; Woodgate, J. 16(1).
Goals – League (36): Crouch 10, Walters 7 (4 pens), Jerome 4, Etherington 3, Huth 3, Delap 2, Shawcross 2, Jones 1, Shotton 1, Upson 1, Whelan 1, own goal 1.
Carling Cup (1): Jones 1.
FA Cup (8): Crouch 2, Huth 2, Jerome 2, Walters 2 (1 pen).
Europa League (17): Jones 4, Crouch 2, Jerome 2, Walters 2 (1 pen), Fuller 1, Pugh 1, Shotton 1, Upson 1, Whelan 1, Whitehead 1, own goal 1.
Ground: Britannia Stadium, Stanley Matthews Way, Stoke-on-Trent, Staffs ST4 4EG. Telephone: (01782) 367 598.
Capacity: 28,383.
Record Attendance: 51,380 v Arsenal, Division 1, 29 March 1937 (at Victoria Ground); 28,218 v Everton, Division 2, 5 January 2002 (at Britannia Stadium).
Manager: Tony Pulis.
Most League Goals: 92, Division 3 (N), 1926–27.

Highest League Scorer in Season: Freddie Steele, 33, Division 1, 1936–37.
Most League Goals in Total Aggregate: Freddie Steele, 142, 1934–49.
Most Capped Player: Gordon Banks, 36 (73), England.
Most League Appearances: Eric Skeels, 506, 1958–76.
Colours: Red and white striped shirts with red sleeves and shoulders, white shorts, white stockings.
Honours – Football League: Division 2 Champions – 1932–33, 1962–63, 1992–93. Division 3 (N) Champions – 1926–27. **Football League Cup:** Winners – 1971–72. **Autoglass Trophy:** Winners – 1992. **Auto Windscreens Shield:** Winners – 2000.

SUNDERLAND   FA PREMIERSHIP

Adams Blair (D)	5 11	11 05	South Shields	8/9/91	Scholar
Angeleri Marcos (D)	6 0	10 10	La Plata	4/7/83	Estudiantes
Armstrong James (M)			Sunderland	10/5/93	Scholar
Bardsley Phillip (D)	5 11	11 13	Salford	28/6/85	Manchester U
Bramble Titus (D)	6 2	13 10	Ipswich	31/7/81	Wigan Ath
Brown Wes (D)	6 1	13 08	Manchester	13/10/79	Manchester U
Campbell Frazier (F)	5 11	12 04	Huddersfield	13/9/87	Manchester U
Cattermole Lee (M)	5 10	11 13	Stockton	21/3/88	Wigan Ath
Colback Jack (M)	5 9	11 05	Killingworth	24/10/89	Scholar
Egan John (D)	6 1	11 11	Cork	20/10/92	Scholar
Elmohamady Ahmed (M)	5 11	12 10	El Mahalla El-Kubra	9/9/87	ENPPI
Gardner Craig (M)	5 10	11 13	Solihull	25/11/86	Birmingham C
Gorrin Alejandro (M)			Tenerife	1/8/93	Scholar
Gyan Asamoah (F)	5 11	12 08	Accra	22/11/85	Rennes
Ji Dong-Won (F)	6 2	12 04	Jeju	28/5/91	Chunnam Dragons
Kilgallon Matthew (D)	6 1	12 10	York	8/1/84	Sheffield U
Knott Billy (M)	5 8	11 02	Canvey Island	28/11/92	Scholar
Laing Louis (D)	5 11	12 00	Newcastle	6/3/93	Scholar
Larsson Sebastian (M)	5 11	11 02	Eskilstuna	6/6/85	Birmingham C
Liddle Michael (D)	5 6	11 00	Hounslow	25/12/89	Scholar
Lynch Craig (F)	5 9	10 01	Chester-le-Street	25/3/92	Scholar
Mandron Mikael (F)			Boulogne	11/10/94	Scholar
Marrs Liam (D)			North Shields	26/11/92	Scholar
McCartney George (D)	5 11	11 02	Belfast	29/4/81	West Ham U
McClean James (M)	5 11	11 00	Derry	22/4/89	Derry C
Meyler David (M)	6 3	11 09	Cork	29/5/89	Cork C
Mignolet Simon (G)	6 4	13 10	St Truiden	6/3/88	St Truiden
Mitchell Adam (M)			Barnard Castle	3/4/93	Scholar
Noble Ryan (F)	6 0	11 00	Sunderland	6/11/91	Scholar
O'Shea John (D)	6 3	13 07	Waterford	30/4/81	Manchester U
Pickford Jordan (G)			Washington	7/3/94	Scholar
Reed Adam (M)	5 5	10 03	Hartlepool	8/5/91	Scholar
Richardson Kieran (M)	5 9	11 13	Greenwich	21/10/84	Manchester U
Sessegnon Stephane (M)	5 8	11 05	Allahe	1/6/84	Paris St Germain
Turner Michael (D)	6 4	13 05	Lewisham	9/11/83	Hull C
Vaughan David (M)	5 7	11 00	Abergele	18/2/83	Blackpool
Watson Jordan (M)			Cyprus	7/4/93	
Westwood Keiren (G)	6 1	13 10	Manchester	23/10/84	Coventry C
Wickham Connor (F)	6 0	14 01	Hereford	31/3/93	Ipswich T
Wilson Ben (G)			Stanley	9/8/92	Scholar

League Appearances: Bardsley, P. 29(2); Bendtner, N. 25(3); Bramble, T. 8; Bridge, W. 3(5); Brown, W. 20; Campbell, F. 6(6); Cattermole, L. 23; Colback, J. 29(6); Elmohamady, A. 7(11); Ferdinand, A. 3; Gardner, C. 22(8); Gordon, C. 1; Gyan, A. 3; Ji, D. 2(17);

Kilgallon, M. 9(1); Kyrgiakos, S. 2(1); Larsson, S. 32; McClean, J. 20(3); Meyler, D. 1(6); Mignolet, S. 29; Noble, R. (2); O'Shea, J. 29; Richardson, K. 26(3); Sessegnon, S. 36; Turner, M. 23(1); Vaughan, D. 17(5); Westwood, K. 8(1); Wickham, C. 5(11).
Goals – League (45): Bendtner 8 (1 pen), Larsson 7, Sessegnon 7, McClean 5, Gardner 3, Ji 2, Richardson 2, Vaughan 2, Bardsley 1, Bramble 1, Brown 1, Campbell 1, Colback 1, Elmohamady 1, Wickham 1, own goals 2.
Carling Cup (0).
FA Cup (8): Bardsley 1, Campbell 1, Colback 1, Larsson 1, McClean 1, Richardson 1, Sessegnon 1, own goal 1.
Ground: Stadium of Light, Sunderland, Tyne and Wear SR5 1SU. Telephone: (0871) 911 1200.
Capacity: 49,000.
Record Attendance: 75,118 v Derby Co, FA Cup 6th rd replay, 8 March 1933 (at Roker Park); 48,353 v Liverpool, FA Premier League, 13 April 2002 (at Stadium of Light). (FA Premier League figure 46,062.)
Manager: Martin O'Neill OBE.
Most League Goals: 109, Division 1, 1935–36.
Highest League Scorer in Season: Dave Halliday, 43, Division 1, 1928–29.
Most League Goals in Total Aggregate: Charlie Buchan, 209, 1911–25.
Most Capped Player: Charlie Hurley, 38 (40), Republic of Ireland.
Most League Appearances: Jim Montgomery, 537, 1962–77.
Colours: Red and white striped shirts, black shorts, black stockings with red tops.
Honours – Football League: FL C Champions – 2004–05, 2006–07. Division 1 Champions – 1891–92, 1892–93, 1894–95, 1901–02, 1912–13, 1935–36, 1995–96, 1998–99. Division 2 Champions – 1975–76. Division 3 Champions – 1987–88. **FA Cup:** Winners – 1937, 1973.

SWANSEA CITY   FA PREMIERSHIP

Agustien Kemy (M)	5 10	11 05	Tilburg	20/8/86	AZ
Alfei Daniel (D)	5 11	12 02	Swansea	23/2/92	Scholar
Allen Joe (M)	5 6	9 10	Carmarthen	14/3/90	Scholar
Bessone Fede (D)	5 11	11 13	Cordoba	23/1/84	Leeds U
Britton Leon (M)	5 6	10 02	Merton	16/9/82	Sheffield U
Cornell David (G)	5 11	11 07	Gorseinon	28/3/91	Scholar
Davies Ben (D)			Neath	24/4/93	Scholar
Dobbie Stephen (F)	5 10	11 00	Glasgow	5/12/82	Queen of the S
Donnelly Rory (F)	6 2	12 10	Belfast	18/2/92	Cliftonville
Donnelly Scott (M)	5 8	11 10	Hammersmith	25/12/87	Aldershot T
Dyer Nathan (M)	5 5	9 00	Trowbridge	29/11/87	Southampton
Edwards Gwion (M)			Carmarthen	1/3/93	Scholar
Gower Mark (M)	5 11	11 12	Edmonton	5/10/78	Southend U
Graham Danny (F)	5 11	12 05	Gateshead	12/8/85	Watford
Lita Leroy (F)	5 7	11 12	DR Congo	28/12/84	Middlesbrough
Lucas Lee (M)	5 11	11 08	Aberdare	10/6/92	Scholar
March Kurtis (M)			Swansea	30/4/93	Scholar
Monk Garry (D)	6 0	12 10	Bedford	6/3/79	Barnsley
Moore Luke (F)	5 11	11 13	Birmingham	13/2/86	WBA
Obeng Curtis (D)	5 6	10 05	Manchester	14/2/89	Wrexham
Orlandi Andrea (M)	6 0	12 01	Barcelona	3/8/84	Alaves
Rangel Angel (D)	5 11	11 12	Barcelona	28/10/82	Terrassa
Richards Jazz (M)	6 1	12 04	Swansea	12/4/91	Scholar
Routledge Wayne (M)	5 6	11 02	Sidcup	7/1/85	Newcastle U
Sinclair Scott (F)	5 10	10 00	Bath	26/3/89	Chelsea
Situ Darnel (D)	6 2	12 02	Rouen	18/3/92	Lens
Tate Alan (D)	6 1	13 05	Seaham	2/9/82	Manchester U
Taylor Neil (D)	5 9	10 02	Ruthin	7/2/89	Wrexham

Tremmel Gerhard (G)	6 3	14 00	Munich	16/11/78	Energie Cottbus
Vorm Michel (G)	6 0	13 03	Nieuwegein	20/10/83	Utrecht
Williams Ashley (D)	6 0	11 02	Wolverhampton	23/8/84	Stockport Co

League Appearances: Agustien, K. 7(6); Allen, J. 31(5); Bessone, F. (1); Britton, L. 35(1); Caulker, S. 26; Dobbie, S. 2(6); Dyer, N. 29(5); Gower, M. 14(6); Graham, D. 32(4); Lita, L. 4(12); McEachran, J. 1(3); Monk, G. 14(2); Moore, L. 3(17); Moras, V. (1); Orlandi, A. 2(1); Rangel, A. 32(2); Richards, J. 6(2); Routledge, W. 17(11); Sigurdsson, G. 17(1); Sinclair, S. 35(3); Tate, A. 1(4); Taylor, N. 35(1); Tremmel, G. 1; Vorm, M. 37; Williams, A. 37.

Goals – League (44): Graham 12 (1 pen), Sinclair 8 (4 pens), Sigurdsson 7, Dyer 5, Allen 4, Lita 2, Moore 2, Orlandi 1, Routledge 1, Williams 1, own goal 1.

Carling Cup (1): own goal 1.

FA Cup (5): Graham 2, Dyer 1, Moore 1, Rangel 1.

Ground: Liberty Stadium, Morfa, Landore, Swansea SA1 2FA. Telephone: (01792) 616 600.

Capacity: 20,520.

Record Attendance: 32,796 v Arsenal, FA Cup 4th rd, 17 February 1968 (at Vetch Field); 19,288 v Yeovil T, FL 1, 11 November 2005 (at Liberty Stadium).

Manager: Michael Laudrup.

Most League Goals: 90, Division 2, 1956–57.

Highest League Scorer in Season: Cyril Pearce, 35, Division 2, 1931–32.

Most League Goals in Total Aggregate: Ivor Allchurch, 166, 1949–58, 1965–68.

Most Capped Player: Ivor Allchurch, 42 (68), Wales.

Most League Appearances: Wilfred Milne, 585, 1919–37.

Colours: All white.

Honours – Football League: FL 1 Winners – 2007–08, Division 3 Champions – 1999–2000. Division 3 (S) Champions – 1924–25, 1948–49. **Autoglass Trophy:** Winners – 1994, 2006. **Football League Trophy:** Winners – 2006. **Welsh Cup:** Winners – 11 times.

SWINDON TOWN

FL CHAMPIONSHIP 1

Benson Paul (F)	6 1	11 01	Southend	12/10/79	Charlton Ath
Bodin Billy (M)	5 11	11 00	Swindon	24/3/92	
Caddis Paul (D)	5 7	10 07	Irvine	19/4/88	Celtic
Cibocchi Alessandro (D)	5 11	11 07	Terni	18/9/82	
Connell Alan (F)	6 0	12 00	Enfield	5/2/83	Bournemouth
Cox Lee (M)	6 1	12 02	Leicester	26/6/90	Inverness CT
De Vita Raffaele (F)	6 0	11 09	Rome	23/9/87	Blackburn R
Devera Joe (D)	6 2	12 00	Southgate	6/2/87	Barnet
Esajas Etienne (F)	5 7	10 03	Amsterdam	4/11/84	Helmond Sp
Ferry Simon (M)	5 8	11 00	Dundee	11/1/88	Celtic
Flint Aiden (D)	6 2	12 00	Pinxton	11/7/89	Alfreton T
Foderingham Wesley (G)	6 1	12 00	Hammersmith	14/1/91	Fulham
Kerrouche Mehdi (F)	5 10	10 10	Douai	11/10/85	Al-Oruba
Lanzano Mattia (G)	6 1	13 05	Grosseto	4/7/90	Gavorrano
Magera Lukas (F)	6 4	14 00	Opava	17/1/83	Timisoara
McCormack Alan (M)	5 8	11 00	Dublin	10/1/84	Charlton Ath
Risser Oliver (M)	6 3	13 10	Windhoek	17/9/80	Lyn
Ritchie Matt (M)	5 8	11 01	Gosport	10/9/89	Portsmouth
Rooney Luke (M)	5 8	11 07	Southwark	28/12/90	Gillingham
Smith Chris (D)			Stoke	12/10/90	Stone Dominoes
Smith Jonathan (M)	6 3	11 02	Preston	17/10/86	York C
Thompson Nathan (D)	5 7	11 02	Chester	9/11/90	Scholar

League Appearances: Abdullah, A. 1(5); Benson, P. 20(2); Boateng, D. 2; Bodin, B. 9(2); Bostock, J. 3; Caddis, P. 39; Cibocchi, A. 11(7); Clarke, L. 2; Comazzi, A. 4; Connell, A.

13(19); Cox, L. 2(5); De Vita, R. 30(8); Devera, J. 28; Esajas, E. 2(4); Ferry, S. 36(8); Flint, A. 28(4); Foderingham, W. 33; Gabilondo, L. 4(6); Holmes, L. 7(3); Jervis, J. 10(2); Kennedy, C. 18; Kerrouche, M. 9(4); Lanzano, M. 5(1); Magera, L. 7(5); McCormack, A. 38(2); McEveley, J. 8; Montano, C. 3(1); Murray, R. 9(11); Ridehalgh, L. 9(2); Risser, O. 23(9); Ritchie, M. 40; Rooney, L. 13(7); Smith, C. (1); Smith, J. 28(10); Smith, P. 8; Storey, M. (4); Tehoue, J. 1(2); Thompson, N. 2(3); Timlin, M. 1.

Goals – League (75): Benson 11, Connell 11, Ritchie 10, Kerrouche 6 (1 pen), Caddis 4 (2 pens), De Vita 4, Bodin 3, Jervis 3, Murray 3, Risser 3, Smith, J. 3, Devera 2, Flint 2, McCormack 2, Rooney 2, Ferry 1, Holmes 1, Kennedy 1 (1 pen), Magera 1, Montano 1, own goal 1.

Carling Cup (2): De Vita 1, Kerrouche 1.

FA Cup (7): Benson 1, Connell 1, De Vita 1, Ferry 1, Flint 1, Kerrouche 1, Ritchie 1.

J Paint Trophy (7): Jervis 2, Caddis 1, Connell 1, Flint 1, Murray 1, Risser 1.

Ground: The County Ground, County Road, Swindon, Wiltshire SN1 2ED. Telephone: (0871) 876 1879.

Capacity: 14,700.

Record Attendance: 32,000 v Arsenal, FA Cup 3rd rd, 15 January 1972.

Manager: Paulo Di Canio.

Most League Goals: 100, Division 3 (S), 1926–27.

Highest League Scorer in Season: Harry Morris, 47, Division 3 (S), 1926–27.

Most League Goals in Total Aggregate: Harry Morris, 216, 1926–33.

Most Capped Player: Rod Thomas, 30 (50), Wales.

Most League Appearances: John Trollope, 770, 1960–80.

Colours: Red shirts with white inserts, red shorts with white inserts, red stockings with white inserts.

Honours – Football League: Division 2 Champions – 1995–96. Division 4 Champions – 1985–86. FL 2 – Champions 2011–12. **Football League Cup:** Winners – 1968–69, 2007–08. **Anglo-Italian Cup:** Winners – 1970.

TORQUAY UNITED

FL CHAMPIONSHIP 2

Ellis Mark (D)	6 2	12 04	Kingsbridge	30/9/88	Bolton W
Halpin Saul (M)	6 1	12 00	Bodmin	31/5/91	Scholar
Howe Rene (F)	6 0	14 03	Bedford	22/10/86	Peterborough U
Lathrope Damon (M)	5 8	10 02	Stevenage	28/10/89	Norwich C
Leadbitter Daniel (D)	6 0	11 00	Newcastle	17/10/90	Newcastle U Scholar
Macklin Lloyd (M)	5 9	12 03	Camberley	2/8/91	Swindon T
Mansell Lee (D)	5 10	11 10	Gloucester	28/10/82	Oxford U
McPhee Chris (F)	5 11	11 09	Eastbourne	20/3/83	Brighton & HA
Morris Ian (D)	6 0	11 05	Dublin	27/2/87	Scunthorpe U
Nicholson Kevin (D)	5 8	12 05	Derby	2/10/80	Notts Co
O'Kane Eunan (M)	5 8	13 04	Derry	10/7/90	Coleraine
Oastler Joe (D)	5 10	11 04	Portsmouth	3/7/90	QPR
Olejnik Robert (G)	6 0	15 06	Vienna	26/11/86	Aston Villa
Rice Martin (G)			Exeter	7/3/86	Truro C
Saah Brian (M)	6 3	12 03	Rush Green	16/12/86	Leyton Orient
Stevens Danny (M)	5 5	9 09	Enfield	26/11/86	Luton T
Yeoman Ashley (F)	5 10	12 01	Kingsbridge	25/2/92	Scholar

League Appearances: Atieno, T. 17(26); Bodin, B. 15(2); Ellis, M. 34(1); Halpin, S. (1); Howe, R. 36(3); Jarvis, R. 3(11); Kee, B. 1(3); Lathrope, D. 35(5); Leadbitter, D. (2); MacDonald, A. 1(1); Macklin, L. 1(3); Mansell, L. 45; McPhee, C. 6(20); Morris, I. 33(4); Nicholson, K. 46; O'Kane, E. 45; Oastler, J. 45; Olejnik, R. 46; Robertson, C. 24(1); Rowe-Turner, L. (21); Saah, B. 35; Stevens, D. 38(3); Yeoman, A. (1).

Goals – League (63): Howe 12 (3 pens), Mansell 12, Stevens 8, Atieno 6, Bodin 5, O'Kane 5, Nicholson 4, Ellis 3, Jarvis 2, McPhee 2, Morris 2, Robertson 1, Saah 1.

Carling Cup (1): Mansell 1.

FA Cup (5): Howe 2, Stevens 2, Nicholson 1.
J Paint Trophy (1): Macklin 1.
Play-Offs (1): Atieno 1.
Ground: Plainmoor Ground, Torquay, Devon TQ1 3PS. Telephone: (01803) 328 666.
Capacity: 6,117.
Record Attendance: 21,908 v Huddersfield T, FA Cup 4th rd, 29 January 1955.
Manager: Martin Ling.
Most League Goals: 89, Division 3 (S), 1956–57.
Highest League Scorer in Season: Sammy Collins, 40, Division 3 (S), 1955–56.
Most League Goals in Total Aggregate: Sammy Collins, 204, 1948–58.
Most Capped Player: Tony Bedeau, 4, Grenada.
Most League Appearances: Dennis Lewis, 443, 1947–59.
Colours: All yellow with blue inserts.
Honours: None.

TOTTENHAM HOTSPUR   FA PREMIERSHIP

Player			Birthplace	Date	Signed from
Archer Jordan (G)			Walthamstow	12/4/93	Margate
Assou-Ekotto Benoit (M)	5 10	10 12	Arras	24/3/84	Lens
Bale Gareth (D)	6 0	11 09	Cardiff	16/7/89	Southampton
Bassong Sebastien (D)	6 2	11 07	Paris	9/7/86	Newcastle U
Bentley David (F)	5 10	11 03	Peterborough	27/8/84	Blackburn R
Bostock John (M)	5 10	11 11	Camberwell	13/10/91	Crystal Palace
Button David (G)	6 3	13 00	Stevenage	27/2/89	Scholar
Byrne Nathan (D)	5 10	10 10	St Albans	5/6/92	Scholar
Carroll Tommy (M)			Watford	28/5/92	Scholar
Caulker Steven (D)	6 3	12 00	Feltham	29/12/91	
Ceballos Cristian (M)			Barcelona	3/12/92	Barcelona Youth
Corluka Vedran (D)	6 3	13 03	Zagreb	9/2/86	Manchester C
Cudicini Carlo (G)	6 1	12 08	Milan	6/9/73	Chelsea
Dawkins Simon (F)	5 10	11 01	Edgware	1/12/87	Scholar
Dawson Michael (D)	6 2	12 02	Leyburn	18/11/83	Nottingham F
Defoe Jermain (F)	5 7	10 04	Beckton	7/10/82	Portsmouth
Falque Iago (M)	5 8	11 00	Vigo	4/4/90	Juventus
Fredericks Ryan (M)	5 8	11 10	Potters Bar	10/10/92	Scholar
Friedel Brad (G)	6 3	14 00	Lakewood	18/5/71	Aston Villa
Gallas William (D)	6 0	12 12	Asnieres	17/8/77	Arsenal
Gallifuoco Giancarlo (M)			Sydney	12/1/94	Sutherland Sharks
Giovani (F)	5 8	12 03	Monterrey	11/5/89	Barcelona
Gomes Heurelho (G)	6 3	12 13	Minas Gerais	15/2/81	PSV Eindhoven
Huddlestone Tom (M)	6 2	11 02	Nottingham	28/12/86	Derby Co
Jenas Jermaine (M)	5 11	11 00	Nottingham	18/2/83	Newcastle U
Kaboul Younes (D)	6 2	13 07	Annemasse	4/1/86	Portsmouth
Kane Harry (F)	6 0	10 00	Chingford	28/7/93	Scholar
Khumalo Bongani (D)	6 2	12 13	Swaziland	6/1/87	Supersport U
Kranjcar Niko (M)	6 1	12 13	Zagreb	13/8/84	Portsmouth
Lancaster Cameron (F)	6 0	11 09	Camden	5/11/92	Scholar
Lennon Aaron (M)	5 6	10 03	Leeds	16/4/87	Leeds U
Livermore Jake (M)	5 9	12 08	Enfield	14/11/89	Scholar
Luongo Massimo (F)	5 8	11 10	Sydney	25/9/92	Rushden & D
Mason Ryan (F)	5 9	10 00	Enfield	13/6/91	Scholar
Modric Luka (M)	5 8	10 03	Zadar	9/9/85	Dinamo Zagreb
Naughton Kyle (M)	5 11	11 07	Sheffield	11/11/88	Sheffield U
Nicholson Jake (M)	6 0	11 07	Harrow	19/7/92	Scholar
Obika Jonathan (F)	6 0	12 00	Enfield	12/9/90	Scholar
Parker Scott (M)	5 9	11 08	Lambeth	13/10/80	West Ham U
Parrett Dean (M)	5 10	11 04	Hampstead	16/11/91	Scholar

Name			Birthplace	Date	Previous club
Pienaar Steven (M)	5 10	10 06	Westbury	17/3/82	Everton
Pritchard Alex (M)			Grays	3/5/93	Scholar
Rose Danny (M)	5 8	11 11	Doncaster	2/6/90	Leeds U
Sandro (M)	6 2	11 11	Riachinho	15/3/89	Internacional
Smith Adam (D)	5 8	10 07	Leytonstone	29/4/91	Scholar
Townsend Andros (M)	6 0	12 00	Chingford	16/7/91	Scholar
Van der Vaart Rafael (M)	5 9	11 09	Heemskerk	11/2/83	Real Madrid
Walker Kyle (D)	5 10	11 07	Sheffield	28/5/90	Sheffield U

League Appearances: Adebayor, E. 32(1); Assou-Ekotto, B. 34; Bale, G. 36; Bassong, S. 1(4); Corluka, V. 1(2); Crouch, P. 1; Dawson, M. 6(1); Defoe, J. 11(14); Friedel, B. 38; Gallas, W. 15; Giovani, (7); Huddlestone, T. (2); Kaboul, Y. 33; King, L. 21; Kranjcar, N. 9(3); Lancaster, C. (1); Lennon, A. 19(4); Livermore, J. 7(17); Modric, L. 36; Nelsen, R. (5); Parker, S. 28(1); Pavlyuchenko, R. (5); Pienaar, S. (2); Rose, D. 3(8); Saha, L. 5(5); Sandro, 17(6); Smith, A. (1); Van der Vaart, R. 28(5); Walker, K. 37.

Goals – League (66): Adebayor 17 (3 pens), Defoe 11, Van der Vaart 11 (1 pen), Bale 9, Modric 4, Lennon 3, Saha 3, Assou-Ekotto 2, Walker 2, Kaboul 1, Kranjcar 1, Pavlyuchenko 1, own goal 1.

Carling Cup (0).

FA Cup (11): Defoe 3, Bale 2, Adebayor 1 (pen), Giovani 1, Nelsen 1, Pavlyuchenko 1, Saha 1, Van der Vaart 1.

Europa League (14): Defoe 3, Pavlyuchenko 2, Bale 1, Giovani 1, Kane 1, Lennon 1, Livermore 1, Modric 1 (pen), Pienaar 1, Townsend 1, Van der Vaart 1.

Ground: White Hart Lane, Bill Nicholson Way, 748 High Road, Tottenham, London N17 0AP. Telephone: (0844) 499 5000.

Capacity: 36,534.

Record Attendance: 75,038 v Sunderland, FA Cup 6th rd, 5 March 1938.

Manager: Andre Villas-Boas.

Most League Goals: 115, Division 1, 1960–61.

Highest League Scorer in Season: Jimmy Greaves, 37, Division 1, 1962–63.

Most League Goals in Total Aggregate: Jimmy Greaves, 220, 1961–70.

Most Capped Player: Pat Jennings, 74 (119), Northern Ireland.

Most League Appearances: Steve Perryman, 655, 1969–86.

Colours: White shirts with black and yellow trim, black shorts, white stockings.

Honours – Football League: Division 1 Champions – 1950–51, 1960–61. Division 2 Champions – 1919–20, 1949–50. **FA Cup:** Winners – 1901 (as non-League club), 1921, 1961, 1962, 1967, 1981, 1982, 1991. **Football League Cup:** Winners – 1970–71, 1972–73, 1998–99, 2007–08. **European Competitions: European Cup-Winners' Cup:** Winners – 1962–63. **UEFA Cup:** Winners – 1971–72, 1983–84.

TRANMERE ROVERS

FL CHAMPIONSHIP 1

Name			Birthplace	Date	Previous club
Akins Lucas (F)	5 10	11 07	Huddersfield	25/2/89	Hamilton A
Bakayogo Zoumana (D)	5 9	10 08	Paris	11/8/86	Millwall
Buchanan David (M)	5 7	11 03	Rochdale	6/5/86	Hamilton A
Goodison Ian (D)	6 1	13 04	St James, Jamaica	21/11/72	Hull C
Holmes Danny (D)	6 0	11 13	Birkenhead	6/1/89	The New Saints
Kay Michael (D)	6 0	11 05	Consett	12/9/89	Sunderland
Kirby Jake (M)	5 11	12 04	Liverpool	9/5/94	Scholar
McChrystal Mark (D)	6 1	13 07	Derry	26/6/84	Lisburn Distillery
McGurk Adam (F)	5 9	12 13	Larne	24/1/89	Aston Villa
Power Max (M)	5 11	11 13	Bebington	27/7/93	Scholar
Robinson Andy (M)	5 8	11 04	Birkenhead	3/11/79	Leeds U
Stockton Cole (F)	6 1	11 11	Huyton	13/3/94	Scholar
Taylor Ash (D)	6 0	12 02	Bromborough	2/9/90	Scholar
Welsh John (M)	5 7	12 02	Liverpool	10/1/84	Hull C
Williams Owain fon (G)	6 1	12 09	Penygroes	17/3/87	Rochdale

League Appearances: Akins, L. 36(8); Bakayogo, Z. 8(18); Baxter, J. 14; Brunt, R. 11(4); Buchanan, D. 41; Cassidy, J. 7(3); Coughlin, A. 1(1); Devaney, M. 16(4); Donaldson, R. 1; Elford-Alliyu, L. 2(2); Goodison, I. 41(2); Holmes, D. 25(1); Kay, M. 4(2); Kirby, J. (1); Labadie, J. 9(18); McChrystal, M. 17(1); McGurk, A. 25(6); Power, M. 2(2); Rachubka, P. 10; Raven, D. 17; Robinson, A. 21(4); Showunmi, E. 21(6); Stockton, C. (1); Taylor, A. 36(1); Tiryaki, M. 16(14); Wallace, J. 18; Weir, R. 29(10); Welsh, J. 43(1); Williams, O. 35.
Goals – League (49): Akins 5, Cassidy 5, Labadie 5 (1 pen), McGurk 4, Robinson 4, Baxter 3, Showunmi 3, Tiryaki 3, Weir 3, Welsh 3, Devaney 2, Taylor 2, Wallace 2, Brunt 1, Buchanan 1, Goodison 1, McChrystal 1, own goal 1.
Carling Cup (0).
FA Cup (0).
J Paint Trophy (5): Taylor 2, McGurk 1, Showunmi 1, Tiryaki 1.
Ground: Prenton Park, Prenton Road West, Birkenhead, Merseyside CH42 9PY. Telephone: (0871) 221 2001.
Capacity: 16,587.
Record Attendance: 24,424 v Stoke C, FA Cup 4th rd, 5 February 1972.
Manager: Ronnie Moore.
Most League Goals: 111, Division 3 (N), 1930–31.
Highest League Scorer in Season: Bunny Bell, 35, Division 3 (N), 1933–34.
Most League Goals in Total Aggregate: Ian Muir, 142, 1985–95.
Most Capped Player: John Aldridge, 30 (69), Republic of Ireland.
Most League Appearances: Harold Bell, 595, 1946–64 (incl. League record 401 consecutive appearances).
Colours: White shirts, white shorts, blue and white hooped stockings.
Honours – Football League: Division 3 (N) Champions – 1937–38. **Welsh Cup:** Winners – 1935. **Leyland Daf Cup:** Winners – 1990.

WALSALL

FL CHAMPIONSHIP 1

Beevers Lee (D)	6 2	11 07	Doncaster	4/12/83	Colchester U
Bowerman George (F)	5 10	10 07	Sedgley	6/11/91	Scholar
Butler Andy (D)	6 0	13 00	Doncaster	4/11/83	Huddersfield T
Chambers Adam (D)	5 10	11 12	Sandwell	20/11/80	Leyton Orient
Grigg Will (M)	5 11	11 00	Solihull	3/7/91	Scholar
Grof David (G)	6 3	14 02	Budapest	17/4/89	Notts Co
Jones Jake (M)			Solihull	6/4/93	Scholar
Paterson Jamie (F)	5 9	10 07	Coventry	20/12/91	Scholar
Sadler Matthew (D)	5 11	11 08	Birmingham	26/2/85	Watford
Smith Manny (D)	6 2	12 02	Birmingham	8/11/88	Scholar
Westlake Darryl (D)	5 9	11 00	Sutton Coldfield	1/3/91	Scholar

League Appearances: Beevers, L. 28(7); Bowerman, G. 3(19); Butler, A. 42; Chambers, A. 26(3); Cuvelier, F. 17(1); Gnakpa, C. 8(12); Grigg, W. 17(12); Grof, D. 22(1); Halliday, A. 2(5); Hurst, K. 30(4); Jarvis, R. 9(10); Lancashire, O. 17(3); Ledesma, E. 9(1); Macken, J. 33(4); Mantom, S. 13; Martin, D. 4; Nicholls, A. 32(13); Paterson, J. 24(10); Peterlin, A. 20(6); Sadler, M. 46; Smith, M. 31(2); Taundry, R. 31(4); Walker, J. 24; Westlake, D. 14(3); Wilson, M. 4.
Goals – League (51): Macken 7 (2 pens), Nicholls 7 (1 pen), Butler 5, Cuvelier 4, Grigg 4, Ledesma 4, Bowerman 3, Mantom 3, Paterson 3, Chambers 2, Hurst 2, Jarvis 2 (1 pen), Gnakpa 1, Lancashire 1, Sadler 1, Smith 1, own goal 1.
Carling Cup (0).
FA Cup (5): Bowerman 1, Gnakpa 1, Macken 1, Nicholls 1, Wilson 1.
J Paint Trophy (3): Hurst 1, Jarvis 1, Taundry 1.
Ground: Banks's Stadium, Bescot Crescent, Walsall WS1 4SA. Telephone: (01922) 622 791.
Capacity: 11,300.

Record Attendance: 25,453 v Newcastle U, Division 2, 29 August 1961 (at Fellows Park); 11,049 v Rotherham U, Division 1, 9 May 2004 (at Bescot Stadium).
Manager: Dean Smith.
Most League Goals: 102, Division 4, 1959–60.
Highest League Scorer in Season: Gilbert Alsop, 40, Division 3 (N), 1933–34 and 1934–35.
Most League Goals in Total Aggregate: Tony Richards, 184, 1954–63; Colin Taylor, 184, 1958–63, 1964–68, 1969–73.
Most Capped Player: Mick Kearns, 15 (18), Republic of Ireland.
Most League Appearances: Colin Harrison, 467, 1964–82.
Colours: Red shirts with black trim, red shorts, red stockings with black tops.
Honours – Football League: FL 2 Champions – 2006–07. Division 4 Champions – 1959–60.

WATFORD   FL CHAMPIONSHIP

Player	Ht	Wt	Birthplace	Birthdate	Club/Source
Assombalonga Britt (F)	5 9	11 13	Kinshasa	6/12/92	Youth
Bennett Dale (D)	5 11	12 02	Enfield	6/1/90	Scholar
Bond Jonathan (G)	6 3	13 03	Hemel Hempstead	19/5/93	Scholar
Bonham Jack (G)			Stevenage	14/9/93	Scholar
Buaben Prince (M)	6 0	11 09	Akosombo	23/4/88	Dundee U
Connolly Kyle (D)			Watford	18/7/94	Youth
Deeney Troy (F)	5 11	12 02	Solihull	29/6/88	Walsall
Dickinson Carl (D)	6 1	12 04	Swadlincote	31/3/87	Stoke C
Doyley Lloyd (D)	5 10	12 13	Whitechapel	1/12/82	Scholar
Eustace John (M)	5 11	11 12	Solihull	3/11/79	Stoke C
Forsyth Craig (M)	6 0	12 00	Carnoustie	24/2/89	Dundee
Garner Joe (F)	5 10	11 02	Blackburn	12/4/88	Nottingham F
Hoban Tommie (D)	6 2	11 13	Walthamstow	24/1/94	Scholar
Hodson Lee (D)	5 11	11 02	Boreham Wood	2/10/91	Scholar
Hogg Jonathan (M)	5 7	10 05	Middlesbrough	6/12/88	Aston Villa
Iwelumo Chris (F)	6 3	15 03	Coatbridge	1/8/78	Burnley
James Tom (D)			Leamington	19/11/88	Stratford T
Jenkins Ross (M)	5 11	12 06	Watford	9/11/90	Scholar
Loach Scott (G)	6 1	13 01	Nottingham	27/5/88	Lincoln C Scholar
Mariappa Adrian (D)	5 10	11 12	Harrow	3/10/86	Scholar
Massey Gavin (F)	5 11	11 06	Watford	14/10/92	Scholar
McGinn Stephen (M)	5 9	10 01	Glasgow	2/12/88	St Mirren
Mensah Bernard (F)			Hounslow	29/12/94	Scholar
Mingoia Piero (M)	5 6	10 12	Enfield	20/10/91	Scholar
Mirfin David (D)	6 3	13 00	Sheffield	18/4/85	Scunthorpe U
Murray Sean (M)	5 9	10 10	Abbots Langley	11/10/93	Scholar
Nosworthy Nyron (D)	6 0	12 08	Brixton	11/10/80	Sunderland
Taylor Martin (D)	6 4	15 02	Ashington	9/11/79	Birmingham C
Thompson Adam (D)	6 2	12 10	Harlow	28/9/92	Scholar
Whichelow Matt (M)	5 7	11 10	Islington	28/9/91	Scholar
Yeates Mark (F)	5 8	13 03	Dublin	11/1/85	Sheffield U

League Appearances: Assombalonga, B. 2(2); Beattie, C. 1(3); Bennett, D. 1(1); Bond, J. (1); Buaben, P. 21(9); Deeney, T. 28(15); Dickinson, C. 38(1); Doyley, L. 33; Eustace, J. 34(5); Forsyth, C. 15(5); Garner, J. 14(8); Gilmartin, R. 2; Hodson, L. 20; Hogg, J. 40; Iwelumo, C. 21(18); Jenkins, R. 4(5); Kacaniklic, A. 11(1); Kightly, M. 11(1); Kuszczak, T. 13; Loach, S. 31; Mariappa, A. 37(2); Massey, G. (3); Mirfin, D. 3(1); Murray, S. 17(1); Nosworthy, N. 32; Sordell, M. 25(1); Taylor, M. 20(2); Trotta, M. 1; Walker, J. (1); Weimann, A. 3; Whichelow, M. (2); Yeates, M. 28(5).

Goals – League (56): Deeney 11 (1 pen), Sordell 8 (2 pens), Murray 7, Eustace 4, Iwelumo 4, Forsyth 3, Kightly 3, Yeates 3, Dickinson 2, Nosworthy 2, Beattie 1, Buaben 1, Garner 1, Kacaniklic 1, Mariappa 1, Taylor 1, own goals 3.
Carling Cup (1): Sordell 1.
FA Cup (4): Forsyth 2, Deeney 1, Sordell 1.
Ground: Vicarage Road Stadium, Vicarage Road, Watford, Herts WD18 0ER. Telephone: (0844) 856 1881.
Capacity: 19,920.
Record Attendance: 34,099 v Manchester U, FA Cup 4th rd (replay), 3 February 1969.
Manager: Gianfranco Zola.
Most League Goals: 92, Division 4, 1959–60.
Highest Scorer in Season: Cliff Holton, 42, Division 4, 1959–60.
Most League Goals in Total Aggregate: Luther Blissett, 148, 1976–83, 1984–88, 1991–92.
Most Capped Players: John Barnes, 31 (79), England; Kenny Jackett, 31, Wales.
Most League Appearances: Luther Blissett, 415, 1976–83, 1984–88, 1991–92.
Colours: Yellow shirts with red and black trim, black shorts, yellow stockings.
Honours – Football League: Division 2 Champions – 1997–98. Division 3 Champions – 1968–69. Division 4 Champions – 1977–78.

WEST BROMWICH ALBION   FA PREMIERSHIP

Name			Birthplace	Date	From
Allan Scott (M)	5 9	11 00	Glasgow	28/11/91	Dundee U
Berahino Saido (F)	5 10	11 13	Burundi	4/8/93	Scholar
Brown Kayleden (M)	6 2	12 08	Derry	15/4/92	Scholar
Brunt Chris (M)	6 1	13 04	Belfast	14/12/84	Sheffield W
Cox Simon (F)	5 10	10 12	Reading	28/4/87	Swindon T
Daniels Donervorn (D)			Montserrat	24/11/93	Scholar
Daniels Luke (G)	6 1	12 10	Bolton	5/1/88	Manchester U Scholar
Dawson Craig (D)	6 0	12 04	Rochdale	6/5/90	Rochdale
Dorrans Graham (M)	5 9	11 07	Glasgow	5/5/87	Livingston
Fortune Marc-Antoine (F)	6 0	11 13	Cayenne	2/7/81	Celtic
Gayle Cameron (D)	5 11	11 00	Birmingham	22/11/92	Scholar
Gera Zoltan (M)	6 0	11 11	Pecs	22/4/79	Fulham
Hurst James (D)	5 8	11 11	Sutton Coldfield	31/1/92	Portsmouth
Jara Gonzalo (D)	5 10	12 02	Chile	29/8/85	Colo Colo
Jones Billy (M)	5 11	13 00	Shrewsbury	24/3/87	Preston NE
Long Shane (F)	5 10	11 02	Co. Tipperary	22/1/87	Reading
Mantom Sam (M)	5 9	11 00	Stourbridge	20/2/92	Scholar
McAuley Gareth (D)	6 3	13 00	Larne	5/12/79	Ipswich T
Morrison James (M)	5 10	10 06	Darlington	25/5/86	Middlesbrough
Mulumbu Youssef (M)	5 9	10 03	Kinshasa	25/1/87	Paris St Germain
Myhill Boaz (G)	6 3	14 06	California	9/11/82	Hull C
Nabi Adil (F)	5 9	10 10	Birmingham	28/2/94	Scholar
O'Neil Liam (D)			Cambridge	31/7/93	Histon
Odemwingie Peter (F)	6 0	11 09	Tashkent	15/7/81	Lokomotiv Moscow
Olsson Jonas (D)	6 4	12 08	Landskrona	10/3/83	NEC Nijmegen
Reid Steven (M)	6 0	12 06	Kingston	10/3/81	Blackburn R
Ridgewell Liam (D)	5 10	10 03	Bexley	21/7/84	Birmingham C
Roofe Kemar (M)			Walsall	6/1/93	Scholar
Sawyers Romaine (M)	5 9	11 00	Birmingham	2/11/91	Scholar
Tamas Gabriel (D)	6 2	12 02	Brasov	9/11/83	Dinamo Bucharest
Thomas Jerome (M)	5 9	11 09	Wembley	23/3/83	Portsmouth
Thorne George (M)	6 2	13 01	Chatham	4/1/93	Scholar
Wood Chris (F)	6 3	12 10	Auckland	7/12/91	

League Appearances: Andrews, K. 8(6); Brunt, C. 25(4); Cox, S. 7(11); Dawson, C. 6(2); Dorrans, G. 16(15); Fortune, M. 12(5); Foster, B. 37; Fulop, M. 1; Gera, Z. 3; Jara, G. 1(3); Jones, B. 17(1); Long, S. 24(8); McAuley, G. 32; Morrison, J. 23(7); Mulumbu, Y. 34(1); Odemwingie, P. 25(5); Olsson, J. 33; Reid, S. 21(1); Ridgewell, L. 13; Scharner, P. 18(11); Shorey, N. 22(3); Tamas, G. 7(1); Tchoyi, S. 6(12); Thomas, J. 26(3); Thorne, G. 1(2).

Goals – League (45): Odemwingie 10, Long 8 (1 pen), Morrison 5, Dorrans 3, Scharner 3, Andrews 2, Brunt 2, Fortune 2, McAuley 2, Olsson 2, Mulumbu 1, Reid 1, Ridgewell 1, Tchoyi 1, Thomas 1, own goal 1.

Carling Cup (5): Fortune 2, Brunt 1 (pen), Cox 1, Thomas 1.

FA Cup (5): Cox 3, Fortune 1, Odemwingie 1.

Ground: The Hawthorns, West Bromwich, West Midlands B71 4LF. Telephone: (0871) 271 1100.

Capacity: 28,003.

Record Attendance: 64,815 v Arsenal, FA Cup 6th rd, 6 March 1937.

Head Coach: Steve Clarke.

Most League Goals: 105, Division 2, 1929–30.

Highest League Scorer in Season: William 'Ginger' Richardson, 39, Division 1, 1935–36.

Most League Goals in Total Aggregate: Tony Brown, 218, 1963–79.

Most Capped Player: Stuart Williams, 33 (43), Wales.

Most League Appearances: Tony Brown, 574, 1963–80.

Colours: Navy blue and white striped shirts, white shorts, white stockings.

Honours – Football League: Division 1 Champions – 1919–20. FL C Champions – 2007–08. Division 2 Champions – 1901–02, 1910–11. **FA Cup:** Winners – 1888, 1892, 1931, 1954, 1968. **Football League Cup:** Winners – 1965–66.

WEST HAM UNITED   FA PREMIERSHIP

Baldock Sam (F)	5 7	10 07	Buckingham	15/3/89	Milton Keynes D
Barrera Pablo (M)	5 9	10 03	Mexico City	21/6/87	UNAM
Cole Carlton (F)	6 3	14 02	Croydon	12/11/83	Chelsea
Collison Jack (M)	6 0	13 10	Watford	2/10/88	Scholar
Demel Guy (D)	6 2	13 12	Paris	13/6/81	Hamburg
Driver Callum (D)	5 8	11 11	Sidcup	23/10/92	Aberdeen
Fanimo Matthias (M)			Lambeth	28/1/94	Scholar
Green Rob (G)	6 3	14 09	Chertsey	18/1/80	Norwich C
Hall Robert (F)	6 2	10 05	Aylesbury	20/10/93	Academy
			Co. Durham	16/12/94	Scholar
Lletget Sebastian (M)	5 10	10 11	San Francisco	3/9/92	
Maynard Nicky (F)	5 11	11 00	Winsford	11/12/86	Bristol C
McCallum Paul (F)	6 3	12 00	Streatham	28/7/93	Dulwich Hamlet
Moncur George (M)	5 9	10 00	Swindon	18/8/93	Scholar
Montano Cristian (F)	5 11	12 00	Cali	11/12/91	Scholar
Morrison Ravel (M)	5 9	11 02	Wythenshawe	2/2/93	Manchester U
Noble Mark (M)	5 11	12 01	West Ham	8/5/87	Scholar
Nolan Kevin (M)	6 0	14 00	Liverpool	24/6/82	Newcastle U
O'Brien Joey (M)	5 11	10 13	Dublin	17/2/86	Bolton W
O'Neil Gary (M)	5 10	11 00	Beckenham	18/5/83	Middlesbrough
Piquionne Frederic (F)	6 2	12 00	New Caledonia	8/12/78	Portsmouth
Potts Danny (D)	5 8	11 00	Barking	13/4/94	Scholar
Reid Winston (D)	6 3	13 10	North Shore	3/7/88	Midtjylland
Ruddock Pelly (M)			Hendon		Boreham Wood
Sears Freddie (F)	5 8	10 01	Hornchurch	27/11/89	Scholar
Spence Jordan (D)	6 2	12 07	Woodford	24/5/90	Scholar
Stech Marek (G)	6 3	14 00	Prague	28/1/90	Scholar
Taylor Matthew (D)	5 11	12 03	Oxford	27/11/81	Bolton W
Tombides Dylan (F)			Perth	8/3/94	Scholar

Tomkins James (D)	6 3	11 10	Basildon	29/3/89	Scholar
Turgott Blair (M)			Bromley	22/5/94	Scholar
Vaz Te Ricardo (F)	6 2	12 07	Lisbon	1/10/86	Barnsley
Vose Dominic (M)			Lambeth	23/11/93	Academy
Wearen Eoin Patrick (D)			Dublin	2/10/92	Scholar

League Appearances: Almunia, M. 4; Baldock, S. 10(13); Barrera, P. (1); Bentley, D. 2(3); Carew, J. 7(12); Cole, C. 28(12); Collins, D. 4(7); Collison, J. 26(5); Demel, G. 7; Diop, P. 14(2); Faubert, J. 28(6); Faye, A. 25(4); Green, R. 42; Hall, R. (3); Ilunga, H. 4; Lansbury, H. 13(9); Maynard, N. 9(5); McCartney, G. 36(2); Morrison, R. (1); Noble, M. 43(2); Nolan, K. 42; Nouble, F. 1(2); O'Brien, J. 27(5); O'Neil, G. 9(7); Parker, S. 4; Piquionne, F. 8(12); Potts, D. 3; Reid, W. 27(1); Sears, F. 2(8); Stanislas, J. (1); Taylor, M. 26(2); Tomkins, J. 42(2); Vaz Te, R. 13(2).
Goals – League (81): Cole 14, Nolan 12, Vaz Te 10 (1 pen), Noble 8 (7 pens), Baldock 5, Collison 4, Tomkins 4, Reid 3, Carew 2, Maynard 2, O'Neil 2, Piquionne 2, Collins 1, Diop 1, Faubert 1, Lansbury 1, McCartney 1, Nouble 1, O'Brien 1, Parker 1, Taylor 1, own goals 4.
Carling Cup (1): Stanislas 1.
FA Cup (0).
Play-Offs (7): Collison 2, Vaz Te 2, Cole 1, Maynard 1, Nolan 1.
Ground: The Boleyn Ground, Upton Park, Green Street, London E13 9AZ. Telephone: (0871) 222 2700.
Capacity: 35,303.
Record Attendance: 42,322 v Tottenham H, Division 1, 17 October 1970.
Manager: Sam Allardyce.
Most League Goals: 101, Division 2, 1957–58.
Highest League Scorer in Season: Vic Watson, 42, Division 1, 1929–30.
Most League Goals in Total Aggregate: Vic Watson, 298, 1920–35.
Most Capped Player: Bobby Moore, 108, England.
Most League Appearances: Billy Bonds, 663, 1967–88.
Colours: Claret shirts with blue trim, white shorts, claret stockings.
Honours – Football League: Division 2 Champions – 1957–58, 1980–81. **FA Cup:** Winners – 1964, 1975, 1980. **European Competitions:** European Cup-Winners' Cup: Winners – 1964–65. **Intertoto Cup:** Winners – 1999.

WIGAN ATHLETIC   FA PREMIERSHIP

Al-Habsi Ali (G)	6 4	12 06	Oman	30/12/81	Bolton W
Alcaraz Antolin (D)	6 0	12 08	Roque Gonzalez	30/7/82	Club Brugge
Beausejour Jean (M)	5 10	12 08	Santiago	1/6/84	Birmingham C
Bingham Rakish (F)			Newham	25/10/93	Scholar
Boothman Steven (M)			Wigan	18/9/92	Scholar
Boselli Mauro (F)	6 0	11 11	Buenos Aires	22/5/85	Estudiantes
Boyce Emmerson (D)	6 0	12 03	Aylesbury	24/9/79	Crystal Palace
Buxton Adam (D)	6 1	12 10	Liverpool	12/5/92	Scholar
Caldwell Gary (D)	5 11	11 10	Stirling	12/4/82	Celtic
Chow Tim (M)			Wigan	18/1/94	Scholar
Crusat Albert (M)	5 5	10 03	Barcelona	13/5/82	Almeria
Cruyff Jessua (D)			Amsterdam	11/3/93	Barcelona Youth
Dawson Adam (M)			Bury	5/10/92	Bury Scholar
Di Santo Franco (F)	6 4	13 01	Mendoza	7/4/89	Chelsea
Dicko Nouha (M)	5 8	11 00	Paris	14/5/92	Strasbourg B
Figueroa Maynor (D)	5 11	12 02	Jutiapa	2/5/83	Victoria La Ceiba
Golobart Roman (D)	6 4	13 10	Barcelona	21/3/92	Espanyol
Gomez Jordi (M)	5 10	11 09	Barcelona	24/5/85	Swansea C
Jones David (M)	5 11	10 10	Southport	4/11/84	Wolverhampton W
Kiernan Rob (D)	6 1	11 13	Rickmansworth	13/1/91	Watford

Langley Josh (M)			Warrington	13/8/92	Scholar
Maloney Shaun (M)	5 7	10 01	Miri	24/1/83	Celtic
McArthur James (M)	5 6	9 13	Glasgow	7/10/87	Hamilton A
McCarthy James (M)	5 11	11 05	Glasgow	12/11/90	Hamilton A
McCormack Jamie (D)			Edinburgh	1/2/92	Hearts Youth
McManaman Callum (F)	5 9	11 02	Huyton	25/4/91	Scholar
Morris Callum (M)			Birkenhead	12/9/92	Scholar
Moses Victor (M)	5 10	11 07	Lagos	12/12/90	Crystal Palace
Mustoe Jordan (M)	5 11	11 11	Birkenhead	28/1/91	Scholar
Nicholls Lee (G)			Huyton	5/10/92	Scholar
Piscu (Adrian Lopez) (D)	6 0	12 00	As Pontes	25/2/87	La Coruna
Redmond Daniel (D)			Liverpool	2/3/91	Scholar
Sammon Conor (F)	5 10	11 11	Dublin	13/4/87	Kilmarnock
Stam Ronnie (M)	5 9	9 11	Breda	18/6/84	Twente
Watson Ben (M)	5 10	10 11	Camberwell	9/7/85	Crystal Palace
Watson Ryan (M)			Crewe	7/7/93	Scholar

League Appearances: Al-Habsi, A. 38; Alcaraz, A. 25; Beausejour, J. 16; Boyce, E. 26; Caldwell, G. 36; Crusat, A. 4(11); Di Santo, F. 24(8); Diame, M. 18(8); Figueroa, M. 37(1); Gohouri, S. 8(2); Gomez, J. 24(4); Jones, D. 13(3); Maloney, S. 8(5); McArthur, J. 18(13); McCarthy, J. 33; McManaman, C. (2); Moses, V. 36(2); Piscu, 5; Rodallega, H. 11(12); Sammon, C. 8(17); Stam, R. 13(7); Van Aanholt, P. 3; Watson, B. 14(7).

Goals – League (42): Di Santo 7, Moses 6, Gomez 5 (2 pens), Boyce 3, Caldwell 3, Diame 3, Maloney 3 (1 pen), McArthur 3, Watson 3 (2 pens), Alcaraz 2, Rodallega 2, Crusat 1, own goal 1.

Carling Cup (1): Watson 1.

FA Cup (1): McManaman 1.

Ground: The DW Stadium, Robin Park Complex, Newtown, Wigan, Lancashire WN5 0UZ. Telephone: (01942) 774 000.

Capacity: 25,138.

Record Attendance: 27,526 v Hereford U, 12 December 1953 (at Springfield Park); 25,133 v Manchester U, FA Premier League, 11 May 2008 (at DW Stadium).

Manager: Roberto Martinez.

Most League Goals: 84, Division 3, 1996–97.

Highest League Scorer in Season: Graeme Jones, 31, Division 3, 1996–97.

Most League Goals in Total Aggregate: Andy Liddell, 70, 1998–2004.

Most Capped Players: Kevin Kilbane, 22 (110), Republic of Ireland; Henri Camara, 22 (99), Senegal.

Most League Appearances: Kevin Langley, 317, 1981–86, 1990–94.

Colours: Blue and white striped shirts with blue sleeves, blue shorts, white stockings.

Honours – Football League: Division 2 Champions – 2002–03. Division 3 Champions – 1996–97. **Freight Rover Trophy:** Winners – 1984–85. **Auto Windscreens Shield:** Winners – 1998–99.

WOLVERHAMPTON WANDERERS   FL CHAMPIONSHIP

Batth Danny (D)	6 3	13 05	Brierley Hill	21/9/90	Scholar
Berra Christophe (D)	6 1	12 10	Edinburgh	31/1/85	Hearts
Cassidy Jake (F)	5 10	11 02	Glan Conwy	9/2/93	Airbus UK
Davis David (M)	5 8	12 03	Smethwick	20/2/91	Scholar
De Vries Dorus (G)	6 1	12 08	Bewerwijk	29/12/80	Swansea C
Doherty Matthew (M)			Dublin	17/1/92	Bohemians
Doyle Kevin (F)	5 11	12 06	Adamstown	18/9/83	Reading
Ebanks-Blake Sylvan (F)	5 10	13 05	Cambridge	29/3/86	Plymouth Arg
Ebanks-Landell Ethan (M)	5 6	11 02	Oldbury	16/12/92	Scholar
Edwards Dave (M)	5 11	11 04	Shrewsbury	3/2/86	Luton T
Elokobi George (D)	5 10	13 02	Cameroon	31/1/86	Colchester U

Fletcher Steven (F)	6 1	12 00	Shrewsbury	26/3/87	Burnley
Foley Kevin (D)	5 9	11 11	Luton	1/11/84	Luton T
Forde Anthony (M)			Limerick	16/11/93	Scholar
Gorman Johnny (M)	5 9	11 00	Sheffield	26/10/92	
Griffiths Leigh (F)	5 07	10 01	Leith	20/8/90	Dundee
Guedioura Adiene (M)	6 1	12 08	La Roche-sur-Yon	12/11/85	Charleroi
Hammill Adam (M)	5 11	11 07	Liverpool	25/1/88	Barnsley
Hennessey Wayne (G)	6 0	11 06	Anglesey	24/1/87	Scholar
Henry Karl (M)	6 0	12 00	Wolverhampton	26/11/82	Stoke C
Hunt Steve (M)	5 9	10 10	Port Laoise	1/8/80	Hull C
Ihiekwe Michael (D)			Liverpool	20/11/92	Scholar
Ikeme Carl (G)	6 2	13 09	Sutton Coldfield	8/6/86	Scholar
Ismail Zeli (M)			Serbia	12/12/93	Scholar
Jarvis Matthew (M)	5 8	11 07	Middlesbrough	22/5/86	Gillingham
Johnson Roger (D)	6 3	11 00	Ashford (Middlesex)	28/4/83	Birmingham C
Jonsson Eggert (D)	6 2	11 05	Reykjavik	18/8/88	Hearts
Kightly Michael (F)	5 10	10 10	Basildon	24/1/86	Southend U
Kostrna Kristian (D)			Trnava	15/12/93	Scholar
McAlinden Liam (F)			Cannock	26/9/93	Scholar
McCarey Aaron (G)			Monaghan	14/1/92	Monaghan U
Mendez-Laing Nathaniel (M)		5 10 11 12		Birmingham 15/4/92	Scholar
Milijas Nenad (M)	6 2	13 09	Belgrade	30/4/83	Red Star Belgrade
Moli David (F)			Kinshasa	30/11/94	Liverpool Scholar
Mouyokolo Steven (D)	6 3	13 08	Melun	24/1/87	Hull C
O'Hara Jamie (M)	5 11	12 04	Dartford	25/9/86	Tottenham H
Price Jack (M)			Shrewsbury	19/12/92	Scholar
Reckord Jamie (D)	5 10	11 11	Wolverhampton	9/3/92	Scholar
Stearman Richard (D)	6 2	10 08	Wolverhampton	19/8/87	Leicester C
Vokes Sam (F)	6 1	13 10	Lymington	21/10/89	Bournemouth
Ward Stephen (D)	5 11	12 02	Dublin	20/8/85	Bohemians
Winnall Sam (F)	5 9	11 04	Wolverhampton	19/1/91	Scholar
Zubar Ronald (D)	6 1	12 08	Guadeloupe	20/9/85	Marseille

League Appearances: Bassong, S. 9; Berra, C. 29(3); Craddock, J. 1; Davis, D. 6(1); De Vries, D. 4; Doherty, M. (1); Doyle, K. 26(7); Ebanks-Blake, S. 8(15); Edwards, D. 24(2); Elokobi, G. 3(6); Fletcher, S. 26(6); Foley, K. 11(5); Forde, A. 3(3); Frimpong, E. 5; Gorman, J. (1); Guedioura, A. 2(8); Hammill, A. 3(6); Hennessey, W. 34; Henry, K. 30(1); Hunt, S. 16(8); Ikeme, C. (1); Jarvis, M. 31(6); Johnson, R. 26(1); Jonsson, E. 2(1); Kightly, M. 14(4); Maierhofer, S. (1); Milijas, N. 6(14); O'Hara, J. 19; Stearman, R. 28(2); Vokes, S. (4); Ward, S. 38; Zubar, R. 14(1).

Goals – League (40): Fletcher 12, Jarvis 8, Doyle 4, Edwards 3, Hunt 3 (3 pens), Kightly 3, Ward 3, O'Hara 2, Ebanks-Blake 1, Zubar 1.

Carling Cup (11): Ebanks-Blake 2, Milijas 2, Edwards 1, Elokobi 1, Guedioura 1, Hammill 1, O'Hara 1, Spray 1, Vokes 1.

FA Cup (0).

Ground: Molineux Stadium, Waterloo Road, Wolverhampton WV1 4QR. Telephone: (0871) 222 2220.

Capacity: 28,565.

Record Attendance: 61,315 v Liverpool, FA Cup 5th rd, 11 February 1939.

Manager: Stale Solbakken.

Most League Goals: 115, Division 2, 1931–32.

Highest League Scorer in Season: Dennis Westcott, 38, Division 1, 1946–47.

Most League Goals in Total Aggregate: Steve Bull, 250, 1986–99.

Most Capped Player: Billy Wright, 105, England (70 consecutive).

Most League Appearances: Derek Parkin, 501, 1967–82.

Colours: Gold shirts with black trim, black shorts, gold stockings.

Honours – Football League: Championship Winners – 2008–09. Division 1 Champions – 1953–54, 1957–58, 1958–59. Division 2 Champions – 1931–32, 1976–77. Division 3 (N) Champions – 1923–24. Division 3 Champions – 1988–89. Division 4 Champions – 1987–88. **FA Cup:** Winners – 1893, 1908, 1949, 1960. **Football League Cup:** Winners – 1973–74, 1979–80. **Texaco Cup:** Winners – 1971. **Sherpa Van Trophy:** Winners – 1988.

WYCOMBE WANDERERS   FL CHAMPIONSHIP 2

Ainsworth Gareth (M)	5 10	12 05	Blackburn	10/5/73	QPR
Basey Grant (D)	6 2	13 12	Bromley	30/11/88	Barnet
Beavon Stuart (F)	5 7	10 10	Reading	5/5/84	Weymouth
Bloomfield Matt (M)	5 9	11 00	Felixstowe	8/2/84	Ipswich T
Bull Nikki (G)	6 2	12 08	Hastings	2/10/81	Brentford
Dunne Charles (F)	5 9	11 09	Lambeth	13/2/93	Scholar
Foster Danny (D)	5 10	12 10	Enfield	23/9/84	Brentford
Grant Joel (F)	6 0	12 01	Acton	26/8/87	Crewe Alex
Johnson Leon (D)	6 1	13 05	Shoreditch	10/5/81	Gillingham
Kewley-Graham Jesse (M)	5 10	11 11	Hounslow	15/6/93	Scholar
Lewis Stuart (M)	5 10	11 06	Welwyn	15/10/87	Dagenham & R
McClure Matt (F)	5 10	11 00	Slough	17/11/91	Scholar
McCoy Marvin (D)	5 11	11 00	Walthamstow	2/10/88	Hereford U
Rendell Scott (F)	6 1	13 00	Ashford (Middlesex)	21/10/86	Peterborough U
Scowen Josh (M)			Cheshunt	28/3/93	Scholar
Stewart Anthony (D)	5 10	12 05	Brixton	18/9/92	Scholar
Winfield Dave (D)	6 3	13 08	Aldershot	24/3/88	Aldershot T

League Appearances: Ainsworth, G. 16(16); Basey, G. 29(3); Beavon, S. 40(3); Benyon, E. 2(7); Betsy, K. 1(2); Bignall, N. (1); Bloomfield, M. 24(7); Bull, N. 46; Doherty, G. 13; Donnelly, S. 16(2); Dunne, C. (3); Eastmond, C. 14; Foster, D. 29; Grant, J. 22(8); Hackett, C. 6(2); Halls, J. 5(2); Harding, B. 3(4); Harper, J. 5; Harris, K. 10(7); Hayes, P. 6; Ibe, J. 2(5); Johnson, L. 24(3); Kewley-Graham, J. (1); Laing, L. 10(1); Lewis, S. 38(3); McClure, M. 3(9); McCoy, M. 24(4); McNamee, A. 11(4); Rendell, S. 2(4); Rowlands, M. 8(2); Sandell, A. 11; Stewart, A. 4; Strevens, B. 29(7); Trotta, M. 8; Tunnicliffe, J. 16(1); Whichelow, M. 4; Winfield, D. 25.

Goals – League (65): Beavon 21, Trotta 8, Hayes 6, Donnelly 4 (2 pens), Grant 4, Strevens 4, Ainsworth 2, Basey 2 (2 pens), Bloomfield 2, McNamee 2, Winfield 2, Doherty 1, Ibe 1, Lewis 1, McClure 1, Rendell 1 (1 pen), Tunnicliffe 1, Whichelow 1, own goal 1.

Carling Cup (4): Beavon 1, Benyon 1 (pen), Donnelly 1, Grant 1.

FA Cup (0).

J Paint Trophy (4): Beavon 3, Betsy 1.

Ground: Adams Park, Hillbottom Road, Sands, High Wycombe HP12 4HJ. Telephone: (01494) 472 100.

Capacity: 10,000.

Record Attendance: 15,850 v St Albans C, FA Amateur Cup 4th rd, 25 February 1950 (at Loakes Park); 9,921 v Fulham, FA Cup 3rd rd, 9 January 2002 (at Adams Park).

Manager: Gary Waddock.

Most League Goals: 72, FL 2, 2005–06.

Highest League Scorer in Season: Scott McGleish, 25, 2007–08.

Most League Goals in Total Aggregate: Nathan Tyson, 42, 2004–06.

Most Capped Player: Mark Rogers, 7, Canada.

Most League Appearances: Steve Brown, 371, 1994–2004.

Colours: Light blue and dark blue quartered shirts, dark blue shorts, light blue stockings.

Honours – GM Vauxhall Conference: Winners – 1993. **FA Trophy:** Winners – 1991, 1993.

YEOVIL TOWN

FL CHAMPIONSHIP 1

Ayling Luke (D)	5 11	10 08	Lambeth	25/8/91	Arsenal
Blizzard Dominic (M)	6 2	12 04	High Wycombe	2/9/83	Bristol R
Edgar Anthony (M)	5 8	11 00	Newham	30/9/90	West Ham U
Haynes-Brown Curtis (D)	6 2	13 00	Ipswich	15/4/89	Lowestoft T
N'Gala Bondz (D)	6 0	12 03	Forest Gate	13/9/89	Plymouth Arg
Upson Edward (M)	5 10	11 06	Bury St Edmunds	21/11/89	Ipswich T
Williams Gavin (M)	5 10	11 05	Pontypridd	20/6/80	Bristol R

League Appearances: Agard, K. 13(16); Ayling, L. 44; Belson, F. 1; Blizzard, D. 24(6); Clifford, C. 6(1); D'Ath, L. 12(2); Dickson, R. 5; Edgar, A. 5(5); Edwards, J. 4; Ehmer, M. 24; Fallon, R. (5); Franks, J. 13(1); Gibson, B. 1(4); Gilbert, K. 3(5); Gilmartin, R. 8; Grounds, J. 13(1); Haynes-Brown, C. 1(9); Hinds, R. 15(1); Huntington, P. 37; Johnson, O. 5(1); Jones, N. 21(1); MacLean, S. 14(6); Massey, G. 8(8); Morris, J. 3(2); N'Gala, B. 24(7); O'Brien, A. 8(5); Obika, J. 24(3); Parrett, D. 9(1); Purse, D. 5; Stech, M. 5; Steer, J. 12; Stewart, G. 1; Upson, E. 40(1); Walker, S. 20; Williams, A. 31(4); Williams, G. 23(5); Woods, M. 2(3); Wotton, P. 22; Youga, K. (1).
Goals – League (59): Williams, A. 16, Agard 6, Obika 4, Williams, G. 4, Blizzard 3, Franks 3, MacLean 3 (1 pen), Massey 3, Upson 3, Huntington 2, N'Gala 2, Wotton 2 (2 pens), D'Ath 1, Dickson 1, Edgar 1, Edwards 1, Hinds 1, Parrett 1, Woods 1, own goal 1.
Carling Cup (0).
FA Cup (5): Upson 2, Blizzard 1, Clifford 1, Williams, A. 1.
J Paint Trophy (2): Ehmer 1, MacLean 1.
Ground: Huish Park, Lufton Way, Yeovil, Somerset BA22 8YF. Telephone: (01935) 423 662.
Capacity: 9,665.
Record Attendance: 16,318 v Sunderland, FA Cup 4th rd, 29 January 1949 (at Huish); 9,527 v Leeds U, FL 1, 25 April 2008 (at Huish Park).
Manager: Gary Johnson.
Most League Goals: 90, FL 2, 2004–05.
Highest League Scorer in Season: Phil Jevons, 27, 2004–05.
Most League Goals in Total Aggregate: Phil Jevons, 42, 2004–06.
Most Capped Players: Andrejs Stolcers, 1 (81), Latvia; Arron Davies, 1, Wales.
Most League Appearances: Terry Skiverton, 195, 2003–09.
Colours: Green and white hooped shirts with green sleeves and black trim, white shorts, white stockings.
Honours – Football League: FL 2 Champions 2004–05. **Football Conference:** Champions – 2002–03. **FA Trophy:** Winners 2001–02.

YORK CITY

FL CHAMPIONSHIP 2

Blair Matty (M)			Warwick	5/7/90	Kidderminster H
Blinkhorn Matthew (F)	6 0	10 10	Blackpool	2/3/85	Sligo R
Bopp Eugen (M)	6 0	12 10	Kiev	5/9/83	Carl Zeiss Jena
Brown Scott (M)	5 9	10 03	Chester	8/5/85	Fleetwood T
Challinor Jon (M)	5 11	11 11	Northampton	2/12/80	Kettering T
Chambers Ashley (F)	5 10	11 07	Leicester	1/3/90	Leicester C
Doig Chris (D)	6 2	12 06	Dumfries	13/2/81	Aldershot T
Fyfield Jamal (D)				17/3/89	Maidenhead U
Ingham Michael (G)	6 4	13 10	Preston	9/7/80	Hereford U
Kerr Scott (M)	5 9	12 10	Leeds	11/12/81	Lincoln C
McGurk David (D)	6 0	11 11	Middlesbrough	30/9/82	Darlington
Meredith James (D)	6 1	11 07	Albury	4/4/88	Shrewsbury T
Moke Adriano (M)	5 9	10 01		11/1/90	Jerez Industrial
Musselwhite Paul (G)	6 2	14 05	Portsmouth	22/12/68	Lincoln C

Oyebanjo Lanre (D)	6 1 11 05	London	27/4/90	Histon
Parslow Daniel (D)	5 11 12 06	Rhymney Valley	11/9/85	Cardiff C
Pilkington Danny (F)	5 9 11 09	Blackburn	25/5/90	Stockport Co
Potts Michael (M)			26/11/91	Blackburn R
Reed Jamie (F)	6 0 12 04	Chester	13/8/87	Bangor C
Smith Chris (D)	5 11 11 00	Derby	30/6/81	Mansfield T
Walker Jason (F)	5 9 11 00	Barrow	21/2/84	Luton T

League Appearances: Ashikodi, 2(6); Blair, 37(4); Blinkhorn, 3(12); Bopp, 1(1); Boucaud, 23; Brown, 6(1); Challinor, 35(4); Chambers, 34(8); Doig, 10; Fyfield, 25(8); Gibson, 8; Henderson, 2(4); Ingham, 43; Kelly, (1); Kerr, 33(1); McGurk, 18(1); McLaughlin, 42(2); Meredith, 43; Moke, 11(15); Musselwhite, 3; Oyebanjo, 19(2); Parslow, 17(10); Pilkington, 10(8); Potts, 2(8); Reed, 17(18); Smith, 31; Swallow, (2); Tonne, 2(1); Walker, 29(1).

Goals – League (81): Walker 18 (3 pens), Blair 10, McLaughlin 10, Reed 10 (1 pen), Chambers 9, Fyfield 3, Moke 3, Smith 3, Challinor 2, Meredith 2, Oyebanjo 2, Pilkington 2, Ashikodi 1, Blinkhorn 1, Boucaud 1, Henderson 1, McGurk 1, Tonne 1, own goal 1.

FA Cup (1): McLaughlin 1.

Play-Offs (4): Blair 2, Chambers 1, own goal 1.

Ground: Bootham Crescent, York YO30 7AQ. Telephone: (01904) 624 447.

Capacity: 9,496.

Record Attendance: 28,123 v Huddersfield T, FA Cup 6th rd, 5 March 1938.

Manager: Gary Mills.

Most League Goals: 96, Division 4, 1983–84.

Highest League Scorer in Season: Bill Fenton, 31, Division 3 (N), 1951–52; Arthur Bottom, 31, Division 3 (N), 1954–55 and 1955–56.

Most League Goals in Total Aggregate: Norman Wilkinson, 125, 1954–66.

Most Capped Player: Peter Scott, 7 (10), Northern Ireland.

Most League Appearances: Barry Jackson, 481, 1958–70.

Colours: Red shirts, navy shorts, navy stockings.

Honours – Football League: Division 4 Champions – 1983–84.

LEAGUE POSITIONS: FA PREMIER from 1992–93 and DIVISION 1 1986–87 to 1991–92

	2010–11	2009–10	2008–09	2007–08	2006–07	2005–06	2004–05	2003–04	2002–03	2001–02	2000–01	1999–2000	1998–99
Arsenal	4	3	4	3	4	4	2	1	2	1	2	2	2
Aston Villa	9	6	6	6	11	16	10	6	16	8	8	6	6
Barnsley	–	–	–	–	–	–	–	–	–	–	–	–	–
Birmingham C	18	9	–	19	–	18	12	10	13	–	–	–	–
Blackburn R	15	10	15	7	10	6	15	15	6	10	–	–	19
Blackpool	19	–	–	–	–	–	–	–	–	–	–	–	–
Bolton W	14	14	13	16	7	8	6	8	17	16	–	–	–
Bradford C	–	–	–	–	–	–	–	–	–	–	20	17	–
Burnley	–	18	–	–	–	–	–	–	–	–	–	–	–
Charlton Ath	–	–	–	–	19	13	11	7	12	14	9	–	18
Chelsea	2	1	3	2	2	1	1	2	4	6	6	5	3
Coventry C	–	–	–	–	–	–	–	–	–	–	19	14	15
Crystal Palace	–	–	–	–	–	–	18	–	–	–	–	–	–
Derby Co	–	–	–	20	–	–	–	–	–	19	17	16	8
Everton	7	8	5	5	6	11	4	17	7	15	16	13	14
Fulham	8	12	7	17	16	12	13	9	14	13	–	–	–
Hull C	–	19	17	–	–	–	–	–	–	–	–	–	–
Ipswich T	–	–	–	–	–	–	–	–	–	18	5	–	–
Leeds U	–	–	–	–	–	–	–	19	15	5	4	3	4
Leicester C	–	–	–	–	–	–	–	18	–	20	13	8	10
Liverpool	6	7	2	4	3	3	5	4	5	2	3	4	7
Luton T	–	–	–	–	–	–	–	–	–	–	–	–	–
Manchester C	3	5	10	9	14	15	8	16	9	–	18	–	–
Manchester U	1	2	1	1	1	2	3	3	1	3	1	1	1
Middlesbrough	–	–	19	13	12	14	7	11	11	12	14	12	9
Millwall	–	–	–	–	–	–	–	–	–	–	–	–	–
Newcastle U	12	–	18	12	13	7	14	5	3	4	11	11	13
Norwich C	–	–	–	–	–	19	–	–	–	–	–	–	20
Nottingham F	–	–	–	–	–	–	–	–	–	–	–	–	20
Notts Co	–	–	–	–	–	–	–	–	–	–	–	–	–
Oldham Ath	–	–	–	–	–	–	–	–	–	–	–	–	–
Oxford U	–	–	–	–	–	–	–	–	–	–	–	–	–
Portsmouth	–	20	14	8	9	17	16	13	–	–	–	–	–
QPR	–	–	–	–	–	–	–	–	–	–	–	–	–
Reading	–	–	–	18	8	–	–	–	–	–	–	–	–
Sheffield U	–	–	–	–	18	–	–	–	–	–	–	–	–
Sheffield W	–	–	–	–	–	–	–	–	–	–	–	19	12
Southampton	–	–	–	–	–	–	20	12	8	11	10	15	17
Stoke C	13	11	12	–	–	–	–	–	–	–	–	–	–
Sunderland	10	13	16	15	–	20	–	–	20	17	7	7	–
Swindon T	–	–	–	–	–	–	–	–	–	–	–	–	–
Tottenham H	5	4	8	11	5	5	9	14	10	9	12	10	11
Watford	–	–	–	–	20	–	–	–	–	–	–	20	–
WBA	11	–	20	–	–	19	17	–	19	–	–	–	–
West Ham U	20	17	9	10	15	9	–	–	18	7	15	9	5
Wigan Ath	16	16	11	14	17	10	–	–	–	–	–	18	16
Wimbledon	–	–	–	–	–	–	–	–	–	–	–	18	16
Wolverhampton W	17	15	–	–	–	–	–	20	–	–	–	–	–

Club	1997–98	1996–97	1995–96	1994–95	1993–94	1992–93	1991–92	1990–91	1989–90	1988–89	1987–88	1986–87
Arsenal	1	3	5	12	4	10	4	1	4	1	6	4
Aston Villa	7	5	4	18	10	2	7	17	2	17	–	22
Barnsley	19	–	–	–	–	–	–	–	–	–	–	–
Birmingham C	–	–	–	–	–	–	–	–	–	–	–	–
Blackburn R	6	13	7	1	2	4	–	–	–	–	–	–
Blackpool	–	–	–	–	–	–	–	–	–	–	–	–
Bolton W	18	–	20	–	–	–	–	–	–	–	–	–
Bradford C	–	–	–	–	–	–	–	–	–	–	–	–
Burnley	–	–	–	–	–	–	–	–	–	–	–	–
Charlton Ath	–	–	–	–	–	–	–	–	19	14	17	19
Chelsea	4	6	11	11	14	11	14	11	5	–	18	14
Coventry C	11	17	16	16	11	15	19	16	12	7	10	10
Crystal Palace	20	–	–	19	–	20	10	3	15	–	–	–
Derby Co	9	12	–	–	–	–	–	20	16	5	15	–
Everton	17	15	6	15	17	13	12	9	6	8	4	1
Fulham	–	–	–	–	–	–	–	–	–	–	–	–
Hull C	–	–	–	–	–	–	–	–	–	–	–	–
Ipswich T	–	–	–	22	19	16	–	–	–	–	–	–
Leeds U	5	11	13	5	5	17	1	4	–	–	–	–
Leicester C	10	9	–	21	–	–	–	–	–	–	–	20
Liverpool	3	4	3	4	8	6	6	2	1	2	1	2
Luton T	–	–	–	–	–	–	20	18	17	16	9	7
Manchester C	–	–	18	17	16	9	5	5	14	–	–	21
Manchester U	2	1	1	2	1	1	2	6	13	11	2	11
Middlesbrough	–	19	12	–	–	21	–	–	–	18	–	–
Millwall	–	–	–	–	–	–	–	–	20	10	–	–
Newcastle U	13	2	2	6	3	–	–	–	–	20	8	17
Norwich C	–	–	–	20	12	3	18	15	10	4	14	5
Nottingham F	–	20	9	3	–	22	8	8	9	3	3	8
Notts Co	–	–	–	–	–	–	21	–	–	–	–	–
Oldham Ath	–	–	–	–	21	19	17	–	–	–	–	–
Oxford U	–	–	–	–	–	–	–	–	–	–	21	18
Portsmouth	–	–	–	–	–	–	–	–	–	–	19	–
QPR	–	–	19	8	9	5	11	12	11	9	5	16
Reading	–	–	–	–	–	–	–	–	–	–	–	–
Sheffield U	–	–	–	–	20	14	9	13	–	–	–	–
Sheffield W	16	7	15	13	7	7	3	–	18	15	11	13
Southampton	12	16	17	10	18	18	16	14	7	13	12	12
Stoke C	–	–	–	–	–	–	–	–	–	–	–	–
Sunderland	–	18	–	–	–	–	–	19	–	–	–	–
Swindon T	–	–	–	–	22	–	–	–	–	–	–	–
Tottenham H	14	10	8	7	15	8	15	10	3	6	13	3
Watford	–	–	–	–	–	–	–	–	–	–	20	9
WBA	–	–	–	–	–	–	–	–	–	–	–	–
West Ham U	8	14	10	14	13	–	22	–	–	19	16	15
Wigan Ath	–	–	–	–	–	–	–	–	–	–	–	–
Wimbledon	15	8	14	9	6	12	13	7	8	12	7	6
Wolverhampton W	–	–	–	–	–	–	–	–	–	–	–	–

LEAGUE POSITIONS: DIVISION 1 from 1992–93, CHAMPIONSHIP from 2004–05 and DIVISION 2 1986–87 to 1991–92

	2010–11	2009–10	2008–09	2007–08	2006–07	2005–06	2004–05	2003–04	2002–03	2001–02	2000–01	1999–2000	1998–99
Aston Villa	–	–	–	–	–	–	–	–	–	–	–	–	–
Barnsley	17	18	20	18	20	–	–	–	–	23	16	4	13
Birmingham C	–	–	2	–	2	–	–	–	–	5	5	5	4
Blackburn R	–	–	–	–	–	–	–	–	–	–	2	11	–
Blackpool	–	6	16	19	–	–	–	–	–	–	–	–	–
Bolton W	–	–	–	–	–	–	–	–	–	–	3	6	6
Bournemouth	–	–	–	–	–	–	–	–	–	–	–	–	–
Bradford C	–	–	–	–	–	–	–	23	19	15	–	–	2
Brentford	–	–	–	–	–	–	–	–	–	–	–	–	–
Brighton & HA	–	–	–	–	–	24	20	–	23	–	–	–	–
Bristol C	15	10	10	4	–	–	–	–	–	–	–	–	24
Bristol R	–	–	–	–	–	–	–	–	–	–	–	–	–
Burnley	8	–	5	13	15	17	13	19	16	7	7	–	–
Bury	–	–	–	–	–	–	–	–	–	–	–	–	22
Cambridge U	–	–	–	–	–	–	–	–	–	–	–	–	–
Cardiff C	4	4	7	12	13	11	16	13	–	–	–	–	–
Charlton Ath	–	–	24	11	–	–	–	–	–	–	–	1	–
Chelsea	–	–	–	–	–	–	–	–	–	–	–	–	–
Colchester U	–	–	–	24	10	–	–	–	–	–	–	–	–
Coventry C	18	19	17	21	17	8	19	12	20	11	–	–	–
Crewe Alex	–	–	–	–	–	22	21	18	–	22	14	19	18
Crystal Palace	20	21	15	5	12	6	–	6	14	10	21	15	14
Derby Co	19	14	18	–	3	20	4	20	18	–	–	–	–
Doncaster R	21	12	14	–	–	–	–	–	–	–	–	–	–
Fulham	–	–	–	–	–	–	–	–	–	–	1	9	–
Gillingham	–	–	–	–	–	–	22	21	11	12	13	–	–
Grimsby T	–	–	–	–	–	–	–	–	24	19	18	20	11
Huddersfield T	–	–	–	–	–	–	–	–	–	–	22	8	10
Hull C	11	–	–	3	21	18	–	–	–	–	–	–	–
Ipswich T	13	15	9	8	14	15	3	5	7	–	–	3	3
Leeds U	7	–	–	–	24	5	14	–	–	–	–	–	–
Leicester C	10	5	–	22	19	16	15	–	2	–	–	–	–
Luton T	–	–	–	–	23	10	–	–	–	–	–	–	–
Manchester C	–	–	–	–	–	–	–	–	–	1	–	2	–
Middlesbrough	12	11	–	–	–	–	–	–	–	–	–	–	–
Millwall	9	–	–	–	–	23	10	10	9	4	–	–	–
Newcastle U	–	1	–	–	–	–	–	–	–	–	–	–	–
Norwich C	2	–	22	17	16	9	–	1	8	6	15	12	9
Nottingham F	6	3	19	–	–	–	23	14	6	16	11	14	–
Notts Co	–	–	–	–	–	–	–	–	–	–	–	–	–
Oldham Ath	–	–	–	–	–	–	–	–	–	–	–	–	–
Oxford U	–	–	–	–	–	–	–	–	–	–	–	–	23
Peterborough U	–	24	–	–	–	–	–	–	–	–	–	–	–
Plymouth Arg	–	23	21	10	11	14	17	–	–	–	–	–	–
Port Vale	–	–	–	–	–	–	–	–	–	–	–	23	21
Portsmouth	16	–	–	–	–	–	–	–	1	17	20	18	19
Preston NE	22	17	6	15	7	4	5	15	12	8	4	–	–
QPR	1	13	11	14	18	21	11	–	–	–	23	10	20

1997–98	1996–97	1995–96	1994–95	1993–94	1992–93	1991–92	1990–91	1989–90	1988–89	1987–88	1986–87	
–	–	–	–	–	–	–	–	–	–	2	–	Aston Villa
–	2	10	6	18	13	16	8	19	7	14	11	Barnsley
7	10	15	–	22	19	–	–	–	23	19	19	Birmingham C
–	–	–	–	–	–	6	19	5	5	5	12	Blackburn R
–	–	–	–	–	–	–	–	–	–	–	–	Blackpool
–	1	–	3	14	–	–	–	–	–	–	–	Bolton W
–	–	–	–	–	–	–	22	12	17	–		Bournemouth
13	21	–	–	–	–	–	–	23	14	4	10	Bradford C
–	–	–	–	–	22	–	–	–	–	–	–	Brentford
–	–	–	–	–	–	23	6	18	19	–	22	Brighton & HA
–	–	–	23	13	15	17	9	–	–	–	–	Bristol C
–	–	–	–	–	24	13	13	–	–	–	–	Bristol R
–	–	–	22	–	–	–	–	–	–	–	–	Burnley
17	–	–	–	–	–	–	–	–	–	–	–	Bury
–	–	–	–	–	23	5	–	–	–	–	–	Cambridge U
–	–	–	–	–	–	–	–	–	–	–	–	Cardiff C
4	15	6	15	11	12	7	16	–	–	–	–	Charlton Ath
–	–	–	–	–	–	–	–	–	1	–	–	Chelsea
–	–	–	–	–	–	–	–	–	–	–	–	Colchester U
–	–	–	–	–	–	–	–	–	–	–	–	Coventry C
11	–	–	–	–	–	–	–	–	–	–	–	Crewe Alex
–	6	3	–	1	–	–	–	–	3	6	6	Crystal Palace
–	–	2	9	6	8	3	–	–	–	–	1	Derby Co
–	–	–	–	–	–	–	–	–	–	–	–	Doncaster R
–	–	–	–	–	–	–	–	–	–	–	–	Fulham
–	–	–	–	–	–	–	–	–	–	–	–	Gillingham
–	22	17	10	16	9	19	–	–	–	–	21	Grimsby T
16	20	8	–	–	–	–	–	–	–	23	17	Huddersfield T
–	–	–	–	–	–	–	24	14	21	15	14	Hull C
5	4	7	–	–	–	1	14	9	8	8	5	Ipswich T
–	–	–	–	–	–	–	–	1	10	7	4	Leeds U
–	–	5	–	4	6	4	22	13	15	13	–	Leicester C
–	–	24	16	20	20	–	–	–	–	–	–	Luton T
22	14	–	–	–	–	–	–	–	2	9	–	Manchester C
2	–	–	1	9	–	2	7	21	–	3	–	Middlesbrough
–	–	22	12	3	7	15	5	–	–	1	16	Millwall
–	–	–	–	–	1	20	11	3	–	–	–	Newcastle U
15	13	16	–	–	–	–	–	–	–	–	–	Norwich C
1	–	–	–	2	–	–	–	–	–	–	–	Nottingham F
–	–	–	24	7	17	–	4	–	–	–	–	Notts Co
–	23	18	14	–	–	–	1	8	16	10	3	Oldham Ath
12	17	–	–	23	14	21	10	17	17	–	–	Oxford U
–	–	–	–	24	10	–	–	–	–	–	–	Peterborough U
–	–	–	–	–	–	22	18	16	18	16	7	Plymouth Arg
19	8	12	17	–	–	24	15	11	–	–	–	Port Vale
20	7	21	18	17	3	9	17	12	20	–	2	Portsmouth
–	–	–	–	–	–	–	–	–	–	–	–	Preston NE
21	9	–	–	–	–	–	–	–	–	–	–	QPR

117

LEAGUE POSITIONS: DIVISION 1 from 1992–93, CHAMPIONSHIP from 2004–05 and DIVISION 2 1986–87 to 1991–92 (cont.)

	2010–11	2009–10	2008–09	2007–08	2006–07	2005–06	2004–05	2003–04	2002–03	2001–02	2000–01	1999–2000	1998–99
Reading	5	9	4	–	–	1	7	9	4	–	–	–	–
Rotherham U	–	–	–	–	–	–	24	17	15	21	–	–	–
Scunthorpe U	24	20	–	23	–	–	–	–	–	–	–	–	–
Sheffield U	23	8	3	9	–	2	8	8	3	13	10	16	8
Sheffield W	–	22	12	16	9	19	–	–	22	20	17	–	–
Shrewsbury T	–	–	–	–	–	–	–	–	–	–	–	–	–
Southampton	–	–	23	20	6	12	–	–	–	–	–	–	–
Southend U	–	–	–	–	22	–	–	–	–	–	–	–	–
Stockport Co	–	–	–	–	–	–	–	–	–	24	19	17	16
Stoke C	–	–	–	2	8	13	12	11	21	–	–	–	–
Sunderland	–	–	–	–	1	–	1	3	–	–	–	–	1
Swansea C	3	7	8	–	–	–	–	–	–	–	–	24	17
Swindon T	–	–	–	–	–	–	–	–	–	–	24	13	15
Tranmere R	–	–	–	–	–	–	–	22	17	18	–	22	–
Walsall	–	–	–	–	–	–	–	–	–	–	–	–	5
Watford	14	16	13	6	–	3	18	16	13	14	9	–	5
WBA	–	2	–	1	4	–	–	2	–	2	6	21	12
West Ham U	–	–	–	–	–	–	6	4	–	–	–	–	–
Wigan Ath	–	–	–	–	–	–	2	7	–	–	–	–	–
Wimbledon	–	–	–	–	–	–	–	24	10	9	8	–	–
Wolverhampton W	–	–	1	7	5	7	9	–	5	3	12	7	7

LEAGUE POSITIONS: DIVISION 2 from 1992–93, LEAGUE 1 from 2004–05 and DIVISION 3 1986–87 to 1991–92

	2010–11	2009–10	2008–09	2007–08	2006–07	2005–06	2004–05	2003–04	2002–03	2001–02	2000–01	1999–2000	1998–99
Aldershot	–	–	–	–	–	–	–	–	–	–	–	–	–
Barnet	–	–	–	–	–	–	–	–	–	–	–	–	–
Barnsley	–	–	–	–	–	5	13	12	19	–	–	–	–
Birmingham C	–	–	–	–	–	–	–	–	–	–	–	–	–
Blackpool	–	–	–	–	3	19	16	14	13	16	–	22	14
Bolton W	–	–	–	–	–	–	–	–	–	–	–	–	–
Bournemouth	6	–	–	21	19	17	8	9	–	21	7	16	7
Bradford C	–	–	–	–	22	11	11	–	–	–	–	–	–
Brentford	11	9	–	–	24	3	4	17	16	3	14	17	–
Brighton & HA	1	13	16	7	18	–	–	4	–	1	–	9	–
Bristol C	–	–	–	–	2	9	7	3	3	7	9	9	–
Bristol R	22	11	11	16	–	–	–	–	–	–	21	7	13
Burnley	–	–	–	–	–	–	–	–	–	22	16	15	–
Bury	–	–	–	–	–	–	–	–	–	24	19	19	–
Cambridge U	–	–	–	–	–	–	–	–	6	4	–	21	–
Cardiff C	–	–	–	–	–	–	–	–	–	–	–	–	–
Carlisle U	12	14	20	4	8	–	–	–	–	–	–	–	–
Charlton Ath	13	4	–	–	–	–	–	–	–	–	–	–	–

1997–98	1996–97	1995–96	1994–95	1993–94	1992–93	1991–92	1990–91	1989–90	1988–89	1987–88	1986–87	
24	18	19	2	–	–	–	–	–	–	22	13	Reading
–	–	–	–	–	–	–	–	–	–	–	–	Rotherham U
–	–	–	–	–	–	–	–	–	–	–	–	Scunthorpe U
6	5	9	8	–	–	–	–	2	–	21	9	Sheffield U
–	–	–	–	–	–	–	3	–	–	–	–	Sheffield W
–	–	–	–	–	–	–	–	–	22	18	18	Shrewsbury T
–	–	–	–	–	–	–	–	–	–	–	–	Southampton
–	24	14	13	15	18	12	–	–	–	–	–	Southend U
8	–	–	–	–	–	–	–	–	–	–	–	Stockport Co
23	12	4	11	10	–	–	–	24	13	11	8	Stoke C
3	–	1	20	12	21	18	–	6	11	–	20	Sunderland
–	–	–	–	–	–	–	–	–	–	–	–	Swansea C
18	19	–	21	–	5	8	21	4	6	12	–	Swindon T
14	11	13	5	5	4	14	–	–	–	–	–	Tranmere R
–	–	–	–	–	–	–	–	–	24	–	–	Walsall
–	–	23	7	19	16	10	20	15	4	–	–	Watford
10	16	11	19	21	–	–	23	20	9	20	15	WBA
–	–	–	–	–	2	–	2	7	–	–	–	West Ham U
–	–	–	–	–	–	–	–	–	–	–	–	Wigan Ath
–	–	–	–	–	–	–	–	–	–	–	–	Wimbledon
9	3	20	4	8	11	11	12	10	–	–	–	Wolverhampton W

1997–98	1996–97	1995–96	1994–95	1993–94	1992–93	1991–92	1990–91	1989–90	1988–89	1987–88	1986–87	
–	–	–	–	–	–	–	–	–	24	20	–	Aldershot
–	–	–	–	24	–	–	–	–	–	–	–	Barnet
–	–	–	–	–	–	–	–	–	–	–	–	Barnsley
–	–	–	1	–	–	2	12	7	–	–	–	Birmingham C
12	7	3	12	20	18	–	–	23	19	10	9	Blackpool
–	–	–	–	–	2	13	4	6	10	–	21	Bolton W
9	16	14	19	17	17	8	9	–	–	–	1	Bournemouth
–	–	6	14	7	10	16	8	–	–	–	–	Bradford C
21	4	15	2	16	–	1	6	13	7	12	11	Brentford
–	–	23	16	14	9	–	–	–	–	2	–	Brighton & HA
2	5	13	–	–	–	–	–	2	11	5	6	Bristol C
5	17	10	4	8	–	–	–	1	5	8	19	Bristol R
20	9	17	–	6	13	–	–	–	–	–	–	Burnley
–	1	–	–	–	–	21	7	5	13	14	16	Bury
–	–	–	20	10	–	–	1	–	–	–	–	Cambridge U
–	–	–	22	19	–	–	–	21	16	–	–	Cardiff C
23	–	21	–	–	–	–	–	–	–	–	22	Carlisle U
–	–	–	–	–	–	–	–	–	–	–	–	Charlton Ath

LEAGUE POSITIONS: DIVISION 2 from 1992–93, LEAGUE 1 from 2004–05 and DIVISION 3 1986–87 to 1991–92 (cont.)

	2010–11	2009–10	2008–09	2007–08	2006–07	2005–06	2004–05	2003–04	2002–03	2001–02	2000–01	1999–2000	1998–99
Cheltenham T	–	–	23	19	17	–	–	–	21	–	–	–	–
Chester C	–	–	–	–	–	–	–	–	–	–	–	–	–
Chesterfield	–	–	–	–	21	16	17	20	20	18	–	24	9
Colchester U	10	8	12	–	–	2	15	11	12	15	17	18	18
Crewe Alex	–	–	22	20	13	–	–	–	2	–	–	–	–
Dagenham & R	21	–	–	–	–	–	–	–	–	–	–	–	–
Darlington	–	–	–	–	–	–	–	–	–	–	–	–	–
Doncaster R	–	–	–	3	11	8	10	–	–	–	–	–	–
Exeter C	8	18	–	–	–	–	–	–	–	–	–	–	–
Fulham	–	–	–	–	–	–	–	–	–	–	–	–	1
Gillingham	–	21	–	22	16	14	–	–	–	–	–	3	4
Grimsby T	–	–	–	–	–	–	–	21	–	–	–	–	–
Hartlepool U	16	20	19	15	–	21	6	6	–	–	–	–	–
Hereford U	–	–	24	–	–	–	–	–	–	–	–	–	–
Huddersfield T	3	6	9	10	15	4	9	–	22	6	–	–	–
Hull C	–	–	–	–	–	–	2	–	–	–	–	–	–
Leeds U	–	2	4	5	–	–	–	–	–	–	–	–	–
Leicester C	–	–	1	–	–	–	–	–	–	–	–	–	–
Leyton Orient	7	17	14	14	20	–	–	–	–	–	–	–	23
Lincoln C	–	–	–	24	–	–	1	10	9	–	22	13	12
Luton T	–	–	–	–	–	–	–	–	–	–	–	–	24
Macclesfield T	–	–	–	–	–	–	–	–	–	–	–	–	3
Manchester C	–	–	–	–	–	–	–	–	23	–	–	–	–
Mansfield T	–	–	–	–	–	–	–	23	–	–	–	–	–
Middlesbrough	–	–	–	–	–	–	–	–	–	–	1	5	10
Millwall	–	3	5	17	10	–	–	–	–	–	–	–	–
Newport Co	–	–	–	–	–	–	–	–	–	–	–	–	22
Northampton T	–	–	21	9	14	–	–	–	24	20	18	–	–
Norwich C	–	1	–	–	–	–	–	–	–	–	–	–	–
Nottingham F	–	–	–	2	4	7	–	23	15	19	8	8	16
Notts Co	19	–	–	–	–	–	–	15	5	9	15	14	20
Oldham Ath	=17	16	10	8	6	10	19	18	11	17	12	24	20
Oxford U	–	–	2	–	–	–	23	–	–	–	–	–	–
Peterborough U	4	–	–	–	–	–	–	1	8	–	–	–	–
Plymouth Arg	23	–	–	23	12	13	18	7	17	14	11	–	–
Port Vale	–	–	–	–	–	–	–	2	4	8	–	–	–
Preston NE	–	–	–	–	–	–	–	–	–	2	3	10	11
QPR	9	–	–	–	–	–	–	–	–	–	2	–	–
Reading	–	–	–	–	23	20	–	–	–	–	–	23	–
Rochdale	–	–	6	–	1	12	22	–	–	–	–	–	–
Rotherham U	–	–	–	–	–	–	5	16	–	–	–	–	–
Rushden & D	15	–	–	–	–	–	–	–	–	–	–	–	–
Scunthorpe U	2	7	–	–	–	–	–	–	–	–	–	–	–
Sheffield U	–	23	8	6	–	1	–	–	–	–	–	–	–
Sheffield W	–	24	18	–	–	–	24	19	14	–	5	5	6
Shrewsbury T	–	–	–	–	–	–	–	–	–	–	–	–	8
Southampton													
Southend U													
Stockport Co													
Stoke C													

1997–98	1996–97	1995–96	1994–95	1993–94	1992–93	1991–92	1990–91	1989–90	1988–89	1987–88	1986–87	
–	–	–	23	–	24	18	19	16	8	15	15	Cheltenham T
10	10	7	–	–	–	–	–	–	22	18	17	Chester C
–	–	–	–	–	–	–	–	–	–	–	–	Chesterfield
–	6	5	3	–	–	–	22	12	–	–	–	Colchester U
–	–	–	–	–	–	–	–	–	–	–	–	Crewe Alex
–	–	–	–	–	–	24	–	–	–	–	23	Dagenham & R
–	–	–	–	–	–	–	–	–	–	24	13	Darlington
–	–	–	–	22	19	20	16	–	–	–	–	Doncaster R
6	–	–	–	21	12	9	21	20	4	9	18	Exeter C
8	11	–	–	–	–	–	–	–	23	13	5	Fulham
3	–	–	–	–	–	–	3	–	–	22	–	Gillingham
–	–	–	–	23	16	11	–	–	–	–	–	Grimsby T
–	–	–	–	–	–	–	–	–	–	–	–	Hartlepool U
–	–	–	5	11	15	3	11	8	14	–	–	Hereford U
–	–	24	8	9	20	14	–	–	–	–	–	Huddersfield T
–	–	–	–	–	–	–	–	–	–	–	–	Hull C
–	–	–	–	–	–	–	–	–	–	–	–	Leeds U
–	–	–	24	18	7	10	13	14	–	–	–	Leicester C
–	–	–	–	–	–	–	–	–	–	–	–	Leyton Orient
17	3	–	–	–	–	–	–	–	–	–	–	Lincoln C
–	–	–	–	–	–	–	–	–	–	–	–	Luton T
–	–	–	–	–	–	–	–	–	–	–	–	Macclesfield T
–	–	–	–	–	–	–	–	–	–	–	–	Manchester C
–	–	–	–	22	–	24	15	15	19	10	–	Mansfield T
–	–	–	–	–	–	–	–	–	–	–	2	Middlesbrough
18	14	–	–	–	–	–	–	–	–	–	–	Millwall
–	–	–	–	–	–	–	–	–	–	–	23	Newport Co
4	–	–	–	–	–	–	22	20	6	–	–	Northampton T
–	–	–	–	–	–	–	–	–	–	–	–	Norwich C
–	–	–	–	–	–	–	–	–	–	–	–	Nottingham F
–	24	4	–	–	–	–	–	3	9	4	7	Notts Co
13	–	–	–	–	–	–	–	–	–	–	–	Oldham Ath
–	–	2	7	–	–	–	–	–	–	–	–	Oxford U
–	21	19	15	–	–	6	–	–	–	–	–	Peterborough U
22	19	–	21	3	14	–	–	–	–	–	–	Plymouth Arg
–	–	–	–	2	3	–	–	–	3	11	12	Port Vale
15	15	–	–	–	21	17	17	19	6	16	–	Preston NE
–	–	–	–	–	–	–	–	–	–	–	–	QPR
–	–	–	–	1	8	12	15	10	18	–	–	Reading
–	–	–	–	–	–	–	–	–	–	–	–	Rochdale
–	23	16	17	15	11	–	23	9	–	21	14	Rotherham U
–	–	–	–	–	–	–	–	–	–	–	–	Rushden & D
–	–	–	–	–	–	–	–	–	–	–	–	Scunthorpe U
–	–	–	–	–	–	–	–	2	–	–	–	Sheffield U
–	–	–	–	–	–	–	–	–	–	–	–	Sheffield W
–	22	18	18	–	–	22	18	11	–	–	–	Shrewsbury T
24	–	–	–	–	–	–	–	–	–	–	–	Southampton
–	2	9	11	4	6	5	–	–	21	17	–	Southend U
–	–	–	–	–	1	4	14	–	–	–	–	Stockport Co
–	–	–	–	–	–	–	–	–	–	–	–	Stoke C

LEAGUE POSITIONS: DIVISION 2 from 1992–93, LEAGUE 1 from 2004–05 and DIVISION 3 1986–87 to 1991–92 (cont.)

	2010-11	2009-10	2008-09	2007-08	2006-07	2005-06	2004-05	2003-04	2002-03	2001-02	2000-01	1999-2000	1998-99
Sunderland	–	–	–	–	–	–	–	–	–	–	–	–	–
Swansea C	–	–	–	1	7	6	–	–	–	–	23	–	–
Swindon T	24	5	15	13	–	23	12	5	10	13	20	–	–
Torquay U	–	–	–	–	–	–	21	–	–	–	–	–	–
Tranmere R	=17	19	7	11	9	18	3	8	7	12	–	–	2
Walsall	20	10	13	12	–	24	14	–	–	–	4	–	2
Watford	–	–	–	–	–	–	–	–	–	–	–	–	–
WBA	–	–	–	–	–	–	–	–	1	10	6	4	6
Wigan Ath	–	–	–	–	–	–	–	–	–	–	–	–	–
Wimbledon	5†	12†	3†	–	–	22†	20†	–	–	–	–	–	–
Wolverhampton W	–	–	–	–	–	–	–	–	–	–	–	–	–
Wrexham	–	–	–	–	–	–	22	13	–	23	10	11	17
Wycombe W	3	22	–	–	–	–	–	24	18	11	13	12	19
Yeovil T	14	15	17	18	5	15	–	–	–	–	–	–	–
York C	–	–	–	–	–	–	–	–	–	–	–	–	21

†As Milton Keynes D

LEAGUE POSITIONS: DIVISION 3 from 1992–93, LEAGUE 2 from 2004–05 and DIVISION 4 1986–87 to 1991–92

	2010-11	2009-10	2008-09	2007-08	2006-07	2005-06	2004-05	2003-04	2002-03	2001-02	2000-01	1999-2000	1998-99
Accrington S	5	15	16	17	20	–	–	–	–	–	–	–	–
Aldershot T	14	6	15	–	–	–	–	–	–	–	24	6	16
Barnet	22	21	17	12	14	18	–	–	–	–	7	–	–
Blackpool	–	–	–	–	–	–	–	–	–	–	–	–	–
Bolton W	–	–	–	–	–	–	–	–	–	–	–	–	–
Boston U	–	–	–	–	23	11	16	11	15	–	–	–	–
Bournemouth	–	2	21	–	–	–	–	–	4	–	–	–	–
Bradford C	18	14	9	10	–	–	–	–	–	–	–	–	1
Brentford	–	–	1	14	–	–	–	–	–	–	1	11	17
Brighton & HA	–	–	–	–	–	–	–	–	–	–	–	–	–
Bristol R	–	–	–	–	6	12	12	15	20	23	–	–	–
Burnley	–	–	–	–	–	–	–	–	–	–	–	–	–
Burton Alb	19	13	–	–	–	–	–	–	–	–	–	–	–
Bury	2	9	4	13	21	19	17	12	7	–	–	–	2
Cambridge U	–	–	–	–	–	–	24	13	12	–	–	–	3
Cardiff C	–	–	–	–	–	–	–	–	–	–	2	–	3
Carlisle U	–	–	–	–	–	1	–	23	22	17	22	23	23
Cheltenham T	17	22	–	–	–	5	14	14	–	4	9	8	–
Chester C	–	–	23	22	18	15	20	–	–	–	–	24	14
Chesterfield	1	8	10	8	–	–	–	–	–	–	3	–	–

*Record expunged

1997–98	1996–97	1995–96	1994–95	1993–94	1992–93	1991–92	1990–91	1989–90	1988–89	1987–88	1986–87	
–	–	–	–	–	–	–	–	–	–	1	–	Sunderland
–	–	22	10	13	5	19	20	17	12	–	–	Swansea C
–	–	1	–	–	–	–	–	–	–	–	3	Swindon T
–	–	–	–	–	23	–	–	–	–	–	–	Torquay U
–	–	–	–	–	–	5	4	–	–	–	–	Tranmere R
19	12	11	–	–	–	–	–	24	–	3	8	Walsall
1	13	–	–	–	–	–	–	–	–	–	–	Watford
–	–	–	–	4	7	–	–	–	–	–	–	WBA
11	–	–	–	–	23	15	10	18	17	7	4	Wigan Ath
–	–	–	–	–	–	–	–	–	1	–	–	Wimbledon
7	8	8	13	12	–	–	–	–	–	–	–	Wolverhampton W
14	18	12	6	–	–	–	–	–	–	–	–	Wrexham
–	–	–	–	–	–	–	–	–	–	–	–	Wycombe W
–	–	–	–	–	–	–	–	–	–	–	–	Yeovil T
16	20	20	9	5	–	–	–	–	–	23	20	York C

1997–98	1996–97	1995–96	1994–95	1993–94	1992–93	1991–92	1990–91	1989–90	1988–89	1987–88	1986–87	
–	–	–	–	–	–	*	23	22	–	–	6	Accrington S
7	15	9	11	–	3	7	–	–	–	–	–	Aldershot T
–	–	–	–	–	–	4	5	–	–	–	–	Barnet
–	–	–	–	–	–	–	–	–	–	–	–	Blackpool
–	–	–	–	–	–	–	–	–	–	3	–	Bolton W
–	–	–	–	–	–	–	–	–	–	–	–	Boston U
–	–	–	–	–	–	–	–	–	–	–	–	Bournemouth
–	–	–	–	–	–	–	–	–	–	–	–	Bradford C
23	23	–	–	–	–	–	–	–	–	–	–	Brentford
–	–	–	–	–	–	–	–	–	–	–	–	Brighton & HA
–	–	–	–	–	–	1	6	16	16	10	22	Bristol R
–	–	–	–	–	–	–	–	–	–	–	–	Burnley
–	–	–	–	–	–	–	–	–	–	–	–	Burton Alb
–	–	3	4	13	7	–	–	–	–	–	–	Bury
16	10	16	–	–	–	–	–	6	8	15	11	Cambridge U
21	7	22	–	–	1	9	13	–	–	2	13	Cardiff C
–	3	–	1	7	18	22	20	8	12	23	–	Carlisle U
14	6	8	–	2	–	–	–	–	–	–	–	Cheltenham T
–	–	–	–	–	–	–	–	–	–	–	–	Chester C
–	–	–	3	8	12	13	18	7	–	–	–	Chesterfield

LEAGUE POSITIONS: DIVISION 3 from 1992–93, LEAGUE 2 from 2004–05 and DIVISION 4 1986–87 to 1991–92 (cont.)

	2010–11	2009–10	2008–09	2007–08	2006–07	2005–06	2004–05	2003–04	2002–03	2001–02	2000–01	1999–2000	1998–99
Colchester U	–	–	–	–	–	–	–	–	–	–	–	–	–
Crewe Alex	10	18	–	–	–	–	–	–	–	–	–	–	–
Dagenham & R	–	7	8	20	–	–	–	–	–	–	–	–	–
Darlington	–	24	12	6	11	8	8	18	14	15	20	4	11
Doncaster R	–	–	–	–	–	–	–	1	–	–	–	–	–
Exeter C	–	–	2	–	–	–	–	–	23	16	19	21	12
Fulham	–	–	–	–	–	–	–	–	–	–	–	–	–
Gillingham	8	–	5	–	–	–	–	–	–	–	–	–	–
Grimsby T	–	23	22	16	15	4	18	–	–	–	–	–	–
Halifax T	–	–	–	–	–	–	–	–	–	24	23	18	10
Hartlepool U	–	–	–	–	2	–	–	–	2	7	4	7	22
Hereford U	21	16	–	3	16	–	–	–	–	–	–	–	–
Huddersfield T	–	–	–	–	–	–	–	4	–	–	–	–	–
Hull C	–	–	–	–	–	–	–	2	13	11	6	14	21
Kidderminster H	–	–	–	–	–	–	23	16	11	11	16	–	–
Leyton Orient	–	–	–	–	–	3	11	19	18	18	5	19	6
Lincoln C	23	20	13	15	5	7	6	7	6	22	18	15	–
Luton T	–	–	24	–	–	–	–	–	–	–	–	–	–
Macclesfield T	15	19	20	19	22	17	5	20	16	13	14	13	–
Maidstone U	–	–	–	–	–	–	–	–	–	–	–	–	–
Mansfield T	–	–	–	23	17	16	13	5	–	3	13	17	8
Morecambe	20	4	11	11	–	–	–	–	–	–	–	–	–
Newport Co	–	–	–	–	–	–	–	–	–	–	–	–	–
Northampton T	16	11	–	–	–	2	7	6	–	–	–	3	–
Notts Co	–	1	19	21	13	21	19	–	–	–	–	–	–
Oxford U	12	–	–	–	–	23	15	9	8	21	–	–	–
Peterborough U	–	–	–	2	10	9	–	–	–	–	–	5	9
Plymouth Arg	–	–	–	–	–	–	–	–	–	1	12	12	13
Port Vale	11	10	18	–	–	–	–	–	–	–	–	–	–
Preston NE	–	–	–	–	–	–	–	–	–	–	–	–	–
Rochdale	–	3	6	5	9	14	9	21	19	5	8	10	19
Rotherham U	9	5	14	9	–	–	–	–	–	–	–	2	–
Rushden & D	–	–	–	–	–	24	22	–	1	6	–	–	–
Scarborough	–	–	–	–	–	–	–	–	–	–	–	–	23
Scunthorpe U	–	–	–	–	–	–	2	9	5	8	10	–	4
Shrewsbury T	4	12	7	18	7	10	21	–	24	9	15	22	15
Southend U	13	–	–	–	–	–	4	17	17	12	11	16	18
Stevenage	6	–	–	–	–	–	–	–	–	–	–	–	–
Stockport Co	24	–	–	4	8	22	–	–	–	–	–	–	–
Swansea C	–	–	–	–	–	–	3	10	21	20	–	–	–
Swindon T	–	–	–	–	3	–	–	–	–	–	–	–	–
Torquay U	7	17	–	–	24	20	–	3	9	19	21	9	20
Tranmere R	–	–	–	–	–	–	–	–	–	–	–	–	–
Walsall	–	–	–	–	1	–	–	–	–	–	–	–	–
Wigan Ath	–	–	–	–	–	–	–	–	–	–	–	–	–
Wimbledon	–	–	–	1†	4†	–	–	–	–	–	–	–	–
Wolverhampton W	–	–	–	–	–	–	–	–	–	–	–	–	–
Wrexham	–	–	–	24	19	13	–	–	–	–	–	–	–
Wycombe W	3	–	3	7	12	6	10	–	–	–	–	–	–
Yeovil T	–	–	–	–	–	–	1	8	–	–	–	–	–
York C	–	–	–	–	–	–	–	24	10	14	17	20	–

†As Milton Keynes D

1997–98	1996–97	1995–96	1994–95	1993–94	1992–93	1991–92	1990–91	1989–90	1988–89	1987–88	1986–87	
4	8	7	10	17	10	–	–	24	22	9	5	Colchester U
–	–	–	–	3	6	6	–	–	3	17	17	Crewe Alex
–	–	–	–	–	–	–	–	–	–	–	–	Dagenham & R
19	18	5	20	21	15	–	1	–	24	13	–	Darlington
24	19	13	9	15	16	21	11	20	23	–	–	Doncaster R
15	22	14	22	–	–	–	–	1	13	22	14	Exeter C
–	2	17	8	–	–	–	–	–	–	–	–	Fulham
–	–	2	19	16	21	11	15	14	–	–	–	Gillingham
–	–	–	–	–	–	–	–	2	9	–	–	Grimsby T
–	–	–	–	–	22	20	22	23	21	18	15	Halifax T
17	20	20	18	–	–	–	3	19	19	16	18	Hartlepool U
–	24	6	16	20	17	17	17	17	15	19	16	Hereford U
22	17	–	–	–	–	–	–	–	–	–	–	Huddersfield T
22	17	–	–	–	–	–	–	–	–	–	–	Hull C
–	–	–	–	–	–	–	–	–	–	–	–	Kidderminster H
11	16	21	–	–	–	–	–	–	6	8	7	Leyton Orient
3	9	18	12	18	8	10	14	10	10	–	24	Lincoln C
–	–	–	–	–	–	–	–	–	–	–	–	Luton T
2	–	–	–	–	–	–	–	–	–	–	–	Macclesfield T
–	–	–	–	–	18	19	5	–	–	–	–	Maidstone U
12	11	19	6	12	–	3	–	–	–	–	–	Mansfield T
–	–	–	–	–	–	–	–	–	–	–	–	Morecambe
–	–	–	–	–	–	–	–	–	–	24	–	Newport Co
–	4	11	17	22	20	16	10	–	–	–	1	Northampton T
1	–	–	–	–	–	–	–	–	–	–	–	Notts Co
–	–	–	–	–	–	–	–	–	–	–	–	Oxford U
10	–	–	–	–	–	4	9	17	7	10	–	Peterborough U
–	–	4	–	–	–	–	–	–	–	–	–	Plymouth Arg
–	–	–	–	–	–	–	–	–	–	–	–	Port Vale
–	–	1	5	5	–	–	–	–	–	–	2	Preston NE
18	14	15	15	9	11	8	12	12	18	21	21	Rochdale
9	–	–	–	–	2	–	–	1	–	–	–	Rotherham U
–	–	–	–	–	–	–	–	–	–	–	–	Rushden & D
6	12	23	21	14	13	12	9	18	5	12	–	Scarborough
8	13	12	7	11	14	5	8	11	4	4	8	Scunthorpe U
13	–	–	–	1	9	–	–	–	–	–	–	Shrewsbury T
–	–	–	–	–	–	–	3	–	–	–	3	Southend U
–	–	–	–	–	–	–	–	–	–	–	–	Stevenage
–	–	–	–	–	–	2	4	20	20	19	–	Stockport Co
20	5	–	–	–	–	–	–	–	–	6	12	Swansea C
–	–	–	–	–	–	–	–	–	–	–	–	Swindon T
5	21	24	13	6	19	–	7	15	14	5	23	Torquay U
–	–	–	–	–	–	–	–	2	14	20	–	Tranmere R
–	–	–	2	10	5	15	16	–	–	–	–	Walsall
–	1	10	14	19	–	–	–	–	–	–	–	Wigan Ath
–	–	–	–	–	–	–	–	–	–	–	–	Wimbledon
–	–	–	–	–	–	–	–	–	–	1	4	Wolverhampton W
–	–	–	–	2	14	24	21	7	11	9	–	Wrexham
–	–	–	4	–	–	–	–	–	–	–	–	Wycombe W
–	–	–	–	–	–	–	–	–	–	–	–	Yeovil T
–	–	–	–	–	4	19	21	13	11	–	–	York C

LEAGUE CHAMPIONSHIP HONOURS

FA PREMIER LEAGUE

Maximum points: 126

	First	Pts	Second	Pts	Third	Pts
1992–93	Manchester U	84	Aston Villa	74	Norwich C	72
1993–94	Manchester U	92	Blackburn R	84	Newcastle U	77
1994–95	Blackburn R	89	Manchester U	88	Nottingham F	77

Maximum points: 114

	First	Pts	Second	Pts	Third	Pts
1995–96	Manchester U	82	Newcastle U	78	Liverpool	71
1996–97	Manchester U	75	Newcastle U*	68	Arsenal*	68
1997–98	Arsenal	78	Manchester U	77	Liverpool	65
1998–99	Manchester U	79	Arsenal	78	Chelsea	75
1999–00	Manchester U	91	Arsenal	73	Leeds U	69
2000–01	Manchester U	80	Arsenal	70	Liverpool	69
2001–02	Arsenal	87	Liverpool	80	Manchester U	77
2002–03	Manchester U	83	Arsenal	78	Newcastle U	69
2003–04	Arsenal	90	Chelsea	79	Manchester U	75
2004–05	Chelsea	95	Arsenal	83	Manchester U	77
2005–06	Chelsea	91	Manchester U	83	Liverpool	82
2006–07	Manchester U	89	Chelsea	83	Liverpool*	68
2007–08	Manchester U	87	Chelsea	85	Arsenal	83
2008–09	Manchester U	90	Liverpool	86	Chelsea	83
2009–10	Chelsea	86	Manchester U	85	Arsenal	75
2010–11	Manchester U	80	Chelsea*	71	Manchester C	71
2011–12	Manchester C*	89	Manchester U	89	Arsenal	70

FOOTBALL LEAGUE CHAMPIONSHIP

Maximum points: 138

	First	Pts	Second	Pts	Third	Pts
2004–05	Sunderland	94	Wigan Ath	87	Ipswich T††	85
2005–06	Reading	106	Sheffield U	90	Watford	81
2006–07	Sunderland	88	Birmingham C	86	Derby Co	84
2007–08	WBA	81	Stoke C	79	Hull C	75
2008–09	Wolverhampton W	90	Birmingham C	83	Sheffield U††	80
2009–10	Newcastle U	102	WBA	91	Nottingham F††	79
2010–11	QPR	88	Norwich C	84	Swansea C*	80
2011–12	Reading	89	Southampton	88	West Ham U	86

DIVISION 1

Maximum points: 138

	First	Pts	Second	Pts	Third	Pts
1992–93	Newcastle U	96	West Ham U*	88	Portsmouth††	88
1993–94	Crystal Palace	90	Nottingham F	83	Millwall††	74
1994–95	Middlesbrough	82	Reading††	79	Bolton W	77
1995–96	Sunderland	83	Derby Co	79	Crystal Palace††	75
1996–97	Bolton W	98	Barnsley	80	Wolverhampton W††	76
1997–98	Nottingham F	94	Middlesbrough	91	Sunderland††	90
1998–99	Sunderland	105	Bradford C	87	Ipswich T††	86
1999–00	Charlton Ath	91	Manchester C	89	Ipswich T	87
2000–01	Fulham	101	Blackburn R	91	Bolton W	87
2001–02	Manchester C	99	WBA	89	Wolverhampton W††	86
2002–03	Portsmouth	98	Leicester C	92	Sheffield U††	80
2003–04	Norwich C	94	WBA	86	Sunderland††	79

FOOTBALL LEAGUE CHAMPIONSHIP 1

Maximum points: 138

	First	Pts	Second	Pts	Third	Pts
2004–05	Luton T	98	Hull C	86	Tranmere R††	79
2005–06	Southend U	82	Colchester U	79	Brentford††	76
2006–07	Scunthorpe U	91	Bristol C	85	Blackpool	83
2007–08	Swansea C	92	Nottingham F	82	Doncaster R	80
2008–09	Leicester C	96	Peterborough U	89	Milton Keynes D††	87
2009–10	Norwich C	95	Leeds U	86	Millwall	85
2010–11	Brighton & HA	95	Southampton	92	Huddersfield T††	87
2011–12	Charlton Ath	101	Sheffield W	93	Sheffield U††	90

DIVISION 2

Maximum points: 138

	First	Pts	Second	Pts	Third	Pts
1992–93	Stoke C	93	Bolton W	90	Port Vale††	89
1993–94	Reading	89	Port Vale	88	Plymouth Arg††	85
1994–95	Birmingham C	89	Brentford††	85	Crewe Alex††	83
1995–96	Swindon T	92	Oxford U	83	Blackpool††	82
1996–97	Bury	84	Stockport Co	82	Luton T††	78
1997–98	Watford	88	Bristol C	85	Grimsby T	72
1998–99	Fulham	101	Walsall	87	Manchester C	82
1999–00	Preston NE	95	Burnley	88	Gillingham	85
2000–01	Millwall	93	Rotherham U	91	Reading††	86
2001–02	Brighton & HA	90	Reading	84	Brentford*††	83
2002–03	Wigan Ath	100	Crewe Alex	86	Bristol C††	83
2003–04	Plymouth Arg	90	QPR	83	Bristol C††	82

FOOTBALL LEAGUE CHAMPIONSHIP 2

Maximum points: 138

	First	Pts	Second	Pts	Third	Pts
2004–05	Yeovil T	83	Scunthorpe U*	80	Swansea C	80
2005–06	Carlisle U	86	Northampton T	83	Leyton Orient	81
2006–07	Walsall	89	Hartlepool U	88	Swindon T	85
2007–08	Milton Keynes D	97	Peterborough U	92	Hereford U	88
2008–09	Brentford	85	Exeter C	79	Wycombe W*	78
2009–10	Notts Co	93	Bournemouth	83	Rochdale	82
2010–11	Chesterfield	86	Bury	81	Wycombe W	80
2011–12	Swindon T	93	Shrewsbury T	88	Crawley T	84

DIVISION 3

Maximum points: 126

	First	Pts	Second	Pts	Third	Pts
1992–93	Cardiff C	83	Wrexham	80	Barnet	79
1993–94	Shrewsbury T	79	Chester C	74	Crewe Alex	73
1994–95	Carlisle U	91	Walsall	83	Chesterfield	81

Maximum points: 138

	First	Pts	Second	Pts	Third	Pts
1995–96	Preston NE	86	Gillingham	83	Bury	79
1996–97	Wigan Ath*	87	Fulham	87	Carlisle U	84
1997–98	Notts Co	99	Macclesfield T	82	Lincoln C	75
1998–99	Brentford	85	Cambridge U	81	Cardiff C	80
1999–00	Swansea C	85	Rotherham U	84	Northampton T	82
2000–01	Brighton & HA	92	Cardiff C	82	Chesterfield¶	80
2001–02	Plymouth Arg	102	Luton T	97	Mansfield T	79
2002–03	Rushden & D	87	Hartlepool U	85	Wrexham	84
2003–04	Doncaster R	92	Hull C	88	Torquay U*	81

* Won or placed on goal average (ratio)/goal difference.
†† Not promoted after play-offs. ¶ 9 pts deducted for irregularities.

FOOTBALL LEAGUE

Maximum points: a 44; *b* 60

	First	*Pts*	*Second*	*Pts*	*Third*	*Pts*
1888–89a	Preston NE	40	Aston Villa	29	Wolverhampton W	28
1889–90a	Preston NE	33	Everton	31	Blackburn R	27
1890–91a	Everton	29	Preston NE	27	Notts Co	26
1891–92b	Sunderland	42	Preston NE	37	Bolton W	36

DIVISION 1 to 1991–92

Maximum points: a 44; *b* 52; *c* 60; *d* 68; *e* 76; *f* 84; *g* 126; *h* 120; *k* 114.

	First	*Pts*	*Second*	*Pts*	*Third*	*Pts*
1892–93c	Sunderland	48	Preston NE	37	Everton	36
1893–94c	Aston Villa	44	Sunderland	38	Derby Co	36
1894–95c	Sunderland	47	Everton	42	Aston Villa	39
1895–96c	Aston Villa	45	Derby Co	41	Everton	39
1896–97c	Aston Villa	47	Sheffield U*	36	Derby Co	36
1897–98c	Sheffield U	42	Sunderland	37	Wolverhampton W*	35
1898–99c	Aston Villa	45	Liverpool	43	Burnley	39
1899–1900d	Aston Villa	50	Sheffield U	48	Sunderland	41
1900–01d	Liverpool	45	Sunderland	43	Notts Co	40
1901–02d	Sunderland	44	Everton	41	Newcastle U	37
1902–03d	The Wednesday	42	Aston Villa*	41	Sunderland	41
1903–04d	The Wednesday	47	Manchester C	44	Everton	43
1904–05d	Newcastle U	48	Everton	47	Manchester C	46
1905–06e	Liverpool	51	Preston NE	47	The Wednesday	44
1906–07e	Newcastle U	51	Bristol C	48	Everton*	45
1907–08e	Manchester U	52	Aston Villa*	43	Manchester C	43
1908–09e	Newcastle U	53	Everton	46	Sunderland	44
1909–10e	Aston Villa	53	Liverpool	48	Blackburn R*	45
1910–11e	Manchester U	52	Aston Villa	51	Sunderland*	45
1911–12e	Blackburn R	49	Everton	46	Newcastle U	44
1912–13e	Sunderland	54	Aston Villa	50	Sheffield W	49
1913–14e	Blackburn R	51	Aston Villa	44	Middlesbrough*	43
1914–15e	Everton	46	Oldham Ath	45	Blackburn R*	43
1919–20f	WBA	60	Burnley	51	Chelsea	49
1920–21f	Burnley	59	Manchester C	54	Bolton W	52
1921–22f	Liverpool	57	Tottenham H	51	Burnley	49
1922–23f	Liverpool	60	Sunderland	54	Huddersfield T	53
1923–24f	Huddersfield T*	57	Cardiff C	57	Sunderland	53
1924–25f	Huddersfield T	58	WBA	56	Bolton W	55
1925–26f	Huddersfield T	57	Arsenal	52	Sunderland	48
1926–27f	Newcastle U	56	Huddersfield T	51	Sunderland	49
1927–28f	Everton	53	Huddersfield T	51	Leicester C	48
1928–29f	Sheffield W	52	Leicester C	51	Aston Villa	50
1929–30f	Sheffield W	60	Derby Co	50	Manchester C*	47
1930–31f	Arsenal	66	Aston Villa	59	Sheffield W	52
1931–32f	Everton	56	Arsenal	54	Sheffield W	50
1932–33f	Arsenal	58	Aston Villa	54	Sheffield W	51
1933–34f	Arsenal	59	Huddersfield T	56	Tottenham H	49
1934–35f	Arsenal	58	Sunderland	54	Sheffield W	49
1935–36f	Sunderland	56	Derby Co*	48	Huddersfield T	48
1936–37f	Manchester C	57	Charlton Ath	54	Arsenal	52
1937–38f	Arsenal	52	Wolverhampton W	51	Preston NE	49

	First	Pts	Second	Pts	Third	Pts
1938–39f	Everton	59	Wolverhampton W	55	Charlton Ath	50
1946–47f	Liverpool	57	Manchester U*	56	Wolverhampton W	56
1947–48f	Arsenal	59	Manchester U*	52	Burnley	52
1948–49f	Portsmouth	58	Manchester U*	53	Derby Co	53
1949–50f	Portsmouth*	53	Wolverhampton W	53	Sunderland	52
1950–51f	Tottenham H	60	Manchester U	56	Blackpool	50
1951–52f	Manchester U	57	Tottenham H*	53	Arsenal	53
1952–53f	Arsenal*	54	Preston NE	54	Wolverhampton W	51
1953–54f	Wolverhampton W	57	WBA	53	Huddersfield T	51
1954–55f	Chelsea	52	Wolverhampton W*	48	Portsmouth*	48
1955–56f	Manchester U	60	Blackpool*	49	Wolverhampton W	49
1956–57f	Manchester U	64	Tottenham H*	56	Preston NE	56
1957–58f	Wolverhampton W	64	Preston NE	59	Tottenham H	51
1958–59f	Wolverhampton W	61	Manchester U	55	Arsenal*	50
1959–60f	Burnley	55	Wolverhampton W	54	Tottenham H	53
1960–61f	Tottenham H	66	Sheffield W	58	Wolverhampton W	57
1961–62f	Ipswich T	56	Burnley	53	Tottenham H	52
1962–63f	Everton	61	Tottenham H	55	Burnley	54
1963–64f	Liverpool	57	Manchester U	53	Everton	52
1964–65f	Manchester U*	61	Leeds U	61	Chelsea	56
1965–66f	Liverpool	61	Leeds U*	55	Burnley	55
1966–67f	Manchester U	60	Nottingham F*	56	Tottenham H	56
1967–68f	Manchester C	58	Manchester U	56	Liverpool	55
1968–69f	Leeds U	67	Liverpool	61	Everton	57
1969–70f	Everton	66	Leeds U	57	Chelsea	55
1970–71f	Arsenal	65	Leeds U	64	Tottenham H*	52
1971–72f	Derby Co	58	Leeds U*	57	Liverpool*	57
1972–73f	Liverpool	60	Arsenal	57	Leeds U	53
1973–74f	Leeds U	62	Liverpool	57	Derby Co	48
1974–75f	Derby Co	53	Liverpool*	51	Ipswich T	51
1975–76f	Liverpool	60	QPR	59	Manchester U	56
1976–77f	Liverpool	57	Manchester C	56	Ipswich T	52
1977–78f	Nottingham F	64	Liverpool	57	Everton	55
1978–79f	Liverpool	68	Nottingham F	60	WBA	59
1979–80f	Liverpool	60	Manchester U	58	Ipswich T	53
1980–81f	Aston Villa	60	Ipswich T	56	Arsenal	53
1981–82g	Liverpool	87	Ipswich T	83	Manchester U	78
1982–83g	Liverpool	82	Watford	71	Manchester U	70
1983–84g	Liverpool	80	Southampton	77	Nottingham F*	74
1984–85g	Everton	90	Liverpool*	77	Tottenham H	77
1985–86g	Liverpool	88	Everton	86	West Ham U	84
1986–87g	Everton	86	Liverpool	77	Tottenham H	71
1987–88h	Liverpool	90	Manchester U	81	Nottingham F	73
1988–89k	Arsenal*	76	Liverpool	76	Nottingham F	64
1989–90k	Liverpool	79	Aston Villa	70	Tottenham H	63
1990–91k	Arsenal†	83	Liverpool	76	Crystal Palace	69
1991–92g	Leeds U	82	Manchester U	78	Sheffield W	75

No official competition during 1915–19 and 1939–46; Regional Leagues operating.
* Won or placed on goal average (ratio)/goal difference.
† 2 pts deducted

Maximum points: a 44; b 56; c 60; d 68; e 76; f 84; g 126; h 132; k 138.

Season					
1892–93a	Small Heath	36	Sheffield U	35	Darwen	30
1893–94b	Liverpool	50	Small Heath	42	Notts Co	39
1894–95c	Bury	48	Notts Co	39	Newton Heath*	38
1895–96c	Liverpool*	46	Manchester C	46	Grimsby T*	42
1896–97c	Notts Co	42	Newton Heath	39	Grimsby T	38
1897–98c	Burnley	48	Newcastle U	45	Manchester C	39
1898–99d	Manchester C	52	Glossop NE	46	Leicester Fosse	45
1899–1900d	The Wednesday	54	Bolton W	52	Small Heath	46
1900–01d	Grimsby T	49	Small Heath	48	Burnley	44
1901–02d	WBA	55	Middlesbrough	51	Preston NE*	42
1902–03d	Manchester C	54	Small Heath	51	Woolwich A	48
1903–04d	Preston NE	50	Woolwich A	49	Manchester U	48
1904–05d	Liverpool	58	Bolton W	56	Manchester U	53
1905–06e	Bristol C	66	Manchester U	62	Chelsea	53
1906–07e	Nottingham F	60	Chelsea	57	Leicester Fosse	48
1907–08e	Bradford C	54	Leicester Fosse	52	Oldham Ath	50
1908–09e	Bolton W	52	Tottenham H*	51	WBA	51
1909–10e	Manchester C	54	Oldham Ath*	53	Hull C*	53
1910–11e	WBA	53	Bolton W	51	Chelsea	49
1911–12e	Derby Co*	54	Chelsea	54	Burnley	52
1912–13e	Preston NE	53	Burnley	50	Birmingham	46
1913–14e	Notts Co	53	Bradford PA*	49	Woolwich A	49
1914–15e	Derby Co	53	Preston NE	50	Barnsley	47
1919–20f	Tottenham H	70	Huddersfield T	64	Birmingham	56
1920–21f	Birmingham*	58	Cardiff C	58	Bristol C	51
1921–22f	Nottingham F	56	Stoke C*	52	Barnsley	52
1922–23f	Notts Co	53	West Ham U*	51	Leicester C	51
1923–24f	Leeds U	54	Bury*	51	Derby Co	51
1924–25f	Leicester C	59	Manchester U	57	Derby Co	55
1925–26f	Sheffield W	60	Derby Co	57	Chelsea	52
1926–27f	Middlesbrough	62	Portsmouth*	54	Manchester C	54
1927–28f	Manchester C	59	Leeds U	57	Chelsea	54
1928–29f	Middlesbrough	55	Grimsby T	53	Bradford PA*	48
1929–30f	Blackpool	58	Chelsea	55	Oldham Ath	53
1930–31f	Everton	61	WBA	54	Tottenham H	51
1931–32f	Wolverhampton W	56	Leeds U	54	Stoke C	52
1932–33f	Stoke C	56	Tottenham H	55	Fulham	50
1933–34f	Grimsby T	59	Preston NE	52	Bolton W*	51
1934–35f	Brentford	61	Bolton W*	56	West Ham U	56
1935–36f	Manchester U	56	Charlton Ath	55	Sheffield U*	52
1936–37f	Leicester C	56	Blackpool	55	Bury	52
1937–38f	Aston Villa	57	Manchester U*	53	Sheffield U	53
1938–39f	Blackburn R	55	Sheffield U	54	Sheffield W	53
1946–47f	Manchester C	62	Burnley	58	Birmingham C	55
1947–48f	Birmingham C	59	Newcastle U	56	Southampton	52
1948–49f	Fulham	57	WBA	56	Southampton	55
1949–50f	Tottenham H	61	Sheffield W*	52	Sheffield U*	52
1950–51f	Preston NE	57	Manchester C	52	Cardiff C	50
1951–52f	Sheffield W	53	Cardiff C*	51	Birmingham C	51
1952–53f	Sheffield U	60	Huddersfield T	58	Luton T	52

	First	Pts	Second	Pts	Third	Pts
1953–54f	Leicester C*	56	Everton	56	Blackburn R	55
1954–55f	Birmingham C*	54	Luton T*	54	Rotherham U	54
1955–56f	Sheffield W	55	Leeds U	52	Liverpool*	48
1956–57f	Leicester C	61	Nottingham F	54	Liverpool	53
1957–58f	West Ham U	57	Blackburn R	56	Charlton Ath	55
1958–59f	Sheffield W	62	Fulham	60	Sheffield U*	53
1959–60f	Aston Villa	59	Cardiff C	58	Liverpool*	50
1960–61f	Ipswich T	59	Sheffield U	58	Liverpool	52
1961–62f	Liverpool	62	Leyton Orient	54	Sunderland	53
1962–63f	Stoke C	53	Chelsea*	52	Sunderland	52
1963–64f	Leeds U	63	Sunderland	61	Preston NE	56
1964–65f	Newcastle U	57	Northampton T	56	Bolton W	50
1965–66f	Manchester C	59	Southampton	54	Coventry C	53
1966–67f	Coventry C	59	Wolverhampton W	58	Carlisle U	52
1967–68f	Ipswich T	59	QPR*	58	Blackpool	58
1968–69f	Derby Co	63	Crystal Palace	56	Charlton Ath	50
1969–70f	Huddersfield T	60	Blackpool	53	Leicester C	51
1970–71f	Leicester C	59	Sheffield U	56	Cardiff C*	53
1971–72f	Norwich C	57	Birmingham C	56	Millwall	55
1972–73f	Burnley	62	QPR	61	Aston Villa	50
1973–74f	Middlesbrough	65	Luton T	50	Carlisle U	49
1974–75f	Manchester U	61	Aston Villa	58	Norwich C	53
1975–76f	Sunderland	56	Bristol C*	53	WBA	53
1976–77f	Wolverhampton W	57	Chelsea	55	Nottingham F	52
1977–78f	Bolton W	58	Southampton	57	Tottenham H*	56
1978–79f	Crystal Palace	57	Brighton & HA*	56	Stoke C	56
1979–80f	Leicester C	55	Sunderland	54	Birmingham C*	53
1980–81f	West Ham U	66	Notts Co	53	Swansea C*	50
1981–82g	Luton T	88	Watford	80	Norwich C	71
1982–83g	QPR	85	Wolverhampton W	75	Leicester C	70
1983–84g	Chelsea*	88	Sheffield W	88	Newcastle U	80
1984–85g	Oxford U	84	Birmingham C	82	Manchester C	74
1985–86g	Norwich C	84	Charlton Ath	77	Wimbledon	76
1986–87g	Derby Co	84	Portsmouth	78	Oldham Ath††	75
1987–88h	Millwall	82	Aston Villa*	78	Middlesbrough	78
1988–89k	Chelsea	99	Manchester C	82	Crystal Palace	81
1989–90k	Leeds U*	85	Sheffield U	85	Newcastle U††	80
1990–91k	Oldham Ath	88	West Ham U	87	Sheffield W	82
1991–92k	Ipswich T	84	Middlesbrough	80	Derby Co	78

No official competition during 1915–19 and 1939–46; Regional Leagues operating.
* Won or placed on goal average (ratio)/goal difference.
†† Not promoted after play-offs.

DIVISION 3 to 1991–92

Maximum points: 92; 138 from 1981–82.

1958–59	Plymouth Arg	62	Hull C	61	Brentford*	57
1959–60	Southampton	61	Norwich C	59	Shrewsbury T*	52
1960–61	Bury	68	Walsall	62	QPR	60
1961–62	Portsmouth	65	Grimsby T	62	Bournemouth*	59
1962–63	Northampton T	62	Swindon T	58	Port Vale	54
1963–64	Coventry C*	60	Crystal Palace	60	Watford	58

	First	Pts	Second	Pts	Third	Pts
1964–65	Carlisle U	60	Bristol C*	59	Mansfield T	59
1965–66	Hull C	69	Millwall	65	QPR	57
1966–67	QPR	67	Middlesbrough	55	Watford	54
1967–68	Oxford U	57	Bury	56	Shrewsbury T	55
1968–69	Watford*	64	Swindon T	64	Luton T	61
1969–70	Orient	62	Luton T	60	Bristol R	56
1970–71	Preston NE	61	Fulham	60	Halifax T	56
1971–72	Aston Villa	70	Brighton & HA	65	Bournemouth*	62
1972–73	Bolton W	61	Notts Co	57	Blackburn R	55
1973–74	Oldham Ath	62	Bristol R*	61	York C	61
1974–75	Blackburn R	60	Plymouth Arg	59	Charlton Ath	55
1975–76	Hereford U	63	Cardiff C	57	Millwall	56
1976–77	Mansfield T	64	Brighton & HA	61	Crystal Palace*	59
1977–78	Wrexham	61	Cambridge U	58	Preston NE*	56
1978–79	Shrewsbury T	61	Watford*	60	Swansea C	60
1979–80	Grimsby T	62	Blackburn R	59	Sheffield W	58
1980–81	Rotherham U	61	Barnsley*	59	Charlton Ath	59
1981–82	Burnley*	80	Carlisle U	80	Fulham	78
1982–83	Portsmouth	91	Cardiff C	86	Huddersfield T	82
1983–84	Oxford U	95	Wimbledon	87	Sheffield U*	83
1984–85	Bradford C	94	Millwall	90	Hull C	87
1985–86	Reading	94	Plymouth Arg	87	Derby Co	84
1986–87	Bournemouth	97	Middlesbrough	94	Swindon T	87
1987–88	Sunderland	93	Brighton & HA	84	Walsall	82
1988–89	Wolverhampton W	92	Sheffield U*	84	Port Vale	84
1989–90	Bristol R	93	Bristol C	91	Notts Co	87
1990–91	Cambridge U	86	Southend U	85	Grimsby T*	83
1991–92	Brentford	82	Birmingham C	81	Huddersfield T	78

Won or placed on goal average (ratio)/goal difference.

DIVISION 4 (1958–1992)

Maximum points: 92; 138 from 1981–82.

	First	Pts	Second	Pts	Third	Pts
1958–59	Port Vale	64	Coventry C*	60	York C	60
1959–60	Walsall	65	Notts Co*	60	Torquay U	60
1960–61	Peterborough U	66	Crystal Palace	64	Northampton T*	60
1961–62†	Millwall	56	Colchester U	55	Wrexham	53
1962–63	Brentford	62	Oldham Ath*	59	Crewe Alex	59
1963–64	Gillingham*	60	Carlisle U	60	Workington	59
1964–65	Brighton & HA	63	Millwall*	62	York C	62
1965–66	Doncaster R*	59	Darlington	59	Torquay U	58
1966–67	Stockport Co	64	Southport*	59	Barrow	59
1967–68	Luton T	66	Barnsley	61	Hartlepools U	60
1968–69	Doncaster R	59	Halifax T	57	Rochdale*	56
1969–70	Chesterfield	64	Wrexham	61	Swansea C	60
1970–71	Notts Co	69	Bournemouth	60	Oldham Ath	59
1971–72	Grimsby T	63	Southend U	60	Brentford	59
1972–73	Southport	62	Hereford U	58	Cambridge U	57
1973–74	Peterborough U	65	Gillingham	62	Colchester U	60
1974–75	Mansfield T	68	Shrewsbury T	62	Rotherham U	59
1975–76	Lincoln C	74	Northampton T	68	Reading	60
1976–77	Cambridge U	65	Exeter C	62	Colchester U*	59

	First	Pts	Second	Pts	Third	Pts
1977–78	Watford	71	Southend U	60	Swansea C*	56
1978–79	Reading	65	Grimsby T*	61	Wimbledon*	61
1979–80	Huddersfield T	66	Walsall	64	Newport Co	61
1980–81	Southend U	67	Lincoln C	65	Doncaster R	56
1981–82	Sheffield U	96	Bradford C*	91	Wigan Ath	91
1982–83	Wimbledon	98	Hull C	90	Port Vale	88
1983–84	York C	101	Doncaster R	85	Reading*	82
1984–85	Chesterfield	91	Blackpool	86	Darlington	85
1985–86	Swindon T	102	Chester C	84	Mansfield T	81
1986–87	Northampton T	99	Preston NE	90	Southend U	80
1987–88	Wolverhampton W	90	Cardiff C	85	Bolton W	78
1988–89	Rotherham U	82	Tranmere R	80	Crewe Alex	78
1989–90	Exeter C	89	Grimsby T	79	Southend U	75
1990–91	Darlington	83	Stockport Co*	82	Hartlepool U	82
1991–92§	Burnley	83	Rotherham U*	77	Mansfield T	77

* Won or placed on goal average (ratio)/goal difference.

† Maximum points: 88 owing to Accrington Stanley's resignation. †† Not promoted after play-offs.

§ Maximum points: 126 owing to Aldershot being expelled.

DIVISION 3—SOUTH (1920–1958)

1920–21 Season as Division 3.

Maximum points: a 84; b 92.

	First		Second		Third	
1920–21a	Crystal Palace	59	Southampton	54	QPR	53
1921–22a	Southampton*	61	Plymouth Arg	61	Portsmouth	53
1922–23a	Bristol C	59	Plymouth Arg*	53	Swansea T	53
1923–24a	Portsmouth	59	Plymouth Arg	55	Millwall	54
1924–25a	Swansea T	57	Plymouth Arg	56	Bristol C	53
1925–26a	Reading	57	Plymouth Arg	56	Millwall	53
1926–27a	Bristol C	62	Plymouth Arg	60	Millwall	56
1927–28a	Millwall	65	Northampton T	55	Plymouth Arg	53
1928–29a	Charlton Ath*	54	Crystal Palace	54	Northampton T*	52
1929–30a	Plymouth Arg	68	Brentford	61	QPR	51
1930–31a	Notts Co	59	Crystal Palace	51	Brentford	50
1931–32a	Fulham	57	Reading	55	Southend U	53
1932–33a	Brentford	62	Exeter C	58	Norwich C	57
1933–34a	Norwich C	61	Coventry C*	54	Reading*	54
1934–35a	Charlton Ath	61	Reading	53	Coventry C	51
1935–36a	Coventry C	57	Luton T	56	Reading	54
1936–37a	Luton T	58	Notts Co	56	Brighton & HA	53
1937–38a	Millwall	56	Bristol C	55	QPR*	53
1938–39a	Newport Co	55	Crystal Palace	52	Brighton & HA	49
1939–46	*Competition cancelled owing to war.*					
1946–47a	Cardiff C	66	QPR	57	Bristol C	51
1947–48a	QPR	61	Bournemouth	57	Walsall	51
1948–49a	Swansea T	62	Reading	55	Bournemouth	52
1949–50a	Notts Co	58	Northampton T*	51	Southend U	51
1950–51b	Nottingham F	70	Norwich C	64	Reading*	57
1951–52b	Plymouth Arg	66	Reading*	61	Norwich C	61
1952–53b	Bristol R	64	Millwall*	62	Northampton T	62
1953–54b	Ipswich T	64	Brighton & HA	61	Bristol C	56

Won or placed on goal average (ratio).

DIVISION 3—NORTH (1921–1958)

Maximum points: a 76; b 84; c 80; d 92.

Won or placed on goal average (ratio).

PROMOTED AFTER PLAY-OFFS

(Not accounted for in previous section)

1986–87 Aldershot to Division 3.

1987–88 Swansea C to Division 3.

1988–89 Leyton Orient to Division 3.

1989–90 Cambridge U to Division 3; Notts Co to Division 2; Sunderland to Division 1.

1990–91 Notts Co to Division 1; Tranmere R to Division 2; Torquay U to Division 3.

1991–92 Blackburn R to Premier League; Peterborough U to Division 1.

1992–93 Swindon T to Premier League; WBA to Division 1; York C to Division 2.

1993–94 Leicester C to Premier League; Burnley to Division 1; Wycombe W to Division 2.

1994–95 Huddersfield T to Division 1.

1995–96 Leicester C to Premier League; Bradford C to Division 1; Plymouth Arg to Division 2.

1996–97 Crystal Palace to Premier League; Crewe Alex to Division 1; Northampton T to Division 2.

1997–98 Charlton Ath to Premier League; Colchester U to Division 2.

1998–99 Watford to Premier League; Scunthorpe to Division 2.

1999–00 Peterborough U to Division 2.

2000–01 Walsall to Division 1; Blackpool to Division 2.

2001–02 Birmingham C to Premier League; Stoke C to Division 1; Cheltenham T to Division 2.

2002–03 Wolverhampton W to Premier League; Cardiff C to Division 1; Bournemouth to Division 2.

2003–04 Crystal Palace to Premier League; Brighton & HA to Division 1; Huddersfield T to Division 2.

2004–05 West Ham U to Premier League; Sheffield W to Football League Championship, Southend U to Football League Championship 1.

2005–06 Watford to Premier League; Barnsley to Football League Championship; Cheltenham T to Football League Championship 1.

2006–07 Derby Co to Premier League; Blackpool to Football League Championship; Bristol R to Football League Championship 1.

2007–08 Hull C to Premier League; Doncaster R to Football League Championship; Stockport Co to Football League Championship 1.

2008–09 Burnley to Premier League; Scunthorpe U to Championship; Gillingham to Championship 1.

2009–10 Blackpool to Premier League; Millwall to Championship; Dagenham & R to Championship 1.

2010–11 Swansea C to Premier League; Peterborough U to Championship; Stevenage to Championship 1.

2010–12 West Ham U to Premier League; Huddersfield T to Championship; Crewe Alex to Championship 1.

RELEGATED CLUBS

FA PREMIER LEAGUE TO DIVISION 1

1992–93 Crystal Palace, Middlesbrough, Nottingham F
1993–94 Sheffield U, Oldham Ath, Swindon T
1994–95 Crystal Palace, Norwich C, Leicester C, Ipswich T
1995–96 Manchester C, QPR, Bolton W
1996–97 Sunderland, Middlesbrough, Nottingham F
1997–98 Bolton W, Barnsley, Crystal Palace
1998–99 Charlton Ath, Blackburn R, Nottingham F
1999–90 Wimbledon, Sheffield W, Watford
2000–01 Manchester C, Coventry C, Bradford C
2001–02 Ipswich T, Derby Co, Leicester C
2002–03 West Ham U, WBA, Sunderland
2003–04 Leicester C, Leeds U, Wolverhampton W

FA PREMIER LEAGUE TO FOOTBALL LEAGUE CHAMPIONSHIP

2004–05 Crystal Palace, Norwich C, Southampton
2005–06 Birmingham C, WBA, Sunderland
2006–07 Sheffield U, Charlton Ath, Watford
2007–08 Reading, Birmingham C, Derby Co
2008–09 Newcastle U, Middlesbrough, WBA
2009–10 Burnley, Hull C, Portsmouth
2010–11 Birmingham C, Blackpool, West Ham U
2011–12 Bolton W, Blackburn R, Wolverhampton W

DIVISION 1 TO DIVISION 2

1898–99 Bolton W and Sheffield W
1899–1900 Burnley and Glossop
1900–01 Preston NE and WBA
1901–02 Small Heath and Manchester C
1902–03 Grimsby T and Bolton W
1903–04 Liverpool and WBA
1904–05 League extended. Bury and
   Notts Co, two bottom clubs in
   First Division, re-elected.
1905–06 Nottingham F and
   Wolverhampton W
1906–07 Derby Co and Stoke C
1907–08 Bolton W and Birmingham C
1908–09 Manchester C and Leicester
   Fosse
1909–10 Bolton W and Chelsea
1910–11 Bristol C and Nottingham F
1911–12 Preston NE and Bury
1912–13 Notts Co and Woolwich Arsenal
1913–14 Preston NE and Derby Co
1914–15 Tottenham H and Chelsea*
1919–20 Notts Co and Sheffield W
1920–21 Derby Co and Bradford PA
1921–22 Bradford C and Manchester U
1922–23 Stoke C and Oldham Ath
1923–24 Chelsea and Middlesbrough
1924–25 Preston NE and Nottingham F
1925–26 Manchester C and Notts Co
1926–27 Leeds U and WBA

1927–28 Tottenham H and Middlesbrough
1928–29 Bury and Cardiff C
1929–30 Burnley and Everton
1930–31 Leeds U and Manchester U
1931–32 Grimsby T and West Ham U
1932–33 Bolton W and Blackpool
1933–34 Newcastle U and Sheffield U
1934–35 Leicester C and Tottenham H
1935–36 Aston Villa and Blackburn R
1936–37 Manchester U and Sheffield W
1937–38 Manchester C and WBA
1938–39 Birmingham C and Leicester C
1946–47 Brentford and Leeds U
1947–48 Blackburn R and Grimsby T
1948–49 Preston NE and Sheffield U
1949–50 Manchester C and
   Birmingham C
1950–51 Sheffield W and Everton
1951–52 Huddersfield T and Fulham
1952–53 Stoke C and Derby Co
1953–54 Middlesbrough and Liverpool
1954–55 Leicester C and Sheffield W
1955–56 Huddersfield T and Sheffield U
1956–57 Charlton Ath and Cardiff C
1957–58 Sheffield W and Sunderland
1958–59 Portsmouth and Aston Villa
1959–60 Luton T and Leeds U
1960–61 Preston NE and Newcastle U
1961–62 Chelsea and Cardiff C

1962–63 Manchester C and Leyton Orient
1963–64 Bolton W and Ipswich T
1964–65 Wolverhampton W and
Birmingham C
1965–66 Northampton T and Blackburn R
1966–67 Aston Villa and Blackpool
1967–68 Fulham and Sheffield U
1968–69 Leicester C and QPR
1969–70 Sunderland and Sheffield W
1970–71 Burnley and Blackpool
1971–72 Huddersfield T and
Nottingham F
1972–73 Crystal Palace and WBA
1973–74 Southampton, Manchester U,
Norwich C
1974–75 Luton T, Chelsea, Carlisle U
1975–76 Wolverhampton W, Burnley,
Sheffield U
1976–77 Sunderland, Stoke C,
Tottenham H
1977–78 West Ham U, Newcastle U,
Leicester C
1978–79 QPR, Birmingham C, Chelsea
1979–80 Bristol C, Derby Co, Bolton W
1980–81 Norwich C, Leicester C, Crystal
Palace
1981–82 Leeds U, Wolverhampton W,
Middlesbrough
1982–83 Manchester C, Swansea C,
Brighton & HA
1983–84 Birmingham C, Notts Co,
Wolverhampton W

1984–85 Norwich C, Sunderland, Stoke C
1985–86 Ipswich T, Birmingham C, WBA
1986–87 Leicester C, Manchester C, Aston
Villa
1987–88 Chelsea**, Portsmouth, Watford,
Oxford U
1988–89 Middlesbrough, West Ham U,
Newcastle U
1989–90 Sheffield W, Charlton Ath,
Millwall
1990–91 Sunderland and Derby Co
1991–92 Luton T, Notts Co, West Ham U
1992–93 Brentford, Cambridge U,
Bristol R
1993–94 Birmingham C, Oxford U,
Peterborough U
1994–95 Swindon T, Burnley, Bristol C,
Notts Co
1995–96 Millwall, Watford, Luton T
1996–97 Grimsby T, Oldham Ath,
Southend U
1997–98 Manchester C, Stoke C, Reading
1998–99 Bury, Oxford U, Bristol C
1999–00 Walsall, Port Vale, Swindon T
2000–01 Huddersfield T, QPR,
Tranmere R
2001–02 Crewe Alex, Barnsley, Stockport
Co
2002–03 Sheffield W, Brighton & HA,
Grimsby T
2003–04 Walsall, Bradford C, Wimbledon

** *Relegated after play-offs.*
* *Subsequently re-elected to Division 1 when League was extended after the War.*

FOOTBALL LEAGUE CHAMPIONSHIP
TO FOOTBALL LEAGUE CHAMPIONSHIP 1

2004–05 Gillingham, Nottingham F, Rotherham U
2005–06 Crewe Alex, Millwall, Brighton & HA
2006–07 Southend U, Luton T, Leeds U
2007–08 Leicester C, Scunthorpe U, Colchester U
2008–09 Norwich C, Southampton, Charlton Ath
2009–10 Sheffield W, Plymouth Arg, Peterborough U
2010–11 Preston NE, Sheffield U, Scunthorpe U
2011–12 Portsmouth, Coventry, Doncaster R

DIVISION 2 TO DIVISION 3

1920–21 Stockport Co
1921–22 Bradford PA and Bristol C
1922–23 Rotherham Co and
Wolverhampton W
1923–24 Nelson and Bristol C
1924–25 Crystal Palace and Coventry C
1925–26 Stoke C and Stockport Co
1926–27 Darlington and Bradford C
1927–28 Fulham and South Shields

1928–29 Port Vale and Clapton Orient
1929–30 Hull C and Notts Co
1930–31 Reading and Cardiff C
1931–32 Barnsley and Bristol C
1932–33 Chesterfield and Charlton Ath
1933–34 Millwall and Lincoln C
1934–35 Oldham Ath and Notts Co
1935–36 Port Vale and Hull C
1936–37 Doncaster R and Bradford C

1937–38 Barnsley and Stockport Co
1938–39 Norwich C and Tranmere R
1946–47 Swansea T and Newport Co
1947–48 Doncaster R and Millwall
1948–49 Nottingham F and Lincoln C
1949–50 Plymouth Arg and Bradford PA
1950–51 Grimsby T and Chesterfield
1951–52 Coventry C and QPR
1952–53 Southampton and Barnsley
1953–54 Brentford and Oldham Ath
1954–55 Ipswich T and Derby Co
1955–56 Plymouth Arg and Hull C
1956–57 Port Vale and Bury
1957–58 Doncaster R and Notts Co
1958–59 Barnsley and Grimsby T
1959–60 Bristol C and Hull C
1960–61 Lincoln C and Portsmouth
1961–62 Brighton & HA and Bristol R
1962–63 Walsall and Luton T
1963–64 Grimsby T and Scunthorpe U
1964–65 Swindon T and Swansea T
1965–66 Middlesbrough and Leyton Orient
1966–67 Northampton T and Bury
1967–68 Plymouth Arg and Rotherham U
1968–69 Fulham and Bury
1969–70 Preston NE and Aston Villa
1970–71 Blackburn R and Bolton W
1971–72 Charlton Ath and Watford
1972–73 Huddersfield T and Brighton & HA
1973–74 Crystal Palace, Preston NE,
        Swindon T
1974–75 Millwall, Cardiff C, Sheffield W
1975–76 Oxford U, York C, Portsmouth
1976–77 Carlisle U, Plymouth Arg,
        Hereford U
1977–78 Blackpool, Mansfield T, Hull C
1978–79 Sheffield U, Millwall, Blackburn R
1979–80 Fulham, Burnley, Charlton Ath
1980–81 Preston NE, Bristol C, Bristol R
1981–82 Cardiff C, Wrexham, Orient
1982–83 Rotherham U, Burnley, Bolton W

1983–84 Derby Co, Swansea C, Cambridge U
1984–85 Notts Co, Cardiff C,
        Wolverhampton W
1985–86 Carlisle U, Middlesbrough, Fulham
1986–87 Sunderland**, Grimsby T,
        Brighton & HA
1987–88 Huddersfield T, Reading, Sheffield
        U**
1988–89 Shrewsbury T, Birmingham C,
        Walsall
1989–90 Bournemouth, Bradford C,
        Stoke C
1990–91 WBA and Hull C
1991–92 Plymouth Arg, Brighton & HA,
        Port Vale
1992–93 Preston NE, Mansfield T,
        Wigan Ath, Chester C
1993–94 Fulham, Exeter C, Hartlepool U,
        Barnet
1994–95 Cambridge U, Plymouth Arg,
        Cardiff C, Chester C, Leyton
        Orient
1995–96 Carlisle U, Swansea C, Brighton &
        HA, Hull C
1996–97 Peterborough U, Shrewsbury T,
        Rotherham U, Notts Co
1997–98 Brentford, Plymouth Arg, Carlisle
        U, Southend U
1998–99 York C, Northampton T, Lincoln
        C, Macclesfield T
1999–00 Cardiff C, Blackpool, Scunthorpe
        U, Chesterfield
2000–01 Bristol R, Luton T, Swansea C,
        Oxford U
2001–02 Bournemouth, Bury, Wrexham,
        Cambridge U
2002–03 Cheltenham T, Huddersfield T,
        Mansfield T, Northampton T
2003–04 Grimsby T, Rushden & D, Notts
        Co, Wycombe W

FOOTBALL LEAGUE CHAMPIONSHIP 1
TO FOOTBALL LEAGUE CHAMPIONSHIP 2

2004–05 Torquay U, Wrexham, Peterborough U, Stockport Co
2005–06 Hartlepool U, Milton Keynes D, Swindon T, Walsall
2006–07 Chesterfield, Bradford C, Rotherham U, Brentford
2007–08 Bournemouth, Gillingham, Port Vale, Luton T
2008–09 Northampton T, Crewe Alex, Cheltenham T, Hereford U
2009–10 Gillingham, Wycombe W, Southend U, Stockport Co
2010–11 Dagenham & R, Bristol R, Plymouth Arg, Swindon T
2011–12 Wycombe W, Chesterfield, Exeter C, Rochdale

DIVISION 3 TO DIVISION 4

1958–59 Rochdale, Notts Co,
Doncaster R, Stockport Co

1959–60 Accrington S, Wrexham,
Mansfield T, York C

1960–61 Chesterfield, Colchester U,
Bradford C, Tranmere R

1961–62 Newport Co, Brentford,
Lincoln C, Torquay U

1962–63 Bradford PA, Brighton & HA,
Carlisle U, Halifax T

1963–64 Millwall, Crewe Alex, Wrexham,
Notts Co

1964–65 Luton T, Port Vale, Colchester U,
Barnsley

1965–66 Southend U, Exeter C, Brentford,
York C

1966–67 Doncaster R, Workington,
Darlington, Swansea T

1967–68 Scunthorpe U, Colchester U,
Grimsby T, Peterborough U
(demoted)

1968–69 Oldham Ath, Crewe Alex,
Hartlepool, Northampton T

1969–70 Bournemouth, Southport,
Barrow, Stockport Co

1970–71 Reading, Bury, Doncaster R,
Gillingham

1971–72 Mansfield T, Barnsley, Torquay U,
Bradford C

1972–73 Rotherham U, Brentford,
Swansea C, Scunthorpe U

1973–74 Cambridge U, Shrewsbury T,
Southport, Rochdale

1974–75 Bournemouth, Tranmere R,
Watford, Huddersfield T

1975–76 Aldershot, Colchester U,
Southend U, Halifax T

1976–77 Reading, Northampton T,
Grimsby T, York C

1977–78 Port Vale, Bradford C,
Hereford U, Portsmouth

1978–79 Peterborough U, Walsall,
Tranmere R, Lincoln C

1979–80 Bury, Southend U, Mansfield T,
Wimbledon

1980–81 Sheffield U, Colchester U,
Blackpool, Hull C

1981–82 Wimbledon, Swindon T,
Bristol C, Chester

1982–83 Reading, Wrexham, Doncaster R,
Chesterfield

1983–84 Scunthorpe U, Southend U,
Port Vale, Exeter C

1984–85 Burnley, Orient, Preston NE,
Cambridge U

1985–86 Lincoln C, Cardiff C,
Wolverhampton W, Swansea C

1986–87 Bolton W**, Carlisle U,
Darlington, Newport Co

1987–88 Doncaster R, York C, Grimsby T,
Rotherham U**

1988–89 Southend U, Chesterfield,
Gillingham, Aldershot

1989–90 Cardiff C, Northampton T,
Blackpool, Walsall

1990–91 Crewe Alex, Rotherham U,
Mansfield T

1991–92 Bury, Shrewsbury T, Torquay U,
Darlington

** *Relegated after play-offs.*

LEAGUE STATUS FROM 1986–1987

RELEGATED FROM LEAGUE	PROMOTED TO LEAGUE
1986–87 Lincoln C	Scarborough
1987–88 Newport Co	Lincoln C
1988–89 Darlington	Maidstone U
1989–90 Colchester U	Darlington
1990–91 —	Barnet
1991–92 —	Colchester U
1992–93 Halifax T	Wycombe W
1993–94 —	—
1994–95 —	—
1995–96 —	—
1996–97 Hereford U	Macclesfield T
1997–98 Doncaster R	Halifax T
1998–99 Scarborough	Cheltenham T
1999–2000 Chester C	Kidderminster H
2000–01 Barnet	Rushden & D
2001–02 Halifax T	Boston U
2002–03 Shrewsbury T, Exeter C	Yeovil T, Doncaster R
2003–04 Carlisle U, York C	Chester C, Shrewsbury T
2004–05 Kidderminster H, Cambridge U	Barnet, Carlisle U
2005–06 Oxford U, Rushden & D	Accrington S, Hereford U
2006–07 Boston U, Torquay U	Dagenham & R, Morecambe
2007–08 Mansfield T, Wrexham	Aldershot T, Exeter C
2008–09 Chester C, Luton T	Burton Alb, Torquay U
2009–10 Grimsby T, Darlington	Stevenage B, Oxford U
2010–11 Lincoln C, Stockport Co	Crawley T, AFC Wimbledon
2011–12 Hereford U, Macclesfield T	Fleetwood T, York C

Did You Know?

There have been many close finishes to top flight championships in the past but arguably none as close as in 2011–12 when Manchester City won it in extra time to deprive Manchester United of the title on goals scored when there were no other differences. Yet there have been five other occasions when teams finished level on points. In 1924 Huddersfield Town edged Cardiff City on goal average (goals scored divided by goals conceded) when a goal either way would have changed it. In 1950 Portsmouth also won on goal average and three years later free-scoring Arsenal were comfortably ahead by the same method. In 1965 it was Manchester United, with a better defensive record, who deprived Leeds United. Even so there was a dramatic climax in 1989 when Arsenal scored a second goal late in the last game against rivals Liverpool to win on goals scored under the goal difference system.

LEAGUE TITLE WINS

FA PREMIER LEAGUE – Manchester U 12, Arsenal 3, Chelsea 3, Blackburn R 1, Manchester C 1.

FOOTBALL LEAGUE CHAMPIONSHIP – Reading 2, Sunderland 2, Newcastle U 1, QPR 1, WBA 1, Wolverhampton W 1.

LEAGUE DIVISION 1 – Liverpool 18, Arsenal 10, Everton 9, Sunderland 8, Aston Villa 7, Manchester U 7, Newcastle U 5, Sheffield W 4, Huddersfield T 3, Leeds U 3, Manchester C 3, Portsmouth 3, Wolverhampton W 3, Blackburn R 2, Burnley 2, Derby Co 2, Nottingham F 2, Preston NE 2, Tottenham H 2; Bolton W, Charlton Ath, Chelsea, Crystal Palace, Fulham, Ipswich T, Middlesbrough, Norwich C, Sheffield U, WBA 1 each.

FOOTBALL LEAGUE CHAMPIONSHIP 1 – Brighton & HA 1, Charlton Ath 1, Leicester C 1, Luton T 1, Norwich C 1, Scunthorpe U 1, Southend U 1, Swansea C 1.

LEAGUE DIVISION 2 – Leicester C 6, Manchester C 6, Birmingham C (one as Small Heath) 5, Sheffield W 5, Derby Co 4, Liverpool 4, Preston NE 4, Ipswich T 3, Leeds U 3, Middlesbrough 3, Notts Co 3, Stoke C 3, Aston Villa 2, Bolton W 2, Burnley 2, Bury 2, Chelsea 2, Fulham 2, Grimsby T 2, Manchester U 2, Millwall 2, Norwich C 2, Nottingham F 2, Tottenham H 2, WBA 2, West Ham U 2, Wolverhampton W 2; Blackburn R, Blackpool, Bradford C, Brentford, Brighton & HA, Bristol C, Coventry C, Crystal Palace, Everton, Huddersfield T, Luton T, Newcastle U, Plymouth Arg, QPR, Oldham Ath, Oxford U, Reading, Sheffield U, Sunderland, Swindon T, Watford, Wigan Ath 1 each.

FOOTBALL LEAGUE CHAMPIONSHIP 2 – Brentford 1, Carlisle U 1, Chesterfield 1, Milton Keynes D 1, Notts Co 1, Swindon T 1, Walsall 1, Yeovil T 1.

LEAGUE DIVISION 3 – Brentford 2, Carlisle U 2, Oxford U 2, Plymouth Arg 2, Portsmouth 2, Preston NE 2, Shrewsbury T 2; Aston Villa, Blackburn R, Bolton W, Bournemouth, Bradford C, Brighton & HA, Bristol R, Burnley, Bury, Cambridge U, Cardiff C, Coventry C, Doncaster R, Grimsby T, Hereford U, Hull C, Leyton Orient, Mansfield T, Northampton T, Notts Co, Oldham Ath, QPR, Reading, Rotherham U, Rushden & D, Southampton, Sunderland, Swansea C, Watford, Wigan Ath, Wolverhampton W, Wrexham 1 each.

LEAGUE DIVISION 4 – Chesterfield 2, Doncaster R 2, Peterborough U 2; Brentford, Brighton & HA, Burnley, Cambridge U, Darlington, Exeter C, Gillingham, Grimsby T, Huddersfield T, Lincoln C, Luton T, Mansfield T, Millwall, Northampton T, Notts Co, Port Vale, Reading, Rotherham U, Sheffield U, Southend U, Southport, Stockport Co, Swindon T, Walsall, Watford, Wimbledon, Wolverhampton W, York C 1 each.

DIVISION 3 (South) – Bristol C 3, Charlton Ath 2, Ipswich T 2, Millwall 2, Notts Co 2, Plymouth Arg 2, Swansea T 2; Brentford, Brighton & HA, Bristol R, Cardiff C, Coventry C, Crystal Palace, Fulham, Leyton Orient, Luton T, Newport Co, Norwich C, Nottingham F, Portsmouth, QPR, Reading, Southampton 1 each.

DIVISION 3 (North) – Barnsley 3, Doncaster R 3, Lincoln C 3, Chesterfield 2, Grimsby T 2, Hull C 2, Port Vale 2, Stockport Co 2; Bradford C, Bradford PA, Darlington, Derby Co, Nelson, Oldham Ath, Rotherham U, Scunthorpe U, Stoke C, Tranmere R, Wolverhampton W 1 each.

FOOTBALL LEAGUE PLAY-OFFS 2011–2012

CHAMPIONSHIP FIRST LEG

Cardiff C	(0) 0	West Ham U	(2) 2
Blackpool	(1) 1	Birmingham C	(0) 0

CHAMPIONSHIP SECOND LEG

West Ham U	(2) 3	Cardiff C	(0) 0
Birmingham C	(0) 2	Blackpool	(1) 2

CHAMPIONSHIP FINAL (at Wembley) Saturday, 19 May 2012

Blackpool (0) 1 *(Ince 48)*

West Ham U (1) 2 *(Cole 35, Vaz Te 87)* 78,523

Blackpool: Gilks; Eardley, Crainey, Ferguson, John Baptiste, Evatt, Angel (Dicko), Dobbie (Bednar), Phillips K (Sylvestre), Ince, Phillips M.
West Ham U: Green; Demel (Faubert), Taylor, Nolan, Reid, Tomkins, O'Neil (McCartney), Noble, Cole, Vaz Te, Collison.
Referee: H. Webb (S. Yorkshire).

LEAGUE ONE FIRST LEG

Stevenage	(0) 0	Sheffield U	(0) 0
Milton Keynes D	(0) 0	Huddersfield T	(1) 2

LEAGUE ONE SECOND LEG

Sheffield U	(0) 1	Stevenage	(0) 0
Huddersfield T	(1) 1	Milton Keynes D	(1) 2

LEAGUE ONE FINAL (at Wembley) Saturday, 26 May 2012

Huddersfield T (0) 0

Sheffield U (0) 0 52,100

Huddersfield T: Smithies; Hunt, Woods, Miller, Clarke P, Morrison, Higginbotham (Roberts), Johnson, Rhodes, Novak (Arfield), Ward (Lee).
Sheffield U: Simonsen; Lowton, Hill, Montgomery (Taylor), Collins, Maguire, Williamson, Doyle, Flynn (O'Halloran), Cresswell (Porter), Quinn.
aet; Huddersfield T won 8-7 on penalties: Miller saved; Williamson saved; Johnson missed; Collins scored; Lee saved; Lowton saved; Clarke P scored; Taylor hit post; Arfield scored; Porter scored; Rhodes scored; Quinn scored; Roberts scored; Maguire scored; Woods scored; Doyle scored; Hunt scored; O'Halloran scored; Morrison scored; Hill scored; Smithies scored; Simonsen missed.

LEAGUE TWO FIRST LEG

Crewe Alex	(0) 1	Southend U	(0) 0
Cheltenham T	(1) 2	Torquay U	(0) 0

LEAGUE TWO SECOND LEG

Southend U	(0) 2	Crewe Alex	(1) 2
Torquay U	(0) 1	Cheltenham T	(0) 2

LEAGUE (at Wembley) Sunday, 27 May 2012

Cheltenham T (0) 0

Crewe Alex (0) 2 *(Powell 15, Moore 82)* 24,029

Cheltenham T: Brown; Jombati, Garbutt, Pack (Penn), Bennett, Elliott, McGlashan, Mohamed, Burgess (Spencer), Goulding (Duffy), Summerfield.
Crewe Alex: Phillips; Tootle, Davis, Westwood, Artell, Dugdale, Mellor, Murphy, Powell (Clayton), Leitch-Smith (Martin C), Moore (Bell).

LEAGUE ATTENDANCES 2011–2012

FA BARCLAYCARD PREMIERSHIP ATTENDANCES

	Average Gate			Season 2011–12	
	2010–11	2011–12	+/–%	Highest	Lowest
Arsenal	60,025	60,000	–0.04	60,111	59,643
Aston Villa	37,193	33,873	–8.93	40,053	30,100
Blackburn Rovers	24,999	22,551	–9.79	26,532	18,003
Bolton Wanderers	22,869	23,669	+3.50	26,901	20,028
Chelsea	41,435	41,478	+0.10	41,830	40,651
Everton	36,038	33,228	–7.80	39,517	29,561
Fulham	25,042	25,293	+1.00	25,700	23,555
Liverpool	42,820	44,253	+3.35	45,071	40,106
Manchester City	45,880	47,044	+2.54	48,000	46,321
Manchester United	75,109	75,387	+0.37	75,627	74,719
Newcastle United	47,717	49,935	+4.65	52,389	42,684
Norwich City	25,386	26,605	+4.80	26,819	26,107
Queens Park Rangers	15,635	17,295	+10.62	18,076	15,195
Stoke City	26,858	27,225	+1.37	27,789	26,500
Sunderland	40,011	39,095	–2.29	47,751	32,296
Swansea City	15,507	19,946	+28.63	20,605	18,985
Tottenham Hotspur	35,703	36,026	+0.90	36,274	35,172
West Bromwich Albion	24,682	24,798	+0.47	26,358	22,474
Wigan Athletic	16,812	18,633	+10.83	22,187	15,796
Wolverhampton Wanderers	27,695	25,682	–7.27	27,494	22,657

FOOTBALL LEAGUE CHAMPIONSHIP ATTENDANCES

	Average Gate			Season 2011–12	
	2010–11	2011–12	+/–%	Highest	Lowest
Barnsley	11,855	10,331	–12.86	17,499	8,900
Birmingham City	25,461	19,126	–24.88	25,516	16,253
Blackpool	15,779	12,764	–19.11	14,141	11,414
Brighton & Hove Albion	7,351	20,027	+172.44	20,968	18,412
Bristol City	14,604	13,907	–4.77	19,003	12,017
Burnley	14,930	14,048	–5.91	17,226	12,355
Cardiff City	23,193	22,100	–4.71	25,109	20,366
Coventry City	16,309	15,118	–7.30	22,240	12,054
Crystal Palace	15,390	15,219	–1.11	21,002	11,853
Derby County	25,892	26,020	+0.49	33,010	22,040
Doncaster Rovers	10,258	9,341	–8.94	12,962	7,572
Hull City	21,168	18,790	–11.23	22,676	16,604
Ipswich Town	19,614	18,266	–6.87	24,763	15,650
Leeds United	27,299	23,283	–14.71	33,366	19,469
Leicester City	23,666	23,036	–2.66	27,720	19,806
Middlesbrough	16,268	17,557	+7.92	27,794	14,366
Millwall	12,438	11,484	–7.67	16,085	9,062
Nottingham Forest	23,274	21,578	–7.29	27,356	12,712
Peterborough United	6,449	9,110	+41.26	13,517	6,351
Portsmouth	15,707	15,015	–4.41	19,879	11,261
Reading	17,681	19,219	+8.70	24,026	15,124
Southampton	22,160	26,419	+19.22	32,363	21,014
Watford	13,151	12,703	–3.41	16,314	10,592
West Ham United	33,492	30,923	–7.67	35,000	25,680

Premiership and Football League attendance averages and highest crowd figures for 2011–12 are unofficial.

FOOTBALL LEAGUE CHAMPIONSHIP 1 ATTENDANCES

| | Average Gate | | | Season 2011–12 | |
	2010–11	2011–12	+/–%	Highest	Lowest
AFC Bournemouth	7,103	5,881	–17.20	8,034	4,563
Brentford	5,172	5,643	+9.11	8,095	4,124
Bury	3,313	3,552	+7.21	6,970	2,072
Carlisle United	5,207	5,247	+0.77	7,721	3,694
Charlton Athletic	15,582	17,401	+11.67	26,749	13,264
Chesterfield	6,972	6,530	–6.34	9,279	5,087
Colchester United	4,246	3,865	–8.97	6,643	2,923
Exeter City	5,393	4,474	–17.04	6,045	3,474
Hartlepool United	2,933	4,960	+69.11	6,800	4,004
Huddersfield Town	13,733	14,144	+2.99	18,646	11,043
Leyton Orient	4,581	4,298	–6.18	6,196	3,258
Milton Keynes Dons	8,512	8,659	+1.73	15,938	6,405
Notts County	6,586	6,807	+3.36	12,410	4,741
Oldham Athletic	4,392	4,432	+0.91	8,032	2,408
Preston North End	11,767	11,820	+0.45	17,518	9,148
Rochdale	3,537	3,108	–12.13	5,361	1,930
Scunthorpe United	5,547	4,339	–21.78	6,047	3,409
Sheffield United	20,632	18,701	–9.36	30,043	15,783
Sheffield Wednesday	17,817	21,336	+19.75	38,082	16,185
Stevenage	2,898	3,558	+22.77	5,351	2,419
Tranmere Rovers	5,467	5,130	–6.16	8,526	4,153
Walsall	3,845	4,274	+11.16	8,603	3,250
Wycombe Wanderers	4,495	4,843	+7.74	7,097	3,259
Yeovil Town	4,291	3,984	–7.15	5,635	3,121

FOOTBALL LEAGUE CHAMPIONSHIP 2 ATTENDANCES

| | Average Gate | | | Season 2011–12 | |
	2010–11	2011–12	+/–%	Highest	Lowest
Accrington Stanley	1,867	1,784	–4.45	3,275	1,308
AFC Wimbledon	3,390	4,294	+26.67	4,634	3,678
Aldershot Town	2,487	2,864	+15.16	4,110	1,871
Barnet	2,249	2,265	+0.71	4,422	1,509
Bradford City	11,127	10,171	–8.59	17,014	2,149
Bristol Rovers	6,253	6,035	–3.49	8,427	5,024
Burton Albion	2,947	2,809	–4.68	3,608	1,714
Cheltenham Town	2,980	3,424	+14.9	5,288	2,035
Crawley Town	2,534	3,256	+28.49	4,723	2,184
Crewe Alexandra	4,119	4,124	+0.12	6,919	3,142
Dagenham & Redbridge	2,769	2,090	–24.52	3,259	1,446
Gillingham	5,230	5,146	–1.61	7,750	3,248
Hereford United	2,516	2,553	+1.47	5,143	1,599
Macclesfield Town	1,816	2,229	+22.74	4,214	1,527
Morecambe	2,647	2,141	–19.12	4,025	1,207
Northampton Town	4,604	4,808	+4.43	6,860	3,643
Oxford United	7,277	7,451	+2.39	11,825	5,653
Plymouth Argyle	8,613	6,828	–20.72	12,836	5,018
Port Vale	5,532	4,819	–12.89	6,356	3,714
Rotherham United	3,667	3,498	–4.61	5,368	2,447
Shrewsbury Town	5,875	5,769	–1.80	9,441	4,871
Southend United	5,344	5,999	+12.26	9,782	4,580
Swindon Town	8,457	8,410	–0.56	12,864	6,304
Torquay United	2,630	2,869	+9.09	4,157	2,018

TRANSFERS 2011–2012

JUNE 2011

		From	*To*
28	Barnett, Tyrone	Macclesfield T	Crawley T
20	Bencherif, Hamza	Macclesfield T	Notts Co
14	Bennett, Elliott	Brighton & HA	Norwich C
6	Buckley, William E.	Watford	Brighton & HA
1	Deering, Sam	Oxford U	Barnet
21	Done, Matthew	Rochdale	Barnsley
30	Gardner, Craig	Birmingham C	Sunderland
29	Green, Daniel R.	Dagenham & R	Charlton Ath
1	Greer, Gordon	Swindon T	Brighton & HA
20	Harrold, Matthew	Shrewsbury T	Bristol R
8	Henderson, Jordan	Sunderland	Liverpool
30	Hobbs, Jack	Leicester C	Hull C
1	Jones, Robert W.	Scunthorpe U	Sheffield W
1	Leigertwood, Mikele B.	QPR	Reading
23	McNulty, Jimmy	Brighton & HA	Barnsley
6	Morison, Steve	Millwall	Norwich C
16	Nolan, Kevin A.J.	Newcastle U	West Ham U
21	Peltier, Lee A.	Huddersfield T	Leicester C
30	Philliskirk, Daniel	Chelsea	Sheffield U
1	Pringle, Benjamin P.	Derby Co	Rotherham U
14	Smith, Jonathan P.	York C	Swindon T
28	Spurr, Thomas	Sheffield W	Doncaster R
29	Stephens, Dale	Oldham Ath	Charlton Ath
29	Wickham, Connor	Ipswich T	Sunderland
30	Wiggins, Rhoys	AFC Bournemouth	Charlton Ath
21	Wiseman, Scott N.K.	Rochdale	Barnsley

TEMPORARY TRANSFERS

29	Addison, Miles V.E.	Derby Co	Barnsley

JULY 2011

7	Adam, Charles G.	Blackpool	Liverpool
5	Ajose, Nicholas O.	Manchester U	Peterborough U
1	Al Habsi, Ali	Bolton W	Wigan Ath
7	Alcock, Craig	Yeovil T	Peterborough U
5	Barrett, Adam	Crystal Palace	AFC Bournemouth
12	Birchall, Adam S.	Dover Ath	Gillingham
6	Brown, Wesley M.	Manchester U	Sunderland
14	Bruna, Gerardo A.B.	Liverpool	Blackpool
1	Carayol, Mustapha	Lincoln C	Bristol R
7	Cisak, Aleksander	Accrington S	Oldham Ath
4	Clichy, Gael	Arsenal	Manchester C
19	Connell, Alan J.	Grimsby T	Swindon T
7	Cork, Jack F.P.	Chelsea	Southampton
20	Daley, Luke A.	Norwich C	Plymouth Arg
15	Dance, James	Crawley T	Luton T
29	Dickinson, Carl	Stoke C	Watford
15	Downing, Stewart	Aston Villa	Liverpool
1	Dunn, Chris	Northampton T	Coventry C
26	Eagles, Christopher M.	Burnley	Bolton W
1	Edmans, Robert M.	Chelmsford C	Dagenham & R
25	Elding, Anthony L.	Rochdale	Grimsby T
25	Emmanuel-Thomas, Jay A.A.	Arsenal	Ipswich T
19	Fairhurst, Waide S.	Doncaster R	Macclesfield T
6	Evina, Cedric D.	Oldham Ath	Charlton Ath
21	Ferguson, Barry	Birmingham C	Blackpool
18	Given, Seamus J.J.	Manchester C	Aston Villa
1	Graham, Daniel A.W.	Watford	Swansea C
18	Greening, Jonathan	Fulham	Nottingham F
1	Gregory, Steven M.	AFC Wimbledon	AFC Bournemouth
8	Gunnarsson, Aron E.M.	Coventry C	Cardiff C
7	Halford, Gregory	Wolverhampton W	Portsmouth
23	Haynes-Brown, Curtis L.	Lowestoft T	Yeovil T

1 Henderson, Darius A.	Sheffield U	Millwall
4 Henderson, Stephen	Bristol C	Portsmouth
29 Hourihane, Conor	Ipswich T	Plymouth Arg
18 Iwelumo, Christopher	Burnley	Watford
12 Johnson, Roger	Birmingham C	Wolverhampton W
1 Jones, Philip A.	Blackburn R	Manchester U
1 Kedwell, Daniel T.	AFC Wimbledon	Gillingham
12 Konchesky, Paul M.	Liverpool	Leicester C
1 Lee, Charlie	Peterborough U	Gillingham
1 Legzdins, Adam R.	Burton Alb	Derby Co
25 Lonergan, Andrew	Preston NE	Leeds U
4 Mackail-Smith, Craig	Peterborough U	Brighton & HA
25 Mason, Joseph	Plymouth Arg	Cardiff C
1 McKenna, Paul S.	Nottingham F	Hull C
26 Mears, Tyrone	Burnley	Bolton W
7 Mills, Matthew C.	Reading	Leicester C
8 Morrison, Michael B.	Sheffield W	Charlton Ath
4 N'Gala, Bondz	Plymouth Arg	Yeovil T
29 N'Zogbia, Charles	Wigan Ath	Aston Villa
1 O'Hara, Jamie	Tottenham H	Wolverhampton W
7 O'Shea, John F.	Manchester U	Sunderland
1 Pearce, Jason D.	AFC Bournemouth	Portsmouth
19 Pilkington, Anthony	Huddersfield T	Norwich C
1 Reed, Jake	Great Yarmouth T	Dagenham & R
1 Reid, Izak G.	Macclesfield T	Morecambe
30 Rice, Martin	Truro C	Torquay U
1 Robinson, Theo	Millwall	Derby Co
1 Schmeichel, Kasper P.	Leeds U	Leicester C
1 Shackell, Jason	Barnsley	Derby Co
1 Smalley, Deane	Oldham Ath	Oxford U
4 St Ledger-Hall, Sean P.	Preston NE	Leicester C
22 Taylor, Matthew S.	Bolton W	West Ham U
14 Taylor, Ryan	Rotherham U	Bristol C
1 Tomlinson, Ben	Worksop T	Macclesfield T
1 Tyson, Nathan	Nottingham F	Derby Co
1 Varney, Luke I.	Derby Co	Portsmouth
15 Vincelot, Romain M.G.	Dagenham & R	Brighton & HA
11 Ward, Daniel C.	Bolton W	Huddersfield T
1 Whelpdale, Chris	Peterborough U	Gillingham
13 Yeates, Mark	Sheffield U	Watford
1 Young, Ashley	Aston Villa	Manchester U
6 Zebroski, Christopher	Torquay U	Bristol R

TEMPORARY TRANSFERS

12 Addison, Miles – Derby Co – Barnsley; 25 Atkinson, Christopher R. – Huddersfield T – Darlington; 28 Batth, Daniel T. – Wolverhampton W – Sheffield W; 12 Benyon, Elliot P. – Swindon T – Wycombe W; 21 Brady, Robert – Manchester U – Hull C; 7 Brodie, Richard J. – Crawley T – Fleetwood T; 14 Carlisle, Clarke J. – Burnley – Preston NE; 18 Cooper, Liam D.I. – Hull C – Huddersfield T; 26 Cullen, Mark – Hull C – Bury; 13 Darby, Stephen – Liverpool – Rochdale; 1 De Laet, Ritchie R.A. – Manchester U – Norwich C; 13 Donnelly, Scott P. – Swansea C – Wycombe W; 26 Ehmer, Maximillian A. – QPR – Yeovil T; 26 Green, Matthew J. – Torquay U – Mansfield T; 21 Gulacsi, Peter – Liverpool – Hull C; 27 Hansen, Martin – Liverpool – Bradford C; 29 Hitchcock, Thomas J. – Blackburn R – Plymouth Arg; 20 Johnson, Damien M. – Plymouth Arg – Huddersfield T; 26 Khumalo, Bongani – Tottenham H – Reading; 14 Logan, Conrad J. – Leicester C. – Rotherham U; 29 Mason, Ryan G. – Tottenham H – Doncaster R; 18 Mee, Benjamin – Manchester C – Burnley; 26 Naughton, Kyle – Tottenham H – Norwich C; 11 N'Diaye, Alassane – Crystal Palace – Southend U; 22 Noble, Liam T. – Sunderland – Carlisle U; 29 Parkes, Thomas P.W. – Leicester C – Burton Alb; 31 Taylor, Jake W.T. – Reading – Aldershot T; 11 Tunnicliffe, Ryan – Manchester U – Peterborough U; 13 Walker, Samuel C. – Chelsea – Northampton T

AUGUST 2011

31 Arteta, Mikel	Everton	Arsenal
12 Ayala, Daniel	Liverpool	Norwich C
30 Baldock, Samuel	Milton Keynes D	West Ham U
26 Barton, Joseph A.	Newcastle U	QPR

31	Beckford, Jermaine P.A.	Everton	Leicester C
4	Campbell, Dudley J.	Blackpool	QPR
2	Cresswell, Aaron	Tranmere R	Ipswich T
31	Crouch, Peter J.	Tottenham H	Stoke C
6	Daley, Luke A.	Norwich C	Plymouth Arg
31	Dann, Scott	Birmingham C	Blackburn R
3	Dickinson, Carl M.	Stoke C	Watford
5	Dikgacoi, Kagisho	Fulham	Crystal Palace
30	Elliot, Robert	Charlton Ath	Newcastle U
31	Elliott, Wade P.	Burnley	Birmingham C
31	Feeney, Liam M.	AFC Bournemouth	Millwall
31	Ferdinand, Anton J.	Sunderland	QPR
11	Fox, Daniel	Burnley	Southampton
31	Garner, Joseph A.	Nottingham F	Watford
3	Goodwillie, David	Dundee U	Blackburn R
24	Gorkss, Kaspars	QPR	Reading
4	Gornell, Terence M.	Accrington S	Shrewsbury T
1	Hamer, Benjamin J.	Reading	Charlton Ath
31	Hargreaves, Owen L.	Manchester U	Manchester C
22	Harley, Ryan	Swansea C	Brighton & HA
31	Harrad, Shaun	Northampton T	Bury
18	Hines, Zavon	West Ham U	Burnley
31	Hogg, Jonathan	Aston Villa	Watford
31	Hutton, Alan	Tottenham H	Aston Villa
5	Ince, Thomas	Liverpool	Blackpool
19	Ings, Daniel W.J.	AFC Bournemouth	Burnley
11	Jose Enrique	Newcastle U	Liverpool
25	Kee, Billy R.	Torquay U	Burton Alb
27	Le Fondre, Adam J.	Rotherham U	Reading
27	Lenihan, Darragh	Middlesbrough	Blackburn R
12	Lines, Christopher J.	Bristol R	Sheffield W
9	Long, Shane P.	Reading	WBA
30	Lowe, Ryan T.	Bury	Sheffield W
26	MacDonald, Charles L.	Brentford	Milton Keynes D
26	MacDonald, Shaun B.	Swansea C	AFC Bournemouth
4	McDermott, Donal	Manchester C	Huddersfield T
31	McDonald, Cody	Norwich C	Coventry C
15	Miller, Ishmael A.	WBA	Nottingham F
23	Miller, Lee A.	Middlesbrough	Carlisle U
22	Mills, Joseph N.	Southampton	Reading
2	Morrison, Michael B.	Sheffield W	Charlton Ath
31	Mozika, Damien	Bury	Scunthorpe U
24	Nasri, Samir	Arsenal	Manchester C
1	N'Gala, Bondz	Plymouth Arg	Yeovil T
31	N'Gog, David	Liverpool	Bolton W
31	N'Guessen, Dany-Gale D.	Leicester C	Millwall
8	Obertan, Gabriel	Manchester C	Newcastle U
11	O'Grady, Christopher J.	Rochdale	Sheffield W
8	Oxlade-Chamberlain, Alexander M.D.	Southampton	Arsenal
31	Pablo Ibanez	WBA	Birmingham C
31	Palacios, Wilson R.	Tottenham H	Stoke C
31	Parker, Scott M.	West Ham U	Tottenham H
3	Pell, Harry D.B.	Bristol R	Hereford U
31	Raul Meireles	Liverpool	Chelsea
5	Raynes, Michael	Scunthorpe U	Rotherham U
31	Revell, Alexander D.	Leyton Orient	Rotherham U
2	Robinson, Anton D.	AFC Bournemouth	Huddersfield T
31	Sinclair, Emile A.	Macclesfield T	Peterborough U
31	Slew, Jordan M.	Sheffield U	Blackburn R
12	Smith, Steven	Norwich C	Preston NE
31	Stanislas, Junior	West Ham U	Burnley
2	Taylor, Ryan P.	Rotherham U	Bristol C
29	Traore, Armand	Arsenal	QPR
5	Treacy, Keith	Preston NE	Burnley

31 Turner, Ben H.	Coventry C	Cardiff C
26 Westcarr, Craig N.	Notts Co	Chesterfield
31 Wright-Philips, Shaun C.	Manchester C	QPR
31 Yakubu, Ayegbeni	Everton	Blackburn R
26 Young, Luke P.	Aston Villa	QPR

TEMPORARY TRANSFERS

31 Abdulla, Ahmed M. – West Ham U – Swindon T; 31 Adeyemi, Thomas O. – Norwich C – Oldham Ath; 4 Almond, Louis J. – Blackpool – Barrow; 12 Andrews, Keith J. – Blackburn R – Ipswich T; 15 Antonio, Michail G. – Reading – Colchester U; 5 Arnold, Steven J.W. – Wycombe W – Hayes & Yeading; 1 Atkins, Ross M. – Derby Co – Burton Alb; 12 Atkinson, William H. – Hull C – Plymouth Arg; 3 Balanta, Angelo J. – QPR – Milton Keynes D; 19 Balkestein, Pim – Brentford – Rochdale; 31 Ball, David M. – Peterborough U – Rochdale; 25 Barkhuizen, Thomas J. – Blackpool – Hereford U; 25 Barnes-Homer, Matt – Luton T – Rochdale; 20 Bates, Jon-jo D. – Dagenham & R – Harrow Bor; 31 Beavers, Mark G. – Sheffield W – Milton Keynes D; 31 Benali, Ahmed – Manchester C – Rochdale; 31 Bender, Thomas J. – Colchester U – Accrington S; 31 Bentley,David M. – Tottenham H – West Ham U; 1 Bergqvist, Jan D. – Aldershot T – Farnborough T; 5 Bignall, Nicholas C. – Reading – Exeter C; 25 Bodin, Billy P. – Swindon T – Torquay U; 4 Bolger, Cian T. – Leicester C – Bristol R; 12 Bond, Jonathan H. – Watford – Brackley T; 10 Breeze, Matthew C. – Peterborough U – Histon; 22 Breimyr, Henrik M. – Aldershot T – Eastleigh; 31 Brown, Jordan – West Ham U – Aldershot T; 16 Brown, Reece – Manchester U – Doncaster R; 11 Bryan, Michael A. – Watford – Bradford C; 25 Butlin, Joey – Walsall – Solihull Moors; 25 Button, David R.E. – Tottenham H – Leyton Orient; 1 Byrne, Nathan W. – Tottenham H – AFC Bournemouth; 31 Byrne, Shane W. – Leicester C – Bury; 19 Cestor, Mike B. – Leyton Orient – Woking; 15 Chamberlain, Elliott C. – Leicester C – Stockport Co; 19 Clarke, Nathan – Huddersfield T – Oldham Ath; 12 Clayton, Harry S. – Crewe Alex – Market Drayton T; 1 Clement, Jordan K. – Aldershot T – Maidenhead U; 18 Clist, Simon J. – Oxford U – Hereford U; 31 Coke, Giles C. – Sheffield W – Bury; 31 Cole, Aaron E. – Derby Co – Eastwood T; 1 Connolly, Reece W. – Aldershot T – Farnborough T; 19 Cornell, David J. – Swansea C – Hereford U; 29 Cort, Leon T.A. – Burnley – Charlton Ath; 26 Daniels, Gregg – Macclesfield T – Newcastle T; 5 Davies, Andrew J. – Stoke C – Crystal Palace; 25 Dean, Luke A. – Bradford C – Hinckley U; 20 Dennis, Louis H. – Dagenham & R – Grays Ath; 31 Devitt, Jamie M. – Hull C – Bradford C; 31 Dixon, Terry N. – Bradford C – FC Halifax T; 11 Doble, Ryan A. – Southampton – AFC Bournemouth; 19 Doughty, Michael E. – QPR – Crawley T; 23 Drinkwater, Daniel N. – Manchester U – Barnsley; 31 Duffy, Shane P.M. – Everton – Scunthorpe U; 25 Eastham, Ashley – Blackpool – Bury; 26 Ellison, James – Burton Alb – Alfreton T; 12 Essam, Connor – Gillingham – Bishop's Stortford; 27 Evans, William G. – Swindon T – Hereford U; 16 Fletcher, Wesleigh J. – Burnley – Accrington S; 5 Forecast, Tommy S. – Southampton – Thurrock; 31 Franks, Jonathan I. – Middlesbrough – Oxford U; 19 Futcher, Benjamin P. – Bury – Mansfield T; 13 Gayle, Dwight D.B. – Dagenham & R – Bishop's Stortford; 20 Gayle, Ian G. – Dagenham & R – Grays Ath; 5 Gibson, Benjamin J. – Middlesbrough – Plymouth Arg; 19 Gilligan, Ryan J. – Northampton T – Newport Co; 17 Gordon, Benjamin L. – Chelsea – Peterborough U; 13 Gough, Conor J.J. – Charlton Ath – Salisbury C; 26 Grella, Michele – Leeds U – Brentford; 31 Griffiths, Jamie – Ipswich T – Plymouth Arg; 26 Grounds, Jonathan M. – Middlesbrough – Chesterfield; 9 Guy, Lewis B. – Milton Keynes D – Oxford U; 20 Harvey, Alex-Ray – Burnley – Fleetwood T; 12 Hassan, Emmanuel – Hartlepool U – Harrogate T; 19 Hawkes, Daren G. – Gillingham – Ramsgate; 12 Haynes, Kyle J. – Cheltenham T – Hednesford T; 22 Hester, Patrick – AFC Bournemouth – Bashley; 27 Hogg, Jonathan – Aston Villa – Watford; 31 Hurst, James – WBA – Blackpool; 3 Ikeme, Carl – Wolverhampton W – Middlesbrough; 15 James-Lewis, Merrick A. – Southend U – Braintree T; 9 Jansson, Oscar – Tottenham H – Bradford C; 26 Johnson, Lee D. – Bristol C – Chesterfield; 4 Johnson, Michael – Manchester C – Leicester C; 30 Johnson, Samuel W. – Port Vale – Stafford R; 3 Kean, Jacob K. – Blackburn R – Rochdale; 16 Keogh, Andrew D. – Wolverhampton W – Leeds U; 26 Kettings, Christopher D. – Blackpool – Birmingham C; 5 Kilbane, Kevin D. – Hull C – Derby Co; 31 King, Simon D.R. – Gillingham – Plymouth Arg; 5 Kinnisburgh, Steven S. – Oxford U – Cambridge U; 19 Lalkovic, Milan – Chelsea – Doncaster R; 26 Lane, Jack F. – Macclesfield T – Newcastle T; 9 Langmead, Kelvin S. – Peterborough U – Northampton T; 31 Lansbury, Henri G. – Arsenal – West Ham U; 5 Lee, Oliver R. – West Ham U – Dagenham & R; 5 Long, Kevin F. – Burnley – Accrington S; 5 LuaLua, Kazenga – Newcastle U – Brighton & HA; 3 Lund, Matthew C. – Stoke C – Oldham Ath; 1 Malone, Scott L. – Wolverhampton W – AFC Bournemouth; 17 Marshall, Ben – Stoke C – Sheffield W; 12 McCartney, George – Sunderland – West Ham U; 12 McClure, Matthew G. – Wycombe W – Hayes & Yeading; 4 McGivern, Ryan – Manchester C – Crystal Palace; 31 McGivern, Ryan – Manchester C –

148

Bristol C; 5 Mendez-Laing, Nathaniel – Wolverhampton W – Sheffield U; 3 Miller, Kern A. – Barnsley – Accrington S; 8 Mills, Daniel P. – Peterborough U – Tamworth; 5 Montano, Cristian A. – West Ham U – Notts Co; 12 Mooney, Jason B. – Wycombe W – Oxford C; 5 Moore, Liam S. – Leicester C – Bradford C; 19 Moult, Louis E. – Stoke C – Accrington S; 19 Murphy, David P. – Reading – Cirencester T; 3 Myhill, Glyn O. – WBA – Birmingham C; 31 Nelson, Mitchell A. – AFC Bournemouth – Lincoln C; 15 Napper, Byron J. – Crawley T – Weymouth; 8 N'Guessen, Dany-Gael D. – Leicester C – Millwall; 24 Norwood, Oliver J. – Manchester U – Scunthorpe U; 5 Obika, Jonathan – Tottenham H – Yeovil T; 25 Osborn, Alexander S. – Dagenham & R – Thurrock; 19 Osborne, Leon A. – Bradford C – Southport; 16 Oyenuga, Kudus – Tottenham H – Bury; 23 Park, Cameron – Middlesbrough – Barnsley; 13 Parsons, Alexander A. – AFC Bournemouth – Wimborne T; 19 Pope, Nicholas D. – Charlton Ath – Harrow Bor; 31 Puncheon, Jason D.I. – Plymouth Arg – QPR; 5 Purkiss, Ben – Oxford U – Darlington; 5 Ramage, Peter I. – QPR – Crystal Palace; 12 Rance, Dean J.R. – Gillingham – Bishop's Stortford; 12 Raymond, Frankie J. – Reading – Eastleigh; 13 Reynolds, Duran-Rhys – Southend U – St Neots T; 31 Richards, Jamie A. – Plymouth Arg – Barnstaple T; 5 Richardson, Michael – Newcastle U – Leyton Orient; 12 Saville, Jack W. – Southampton – Hayes & Yeading; 11 Severn, James A.R.M. – Derby Co – Eastwood T; 3 Shea, James – Arsenal – Dagenham & R; 31 Simpson, Jay-Alistaire F. – Hull C – Millwall; 16 Smith, Adam J. – Tottenham H – Milton Keynes D; 3 Spence, Jordan J. – West Ham U – Bristol C; 1 Spencer, James C. – Huddersfield T – Cheltenham T; 3 Steer, Jed J. – Norwich C – Yeovil T; 25 Stephenson, Darren C.A. – Bradford C – Hinckley U; 19 Stephenson, Timothy J. – AFC Bournemouth – Weymouth; 5 Stockdale, David A. – Fulham – Ipswich T; 13 Strugnell, Daniel – AFC Bournemouth – Wimborne T; 31 Swallow, Ben – Bristol R – Bath C; 12 Tavernier, James H. – Newcastle U – Carlisle U; 1 Taylor, Jake W.T. – Reading – Aldershot T; 19 Thomas, Daniel – AFC Bournemouth – Welling U; 12 Thomas, Michael D. – Macclesfield – Leek T; 25 Thompson, Adam L. – Watford – Brentford; 31 Timlin, Michael A. – Swindon T – Southend U; 3 Trippier, Kieran J. – Manchester C – Burnley; 5 Tunchev, Aleksandar – Leicester C – Crystal Palace; 23 Turner, Jake S.P. – Scunthorpe U – Brigg T; 31 Waghorn, Martyn T. – Leicester C – Hull C; 30 Walker, Joshua – Watford – Stevenage; 26 Weimann, Andreas – Aston Villa – Watford; 11 Weir, Tyler C. – Hereford U – Gloucester C; 13 Wilkinson, Luke A. – Dagenham & R – Boreham Wood; 30 Williams, Brett A. – Reading – Rotherham U; 5 Wood, Chris – WBA – Birmingham C; 26 Vine, Rowan L. – QPR – Exeter C; 31 Winn, Peter H. – Stevenage – Cambridge U; 26 Winnall, Sam T. – Wolverhampton W – Hereford U; 15 Woodley, Aaron R. – Oxford U – Banbury U; 26 Woodyard, Alexander J. – Southend U – Farnborough; 20 Wootton, Lee S. – Dagenham & R – Harrow Bor; 3 Wootton, Scott J. – Manchester U – Peterborough U; 1 Worsfold, Max N. – Aldershot T – Maidenhead U

SEPTEMBER 2011 TEMPORARY TRANSFERS

8 Adams, Blair – Sunderland – Brentford; 16 Agdestein, Torbjorn – Brighton & HA – Bath C; 22 Ajose, Nicholas – Peterborough U – Scunthorpe U; 30 Almunia, Manuel – Arsenal – West Ham U; 9 Alnwick, Ben R. – Tottenham H – Leyton Orient; 23 Amoo, David O.S. – Liverpool – Bury; 29 Andrade, Bruno M.C. – QPR – Aldershot T; 1 Arnold, Steven J.W. – Wycombe W – Hayes & Yeading; 9 Asante, Kyle E.K. – Southend U – Concord R; 8 Baggridge, Rhys W. – Yeovil T – Gillingham T; 30 Baldock, George H.I. – Milton Keynes D – Northampton T; 8 Banton, Jason – Leicester C – Burton Alb; 23 Baxter, Jose – Everton – Tranmere R; 30 Borrowdale, Gary I. – QPR – Barnet; 10 Brooke, Ryan M. – Oldham Ath – Barrow; 23 Brown, Alexander S. – Gillingham – Whitstable T; 22 Burrow, Jordan – Chesterfield – Boston U; 8 Butland, Jack – Birmingham C – Cheltenham T; 20 Bywater, Stephen – Derby Co – Sheffield W; 30 Canham, Sean – Hereford U – Bath C; 19 Carey, Lewis T. – Bristol C – Gloucester C; 12 Carson, Trevor – Sunderland – Bury; 23 Chilvers, Liam C. – Notts Co – Port Vale; 22 Clark, Matthew W. – Swindon T – Oxford C; 9 Clarke, Leon M. – Swindon T – Chesterfield; 9 Clarke, Thomas – Huddersfield T – Leyton Orient; 16 Clarkson, David – Bristol C – Brentford; 9 Clough, Charlie – Bristol R – Bath C; 9 Collins, Daniel – Stoke C – Ipswich T; 24 Davies, Andrew J. – Stoke C – Bradford C; 30 Davisson, Benjamin J. – Charlton Ath – Welling U; 22 Dawson, Aaron P. – Exeter C – Tiverton T; 19 Deards, Connor A.J. – Walsall – Redditch U; 23 Dempster, John – Crawley T – Kettering T; 16 Donaldson, Ryan M. – Newcastle U – Tranmere R; 9 Donnelly, George – Fleetwood T – Macclesfield T; 15 Drury, Andrew M. – Ipswich T – Crawley T; 13 Eastman, Thomas M. – Colchester U – Crawley T; 30 Elder, Nathan – Hayes & Yeading – Hereford U; 23 Forecast, Tommy S. – Southampton – Bromley; 23 Franks, Fraser G. – AFC Wimbledon – Hayes & Yeading; 8 Furzer, Jack L. – Exeter C – Bideford; 23 Gallinagh, Andrew A.R. – Cheltenham T – Bath C; 29 Garbutt, Luke – Everton – Cheltenham T; 9 Griffiths, Scott R. – Peterborough U – Crawley T; 12 Hall, Robert – West Ham U – Oxford U; 19 Hassan, Emmanuel – Hartlepool U – Whitby T; 16 Haworth, Andrew A.D. – Bury – Oxford U; 29 Hewitt, Troy R. – QPR – Dagenham & R; 24 Hill, Clinton S. – QPR –

Nottingham F; 20 Hollis, Haydn J. – Notts Co – Barrow; 26 Howard, Ryan R.W.B. –
Reading – Millwall; 16 Isaac, Chez J.T. – Watford – Boreham Wood; 13 Jackson, Marlon M.
– Bristol C – Northampton T; 9 Jarvis, Nathaniel S. – Cardiff C – Newport Co; 29 Jervis,
Jake M. – Birmingham C – Swindon T; 26 Johnson, Oliver T. – Norwich C – Yeovil T; 5
Johnstone, Samuel L. – Manchester U – Scunthorpe U; 30 Kennedy, Thomas G. – Leicester
C – Peterborough U; 30 Kewley-Graham, Jesse J. – Wycombe W – Staines T; 19 Kovacs,
Janos – Hereford U – Luton T; 16 Lacey, Patrick S. – Bradford C – Vauxhall Motors; 8
Llera, Miguel A. – Charlton Ath – Brentford; 10 Lovelock, Thomas J. – Leyton Orient –
Chertsey T; 16 Mambo, Yado M. – Charlton Ath – Ebbsfleet U; 13 Martin, David J. –
Derby Co – Walsall; 12 Massey, Gavin A. – Watford – Yeovil T; 16 McGoldrick, David J. –
Nottingham F – Sheffield W; 9 McNaughton, Callum J. – West Ham C – AFC Wimbledon;
23 Milton, Harry T. – Milton Keynes D – Aveley; 23 Mitchell, Liam – Notts Co – Lewes; 16
Montgomery, Graeme – Aldershot T – Eastleigh; 24 Morrison, Clinton H. – Sheffield W –
Milton Keynes D; 23 Mukendi, Vinny K. – Macclesfield T – Southport; 23 Murphy, David
P. – Reading – Hungerford T; 9 Nesbitt, Teddy – Southend U – Concord R; 23 Nicholas,
George A. – Notts Co – Lewes; 23 Norburn, Oliver L. – Leicester C – Bristol R; 16 Nouble,
Frank H. – West Ham U – Gillingham; 2 Okus, Conor E. – Dagenham & R – Havant &
W'ville; 30 Osei-Kuffour, Jonathan – Bristol R – Gillingham; 23 Parish, Elliott C. – Aston
Villa – Cardiff C; 21 Parkin, Jonathan – Cardiff C – Doncaster R; 13 Pentney, Carl –
Colchester U – Chelmsford C; 23 Peters, Jaime B. – Ipswich T – AFC Bournemouth; 12
Pittman, Jon P. – Oxford U – Crawley T; 23 Pugh, Daniel A. – Stoke C – Leeds U; 15
Purcell, Tadhg – Northampton T – Darlington; 9 Purkiss, Ben – Oxford U – Darlington; 30
Raglan, Charles J.C. – Port Vale – Hinckley U; 29 Reed, Adam M. – Sunderland –
Bradford C; 28 Ridehalgh, Liam – Huddersfield T – Swindon T; 27 Riise, Bjorn H.S. –
Fulham – Portsmouth; 29 Rowe, Dominic R. – Bradford C – Barrow; 26 Rowlands, Martin
C. – QPR – Wycombe W; 8 Sekajja, Ibra – Crystal Palace – Kettering T; 30 Shelvey, Jonjo –
Liverpool – Blackpool; 10 Simpson, Robbie – Huddersfield T – Oldham Ath; 16 Smith,
Adam C. – Leicester C – Chesterfield; 23 Smith, Ben P. – Crawley T – Kettering T; 9
Stockford, Lewis J. – Portsmouth – Salisbury C; 27 Swinglehurst, Steven – Carlisle U –
Kendal T; 16 Tallack, Lewis J. – Portsmouth – Dorchester T; 21 Taylor, Jake W.T. – Reading
– Exeter C; 19 Tchuimeni-Nimely, Alex – Manchester C – Middlesbrough; 10 Thomas,
Wesley A.N. – Crawley T – AFC Bournemouth; 12 Tunchev, Aleksandar – Leicester C –
Crystal Palace; 30 Wabara, Reece – Manchester C – Ipswich T; 23 Walker, Paul H. –
Northampton T – Brackley T; 26 Warren, Freddie R. – Charlton Ath – Kettering T; 2
Watson, Karlton A.J. – Nottingham F – Eastwood T; 15 Whichelow, Matthew R. – Watford
– Exeter C; 8 White, Andrew I. – Crewe Alex – Stafford R; 23 Whiteley, Lewis – Notts Co –
Bishop's Stortford; 13 Williams, Marcus V. – Reading – Sheffield U

OCTOBER 2011

5 Fogden, Wesley K.	Havant & W'ville	AFC Bournemouth
20 Sheringham, Charles E.W.	Dartford	AFC Bournemouth

TEMPORARY TRANSFERS
13 Agyemang, Patrick – QPR – Millwall; 28 Asante, Kyle E.K. – Southend U – Canvey
Island; 6 Basey, Grant W. – Peterborough U – Wycombe W; 25 Beattie, Craig – Swansea C
– Watford; 27 Bennett, Dale O. – Watford – Brentford; 21 Berahino, Saldo – WBA –
Northampton T; 25 Bignall, Nicholas C. – Reading – Wycombe W; 21 Bird, David A. –
Cheltenham T – Kidderminster H; 28 Blake, Ryan G. – Brentford – Farnborough T; 22
Boateng, Michael K.A. – Bristol R – Tonbridge Angels; 14 Boden, Scott D. – Chesterfield –
Macclesfield T; 14 Branston, Guy P.B. – Bradford C – Rotherham U; 21 Brown, Connor A.
– Sheffield U – Eastwood T; 7 Brunt, Thomas J. – Gillingham – Ashford U; 5 Clarke, Lewis
P. – Yeovil T – Poole T; 14 Clarke, William C. – Blackpool – Sheffield U; 27 Cook, Steve A.
– Brighton & HA – AFC Bournemouth; 22 Cox, Samuel P. – Barnet – Boreham Wood; 25
Cunningham, Gregory R. – Manchester C – Nottingham F; 25 Daniels, Luke M. – WBA –
Southend U; 25 Davies, Callum J. – Gillingham – Thurrock; 27 Davies, Scott M.E. –
Crawley T – Aldershot T; 6 Day, Joseph D. – Peterborough U – Alfreton T; 3 Dean, Luke
A. – Bradford C – Harrogate T; 14 Dobie, Luke J. – Middlesbrough – Accrington S; 31
Donnelly, George – Fleetwood T – Macclesfield T; 28 Dovey, Jack M. – Southampton –
Eastleigh; 14 Dunne, Charles – Wycombe W – Staines T; 21 Eccleston, Nathan – Liverpool
– Rochdale; 14 Foderingham, Wesley A. – Crystal Palace – Swindon T; 14 Gayle, Ian G. –
Dagenham & R – Kingstonian; 20 Green, Michael J. – Port Vale – Eastleigh; 14 Harley, Jon
– Notts Co – Rotherham U; 24 Harper, Stephen A. – Newcastle U – Brighton & HA; 14
Hatfield, William H. – Leeds U – Accrington S; 14 Helan, Jeremy – Manchester C –
Carlisle U; 21 Holland, Jack – Crystal Palace – Farnborough T; 4 Ilunga, Herita – West
Ham U – Doncaster R; 18 Jackson, Ryan O. – AFC Wimbledon – Fleetwood T; 21 James,
Kingsley S. – Port Vale – Chasetown; 21 Jara, Gonzalo A.R. – WBA – Brighton & HA; 13
Kightly, Michael J. – Wolverhampton W – Watford; 13 Kirkland, Christopher E. – Wigan

150

Ath – Doncaster R; 6 Leslie, Steven – Shrewsbury T – Hereford U; 13 Losasso, Charlie C. – Reading – Salisbury C; 6 Lynch, David C.W. – Burnley – Droylsden; 22 McLaggon, Kayne S. – Bristol R – Tonbridge Angels; 17 McManaman, Callum H. – Wigan Ath – Blackpool; 17 McManaman, Callum H. – Wigan Ath – Blackpool; 16 Mambo, Yado M. – Charlton Ath – Ebbsfleet U; 7 Mekki, Adam R. – Aldershot T – Dorchester T; 13 Montano, Cristian A.C. – West Ham U – Swindon T; 10 Nelson, Mitchell A. – AFC Bournemouth – Lincoln C; 28 Niven, Derek – Chesterfield – Northampton T; 28 Nosworthy, Nyron – Sunderland – Watford; 7 Ntlhe, Kgosietsile – Peterborough U – St Albans C; 1 Oakley, Matthew – Leicester C – Exeter C; 21 Orenuga, Femi K. – Everton – Notts Co; 7 Overson, Dean J. – Burnley – Vauxhall Motors; 27 Paynter, William P. – Leeds U – Brighton & HA; 14 Phillips, Matthew – Blackpool – Sheffield U; 21 Philliskirk, Daniel – Sheffield U – Oxford U; 20 Potter, Luke A. – Barnsley – Alfreton T; 21 Purse, Darren J. – Millwall – Yeovil T; 7 Radford, Oscor S. – Doncaster R – Matlock T; 28 Razak, Abdul – Manchester C – Portsmouth; 7 Redwood, Leon N. – Brighton & HA – Dover Ath; 21 Reece, Charles T. – Bristol R – Gloucester C; 7 Rendell, Scott D. – Wycombe W – Bristol R; 3 Reynolds, Duran-Rhys – Dagenham & R – Met Police; 7 Robinson, Adam J. – Bradford C – Blyth Spartans; 21 Rodney, Nialle – Bradford C – Darlington; 10 Sandell, Andrew – Wycombe W – Forest Green R; 7 Scott, Mark J. – Swindon T – Oxford C; 21 Scowen, Josuha C. – Wycombe W – Hemel Hempstead T; 7 Smith, Nathan A. – Mansfield T – Aldershot T; 4 Spray, James M.K.T. – Wolverhampton W – Accrington S; 28 Spear, Ray B.K. – Torquay U – Bideford; 14 Stech, Marek – West Ham U – Yeovil T; 7 Stephenson, Darren C.A. – Bradford C – Woodley Sp; 14 Stockford, Lewis J. – Portsmouth – Salisbury C; 7 Taylor, Alistair W. – Barnsley – Worksop T; 7 Thalassitis, Michael – Stevenage – Boreham Wood; 21 Thompson, Curtis L. – Nots Co – Lincoln C; 12 Vose, Dominic J.S. – West Ham U – Braintree T; 13 Wassmer, Charlie – Crawley T – Fleetwood T; 13 Wilson, Glenn M. – Crawley T – Fleetwood T; 28 Wilson, Mark A. – Doncaster R – Walsall; 28 Woodley, Jordan A. – Brighton & HA – Hastings U

NOVEMBER 2011

16 LuaLua, Kazenga   Newcastle U   Brighton & HA

TEMPORARY TRANSFERS

24 Aldred, Thomas M. – Colchester U – Torquay U; 24 Amadi Holloway, Aaron J. – Bristol C – Bath C; 22 Aneke, Chukwuemeka, A.A. – Arsenal – Stevenage; 24 Assombalonga, Britt – Watford – Wealdstone; 22 Baker, Nathan L. – Aston Villa – Millwall; 24 Ball, David M. – Peterborough U – Rochdale; 24 Banks, Oliver – Rotherham U – Buxton; 24 Baseya, Cedric – Reading – Barnet; 24 Baxendale, James – Doncaster R – Buxton; 17 Bergkamp, Roland A.M. – Brighton & HA – Rochdale; 22 Beye, Habib – Aston Villa – Doncaster R; 24 Bidwell, Jake – Everton – Brentford; 4 Bignot, Paul J. – Blackpool – Plymouth Arg; 4 Bond, Jonathan H. – Watford – Forest Green R; 24 Bruce, Alex S. – Leeds U – Huddersfield T; 24 Bryan, Joseph E. – Bristol C – Bath C; 17 Bubb, Bradley – Aldershot T – Basingstoke T; 4 Bunn, Harry – Manchester C – Rochdale; 18 Butlin, Joey – Walsall – Sutton Coldfield T; 24 Chadwick, Nicholas G. – Stockport Co – Plymouth Arg; 24 Chantler, Christopher S. – Manchester C – Carlisle U; 24 Charnock, Kieran J. – Morecambe – Fleetwood T; 23 Clayton, Harry S. – Crewe Alex – Stafford R; 4 Clifford, Conor – Chelsea – Yeovil T; 12 Clowes, Robert N. – Yeovil T – Wimborne T; 24 Cole, Aaron E. – Derby Co – Stockport Co; 18 Collins, Daniel – Stoke C – Ipswich T; 18 Connerton, Jordan S. – Crewe Alex – Kendal T; 24 Cook, Lee – QPR – Leyton Orient; 24 Craig, Tony A. – Millwall – Leyton Orient; 24 Cunnington – Adam – Kettering T – Dagenham & R; 24 Daniels, Charlie – Leyton Orient – AFC Bournemouth; 19 Davies, Andrew J. – Stoke C – Bradford C; 18 Davisson, Benjamin J. – Charlton Ath – Welling U; 17 Day, Jamie R. – Crawley T – Aldershot T; 24 Dean, Harlee J. – Southampton – Brentford; 22 Dempster, John – Crawley T – Mansfield T; 11 Dorman, Andrew J. – Crystal Palace – Bristol R; 3 Downing, Paul – WBA – Barnet; 24 Doyle, Nathan L.R. – Barnsley – Preston NE; 4 Elder, Nathan – Hayes & Yeading – Hereford U; 10 Ellison, James – Burton Alb – Chester; 15 Ephraim, Hogan – QPR – Charlton Ath; 1 Evans, Micah – Blackburn R – Accrington S; 24 Farah, Ibrahim H. – Cardiff C – Tamworth; 4 Fisher, Thomas M. – Macclesfield T – Hyde U; 24 Fletcher, Wesleigh J. – Burnley – Crewe Alex; 8 Forte, Jonathan R.J. – Southampton – Preston NE; 24 Fortune, Marc-Antoine – WBA – Doncaster R; 8 Francis, Simon C. – Charlton Ath – AFC Bournemouth; 17 Freeman, Luke A. – Arsenal – Stevenage; 24 Gardner, Gary – Aston Villa – Coventry C; 21 Geohaghon, Exodus I. – Darlington – Dagenham & R; 24 Gilmartin, Rene – Watford – Yeovil T; 17 Goodman, Jake O. – Millwall – Staines T; 24 Goulon, Herold – Blackburn R – Doncaster R; 11 Gray, Daniel E. – Chesterfield – Macclesfield T; 24 Griffiths, Scott R. – Peterborough U – Chesterfield; 24 Guthrie, Kurtis O. – Accrington S – Southport; 24 Guy, Lewis R. – Milton Keynes D – Oxford U; 24 Hackett, Christopher J. – Millwall – Exeter C; 16 Hall, Robert – West Ham U – Oxford U; 24 Halliday, Andrew – Middlesbrough – Walsall; 11 Halstead,

151

Mark J. – Blackpool – Stockport Co; 3 Hector, Michael A.J. – Reading – Barnet; 24 Hemmings, Ashley J. – Wolverhampton W – Plymouth Arg; 24 Henry, Charles – Luton T – Aldershot T; 4 Holden, Dean T.J. – Chesterfield – Rochdale; 24 Holland, Jack – Crystal Palace – Farnborough T; 8 Hoskins, Samuel T. – Southampton – Preston NE; 22 Hudson, Daniel A. – Bury – Mossley; 18 Hurst, James – WBA – Shrewsbury T; 10 Ikeme, Carl – Wolverhampton W – Doncaster R; 24 Jackson, Marlon M. – Bristol C – Cheltenham T; 24 Jarvis, Nathaniel S. – Cardiff C – Newport Co; 4 Johnson, Paul A. – Hartlepool U – Workington; 11 Jones, Jake – Walsall – Redditch U; 24 Keinan, Dekel – Cardiff C – Crystal Palace; 1 Kettings, Christopher D. – Blackpool – Woodley Sp; 4 Kovacs, Janos – Hereford U – Luton T; 21 Llera, Miguel A. – Blackpool – Sheffield W; 11 Lovelock, Thomas J. – Leyton Orient – Chertsey T; 18 Lovelock, Thomas J. – Leyton Orient – Farnborough T; 24 Lowry, Jamie – Chesterfield – Crewe Alex; 24 Lowry, Shane T. – Aston Villa – Millwall; 24 MacDonald, Angus – Reading – Basingstoke T; 24 Madjo, Guy B. – Stevenage – Port Vale; 3 Mancini, Andreas – Manchester C – Oldham Ath; 18 Martin, Christopher H. – Norwich C – Crystal Palace; 24 Mattock, Joseph W. – WBA – Portsmouth; 23 McCallum, Gavin K. – Lincoln C – Barnet; 4 McCarthy, Alex S. – Reading – Leeds U; 24 McCarthy, Luke J. – Bury – Grimsby T; 24 McCombe, Jamie P. – Huddersfield T – Preston NE; 24 McNamee, Anthony – Milton Keynes D – Wycombe W; 17 Montano, Cristian A. – West Ham U – Dagenham & R; 24 Murray, Ronan M. – Ipswich T – Swindon T; 24 Myrie-Williams, Jennison – Stevenage – Port Vale; 15 Naylor, Tom – Mansfield T – Derby Co; 9 Obadeyi, Temitope – Bolton W – Chesterfield; 24 O'Connor, Shane E. – Ipswich T – Port Vale; 4 Owusu, Lloyd M. – Barnet – Hayes & Yeading; 17 Panther, Emmanuel – Aldershot T – Grimsby T; 17 Parish, Elliott C. – Aston Villa – Cardiff C; 23 Parkin, Jonathan – Cardiff C – Huddersfield T; 4 Pearson, Gregory C. – Huddersfield – Blyth Spartans; 24 Pearson, Gregory E. – Burton Alb – Aldershot T; 4 Pearson, Stephen P. – Derby Co – Bristol C; 24 Peniket, Richard J. – Fulham – Hereford U; 14 Pentney, Carl – Colchester U – Hayes & Yeading; 4 Pinney, Nathaniel B. – Crystal Palace – Ebbsfleet U; 23 Priskin, Tamas – Ipswich T – Derby Co; 18 Pugh, Daniel A. – Stoke C – Leeds U; 24 Purse, Darren J. – Millwall – Plymouth Arg; 24 Rachubka, Paul S. – Leeds U – Tranmere R; 22 Ranger, Nile – Newcastle U – Barnsley; 18 Ravenhill, Richard J. – Notts Co – Bradford C; 24 Reach, Adam M. – Middlesbrough – Darlington; 24 Reid, Bobby – Bristol C – Cheltenham T; 3 Ribeiro, Christian M. – Bristol C – Carlisle U; 24 Rodney, Nialle – Bradford C – Mansfield T; 24 Russell, Darel F.R. – Preston NE – Charlton Ath; 25 Said, Abdul K.H. – Swindon T – Fairford T; 7 Saville, Jack W. – Southampton – Barnet; 3 Scapuzzi, Luca – Manchester C – Oldham Ath; 25 Scott, Mark J. – Swindon T – Salisbury C; 25 Smith, Ben P. – Crawley T – Woking; 23 Smith, Nathan A. – Mansfield T – Aldershot T; 4 Soderberg, Ole P. – Newcastle U – Chesterfield; 18 Spillane, Michael E. – Brentford – Dagenham & R; 4 Stockley, Jayden C. – AFC Bournemouth – Accrington S; 15 Sutherland, Craig S. – Blackpool – Plymouth Arg; 22 Tavernier, James H. – Newcastle U – Sheffield W; 4 Thomas, Casey K. – Swansea C – Colchester U; 24 Thorne, George L.E. – WBA – Portsmouth; 24 Townsend, Conor S. – Hull C – Grimsby T; 3 Trotman, Neal A. – Rochdale – Chesterfield; 24 Trotta, Marcello – Fulham – Wycombe W; 18 Vokes, Samuel M. – Wolverhampton W – Burnley; 3 Wallace, James R. – Everton – Shrewsbury T; 24 Watt, Herschel O.S. – Arsenal – Sheffield W; 8 Wildig, Aaron K. – Cardiff C – Shrewsbury T'; 24 Wood, Samuel J. – Brentford – Rotherham U; 2 Woodyard, Alexander J. – Southend U – Farnborough T

DECEMBER 2011 TEMPORARY TRANSFERS

13 Baggridge, Rhys W. – Yeovil T – Poole T; 6 Carey, Lewis T. – Bristol C – Gloucester C; 7 Chamberlain, Elliott C. – Leicester C – AFC Telford U; 8 Cudworth, Jack R. – Macclesfield T – Colwyn Bay; 1 Dodd, Adam J. – Blackpool – Altrincham; 16 Ebigbeyi-Popo, Tosan E. – Charlton Ath – Chelmsford C; 16 Essam, Connor – Gillingham – Dartford; 12 Evans, Jack P. – Gillingham – Welling U; 14 Gough, Conor J.J. – Charlton Ath – Eastbourne Bor; 16 Gray, Reece A. – Rochdale – Hyde U; 5 Hawkes, Daren G. – Gillingham – Maidstone U; 9 James-Lewis, Merrick A. – Southend U – Bishop's Stortford; 15 Lacey, Patrick S. – Bradford C – Vauxhall Motors; 16 Lane, Jack F. – Macclesfield T – Woodley Sp; 1 Locke, Simon J. – Reading – Forest Green R; 1 Macklin, Lloyd J. – Torquay U – Salisbury C; 2 McLaren, Connor G.D. – Millwall – Lewes; 2 McLellan, Michael – Preston NE – Workington; 2 Milton, Harry T. – Milton Keynes D – Aveley; 23 Muggeridge, Henry J. – Bristol C – Cleveland T; 5 Nelson, Mitchell A. – AFC Bournemouth – Lincoln C; 16 Parkinson, Daniel J. – Morecambe – Colwyn Bay; 24 Pavett, Jordan L. – Swindon T – Heybridge Swifts; 23 Pentney, Carl – Colchester U – Hayes & Yeading; 22 Pope, Nicholas D. – Charlton Ath – Welling U; 9 Sekajja, Ibra – Crystal Palace – Bromley; 20 Stephenson, Darren C.A. – Bradford C – Woodley Sp; 21 Tomsett, Liam R. – Blackpool – Altrincham; 2 Warren, Freddie R. – Charlton Ath – Bromley; 12 Wint, Aron L. – Scunthorpe U – Belper T

152

JANUARY 2012

31 Bamford, Patrick J.	Nottingham F	Chelsea
1 Basey, Grant W.	Peterborough U	Wycombe W
25 Beausejour, Jean A.E.	Birmingham C	Wigan Ath
31 Bennett, Ryan	Peterborough U	Norwich C
2 Benson, Paul A.	Charlton Ath	Swindon T
1 Benyon, Elliot P.	Swindon T	Southend U
16 Cahill, Gary J.	Bolton W	Chelsea
6 Chantler, Christopher S.	Manchester C	Carlisle U
1 Clarke, Leon M.	Swindon T	Charlton Ath
5 Cook, Steve A.	Brighton & HA	AFC Bournemouth
9 Dagnall, Christopher	Scunthorpe U	Barnsley
5 Daniels, Charlie	Leyton Orient	AFC Bournemouth
31 Dawson, Stephen J.	Leyton Orient	Barnsley
20 Drinkwater, Daniel N.	Manchester U	Leicester C
1 Evans, William G.	Swindon T	Hereford U
10 Foderingham, Wesley A.	Crystal Palace	Swindon T
1 Francis, Simon C.	Charlton Ath	AFC Bournemouth
12 Freeman, Luke A.	Arsenal	Stevenage
13 Gibson, Darron	Manchester U	Everton
30 Golbourne, Julio S.	Exeter C	Barnsley
31 Harding, Benjamin S.	Wycombe W	Northampton T
13 Harrison, Byron J.	Stevenage	AFC Wimbledon
13 Haynes, Danny L.	Barnsley	Charlton Ath
3 Holden, Dean T.J.	Chesterfield	Rochdale
20 Holroyd, Christopher	Rotherham U	Preston NE
23 Howson, Jonathan M.	Leeds U	Norwich C
17 Hreidarsson, Hermann	Portsmouth	Coventry C
12 Jones, Michael D.	Bury	Sheffield W
17 Jutkiewicz, Lukas I.P.	Coventry C	Middlesbrough
31 Keogh, Andrew D.	Wolverhampton W	Millwall
30 Lowry, Shane T.	Aston Villa	Millwall
20 Madjo, Guy B.	Stevenage	Aldershot T
6 Malone, Scott L.	Wolverhampton W	AFC Bournemouth
31 Marshall, Ben	Stoke C	Leicester C
5 Martin, David J.	Derby Co	Southend U
31 Mathurin-Harris, Kadeem R.	Wycombe W	Cardiff C
31 Maynard, Nicholas D.	Bristol C	West Ham U
31 McDermott, Donal	Huddersfield T	AFC Bournemouth
20 McGlashan, Jermain	Aldershot T	Cheltenham T
13 McNaughton, Callum J.	West Ham U	AFC Wimbledon
20 Mee, Benjamin T.	Manchester C	Burnley
31 Morgan, Westley N.	Nottingham F	Leicester C
31 Morrison, Ravel R.	Manchester U	West Ham U
12 Noble, Liam T.	Sunderland	Carlisle U
12 Nosworthy, Nyron	Sunderland	Watford
26 Onuoha, Chinedum	Manchester C	QPR
31 Orr, Bradley J.	QPR	Blackburn R
13 Osei-Kuffour, Jonathan	Bristol R	Gillingham
5 Parish, Elliott C.	Aston Villa	Cardiff C
27 Procter, Andrew J.	Accrington S	Preston NE
3 Pugh, Daniel A.	Stoke C	Leeds U
31 Ridgewell, Liam M.	Birmingham C	WBA
31 Robertson, Christopher	Torquay U	Preston NE
20 Rooney, Luke W.	Gillingham	Swindon T
31 Saha, Louis	Everton	Tottenham H
31 Sharp, Billy L.	Doncaster R	Southampton
31 Sordell, Marvin A.	Watford	Bolton W
1 Thomas, Wesley A.N.	Crawley T	AFC Bournemouth
5 Timlin, Michael A.	Swindon T	Southend U
13 Trippier, Kieran J.	Manchester C	Burnley
5 Trotman, Neal A.	Rochdale	Chesterfield
30 Tubbs, Matthew S.	Crawley T	AFC Bournemouth
31 Vaz Te, Ricardo J.	Barnsley	West Ham U
31 Veseli, Frederic	Manchester C	Manchester U
31 Williams, Ryan D.	Portsmouth	Fulham
31 Zamora, Robert L.	Fulham	QPR

TEMPORARY TRANSFERS

5 Abdulla, Ahmed M. – West Ham U – Dagenham & R; 2 Adams, Blair – Sunderland – Northampton T; 1 Addison, Miles – Derby Co – Barnsley; 5 Adeyemi, Thomas O. – Norwich C – Oldham Ath; 31 Ajose, Nicholas – Peterborough U – Chesterfield; 20 Alabi, Rasheed T. – Millwall – Hampton & Richmond Bor; 31 Almond, Louis J. – Blackpool – Lincoln C; 30 Aneke, Chukwuemeka A.A. – Arsenal – Stevenage; 1 Asante, Akwasi – Birmingham C – Northampton T; 27 Asante, Kyle E.K. – Southend U – Thurrock; 26 Atkinson, William H. – Hull C – Bradford C; 12 Banks, Oliver I. – Rotherham U – Stalybridge C; 9 Barkhuizen, Thomas J. – Blackpool – Hereford U; 21 Boateng, Daniel – Arsenal – Swindon T; 31 Bassong, Sebastian A. – Tottenham H – Wolverhampton W; 3 Batth, Daniel T. – Wolverhampton W – Sheffield W; 19 Bembo Leta, Djenny – Oldham Ath – Stalybridge C; 1 Bennett, Dale O. – Watford – Brentford; 31 Bennett, Ryan – Norwich C – Peterborough U; 26 Bignot, Paul J. – Blackpool – Plymouth Arg; 19 Blake, Ryan G. – Brentford – Hampton & Richmond Bor; 1 Bogdanovic, Daniel – Blackpool – Rochdale; 2 Bolger, Cian T. – Leicester C – Bristol R; 30 Bostock, John – Tottenham H – Sheffield W; 6 Bradley, Sonny – Hull C – Aldershot T; 26 Breeze, Matthew C. – Peterborough U – Histon; 31 Bridge, Wayne M. – Manchester C – Sunderland; 31 Brooke, Ryan M. – Oldham Ath – AFC Telford U; 6 Brown, Troy A.F. – Rotherham U – Aldershot T; 26 Brunt, Ryan S. – Stoke C – Tranmere R; 27 Brunt, Thomas J. – Gillingham – Leatherhead; 9 Bubb, Bradley – Aldershot T – Eastleigh; 3 Bunn, Harry – Manchester C – Preston NE; 2 Button, David R.E. – Tottenham H – Doncaster R; 26 Cadogan, Kieron J.N. – Crystal Palace – Rotherham U; 31 Cairns, Alex T. – Leeds U – Barrow; 1 Canham, Sean – Hereford U – Bath C; 13 Carey, Lewis T. – Bristol C – Gloucester C; 31 Carlisle, Clarke J. – Burnley – Northampton T; 20 Carroll, Thomas J. – Tottenham H – Derby Co; 13 Carson, Trevor – Sunderland – Hull C; 13 Cestor, Mike B. – Leyton Orient – Woking; 27 Chapman, Adam – Oxford U – Newport Co; 27 Chenoweth, Oliver R. – Plymouth Arg – Truro C; 1 Chicksen, Adam T. – Milton Keynes D – Leyton Orient; 27 Clarke, Lewis P. – Yeovil T – Weymouth; 20 Clay, Craig W. – Chesterfield – Alfreton T; 23 Clayton, Harry S. – Crewe Alex – Newcastle T; 27 Clowes, Robert N. – Yeovil T – Bridgwater T; 13 Coke, Giles C. – Sheffield W – Bury; 13 Collins, Charlie J. – Milton Keynes D – Aldershot T; 27 Connerton, Jordan S. – Crewe Alex – Nantwich T; 31 Connolly, Matthew T.M. – QPR – Reading; 19 Cook, Jordan A. – Sunderland – Carlisle U; 27 Cox, Samuel P. – Barnet – Boreham Wood; 9 Cuff, Sean A. – Sheffield U – Cambridge U; 1 Cunningham, Gregory R. – Manchester C – Nottingham F; 27 Cuvelier, Florent – Stoke C – Walsall; 30 Darikwa, Tendayi D. – Chesterfield – Hinckley U; 3 Davies, Andrew J. – Stoke C – Bradford C; 14 Davis, David L. – Wolverhampton W – Chesterfield; 2 Day, Joseph D. – Peterborough U – Alfreton T; 6 Dean, Harlee J. – Southampton – Brentford; 3 Deards, Connor A.J. – Walsall – Hinckley U; 23 Delfouneso, Nathan – Aston Villa – Leicester C; 20 Delph, Fabian – Aston Villa – Leeds U; 27 Dicko, Nouha – Wigan Ath – Blackpool; 9 Dickson, Ryan A. – Southampton – Yeovil T; 17 Doble, Ryan A. – Southampton – Bury; 30 Dorman, Andrew J. – Crystal Palace – Bristol R; 1 Downes, Aaron T. – Chesterfield – Bristol R; 7 Drinkwater, Daniel N. – Manchester U – Barnsley; 5 Driver, Callum C.J. – West Ham U – Burton Alb; 6 Dumbuya, Mustapha S.M. – Doncaster R – Crystal Palace; 16 Ebigbeyi-Popo, Tosan E. – Charlton Ath – Chelmsford C; 12 Edwards, Joseph R. – Bristol C – Yeovil T; 7 Egan, John – Sunderland – Crystal Palace; 16 Elford-Alliyu, Lateef – WBA – Tranmere R; 12 Euell, Jason J. – Charlton Ath – AFC Wimbledon; 20 Falque, Yago – Tottenham H – Southampton; 20 Fisher, Thomas M. – Macclesfield T – Droylsden; 27 Forte, Jonathan R.J. – Southampton – Notts Co; 13 Freeman, Kieron S. – Nottingham F – Notts Co; 1 Frimpong, Emmanuel Y. – Arsenal – Wolverhampton W; 20 Futcher, Benjamin P. – Bury – AFC Telford U; 20 Gayle, Ian G. – Dagenham & R – Kingstonian; 31 Gough, Conor J.J. – Charlton Ath – Eastbourne Bor; 10 Griffiths, Scott R. – Peterborough U – Rotherham U; 30 Guedioura, Adlene – Wolverhampton W – Nottingham F; 17 Hajrovic, Sead – Arsenal – Barnet; 1 Harding, Benjamin S. – Wycombe W – Northampton T; 25 Harper, James A.J. – Hull C – Wycombe W; 1 Harrop, Max – Bury – Blyth S; 10 Harvey, Alex-Ray – Burnley – Barrow; 31 Hawley, Karl L. – Notts Co – Crawley T; 12 Haworth, Andrew A.D. – Bury – Bradford C; 3 Hector, Michael A.J. – Reading – Barnet; 13 Hemmings, Ashley J. – Wolverhampton W – Plymouth Arg; 31 Higginbotham, Daniel J. – Stoke C – Nottingham F; 31 Hoskins, William R. – Brighton & HA – Sheffield U; 27 Hoyte, Gavin A. – Arsenal – AFC Wimbledon; 23 Hubbins, Luke A. – Birmingham C – Tamworth; 27 Hudson, Daniel A. – Bury – Mossley; 6 Hughes, Caspar D.S. – Crewe Alex – Chasetown; 11 Hurst, James – WBA – Chesterfield; 1 Isaac, Chaz J.T. – Watford – Tamworth; 10 Jackson, Josef J. – Burnley – Barrow; 31 Jackson, Ryan O. – AFC Wimbledon – Cambridge U; 31 Jara, Gonzalo A. – WBA – Brighton & HA; 1 Jarvis, Nathaniel S. – Cardiff C – Newport Co; 1 Jervis, Jake M. – Birmingham C – Preston NE; 26 Johnson, Brett – AFC Wimbledon – Cambridge U; 13 Jones, Reece N. – AFC Wimbledon – Carshalton Ath; 14 Jutkiewicz, Lukas I.P. – Coventry C – Middlesbrough; 30 Kacaniklic, Alexander – Fulham – Watford; 1

154

Kane, Harry – Tottenham H – Millwall; 27 Kettings, Christopher D. – Blackpool – Morecambe; 27 Kiernan, Brendan J. – AFC Wimbledon – Braintree T; 14 King, Joshua C.K. – Manchester U – Hull C; 13 Knott, Billy S. – Sunderland – AFC Wimbledon; 2 Kurucz, Peter – West Ham U – Rochdale; 17 Laing, Louis M. – Sunderland – Wycombe W; 27 Long, Kevin F. – Burnley – Rochdale; 1 Losasso, Charlie C. – Reading – Salisbury C; 27 Lucas, Lee P. – Swansea C – Burton Alb; 30 Lund, Matthew C. – Stoke C – Bristol R; 10 Lynch, David C.W. – Burnley – Stalybridge C; 1 Macheda, Federico – Manchester U – QPR; 31 Mainwaring, Matthew T. – Hull C – Stockport Co; 5 Mannone, Vito – Arsenal – Hull C; 27 Marrow, Alexander J. – Crystal Palace – Preston NE; 27 Marshall, Marcus J.L. – Rotherham U – Macclesfield T; 6 Martin, Christopher H. – Norwich C – Crystal Palace; 1 Mason, Ryan G. – Tottenham H – Millwall; 19 Massey, Gavin A. – Watford – Colchester U; 31 Mattock, Joseph W. – WBA – Brighton & HA; 12 McAllister, David J. – Sheffield U – Shrewsbury T; 20 McAllister, James R. – Bristol C – Preston NE; 31 McCallum, Paul L.M. – West Ham U – Rochdale; 10 McCarthy, Alex S. – Reading – Ipswich T; 31 McDonald, Alex – Burnley – Plymouth Arg; 13 McQuilkin, James R.L. – Hereford U – Kidderminster H; 20 McQuoid, Joshua J.B. – Millwall – Burnley; 13 McShane, Paul D. – Hull C – Crystal Palace; 13 Mills, Daniel P. – Peterborough U – Kettering T; 5 Mingoia, Pietro – Watford – Brentford; 12 Minshull, Lee B. – AFC Wimbledon – Newport Co; 31 Mirfin, David M. – Watford – Scunthorpe U; 30 Miyaichi, Ryo – Arsenal – Bolton W; 10 Moncur, George – West Ham U – AFC Wimbledon; 24 Morrison, Sean J. – Reading – Huddersfield T; 19 Mukendi, Vinny K. – Macclesfield T – Southport; 30 Murphy, Rhys P.E. – Arsenal – Preston NE; 20 Murray, Ronan M. – Ipswich T – Swindon T; 31 Mustoe, Jordan D. – Wigan Ath – Barnet; 27 Nesbitt, Teddy – Southend U – Great Wakering R; 6 Nichols, Tom A. – Exeter C – Dorchester T; 19 Noble, Ryan – Sunderland – Derby Co; 31 Norwood, Oliver J. – Manchester U – Coventry C; 6 Nsiala, Aristote – Everton – Accrington S; 10 Obika, Jonathan – Tottenham H – Yeovil T; 27 Obita, Jordan J. – Reading – Barnet; 1 O'Brien, Aiden A. – Millwall – Staines T; 12 Odubajo, Moses A.A.J. – Leyton Orient – Sutton U; 3 Ormerod, Brett R. – Blackpool – Rochdale; 27 Palmer, Ashley J. – Scunthorpe U – Southport; 26 Parker, Ben B.C. – Leeds U – Carlisle U;20 Parkes, Jordan D. – Barnet – Farnborough T; 31 Parkin, Jonathan – Cardiff C – Scunthorpe U; 13 Parrett, Dean G. – Tottenham H – Yeovil T; 18 Parsons, Alexander A. – AFC Bournemouth – Bashley; 6 Paterson, Matthew – Southend U – Forest Green R; 12 Payne, Joshua J. – Oxford U – Aldershot T; 13 Pearson, Gregory E. – Burton Alb – Crewe Alex; 31 Pienaar, Steven – Tottenham H – Everton; 9 Pinney, Nathaniel B. – Crystal Palace – Ebbsfleet U; 1 Poke, Michael H. – Brighton & HA – Bristol R; 20 Procter, Andrew J. – Accrington S – Preston NE; 10 Ray, George E. – Crewe Alex – Leek T; 30 Reckord, Jamie – Wolverhampton W – Scunthorpe U; 27 Redshaw, Jack – Morecambe – Altrincham; 31 Rendell, Scott D. – Wycombe W – Oxford U; 2 Reynolds, Duran-Rhys – Dagenham & R – Met Police; 13 Ribeiro, Christian M. – Bristol C – Scunthorpe U; 6 Ridehalgh, Liam – Huddersfield T – Chesterfield; 5 Russell, Darel F.R. – Preston NE – Charlton Ath; 12 Sampson, Jack – Bolton W – Southend U; 27 Sawyers, Romaine T. – WBA – Shrewsbury T; 31 Shephard, Christopher J. – Exeter C – Bath C; 2 Simpson, Robbie – Huddersfield T – Oldham Ath; 19 Smalley, Deane A.M. – Oxford U – Bradford C; 6 Smith, Adam C. – Leicester C – Lincoln C; 31 Smith, Adam J. – Tottenham H – Leeds U; 30 Smith, Alan – Newcastle U – Milton Keynes D; 31 Smith, Ben P. – Crawley T – Aldershot T; 25 Smith, Korey A. – Norwich C – Barnsley; 17 Smith, Michael J. – Charlton Ath – Accrington S; 3 Spencer, James C. – Huddersfield T – Cheltenham T; 27 Stephenson, Darren C.A. – Bradford C – Stocksbridge PS; 6 Stewart, Damion D. – Bristol C – Notts Co; 31 Symes, Michael – AFC Bournemouth – Rochdale; 27 Taiwo, Soloman O. – Cardiff C – Leyton Orient; 31 Tavernier, James H. – Newcastle U – Milton Keynes D; 1 Taylor, Charles J. – Leeds U – Bradford C; 31 Taylor, Jake W.T. – Reading – Exeter C; 2 Taylor, Rhys F. – Chelsea – Rotherham U; 13 Tchuimeni-Nimely, Alex – Manchester C – Coventry C; 6 Thomas Daniel A. – AFC Bournemouth – AFC Totton; 6 Thompson, Daniel A. – Portsmouth – Havant & W'ville; 6 Ting, Daniel S. – Crewe Alex – Market Drayton; 13 Tomlin, Gavin G. – Dagenham & R – Gillingham; 25 Tonge, Michael W.E. – Stoke C – Barnsley; 31 Tonne, Erik – Sheffield U – York C; 1 Townsend, Andros – Tottenham H – Leeds U; 31 Tsoumou, Hama J.F. – Preston NE – Plymouth Arg; 23 Turnbull, Paul D. – Northampton T – Stockport Co; 31 Ugwu, Chigozie E. – Reading – Ebbsfleet U; 30 Vokes, Samuel M. – Wolverhampton W – Brighton & HA; 13 Walker, Joshua – Watford – Scunthorpe U; 19 Walker, Samuel C. – Chelsea – Yeovil T; 20 Wallace, James R. – EvertonT – Tranmere R; 1 Walsh, Phillip – Dagenham & R – Hayes & Yeading; 27 Watt, Herschel O.S. – Arsenal – Crawley T; 20 Weale, Christopher – Leicester C – Northampton T; 5 Wearen, Eoin P. – West Ham U – Dagenham & R; 9 Weir, Tyler C. – Hereford U – Worcester C; 31 Whichelow, Matthew R. – Watford – Wycombe W; 19 Wildig, Aaron K. – Cardiff C – Shrewsbury T; 1 Wilson, Callum E.G. – Coventry C – Tamworth; 1 Wilson, Daniel – Liverpool – Blackpool; 13 Wood, Chris – WBA – Bristol C; 12 Wood, Samuel J. –

Brentford – Rotherham U; 27 Woodley, Aaron R. – Oxford U – Oxford C; Wootton, Scott
J. – Manchester U – Nottingham F

FEBRUARY 2012 TEMPORARY TRANSFERS

24 Abadaki, Godwin O.E. – Rochdale – Hyde U; 24 Addison, Miles – Derby Co – AFC
Bournemouth; 24 Allan, Scott – WBA – Portsmouth; 23 Annerson, Jamie P. – Rotherham
U – Bradford C; 17 Anthony, Byron – Bristol R – Hereford U; 24 Antonio, Michail G. –
Reading – Sheffield W; 17 Arnott, Craig W. – Colchester U – Leiston; 8 Assombalonga,
Britt C. – Wealdstone – Watford; 10 Assombalonga, Britt C. – Watford – Braintree T; 17
Assulin, Gai – Manchester C – Brighton & HA; 21 Barnett, Tyrone – Crawley T –
Peterborough U; 21 Batt, Shaun A.S.P. – Millwall – Crawley T; 10 Berahino, Saido – WBA
– Brentford; 23 Bond, Jonathan H. – Watford – Dagenham & R; 15 Bonham, Jack E. –
Watford – Harrow Borough; 8 Briggs, Matthew – Fulham – Peterborough U; 15 Brisley,
Shaun R. – Macclesfield – Peterborough U; 21 Butland, Jack – Birmingham C –
Cheltenham T; 24 Carson, Trevor – Sunderland – Bury; 24 Connolly, Mark G. – Bolton W –
Macclesfield T; 22 Cronin, Lance – Bristol R – Ebbsfleet U; 9 D'Ath, Lawson M. –
Reading – Yeovil T; 24 Davis, Sean – Bolton W – Bristol C; 17 Devitt, Jamie M. – Hull C –
Accrington S; 10 Dickson, Ryan A. – Southampton – Leyton Orient; 24 Doherty, Gary
M.T. – Charlton Ath – Wycombe W; 20 Duke, Matthew – Bradford C – Northampton T; 21
Eastmond, Craig L. – Arsenal – Wycombe W; 21 Elford-Alliyu, Lateef – WBA – Bury; 9
Elokobi, George N. – Wolverhampton W – Nottingham F; 17 Euell, Jason J. – Charlton Ath
– AFC Wimbledon; 23 Forshaw, Adam – Everton – Brentford; 22 Franks, Jonathan I. –
Middlesbrough – Yeovil T; 12 Freeman, Kieron S. – Nottingham F – Notts Co; 20 Futcher,
Benjamin P. – Bury – Macclesfield T; 7 Gallagher, Jake F. – Millwall – Staines T; 9 Gibson,
Benjamin J. – Middlesbrough – York C; 16 Gilmartin, Rene – Watford – Crawley T; 24
Gray, Reece A. – Rochdale – Hyde U; 29 Gregory, Corey L. – Sheffield U – Leicester C; 22
Grounds, Jonathan M. – Middlesbrough – Yeovil T; 21 Hackett, Christopher J. – Millwall –
Wycombe W; 8 Harrad, Shaun – Bury – Rotherham U; 10 Hawkes, Daren G. – Maidstone
U – Gillingham; 24 Hayes, Paul E. – Charlton Ath – Wycombe W; 2 Hoban, Thomas M. –
Watford – Wealdstone; 15 Hollis, Haydn J. – Notts Co – Hinckley U; 13 Holmes, Lee D. –
Southampton – Oxford U; 24 Huseklepp, Erik – Portsmouth – Birmingham C; 24 Jones,
Reece N. – AFC Wimbledon – Hampton & Richmond Bor; 9 Kerrouche, Mehdi –
Swindon T – Oxford U; 3 Koral, Michael D. – Crewe Alex – Congleton T; 22 Kuszczak,
Tomasz – Manchester U – Watford; 17 Lee, Oliver R. – West Ham U – Gillingham; 24
Liddle, Michael W. – Sunderland – Accrington S; 9 MacDonald, Angus L. – Reading –
Torquay U; 24 Mainwaring, Matthew T. – Hull C – Stockport Co; 27 McGinty, Sean A. –
Manchester U – Morecambe; 14 McManus, Stephen – Middlesbrough – Bristol C; 8
Montano, Cristian A. – West Ham U – Notts Co; 17 Mulley, James A. – AFC Wimbledon –
Hayes & Yeading; 10 Murphy, Darren – Stevenage – Aldershot T; 24 Nicholls, Lee A. –
Wigan Ath – Accrington S; 24 O'Donnell, Richard M. – Sheffield W – Macclesfield T; 7
Osborn, Alexander S. – Dagenham & R – Chelmsford C; 10 Parkes, Thomas P.W. –
Leicester C – Bristol R; 24 Parkinson, Daniel J. – Morecambe – Vauxhall Motors; 28
Raglan, Charles J.C. – Port Vale – Chasetown; 24 Ramsey-Dickson, Kristian – Burton Alb
– Mickleover Sp; 17 Razaak, Abdul – Manchester C – Brighton & HA; 1 Reece, Charles T. –
Bristol R – Tamworth; 23 Reeves, Benjamin N. – Southampton – Dagenham & R; 20 Scott,
Mark J. – Swindon T – Salisbury C; 17 Sears, Fred – West Ham U – Colchester U; 14 Silva,
Brito E.T. – Liverpool – Northampton T; 24 Stech, Marek – West Ham U – Leyton Orient;
15 Stockford, Lewis J. – Portsmouth – AFC Totton; 11 Taylor, Lyle J.A. – AFC
Bournemouth – Hereford U; 17 Thalassitis, Michael – Stevenage – Hayes & Yeading; 9
Thompson, Adam L. – Watford – Brentford; 18 Thorne, George L.E. – WBA – Portsmouth;
24 Ting, Daniel S. – Crewe Alex – Market Drayton T; 24 Townsend, Andros – Tottenham H
– Birmingham C; 23 Trotta, Marcello – Fulham – Watford; 9 Tunnicliffe, James M. –
Wycombe W – Crewe Alex; 17 Vilhete, Mauro A.D.S. – Barnet – Boreham Wood; 10
Vuckic, Haris – Newcastle U – Cardiff C; 18 Walker, Joshua – Watford – Scunthorpe U; 21
Walshe, Carl D. – Portsmouth – Frome T; 20 Warren, Freddie R. – Charlton Ath – Hayes &
Yeading; 3 White, Andrew I. – Crewe Alex – Nantwich T; 24 Wilkinson, Luke A. –
Dagenham & R – Dartford; 10 Williams, Brett A. – Reading – Northampton T; 1 Worsfold,
Max N. – Aldershot T – Dorchester T

MARCH 2012

13 Payne, Joshua J.   Oxford U   Aldershot T

TEMPORARY TRANSFERS

20 Adebola, Bamberdele – Hull C – Notts Co; 13 Adeyemi, Thomas O. – Norwich C –
Oldham Ath; 2 Adjei, Samuel – Newcastle U – Hartlepool U; 22 Afobe, Benik – Arsenal –
Reading; 9 Agyemang, Patrick – QPR – Stevenage; 6 Ainsworth, Lionel G.R. –
Shrewsbury T – Burton Alb; 17 Akinde, John J.A. – Crawley T – Dagenham & R; 8
Alexander, Gary G. – Brentford – Crawley T; 22 Aley, Zachery G. – Blackburn R –

Macclesfield T; 29 Allinson, Lloyd J. – Huddersfield T – Ilkeston T; 21 Amoo, David O.S. – Liverpool – Bury; 2 Andrew, Calvin H. – Crystal Palace – Leyton Orient; 16 Andrew, Daniel K. – Cheltenham T – Mansfield T; 22 Aneke, Chukwuemeka A.A. – Arsenal – Preston NE; 20 Anthony, Byron – Bristol R – Hereford U; 16 Arismendi, Hugo D. – Stoke C – Huddersfield T; 23 Baggridge, Rhys W. – Yeovil T – Weymouth; 22 Baldock, George H.I. – Milton Keynes D – Tamworth; 16 Baldwin, Patrick M. – Southend U – Exeter C; 9 Balkestein, Pim – Brentford – AFC Wimbledon; 15 Ball, Matthew – Norwich C – Macclesfield T; 12 Baudry, Mathieu M.G. – AFC Bournemouth – Dagenham & R; 22 Baxendale, James R. – Doncaster R – Hereford U; 3 Belford, Cameron D. – Bury – Southend U; 13 Bellamy, Liam J. – Brentford – Ebbsfleet U; 2 Bergqvist, Jan D. – Aldershot T – Farnborough T; 22 Bikey, Andre S. – Burnley – Bristol C; 22 Bodin, Billy P. – Swindon T – Crewe Alex; 22 Bogdanovic, Daniel – Blackpool – Notts Co; 22 Bond, Jonathan H. – Watford – Bury; 22 Bostock, John – Tottenham H – Swindon T; 2 Brown, Connor A. – Sheffield U – Hinckley U; 2 Brown, Reece – Manchester U – Oldham Ath; 27 Built, Michael C. – Northampton T – Bedford T; 16 Bunn, Harry – Manchester C – Oldham Ath; 22 Burgess, Benjamin K. – Notts Co – Cheltenham T; 9 Burns, Andrew – Bradford C – Harrogate T; 20 Button, David R.E. – Tottenham H – Barnsley; 8 Campbell-Ryce, Jamal J. – Bristol C – Leyton Orient; 6 Carr, Matthew D. – Oldham Ath – Woodley Sp; 16 Cassidy, Jake A. – Wolverhampton W – Tranmere R; 21 Cestor, Mike – Leyton Orient – Woking; 22 Chambers, James A. – Doncaster R – Hereford U; 17 Clarke, Leon M. – Charlton Ath – Crawley T; 9 Clarke, Nathan – Huddersfield T – Bury; 9 Clough, Charlie – Bristol R – AFC Telford U; 22 Clucas, Martin S. – Preston NE – Burton Alb; 22 Collins, Charlie J. – Milton Keynes D – Tamworth; 9 Collins, Daniel – Stoke C – West Ham U; 16 Collins, Lee – Port Vale – Barnsley; 9 Connelly, Seamus J. – Sheffield U – Alfreton T; 2 Connerton, Jordan S. – Crewe Alex – Workington; 22 Cook, Jordan A. – Sunderland – Carlisle U; 20 Cook, Lee – QPR – Charlton Ath; 9 Crooks, Matt D.R. – Huddersfield T – AFC Halifax T; 22 Cudworth, Jack R. – Macclesfield T – Barrow; 16 Cuff, Sean – Sheffield W – Worksop T; 22 Cummings, Warren T. – AFC Bournemouth – Crawley T; 8 Cunnington, Adam – Dagenham & R – Alfreton T; 2 Cureton, Jamie – Leyton Orient – Exeter C; 22 Curran, Craig – Carlisle U – Morecambe; 16 Dagnall, Christopher – Barnsley – Bradford C; 20 Dalla Valle, Lauri – Fulham – Exeter C; 22 Darlow, Karl – Nottingham F – Newport Co; 20 Dean, Luke – Bradford C – Harrogate T; 22 Dobbie, Stephen – Swansea C – Blackpool; 5 Doughty, Michael E. – QPR – Aldershot T; 21 Eastham, Ashley – Blackpool – Bury; 22 Eastwood, Freddy – Coventry C – Southend U; 22 Edmans, Robert M. – Dagenham & R – Dover Ath; 9 Edwards, Philip L. – Stevenage – Rochdale; 6 Egan, John – Sunderland – Sheffield U; 16 Ehmer, Maximilian A. – QPR – Preston NE; 22 Ephraim, Hogan – QPR – Bristol C; 22 Evans, Daniel J. – Crawley T – Hayes & Yeading; 9 Fisher, Thomas M. – Macclesfield T – Drolysden; 22 Fletcher, Steven M. – AFC Bournemouth – Plymouth Arg; 21 Franks, Fraser G. – AFC Wimbledon – Newport Co; 29 Gallagher, Jake F. – Millwall – Met Police; 22 Gibson, William – Yeovil T – Braintree T; 9 Godden, Matthew J. – Scunthorpe U – Gainsborough T; 16 Grant, Robert – Scunthorpe U – Accrington S; 9 Green, Daniel J. – Dagenham & R – Dover Ath; 29 Guthrie, Jonathan N. – Crewe Alex – Leek T; 16 Hall, Robert – West Ham U – Milton Keynes D; 22 Hamilton, Bradley – Colchester U – Chelmsford C; 1 Hammill, Adam – Wolverhampton W – Middlesbrough; 16 Hannah, Ross – Bradford C – AFC Halifax T; 6 Harriott, Matthew A. – Sheffield U – Burton Alb; 22 Harris, Louis D. – Wolverhampton W – Notts Co; 16 Henderson, Stephen – Portsmouth – West Ham U; 22 Higginbotham, Kallum M. – Huddersfield T – Barnsley; 6 Hill, Matthew C. – Blackpool – Sheffield U; 2 Hills, Lee M. – Crystal Palace – Southend U; 22 Hines, Zavon – Burnley – AFC Bournemouth; 5 Hoban, Thomas M. – Watford – Wealdstone; 22 Hollis, Haydn J. – Notts Co – Darlington; 16 Holmes,Lee D. – Southampton – Swindon T; 3 Holness, Charlie H.V. – Crystal Palace – Leatherhead; 15 Hoskins, Samuel T. – Southampton – Rotherham U; 2 Hudson, Daniel A. – Bury – Mossley; 2 Hughes, Casper D.S. – Crewe Alex – Nantwich T; 2 Ikeme, Carl – Wolverhampton W – Doncaster R; 2 James, Lloyd R.S. – Colchester U – Crawley T; 16 James-Lewis, Merrick – Southend U – Carshalton Ath; 1 Jarvis, Ryan R. – Walsall – Torquay U; 16 Johnson, Paul A. – Hartlepool U – Darlington; 22 Keinan, Dekel – Cardiff C – Bristol C; 16 Kiernan, Robert S. – Wigan Ath – Accrington S; 6 Lane, Jack F. – Macclesfield T – Leek T; 12 Lascelles, Jamaal – Nottingham F – Stevenage; 6 Lawrence, Liam – Portsmouth – Cardiff C; 20 Legzdins, Adam R. – Derby Co – Burton Alb; 9 Lewis, Theo A. – Cheltenham T – Gloucester C; 10 MacDonald, Alex – Burnley – Plymouth Arg; 22 MacLean, Steven – Yeovil T – Cheltenham T; 9 Maguire, Christopher – Derby Co – Portsmouth; 4 Mantom, Samuel S. – WBA – Walsall; 16 Massey, Gavin A. – Watford – Colchester U; 10 May, Ben S. – Stevenage – Barnet; 22 McAleny, Conor M. – Everton – Scunthorpe U; 22 McConville, Sean J. – Stockport Co – Rochdale; 9 McDermott, Sean – Arsenal – Leeds U; 22 McEveley, James – Barnsley – Swindon T; 1 McGleish, Scott – Bristol R – Barnet; 20 McLaren, Connor G.D. – Millwall – Welling U; 2 McLaughlin,

Conor G. – Preston NE – Shrewsbury T; 22 Meadows, Daniel T. – Nottingham F – Alfreton T; 22 Mingoia, Pietro – Watford – Hayes & Yeading; 22 Molesley, Mark – AFC Bournemouth – Aldershot T; 16 Montano, Cristian A.C. – West Ham U – Oxford U; 19 Montgomery, Nicholas A. – Sheffield U – Millwall; 8 Morgan, Dean L. – Chesterfield – Oxford U; 22 Morris, Joshua F. – Blackburn R – Yeovil T; 22 Morrison, Clinton H. – Sheffield W – Brentford; 16 Moussa, Franck – Leicester C – Chesterfield; 29 Mulley, James A. – AFC Wimbledon – Wealdstone; 16 Mullins, Hayden – Portsmouth – Reading; 12 Nappa, Byron J. – Crawley T – Weymouth; 9 Nesbitt, Teddy – Southend U – Thurrock; 19 N'Guessen, Diombo D-G. – Millwall – Charlton Ath; 20 Noble, Ryan – Sunderland – Hartlepool U; 8 Nouble, Frank H. – West Ham U – Barnsley; 23 Nyoni, Cecil – Sheffield W – Frickley Ath; 15 Obadeyi, Temitope – Bolton W – Rochdale; 2 Obita, Jordan J. – Reading – Gillingham; 13 O'Brien, Aiden A. – Millwall – Hayes & Yeading; 22 O'Halloran, Michael F. – Bolton W – Sheffield U; 26 Overson, Dean J. – Bradford C – Bradford PA; 9 Palmer, Ashley – Scunthorpe U – Harrogate T; 8 Parker, Joshua K.S. – Oldham Ath – Dagenham & R; 17 Parkin, Jonathan – Cardiff C – Scunthorpe U; 10 Payne, Sanchez – Leeds U – Buxton; 21 Pell, Harry D.B. – Hereford U – Cambridge U; 6 Piquionne, Frederic – West Ham U – Doncaster R; 1 Porter, Max – AFC Wimbledon – Newport Co; 6 Rachubka, Paul S. – Leeds U – Leyton Orient; 1 Ramage, Peter I. – QPR – Birmingham C; 2 Rance, Dean J.R. – Gillingham – Dover Ath; 22 Ranger, Nile – Newcastle U – Sheffield W; 9 Reed, Adam M. – Sunderland – Leyton Orient; 22 Rekik, Kerim – Manchester C – Portsmouth; 6 Roberts, Adam J. – Macclesfield T – Leek T; 22 Roberts, Connor S. – Everton – Colwyn Bay; 6 Robinson, Paul P. – Bolton W – Leeds U; 14 Sam, Lloyd E. – Leeds U – Notts Co; 22 Scapuzzi, Luca – Manchester C – Portsmouth; 13 Sinclair, Robert J. – Stevenage – Aldershot T; 3 Slew, Jordan M. – Blackburn R – Stevenage; 14 Smith, Mathieu – Oldham Ath – Macclesfield T; 13 Stephenson, Darren C.A. – Bradford C – Southport; 2 Stewart, Jonathan – Burnley – Alfreton T; 30 Stockford, Lewis J. – Portsmouth – AFC Totton; 2 Strugnell, Daniel – AFC Bournemouth – Bashley; 2 Strutton, Charles – AFC Wimbledon – Maidenhead U; 13 Tallack, Lewis J. – Portsmouth – Poole T; 13 Taylor, Maik S. – Leeds U – Millwall; 8 Tehoue, Jonathan – Leyton Orient – Swindon T; 1 Tiryaki, Mustafa – Tranmere R – Cambridge U; 22 Tounkara, Oumare – Sunderland – Oldham Ath; 22 Treacy, Keith – Burnley – Sheffield W; 22 Vine, Rowan L. – QPR – Gillingham; 6 Walker, Mitchell C.A. – Brighton & HA – Eastbourne Bor; 21 Wallace, Jed F. – Portsmouth – Farnborough T; 17 Wassmer, Charlie – Crawley T – Dagenham & R; 22 Wickham, Arron L. – Crawley T – Hayes & Yeading; 25 Wilkinson, Luke A. – Dagenham & R – Dartford; 21 Wilson, Glenn M. – Crawley T – Woking; 9 Wilson, Ross S. – Burnley – Silsden; 8 Winn, Peter H. – Stevenage – Grimsby T; 5 Wint, Aron L. – Scunthorpe U – FC Halifax T; 22 Wright, Andrew D. – Scunthorpe U – Grimsby T; 9 Wyke, Charles T. – Middlesbrough – Kettering T; 22 Yennaris, Nicholas – Arsenal – Notts Co

APRIL 2012

30 Barnett, Tyrone   Crawley T   Peterborough U

TEMPORARY TRANSFERS

20 Allan, Scott – WBA – Portsmouth; 15 Ball, Matthew – Norwich C – Macclesfield T; 15 Baudry, Mathieu – AFC Bournemouth – Dagenham & R; 11 Bellamy, Liam J. – Brentford – Ebbsfleet U; 1 Brown, Reece – Manchester U – Oldham Ath; 9 Burns, Andrew J. – Bradford C – Harrogate T; 16 Button, David R. – Tottenham H – Barnsley; 4 Cassidy, Jake A. – Wolverhampton W – Tranmere R; 4 Clarke, Oliver A. – Bristol R – Cleveland T; 10 Conneely, Seamus – Sheffield U – Alfreton T; 11 Crooks, Matt – Huddersfield T – FC Halifax T; 1 Cummings, Warren T. – AFC Bournemouth – Crawley T; 10 Cunnington, Adam P. – Dagenham & R – Alfreton T; 10 D'Ath, Lawson M. – Reading – Yeovil T; 20 Dean, Luke A. – Bradford C – Harrogate T; 4 Dummett, Paul – Newcastle U – Gateshead; 10 Fisher, Thomas – Macclesfield T – Droylsden; 22 Gibson, William M.H. – Yeovil T – Braintree T; 29 Guthrie, John – Crewe Alex – Leek T; 1 Hajrovic, Sead – Arsenal – Barnet; 11 Hoban, Thomas – Watford – Wealdstone; 3 Hughes, Casper – Crewe Alex – Nantwich T; 8 Ikeme, Carl – Wolverhampton W – Doncaster R; 1 James, Lloyd S.R. – Colchester U – Crawley T; 10 Knott, Billy S. – Sunderland – AFC Wimbledon; 8 Lewis, Theo A. – Cheltenham T – Gloucester C; 5 Maguire, Christopher – Derby Co – Portsmouth; 3 Mantom, Sam – WBA – Walsall; 1 McAllister, David – Sheffield U – Shrewsbury T; 7 McGleish, Scott – Bristol R – Barnet; 29 McLaren, Connor G.D. – Millwall – Welling U; 10 Moncur, George – West Ham U – AFC Wimbledon; 16 Montano, Cristian A. – West Ham U – Oxford U; 27 Mooney, Jason – Wycombe W – Oxford C; 10 Morgan, Dean – Chesterfield – Oxford U; 10 Nouble, Frank H. – West Ham U – Barnsley; 22 Nyoni, Cecil – Sheffield W – Frickley Ath; 10 Palmer, Ashley J. – Scunthorpe U – Harrogate T; 8 Parker, Joshua K.S. – Oldham Ath – Dagenham & R; 7 Rachubka, Paul S. – Leeds U – Leyton Orient; 1 Ramsey-Dickson, Kristian – Burton Alb – Mickleover Sp; 1 Reckord, Jamie – Wolverhampton W – Scunthorpe U; 19 Rekik, Karim – Manchester C – Portsmouth; 28

Ripley, Connor J. – Middlesbrough – Oxford U; 10 Robinson, Paul P. – Bolton W – Leeds U; 1 Strugnell, Daniel S. – AFC Bournemouth – Bashley; 1 Strutton, Charles – AFC Wimbledon – Maidenhead U; 13 Tallack, Lewis – Portsmouth – Poole T; 1 Taylor, Jake W.T. – Reading – Exeter C; 11 Thompson, Adam L. – Watford – Brentford; 22 Treacy, Keith P. – Burnley – Sheffield W

MAY 2012

8 Brisley, Shaun R.	Macclesfield T	Peterborough U
10 Collins, Lee	Port Vale	Barnsley
15 Donnelly, George	Macclesfield T	Rochdale
8 Pearce, Jason D.	Portsmouth	Leeds U

TEMPORARY TRANSFERS

4 Gough, Conor J.J. – Charlton Ath – Bristol R; 5 Martinez, Damain E. – Arsenal – Oxford U

FOREIGN TRANSFERS 2011–2012

JULY/AUGUST 2011	*From*	*To*
Aguero, Sergio	Atletico Madrid	Manchester C
Cabaye, Yohan	Lille	Newcastle U
Coates, Sebastian	Nacional	Liverpool
Crusat, Albert	Almeria	Wigan Ath
De Gea, David	Atletico Madrid	Manchester U
Drenthe, Royston	Real Madrid	Everton
Formica, Mauro	Newell's Old Boys	Blackburn R
Gecov, Marcel	Slovan Liberec	Fulham
Gervinho	Lille	Arsenal
Grygera, Zdenek	Juventus	Fulham
Ji, Dong-Won	Chunnam Dragons	Sunderland
Kasami, Pajtim	Palermo	Fulham
Lukaku, Romelu	Anderlecht	Chelsea
Mata, Juan	Valencia	Chelsea
Marveaux, Sylvain	Rennes	Newcastle U
Mertesacker, Per	Werder Bremen	Arsenal
Moras, Vangelis	Bologna	Swansea C
Park, Chu-Young	Monaco	Arsenal
Perone, Bruno	Tombense	QPR
Petrovic, Radosav	Partizan Belgrade	Blackburn R
Romeu, Oriol	Barcelona	Chelsea
Ruiz, Bryan	Twente	Fulham
Sa, Orlando	Porto	Fulham
Santon, Davide	Internazionale	Newcastle U
Santos, Andre	Fenerbahce	Arsenal
Savic, Stefan	Partizan Belgrade	Manchester C
Stracqualursi, Denis	Tigre	Everton
Vellios, Apostolos	Iraklis	Everton
Vorm, Michel	Utrecht	Swansea C
Vukcevic, Simon	Sporting Lisbon	Blackburn R
JANUARY/FEBRUARY 2012		
Cisse, Papisse Demba	Freiburg	Newcastle U
Diakite, Samba	Nancy	QPR
Diarra, Mahamadou	Monaco	Fulham
Frei, Kerim	Grasshoppers	Fulham
Jelavic, Nikica	Rangers	Everton
Jonsson, Eggert	Hearts	Wolverhampton W
Kasami, Pajtim	Palermo	Fulham
Miyaichi, Ryo	Arsenal	Bolton W
Modeste, Anthony	Bordeaux	Blackburn R
Olsson, Marcus	Halmstad	Blackburn R
Pizzaro, David	Roma	Manchester C
Pogrebnyak, Pavel	Stuttgart	Fulham
Ream, Tim	New York Red Bulls	Bolton W
Tremmel, Gerhard	Salzburg	Swansea C
Vuckic, Haris	Domzale	Newcastle U

MILESTONES 2011–2012

FEBRUARY
26   Carling Cup final: Liverpool 2 Cardiff C 2.
      (Liverpool won 3-2 on penalties).

MARCH
18   Scottish Communities Cup final: Kilmarnock 1 Celtic 0.
25   Johnstone's Paint Trophy final: Chesterfield 2 Swindon Town 0.

APRIL
1   Ramsdens Cup final: Falkirk 1 Hamilton Academical 0.
7   Celtic Scottish Premier League Champions.
      Alloa Athletic promoted to Scottish League Division 2.
10   Ross County promoted to Scottish Premier League.
14   Charlton Athletic promoted to Football League Championship.
      Doncaster Rovers relegated to Football League One.
      Fleetwood Town promoted to Football League Two as Blue Square Premier champions.
      Darlington, Kettering Town and Bath City relegated from Blue Square Premier.
17   Reading promoted to Premier League.
21   Portsmouth and Coventry City relegated to Football League One.
      Charlton Athletic Football League One Champions.
      Swindon Town promoted to Football League One.
      Rochdale relegated to Football League Two.
      Cowdenbeath promoted to Scottish League Division 1.
      The New Saints Welsh Premier League Champions.
22   Wolverhampton Wanderers relegated to Football League Championship.
28   Southampton promoted to Premier League.
      Swindon Town Football League Two Champions.
      Shrewsbury Town promoted to Football League One.
      Chesterfield, Exeter City and Wycombe Wanderers relegated to Football League Two.
      Macclesfield Town relegated to Blue Square Premier.
      Queen of the South relegated to Scottish League Division 2.
      Stirling Albion relegated to Scottish League Division 3.
      Hayes & Yeading relegated from Blue Square Premier.
      Welsh Premier League Cup final: Afan Lido 1 Newtown 1.
      (Afan Lido won 4-3 on penalties).

MAY
5   FA Cup final: Chelsea 2 Liverpool 1.
      Sheffield Wednesday promoted to Football League Championship.
      Crawley Town promoted to Football League One.
      Hereford United relegated to Blue Square Premier.
      Welsh Cup final: The New Saints 2 Cefn Druids 0.
7   Blackburn Rovers relegated to Football League Championship.
      Dunfermline Athletic relegated to Scottish League Division 1.
9   Europa League final: Atletico Madrid 3 Athletic Bilbao 0.
12   FA Trophy final: York City 2 Newport County 0.
      Ayr United relegated to Scottish League Division 2.
13   Manchester City Premier League Champions.
      Bolton Wanderers relegated to Football League Championship.
      FA Vase final: Dunston UTS 2 West Auckland Town 0.
19   Champions League final: Bayern Munich 1 Chelsea 1.
      (Chelsa won 4-3 on penalties).
      Championship Play-off final: West Ham United 2 Birmingham C 1.
      (West Ham United promoted to Premier League).
      William Hill Scottish Cup final: Hearts 5 Hibernian 1.
20   Blue Square Play-off final: York City 2 Luton Town 1
      (York City promoted to Football League Two).
      Dumbarton promoted to Scottish League Division 1.
      Albion Rovers retain Scottish League Division 2 status.
26   Football League One Play-off final: Huddersfield Town 0 Sheffield United 0.
      (Huddersfield Town won 8-7 on penalties and promoted to Football League Championship).
      Women's FA Cup final: Birmingham City 1 Chelsea 1.
      (Birmingham City won 3-2 on penalties).

THE FA CUP 2011–2012

FIRST ROUND

Cambridge U	(0) 2	Wrexham	(1) 2
AFC Totton	(3) 8	Bradford PA	(1) 1
AFC Wimbledon	(0) 0	Scunthorpe U	(0) 0
Alfreton T	(0) 0	Carlisle U	(4) 4
Barrow	(1) 1	Rotherham U	(0) 2
Blyth Spartans	(0) 0	Gateshead	(1) 2
Bournemouth	(1) 3	Gillingham	(1) 3
Bradford C	(0) 1	Rochdale	(0) 0
Brentford	(1) 1	Basingstoke T	(0) 0
Bristol R	(1) 3	Corby T	(0) 1
Bury	(0) 0	Crawley T	(0) 2
Chelmsford C	(2) 4	AFC Telford U	(0) 0
Chesterfield	(0) 1	Torquay U	(1) 3
Crewe Alex	(1) 1	Colchester U	(0) 4
Dagenham & R	(1) 1	Bath C	(1) 1
East Thurrock U	(0) 0	Macclesfield T	(1) 3
Exeter C	(0) 1	Walsall	(1) 1
Fleetwood T	(1) 2	Wycombe W	(0) 0
Hartlepool U	(0) 0	Stevenage	(1) 1
Hereford U	(0) 0	Yeovil T	(1) 3
Hinckley U	(0) 2	Tamworth	(0) 2
Leyton Orient	(1) 3	Bromley	(0) 0
Luton T	(0) 1	Northampton T	(0) 0
Maidenhead U	(1) 1	Aldershot T	(0) 1
Milton Keynes D	(2) 6	Nantwich T	(0) 0
Newport Co	(0) 0	Shrewsbury T	(1) 1
Notts Co	(1) 4	Accrington S	(0) 1
Oldham Ath	(3) 3	Burton Alb	(0) 1
Plymouth Arg	(1) 3	Stourbridge	(1) 3
Port Vale	(0) 0	Grimsby T	(0) 0
Preston NE	(0) 0	Southend U	(0) 0
Redbridge	(0) 0	Oxford C	(0) 0
Salisbury C	(1) 3	Arlesey T	(1) 1
Sheffield U	(2) 3	Oxford U	(0) 0
Southport	(0) 1	Barnet	(0) 2
Sutton U	(0) 1	Kettering T	(0) 0
Swindon T	(2) 4	Huddersfield T	(1) 1
Tranmere R	(0) 0	Cheltenham T	(1) 1
FC Halifax T	(0) 0	Charlton Ath	(1) 4
Morecambe	(0) 1	Sheffield W	(1) 2

FIRST ROUND REPLAYS

Aldershot T	(2) 2	Maidenhead U	(0) 0
Gillingham	(1) 3	Bournemouth	(0) 2
Grimsby T	(0) 1	Port Vale	(0) 0
Oxford C	(1) 1	Redbridge	(0) 2
(aet.)			
Scunthorpe U	(0) 0	AFC Wimbledon	(0) 1
Southend U	(0) 1	Preston NE	(0) 0
Stourbridge	(0) 2	Plymouth Arg	(0) 0
Tamworth	(0) 1	Hinckley U	(0) 0
Wrexham	(0) 2	Cambridge U	(0) 1
Bath C	(0) 1	Dagenham & R	(1) 3
(aet.)			

| Walsall | (0) 3 | Exeter C | (1) 2 |

(aet.)

SECOND ROUND

Fleetwood T	(0) 2	Yeovil T	(1) 2
Barnet	(0) 1	Milton Keynes D	(1) 3
Bradford C	(2) 3	AFC Wimbledon	(0) 1
Brentford	(0) 0	Wrexham	(1) 1
Charlton Ath	(0) 2	Carlisle U	(0) 0
Chelmsford C	(1) 1	Macclesfield T	(0) 1
Colchester U	(0) 0	Swindon T	(0) 1
Crawley T	(2) 5	Redbridge	(0) 0
Dagenham & R	(0) 1	Walsall	(0) 1
Gateshead	(0) 1	Tamworth	(1) 2
Leyton Orient	(0) 0	Gillingham	(1) 1
Luton T	(1) 2	Cheltenham T	(2) 4
Salisbury C	(0) 0	Grimsby T	(0) 0
Sheffield U	(0) 3	Torquay U	(1) 2
Sheffield W	(0) 1	Aldershot T	(0) 0
Shrewsbury T	(0) 2	Rotherham U	(1) 1
Southend U	(0) 1	Oldham Ath	(1) 1
Stourbridge	(0) 0	Stevenage	(0) 3
AFC Totton	(0) 1	Bristol R	(3) 6
Sutton U	(0) 0	Notts Co	(1) 2

SECOND ROUND REPLAYS

Grimsby T	(0) 2	Salisbury C	(0) 3

(aet.)

Oldham Ath	(0) 1	Southend U	(0) 0
Walsall	(0) 0	Dagenham & R	(0) 0

(aet; Dagenham & R won 3-2 on penalties.)

Yeovil T	(0) 0	Fleetwood T	(1) 2
Macclesfield T	(1) 1	Chelmsford C	(0) 0

THIRD ROUND

Liverpool	(2) 5	Oldham Ath	(1) 1
Barnsley	(1) 2	Swansea C	(1) 4
Birmingham C	(0) 0	Wolverhampton W	(0) 0
Brighton & HA	(0) 1	Wrexham	(0) 1
Bristol R	(0) 1	Aston Villa	(1) 3
Coventry C	(1) 1	Southampton	(0) 2
Crawley T	(0) 1	Bristol C	(0) 0
Dagenham & R	(0) 0	Millwall	(0) 0
Derby Co	(1) 1	Crystal Palace	(0) 0
Doncaster R	(0) 0	Notts Co	(1) 2
Everton	(1) 2	Tamworth	(0) 0
Fleetwood T	(0) 1	Blackpool	(1) 5
Fulham	(1) 4	Charlton Ath	(0) 0
Gillingham	(1) 1	Stoke C	(2) 3
Hull C	(2) 3	Ipswich T	(0) 1
Macclesfield T	(1) 2	Bolton W	(1) 2
Middlesbrough	(1) 1	Shrewsbury T	(0) 0
Milton Keynes D	(0) 1	QPR	(0) 1
Newcastle U	(0) 2	Blackburn R	(1) 1
Norwich C	(2) 4	Burnley	(1) 1
Nottingham F	(0) 0	Leicester C	(0) 0

Reading	(0) 0	Stevenage	(1) 1
Sheffield U	(1) 3	Salisbury C	(0) 1
Swindon T	(1) 2	Wigan Ath	(1) 1
Tottenham H	(2) 3	Cheltenham T	(0) 0
Watford	(2) 4	Bradford C	(1) 2
WBA	(2) 4	Cardiff C	(1) 2
Chelsea	(0) 4	Portsmouth	(0) 0
Manchester C	(0) 2	Manchester U	(3) 3
Peterborough U	(0) 0	Sunderland	(0) 2
Sheffield W	(0) 1	West Ham U	(0) 0
Arsenal	(0) 1	Leeds U	(0) 0

THIRD ROUND REPLAYS

Bolton W	(2) 2	Macclesfield T	(0) 0
Leicester C	(2) 4	Nottingham F	(0) 0
Millwall	(2) 5	Dagenham & R	(0) 0
QPR	(0) 1	Milton Keynes D	(0) 0
Wolverhampton W	(0) 0	Birmingham C	(0) 1
Wrexham	(1) 1	Brighton & HA	(0) 1

(aet; Brighton & HA won 5-4 on penalties.)

FOURTH ROUND

Everton	(1) 2	Fulham	(1) 1
Watford	(0) 0	Tottenham H	(1) 1
Blackpool	(0) 1	Sheffield W	(0) 1
Bolton W	(1) 2	Swansea C	(1) 1
Brighton & HA	(0) 1	Newcastle U	(0) 0
Derby Co	(0) 0	Stoke C	(1) 2
Hull C	(0) 0	Crawley T	(0) 1
Leicester C	(1) 2	Swindon T	(0) 0
Liverpool	(1) 2	Manchester U	(1) 1
Millwall	(0) 1	Southampton	(1) 1
QPR	(0) 0	Chelsea	(0) 1
Sheffield U	(0) 0	Birmingham C	(2) 4
Stevenage	(1) 1	Notts Co	(0) 0
WBA	(0) 1	Norwich C	(1) 2
Arsenal	(0) 3	Aston Villa	(2) 2
Sunderland	(0) 1	Middlesbrough	(1) 1

FOURTH ROUND REPLAYS

Sheffield W	(0) 0	Blackpool	(2) 3
Southampton	(1) 2	Millwall	(1) 3
Middlesbrough	(0) 1	Sunderland	(1) 2

(aet.)

FIFTH ROUND

Chelsea	(0) 1	Birmingham C	(1) 1
Everton	(2) 2	Blackpool	(0) 0
Millwall	(0) 0	Bolton W	(1) 2
Norwich C	(1) 1	Leicester C	(1) 2
Sunderland	(1) 2	Arsenal	(0) 0
Crawley T	(0) 0	Stoke C	(1) 2
Liverpool	(2) 6	Brighton & HA	(1) 1
Stevenage	(0) 0	Tottenham H	(0) 0

FIFTH ROUND REPLAYS

| Birmingham C | (0) 0 | Chelsea | (0) 2 |
| Tottenham H | (1) 3 | Stevenage | (1) 1 |

SIXTH ROUND

Everton	(1) 1	Sunderland	(1) 1
Chelsea	(2) 5	Leicester C	(0) 2
Liverpool	(1) 2	Stoke C	(1) 1
Tottenham H	(1) 1	Bolton W	(1) 1

(Abandoned 41 minutes; Muamba suffered serious cardiac event.)

| Tottenham H | (0) 3 | Bolton W | (0) 1 |

SIXTH ROUND REPLAY

| Sunderland | (0) 0 | Everton | (1) 2 |

SEMI-FINALS

| Liverpool | (0) 2 | Everton | (1) 1 |
| Tottenham H | (0) 1 | Chelsea | (1) 5 |

THE FA CUP FINAL

Saturday, 5 May 2012

(at Wembley Stadium, attendance 89,102)

Chelsea (1) 2   Liverpool (0) 1

Chelsea: Cech; Bosingwa, Cole, Mikel, Terry, Ivanovic, Ramires (Raul Meireles), Lampard, Kalou, Drogba, Mata (Malouda).
Scorers: Ramires 11, Drogba 52.

Liverpool: Reina; Johnson, Jose Enrique, Spearing (Carroll), Agger, Skrtel, Henderson, Gerrard, Suarez, Bellamy (Kuyt), Downing.
Scorer: Carroll 64.

Referee: P. Dowd (Staffordshire).

Did You Know?

While records continue to be broken in the FA Cup, it is most unusual for such an event to occur twice in the same match. Yet on 12 November 2011 in a First Round proper tie between Milton Keynes Dons and Nantwich Town, first one substitute George Williams coming on in the 75th minute became the youngest to score in the FA Cup at such a stage at 16 years two months and five days, then the youngest to receive a booking as well as adding MK Dons' youngest marksman and player to his CV. However, three minutes later, Brendon Galloway was brought on for his first game at 15 years seven months and 26 days, thus becoming the club's youngest debutant and also the FA Cup's youngest entrant. Though Nantwich were beaten 6-0 it was the first time in the club's history that they had reached the First Round proper in 127 years and a record of their own of which to be proud.

PAST FA CUP FINALS

Details of one goalscorer is not available in 1878.

1872	The Wanderers...............1		Royal Engineers.....................0	
	Betts			
1873	The Wanderers...............2		Oxford University.....................0	
	Kinnaird, Wollaston			
1874	Oxford University.................2		Royal Engineers.....................0	
	Mackarness, Patton			
1875	Royal Engineers......................1		Old Etonians..............................1*	
	Renny-Tailyour		*Bonsor*	
Replay	Royal Engineers......................2		Old Etonians..............................0	
	Renny-Tailyour, Stafford			
1876	The Wanderers...............1		Old Etonians..............................1*	
	Edwards		*Bonsor*	
Replay	The Wanderers...............3		Old Etonians..............................0	
	Wollaston, Hughes 2			
1877	The Wanderers...............2		Oxford University.....................1*	
	Lindsay, Kenrick		*Kinnaird (og)*	
1878	The Wanderers...............3		Royal Engineers.....................1	
	Kenrick 2, Kinnaird		*Unknown*	
1879	Old Etonians................................1		Clapham Rovers.........................0	
	Clerke			
1880	Clapham Rovers........................1		Oxford University.....................0	
	Lloyd-Jones			
1881	Old Carthusians..........................3		Old Etonians..............................0	
	Wyngard, Parry, Todd			
1882	Old Etonians................................1		Blackburn Rovers 0	
	Anderson			
1883	Blackburn Olympic....................2		Old Etonians..............................1*	
	Costley, Matthews		*Goodhart*	
1884	Blackburn Rovers 2		Queen's Park, Glasgow 1	
	Sowerbutts, Forrest		*Christie*	
1885	Blackburn Rovers 2		Queen's Park, Glasgow 0	
	Forrest, Brown			
1886	Blackburn Rovers 0		West Bromwich Albion 0	
Replay	Blackburn Rovers 2		West Bromwich Albion 0	
	Brown, Sowerbutts			
1887	Aston Villa 2		West Bromwich Albion 0	
	Hunter, Hodgetts			
1888	West Bromwich Albion 2		Preston NE....................1	
	Woodhall, Bayliss		*Dewhurst*	
1889	Preston NE....................3		Wolverhampton W 0	
	Dewhurst, J. Ross, Thompson			
1890	Blackburn Rovers 6		Sheffield W.....................1	
	Walton, John Southworth, Lofthouse, Townley 3		*Bennett*	
1891	Blackburn Rovers 3		Notts Co 1	
	Dewar, John Southworth, Townley		*Oswald*	
1892	West Bromwich Albion 3		Aston Villa 0	
	Geddes, Nicholls, Reynolds			
1893	Wolverhampton W 1		Everton.....................0	
	Allen			

Year	Winner	Score	Runner-up	Score
1894	Notts Co *Watson, Logan 3*	4	Bolton W *Cassidy*	1
1895	Aston Villa *J. Devey*	1	West Bromwich Albion	0
1896	Sheffield W *Spiksley 2*	2	Wolverhampton W *Black*	1
1897	Aston Villa *Campbell, Wheldon, Crabtree*	3	Everton *Boyle, Bell*	2
1898	Nottingham F *Cape 2, McPherson*	3	Derby Co *Bloomer*	1
1899	Sheffield U *Bennett, Beers, Almond, Priest*	4	Derby Co *Boag*	1
1900	Bury *McLuckie 2, Wood, Plant*	4	Southampton	0
1901	Tottenham H *Brown 2*	2	Sheffield U *Bennett, Priest*	2
Replay	Tottenham H *Cameron, Smith, Brown*	3	Sheffield U *Priest*	1
1902	Sheffield U *Common*	1	Southampton *Wood*	1
Replay	Sheffield U *Hedley, Barnes*	2	Southampton *Brown*	1
1903	Bury *Ross, Sagar, Leeming 2, Wood, Plant*	6	Derby Co	0
1904	Manchester C *Meredith*	1	Bolton W	0
1905	Aston Villa *Hampton 2*	2	Newcastle U	0
1906	Everton *Young*	1	Newcastle U	0
1907	Sheffield W *Stewart, Simpson*	2	Everton *Sharp*	1
1908	Wolverhampton W *Hunt, Hedley, Harrison*	3	Newcastle U *Howey*	1
1909	Manchester U *A. Turnbull*	1	Bristol C	0
1910	Newcastle U *Rutherford*	1	Barnsley *Tufnell*	1
Replay	Newcastle U *Shepherd 2 (1 pen)*	2	Barnsley	0
1911	Bradford C	0	Newcastle U	0
Replay	Bradford C *Speirs*	1	Newcastle U	0
1912	Barnsley	0	West Bromwich Albion	0
Replay	Barnsley *Tufnell*	1	West Bromwich Albion	0*
1913	Aston Villa *Barber*	1	Sunderland	0
1914	Burnley *Freeman*	1	Liverpool	0
1915	Sheffield U *Simmons, Masterman, Kitchen*	3	Chelsea	0

166

1920	Aston Villa 1	Huddersfield T 0*
	Kirton	
1921	Tottenham H...............................1	Wolverhampton W 0
	Dimmock	
1922	Huddersfield T 1	Preston NE.......................................0
	Smith (pen)	
1923	Bolton W 2	West Ham U 0
	Jack, J.R. Smith	
1924	Newcastle U 2	Aston Villa 0
	Harris, Seymour	
1925	Sheffield U 1	Cardiff C...0
	Tunstall	
1926	Bolton W 1	Manchester C...................................0
	Jack	
1927	Cardiff C.......................................1	Arsenal 0
	Ferguson	
1928	Blackburn Rovers 3	Huddersfield T 1
	Roscamp 2, McLean	*A. Jackson*
1929	Bolton W 2	Portsmouth.......................................0
	Butler, Blackmore	
1930	Arsenal...2	Huddersfield T 0
	James, Lambert	
1931	West Bromwich Albion 2	Birmingham 1
	W.G. Richardson 2	*Bradford*
1932	Newcastle U 2	Arsenal...1
	Allen 2	*John*
1933	Everton...3	Manchester C...................................0
	Stein, Dean, Dunn	
1934	Manchester C...............................2	Portsmouth.......................................1
	Tilson 2	*Rutherford*
1935	Sheffield W..................................4	West Bromwich Albion 2
	Rimmer 2, Palethorpe, Hooper	*Boyes, Sandford*
1936	Arsenal...1	Sheffield U 0
	Drake	
1937	Sunderland...................................3	Preston NE.......................................1
	Gurney, Carter, Burbanks	*F. O'Donnell*
1938	Preston NE...................................1	Huddersfield T 0*
	Mutch (pen)	
1939	Portsmouth...................................4	Wolverhampton W 1
	Parker 2, Barlow, Anderson	*Dorsett*
1946	Derby Co.......................................4	Charlton Ath.....................................1*
	H. Turner (og), Doherty, Stamps 2	*H. Turner*
1947	Charlton Ath.................................1	Burnley...0*
	Duffy	
1948	Manchester U 4	Blackpool 2
	Rowley 2, Pearson, Anderson	*Shimwell (pen), Mortensen*
1949	Wolverhampton W 3	Leicester C.......................................1
	Pye 2, Smyth,	*Griffiths*
1950	Arsenal...2	Liverpool..0
	Lewis 2	
1951	Newcastle U 2	Blackpool 0
	Milburn 2	

Year	Winner	Score	Runner-up	Score
1952	Newcastle U *G. Robledo*	1	Arsenal	0
1953	Blackpool *Mortensen 3, Perry*	4	Bolton W *Lofthouse, Moir, Bell*	3
1954	West Bromwich Albion *Allen 2 (1 pen), Griffin*	3	Preston NE *Morrison, Wayman*	2
1955	Newcastle U *Milburn, Mitchell, Hannah*	3	Manchester C *Johnstone*	1
1956	Manchester C *Hayes, Dyson, Johnstone*	3	Birmingham C *Kinsey*	1
1957	Aston Villa *McParland 2*	2	Manchester U *T. Taylor*	1
1958	Bolton W *Lofthouse 2*	2	Manchester U	0
1959	Nottingham F *Dwight, Wilson*	2	Luton T *Pacey*	1
1960	Wolverhampton W *McGrath (og), Deeley 2*	3	Blackburn Rovers	0
1961	Tottenham H *Smith, Dyson*	2	Leicester C	0
1962	Tottenham H *Greaves, Smith, Blanchflower (pen)*	3	Burnley *Robson*	1
1963	Manchester U *Herd 2, Law*	3	Leicester C *Keyworth*	1
1964	West Ham U *Sissons, Hurst, Boyce*	3	Preston NE *Holden, Dawson*	2
1965	Liverpool *Hunt, St John*	2	Leeds U *Bremner*	1*
1966	Everton *Trebilcock 2, Temple*	3	Sheffield W *McCalliog, Ford*	2
1967	Tottenham H *Robertson, Saul*	2	Chelsea *Tambling*	1
1968	West Browmich Albion *Astle*	1	Everton	0*
1969	Manchester C *Young*	1	Leicester C	0
1970	Chelsea *Houseman, Hutchinson*	2	Leeds U *Charlton, Jones*	2*
Replay	Chelsea *Osgood, Webb*	2	Leeds U *Jones*	1*
1971	Arsenal *Kelly, George*	2	Liverpool *Heighway*	1*
1972	Leeds U *Clarke*	1	Arsenal	0
1973	Sunderland *Porterfield*	1	Leeds U	0
1974	Liverpool *Keegan 2, Heighway*	3	Newcastle	0
1975	West Ham U *A. Taylor 2*	2	Fulham	0
1976	Southampton *Stokes*	1	Manchester U	0
1977	Manchester U *Pearson, J. Greenhoff*	2	Liverpool *Case*	1

1978	Ipswich T	1	Arsenal	0
	Osborne			
1979	Arsenal	3	Manchester U	2
	Talbot, Stapleton, Sunderland		McQueen, McIlroy	
1980	West Ham U	1	Arsenal	0
	Brooking			
1981	Tottenham H	1	Manchester C	1*
	Hutchison (og)		Hutchison	
Replay	Totteham H	3	Manchester C	2
	Villa 2, Crooks		MacKenzie, Reeves (pen)	
1982	Tottenham H	1	QPR	1*
	Hoddle		Fenwick	
Replay	Tottenham H	1	QPR	0
	Hoddle (pen)			
1983	Manchester U	2	Brighton & HA	2*
	Stapleton, Wilkins		Smith, Stevens	
Replay	Manchester U	4	Brighton & HA	0
	Robson 2, Whiteside, Muhren (pen)			
1984	Everton	2	Watford	0
	Sharp, Gray			
1985	Manchester U	1	Everton	0*
	Whiteside			
1986	Liverpool	3	Everton	1
	Rush 2, Johnston		Lineker	
1987	Coventry C	3	Tottenham H	2*
	Bennett, Houchen, Mabbutt (og)		C. Allen, Kilcline (og)	
1988	Wimbledon	1	Liverpool	0
	Sanchez			
1989	Liverpool	3	Everton	2*
	Aldridge, Rush 2		McCall 2	
1990	Manchester U	3	Crystal Palace	3*
	Robson, Hughes 2		O'Reilly, Wright 2	
Replay	Manchester U	1	Crystal Palace	0
	Martin			
1991	Tottenham H	2	Nottingham F	1*
	Stewart, Walker (og)		Pearce	
1992	Liverpool	2	Sunderland	0
	Thomas, Rush			
1993	Arsenal	1	Sheffield W	1*
	Wright		Hirst	
Replay	Arsenal	2	Sheffield W	1*
	Wright, Linighan		Waddle	
1994	Manchester U	4	Chelsea	0
	Cantona 2 (2 pens), Hughes, McClair			
1995	Everton	1	Manchester U	0
	Rideout			
1996	Manchester U	1	Liverpool	0
	Cantona			
1997	Chelsea	2	Middlesbrough	0
	Di Matteo, Newton			
1998	Arsenal	2	Newcastle U	0
	Overmars, Anelka			

1999	Manchester U 2	Newcastle U 0
	Sheringham, Scholes	
2000	Chelsea 1	Aston Villa 0
	Di Matteo	
2001	Liverpool.............................2	Arsenal 1
	Owen 2	Ljungberg
2002	Arsenal 2	Chelsea 0
	Parlour, Ljungberg	
2003	Arsenal 1	Southampton 0
	Pires	
2004	Manchester U 3	Millwall...0
	Ronaldo, Van Nistelrooy 2 (1 pen)	
2005	Arsenal 0	Manchester U 0*
	Arsenal won 5-4 on penalties	
2006	Liverpool.............................3	West Ham U 3*
	Cisse, Gerrard 2	Carragher (og), Ashton, Konchesky
	Liverpool won 3-1 on penalties	
2007	Chelsea 1	Manchester U 0*
	Drogba	
2008	Portsmouth............................1	Cardiff C...0
	Kanu	
2009	Chelsea 2	Everton..1
	Drogba, Lampard	Saha
*After extra time		
2010	Chelsea 1	Portsmouth...0
	Drogba	
2011	Manchester C............................1	Stoke C 0
	Y. Toure	
2012	Chelsea 2	Liverpool..1
	Ramires, Drogba	Carroll

FA CUP ATTENDANCES 1969–2012

	Total	No. of matches	Average per match		Total	No. of matches	Average per match
2011–12	1,987,740	151	13,164	1989–90	2,190,463	170	12,885
2010–11	1,996,935	150	13,313	1988–89	1,966,318	164	12,173
2009–10	1,884,421	151	12,480	1987–88	2,050,585	155	13,229
2008–09	2,131,669	163	13,078	1986–87	1,877,400	165	11,378
2007–08	2,011,320	152	13,232	1985–86	1,971,951	168	11,738
2006–07	2,218,846	158	14,043	1984–85	1,909,359	157	12,162
2005–06	1,966,638	160	12,291	1983–84	1,941,400	166	11,695
2004–05	1,999,752	146	13,697	1982–83	2,209,625	154	14,348
2003–04	1,870,103	149	12,551	1981–82	1,840,955	160	11,506
2002–03	1,850,326	150	12,336	1980–81	2,756,800	169	16,312
2001–02	1,809,093	148	12,224	1979–80	2,661,416	163	16,328
2000–01	1,804,535	151	11,951	1978–79	2,604,002	166	15,687
1999–2000	1,700,913	158	10,765	1977–78	2,594,578	160	16,216
1998–99	2,107,947	155	13,599	1976–77	2,982,102	174	17,139
1997–98	2,125,696	165	12,883	1975–76	2,759,941	161	17,142
1996–97	1,843,998	151	12,211	1974–75	2,968,903	172	17,261
1995–96	2,046,199	167	12,252	1973–74	2,779,952	167	16,646
1994–95	2,015,249	161	12,517	1972–73	2,928,975	160	18,306
1993–94	1,965,146	159	12,359	1971–72	3,158,562	160	19,741
1992–93	2,047,670	161	12,718	1970–71	3,220,432	162	19,879
1991–92	1,935,340	160	12,095	1969–70	3,026,765	170	17,805
1990–91	2,038,518	162	12,583				

SUMMARY OF FA CUP WINNERS SINCE 1872

Manchester United	11
Arsenal	10
Tottenham Hotspur	8
Aston Villa	7
Chelsea	7
Liverpool	7
Blackburn Rovers	6
Newcastle United	6
Everton	5
Manchester City	5
The Wanderers	5
West Bromwich Albion	5
Bolton Wanderers	4
Sheffield United	4
Wolverhampton Wanderers	4
Sheffield Wednesday	3
West Ham United	3
Bury	2
Nottingham Forest	2
Old Etonians	2
Portsmouth	2
Preston North End	2
Sunderland	2
Barnsley	1
Blackburn Olympic	1
Blackpool	1
Bradford City	1
Burnley	1
Cardiff City	1
Charlton Athletic	1
Clapham Rovers	1
Coventry City	1
Derby County	1
Huddersfield Town	1
Ipswich Town	1
Leeds United	1
Notts County	1
Old Carthusians	1
Oxford University	1
Royal Engineers	1
Southampton	1
Wimbledon	1

APPEARANCES IN FA CUP FINAL

Manchester United	18
Arsenal	17
Liverpool	14
Everton	13
Newcastle United	13
Chelsea	11
Aston Villa	10
West Bromwich Albion	10
Manchester City	9
Tottenham Hotspur	9
Blackburn Rovers	8
Wolverhampton Wanderers	8
Bolton Wanderers	7
Preston North End	7
Old Etonians	6
Sheffield United	6
Sheffield Wednesday	6
Huddersfield Town	5
Portsmouth	5
The Wanderers	5
West Ham United	5
Derby County	4
Leeds United	4
Leicester City	4
Oxford University	4
Royal Engineers	4
Southampton	4
Sunderland	4
Blackpool	3
Burnley	3
Cardiff City	3
Nottingham Forest	3
Barnsley	2
Birmingham City	2
Bury	2
Charlton Athletic	2
Clapham Rovers	2
Notts County	2
Queen's Park (Glasgow)	2
Blackburn Olympic	1
Bradford City	1
Brighton & Hove Albion	1
Bristol City	1
Coventry City	1
Crystal Palace	1
Fulham	1
Ipswich Town	1
Luton Town	1
Middlesbrough	1
Millwall	1
Old Carthusians	1
Queens Park Rangers	1
Stoke C.	1
Watford	1
Wimbledon	1

CARLING CUP 2011–2012

PRELIMINARY ROUND

Crawley T	(1) 3	AFC Wimbledon	(1) 2

FIRST ROUND

Accrington S	(0) 0	Scunthorpe U	(0) 2
Barnsley	(0) 0	Morecambe	(0) 2
Bournemouth	(2) 5	Dagenham & R	(0) 0
Brighton & HA	(0) 1	Gillingham	(0) 0
Burnley	(0) 6	Burton Alb	(0) 3
(aet.)			
Bury	(1) 3	Coventry C	(1) 1
Cheltenham T	(1) 1	Milton Keynes D	(1) 4
Derby Co	(0) 2	Shrewsbury T	(3) 3
Doncaster R	(2) 3	Tranmere R	(0) 0
Exeter C	(0) 2	Yeovil T	(0) 0
Hartlepool U	(0) 1	Sheffield U	(1) 1
(aet; Sheffield U won 4-3 on penalties.)			
Hereford U	(0) 1	Brentford	(0) 0
Hull C	(0) 0	Macclesfield T	(1) 2
Ipswich T	(1) 1	Northampton T	(1) 2
Leeds U	(0) 3	Bradford C	(1) 2
Nottingham F	(1) 3	Notts Co	(1) 3
(aet; Nottingham F won 4-3 on penalties.)			
Oldham Ath	(1) 1	Carlisle U	(0) 1
(aet; Carlisle U won 4-2 on penalties.)			
Plymouth Arg	(0) 0	Millwall	(1) 1
Port Vale	(1) 2	Huddersfield T	(2) 4
Portsmouth	(0) 0	Barnet	(1) 1
Preston NE	(1) 3	Crewe Alex	(2) 2
Rochdale	(1) 3	Chesterfield	(1) 2
(aet.)			
Rotherham U	(1) 1	Leicester C	(1) 4
Southampton	(2) 4	Torquay U	(1) 1
Southend U	(1) 1	Leyton Orient	(1) 1
(aet; Leyton Orient won 4-3 on penalties.)			
Stevenage	(1) 3	Peterborough U	(1) 4
(aet.)			
Walsall	(0) 0	Middlesbrough	(2) 3
Wycombe W	(2) 3	Colchester U	(2) 3
(aet; Wycombe W won 5-4 on penalties.)			
Oxford U	(1) 1	Cardiff C	(1) 3
(aet.)			
Sheffield W	(0) 0	Blackpool	(0) 0
(aet; Sheffield W won 4-2 on penalties.)			
Bristol R	(1) 1	Watford	(1) 1
(aet; Bristol R won 4-2 on penalties.)			
Charlton Ath	(1) 2	Reading	(0) 1
Crystal Palace	(0) 2	Crawley T	(0) 0
Bristol C	(0) 0	Swindon T	(0) 1
West Ham U	(1) 1	Aldershot T	(0) 2

SECOND ROUND

Aston Villa	(0) 2	Hereford U	(0) 0
Bournemouth	(0) 1	WBA	(2) 4

Brighton & HA	(0) 1	Sunderland	(0) 0
(aet.)			
Burnley	(1) 3	Barnet	(0) 2
(aet.)			
Bury	(1) 2	Leicester C	(1) 4
Cardiff C	(2) 5	Huddersfield T	(0) 3
(aet.)			
Doncaster R	(1) 1	Leeds U	(1) 2
Millwall	(2) 2	Morecambe	(0) 0
Northampton T	(0) 0	Wolverhampton W	(2) 4
Norwich C	(0) 0	Milton Keynes D	(2) 4
QPR	(0) 0	Rochdale	(1) 2
Shrewsbury T	(1) 3	Swansea C	(1) 1
Wycombe W	(0) 1	Nottingham F	(2) 4
Blackburn R	(3) 3	Sheffield W	(0) 1
Bolton W	(0) 2	Macclesfield T	(1) 1
Everton	(3) 3	Sheffield U	(1) 1
Exeter C	(0) 1	Liverpool	(1) 3
Peterborough U	(0) 0	Middlesbrough	(2) 2
Scunthorpe U	(1) 1	Newcastle U	(0) 2
(aet.)			
Aldershot T	(1) 2	Carlisle U	(0) 0
Leyton Orient	(2) 3	Bristol R	(0) 2
Swindon T	(0) 1	Southampton	(2) 3
Charlton Ath	(0) 0	Preston NE	(1) 2
Crystal Palace	(2) 2	Wigan Ath	(0) 1

THIRD ROUND

Aldershot T	(0) 2	Rochdale	(1) 1
Arsenal	(1) 3	Shrewsbury T	(1) 1
Aston Villa	(0) 0	Bolton W	(0) 2
Blackburn R	(1) 3	Leyton Orient	(0) 2
Burnley	(0) 2	Milton Keynes D	(1) 1
Crystal Palace	(1) 2	Middlesbrough	(0) 1
Leeds U	(0) 0	Manchester U	(3) 3
Nottingham F	(0) 3	Newcastle U	(1) 4
(aet.)			
Stoke C	(0) 0	Tottenham H	(0) 0
(aet; Stoke C won 7-6 on penalties.)			
Wolverhampton W	(3) 5	Millwall	(0) 0
Brighton & HA	(0) 1	Liverpool	(1) 2
Cardiff C	(1) 2	Leicester C	(1) 2
(aet; Cardiff C won 7-6 on penalties.)			
Chelsea	(0) 0	Fulham	(0) 0
(aet; Chelsea won 4-3 on penalties.)			
Everton	(0) 2	WBA	(0) 1
(aet.)			
Manchester C	(2) 2	Birmingham C	(0) 0
Southampton	(1) 2	Preston NE	(0) 1

FOURTH ROUND

Aldershot T	(0) 0	Manchester U	(2) 3
Arsenal	(0) 2	Bolton W	(0) 1
Cardiff C	(1) 1	Burnley	(0) 0
Crystal Palace	(0) 2	Southampton	(0) 0
Blackburn R	(1) 4	Newcastle U	(0) 3
(aet.)			

Everton	(0) 1	Chelsea	(1) 2
(aet.)			
Stoke C	(1) 1	Liverpool	(0) 2
Wolverhampton W	(1) 2	Manchester C	(3) 5

QUARTER-FINALS

Arsenal	(0) 0	Manchester C	(0) 1
Cardiff C	(1) 2	Blackburn R	(0) 0
Chelsea	(0) 0	Liverpool	(0) 2
Manchester U	(0) 1	Crystal Palace	(0) 2
(aet.)			

SEMI-FINAL FIRST LEG

| Crystal Palace | (1) 1 | Cardiff C | (0) 0 |
| Manchester C | (0) 0 | Liverpool | (1) 1 |

SEMI-FINAL SECOND LEG

Cardiff C	(1) 1	Crystal Palace	(0) 0
(aet; Cardiff C won 3-1 on penalties.)			
Liverpool	(1) 2	Manchester C	(1) 2

THE CARLING CUP FINAL

Sunday, 26 February 2012

Cardiff C (1) 2   Liverpool (0) 2

(at Wembley Stadium, attendance 89,044)

Cardiff C: Heaton; McNaughton (Blake), Taylor, Gunnarsson, Hudson (Gerrard), Turner, Cowie, Whittingham, Miller, Gestede, Mason (Kiss).
Scorers: Mason 19, Turner 118.

Liverpool: Reina; Johnson, Jose Enrique, Skrtel, Agger (Carragher), Adam, Henderson (Bellamy), Gerrard, Carroll (Kuyt), Suarez, Downing.
Scorers: Skrtel 60, Kuyt 108.

aet; Liverpool won 3-2 on penalties.

Referee: M. Clattenburg (Tyne & Wear).

Did You Know?

Without the expansion of floodlights in England during the late 1950s it is doubtful whether a League Cup competition would have been possible since the only viable way for it to function properly in the football calendar was in midweek evenings. Since its debut in 1960–61, there have been many changes to the original concept and a fluctuation in overall attendances when two-legged ties were a feature. The highest average attendance was achieved in 1971–72 when the 123 matches produced a figure of 19,489. There were seasons where more games were played, the record being established in 1979–80 when 169 were completed. As to the highest aggregate attendance, this was of course attained in 1971–72 at 2,397,154. Now with the slimmed down version without replays the average crowds have remained at a sustainable level and for 2012–13 there will be a new sponsor, too, Capital One.

PAST LEAGUE CUP FINALS

Played as two legs up to 1966

1961	Rotherham U....................2	Aston Villa.........................0	
	Webster, Kirkman		
	Aston Villa.......................3	Rotherham U......................0*	
	O'Neill, Burrows, McParland		
1962	Rochdale..........................0	Norwich C..........................3	
	Lythgoe 2, Punton		
	Norwich C........................1	Rochdale.............................0	
	Hill		
1963	Birmingham C...................3	Aston Villa.........................1	
	Leek 2, Bloomfield	*Thomson*	
	Aston Villa.......................0	Birmingham C......................0	
1964	Stoke C............................1	Leicester C.........................1	
	Bebbington	*Gibson*	
	Leicester C.......................3	Stoke C..............................2	
	Stringfellow, Gibson, Riley	*Viollet, Kinnell*	
1965	Chelsea............................3	Leicester C.........................2	
	Tambling, Venables (pen),	*Appleton, Goodfellow*	
	McCreadie		
	Leicester C.......................0	Chelsea...............................0	
1966	West Ham U 2	WBA...................................1	
	Moore, Byrne	*Astle*	
	WBA.................................4	West Ham U 1	
	Kaye, Brown, Clark, Williams	*Peters*	
1967	QPR..................................3	WBA...................................2	
	Morgan R, Marsh, Lazarus	*Clark C 2*	
1968	Leeds U 1	Arsenal...............................0	
	Cooper		
1969	Swindon T 3	Arsenal...............................1*	
	Smart, Rogers 2	*Gould*	
1970	Manchester C....................2	WBA...................................1*	
	Doyle, Pardoe	*Astle*	
1971	Tottenham H......................2	Aston Villa.........................0	
	Chivers 2		
1972	Chelsea............................1	Stoke C..............................2	
	Osgood	*Conroy, Eastham*	
1973	Tottenham H......................1	Norwich C..........................0	
	Coates		
1974	Wolverhampton W 2	Manchester C......................1	
	Hibbitt, Richards	*Bell*	
1975	Aston Villa.......................1	Norwich C..........................0	
	Graydon		
1976	Manchester C....................2	Newcastle U........................1	
	Barnes, Tueart	*Gowling*	
1977	Aston Villa.......................0	Everton...............................0	
Replay	Aston Villa.......................1	Everton...............................1*	
	Kenyon (og)	*Latchford*	
Replay	Aston Villa.......................3	Everton...............................2*	
	Little 2, Nicholl	*Latchford, Lyons*	
1978	Nottingham F.....................0	Liverpool............................0*	
Replay	Nottingham F.....................1	Liverpool............................0	
	Robertson (pen)		

1979	Nottingham F	3	Southampton	2
	Birtles 2, Woodcock		Peach, Holmes	
1980	Wolverhampton W	1	Nottingham F	0
	Gray			
1981	Liverpool	1	West Ham U	1*
	Kennedy A		Stewart (pen)	
Replay	Liverpool	2	West Ham U	1
	Dalglish, Hansen		Goddard	
1982	Liverpool	3	Tottenham H	1*
	Whelan 2, Rush		Archibald	
1983	Liverpool	2	Manchester U	1*
	Kennedy A, Whelan		Whiteside	
1984	Liverpool	0	Everton	0*
Replay	Liverpool	1	Everton	0
	Souness			
1985	Norwich C	1	Sunderland	0
	Chisholm (og)			
1986	Oxford U	3	QPR	0
	Hebberd, Houghton, Charles			
1987	Arsenal	2	Liverpool	1
	Nicholas 2		Rush	
1988	Luton T	3	Arsenal	2
	Stein B 2, Wilson		Hayes, Smith	
1989	Nottingham F	3	Luton T	1
	Clough 2, Webb		Harford	
1990	Nottingham F	1	Oldham Ath	0
	Jemson			
1991	Sheffield W	1	Manchester U	0
	Sheridan			
1992	Manchester U	1	Nottingham F	0
	McClair			
1993	Arsenal	2	Sheffield W	1
	Merson, Morrow		Harkes	
1994	Aston Villa	3	Manchester U	1
	Atkinson, Saunders 2 (1 pen)		Hughes	
1995	Liverpool	2	Bolton W	1
	McManaman 2		Thompson	
1996	Aston Villa	3	Leeds U	0
	Milosevic, Taylor, Yorke			
1997	Leicester C	1	Middlesbrough	1*
	Heskey		Ravanelli	
Replay	Leicester C	1	Middlesbrough	0*
	Claridge			
1998	Chelsea	2	Middlesbrough	0*
	Sinclair, Di Matteo			
1999	Tottenham H	1	Leicester C	0
	Nielsen			
2000	Leicester C	2	Tranmere R	1
	Elliott 2		Kelly	
2001	Liverpool	1	Birmingham C	1
	Fowler		Purse (pen)	

Liverpool won 5-4 on penalties.

| 2002 | Blackburn | 2 | Tottenham H | 1 |
| | Jansen, Cole | | Ziege | |

2003	Liverpool 2	Manchester U 0
	Gerrard, Owen	
2004	Middlesbrough 2	Bolton W 1
	Job, Zenden (pen)	Davies
2005	Chelsea 3	Liverpool...2*
	Gerrard (og), Drogba, Kezman	Riise, Nunez
2006	Manchester U 4	Wigan Ath 0
	Rooney 2, Saha, Ronaldo	
2007	Chelsea 2	Arsenal 1
	Drogba 2	Walcott
2008	Tottenham H..................................2	Chelsea 1*
	Berbatov, Woodgate	Drogba
2009	Manchester U 0	Tottenham H...................................0*
	Manchester U won 4-1 on penalties.	
2010	Manchester U 2	Aston Villa 1
	Owen, Rooney	Milner (pen)
2011	Birmingham C 2	Arsenal 1
	Zigic, Martins	Van Persie
2012	Liverpool.......................................2	Cardiff...2*
	Skrtel, Kuyt	Mason, Turner
	Liverpool won 3-2 on penalties.	

*After extra time

LEAGUE CUP ATTENDANCES 1960–2012

	Total	No. of matches	Average per match		Total	No. of matches	Average per match
2011–12	1,209,684	93	13,007	1985–86	1,579,916	163	9,693
2010–11	1,197,917	93	12,881	1984–85	1,876,429	167	11,236
2009–10	1,376,405	93	14,800	1983–84	1,900,491	168	11,312
2008–09	1,329,753	93	14,298	1982–83	1,679,756	160	10,498
2007–08	1,332,841	94	14,179	1981–82	1,880,682	161	11,681
2006–07	1,098,403	93	11,811	1980–81	2,051,576	161	12,743
2005–06	1,072,362	93	11,531	1979–80	2,322,866	169	13,745
2004–05	1,313,693	93	14,216	1978–79	1,825,643	139	13,134
2003–04	1,267,729	93	13,631	1977–78	2,038,295	148	13,772
2002–03	1,242,478	92	13,505	1976–77	2,236,636	147	15,215
2001–02	1,076,390	93	11,574	1975–76	1,841,735	140	13,155
2000–01	1,501,304	154	9,749	1974–75	1,901,094	127	14,969
1999–2000	1,354,233	153	8,851	1973–74	1,722,629	132	13,050
1998–99	1,555,856	153	10,169	1972–73	1,935,474	120	16,129
1997–98	1,484,297	153	9,701	1971–72	2,397,154	123	19,489
1996–97	1,529,321	163	9,382	1970–71	2,035,315	116	17,546
1995–96	1,776,060	162	10,963	1969–70	2,299,819	122	18,851
1994–95	1,530,478	157	9,748	1968–69	2,064,647	118	17,497
1993–94	1,744,120	163	10,700	1967–68	1,671,326	110	15,194
1992–93	1,558,031	161	9,677	1966–67	1,394,553	118	11,818
1991–92	1,622,337	164	9,892	1965–66	1,205,876	106	11,376
1990–91	1,675,496	159	10,538	1964–65	962,802	98	9,825
1989–90	1,836,916	168	10,934	1963–64	945,265	104	9,089
1988–89	1,552,780	162	9,585	1962–63	1,029,893	102	10,097
1987–88	1,539,253	158	9,742	1961–62	1,030,534	104	9,909
1986–87	1,531,498	157	9,755	1960–61	1,204,580	112	10,755

JOHNSTONE'S PAINT TROPHY 2011–2012

NORTHERN SECTION FIRST ROUND

Bradford C (0) 0 — Sheffield W (0) 0
(Bradford C won 3-1 on penalties.)
Burton Alb (0) 1 — Sheffield U (0) 2
Bury (0) 0 — Crewe Alex (0) 0
(Crewe Alex won 4-2 on penalties.)
Northampton T (1) 1 — Huddersfield T (1) 2
Scunthorpe U (0) 2 — Hartlepool U (0) 0
Tranmere R (0) 1 — Port Vale (0) 1
(Tranmere R won 4-2 on penalties.)
Walsall (2) 2 — Shrewsbury T (0) 1
Accrington S (1) 3 — Carlisle U (0) 2

SOUTHERN SECTION FIRST ROUND

Bournemouth (1) 4 — Hereford U (1) 1
Cheltenham T (2) 2 — Torquay U (0) 1
Colchester U (1) 1 — Barnet (2) 3
Exeter C (1) 1 — Plymouth Arg (0) 1
(Exeter C won 3-0 on penalties.)
Milton Keynes D (2) 3 — Brentford (1) 3
(Brentford won 4-3 on penalties.)
Southend U (1) 1 — Crawley T (0) 0
Wycombe W (1) 3 — Bristol R (0) 1
Leyton Orient (0) 1 — Dagenham & R (0) 1
(Dagenham & R won 14-13 on penalties.)

NORTHERN SECTION SECOND ROUND

Huddersfield T (0) 2 — Bradford C (0) 2
(Bradford C won 4-3 on penalties.)
Morecambe (0) 2 — Preston NE (2) 2
(Preston NE won 7-6 on penalties.)
Notts Co (1) 1 — Chesterfield (0) 3
Rochdale (0) 1 — Walsall (0) 1
(Rochdale won 3-1 on penalties.)
Rotherham U (0) 1 — Sheffield U (1) 2
Scunthorpe U (0) 0 — Oldham Ath (1) 1
Crewe Alex (0) 1 — Macclesfield T (0) 0
Accrington S (0) 0 — Tranmere R (1) 1

SOUTHERN SECTION SECOND ROUND

AFC Wimbledon (0) 2 — Stevenage (1) 2
(AFC Wimbledon won 4-3 on penalties.)
Aldershot T (0) 1 — Oxford U (0) 2
Bournemouth (3) 3 — Yeovil T (0) 2
Dagenham & R (0) 1 — Southend U (1) 3
Exeter C (0) 1 — Swindon T (2) 2
Gillingham (1) 1 — Barnet (1) 3
Wycombe W (0) 1 — Cheltenham T (1) 3
Charlton Ath (0) 0 — Brentford (2) 3

NORTHERN SECTION QUARTER-FINALS

Oldham Ath (1) 3 — Crewe Alex (0) 1
Rochdale (0) 1 — Preston NE (1) 1
(Preston NE won 4-2 on penalties.)
Sheffield U (1) 1 — Bradford C (1) 1
(Bradford C won 6-5 on penalties.)
Chesterfield (1) 4 — Tranmere R (1) 3

SOUTHERN SECTION QUARTER-FINALS

Brentford	(2) 6	Bournemouth	(0) 0
Cheltenham T	(0) 0	Barnet	(1) 2
Oxford U	(0) 0	Southend U	(1) 1
Swindon T	(0) 1	AFC Wimbledon	(0) 1

(Swindon T won 3-1 on penalties.)

NORTHERN SECTION SEMI-FINAL

Oldham Ath	(0) 2	Bradford C	(0) 0
Preston NE	(1) 1	Chesterfield	(1) 1

(Chesterfield won 4-2 on penalties.)

SOUTHERN SECTION SEMI-FINAL

Barnet	(0) 0	Brentford	(0) 0

(Barnet won 5-3 on penalties.)

Southend U	(0) 1	Swindon T	(0) 2

NORTHERN SECTION FINAL FIRST LEG

Chesterfield	(0) 2	Oldham Ath	(0) 1

NORTHERN SECTION FINAL SECOND LEG

Oldham Ath	(0) 0	Chesterfield	(0) 1

SOUTHERN SECTION FINAL FIRST LEG

Barnet	(0) 1	Swindon T	(1) 1

SOUTHERN SECTION FINAL SECOND LEG

Swindon T	(1) 1	Barnet	(0) 0

JOHNSTONE'S PAINT TROPHY FINAL

Sunday, 25 March 2012

(at Wembley Stadium, attendance 49,602)

Chesterfield (0) 2   Swindon T (0) 0

Chesterfield: Lee; Hurst, Smith, Moussa (Randall), Thompson, Ford, Talbot, Allott, Lester (Westcarr), Bowery (Boden), Mendy.

Scorers: Risser 47 (og), Westcarr 90.

Swindon T: Foderingham; Devera, McEveley (Cibocchi), Smith J (Bostock), Risser (Murray), McCormack, Ritchie, Ferry, Benson, Connell, Holmes.

Referee: T. Bates (Staffordshire).

THE FA COMMUNITY SHIELD 2011

Manchester C (2) 2   Manchester U (0) 3

At Wembley Stadium, 7 August 2011, attendance 77,169

Manchester C: Hart; Richards, Kolarov (Clichy 73), De Jong, Lescott, Kompany, Silva, Toure Y, Balotelli (Barry 59), Dzeko, Milner (Johnson A 67).
Scorers: Lescott 38, Dzeko 45.

Manchester United: De Gea; Smalling, Evra (Rafael 71), Carrick (Jones 46), Ferdinand (Evans J 46), Vidic (Cleverley 46), Young, Anderson, Welbeck (Berbatov 89), Rooney, Nani.
Scorers: Smalling 52, Nani 58, 90.

Referee: P. Dowd (Staffordshire).

SCOTTISH LEAGUE TABLES 2011–2012

(P) Promoted into division at end of 2010–11 season.
(R) Relegated into division at end of 2010–11 season.

Clydesdale Bank Scottish

Premier League	P	W	D	L	F	A	W	D	L	F	A	W	D	L	F	A	GD	Pts
			Total						Home						Away			
1 Celtic	38	30	3	5	84	21	17	1	1	41	6	13	2	4	43	15	63	93
2 Rangers*	38	26	5	7	77	28	12	5	2	38	14	14	0	5	39	14	49	73
3 Motherwell	38	18	8	12	49	44	9	3	7	27	24	9	5	5	22	20	5	62
4 Dundee U	38	16	11	11	62	50	8	6	5	27	16	8	5	6	35	34	12	59
5 Hearts	38	15	7	16	45	43	11	0	8	30	19	4	7	8	15	24	2	52
6 St Johnstone	38	14	8	16	43	50	6	2	10	20	30	8	6	6	23	20	–7	50
7 Kilmarnock	38	11	14	13	44	61	7	7	6	29	35	4	7	7	15	26	–17	47
8 St Mirren	38	9	16	13	39	51	6	6	7	23	25	3	10	6	16	26	–12	43
9 Aberdeen	38	9	14	15	36	44	6	8	5	22	16	3	6	10	14	28	–8	41
10 Inverness CT	38	10	9	19	42	60	5	5	9	19	27	5	4	10	23	33	–18	39
11 Hibernian	38	8	9	21	40	67	2	7	10	17	30	6	2	11	23	37	–27	33
12 Dunfermline Ath (P)	38	5	10	23	40	82	1	7	11	22	44	4	3	12	18	38	–42	25

Rangers deducted 10 points; Top 6 teams split after 33 games.

Irn-Bru Scottish

First Division	P	W	D	L	F	A	W	D	L	F	A	W	D	L	F	A	GD	Pts
			Total						Home						Away			
1 Ross Co	36	22	13	1	72	32	11	7	0	40	14	11	6	1	32	18	40	79
2 Dundee	36	15	10	11	53	43	7	5	6	25	20	8	5	5	28	23	10	55
3 Falkirk	36	13	13	10	53	43	9	6	3	29	21	4	7	7	24	27	5	52
4 Hamilton A (R)	36	14	7	15	55	56	8	3	7	33	30	6	4	8	22	26	–1	49
5 Livingston (P)	36	13	9	14	56	54	5	6	7	26	29	8	3	7	30	25	2	48
6 Partick Th	36	12	11	13	50	39	7	6	5	27	16	5	5	8	23	23	11	47
7 Raith R	36	11	11	14	46	49	7	4	7	24	21	4	7	7	22	28	–3	44
8 Morton	36	10	12	14	40	55	5	5	8	24	29	5	7	6	16	26	–15	42
9 Ayr U (P)	36	9	11	16	44	67	5	7	6	22	25	4	4	10	22	42	–23	38
10 Queen of the S	36	7	11	18	38	64	6	5	7	21	31	1	6	11	17	33	–26	32

Irn-Bru Scottish

Second Division	P	W	D	L	F	A	W	D	L	F	A	W	D	L	F	A	GD	Pts
			Total						Home						Away			
1 Cowdenbeath (R)	36	20	11	5	68	29	13	4	1	37	10	7	7	4	31	19	39	71
2 Arbroath (P)	36	17	12	7	76	51	10	5	3	44	23	7	7	4	32	28	25	63
3 Dumbarton¶	36	17	7	12	61	61	10	2	6	30	30	7	5	6	31	31	0	58
4 Airdrie U	36	14	10	12	68	60	9	4	5	43	30	5	6	7	25	30	8	52
5 Stenhousemuir	36	15	6	15	54	49	9	2	7	32	23	6	4	8	22	26	5	51
6 East Fife	36	14	6	16	55	57	7	4	7	27	29	7	2	9	28	28	–2	48
7 Forfar Ath	36	11	9	16	59	72	6	5	7	33	34	5	4	9	26	38	–13	42
8 Brechin C	36	10	11	15	47	62	5	6	7	24	30	5	5	8	23	32	–15	41
9 Albion R (P)	36	10	7	19	43	66	6	6	6	25	22	4	1	13	18	44	–23	37
10 Stirling Alb (R)	36	9	7	20	46	70	4	5	9	22	29	5	2	11	24	41	–24	34

¶*Dumbarton promoted via play-offs.*

Irn-Bru Scottish

Third Division	P	W	D	L	F	A	W	D	L	F	A	W	D	L	F	A	GD	Pts
			Total						Home						Away			
1 Alloa Ath (R)	36	23	8	5	70	39	13	4	1	43	13	10	4	4	27	26	31	77
2 Queen's Park	36	19	6	11	70	48	10	4	4	41	17	9	2	7	29	31	22	63
3 Stranraer	36	17	7	12	77	57	10	2	6	43	33	7	5	6	34	24	20	58
4 Elgin C	36	16	9	11	68	60	11	3	4	43	17	5	6	7	25	43	8	57
5 Peterhead (R)	36	15	6	15	51	53	7	5	6	25	23	8	1	9	26	30	–2	51
6 Annan Ath	36	13	10	13	53	53	7	5	6	28	26	6	5	7	25	27	0	49
7 Berwick R	36	12	12	12	61	58	6	5	7	30	28	6	7	5	31	30	3	48
8 Montrose	36	11	5	20	58	75	7	3	8	34	33	4	2	12	24	42	–17	38
9 Clyde	36	8	11	17	35	50	5	5	8	24	23	3	6	9	11	27	–15	35
10 East Stirling	36	6	6	24	38	88	5	4	9	24	33	1	2	15	14	55	–50	24

CLYDESDALE BANK SCOTTISH PREMIER LEAGUE RESULTS 2011–12

	Aberdeen	Celtic	Dundee U	Dunfermline Ath	Hearts	Hibernian	Inverness CT	Kilmarnock	Motherwell	Rangers	St Johnsone	St Mirren
Aberdeen	—	0-1 1-1	3-1 3-1	4-0 1-0	0-0	1-0 1-2†	2-1 0-1	2-2 0-0	1-2	1-2	0-0 0-0	2-2 0-0†
Celtic	2-1	—	5-1 2-1	2-1 2-0	1-0 5-0*	0-0	2-0 1-0	2-1	4-0 1-0	1-0 3-0*	0-1 2-0 1-0*	5-0
Dundee U	1-2	0-1 1-0*	—	0-1 3-0	1-0 2-2*	3-1	3-1 3-0	1-1 4-0	1-3 1-1	0-4 1-4	0-0	1-1 0-0
Dunfermline Ath	3-3 3-0†	0-3	1-4	—	0-2 1-2	2-2 2-3	3-3 1-1	1-1 1-2†	2-4 0-2	0-2 1-2	0-3	2-0 5-2
Hearts	3-0 3-0	0-2 0-4	0-1 0-2	4-0	—	1-3	2-1	0-1	1-0 3-0	1-1 1-2	1-2 2-0*	1-2 0-0
Hibernian	0-0 0-0	0-2 0-5	0-1 0-2	0-1	2-0 2-0	—	1-1	1-1	4-1 1-3	1-0 4-0	3-2 2-3	2-3 1-0†
Inverness CT	2-1 0-2†	0-2	3-3 0-2	1-1	1-1 1-0	0-1 2-3 2-0†	—	2-1 1-1	3-0 0-1	0-2 1-4	0-1	2-1 0-0
Kilmarnock	2-0 1-1†	3-3 0-6	1-1	3-2 0-3	0-0 1-1	4-1 1-3	3-6 4-3†	—	0-0 2-0	1-0	1-2 0-0	2-1
Motherwell	1-0 1-0	1-2	0-0 0-2*	3-1	1-0 3-0	4-3	3-0 0-1	2-1 1-1	—	0-3 1-2	0-3 3-2 5-1*	1-1
Rangers	2-0 1-1	4-2 3-2	3-1 1-2	2-1	1-1 1-2	1-0 4-0	2-1	2-0 0-1	3-0 0-0*	—	0-3 3-2 5-1*	0-2†
St Johnstone	1-2	0-2	3-3 1-5 0-2*	0-1 3-1	2-0 2-1	3-1	2-0 0-0	2-0	0-3	0-2 1-2 0-4*	—	1-1 3-1
St Mirren	1-0 1-1	0-2 0-2	2-2	4-4†	0-0	2-3 1-0†	1-2 0-1†	3-0 4-2	0-1 0-0	2-1	0-0 0-3	—

Splits after 33 games. Post-split matches, *top half, †bottom half.

IRN BRU SCOTTISH LEAGUE—DIVISION ONE RESULTS 2011–2012

	Ayr U	Dundee	Falkirk	Hamilton A	Livingston	Morton	Partick Th	Queen of S	Raith R	Ross Co
Ayr U	— —	1-3 3-2	2-2 1-0	1-2 2-2	0-0 3-1	0-1 0-0	0-0 1-3	1-0 1-1	2-1 1-1	2-3 1-3
Dundee	1-1 4-1	— —	4-2 3-1	0-1 2-2	3-0 1-0	0-1 0-1	0-1 0-3	2-1 1-1	1-0 1-1	1-2 1-1
Falkirk	0-0 3-2	2-1 1-1	— —	0-0 3-0	4-3 2-5	1-0 0-2	2-1 1-1	1-0 3-0	2-0 2-3	1-1 1-1
Hamilton A	2-3 3-2	1-6 3-1	0-1 0-1	— —	1-1 0-1	1-2 4-3	1-0 2-2	3-1 3-0	2-2 2-1	5-1 0-2
Livingston	1-2 0-1	4-2 2-3	1-1 1-2	1-0 0-4	— —	1-1 0-0	2-1 3-1	2-2 2-2	1-1 4-0	0-3 1-3
Morton	4-1 3-1	1-2 0-2	3-2 0-0	0-2 1-2	2-1 1-3	— —	1-2 1-0	2-2 2-2	1-1 1-3	0-2 1-1
Partick Th	4-0 4-2	0-1 0-0	2-2 1-1	1-1 2-0	2-1 2-3	5-0 0-0	— —	2-1 1-0	0-1 1-1	0-1 0-1
Queen of S	4-1 2-1	0-0 1-1	1-5 0-0	1-0 1-2	0-2 0-4	4-1 2-1	0-0 0-5	— —	1-3 1-0	0-0 3-5
Raith R	0-1 2-2	0-1 0-1	1-0 2-2	3-2 2-1	0-1 0-3	1-1 5-0	2-0 2-1	0-2 3-1	— —	0-1 1-1
Ross Co	4-0 1-1	1-1 3-0	3-1 2-1	1-0 5-1	1-1 3-0	0-0 2-2	2-2 3-0	2-0 2-1	4-2 1-1	— —

IRN BRU SCOTTISH LEAGUE—DIVISION TWO RESULTS 2011–2012

	Aidrie U	Albion R	Arbroath	Brechin C	Cowdenbeath	Dumbarton	East Fife	Forfar Ath	Stenhousemuir	Stirling Alb
Airdrie U	— —	4-0 1-0	3-3 2-0	2-3 4-1	1-5 1-1	3-0 2-3	1-3 2-0	4-4 3-0	5-2 0-3	1-1 4-1
Albion R	7-2 0-1	— —	1-0 1-1	1-2 0-1	3-3 1-0	3-1 1-1	0-3 1-1	1-0 2-2	1-1 1-0	0-1 1-2
Arbroath	3-1 2-2	6-2 6-1	— —	1-1 2-3	1-1 1-1	4-3 2-0	3-0 2-2	4-1 0-1	1-0 0-2	4-2 2-0
Brechin C	1-1 1-1	1-4 2-1	2-3 1-1	— —	1-0 2-2	3-3 2-2	0-2 1-3	0-1 2-1	2-0 1-0	1-3 1-2
Cowdenbeath	2-0 0-0	2-1 3-0	0-0 2-3	3-1 1-0	— —	0-0 4-1	3-2 4-0	0-1 3-2	2-0 1-0	2-0 4-1
Dumbarton	1-1 2-1	2-1 1-0	3-4 3-2	1-0 4-2	0-4 0-2	— —	3-0 0-4	1-1 1-0	3-0 0-2	1-5 4-1
East Fife	2-0 2-0	2-0 1-2	2-2 1-3	1-1 2-2	1-3 0-1	0-6 1-2	— —	4-3 4-0	1-3 1-1	1-0 1-0
Forfar Ath	3-2 2-3	0-2 4-0	1-1 2-4	0-0 4-1	2-2 1-0	0-2 1-1	3-2 1-4	— —	2-3 1-2	2-2 4-3
Stenhousemuir	1-1 0-3	3-0 1-2	2-0 1-3	1-1 2-1	3-1 0-2	3-1 1-2	2-1 1-0	2-3 1-2	— —	4-0 4-0
Stirling Alb	1-4 0-2	2-2 3-0	0-1 1-1	1-0 2-3	1-1 0-2	0-1 1-2	1-0 0-1	2-4 2-2	2-2 3-1	— —

IRN BRU SCOTTISH LEAGUE—DIVISION THREE RESULTS 2011–2012

	Alloa Ath	Annan Ath	Berwick R	Clyde	East Stirling	Elgin C	Montrose	Peterhead	Queen's Park	Stranraer
Alloa Ath	— / —	1-0 / 1-1	1-1 / 0-1	2-2 / 1-0	1-1 / 5-1	3-0 / 8-1	4-2 / 2-0	2-1 / 3-1	1-0 / 4-0	1-0 / 3-1
Annan Ath	2-0 / 1-2	— / —	2-2 / 2-1	1-0 / 1-0	3-0 / 2-2	1-1 / 1-1	2-1 / 1-2	2-0 / 0-3	5-2 / 2-3	0-3 / 1-3
Berwick R	2-2 / 5-0	0-1 / 1-3	— / —	0-2 / 3-0	4-2 / 0-2	1-1 / 3-3	1-2 / 2-2	2-1 / 0-1	2-0 / 1-4	2-2 / 1-0
Clyde	0-1 / 1-1	0-0 / 1-1	1-4 / 2-2	— / —	7-1 / 3-0	1-2 / 0-2	1-0 / 1-2	2-0 / 0-1	0-2 / 1-2	1-1 / 2-1
East Stirling	0-1 / 1-3	1-0 / 0-4	1-3 / 2-1	1-1 / 0-1	— / —	1-1 / 2-2	1-0 / 3-1	0-2 / 6-3	1-3 / 1-2	1-3 / 2-2
Elgin C	5-0 / 3-0	3-0 / 1-2	4-1 / 4-0	0-3 / 1-1	2-0 / 3-1	— / —	3-1 / 2-1	6-1 / 1-2	2-0 / 1-1	1-1 / 1-2
Montrose	1-1 / 0-2	2-3 / 1-1	3-5 / 1-1	4-0 / 5-0	2-1 / 3-1	3-0 / 2-3	— / —	2-1 / 1-3	0-1 / 3-1	0-6 / 1-3
Peterhead	1-1 / 0-1	2-3 / 3-2	1-0 / 1-2	0-0 / 1-1	1-0 / 2-0	1-3 / 3-0	2-3 / 2-1	— / —	1-1 / 2-1	1-3 / 1-1
Queen's Park	1-3 / 1-2	0-0 / 2-0	1-1 / 2-2	3-0 / 3-0	2-0 / 5-1	6-0 / 1-3	3-1 / 5-0	1-1 / 0-1	— / —	2-0 / 3-2
Stranraer	2-3 / 0-4	4-2 / 4-2	2-1 / 1-3	0-0 / 1-0	6-0 / 4-1	1-0 / 5-2	4-4 / 3-1	2-1 / 0-3	2-3 / 2-3	— / —

ABERDEEN

Ground: Pittodrie Stadium, Aberdeen AB24 5QH (01224) 650400
Ground capacity: 21,421 (all seated). **Colours:** All red.
Manager: Craig Brown.
League Appearances: Anderson, R. 4(2); Arnason, K. 31(2); Brown, J. 20; Chalali, M. 4(12); Clark, C. 16(8); Considine, A. 36; Fallon, R. 18(4); Foster, R. 22; Fraser, R. (3); Fyvie, F. 26(1); Gonzalez, D. 14; Hughes, S. 3(2); Jack, R. 30(1); Langfield, J. 4; Low, N. (2); Mackie, D. 8(11); Magennis, J. 13(10); Masson, J. 3(1); Mawene, Y. 19(3); McArdle, R. 20(5); McManus, D. (2); Megginson, M. 7(9); Milsom, R. 22; Osbourne, I. 22(1); Paton, M. (2); Pawlett, P. 5(16); Rae, G. 12; Reynolds, M. 16; Robertson, C. 9; Smith, C. (2); Uchechi, D. (1); Vernon, S. 34(1).
Goals – League (36): Vernon 11 (1 pen), Arnason 3, Considine 3, Jack 3, Fallon 2, Mawene 2, Chalali 1, Clark 1, Foster 1, Fyvie 1, Mackie 1, Magennis 1, Masson 1, Milsom 1, own goals 4.
Scottish Cup (10): Fallon 4, Vernon 2, Chalili 1, Considine 1, Fyvie 1, Megginson 1.
Scottish Communities Cup (4): Mackie 2, Fallon 1, McArdle 1.
Honours – Division 1: Champions – 1954–55, **Premier Division:** Champions – 1979–80, 1983–84, 1984–85. **Scottish Cup winners** 1947, 1970, 1982, 1983, 1984, 1986, 1990. **League Cup winners** 1956, 1977, 1986, 1990, 1996. **European Cup-Winners' Cup winners** 1983.

AIRDRIE UNITED

Ground: Shyberry Excelsior Stadium, Airdrie ML6 8QZ (01236) 622000
Postal address: 60 St Enoch Square, Glasgow G1 4AG.
Ground capacity: 10,171. **Colours:** White shirts with red trim, white shorts, white stockings.
Manager: Jimmy Boyle.
League Appearances: Adam, G. 14; Bain, J. 31(3); Blockley, N. 19(4); Boyle, J. 12(14); Burns, D. 1; Devlin, R. 6(9); Donnelly, R. 33; Duncan, A. 1(1); Fairley, C. 12; Goodall, G. 2(1); Green, K. 4(1); Hill, C. 4(3); Holmes, D. 21(11); Johnston, P. 9(4); Keast, F. 7(7); Lamie, R. 7(3); Lilley, D. 31; Lovering, P. 25(1); Lynch, S. 29; MacDonald, C. 14; Malone, C. 5(1); McKane, P. 9; McLaren, W. 20(3); McNeil, E. 6; Morton, S. 4(5); Owens, G. 11(9); Sally, S. 1(10); Stallard, K. 29(2); Stephenson, J. 28(3); Watt, L. (1); Woodburn, A. 1.
Goals – League (68): Donnelly 21, McLaren 8, Lovering 7 (4 pens), Boyle 6, Lynch 6, Stephenson 5 (1 pen), Holmes 4, Bain 2, Blockley 2, Johnston 2, Owens 2 (1 pen), MacDonald 1, Morton 1, Sally 1.
Scottish Cup (13): Boyle 3, Donnelly 3, Stevenson 3, Lovering 2 (1 pen), Holmes 1, McLaren 1.
Scottish Communities Cup (7): Donnelly 3, Owens 2 (2 pens), Bain 1, Holmes 1.
Ramsdens Cup (0).
Play-Offs (5): Holmes 3, Bain 1, McLaren 1.
Honours – Second Division: Champions – 2003–04. **League Challenge Cup winners** 2008–09.

ALBION ROVERS

Ground: Cliffhill Stadium, Main Street, Coatbridge ML5 3RB (01236) 606334
Ground capacity: 1,249 (seated: 489). **Colours:** All red.
Manager: Paul Martin.
League Appearances: Acqua, L. (13); Boyle, C. 18(4); Canning, S. 8; Chaplain, S. 26(4); Crawford, D. 1; Dempsie, A. 1; Donnelly, C. 18; Donnelly, R. 4; Fahey, C. 6(2); Ferry, D. 5(2); Gaston, D. 29(1); Gemmell, J. 28(1); Gilmartin, J. 5(10); Halsman, J. 7; Hamilton, C. 1(6); Hunter, R. 1; Lawless, S. 10; Love, R. 25(9); Lumsden, T. 22; Marriott, S. 16(6); McGowan, J. 1; McKay, D. 5(3); McStay, R. 24(8); O'Byrne, M. 30(1); Pierce, S. 1; Quinn,

P. (2); Reid, A. 35; Reilly, T. (5); Russell, B. 20(1); Scott, A. 7(7); Stevenson, A. 33(1); Werndly, J. 9(3).

Goals – League (43): Gemmell 9, Love 9, Chaplain 7 (1 pen), Lawless 3, O'Byrne 3, Werndly 3, Boyle 2, McStay 2, Acqua 1, Ferry 1, Gilmartin 1, Halsman 1, Russell 1.

Scottish Cup (0).

Scottish Communities Cup (2): Boyle 1, Chaplain 1 (pen).

Ramsdens Cup (0).

Play-Offs (5): Chaplain 3 (1 pen), Gemmell 1, Love 1.

Honours – Division II: Champions – 1933–34. **Second Division:** Champions 1988–89.

ALLOA ATHLETIC

Ground: Recreation Park, Alloa FK10 1RY (01259) 722695

Ground capacity: 3,100. **Colours:** Gold shirts with black trim, black shorts, black stockings.

Player-Manager: Paul Hartley.

League Appearances: Bain, S. 30; Caddis, R. (2); Campbell, C. 1(14); Cawley, K. 32(3); Docherty, M. 22(7); Doyle, M. 36; Forrest, F. 3(2); Gordon, B. 32(1); Harding, R. 35; Holmes, G. 33(1); Howarth, S. (2); Innes, P. 3(4); Locke, N. 1; Masterton, S. 8(6); May, S. 22; McCord, Ross 10(18); McCord, Ryan 32; McCullagh, M. 9(4); McDowall, C. 6(2); McHattie, K. 5; McKinnon, R. 16; O'Brien, K. 1(1); One, A. 3(11); Smith, S. 3; Winters, R. 20(7); Wright, M. 1(6); Young, D. 32.

Goals – League (70): May 19, McCord, Ryan 11 (3 pens), Cawley 9, Gordon 5, Winters 5, Docherty 4, Campbell 3, Holmes 3, Doyle 2, Young 2, Harding 1, Masterton 1, McCord, Ross 1, McKinnon 1, One 1, own goals 2.

Scottish Cup (2): Cawley 1, Masterton 1.

Scottish Communities Cup (0).

Ramsdens Cup (2): McCord, Ross 1, Wright 1.

Honours – Division II: Champions – 1921–22. **Third Division:** Champions – 1997–98, 2011–12. **League Challenge Cup winners** 1999–2000.

ANNAN ATHLETIC

Ground: Galabank, North Street, Annan DG12 5DQ (01461) 204108

Ground capacity: 3,000 (426 seated). **Colours:** Gold shirts with black trim, black shorts, gold stockings.

Manager: Harry Cairney.

League Appearances: Aitken, A. 3; Atkinson, J. (3); Bell, G. 16(5); Cox, D. 31; Gibson, S. 23; Gilfillan, B. 8(12); Harty, I. 11(2); Holms, R. (1); Jardine, C. 26(3); MacBeth, J. 9(10); McGowan, M. 35; McKechnie, J. 18(9); McKenna, B. 12(2); Mitchell, A. 25; Mitchell, D. 8(6); Muirhead, A. 26(1); Neilson, K. 2(3); O'Connor, S. 23(4); Sloan, S. 30(6); Steele, J. 19(9); Summersgill, C. 11; Swinglehurst, S. 13(1); Underwood, L. (1); Watson, P. 34; Wild, G. 2(1); Winters, D. 11(6).

Goals – League (53): Gibson 7, Muirhead 7 (6 pens), O'Connor 7, Cox 5, McKechnie 5, Harty 4 (2 pens), Steele 4, Winters 4, Bell 3, Sloan 3, McGowan 1, Swinglehurst 1, Underwood 1, Watson, P. 1.

Scottish Cup (4): Cox 1, Gilfillan 1, Muirhead 1, Watson, P. 1.

Scottish Communities Cup (1): Cox 1.

Ramsdens Cup (7): Harty 4, Cox 2, Muirhead 1.

Honours – East of Scotland Premier League: Winners (4). **East of Scotland League Cup:** Winners (1). **East of Scotland Div 1:** Winners (1). **South of Scotland League:** Winners (2). **South of Scotland League Cup:** Winners (4). **Scottish Challenge Cup South:** Winners (1). **Scottish Qualifying Cup South:** Winners (1).

ARBROATH

Ground: Gayfield Park, Arbroath DD11 1QB (01241) 872157
Ground capacity: 4,165 (860 seated; 3,305 standing). **Colours:** Maroon shirts with white trim, white shorts, white stockings.
Manager: Paul Sheerin.
League Appearances: Ardallany, P. 4(6); Baxter, M. 29; Birse, C. 1(2); Brown, K. 5(4); Bryce, L. (10); Busch, B. 19(1); Caddis, L. 10(10); Connelly, C. 1; Doris, S. 33; Elfverson, J. (5); Falkingham, J. 34(1); Gibson, K. 13(14); Girvan, G. 4(1); Hill, D. 35; Innes, C. 12; Kerr, B. 33(2); Mair, J. 1(2); Malcolm, S. 31; McAnespie, K. 24(1); McWalter, K. (1); Monti, C. 2; Robertson, D. (1); Samuel, C. 8(5); Sheerin, P. 27(3); Sibanda, L. 19(15); Strachan, M. (1); Swankie, G. 28(5); Wedderburn, C. 22(5); White, M. 1.
Goals – League (76): Doris 21 (8 pens), Swankie 11, Falkingham 8, Sibanda 8, Sheerin 6 (2 pens), Malcolm 5, McAnespie 4, Samuel 4, Caddis 3, Gibson 2, Innes 2, Bryce 1, own goal 1.
Scottish Cup (1): Sheerin 1 (pen).
Scottish Communities Cup (0).
Ramsdens Cup (1): Elfverson 1.
Play-Offs (1): Malcolm 1.
Honours – Third Division: Champions – 2010-11.

AYR UNITED

Ground: Somerset Park, Ayr KA8 9NB (01292) 263435
Ground capacity: 10,185 (1,597 seated). **Colours:** Black and white halved shirts, white shorts , white stockings with black trim.
Manager: Mark Roberts.
League Appearances: Armstrong, G. 2(2); Burke, A. 1(2); Campbell, M. 7(2); Connolly, R. 1(8); Crawford, R. 1; Cuthbert, K. 35; Dodd, A. 13(3); Duff, S. 3; Geggan, A. 34; Higgins, S. 1; Hutchinson, S. 1(1); Longridge, J. 1(1); Malone, E. 31; McGill, D. 1; McGowan, M. 33; McKernan, J. 16(4); McManus, T. 2(3); McWilliams, R. 1; Moffat, M. 31(5); Parker, K. 14(2); Paterson, R. 1(1); Roberts, M. 27(8); Robertson, J. 27; Robertson, R. 9(11); Smith, C. 34; Tiffoney, J. 28(2); Tomsett, L. 15(1); Trouten, A. 16(7); Wardlaw, G. 10(15); Wyllie, A. (1).
Goals – League (44): Moffat 8, Roberts 8 (4 pens), Parker 5, Malone 4, McGowan 4, Geggan 3, Dodd 2, Robertson, R. 2, Wardlaw 2, Robertson, J. 1, Smith 1, Tiffoney 1, Tomsett 1, Trouten 1, own goal 1.
Scottish Cup (8): Trouten 3 (1 pen), Geggan 2, McGowan 1, Roberts 1 (pen), Robertson, R. 1.
Scottish Communities Cup (6): Roberts 2, Malone 1, Smith 1, Trouten 1, Wardlaw 1.
Ramsdens Cup (5): Campbell 1, Geggan 1, McKernan 1, Paterson 1, Robertson, R. 1.
Play-Off (1): Geggan 1.
Honours – Division II: Champions – 1911–12, 1912–13, 1927–28, 1936–37, 1958–59, 1965–66. **Second Division:** Champions – 1987–88, 1996–97.

BERWICK RANGERS

Ground: Shielfield Park, Berwick-on-Tweed TD15 2EF (01289) 307424
Ground capacity: 4,131. **Colours:** Black shirt with broad gold vertical stripes, black shorts, black stockings.
Manager: Ian Little.
League Appearances: Barclay, J. 29; Bejaoui, Y. 7; Currie, L. 33; Currie, P. 4; Deland, M. 13(5); Ferguson, J. 5(7); Forster, J. 10; Gray, D. 16(14); Gray, R. 17(1); Greenhill, D. 18(8); Gribben, D. 18(9); Handling, D. 7; Lavery, D. 2(6); Little, I. 4; McDonald, K. 29(1); McGlinchey, C. 10(1); McLaren, F. 15(10); McLean, A. 24(3); McLeod, C. 14; Miller, B.

(4); Noble, S. 24(8); Notman, S. 29; Ponton, A. 1(1); Smith, D. 1(3); Smith, E. 7(6); Thompson, S. 18; Townsley, C. 28; Tulloch, S. 4; Walker, R. 9(7).

Goals – League (61): Gribben 10 (2 pens), Gray, D. 7 (1 pen), Handling 7, McLaren 6, Noble 6, Currie, L. 4 (1 pen), Currie, P. 3 (1 pen), Greenhill 3, Deland 2, Forster 2, McDonald 2, Ferguson 1, Gray, R. 1, McLean 1, McLeod 1, Notman 1, Smith, E. 1, Walker 1, own goals 2.

Scottish Cup (0).

Scottish Communities Cup (3): Currie, P. 1, Gray, D. 1, Noble 1.

Ramsdens Cup (4): Currie, L. 2, Gray, D. 1, Greenhill 1, McDonald 1.

Honours – Second Division: Champions – 1978–79. **Third Division:** Champions – 2006–07.

BRECHIN CITY

Ground: Glebe Park, Brechin DD9 6BJ (01356) 622856

Ground capacity: 3,960. **Colours:** Red shirts with white trim, white shorts, red stockings.

Manager: Jim Weir.

League Appearances: Adam, M. 1; Brady, G. 25(3); Buist, S. 30(1); Carcary, D. 2(9); Crawford, S. 9(11); Dunlop, M. 32; Fusco, G. 20(9); Hodge, B. 23(2); Janczyk, N. 12; King, C. 13(11); Lindsay, J. 9; Lister, J. 15(11); McClune, D. 6(6); McKenna, D. 23(11); McKenzie, R. 16(1); McLauchlan, G. 8(1); McLean, P. 30; McManus, P. 24(6); Molloy, C. 31; Moyes, E. 14(1); Nelson, C. 34; Scott, D. 2; Smith, S. 11(1); Webster, S. 1; Weir, G. 5(7).

Goals – League (47): McManus 15 (3 pens), McKenzie 7 (2 pens), King 5 (2 pens), Lister 4, McKenna 4, Buist 3, Hodge 2, Brady 1, Dunlop 1, Fusco 1, McLean 1, Molloy 1, Moyes 1, own goal 1.

Scottish Cup (4): McManus 2, King 1, Molloy 1.

Scottish Communities Cup (2): King 1, McKenna 1.

Ramsdens Cup (1): McKenna 1.

Honours – Second Division: Champions – 1982–83, 1989–90, 2004–05. **Third Division:** Champions – 2001–02. **C Division:** Champions – 1953–54.

CELTIC

Ground: Celtic Park, Glasgow G40 3RE (0871) 226 1888

Ground capacity: 60,355 (all seated). **Colours:** Emerald green and white hooped shirts, white shorts with emerald green trim, whie stockings with emerald green trim.

Manager: Neil Lennon.

League Appearances: Bangura, M. 2(8); Blackman, A. 1(2); Brown, S. 20(2); Brozek, P. 1(2); Cha, D. 11(4); Commons, K. 16(8); El Kaddouri, B. 5(1); Forrest, J. 23(6); Forster, F. 33; Hooper, G. 34(3); Ibrahim, R. (1); Izaguirre, E. 9(3); Kayal, B. 18(1); Ki, S. 21(9); Ledley, J. 31(1); Loovens, G. 11; Lustig, M. 3(1); Majstorovic, D. 15(2); Maloney, S. 1(2); Matthews, A. 25(2); McCourt, P. (13); McGeouch, D. 1(5); Mulgrew, C. 29(1); Rogne, T. 15(2); Samaras, G. 20(6); Stokes, A. 25(9); Twardzik, F. (1); Wanyama, V. 24(5); Watt, T. (3); Wilson, K. 14(1); Wilson, M. 5(2); Zaluska, L. 5.

Goals – League (84): Hooper 24 (1 pen), Stokes 12, Mulgrew 8, Forrest 7, Ledley 7, Ki 6, Samaras 4, Wanyama 4, Brown 3 (1 pen), Watt 2, Cha 1, Commons 1, El Kaddouri 1, Loovens 1, McGeouch 1, Rogne 1, own goal 1.

Scottish Cup (10): Stokes 4, Brown 2 (2 pens), Samaras 2, Hooper 1, Ledley 1.

Scottish Communities Cup (9): Stokes 3, Forrest 2, Hooper 2, Brown 1 (pen), own goal 1.

Europa League (7): Hooper 2, Stokes 2, Ki 1 (pen), Ledley 1, Mulgrew 1.

Honours – Division I: Champions – 1892–93, 1893–94, 1895–96, 1897–98, 1904–05, 1905–06, 1906–07, 1907–08, 1908–09, 1909–10, 1913–14, 1914–15, 1915–16, 1916–17, 1918–19, 1921–22, 1925–26, 1935–36, 1937–38, 1953–54, 1965–66, 1966–67, 1967–68, 1968–69, 1969–70, 1970–71, 1971–72, 1972–73, 1973–74. **Premier Division:** Champions – 1976–77, 1978–79, 1980–81, 1981–82, 1985–86, 1987–88, 1997–98. **Premier League:** 2000–01, 2001–02, 2003–04, 2005–06, 2006–07, 2007–08, 2011–12. **Scottish Cup winners**

1892, 1899, 1900, 1904, 1907, 1908, 1911, 1912, 1914, 1923, 1925, 1927, 1931, 1933, 1937, 1951, 1954, 1965, 1967, 1969, 1971, 1972, 1974, 1975, 1977, 1980, 1985, 1988, 1989, 1995, 2001, 2004, 2005, 2007, 2011. **League Cup winners** 1957, 1958, 1966, 1967, 1968, 1969, 1970, 1975, 1983, 1998, 2000, 2001, 2004, 2006, 2009. **European Cup winners** 1967.

CLYDE

Ground: Broadwood Stadium, Cumbernauld G68 9NE (01236) 451511
Ground capacity: 8,006. **Colours:** Red and white halved shirts, black shorts, red stockings.
Manager: Jim Duffy.
League Appearances: Archdeacon, M. 1(11); Brannan, K. 9; Brown, G. 19(4); Combe, A. 1; Crawford, D. 12; Cusack, L. 18; Daw, K. (2); Dickie, G. 1(1); Feely, N. 12; Finlayson, K. 1; Fitzpatrick, D. (4); Fulton, D. 1(1); Gallagher, D. 25; Gray, I. 30(2); Hay, P. 29; Irvine, C. 1(8); Kane, R. 10(15); Marr, J. 16(1); McDonald, S. 18(10); McMullan, P. 1(3); McQueen, B. 29; Mental, F. 11; Neill, J. 33; Oliver, M. 17(12); Pollock, J. 8(1); Ramsay, D. 2(3); Scullion, P. 14(7); Sharp, L. 35; Sloss, J. 4(5); Sweeney, J. 32(1); White, J. 6.
Goals – League (35): Neill 7, Cusack 5, Sweeney 5 (3 pens), McDonald 3, Brown 2, Gallagher 2, Pollock 2, Archdeacon 1, Brannan 1, Oliver 1, Scullion 1, Sloss 1, White 1, own goals 3.
Scottish Cup (1): Neill 1.
Scottish Communities Cup (4): Archdeacon 1, Gray 1, Sweeney 1 (pen), own goal 1.
Ramsdens Cup (3): McDonald 2, Fitzpatrick 1.
Honours – Division II: Champions – 1904–05, 1951–52, 1956–57, 1961–62, 1972–73.
Second Division: Champions – 1977–78, 1981–82, 1992–93, 1999–2000. **Scottish Cup winners** 1939, 1955, 1958. **League Challenge Cup winners** 2006–07.

COWDENBEATH

Ground: Central Park, Cowdenbeath KY4 9QQ (01383) 610166
Ground capacity: 4,370 (1,431 seated). **Colours:** Royal blue shirts, white shorts, red stockings.
Manager: Colin Cameron.
League Appearances: Adamson, K. 30(1); Armstrong, J. 33(1); Bejaoui, Y. 5; Brett, D. 16(1); Byrne, P. (2); Cameron, C. 20(2); Coult, L. 20(12); Cowan, D. 15; Cusack, L. 5(8); Fisher, G. 9(1); Flynn, T. 30; Linton, S. 30(3); Lyle, D. 12(6); Makel, L. 1(2); Mbu, J. 31; McKenzie, M. 31(5); Miller, K. 2(3); Milne, L. 2(5); Morton, J. 12(6); Naismith, K. 7(2); O'Brien, T. 11(4); Ramsay, M. 19(5); Robertson, J. 35; Stewart, G. 16(13); Wilson, L. 1; Winter, C. 3(6).
Goals – League (68): McKenzie 18 (1 pen), Coult 13, Morton 6 (1 pen), Ramsay 6 (2 pens), Stewart 6, Robertson 5, Linton 4, Mbu 2, Naismith 2 (1 pen), Adamson 1, Armstrong 1, Cameron 1, Lyle 1, O'Brien 1, own goal 1.
Scottish Cup (5): Robertson 2, Coult 1, Linton 1, Stewart 1.
Scottish Communities Cup (2): Ramsey 2.
Ramsdens Cup (1): Coult 1.
Honours – Division II: Champions – 1913–14, 1914–15, 1938–39. **Second Division:** Champions – 2011–12. **Third Division:** Champions – 2005–06.

DUMBARTON

Ground: Dumbarton Football Stadium, Castle Road, Dumbarton G82 1JJ (01389) 762569/767864
Ground capacity: 2,025. **Colours:** White with yellow and black horizontal striped shirts, white shorts, white stockings.
Manager: Alan Adamson.

League Appearances: Agnew, S. 35; Borris, R. 6(10); Brannan, K. 1(10); Creaney, J. 32; Dargo, C. 7(2); Ewings, J. 9; Finnie, R. 11(3); Gastal, A. 1; Gilhaney, M. 33(1); Graham, A. 10(7); Gray, D. 2(1); Grindlay, S. 26; Hempstead, J. 1(1); Kennedy, D. 7(1); Lemont, M. 7(5); Lithgow, A. 32; Lyden, J. 5(1); McBride, M. 5; McKell, G. 1(1); McKinnon, R. 6(1); McNiff, M. 28(1); Metcalf, R. (1); Monaghan, A. 1; Mptata, A. 2(2); Nicoll, K. 26(3); Nugent, P. 30(3); Prunty, B. 32(1); Ramage, G. (5); Thomson, G. (1); Walker, P. 22(14); Wallace, A. 16(6); Winters, D. 2(10).
Goals – League (61): Prunty 14 (1 pen), Agnew 13, Gilhaney 7 (1 pen), Dargo 5, Lithgow 4, Walker 3, Graham 2, Lyden 2, McNiff 2, McBride 1, McKinnon 1, Nicoll 1, Thomson 1, Winters 1, own goals 4.
Scottish Cup (0).
Scottish Communities Cup (0).
Ramsdens Cup (3): Gilhaney 1 (pen), Prunty 1, Walker 1.
Play-Offs (8): Wallace 3, Dargo 2, Prunty 2, Gilhaney 1.
Honours – Division I: Champions – 1890–91 (Shared), 1891–92. **Division II:** Champions – 1910–11, 1971–72. **Second Division:** Champions – 1991–92. **Third Division:** Champions – 2008–09. **Scottish Cup winners** 1883.

DUNDEE

Ground: Dens Park, Dundee DD3 7JY (01382) 889966
Ground capacity: 11,760 (all seated). **Colours:** Navy blue shirts with one white and red band, white shorts, navy blue stockings.
Manager: Barry Smith.
League Appearances: Bayne, G. 7(11); Benedictis, K. 11(3); Chisholm, R. 13(5); Conroy, R. 32(3); Douglas, R. 36; Elliot, C. 1(5); Finnigan, C. 4(1); Fotheringham, M. 2(6); Gibson, J. (1); Harkins, G. 1; Hyde, J. 14(12); Irvine, G. 35; Lockwood, M. 34; Masterton, S. (1); McBride, K. 11; McCluskey, J. 20(8); McGregor, N. 26(1); McIntosh, L. 11(7); McKeown, C. 23(4); Milne, S. 30(1); O'Donnell, S. 33; Rae, G. 12(1); Reid, J. 1; Riley, N. 19(6); Weston, R. 20(5).
Goals – League (53): Conroy 11 (4 pens), Milne 11 (1 pen), Hyde 6, Riley 4, Finnigan 3, Lockwood 3 (2 pens), McCluskey 3, O'Donnell 3, Rae 3, Irvine 1, McGregor 1, McIntosh 1, Reid 1, Weston 1, own goal 1.
Scottish Cup (4): Milne 2, Conroy 1, Rae 1.
Scottish Communities Cup (4): Milne 2, Lockwood 1 (pen), McCluskey 1.
Ramsdens Cup (2): Milne 1, O'Donnell 1.
Honours – Division I: Champions – 1961–62. **First Division:** Champions – 1978–79, 1991–92, 1997–98. **Division II:** Champions – 1946–47. **Scottish Cup winners** 1910. **League Cup winners** 1952, 1953, 1974. **League Challenge Cup winners** 2009-10, **B&Q (Centenary) Cup winners** 1991.

DUNDEE UNITED

Ground: Tannadice Park, Dundee DD3 7JW (01382) 833166
Ground capacity: 14,223. **Colours:** Tangerine shirts with black trim, black shorts, tangerine stockings with black hoop.
Manager: Peter Houston.
League Appearances: Allan, S. 4(4); Armstrong, S. 11(12); Dalla Valle, L. 5(7); Daly, J. 35(1); Dillon, S. 26(2); Dixon, P. 37; Douglas, B. 5(5); Dow, R. 3(7); Flood, W. 30(2); Gauld, R. (1); Goodwillie, D. 1; Gunning, G. 29(2); Kenneth, G. 20(5); Lacny, M. (4); Mackay-Steven, G. 24(7); Marsh-Brown, K. (1); Neilson, R. 21; Pernis, D. 38; Rankin, J. 38; Robertson, S. 34(3); Russell, J. 33(4); Ryan, R. 2(12); Severin, S. 2; Swanson, D. 6(8); Watson, K. 14(3).
Goals – League (62): Daly 19 (1 pen), Russell 9, Robertson 6, Mackay-Steven 4, Rankin 4, Dalla Valle 3, Dixon 3, Swanson 3, Gunning 2, Armstrong 1, Douglas 1, Flood 1, Lacny 1, Watson 1, own goals 4.

Scottish Cup (8): Russell 4, Gunning 1, Mackay-Steven 1, Rankin 1, Robertson 1.
Scottish Communities Cup (4): Daly 2, Dow 1, Russell 1.
Europa League (3): Daly 1 (pen), Goodwillie 1, Watson 1.
Honours – Premier Division: Champions – 1982–83. **Division II:** Champions – 1924–25, 1928–29. **Scottish Cup winners** 1994, 2010. **League Cup winners** 1980, 1981.

DUNFERMLINE ATHLETIC

Ground: East End Park, Dunfermline KY12 7RB (01383) 724295
Ground capacity: 12,509. **Colours:** Black and white striped shirts, white shorts, white stockings.
Player-Manager: Jim Jefferies.
League Appearances: Barrowman, A. 13(9); Boyle, P. 20(1); Buchanan, L. 14(13); Burns, P. 21(4); Cardle, J. 24(12); Clarke, P. (3); Dowie, A. 30; Easton, C. 3; Fernandez, B. 1; Gallacher, P. 18; Graham, D. 33(5); Hardie, M. 18(10); Hutton, K. 8(1); Keddie, A. 36; Kerr, M. 13; Kirk, A. 23(13); Mason, G. 32; McCann, A. 22(1); McDougall, S. 2(10); McMillan, J. 11; Phinn, N. (1); Potter, J. 15(1); Rutkiewicz, K. 8; Smith, C. 14; Thomson, J. 12; Thomson, R. 11(14); Turner, I. 5; Willis, P. 11(10).
Goals – League (40): Kirk 11, Cardle 8, Buchanan 5 (1 pen), Barrowman 3, Burns 2, Graham 2, Thomson, R. 2, Hardie 1, McCann 1, McMillan 1, Thomson, J. 1, Willis 1, own goals 2.
Scottish Cup (2): Barrowman 2.
Scottish Communities Cup (3): Barrowman 1, Buchanan 1, Kirk 1.
Honours – First Division: Champions – 1988–89, 1995–96, 2010-11. **Division II:** Champions – 1925–26. **Second Division:** Champions – 1985–86. **Scottish Cup winners** 1961, 1968.

EAST FIFE

Ground: Bayview Park, Methil, Fife KY8 3RW (01333) 426323
Ground capacity: 1992. **Colours:** Black shirts with gold sleeves, black shorts with gold trim, black stockings.
Manager: Gordon Durie.
League Appearances: Brown, M. 15(1); Brown, R. 8(1); Campbell, S. 22; Collier, A. (1); Cook, A. 22(4); Cowan, D. 2(1); Dalziel, S. 10(16); Devlin, J. (1); Durie, S. 29(1); Hislop, S. 14(13); Innes, C. 1; Janczyk, N. 16(2); Johnstone, C. 16(12); Linn, R. 35; Martin, J. (3); McCormack, D. 16; McQuade, P. 3(9); Muir, D. 25(6); Ogleby, R. 13(1); Ovenstone, J. 19(4); Park, M. 14; Ridgers, M. 13; Sloan, R. 16(16); Smith, D. 26(4); Wallace, R. 32; White, D. 27; Young, L. 2(1).
Goals – League (55): Wallace 20 (2 pens), Sloan 8 (4 pens), Linn 7, Johnstone 5, Muir 4, Dalziel 3, Hislop 3, Ogleby 2, Cook 1, Ovenstone 1, own goal 1.
Scottish Cup (5): Ogleby 2, Linn 1, Sloan 1, Wallace 1.
Scottish Communities Cup (7): Wallace 2, Dalziel 1, Linn 1, Ogleby 1, Park 1, Sloan 1.
Ramsdens Cup (9): Wallace 4, Ogleby 3 (1 pen), Linn 1, Young 1.
Honours – Division II: Champions – 1947–48. **Third Division:** Champions – 2007–08. **Scottish Cup winners** 1938. **League Cup winners** 1948, 1950, 1954.

EAST STIRLINGSHIRE

Ground: Ochilview Park, Gladstone Road, Stenhousemuir FK5 4QL – club moving to new premises. Present contact: 202 Stirling Road, Larbert, Falkirk FK5 3NJ (01324) 557 862
Ground capacity: 3776 (626 seated). **Colours:** Black and white hooped shirts, black shorts, black and white hooped stockings.

Head Coach: John Coughlin.
League Appearances: Antell, C. 35; Benton, J. 5(2); Beveridge, S. 11; Campbell, J. (1); Cane, D. 25(1); Chisholm, I. 18(2); Coyne, B. 11; Devlin, R. 10(2); Dingwall, J. 27(2); Frances, R. 15; Fulton, S. 2(6); Gibson, N. (8); Gillespie, K. 1(6); Glasgow, J. (2); Gordon, C. (1); Hay, G. 1; Horner, L. 25; Hunter, M. 30(2); Jackson, S. 31(2); Love, A. 13(2); Love, S. (3); Lurinsky, A. 20(7); Maxwell, S. 26(2); Ramage, G. 3(7); Savage, J. 1(2); Scott, C. 5(3); Sheerin, J. 9(10); Stirling, A. 35; Tart, S. (4); Team, F. 5(13); Turner, K. 28(5); Winter, C. 4.
Goals – League (38): Turner 6, Coyne 5 (1 pen), Lurinsky 5 (2 pens), Stirling 5, Maxwell 4, Horner 2, Hunter 2, Love, A. 2 (1 pen), Beveridge 1, Devlin 1, Dingwall 1, Gibson 1, Jackson 1 (1 pen), Ramage 1, Sheerin 1.
Scottish Cup (4): Coyne 1, Gibson 1, Stirling 1, Team 1.
Scottish Communities Cup (0).
Ramsdens Cup (2): Love, A. 1, Turner 1.
Honours – Division II: Champions – 1931–32. **C Division:** Champions – 1947–48.

ELGIN CITY

Ground: Borough Briggs, Elgin IV30 1AP (01343) 551114
Ground capacity: 3,927 (478 seated). **Colours:** Black and white striped shirts, black shorts, red stockings.
Manager: Ross Jack.
Scottish Cup (7): Gunn 3, Crooks 2, Millar 1, Wilson 1 (pen).
CIS Cup (3): Gunn 2 (1 pen), Millar 1.
Alba Challenge Cup (1): Gunn 1.
League Appearances: Beveridge, G. 20(9); Calder, J. 3(2); Cameron, B. 26(1); Clark, A. 33; Cooper, A. 8; Crooks, J. 12(19); Duff, J. 32(1); Durnan, M. 15(2); Edwards, S. 1(4); Forbes, F. (1); Frizzel, C. 2(6); Gunn, C. 30(4); Halford, L. (1); Innes, G. (2); Kaczan, P. 11; Lawrie, B. (8); Leslie, S. 28(1); MacPhee, A. 30(3); McLean, C. (2); McMullan, P. 9(9); Millar, P. 17(7); Moore, D. 31; Nicolson, M. 35; Niven, D. 34(1); O'Donoghue, R. 16(8); Wilson, B. 3(8).
Goals – League (68): Gunn 18 (1 pen), Millar 7, MacPhee 6 (1 pen), Crooks 5, Leslie 5 (2 pens), Beveridge 4, Nicolson 4, Niven 4, Cameron 3, Duff 2, Durnan 2, O'Donoghue 2, Moore 1, Wilson 1, own goals 4.
Scottish Cup (7): Gunn 3, Cameron 1, Crooks 1, Nicolson 1, own goal 1.
Scottish Communities Cup (1): Cameron 1.
Ramsdens Cup (2): Cameron 1, Leslie 1.
Play-Offs (1): Millar 1.
Honours – Nil.

FALKIRK

Ground: Brockville Park, Falkirk FK1 5AX (01324) 624121
Ground capacity: 8,000. **Colours:** Navy blue shirts with white seams, white shorts, white stockings.
Manager: Steven Pressley.
League Appearances: Alston, B. 14(10); Bennett, R. 8(10); Bowman, G. 1(1); Brisbane, S. (2); Dick, L. (1); Dods, D. 34; Duffie, K. 30; El Alaguie, F. 33; Faulds, K. 4(5); Fulton, D. 4(2); Fulton, J. 23(9); Gibson, W. 10(2); Graham, A. (3); Higginbotham, K. 20; Kingsley, S. 8(7); McGovern, M. 35; Millar, M. 33; Millar, R. 1(4); Murdoch, S. 25(1); Scobbie, T. 30; Sibbald, C. 22(4); Wallace, M. 32(2); Weatherston, D. 25(1); White, J. 4(6).
Goals – League (53): El Alaguie 18, Millar, M. 6 (3 pens), Alston 5, Dods 5, Higginbotham 5, Weatherston 4, Sibbald 2, Wallace 2, Duffie 1, Fulton, J. 1, Gibson 1, Scobbie 1 (1 pen), own goals 2.
Scottish Cup (3): Alston 1, Dods 1, El Alagui 1.

Scottish Communities Cup (12): El Alagui 5, Fulton, J. 2, Graham 1, Higginbotham 1, Millar, M. 1, Sibbald 1, own goal 1.

Ramsdens Cup (11): El Alagui 3, Dods 2, Higginbotham 2, Millar, M. 2, Bennett 1, Sibbald 1.

Honours – Division II: Champions – 1935–36, 1969–70, 1974–75. **First Division:** Champions – 1990–91, 1993–94, 2002–03, 2004–05. **Second Division:** Champions – 1979–80. **Scottish Cup winners** 1913, 1957. **B&Q Cup winners** 1994. **League Challenge Cup winners** 1998, 2005, 2011–12.

FORFAR ATHLETIC

Ground: Station Park, Carseview Road, Forfar DD8 3BT (01307) 463576

Ground capacity: 5,177 (739 seated). **Colours:** Sky blue and white striped shirts, white shorts, white stockings.

Manager: Dick Campbell.

League Appearances: Bishop, J. 8; Bolocheweckyj, M. 16(8); Brown, J. 3(1); Bryce, L. (3); Byers, K. 13(16); Campbell, I. 21(1); Campbell, R. 12(11); Coyne, B. 9(7); Crawford, S. 11; Fotheringham, M. 22(4); Gibson, G. 4(12); Girvan, G. (1); Hegarty, C. 20(4); Hilson, D. 19; Langfield, J. 2; Low, N. 28(1); McCallum, M. 10; McCulloch, M. 28; McHugh, A. 6; Motion, K. 13(12); Mowat, D. 20(3); Paterson, G. 20(1); Ried, D. (1); Ross, G. 27(3); Sellars, B. 2(2); Shaughnessy, J. 26; Templeman, C. 32(1); Tulloch, S. 13(2); Wilson, C. 11(6).

Goals – League (59): Templeman 16 (2 pens), Fotheringham 8 (1 pen), Byers 7, Low 6, Coyne 5, Motion 3, Shaughnessy 3, Crawford 2, Hilson 2, Ross 2, McCulloch 1, Mowat 1, Tulloch 1, own goals 2.

Scottish Cup (4): Templeman 2, Gibson 1, Ross 1.

Scottish Communities Cup (2): Crawford 1, Templeman 1.

Ramsdens Cup (1): Gibson 1.

Honours – Second Division: Champions – 1983–84. **Third Division:** Champions – 1994–95.

HAMILTON ACADEMICAL

Ground: New Douglas Park, Cadzow Avenue, Hamilton ML3 0FT (01698) 368650

Ground capacity: 6,078. **Colours:** Red and white hooped shirts, white shorts, white stockings.

Manager: Billy Reid.

League Appearances: Anderson, G. 7(13); Canning, M. 31(1); Cerny, T. 11; Chambers, J. 5(5); Christie, S. 3; Coombe, A. 1; Crawford, A. 16(3); Currie, B. 3(1); Currie, P. 3(6); Devlin, M. 1(2); Fraser, G. 3(1); Gillespie, G. 12(4); Gordon, Z. 7(1); Hendrie, s. 22(3); Hopkirk, D. 1(2); Hutton, D. 18(1); Imrie, D. 18(1); Jivanda, J. 1; Kilday, L. 13; Kirkpatrick, J. 2(5); Longridge, L. 1(1); Lyle, D. 3(6); MacGregor, G. (1); Martin, J. 1; McAlister, J. 36; McBride, K. 5(1); McGlinchey, C. 1; McLaren, W. (3); McLaughlin, M. 23; McShane, J. 17; Mensing, S. 34; Millar, K. 2; Neil, A. 17; Paterson, M. 10(4); Redmond, D. 18; Routledge, J. 15(1); Ryan, A. 13(8); Smith, G. 3; Spence, G. 11(18); Stewart, M. 8(5); Watson, C. (1); Wilkie, K. (1).

Goals – League (55): McShane 9, McLaughlin 7, Imrie 5, Redmond 5, Spence 5, Ryan 4, Anderson 3, Mensing 3, Crawford 2, Currie, P. 2 (1 pen), Paterson 2, Routledge 2, Canning 1, Chambers 1 (1 pen), Lyle 1, McAlister 1, Stewart 1, own goal 1.

Scottish Cup (0).

Scottish Communities Cup (1): Chambers 1 (pen).

Ramsdens Cup (6): Chambers 1 (pen), Crawford 1, Hopkirk 1, McLaughlin 1, Mensing 1, Spence 1.

Honours – First Division: Champions – 1985–86, 1987–88, 2007–08. **Division II:** Champions – 1903–04. **Division III:** Champions – 2000–01. **B&Q Cup winners** 1992, 1993.

HEART OF MIDLOTHIAN

Ground: Tynecastle Park, McLeod Street, Edinburgh EH11 2NL (0871) 663 1874
Ground capacity: 17,402. **Colours:** Maroon shirts with white panels, white shorts with maroon side panels, maroon stockings with white tops.
Manager: TBA.
League Appearances: Barr, D. 13(2); Beattie, C. 4(1); Black, I. 28(1); Driver, A. 15(6); Elliott, S. 19(7); Glen, G. 4(4); Grainger, D. 27; Hamill, J. 28(1); Holt, J. 1(1); Jonsson, E. 14(2); Kello, M. 20; MacDonald, J. 17(1); McGowan, R. 23(5); McHattie, K. (1); Mrowiec, A. 27(2); Novikovas, A. 4(11); Obua, D. 11(8); Prychynenko, D. (3); Ridgers, M. 1(1); Robinson, S. 14(6); Santana, S. 3(10); Skacel, R. 19(10); Smith, G. (6); Stevenson, R. 15(4); Sutton, J. 9(5); Taouil, M. 15(9); Templeton, D. 20(7); Webster, A. 31; Zaliukas, M. 36.
Goals – League (45): Skacel 11, Webster 4, Elliott 3, Sutton 3, Black 2, Hamill 2 (1 pen), McGowan 2, Novikovas 2, Santana 2, Stevenson 2, Taouil 2, Templeton 2, Barr 1, Beattie 1, Glen 1, Holt 1, Jonsson 1, Obua 1, Zaliukas 1, own goal 1.
Scottish Cup (14): Skacel 5, Beattie 2 (1 pen), Hamill 2 (1 pen), Barr 1, Grainger 1 (pen), Smith 1, Templeton 1, Zaliukas 1.
Scottish Communities Cup (1): Robinson 1.
Europa League (5): Stevenson 2, Driver 1, Hamill 1 (pen), Skacel 1.
Honours – Division I: Champions – 1894–95, 1896–97, 1957–58, 1959–60. **First Division:** Champions – 1979–80. **Scottish Cup winners** 1891, 1896, 1901, 1906, 1956, 1998, 2006, 2012.
League Cup winners 1955, 1959, 1960, 1963.

HIBERNIAN

Ground: Easter Road Stadium, 12 Albion Place, Edinburgh EH7 5QG (0131) 661 2159
Ground capacity: 17,400. **Colours:** Green shirts with white sleeves, white shorts, white stockings.
Manager: Pat Fenlon.
League Appearances: Agogo, J. 9(3); Airey, P. (1); Booth, C. 10(2); Brown, M. 7; Caldwell, R. (1); Claros, J. 10; Crawford, D. (2); De Graaf, E. (1); Doherty, M. 11(2); Doyle, E. 6(7); Francomb, G. 11(3); Galbraith, D. 7(9); Grant, P. 1; Griffiths, L. 24(6); Hanlon, P. 35; Hart, M. 6; Kujabi, P. 12(1); McPake, J. 11; Murray, I. 13(2); O'Connor, G. 27(6); O'Donovan, R. 5(9); O'Hanlon, S. 22; Osbourne, I. 29(1); Palsson, V. 12(3); Scott, M. 8(7); Soares, T. 9(1); Sodje, A. (12); Sproule, I. 26(8); Stack, G. 30; Stanton, S. (2); Stephens, D. 14(3); Stevenson, L. 27(2); Thornhill, M. 5(1); Towell, R. 11(3); Wotherspoon, D. 20(10).
Goals – League (40): O'Connor 12 (2 pens), Griffiths 8 (1 pen), Sproule 3, Doherty 2, Hanlon 2, O'Hanlon 2, Soares 2, Agogo 1, Booth 1, Doyle 1, O'Donovan 1, Osbourne 1, Towell 1, own goals 3.
Scottish Cup (9): Griffiths 3 (1 pen), Doyle 2, McPake 1, O'Connor 1, O'Donovan 1, Wotherspoon 1.
Scottish Communities Cup (8): O'Connor 3, Scott 2, Sodje 1, Sproule 1, own goal 1.
Honours – Division I: Champions – 1902–03, 1947–48, 1950–51, 1951–52. **First Division:** Champions – 1980–81, 1998–99. **Division II:** Champions – 1893–94, 1894–95, 1932–33.
Scottish Cup winners 1887, 1902. **League Cup winners** 1973, 1992, 2007.

INVERNESS CALEDONIAN THISTLE

Ground: Tulloch Caledonian Stadium, Stadium Road, Inverness IV1 1FF (01463) 715816
Ground capacity: 7,780. **Colours:** Blue shirts with red stripes, blue shorts, blue stockings with red tops.
Manager: Terry Butcher.

League Appearances: Aldred, T. 2(2); Chippendale, A. 1(4); Cox, L. 4(3); Davis, D. 14; Doran, A. 7(3); Esson, R. 33; Foran, R. 37; Gillet, K. 25; Gnakpa, C. 2(5); Golobart, R. 18(4); Hayes, J. 25(1); Hogg, C. 9; McKay, W. 17(5); Meekings, J. 18(1); Morrison, G. 3(1); Piermayr, T. 16(4); Proctor, D. 9(8); Ross, N. 18(11); Shinnie, A. 15(4); Shinnie, G. 25(1); Sutherland, S. 9(19); Tade, G. 30(6); Tansey, G. 33(3); Tokely, R. 28(1); Tudur-Jones, O. 8(7); Tuffey, J. 5; Williams, S. 6(3); Winnall, S. 1(1).
Goals – League (42): Tade 9, Hayes 7 (1 pen), Shinnie, A. 7, Tansey 4 (1 pen), McKay 3, Foran 2, Golobart 2, Ross 2, Williams 2, Davis 1, Shinnie, G. 1, Sutherland 1, Tokely 1.
Scottish Cup (4): Hayes 2, Shinnie, A. 1, Tansey 1.
Scottish Communities Cup (0).
Honours – First Division: Champions – 2003–04, 2009-10. **Third Division:** Champions – 1996–97. **League Challenge Cup winners** 2004.

KILMARNOCK

Ground: Rugby Park, Kilmarnock KA1 2DP (01563) 525184
Ground capacity: 18,128. **Colours:** Light and dark blue striped shirts, dark blue shorts with light blue stripes, white stockings with dark blue tops.
Manager: Kenny Shiels.
League Appearances: Ada, P. 3; Barbour, R. 1(1); Bell, C. 32; Buijs, D. 12(2); Clancy, T. 1; Davidson, R. (1); Dayton, J. 13(16); Fisher, G. 3(3); Fowler, J. 34(3); Galan, J. (4); Gordon, B. 17; Gros, W. 2(6); Harkins, G. 29(1); Hay, G. 20(4); Heffernan, P. 26(3); Hutchinson, R. 3(1); Jaakkola, A. 5; Johnson, L. 7(2); Johnston, C. (2); Kelly, L. 33(1); Kennedy, M. 2(9); Kroca, Z. 13(1); Letheren, K. 1(1); McKeown, R. 18; Nelson, M. 15; O'Leary, R. 7(1); Panikvar, L. 2; Pascali, M. 24; Pursehouse, A. 8; Racchi, D. 9(10); Shiels, D. 33(2); Silva, D. 3(13); Sissoko, M. 24(3); Toshney, L. 12; Van Tornhout, D. 6(5); Winchester, J. (2).
Goals – League (44): Shiels 13 (3 pens), Heffernan 11 (2 pens), Dayton 3, Fowler 3, Pascali 3, Racchi 2, Harkins 1, Kelly 1, Kroca 1, McKeown 1, Nelson 1, Van Tornhout 1, Winchester 1, own goals 2.
Scottish Cup (3): Heffernan 1, Pascali 1, Shiels 1.
Scottish Communities Cup (9): Heffernan 3, Harkins 2, Hutchinson 1, Shiels 1, Sissoko 1, Van Tournhout 1.
Honours – Division I: Champions – 1964–65. **Division II:** Champions – 1897–98, 1898–99. **Scottish Cup winners** 1920, 1929, 1997. **Scottish League Cup winners** 2011–12.

LIVINGSTON

Ground: The Braidwood Motor Company Stadium, Almondvale Stadium Road, Livingston EH54 7DN (01506) 417 000
Ground capacity: 10,005. **Colours:** Yellow shirts, black shorts, yellow stockings.
Manager: John Hughes.
League Appearances: Barr, B. 34(2); Barr, C. 35; Beaumont, J. (2); Boulding, R. 12(13); Brown, J. 8(2); Cummings, D. 5(6); Deuchar, K. 14(5); Doherty, R. 8(3); Downie, J. (1); Easton, D. (2); Fordyce, C. 8(2); Fotheringham, M. 11; Fox, L. 21(1); Gray, L. (2); Jacobs, Keaghan 30(1); Jacobs, Kyle 29(5); MacDonald, C. 1(3); McCann, K. 10; McNeil, A. 36; McNulty, M. 25(5); Ross, M. 8; Russell, I. 17(9); Russle, A. (8); Scott, M. 1; Scougall, S. 20(4); Sinclair, D. 6(8); Talbot, J. 25; Travis, M. (1); Watson, P. 32.
Goals – League (56): Boulding 11 (1 pen), McNulty 11 (1 pen), Russell, I. 8 (4 pens), Barr, B. 4, Deuchar 4, Jacobs, Keaghan 4, Jacobs, Kyle 3, Barr, C. 2, Fotheringham 2, Sinclair 2, Cummings 1, Fox 1, Scougall 1, Watson 1, own goal 1.
Scottish Cup (7): McNulty 4, Barr, R. 1, Boulding 1, Deuchar 1.
Scottish Communities Cup (6): Russell, I. 2, Boulding 1, Jacobs, Keaghan 1, McNulty 1, Talbot 1.
Ramsdens Cup (12): Deuchar 3, Russell, I. 3, Barr, R. 2, Scougall 1, Sinclair 1, own goals 2.

Honours – First Division: Champions – 2000–01. **Second Division:** Champions – 1986–87, 1998–99, 2010–11. **Third Division:** Champions – 1995–96, 2009-10. **League Cup winners** 2004.

MONTROSE

Ground: Links Park, Montrose DD10 8QD (01674) 673200
Ground capacity: 3,292. **Colours:** Royal blue shirts with white trim, white shorts with blue trim, blue stockings with white trim.
Player Manager: Stuart Garden.
League Appearances: Andrews, M. 25; Boyle, M. 36; Brown, K. 1; Cameron, D. 34; Campbell, A. 28; Crawford, J. 23(5); Crighton, S. 25(1); Dimilta, D. (6); Johnston, S. 28(4); Lunan, P. 20(2); Masson, T. 30(3); Masterton, S. 1; McGowan, D. 11(4); McNalley, S. 25(5); McPhee, S. 4(16); Pierce, S. 8(6); Smart, J. 21(1); Winter, J. 31(2); Wood, G. 12(4); Wood, S. 11; Young, L. 22.
Goals – League (58): Boyle 22, Winter 9 (2 pens), Johnston 5, Crawford 3 (1 pen), Masson 3, Pierce 3 (2 pens), Cameron 2, Campbell 2, McGowan 2, Wood, G. 2, Crighton 1, Lunan 1, McNalley 1, Smart 1, own goal 1.
Scottish Cup (5): Winter 2 (1 pen), Lunan 1, Masson 1, Pierce 1.
Scottish Communities Cup (1): Winter 1.
Ramsdens Cup (1): McPhee 1.
Honours – Second Division: Champions – 1984–85.

MORTON

Ground: Cappielow Park, Sinclair St, Greenock PA15 2TY (01475) 723571
Ground capacity: 11,612. **Colours:** Blue and white hooped shirts, white shorts with blue trim, blue stockings with white trim.
Manager: Allan Moore.
League Appearances: Bachirou, F. 28(2); Campbell, A. 16(16); Cervi, D. 7; Combe, A. 10; Di Giacomo, P. 16(8); Evans, G. 31(2); Fitzharris, S. 3(7); Flannigan, I. 3(1); Forsyth, R. 26; Frizzell, A. (1); Graham, A. 25(2); Hawke, L. (2); Jackson, A. 20(9); Kasubandi, J. (2); Little, C. 1; MacDonald, P. 30(5); McCaffrey, S. 6; McCann, K. 10(1); McGeouch, D. 13(13); McGinley, M. 2; O'Brien, D. 32; O'Ware, T. 13(1); Ramsay, C. (1); Smyth, M. 28; Stewart, C. 17; Tidser, M. 22(3); Weatherson, P. 19(12); Young, D. 18(1).
Goals – League (40): MacDonald 10 (2 pens), O'Brien 6, Campbell 5, Jackson 5, Weatherson 3 (2 pens), Di Giacomo 2, McGeouch 2, Tidser 2, Bachirou 1, Hawke 1, Smyth 1, Young 1, own goal 1.
Scottish Cup (6): MacDonald 2 (1 pen), Campbell 1, Jackson 1, O'Brien 1, Weatherson 1.
Scottish Communities Cup (6): Jackson 2, Di Giacomo 1, MacDonald 1, Tidser 1, Weatherson 1.
Ramsdens Cup (14): Di Giacomo 5, Jackson 4, MacDonald 2, Campbell 1, O'Brien 1, Weatherson 1.
Honours – First Division: Champions – 1977–78, 1983–84, 1986–87. **Division II:** Champions – 1949–50, 1963–64, 1966–67. **Second Division:** Champions – 1994–95, 2006–07. **Third Division:** Champions 2002–03. **Scottish Cup winners** 1922.

MOTHERWELL

Ground: Fir Park, Motherwell ML1 2QN (01698) 333333
Ground capacity: 13,742. **Colours:** Amber shirts with maroon band, amber shorts with maroon strip, amber stockings with maroon tops.
Manager: Stuart McCall.

League Appearances: Carswell, S. 4(10); Clancy, T. 24(2); Craigan, S. 24(2); Cummins, A. 1; Daley, O. 11(14); Forbes, R. 1(3); Hammell, S. 37; Hateley, T. 38; Higdon, M. 35; Hughes, S. 2(2); Humphrey, C. 23(12); Hutchinson, S. 29(1); Jennings, S. 33(1); Lasley, K. 32; Law, N. 38; McHugh, R. 1(8); Murphy, J. 32(4); Ojamaa, H. 12(6); Page, J. 2(2); Randolph, D. 38; Saunders, S. 1(1); Smith, G. (1).

Goals – League (49): Higdon 14 (4 pens), Murphy 9, Ojamaa 7, Lasley 4, Law 4, Daley 2, Hammell 2, Hateley 2, Humphrey 2, Hutchinson 1, McHugh 1, own goal 1.

Scottish Cup (11): Murphy 4, Law 2, Ojamaa 2, Daley 1, Hateley 1, Hutchinson 1.

Scottish Communities Cup (6): Higdon 2, Hateley 1, Lasley 1, Law 1, Lawless 1.

Honours – Division I: Champions – 1931–32. **First Division:** Champions – 1981–82, 1984–85. **Division II:** Champions – 1953–54, 1968–69. **Scottish Cup winners** 1952, 1991. **League Cup winners** 1951.

PARTICK THISTLE

Ground: Firhill Stadium, Glasgow G20 7AL (0141) 579 1971

Ground capacity: 13,141. **Colours:** Yellow shirts with thin red strips, black shorts, black stockings.

Manager: Jackie McNamara.

League Appearances: Archibald, A. 33; Balatoni, C. 21(3); Bannigan, S. 9(5); Burns, K. 1(4); Cairney, P. 35; Campbell, J. (2); Cole, D. 6; Dargo, C. 3(1); Doolan, K. 28(6); Elliot, C. 18(11); Erskine, C. 23(12); Flannigan, I. 2(3); Fox, S. 31; Griffin, G. (2); Halsman, B. 1; Hutton, K. 12; Kinniburgh, W. 4(1); Lindsay, J. (1); McAleer, C. (1); McGuigan, M. 4(3); Naismith, K. 4(4); O'Donnell, S. 28(3); Paton, P. 33; Robertson, S. 18(3); Rowson, D. 28(1); Scully, R. 5; Sekhon, A. 1; Sinclair, A. 29; Stewart, T. 8(13); Welsh, S. 10(2); Wilson, D. 1.

Goals – League (50): Doolan 13 (1 pen), Cairney 11 (4 pens), Erskine 7, Elliot 5, Rowson 3, McGuigan 2, O'Donnell 2, Welsh 2, Balatoni 1, Bannigan 1, Sinclair 1, Stewart 1, own goal 1.

Scottish Cup (5): Cairney 3, Elliot 1, Erskline 1.

Scottish Communities Cup (1): Cairney 1.

Ramsdens Cup (2): Rowson 1, Stewart 1.

Honours – First Division: Champions – 1975–76, 2001–02. **Division II:** Champions – 1896–97, 1899–1900, 1970–71. **Second Division:** Champions 2000–01. **Scottish Cup winners** 1921. **League Cup winners** 1972.

PETERHEAD

Ground: Balmoor Stadium, Balmoor Terrace, Peterhead AB42 1EQ (01779) 478256

Ground capacity: 3,250 (1,000 seated). **Colours:** Royal blue shirts with two white stripes, white shorts, royal blue stockings.

Manager: Jim McInally.

League Appearances: Bavidge, M. 26(6); Bishop, J. 3; Conway, A. 4(5); Davidson, L. 8(11); Deasley, B. 23(6); Donald, D. 34(2); Duffy, N. 1; Duncan, R. 5; Jarvie, P. 17; Jellema, R. 18(3); Kelly, D. (1); MacDonald, C. 31(1); McAllister, R. 33(1); McBain, R. 29; Rattray, A. 4(2); Redman, J. 33; Robertson, S. (4); Ross, D. 14(9); Ross, S. 22(2); Sellars, B. 8; Sharp, G. 20(8); Smith, R. 6(2); Strachan, R. 26(2); Tully, C. 10(1); Watson, P. 5(1); Webster, G. 5(2); Wood, G. 3(1); Wyness, D. 8(21).

Goals – League (51): McAllister 20 (7 pens), Bavidge 8, Deasley 4, Redman 3, MacDonald 2, McBain 2, Ross, S. 2, Sharp 2, Ross, D. 1, Sellars 1, Strachan 1, Tully 1, Webster 1, Wyness 1, own goals 2.

Scottish Cup (6): Bavidge 2, McAllister 1, MacDonald 1, Redman 1, Ross, S. 1.

Scottish Communities Cup (0).

Ramsdens Cup (4): McAllister 2 (1 pen), Deasley 1, Redman 1.

Honours – None.

QUEEN OF THE SOUTH

Ground: Palmerston Park, Dumfries DG2 9BA (01387) 254853
Ground capacity: 6,412. **Colours:** Royal blue shirts with white trim, royal blue shorts, royal blue stockings.
Manager: Gus MacPherson.
League Appearances: Black, S. 3(3); Brighton, T. 15(6); Campbell, M. 15; Carmichael, D. 27(7); Clark, N. 19(11); Higgins, C. 31(1); Holt, K. 13(4); Johnston, A. 31; McCusker, M. (7); McGuffie, R. 26(4); McKenna, S. 24(6); McKenzie, R. 2; McLaughlin, S. 35; McShane, I. 1(3); Orsi, D. 1(1); Parkin, S. 15; Potter, J. 12(1); Reid, A. 23(5); Reid, C. 26; Reilly, G. 3(11); Robinson, L. 34; Simmons, S. 23(6); Smith, K. 17(6); Smylie, R. (8).
Goals – League (38): Parkin 6, McLaughlin 5 (1 pen), Smith 5 (1 pen), Brighton 4, Carmichael 4, McGuffie 3 (1 pen), Johnston 2, McKenna 2, Reilly 2, Simmons 2, Campbell 1, Higgins 1, Potter 1.
Scottish Cup (3): Carmichael 1, McGuffie 1 (pen), McLaughlin 1.
Scottish Communities Cup (5): Brighton 2, Carmichael 1, Clark 1, Johnston 1.
Ramsdens Cup (0).
Honours – Division II: Champions – 1950–51. **Second Division:** Champions – 2001–02.
League Challenge Cup winners 2003.

QUEEN'S PARK

Ground: Hampden Park, Glasgow G42 9BA (0141) 632 1275
Ground capacity: 52,000. **Colours:** White shirts with thin black hoops, white shorts, white stockings.
Head Coach: Gardner Spiers.
League Appearances: Anderson, D. 29; Baillie, S. 2; Bradley, P. 12(1); Brough, J. 22; Burns, S. 20(6); Capuano, G. 5(1); Daly, M. 18(12); Gallagher, P. 10(7); Kennedy, K. (1); Lauchlan, G. 1; Little, R. 33; Lockhead, B. (1); Longworth, J. 33(2); McBride, M. 29; McGinn, P. 34; McVey, C. (1); Meggatt, D. 31; Murray, D. 19(7); Parry, N. 34; Quinn, T. 6(15); Ronald, O. 7(12); Smith, C. 14(13); Stewart, P. 4(6); Strain, A. 2; Urquhart, A. 2; Watt, I. 29(3).
Goals – League (70): Longworth 20, Daly 10, McBride 8 (3 pens), Smith 8, Quinn 7, Watt 7, Murray 4, Burns 3, Brough 1, Ronald 1, own goal 1.
Scottish Cup (7): Smith 3, Burns 1, Longworth 1, McBride 1 (pen), Murray 1.
Scottish Communities Cup (1): Daly 1.
Ramsdens Cup (0).
Play-Offs (1): Quinn 1.
Honours – Second Division: Champions – 1980–81. **Third Division:** Champions – 1999–2000. **Scottish Cup winners** 1874, 1875, 1876, 1880, 1881, 1882, 1884, 1886, 1890, 1893.

RAITH ROVERS

Ground: Stark's Park, Pratt Street, Kirkcaldy KY1 1SA (01592) 263514
Ground capacity: 10,104 (all seated). **Colours:** Navy blue shirts with white trim, white shorts, white stockings.
Manager: John McGlynn.
League Appearances: Baird, J. 34(1); Callachan, R. 1(5); Casalinuovo, D. 9(6); Clarke, P. 7(8); Davidson, I. 21(2); Donaldson, R. 21; Dyer, W. 30(4); Ellis, L. 30(2); Graham, B. 19(5); Hamill, J. 30(3); Hill, D. 28(1); Holt , J. 3(2); Laidlaw, R. 2; McBride, S. 1(3); McGurn, D. 34; Murray, G. 36; Prychynenko, D. 4(1); Reynolds, S. 1(10); Smith, D. 6(2); Stewart, J. 1(3); Thomson, D. 6(8); Thomson, J. 9; Vaughan, L. (1); Walker, A. 36; Walker, J. 10(13); Williamson, I. 17(10); Wilson, C. (1).
Goals – League (46): Graham 11 (1 pen), Baird 10, Clarke 4 (1 pen), Casalinuovo 3, Hamill 3, Walker, A. 3, Walker, J. 3, Murray 2, Ellis 1, Holt 1, Prychynenko 1, Reynolds 1, Smith 1, Williamson 1, own goal 1.

Scottish Cup (1): Clarke 1.
Scottish Communities Cup (4): Baird 1, Thomson 1, Walker, A. 1, Williamson 1.
Ramsdens Cup (2): Baird 2.
Honours – First Division: Champions – 1992–93, 1994–95. **Second Division:** Champions – 2002–03, 2008–09. **Division II:** Champions – 1907–08, 1909–10 (Shared), 1937–38, 1948–49.
League Cup winners 1995.

RANGERS

Ground: Ibrox Stadium, Glasgow G51 2XD (0871) 702 1972.
New club: The Rangers Football Club Ltd from June 2012.
Ground capacity: 51,082. **Colours:** Royal blue shirts with red and white trim, white shorts, black stockings with red tops.
Manager: Ally McCoist.
League Appearances: Alexander, N. 1; Aluko, S. 19(2); Bartley, K. 18(1); Bedoya, A. 5(7); Bendiksen, T. 1(2); Bocanegra, C. 29; Bougherra, M. 2; Broadfoot, K. 11(5); Celik, M. (5); Davis, S. 33; Edu, M. 34(2); Fleck, J. (4); Goian, D. 33; Healy, D. 6(5); Hemmings, K. (4); Jelavic, N. 21(1); Juanma Ortiz, P. 5(5); Kerkar, S. 5(10); Lafferty, K. 14(6); Little, A. 6(4); McCabe, R. 8(1); McCulloch, L. 20(6); McGregor, A. 37; McKay, B. (1); McKay, M. 2(1); McMillan, J. 1(1); Mitchell, A. 1(1); Naismith, S. 11; Ness, J. 3(2); Papac, S. 21; Perry, R. 8(4); Wallace, L. 26(2); Whittaker, S. 24(1); Wylde, G. 13(8).
Goals – League (77): Jelavic 15 (5 pens), Aluko 12, Naismith 9, Lafferty 7 (1 pen), Davis 5, Little 5, McCulloch 5, Edu 3, Healy 3, Bocanegra 2, Wallace 2, Whittaker 2, Wylde 2, Bedoya 1, Kerkar 1, Ness 1, own goals 2.
Scottish Cup (4): Healy 1, Jelavic 1, Kerkar 1, own goal 1.
Scottish Communities Cup (2): Goian 1, Jelavic 1.
Champions League (1): Jelavic 1.
Europa League (2): Bocanegra 1, Juanma Ortiz 1.
Honours – Division I: Champions – 1890–91 (Shared), 1898–99, 1899–1900, 1900–01, 1901–02, 1910–11, 1911–12, 1912–13, 1917–18, 1919–20, 1920–21, 1922–23, 1923–24, 1924–25, 1926–27, 1927–28, 1928–29, 1929–30, 1930–31, 1932–33, 1933–34, 1934–35, 1936–37, 1938–39, 1946–47, 1948–49, 1949–50, 1952–53, 1955–56, 1956–57, 1958–59, 1960–61, 1962–63, 1963–64, 1974–75. **Premier Division:** Champions – 1975–76, 1977–78, 1986–87, 1988–89, 1989–90, 1990–91, 1991–92, 1992–93, 1993–94, 1994–95, 1995–96, 1996–97. **Premier League:** Champions – 1998–99, 1999–2000, 2002–03, 2004–05, 2008–09, 2009–10, 2010–11. **Scottish Cup winners** 1894, 1897, 1898, 1903, 1928, 1930, 1932, 1934, 1935, 1936, 1948, 1949, 1950, 1953, 1960, 1962, 1963, 1964, 1966, 1973, 1976, 1978, 1979, 1981, 1992, 1993, 1996, 2000, 2002, 2003, 2008, 2009. **League Cup winners** 1947, 1949, 1961, 1962, 1964, 1965, 1971, 1976, 1978, 1979, 1982, 1984, 1985, 1987, 1988, 1989, 1991, 1993, 1994, 1997, 1999, 2002, 2003, 2005, 2008, 2010, 2011. **European Cup-Winners' Cup winners** 1972.

ROSS COUNTY

Ground: Victoria Park Stadium, Jubilee Road, Dingwall IV15 9QZ (01349) 860860
Ground capacity: 6,700. **Colours:** Navy blue shirts with white V, navy blue shorts with white flashes, navy blue stockings with white ring.
Manager: Derek Adam.
League Appearances: Boyd, S. 34(1); Brittain, R. 34(1); Byrne, K. 1(12); Corcoran, M. 6(26); Craig, S. 7(18); Duncan, R. (4); Fitzpatrick, M. 13; Flynn, J. 3(4); Fraser, M. 36; Gardyne, M. 30(4); Kettlewell, S. 27(1); Lawson, R. 31(2); McMenamin, C. 34; Miller, G. 36; Morrison, S. 23(1); Morrow, S. 4(7); Munro, G. 35; Quinn, R. 15(13); Vigurs, I. 27(3).
Goals – League (72): McMenamin 19, Gardyne 13, Brittain 10 (4 pens), Kettlewell 5, Vigurs 5, Craig 4, Morrow 3, Quinn 3, Boyd 2, Byrne 2, Lawson 2, Munro 2, Miller 1, own goal 1.

Scottish Cup (13): Gardyne 4, Brittain 2 (2 pens), Byrne 2, Vigurs 2, Craig 1, Lawson 1, Morrow 1.
Scottish Communities Cup (4): Craig 1, Flynn 1, Gardyne 1, McMenamin 1.
Ramsdens Cup (1): Morrison 1.
Honours – First Division: 2011–12. **Second Division:** Champions – 2007–08. **Third Division:** Champions – 1998–99. **League Challenge Cup winners** 2007, 2011.

ST JOHNSTONE

Ground: McDiarmid Park, Crieff Road, Perth PH1 2SJ (01738) 459090
Ground capacity: 10,673. **Colours:** Royal blue shirts, white shorts, royal blue stockings.
Manager: Steve Lomas.
League Appearances: Adams, J. 6(1); Anderson, S. 26(3); Compton, J. (3); Craig, L. 36; Croft, L. 10(1); Davidson, C. 26; Davidson, M. 24(2); Enckelman, P. 25; Finnigan, C. 3(8); Gibson, W. 1(10); Haber, M. 14(17); Higgins, S. (3); Keatings, J. (4); MacKay, D. 36; Mannus, A. 13; May, S. (1); Maybury, A. 15(7); McCracken, D. 27(1); Millar, C. 26(4); Moon, K. 13(6); Morris, J. 28; Oyenuga, K. (1); Parkin, S. 1(1); Riordan, D. 2(2); Robertson, D. 10(6); Sandaza, F. 28(1); Sheridan, C. 25(3); Wright, F. 23.
Goals – League (43): Sandaza 14 (4 pens), Craig 7 (1 pen), Sheridan 4, Croft 3, MacKay 3, Davidson, M. 2, Haber 2, Anderson 1, Davidson, C. 1, Maybury 1 (1 pen), McCracken 1, Morris 1, own goals 3.
Scottish Cup (4): Davidson, M. 2, Sheridan 1, Sandaza 1.
Scottish Communities Cup (3): Sandaza 2, Wright 1.
Honours – First Division: Champions – 1982–83, 1989–90, 1996–97, 2008–09. **Division II:** Champions – 1923–24, 1959–60, 1962–63. **League Challenge Cup winners** 2008.

ST MIRREN

Ground: St Mirren Park, Greenhill Road, Paisley PA3 1RU (0141) 889 2558
Ground capacity: 10,476 (all seated). **Colours:** Black and white striped shirts, white shorts, white stockings.
Manager: Danny Lennon.
League Appearances: Barron, D. 12(5); Carey, G. 20(9); Goodwin, J. 31; Haddad, I. 4(6); Hasselbaink, N. 22(12); Imrie, D. 12(2); Mair, L. 34; McAusland, M. 31(1); McGowan, P. 37; McGregor, D. 6(3); McKee, J. (2); McLean, K. 24(4); McQuade, P. (1); McShane, J. 1(9); Mooy, A. 3(5); Murray, H. 1(6); Naismith, J. (2); Reilly, T. (4); Samson, C. 38; Teale, G. 21(13); Tesselaar, J. 33; Thompson, S. 34(1); Thomson, S. 19(5); Van Zanten, D. 35.
Goals – League (39): Thompson 13, McGowan 8 (2 pens), Hasselbaink 6, McLean 4, Carey 2, Thomson 2, Goodwin 1, Mair 1, McAusland 1, Mooy 1.
Scottish Cup (6): Carey 2, Hasselbaink 1, Teale 1, Thompson 1, own goal 1.
Scottish Communities Cup (6): Thompson 2, Goodwin 1, Hasselbaink 1 (pen), Teale 1, own goal 1.
Honours – First Division: Champions – 1976–77, 1999–2000, 2005–06. **Division II:** Champions – 1967–68. **Scottish Cup winners** 1926, 1959, 1987.
League Challenge Cup winners 2005–06.

STENHOUSEMUIR

Ground: Ochilview Park, Stenhousemuir FK5 4QL (01324) 562992
Ground capacity: 3,776 (626 seated). **Colours:** Maroon shirts with light blue trim, white shorts, maroon stockings.
Manager: Dave Irons.
League Appearances: Anderson, K. 6(1); Brown, A. 27(1); Campbell, J. 6(1); Corrigan, M. 19; Deuchar, K. 6(3); Devlin, M. 12(1); Devlin, N. 6; Dickson, S. 15(10); Ferguson, B.

31; Fitzharris, S. 2(1); Fraser, S. (3); Hamilton, C. 6(2); Hamilton, J. (2); Kean, S. 36; Lawson, A. 5(4); Lyle, W. 27(2); McCafferty, J. 1(4); McCluskey, C. 8; McHale, P. 12(5); McKinlay, K. 26(3); McMillan, R. 29(1); Miller, K. 5; Murray, S. 22(8); Paton, E. 24(2); Plenderleith, G. (4); Quinn, P. 2(11); Rodgers, A. 28(5); Shaw, D. 1; Smith, G. 5(5); Thomson, I. 29(5).
Goals – League (54): Rodgers 14, Kean 10, Ferguson 7 (2 pens), McMillan 4, Thomson 4, Anderson 3, Smith 3, Dickson 2, Campbell 1, Hamilton, C. 1, McHale 1, Murray 1, Paton 1 (1 pen), Quinn 1, own goal 1.
Scottish Cup (4): Rodgers 3, Kean 1.
Scottish Communities Cup (3): Paton 2, Lyle 1.
Ramsdens Cup (1): Kean 1.
Honours – Second Division: Champions – 2009–10. **League Challenge Cup winners** 1996.

STIRLING ALBION

Ground: Forthbank Stadium, Springkerse, Stirling FK7 7UJ (01786) 450399
Ground capacity: 3,808. **Colours:** All red with white trim.
Manager: Greg McDonald.
League Appearances: Allison, B. 28; Ashe, D. (2); Bonar, L. 9(7); Brass, G. 1(1); Cleland, J. 1; Cook, A. 24(9); Crawley, J. 26(3); Davidson, S. 8(5); Davieson, S. 19(1); Day, S. (3); Dillon, S. 15(2); Fagan, S. 21(1); Ferry, M. 19(2); Filler, S. 13(1); Flood, J. 10(12); Jacobs, D. 26(6); Kelbie, K. 10(4); McCulloch, M. 18(2); McCunnie, J. 7(1); McDonald, G. (1); McGeachie, R. 1; McLeish, C. 13(5); McPherson, D. 3(6); McSorley, D. 22(3); Nicholas, S. 1(9); Reidford, C. 22; Smith, D. 29(4); Thom, G. 34; Weir, G. 16(1).
Goals – League (46): Cook 8 (1 pen), Davieson 6 (2 pens), Ferry 6, Smith 4, Thom 4, Davidson 3, Dillon 2, Flood 2, Kelbie 2, McSorley 2, Bonar 1, Brass 1, Crawley 1, Day 1, Jacobs 1, McLeish 1, own goal 1.
Scottish Cup (1): Smith 1.
Scottish Communities Cup (0).
Ramsdens Cup (3): Bonar 2 (1 pen), McPherson 1.
Honours – Division II: Champions – 1952–53, 1957–58, 1960–61, 1964–65. **Second Division:** Champions – 1976–77, 1990–91, 1995–96, 2009–10.

STRANRAER

Ground: Stair Park, Stranraer DG9 8BS (01776) 703271
Ground capacity: 5,600. **Colours:** Royal blue shirts with white trim, white shorts with royal blue trim, royal blue stockings.
Manager: Keith Knox.
League Appearances: Agnew, D. (4); Aitken, C. 24(2); Belkouche, Z. 5(1); Borris, R. 8; Carnaghan, A. (1); Cochrane, A. (4); Dougan, B. (1); Durnan, M. 4; Gallagher, G. 24(3); Grehan, M. 22(5); Kane, J. 29(3); Kennedy, R. 2; Malcolm, C. 34(1); Marshall, R. 12(1); McColm, S. 16(16); McGregor, D. 25; McKeown, F. 33; Mitchell, Danny 6(3); Mitchell, David 24; Moore, M. 9(22); Murphy, P. 2(2); Noble, S. 30(1); Shepherd, N. 12(12); Stirling, S. 24(2); Taggart, S. 24; Winter, S. 27(8).
Goals – League (77): Malcolm 15, Moore 12, Stirling 12 (3 pens), Aitken 9 (4 pens), McColm 9, Winter 7, Grehan 5, McKeown 2, Taggart 2, Gallagher 1, Noble 1, Shepherd 1, own goal 1.
Scottish Cup (10): Winter 3, Grehan 2, Malcolm 2, Aitken 1, McColm 1, McKeown 1.
Scottish Communities Cup (1): Gallagher 1.
Ramsdens Cup (0).
Play-Offs (8): Grehan 2, Malcolm 2, Winter 2, McKeown 1, Moore 1.
Honours – Second Division: Champions – 1993–94, 1997–98. **Third Division:** Champions – 2003–04. **League Challenge Cup winners** 1997.

SCOTTISH LEAGUE HONOURS

*On goal average (ratio)/difference. †Held jointly after indecisive play-off.
‡Won on deciding match. ¶Two points deducted for fielding ineligible player.
Competition suspended 1940–45 during war; Regional Leagues operating.
‡‡Two points deducted for registration irregularities. §Not promoted after play-offs.
§§Ten points deducted for entering administration.

PREMIER LEAGUE

Maximum points: 108

	First	Pts	Second	Pts	Third	Pts
1998–99	Rangers	77	Celtic	71	St Johnstone	57
1999–00	Rangers	90	Celtic	69	Hearts	54

Maximum points: 114

		Pts		Pts		Pts
2000–01	Celtic	97	Rangers	82	Hibernian	66
2001–02	Celtic	103	Rangers	85	Livingston	58
2002–03	Rangers*	97	Celtic	97	Hearts	63
2003–04	Celtic	98	Rangers	81	Hearts	68
2004–05	Rangers	93	Celtic	92	Hibernian*	61
2005–06	Celtic	91	Hearts	74	Rangers	73
2006–07	Celtic	84	Rangers	72	Aberdeen	65
2007–08	Celtic	89	Rangers	86	Motherwell	60
2008–09	Rangers	86	Celtic	82	Hearts	59
2009–10	Rangers	87	Celtic	81	Dundee U	63
2010–11	Rangers	93	Celtic	92	Hearts	63
2011–12	Celtic	93	Rangers§§	73	Motherwell	62

PREMIER DIVISION

Maximum points: 72

		Pts		Pts		Pts
1975–76	Rangers	54	Celtic	48	Hibernian	43
1976–77	Celtic	55	Rangers	46	Aberdeen	43
1977–78	Rangers	55	Aberdeen	53	Dundee U	40
1978–79	Celtic	48	Rangers	45	Dundee U	44
1979–80	Aberdeen	48	Celtic	47	St Mirren	42
1980–81	Celtic	56	Aberdeen	49	Rangers*	44
1981–82	Celtic	55	Aberdeen	53	Rangers	43
1982–83	Dundee U	56	Celtic*	55	Aberdeen	55
1983–84	Aberdeen	57	Celtic	50	Dundee U	47
1984–85	Aberdeen	59	Celtic	52	Dundee U	47
1985–86	Celtic*	50	Hearts	50	Dundee U	47

Maximum points: 88

		Pts		Pts		Pts
1986–87	Rangers	69	Celtic	63	Dundee U	60
1987–88	Celtic	72	Hearts	62	Rangers	60

Maximum points: 72

		Pts		Pts		Pts
1988–89	Rangers	56	Aberdeen	50	Celtic	46
1989–90	Rangers	51	Aberdeen*	44	Hearts	44
1990–91	Rangers	55	Aberdeen	53	Celtic*	41

	First	Pts	Second	Pts	Third	Pts

Maximum points: 88

1991–92	Rangers	72	Hearts	63	Celtic	62
1992–93	Rangers	73	Aberdeen	64	Celtic	60
1993–94	Rangers	58	Aberdeen	55	Motherwell	54

Maximum points: 108

1994–95	Rangers	69	Motherwell	54	Hibernian	53
1995–96	Rangers	87	Celtic	83	Aberdeen*	55
1996–97	Rangers	80	Celtic	75	Dundee U	60
1997–98	Celtic	74	Rangers	72	Hearts	67

FIRST DIVISION

Maximum points: 52

| 1975–76 | Partick Th | 41 | Kilmarnock | 35 | Montrose | 30 |

Maximum points: 78

1976–77	St Mirren	62	Clydebank	58	Dundee	51
1977–78	Morton*	58	Hearts	58	Dundee	57
1978–79	Dundee	55	Kilmarnock*	54	Clydebank	54
1979–80	Hearts	53	Airdrieonians	51	Ayr U*	44
1980–81	Hibernian	57	Dundee	52	St Johnstone	51
1981–82	Motherwell	61	Kilmarnock	51	Hearts	50
1982–83	St Johnstone	55	Hearts	54	Clydebank	50
1983–84	Morton	54	Dumbarton	51	Partick Th	46
1984–85	Motherwell	50	Clydebank	48	Falkirk	45
1985–86	Hamilton A	56	Falkirk	45	Kilmarnock	44

Maximum points: 88

| 1986–87 | Morton | 57 | Dunfermline Ath | 56 | Dumbarton | 53 |
| 1987–88 | Hamilton A | 56 | Meadowbank Th | 52 | Clydebank | 49 |

Maximum points: 78

1988–89	Dunfermline Ath	54	Falkirk	52	Clydebank	48
1989–90	St Johnstone	58	Airdrieonians	54	Clydebank	44
1990–91	Falkirk	54	Airdrieonians	53	Dundee	52

Maximum points: 88

1991–92	Dundee	58	Partick Th*	57	Hamilton A	57
1992–93	Raith R	65	Kilmarnock	54	Dunfermline Ath	52
1993–94	Falkirk	66	Dunfermline Ath	65	Airdrieonians	54

Maximum points: 108

1994–95	Raith R	69	Dunfermline Ath*	68	Dundee	68
1995–96	Dunfermline Ath	71	Dundee U*	67	Morton	67
1996–97	St Johnstone	80	Airdrieonians	60	Dundee*	58
1997–98	Dundee	70	Falkirk	65	Raith R*	60
1998–99	Hibernian	89	Falkirk	66	Ayr U	62
1999–00	St Mirren	76	Dunfermline Ath	71	Falkirk	68
2000–01	Livingston	76	Ayr U	69	Falkirk	56
2001–02	Partick Th	66	Airdrieonians	56	Ayr U	52

	First	*Pts*	*Second*	*Pts*	*Third*	*Pts*
2002–03	Falkirk	81	Clyde	72	St Johnstone	67
2003–04	Inverness CT	70	Clyde	69	St Johnstone	57
2004–05	Falkirk	75	St Mirren*	60	Clyde	60
2005–06	St Mirren	76	St Johnstone	66	Hamilton A	59
2006–07	Gretna	66	St Johnstone	65	Dundee*	53
2007–08	Hamilton A	76	Dundee	69	St Johnstone	58
2008–09	St Johnstone	65	Partick Th	55	Dunfermline Ath	51
2009–10	Inverness CT	73	Dundee	61	Dunfermline Ath	58
2010–11	Dunfermline Ath	70	Raith R	60	Falkirk	58
2011–12	Ross Co	79	Dundee	55	Falkirk	52

SECOND DIVISION

Maximum points: 52

	First	*Pts*	*Second*	*Pts*	*Third*	*Pts*
1975–76	Clydebank*	40	Raith R	40	Alloa Ath	35

Maximum points: 78

	First	*Pts*	*Second*	*Pts*	*Third*	*Pts*
1976–77	Stirling Alb	55	Alloa Ath	51	Dunfermline Ath	50
1977–78	Clyde*	53	Raith R	53	Dunfermline Ath	48
1978–79	Berwick R	54	Dunfermline Ath	52	Falkirk	50
1979–80	Falkirk	50	East Stirling	49	Forfar Ath	46
1980–81	Queen's Park	50	Queen of the S	46	Cowdenbeath	45
1981–82	Clyde	59	Alloa Ath*	50	Arbroath	50
1982–83	Brechin C	55	Meadowbank Th	54	Arbroath	49
1983–84	Forfar Ath	63	East Fife	47	Berwick R	43
1984–85	Montrose	53	Alloa Ath	50	Dunfermline Ath	49
1985–86	Dunfermline Ath	57	Queen of the S	55	Meadowbank Th	49
1986–87	Meadowbank Th	55	Raith R*	52	Stirling Alb*	52
1987–88	Ayr U	61	St Johnstone	59	Queen's Park	51
1988–89	Albion R	50	Alloa Ath	45	Brechin C	43
1989–90	Brechin C	49	Kilmarnock	48	Stirling Alb	47
1990–91	Stirling Alb	54	Montrose	46	Cowdenbeath	45
1991–92	Dumbarton	52	Cowdenbeath	51	Alloa Ath	50
1992–93	Clyde	54	Brechin C*	53	Stranraer	53
1993–94	Stranraer	56	Berwick R	48	Stenhousemuir*	47

Maximum points: 108

	First	*Pts*	*Second*	*Pts*	*Third*	*Pts*
1994–95	Morton	64	Dumbarton	60	Stirling Alb	58
1995–96	Stirling Alb	81	East Fife	67	Berwick R	60
1996–97	Ayr U	77	Hamilton A	74	Livingston	64
1997–98	Stranraer	61	Clydebank	60	Livingston	59
1998–99	Livingston	77	Inverness CT	72	Clyde	53
1999–00	Clyde	65	Alloa Ath	64	Ross County	62
2000–01	Partick Th	75	Arbroath	58	Berwick R*	54
2001–02	Queen of the S	67	Alloa Ath	59	Forfar Ath	53
2002–03	Raith R	59	Brechin C	55	Airdrie U	54
2003–04	Airdrie U	70	Hamilton A	62	Dumbarton	60
2004–05	Brechin C	72	Stranraer	63	Morton	62
2005–06	Gretna	88	Morton§	70	Peterhead*§	57
2006–07	Morton	77	Stirling Alb	69	Raith R§	62

	First	Pts	Second	Pts	Third	Pts
2007–08	Ross Co	73	Airdrie U	66	Raith R§	60
2008–09	Raith R	76	Ayr U	74	Brechin C§	62
2009–10	Stirling Alb*	65	Alloa Ath§	65	Cowdenbeath	59
2010–11	Livingston	82	Ayr U*	59	Forfar§	59
2011–12	Cowdenbeath	71	Arbroath§	63	Dumbarton	58

THIRD DIVISION

Maximum points: 108

	First	Pts	Second	Pts	Third	Pts
1994–95	Forfar Ath	80	Montrose	67	Ross Co	60
1995–96	Livingston	72	Brechin C	63	Caledonian Th	57
1996–97	Inverness CT	76	Forfar Ath*	67	Ross Co	67
1997–98	Alloa Ath	76	Arbroath	68	Ross Co*	67
1998–99	Ross Co	77	Stenhousemuir	64	Brechin C	59
1999–00	Queen's Park	69	Berwick R	66	Forfar Ath	61
2000–01	Hamilton A*	76	Cowdenbeath	76	Brechin C	72
2001–02	Brechin C	73	Dumbarton	61	Albion R	59
2002–03	Morton	72	East Fife	71	Albion R	70
2003–04	Stranraer	79	Stirling Alb	77	Gretna	68
2004–05	Gretna	98	Peterhead	78	Cowdenbeath	51
2005–06	Cowdenbeath*	76	Berwick R§	76	Stenhousemuir§	73
2006–07	Berwick R	75	Arbroath§	70	Queen's Park	68
2007–08	East Fife	88	Stranraer	65	Montrose§	59
2008–09	Dumbarton	67	Cowdenbeath§	63	East Stirling§	61
2009–10	Livingston	78	Forfar Ath	63	East Stirling§	61
2010–11	Arbroath	66	Albion R	61	Queen's Park*§	59
2011–12	Alloa Ath	77	Queen's Park§	63	Stranraer§	58

DIVISION 1 to 1974–75

Maximum points: a 36; b 44; c 40; d 52; e 60; f 68; g 76; h 84.

	First	Pts	Second	Pts	Third	Pts
1890–91a	Dumbarton†	29	Rangers†	29	Celtic	21
1891–92b	Dumbarton	37	Celtic	35	Hearts	34
1892–93a	Celtic	29	Rangers	28	St Mirren	20
1893–94a	Celtic	29	Hearts	26	St Bernard's	23
1894–95a	Hearts	31	Celtic	26	Rangers	22
1895–96a	Celtic	30	Rangers	26	Hibernian	24
1896–97a	Hearts	28	Hibernian	26	Rangers	25
1897–98a	Celtic	33	Rangers	29	Hibernian	22
1898–99a	Rangers	36	Hearts	26	Celtic	24
1899–1900a	Rangers	32	Celtic	25	Hibernian	24
1900–01c	Rangers	35	Celtic	29	Hibernian	25
1901–02a	Rangers	28	Celtic	26	Hearts	22
1902–03b	Hibernian	37	Dundee	31	Rangers	29
1903–04d	Third Lanark	43	Hearts	39	Celtic*	38
1904–05d	Celtic‡	41	Rangers	41	Third Lanark	35
1905–06e	Celtic	49	Hearts	43	Airdrieonians	38
1906–07f	Celtic	55	Dundee	48	Rangers	45
1907–08f	Celtic	55	Falkirk	51	Rangers	50
1908–09f	Celtic	51	Dundee	50	Clyde	48

	First	Pts	Second	Pts	Third	Pts
1909–10f	Celtic	54	Falkirk	52	Rangers	46
1910–11f	Rangers	52	Aberdeen	48	Falkirk	44
1911–12f	Rangers	51	Celtic	45	Clyde	42
1912–13f	Rangers	53	Celtic	49	Hearts*	41
1913–14g	Celtic	65	Rangers	59	Hearts*	54
1914–15g	Celtic	65	Hearts	61	Rangers	50
1915–16g	Celtic	67	Rangers	56	Morton	51
1916–17g	Celtic	64	Morton	54	Rangers	53
1917–18f	Rangers	56	Celtic	55	Kilmarnock*	43
1918–19f	Celtic	58	Rangers	57	Morton	47
1919–20h	Rangers	71	Celtic	68	Motherwell	57
1920–21h	Rangers	76	Celtic	66	Hearts	50
1921–22h	Celtic	67	Rangers	66	Raith R	51
1922–23g	Rangers	55	Airdrieonians	50	Celtic	46
1923–24g	Rangers	59	Airdrieonians	50	Celtic	46
1924–25g	Rangers	60	Airdrieonians	57	Hibernian	52
1925–26g	Celtic	58	Airdrieonians*	50	Hearts	50
1926–27g	Rangers	56	Motherwell	51	Celtic	49
1927–28g	Rangers	60	Celtic*	55	Motherwell	55
1928–29g	Rangers	67	Celtic	51	Motherwell	50
1929–30g	Rangers	60	Motherwell	55	Aberdeen	53
1930–31g	Rangers	60	Celtic	58	Motherwell	56
1931–32g	Motherwell	66	Rangers	61	Celtic	48
1932–33g	Rangers	62	Motherwell	59	Hearts	50
1933–34g	Rangers	66	Motherwell	62	Celtic	47
1934–35g	Rangers	55	Celtic	52	Hearts	50
1935–36g	Celtic	66	Rangers*	61	Aberdeen	61
1936–37g	Rangers	61	Aberdeen	54	Celtic	52
1937–38g	Celtic	61	Hearts	58	Rangers	49
1938–39g	Rangers	59	Celtic	48	Aberdeen	46
1946–47e	Rangers	46	Hibernian	44	Aberdeen	39
1947–48e	Hibernian	48	Rangers	46	Partick Th	36
1948–49e	Rangers	46	Dundee	45	Hibernian	39
1949–50e	Rangers	50	Hibernian	49	Hearts	43
1950–51e	Hibernian	48	Rangers*	38	Dundee	38
1951–52e	Hibernian	45	Rangers	41	East Fife	37
1952–53e	Rangers*	43	Hibernian	43	East Fife	39
1953–54e	Celtic	43	Hearts	38	Partick Th	35
1954–55e	Aberdeen	49	Celtic	46	Rangers	41
1955–56f	Rangers	52	Aberdeen	46	Hearts*	45
1956–57f	Rangers	55	Hearts	53	Kilmarnock	42
1957–58f	Hearts	62	Rangers	49	Celtic	46
1958–59f	Rangers	50	Hearts	48	Motherwell	44
1959–60f	Hearts	54	Kilmarnock	50	Rangers*	42
1960–61f	Rangers	51	Kilmarnock	50	Third Lanark	42
1961–62f	Dundee	54	Rangers	51	Celtic	46
1962–63f	Rangers	57	Kilmarnock	48	Partick Th	46
1963–64f	Rangers	55	Kilmarnock	49	Celtic*	47

	First	Pts	Second	Pts	Third	Pts
1964–65f	Kilmarnock*	50	Hearts	50	Dunfermline Ath	49
1965–66f	Celtic	57	Rangers	55	Kilmarnock	45
1966–67f	Celtic	58	Rangers	55	Clyde	46
1967–68f	Celtic	63	Rangers	61	Hibernian	45
1968–69f	Celtic	54	Rangers	49	DunfermlineAth	45
1969–70f	Celtic	57	Rangers	45	Hibernian	44
1970–71f	Celtic	56	Aberdeen	54	St Johnstone	44
1971–72f	Celtic	60	Aberdeen	50	Rangers	44
1972–73f	Celtic	57	Rangers	56	Hibernian	45
1973–74f	Celtic	53	Hibernian	49	Rangers	48
1974–75f	Rangers	56	Hibernian	49	Celtic	45

DIVISION 2 to 1974–75

Maximum points: a 76; b 72; c 68; d 52; e 60; f 36; g 44.

	First	Pts	Second	Pts	Third	Pts
1893–94f	Hibernian	29	Cowlairs	27	Clyde	24
1894–95f	Hibernian	30	Motherwell	22	Port Glasgow	20
1895–96f	Abercorn	27	Leith Ath	23	Renton	21
1896–97f	Partick Th	31	Leith Ath	27	Kilmarnock*	21
1897–98f	Kilmarnock	29	Port Glasgow	25	Morton	22
1898–99f	Kilmarnock	32	Leith Ath	27	Port Glasgow	25
1899–1900f	Partick Th	29	Morton	28	Port Glasgow	20
1900–01f	St Bernard's	25	Airdrieonians	23	Abercorn	21
1901–02g	Port Glasgow	32	Partick Th	31	Motherwell	26
1902–03g	Airdrieonians	35	Motherwell	28	Ayr U*	27
1903–04g	Hamilton A	37	Clyde	29	Ayr U	28
1904–05g	Clyde	32	Falkirk	28	Hamilton A	27
1905–06g	Leith Ath	34	Clyde	31	Albion R	27
1906–07g	St Bernard's	32	Vale of Leven*	27	Arthurlie	27
1907–08g	Raith R	30	Dumbarton‡‡	27	Ayr U	27
1908–09g	Abercorn	31	Raith R*	28	Vale of Leven	28
1909–10g	Leith Ath‡	33	Raith R	33	St Bernard's	27
1910–11g	Dumbarton	31	Ayr U	27	Albion R	25
1911–12g	Ayr U	35	Abercorn	30	Dumbarton	27
1912–13d	Ayr U	34	Dunfermline Ath	33	East Stirling	32
1913–14g	Cowdenbeath	31	Albion R	27	Dunfermline Ath*	26
1914–15d	Cowdenbeath*	37	St Bernard's*	37	Leith Ath	37
1921–22a	Alloa Ath	60	Cowdenbeath	47	Armadale	45
1922–23a	Queen's Park	57	Clydebank ¶	50	St Johnstone ¶	45
1923–24a	St Johnstone	56	Cowdenbeath	55	Bathgate	44
1924–25a	Dundee U	50	Clydebank	48	Clyde	47
1925–26a	Dunfermline Ath	59	Clyde	53	Ayr U	52
1926–27a	Bo'ness	56	Raith R	49	Clydebank	45
1927–28a	Ayr U	54	Third Lanark	45	King's Park	44
1928–29b	Dundee U	51	Morton	50	Arbroath	47
1929–30a	Leith Ath*	57	East Fife	57	Albion R	54
1930–31a	Third Lanark	61	Dundee U	50	Dunfermline Ath	47
1931–32a	East Stirling*	55	St Johnstone	55	Raith R*	46
1932–33c	Hibernian	54	Queen of the S	49	Dunfermline Ath	47

First	Pts	Second	Pts	Third	Pts
1933–34*c* Albion R	45	Dunfermline Ath*	44	Arbroath	44
1934–35*c* Third Lanark	52	Arbroath	50	St Bernard's	47
1935–36*c* Falkirk	59	St Mirren	52	Morton	48
1936–37*c* Ayr U	54	Morton	51	St Bernard's	48
1937–38*c* Raith R	59	Albion R	48	Airdrieonians	47
1938–39*c* Cowdenbeath	60	Alloa Ath*	48	East Fife	48
1946–47*d* Dundee	45	Airdrieonians	42	East Fife	31
1947–48*e* East Fife	53	Albion R	42	Hamilton A	40
1948–49*e* Raith R*	42	Stirling Alb	42	Airdrieonians*	41
1949–50*e* Morton	47	Airdrieonians	44	Dunfermline Ath*	36
1950–51*e* Queen of the S*	45	Stirling Alb	45	Ayr U*	36
1951–52*e* Clyde	44	Falkirk	43	Ayr U	39
1952–53*e* Stirling Alb	44	Hamilton A	43	Queen's Park	37
1953–54*e* Motherwell	45	Kilmarnock	42	Third Lanark*	36
1954–55*e* Airdrieonians	46	Dunfermline Ath	42	Hamilton A	39
1955–56*b* Queen's Park	54	Ayr U	51	St Johnstone	49
1956–57*b* Clyde	64	Third Lanark	51	Cowdenbeath	45
1957–58*b* Stirling Alb	55	Dunfermline Ath	53	Arbroath	47
1958–59*b* Ayr U	60	Arbroath	51	Stenhousemuir	46
1959–60*b* St Johnstone	53	Dundee U	50	Queen of the S	49
1960–61*b* Stirling Alb	55	Falkirk	54	Stenhousemuir	50
1961–62*b* Clyde	54	Queen of the S	53	Morton	44
1962–63*b* St Johnstone	55	East Stirling	49	Morton	48
1963–64*b* Morton	67	Clyde	53	Arbroath	46
1964–65*b* Stirling Alb	59	Hamilton A	50	Queen of the S	45
1965–66*b* Ayr U	53	Airdrieonians	50	Queen of the S	47
1966–67*a* Morton	69	Raith R	58	Arbroath	57
1967–68*b* St Mirren	62	Arbroath	53	East Fife	49
1968–69*b* Motherwell	64	Ayr U	53	East Fife*	48
1969–70*b* Falkirk	56	Cowdenbeath	55	Queen of the S	50
1970–71*b* Partick Th	56	East Fife	51	Arbroath	46
1971–72*b* Dumbarton*	52	Arbroath	52	Stirling Alb	50
1972–73*b* Clyde	56	Dumfermline Ath	52	Raith R*	47
1973–74*b* Airdrieonians	60	Kilmarnock	58	Hamilton A	55
1974–75*a* Falkirk	54	Queen of the S*	53	Montrose	53

Elected to Division 1: 1894 Clyde; 1895 Hibernian; 1896 Abercorn; 1897 Partick Th; 1899 Kilmarnock; 1900 Morton and Partick Th; 1902 Port Glasgow and Partick Th; 1903 Airdrieonians and Motherwell; 1905 Falkirk and Aberdeen; 1906 Clyde and Hamilton A; 1910 Raith R; 1913 Ayr U and Dumbarton.

From 1946–47 to 1955–56 the two divisions were known as A and B. A division 3 had existed for three years from 1923–24 and was revived for three more seasons from 1946–47 as Division C when it included reserve teams.

RELEGATED CLUBS

From Premier League

1998–99 Dunfermline Ath
1999–00 *No relegated team*
2000–01 St Mirren
2001–02 St Johnstone
2002–03 *No relegated team*
2003–04 Partick Th
2004–05 Dundee

2005–06 Livingston
2006–07 Dunfermline Ath
2007–08 Gretna
2008–09 Inverness CT
2009–10 Falkirk
2010–11 Hamilton A
2011–12 Dunfermline Ath

From Premier Division

1974–75 *No relegation due to League
    reorganisation*
1975–76 Dundee, St Johnstone
1976–77 Hearts, Kilmarnock
1977–78 Ayr U, Clydebank
1978–79 Hearts, Motherwell
1979–80 Dundee, Hibernian
1980–81 Kilmarnock, Hearts
1981–82 Partick Th, Airdrieonians
1982–83 Morton, Kilmarnock
1983–84 St Johnstone, Motherwell
1984–85 Dumbarton, Morton
1985–86 *No relegation due to League
    reorganisation*

1986–87 Clydebank, Hamilton A
1987–88 Falkirk, Dunfermline Ath,
    Morton
1988–89 Hamilton A
1989–90 Dundee
1990–91 None
1991–92 St Mirren, Dunfermline Ath
1992–93 Falkirk, Airdrieonians
1993–94 *See footnote*
1994–95 Dundee U
1995–96 Partick Th, Falkirk
1996–97 Raith R
1997–98 Hibernian

From Division 1

1974–75 *No relegation due to League
    reorganisation*
1975–76 Dunfermline Ath, Clyde
1976–77 Raith R, Falkirk
1977–78 Alloa Ath, East Fife
1978–79 Montrose, Queen of the S
1979–80 Arbroath, Clyde
1980–81 Stirling Alb, Berwick R
1981–82 East Stirling, Queen of the S
1982–83 Dunfermline Ath, Queen's Park
1983–84 Raith R, Alloa Ath
1984–85 Meadowbank Th, St Johnstone
1985–86 Ayr U, Alloa Ath
1986–87 Brechin C, Montrose
1987–88 East Fife, Dumbarton
1988–89 Kilmarnock, Queen of the S
1989–90 Albion R, Alloa Ath
1990–91 Clyde, Brechin C
1991–92 Montrose, Forfar Ath
1992–93 Meadowbank Th, Cowdenbeath

1993–94 *See footnote*
1994–95 Ayr U, Stranraer
1995–96 Hamilton A, Dumbarton
1996–97 Clydebank, East Fife
1997–98 Partick Th, Stirling Alb
1998–99 Hamilton A, Stranraer
1999–00 Clydebank
2000–01 Morton, Alloa Ath
2001–02 Raith R
2002–03 Alloa Ath, Arbroath
2003–04 Ayr U, Brechin C
2004–05 Partick Th, Raith R
2005–06 Stranraer, Brechin C
2006–07 Airdrie U, Ross Co
2007–08 Stirling Alb
2008–09 Clyde
2009–10 Airdrie U, Ayr U
2010–11 Cowdenbeath, Stirling Alb
2011–12 Ayr U, Queen of the S

From Division 2

1994–95 Meadowbank Th, Brechin C
1995–96 Forfar Ath, Montrose
1996–97 Dumbarton, Berwick R
1997–98 Stenhousemuir, Brechin C
1998–99 East Fife, Forfar Ath
1999–00 Hamilton A**
2000–01 Queen's Park, Stirling Alb
2001–02 Morton
2002–03 Stranraer, Cowdenbeath

2003–04 East Fife, Stenhousemuir
2004–05 Arbroath, Berwick R
2005–06 Dumbarton
2006–07 Stranraer, Forfar Ath
2007–08 Cowdenbeath, Berwick R
2008–09 Stranraer, Queen's Park
2009–10 Arbroath, Clyde
2010–11 Alloa Ath, Peterhead
2011–12 Stirling Alb

From Division 1 1973–74

1921–22 *Queen's Park, Dumbarton, Clydebank
1922–23 Albion R, Alloa Ath
1923–24 Clyde, Clydebank
1924–25 Third Lanark, Ayr U
1925–26 Raith R, Clydebank
1926–27 Morton, Dundee U
1927–28 Dunfermline Ath, Bo'ness
1928–29 Third Lanark, Raith R
1929–30 St Johnstone, Dundee U
1930–31 Hibernian, East Fife
1931–32 Dundee U, Leith Ath
1932–33 Morton, East Stirling
1933–34 Third Lanark, Cowdenbeath
1934–35 St Mirren, Falkirk
1935–36 Airdrieonians, Ayr U
1936–37 Dunfermline Ath, Albion R
1937–38 Dundee, Morton
1938–39 Queen's Park, Raith R
1946–47 Kilmarnock, Hamilton A
1947–48 Airdrieonians, Queen's Park
1948–49 Morton, Albion R
1949–50 Queen of the S, Stirling Alb
1950–51 Clyde, Falkirk

1951–52 Morton, Stirling Alb
1952–53 Motherwell, Third Lanark
1953–54 Airdrieonians, Hamilton A
1954–55 *No clubs relegated*
1955–56 Stirling Alb, Clyde
1956–57 Dunfermline Ath, Ayr U
1957–58 East Fife, Queen's Park
1958–59 Queen of the S, Falkirk
1959–60 Arbroath, Stirling Alb
1960–61 Ayr U, Clyde
1961–62 St Johnstone, Stirling Alb
1962–63 Clyde, Raith R
1963–64 Queen of the S, East Stirling
1964–65 Airdrieonians, Third Lanark
1965–66 Morton, Hamilton A
1966–67 St Mirren, Ayr U
1967–68 Motherwell, Stirling Alb
1968–69 Falkirk, Arbroath
1969–70 Raith R, Partick Th
1970–71 St Mirren, Cowdenbeath
1971–72 Clyde, Dunfermline Ath
1972–73 Kilmarnock, Airdrieonians
1973–74 East Fife, Falkirk

*Season 1921–22 – only 1 club promoted, 3 clubs relegated.
**15 pts deducted for failing to field a team.*

Scottish League championship wins: Rangers 54, Celtic 43, Aberdeen 4, Hearts 4, Hibernian 4, Dumbarton 2, Dundee 1, Dundee U 1, Kilmarnock 1, Motherwell 1, Third Lanark 1.

The Scottish Football League was reconstructed into three divisions at the end of the 1974–75 season, so the usual relegation statistics do not apply. Further reorganization took place at the end of the 1985–86 season. From 1986–87, the Premier and First Division had 12 teams each. The Second Division remained at 14. From 1988–89, the Premier Division reverted to 10 teams, and the First Division to 14 teams but in 1991–92 the Premier and First Division reverted to 12. At the end of the 1997–98 season, the top nine clubs in Premier Division broke away from the Scottish League to form a new competition, the Scottish Premier League, with the club promoted from Division One. At the end of the 1999–2000 season two teams were added to the Scottish League. There was no relegation from the Premier League but two promoted from the First Division and three from each of the Second and Third Divisions. One team was relegated from the First Division and one from the Second Division, leaving 12 teams in each division. In season 2002–03, Falkirk were not promoted to the Premier League due to the failure of their ground to meet League standards. Inverness CT were promoted after a previous refusal in 2003–04 because of ground sharing. At the end of 2005–06 the Scottish League introduced play-offs for the team finishing second from the bottom of Division 1 against the winners of the second, third and fourth finishing teams in Division 2 and with a similar procedure for Division 2 and Division 3.

SCOTTISH LEAGUE PLAY-OFFS 2011–2012

■ *Denotes player sent off.*

DIVISION 1 SEMI-FINALS FIRST LEG

Airdrie U	(0) 0	Ayr U	(0) 0
Dumbarton	(1) 2	Arbroath	(1) 1

DIVISION 1 SEMI-FINALS SECOND LEG

Arbroath	(0) 0	Dumbarton	(0) 0
Ayr U	(0) 1	Airdrie U	(0) 3

DIVISION 1 FINAL FIRST LEG Wednesday, 16 May 2012

Dumbarton (2) 2 *(Prunty 29, Wallace 32)*

Airdrie U (1) 1 *(Bain 42)*   1746

Dumbarton: Grindlay; Nugent■, Creaney, Lithgow, Wallace (Gray), Agnew, Nicoll, McNiff, Gilhaney (Lamont), Prunty, Walker (Graham).
Airdrie U: Adam; Stallard, Lovering, MacDonald (McNeil), Lilley, Lynch, Bain (McLaren), Blockley, Stevenson, Holmes, Donnelly (Boyle).

DIVISION 1 FINAL SECOND LEG Sunday, 20 May 2012

Airdrie U (1) 1 *(Holmes 35)*

Dumbarton (3) 4 *(Dargo 9, 21, Gilhaney 45, Wallace 65)*   2914

Airdrie U: Adam; McNeil, Stallard (Lamie), Lilley, Lovering, Stevenson, Lynch (Bain■), Blockley, McLaren, Holmes, Donnelly (Boyle).
Dumbarton: Grindlay; Finnie, Lithgow, Creaney, McNiff, Wallace, Nicoll, Gilhaney (Lamont), Agnew, Prunty (Graham), Dargo (Walker).

DIVISION 2 SEMI-FINALS FIRST LEG

Elgin C	(0) 1	Albion R	(0) 0
Stranraer	(2) 3	Queen's Park	(0) 1

DIVISION 2 SEMI-FINALS SECOND LEG

Albion R	(0) 2	Elgin C	(0) 0
Queen's Park	(0) 0	Stranraer	(2) 2

DIVISION 2 FINAL FIRST LEG Wednesday, 16 May 2012

Stranraer (1) 2 *(McKeown 39, Moore 90)*

Albion R (0) 0   506

Stranraer: David Mitchell; Taggart, McKeown, McGregor, Gallagher, Noble, Winter, Aitken, Stirling, Malcolm, Grehan (Moore).
Albion R: Gaston; Donnelly, Lumsden, O'Byrne, Russell, Stevenson, Canning, McStay, Boyle (Marriott), Pierce (Love), Gemmell.

DIVISION 2 FINAL SECOND LEG Sunday, 20 May 2012

Albion R (3) 3 *(Chaplain 6, 33 (pen), Love 25)*

Stranraer (1) 1 *(Grehan 27)*   1008

Albion R: Gaston; Reid, Donnelly, Stevenson, O'Byrne, Ferry (Werndly), Boyle (Russell), Love, Canning, Chaplain (McStay), Acqua.
Stranraer: David Mitchell; Taggart, McGregor, McKeown, Noble, Winter (Borris), Aitken, Stirling, Gallagher (McColm), Malcolm (Moore), Grehan.
aet; Albion R won 5-3 on penalties.

PAST SCOTTISH LEAGUE CUP FINALS

1946–47	Rangers	4	Aberdeen	0
1947–48	East Fife	0 4	Falkirk	0* 1
1948–49	Rangers	2	Raith Rovers	0
1949–50	East Fife	3	Dunfermline	0
1950–51	Motherwell	3	Hibernian	0
1951–52	Dundee	3	Rangers	2
1952–53	Dundee	2	Kilmarnock	0
1953–54	East Fife	3	Partick Th	2
1954–55	Hearts	4	Motherwell	2
1955–56	Aberdeen	2	St Mirren	1
1956–57	Celtic	0 3	Partick Th	0 0
1957–58	Celtic	7	Rangers	1
1958–59	Hearts	5	Partick Th	1
1959–60	Hearts	2	Third Lanark	1
1960–61	Rangers	2	Kilmarnock	0
1961–62	Rangers	1 3	Hearts	1 1
1962–63	Hearts	1	Kilmarnock	0
1963–64	Rangers	5	Morton	0
1964–65	Rangers	2	Celtic	1
1965–66	Celtic	2	Rangers	1
1966–67	Celtic	1	Rangers	0
1967–68	Celtic	5	Dundee	3
1968–69	Celtic	6	Hibernian	2
1969–70	Celtic	1	St Johnstone	0
1970–71	Rangers	1	Celtic	0
1971–72	Partick Th	4	Celtic	1
1972–73	Hibernian	2	Celtic	1
1973–74	Dundee	1	Celtic	0
1974–75	Celtic	6	Hibernian	3
1975–76	Rangers	1	Celtic	0
1976–77	Aberdeen	2	Celtic	1
1977–78	Rangers	2	Celtic	1*
1978–79	Rangers	2	Aberdeen	1
1979–80	Aberdeen	0 0	Dundee U	0* 3
1980–81	Dundee	0	Dundee U	3
1981–82	Rangers	2	Dundee U	1
1982–83	Celtic	2	Rangers	1
1983–84	Rangers	3	Celtic	2
1984–85	Rangers	1	Dundee U	0
1985–86	Aberdeen	3	Hibernian	0
1986–87	Rangers	2	Celtic	1
1987–88	Rangers†	3	Aberdeen	3*
1988–89	Aberdeen	2	Rangers	3*
1989–90	Aberdeen	2	Rangers	1
1990–91	Rangers	2	Celtic	1
1991–92	Hibernian	2	Dunfermline Ath	0
1992–93	Rangers	2	Aberdeen	1*
1993–94	Rangers	2	Hibernian	1
1994–95	Raith R†	2	Celtic	2*
1995–96	Aberdeen	2	Dundee	0
1996–97	Rangers	4	Hearts	3
1997–98	Celtic	3	Dundee U	0
1998–99	Rangers	2	St Johnstone	1

1999–2000	Celtic	2	Aberdeen	0
2000–01	Celtic	3	Kilmarnock	0
2001–02	Rangers	4	Ayr U	0
2002–03	Rangers	2	Celtic	1
2003–04	Livingston	2	Hibernian	0
2004–05	Rangers	5	Motherwell	1
2005–06	Celtic	3	Dunfermline Ath	0
2006–07	Hibernian	5	Kilmarnock	1
2007–08	Rangers†	2	Dundee U	2*
2008–09	Celtic	2	Rangers	0*
2009–10	Rangers	1	St Mirren	0
2010–11	Rangers	2	Celtic	1*
2011–12	Kilmarnock	1	Celtic	0

†*Won on penalties *After extra time*

PAST LEAGUE CHALLENGE FINALS

1990–91	Dundee	3	Ayr U	2
1991–92	Hamilton A	1	Ayr U	0
1992–93	Hamilton A	3	Morton	2
1993–94	St Mirren	9	Falkirk	3
1994–95	Airdrieonians	3	Dundee	2
1995–96	Stenhousemuir	0	Dundee U	0
	(aet; Stenhousemuir won 5-4 on penalties.)			
1996–97	Stranraer	1	St Johnstone	0
1997–98	Falkirk	1	Qeeen of the S	0
1998–99	no competition			
1999–2000	Alloa Ath	4	Inverness CT	4
	(aet; Alloa Ath won 5-4 on penalties.)			
2000–01	Airdrieonians	2	Livingston	2
	(aet; Airdrieonians won 3-2 on penalties.)			
2001–02	Airdrieonians	2	Alloa Ath	1
2002–03	Queen of the S	2	Brechin C	0
2003–04	Inverness CT	2	Airdrie U	0
2004–05	Falkirk	2	Ross Co	1
2005–06	St Mirren	2	Hamilton A	1
2006–07	Ross Co	1	Clyde	1
	(aet; Ross Co won 5-4 on penalties.)			
2007–08	St Johnstone	3	Dunfermline Ath	2
2008–09	Airdrie	2	Ross Co	2
	(aet; Airdrie U won 3-2 on penalties.)			
2009–10	Dundee	3	Inverness CT	2
2010–11	Ross Co	2	Queen of the S	0
2011–12	Falkirk	1	Hamilton A	0

SCOTTISH COMMUNITIES LEAGUE CUP 2011–2012

FIRST ROUND

Airdrie U	(2) 5	Stirling Alb	(0) 0
Albion R	(1) 2	Falkirk	(1) 4
Alloa Ath	(0) 0	Morton	(1) 3
Annan Ath	(1) 1	Dunfermline Ath	(1) 2
Brechin C	(1) 2	Clyde	(1) 4
(aet.)			
Cowdenbeath	(2) 2	Stenhousemuir	(1) 2
(aet; Stenhousemuir won 4-3 on penalties.)			
Dumbarton	(0) 0	Dundee	(0) 4
East Fife	(0) 2	Elgin C	(0) 1
East Stirling	(0) 0	Ayr U	(2) 3
Forfar Ath	(1) 2	Peterhead	(0) 0
Livingston	(4) 6	Arbroath	(0) 0
Montrose	(1) 1	Raith R	(1) 4
Partick Th	(1) 1	Berwick R	(1) 3
Queen of the S	(1) 2	Stranraer	(1) 1
Ross Co	(0) 2	Queen's Park	(1) 1

SECOND ROUND

Aberdeen	(1) 1	Dundee	(0) 0
Airdrie U	(2) 2	Raith R	(0) 0
East Fife	(1) 2	Dunfermline Ath	(1) 1
Hamilton A	(1) 1	Ross Co	(0) 2
Hibernian	(2) 5	Berwick R	(0) 0
Morton	(2) 3	St Mirren	(1) 4
Queen of the S	(1) 3	Forfar Ath	(0) 0
Ayr U	(0) 1	Inverness CT	(0) 0
Clyde	(0) 0	Motherwell	(2) 4
Falkirk	(0) 3	Stenhousemuir	(1) 1
St Johnstone	(3) 3	Livingston	(0) 0

THIRD ROUND

Aberdeen	(1) 3	East Fife	(1) 3
(aet; East Fife won 4-3 on penalties.)			
Airdrie U	(0) 0	Dundee U	(1) 2
Kilmarnock	(2) 5	Queen of the S	(0) 0
Motherwell	(2) 2	Hibernian	(1) 2
(aet; Hibernian won 7-6 on penalties.)			
St Johnstone	(0) 0	St Mirren	(2) 2
Ayr U	(0) 1	Hearts	(0) 1
(aet; Ayr U won 4-1 on penalties.)			
Falkirk	(0) 3	Rangers	(0) 2
Ross Co	(0) 0	Celtic	(1) 2

QUARTER-FINALS

Dundee U	(0) 2	Falkirk	(0) 2
(aet; Falkirk won 5-4 on penalties.)			
Kilmarnock	(0) 2	East Fife	(0) 0
St Mirren	(0) 0	Ayr U	(0) 1
Hibernian	(1) 1	Celtic	(0) 4

SEMI-FINALS

Ayr U	(0) 0	Kilmarnock	(0) 1
(aet.)			
Falkirk	(1) 1	Celtic	(1) 3

FINAL

Celtic	(0) 0	Kilmarnock	(0) 1

RAMSDENS LEAGUE CHALLENGE CUP 2011–2012

FIRST ROUND NORTH-EAST

Arbroath	(0) 1	Dundee	(0) 2
Brechin C	(1) 1	Falkirk	(2) 2
Deveronvale	(0) 1	Stirling Alb	(1) 3
Forfar Ath	(1) 1	Buckie Th	(1) 1
(aet; Forfar Ath won 5-4 on penalties.)			
Montrose	(0) 1	East Fife	(3) 6
Peterhead	(1) 2	Alloa Ath	(1) 2
(aet; Peterhead won 5-4 on penalties.)			
Raith R	(0) 2	Cowdenbeath	(0) 1
Ross Co	(1) 1	Elgin C	(1) 2

FIRST ROUND SOUTH-WEST

Airdrie U	(0) 0	Livingston	(0) 5
Albion R	(0) 0	Annan Ath	(1) 2
Ayr U	(0) 2	Queen of the S	(0) 0
(aet.)			
Clyde	(1) 2	Berwick R	(2) 2
(aet; Berwick R won 4-3 on penalties.)			
Partick Th	(1) 2	Stenhousemuir	(0) 1
Queen's Park	(0) 0	Hamilton A	(0) 2
Stranraer	(0) 0	Morton	(2) 8
Dumbarton	(0) 3	East Stirling	(0) 2

SECOND ROUND

Annan Ath	(2) 4	Peterhead	(0) 2
Ayr U	(1) 3	Raith R	(0) 0
Dumbarton	(0) 0	Berwick R	(0) 2
East Fife	(0) 2	Elgin C	(0) 0
Falkirk	(1) 1	Dundee	(0) 0
Forfar Ath	(0) 0	Morton	(0) 5
Hamilton A	(0) 1	Partick Th	(0) 0
Livingston	(3) 5	Stirling Alb	(0) 0

QUARTER-FINALS

Ayr U	(0) 0	Annan Ath	(0) 1
Berwick R	(0) 1	Livingston	(1) 2
East Fife	(1) 1	Falkirk	(1) 4
Hamilton A	(2) 2	Morton	(1) 1

SEMI-FINALS

| Annan Ath | (0) 0 | Falkirk | (3) 3 |
| Hamilton A | (1) 1 | Livingston | (0) 0 |

FINAL

| Falkirk | (1) 1 | Hamilton A | (0) 0 |

WILLIAM HILL SCOTTISH CUP 2011–2012

FIRST ROUND

Rothes v Clachnacuddin	0-3
Fort William v Bo'ness U	0-4
Edinburgh C v Brora R	3-0
Nairn Co v Selkirk	2-1
Fraserburgh v Civil Service S	4-3
Wigtown & B v Preston Ath	2-0
Lossiemouth v Auchinleck T	1-2
Huntly v Newton Stewart	6-1
Forres Mechs v Irvine Meadow	2-2, 3-6
Dalbeattie Star v Inverurie Loco W	1-6
Wick Acad v Coldstream	9-1
Glasgow Univ v Cove R	0-4
Vale of Leithen v Girvan	1-0
Gala Fairydean v Hawick R A	8-1
Culter v Burntisland S	4-0
Edinburgh Univ v Whitehill Wel	0-3
St Cuthbert W v Keith	0-2

Golspie S received a bye.

SECOND ROUND

Clachnacuddin v Inverurie Loco W	1-1, 2-3
Vale of Leithen v Cove R	3-2
Gala Fairydean v Golspie S	5-2
Bo'ness U v Whitehill Wel	2-1
Fraserburgh v Elgin C	0-0, 2-5
Wigtown & B v Stranraer	0-9
Peterhead v Nairn Co	2-0
Wick Acad v Keith	0-1
Culter v Spartans	0-2

Spartans expelled for fielding an ineligible player.

Alloa Ath v Annan Ath	2-2, 0-2
Deveronvale v Berwick R	4-0
Auchinleck T v Threave R	8-1
East Stirling v Buckie T	1-1, 4-2
Huntly v Queen's Park	0-3
Montrose v Clyde	2-1
Edinburgh C v Irvine Meadow	0-1

THIRD ROUND

Airdrie U	(5) 11	Gala Fairydean	(0) 0
Auchinleck T	(1) 3	Vale of Leithen	(1) 1
Ayr U	(1) 2	Montrose	(1) 2
Bo'ness U	(0) 0	Cowdenbeath	(1) 3
Brechin C	(1) 3	Dumbarton	(0) 0
Culter	(1) 1	Partick Th	(1) 1
East Fife	(2) 5	East Stirling	(0) 0
Elgin C	(1) 1	Queen's Park	(0) 1
Inverurie Loco W	(1) 2	Peterhead	(3) 4
Irvine Meadow	(0) 0	Livingston	(4) 6
Keith	(0) 0	Arbroath	(0) 1
Morton	(3) 5	Deveronvale	(1) 1
Ross Co	(2) 4	Albion R	(0) 0
Stenhousemuir	(4) 4	Annan Ath	(0) 0
Stirling Alb	(1) 1	Dundee	(1) 2
Stranraer	(0) 1	Forfar Ath	(1) 1

THIRD ROUND REPLAYS

Forfar Ath	(0) 3	Stranraer	(0) 0
Partick Th	(3) 4	Culter	(0) 0
Queen's Park	(2) 3	Elgin C	(0) 1
Montrose	(0) 1	Ayr U	(1) 2

FOURTH ROUND

Airdrie U	(0) 2	Dundee U	(2) 6
Cowdenbeath	(1) 2	Hibernian	(2) 3
Dundee	(0) 1	Kilmarnock	(1) 1
Falkirk	(2) 2	East Fife	(0) 0
Forfar Ath	(0) 0	Aberdeen	(2) 4
Hearts	(0) 1	Auchinleck T	(0) 0
Inverness CT	(0) 1	Dunfermline Ath	(1) 1
Livingston	(1) 1	Ayr U	(1) 2
Motherwell	(2) 4	Queen's Park	(0) 0
Partick Th	(0) 0	Queen of the S	(0) 1
Raith R	(1) 1	Morton	(0) 2
Ross Co	(1) 7	Stenhousemuir	(0) 0
St Johnstone	(1) 2	Brechin C	(1) 1
St Mirren	(0) 0	Hamilton A	(0) 0
Arbroath	(0) 0	Rangers	(2) 4
Peterhead	(0) 0	Celtic	(1) 3

FOURTH ROUND REPLAYS

Kilmarnock	(2) 2	Dundee	(0) 1
Dunfermline Ath	(1) 1	Inverness CT	(0) 3
(aet.)			
Hamilton A	(0) 0	St Mirren	(1) 1

FIFTH ROUND

Aberdeen	(0) 1	Queen of the S	(0) 1
Hibernian	(1) 1	Kilmarnock	(0) 0
Inverness CT	(0) 0	Celtic	(1) 2
Motherwell	(5) 6	Morton	(0) 0
St Mirren	(1) 1	Ross Co	(1) 1
Hearts	(1) 1	St Johnstone	(0) 1
Rangers	(0) 0	Dundee U	(2) 2
Ayr U	(1) 2	Falkirk	(1) 1

FIFTH ROUND REPLAYS

Queen of the S	(0) 1	Aberdeen	(1) 2
Ross Co	(0) 1	St Mirren	(1) 2
St Johnstone	(0) 1	Hearts	(0) 2
(aet.)			

QUARTER-FINALS

Ayr U	(0) 0	Hibernian	(2) 2
Hearts	(1) 2	St Mirren	(1) 2
Dundee U	(0) 0	Celtic	(0) 4
Motherwell	(0) 1	Aberdeen	(2) 2

QUARTER-FINAL REPLAY

St Mirren	(0) 0	Hearts	(1) 2

SEMI-FINALS

Aberdeen	(0) 1	Hibernian	(1) 2
Celtic	(0) 1	Hearts	(0) 2

FINAL

Hibernian	(1) 1	Hearts	(2) 5

PAST SCOTTISH CUP FINALS

1874	Queen's Park	2	Clydesdale	0
1875	Queen's Park	3	Renton	0
1876	Queen's Park	1 2	Third Lanark	1 0
1877	Vale of Leven	0 1 3	Rangers	0 1 2
1878	Vale of Leven	1	Third Lanark	0
1879	Vale of Leven	1	Rangers	1
	Vale of Leven awarded cup, Rangers did not appear for replay			
1880	Queen's Park	3	Thornlibank	0
1881	Queen's Park	2 3	Dumbarton	1 1
	Replayed because of protest			
1882	Queen's Park	2 4	Dumbarton	2 1
1883	Dumbarton	2 2	Vale of Leven	2 1
1884	*Queen's Park awarded cup when Vale of Leven did not appear for the final*			
1885	Renton	0 3	Vale of Leven	0 1
1886	Queen's Park	3	Renton	1
1887	Hibernian	2	Dumbarton	1
1888	Renton	6	Cambuslang	1
1889	Third Lanark	3 2	Celtic	0 1
	Replayed because of protest			
1890	Queen's Park	1 2	Vale of Leven	1 1
1891	Hearts	1	Dumbarton	0
1892	Celtic	1 5	Queen's Park	0 1
	Replayed because of protest			
1893	Queen's Park	2	Celtic	1
1894	Rangers	3	Celtic	1
1895	St Bernards	3	Renton	1
1896	Hearts	3	Hibernian	1
1897	Rangers	5	Dumbarton	1
1898	Rangers	2	Kilmarnock	0
1899	Celtic	2	Rangers	0
1900	Celtic	4	Queen's Park	3
1901	Hearts	4	Celtic	3
1902	Hibernian	1	Celtic	0
1903	Rangers	1 0 2	Hearts	1 0 0
1904	Celtic	3	Rangers	2
1905	Third Lanark	0 3	Rangers	0 1
1906	Hearts	1	Third Lanark	0
1907	Celtic	3	Hearts	0
1908	Celtic	5	St Mirren	1
1909	*After two drawn games between Celtic and Rangers, 2-2, 1-1, there was a riot and the cup was withheld*			
1910	Dundee	2 0 2	Clyde	2 0 1
1911	Celtic	0 2	Hamilton Acad	0 0
1912	Celtic	2	Clyde	0
1913	Falkirk	2	Raith R	0
1914	Celtic	0 4	Hibernian	0 1
1920	Kilmarnock	3	Albion R	2
1921	Partick Th	1	Rangers	0
1922	Morton	1	Rangers	0
1923	Celtic	1	Hibernian	0
1924	Airdrieonians	2	Hibernian	0
1925	Celtic	2	Dundee	1
1926	St Mirren	2	Celtic	0
1927	Celtic	3	East Fife	1
1928	Rangers	4	Celtic	0
1929	Kilmarnock	2	Rangers	0
1930	Rangers	0 2	Partick Th	0 1

Year	Winner	Score	Runner-up	Score
1931	Celtic	2 4	Motherwell	2 2
1932	Rangers	1 3	Kilmarnock	1 0
1933	Celtic	1	Motherwell	0
1934	Rangers	5	St Mirren	0
1935	Rangers	2	Hamilton A	1
1936	Rangers	1	Third Lanark	0
1937	Celtic	2	Aberdeen	1
1938	East Fife	1 4	Kilmarnock	1 2
1939	Clyde	4	Motherwell	0
1947	Aberdeen	2	Hibernian	1
1948	Rangers	1 1	Morton	1 0
1949	Rangers	4	Clyde	1
1950	Rangers	3	East Fife	0
1951	Celtic	1	Motherwell	0
1952	Motherwell	4	Dundee	0
1953	Rangers	1 1	Aberdeen	1 0
1954	Celtic	2	Aberdeen	1
1955	Clyde	1 1	Celtic	1 0
1956	Hearts	3	Celtic	1
1957	Falkirk	1 2	Kilmarnock	1 1
1958	Clyde	1	Hibernian	0
1959	St Mirren	3	Aberdeen	1
1960	Rangers	2	Kilmarnock	0
1961	Dunfermline Ath	0 2	Celtic	0 0
1962	Rangers	2	St Mirren	0
1963	Rangers	1 3	Celtic	1 0
1964	Rangers	3	Dundee	1
1965	Celtic	3	Dunfermline Ath	2
1966	Rangers	0 1	Celtic	0 0
1967	Celtic	2	Aberdeen	0
1968	Dunfermline Ath	3	Hearts	1
1969	Celtic	4	Rangers	0
1970	Aberdeen	3	Celtic	1
1971	Celtic	1 2	Rangers	1 1
1972	Celtic	6	Hibernian	1
1973	Rangers	3	Celtic	2
1974	Celtic	3	Dundee U	0
1975	Celtic	3	Airdrieonians	1
1976	Rangers	3	Hearts	1
1977	Celtic	1	Rangers	0
1978	Rangers	2	Aberdeen	1
1979	Rangers	0 0 3	Hibernian	0 0 2
1980	Celtic	1	Rangers	0
1981	Rangers	0 4	Dundee U	0 1 (aet)
1982	Aberdeen	4	Rangers	1 (aet)
1983	Aberdeen	1	Rangers	0 (aet)
1984	Aberdeen	2	Celtic	1 (aet)
1985	Celtic	2	Dundee U	1
1986	Aberdeen	3	Hearts	0
1987	St Mirren	1	Dundee U	0 (aet)
1988	Celtic	2	Dundee U	1
1989	Celtic	1	Rangers	0
1990	Aberdeen	0	Celtic	0
	(aet; Aberdeen won 9-8 on penalties)			
1991	Motherwell	4	Dundee U	3 (aet)
1992	Rangers	2	Airdrieonians	1
1993	Rangers	2	Aberdeen	1
1994	Dundee U	1	Rangers	0
1995	Celtic	1	Airdrieonians	0

1996	Rangers	5	Hearts	1
1997	Kilmarnock	1	Falkirk	0
1998	Hearts	2	Rangers	1
1999	Rangers	1	Celtic	0
2000	Rangers	4	Aberdeen	0
2001	Celtic	3	Hibernian	0
2002	Rangers	3	Celtic	2
2003	Rangers	1	Dundee	0
2004	Celtic	3	Dunfermline Ath	1
2005	Celtic	1	Dundee U	0
2006	Hearts	1	Gretna	1
	(aet; Hearts won 4-2 on penalties)			
2007	Celtic	1	Dunfermline Ath	0
2008	Rangers	3	Queen of the S	2
2009	Rangers	1	Falkirk	0
2010	Dundee U	3	Ross Co	0
2011	Celtic	3	Motherwell	0
2012	Hearts	5	Hibernian	1

PRESS AND JOURNAL HIGHLAND LEAGUE 2011–2012

						Total					Home					Away			
	P	W	D	L	F	A	W	D	L	F	A	W	D	L	F	A	GD	Pts
1 Forres Mechanics	34	24	5	5	85	35	14	2	1	44	18	10	3	4	41	17	50	77
2 Cove Rangers	34	23	7	4	93	33	12	4	1	50	14	11	3	3	43	19	60	76
3 Nairn County	34	19	9	6	92	43	10	4	3	51	23	9	5	3	41	20	49	66
4 Inverurie Locos	34	20	5	9	70	35	10	2	5	34	16	10	3	4	36	19	35	65
5 Buckie Thistle	34	18	7	9	79	45	10	4	3	41	20	8	3	6	38	25	34	61
6 Fraserburgh	34	17	8	9	79	63	12	2	3	45	28	5	6	6	34	35	16	59
7 Deveronvale	34	17	4	13	75	50	9	2	6	36	21	8	2	7	39	29	25	55
8 Wick Academy	34	16	7	11	77	55	10	5	2	52	23	6	2	9	25	32	22	55
9 Keith	34	16	6	12	85	57	8	3	6	43	24	8	3	6	42	33	28	54
10 Clachnacuddin	34	14	8	12	79	65	10	1	6	47	29	4	7	6	32	36	14	50
11 Formartine Utd	34	14	7	13	62	60	9	4	4	36	25	5	3	9	26	35	2	49
12 Lossiemouth	34	15	4	15	51	52	8	1	8	28	30	7	3	7	23	22	–1	49
13 Huntly	34	14	4	16	50	67	7	4	6	26	28	7	0	10	24	39	–17	46
14 Turriff United	34	13	4	17	61	64	8	3	6	34	25	5	1	11	27	39	–3	43
15 Rothes	34	7	5	22	31	80	4	2	11	17	40	3	3	11	14	40	–49	26
16 Brora	34	6	2	26	33	115	4	2	11	24	49	2	0	15	9	66	–82	20
17 Strathspey Thistle	34	3	2	29	27	102	3	0	14	13	45	0	2	15	14	57	–75	11
18 Fort William	34	1	4	29	14	122	0	4	13	7	57	1	0	16	7	65	–108	7

CENTRAL TAXIS EAST OF SCOTLAND LEAGUE PREMIER DIVISION 2011–2012

	P	W	D	L	F	A	GD	Pts
1 Stirling University	22	16	3	3	74	32	42	51
2 Spartans	22	16	3	3	66	28	38	51
3 Whitehill Welfare	22	12	3	7	45	34	11	39
4 Edinburgh University	22	10	3	9	38	26	12	33
5 Edinburgh City	22	10	3	9	41	39	2	33
6 Gretna 2008	22	9	6	7	40	46	–6	33
7 Civil Service Strollers	22	10	1	11	38	46	–8	31
8 Vale of Leithen	22	9	1	12	49	47	2	28
9 Tynecastle	22	8	3	11	33	52	–19	27
10 Lothian Thistle Hutchison Vale	22	6	3	13	36	50	–14	21
11 Leith Athletic	22	5	4	13	32	59	–27	19
12 Selkirk	22	3	3	16	24	57	–33	12

CORBETTSPORTS.COM WELSH PREMIER LEAGUE 2011–2012

			Total					Home					Away				
	P	W	D	L	F	A	W	D	L	F	A	W	D	L	F	A	GD	Pts
1 The New Saints	32	23	5	4	75	31	12	2	2	46	19	11	3	2	29	12	44	74
2 Bangor C	32	22	3	7	72	45	11	2	3	40	25	11	1	4	32	20	27	69
3 Neath Ath	32	18	8	6	60	36	11	2	3	34	16	7	6	3	26	20	24	62
4 Llanelli	32	18	5	9	63	37	9	1	6	33	19	9	4	3	30	18	26	59
5 Bala T	32	14	7	11	48	41	6	5	5	24	17	8	2	6	24	24	7	49
6 Prestatyn T	32	8	4	20	41	63	5	2	9	21	32	3	2	11	20	31	–22	28
7 Airbus UK Broughton	32	10	9	13	48	50	6	6	4	29	25	4	3	9	19	25	–2	39
8 Aberystwyth T	32	8	10	14	45	50	4	6	6	23	26	4	4	8	22	24	–5	33
9 Port Talbot T	32	8	9	15	39	51	6	4	6	21	22	2	5	9	18	29	–12	33
10 Afan Lido	32	7	11	14	40	55	5	5	6	18	20	2	6	8	22	35	–15	32
11 Carmarthen T	32	10	2	20	33	67	8	1	7	22	25	2	1	13	11	42	–34	32
12 Newtown	32	7	5	20	44	82	5	3	8	20	31	2	2	12	24	51	–38	23

Top 6 teams split after 22 games. Aberystwyth T deducted 1 point. Newtown deducted 3 points.

NORTHERN IRELAND CARLING PREMIERSHIP 2011–2012

			Total					Home					Away				
	P	W	D	L	F	A	W	D	L	F	A	W	D	L	F	A	GD	Pts
1 Linfield	38	27	4	7	79	29	16	2	2	43	8	11	2	5	36	21	50	85
2 Portadown	38	22	5	11	72	47	10	3	4	34	20	12	2	7	38	27	25	71
3 Cliftonville	38	21	6	11	83	62	11	2	6	43	33	10	4	5	40	29	21	69
4 Coleraine	38	18	12	8	61	38	11	5	3	33	18	7	7	5	28	20	23	66
5 Crusaders	38	18	10	10	63	47	9	6	5	34	25	9	4	5	29	22	16	64
6 Glentoran	38	16	9	13	67	52	6	5	7	30	31	10	4	6	37	21	15	57
7 Ballymena U	38	14	8	16	66	71	3	6	10	26	42	11	2	6	40	29	–5	50
8 Donegal Celtic	38	12	5	21	44	80	4	3	12	20	40	8	2	9	24	40	–36	41
9 Dungannon Swifts	38	8	11	19	42	71	5	5	10	23	42	3	6	9	19	29	–29	35
10 Glenavon	38	8	10	20	60	71	7	2	9	29	28	1	8	11	31	43	–11	34
11 Lisburn Distillery	38	8	8	22	56	84	4	1	15	26	47	4	7	7	30	37	–28	32
12 Carrick Rangers	38	7	10	21	50	91	2	9	8	27	41	5	1	13	23	50	–41	31

Top 6 teams split after 33 games.

REPUBLIC OF IRELAND LEAGUE 2011

			Total					Home					Away				
	P	W	D	L	F	A	W	D	L	F	A	W	D	L	F	A	GD	Pts
1 Shamrock Rovers	36	23	8	5	69	24	13	3	2	43	11	10	5	3	26	13	+45	77
2 Sligo Rovers	36	22	7	7	73	19	13	2	3	44	10	9	5	4	29	9	+54	73
3 Derry City	36	18	14	4	63	23	9	8	1	34	7	9	6	3	29	16	+40	68
4 St Patrick's Ath	36	17	12	7	62	35	8	9	1	36	18	9	3	6	26	17	+27	63
5 Bohemians	36	17	9	10	39	27	7	4	7	15	14	10	5	3	24	13	+12	60
6 Bray Wanderers	36	15	6	15	53	50	7	1	10	23	27	8	5	5	30	23	+3	51
7 Dundalk	36	11	11	14	50	53	6	6	6	25	22	5	5	8	25	31	–3	44
8 UCD	36	10	4	22	42	80	8	1	9	27	31	2	3	13	15	49	–38	34
9 Drogheda United	36	7	4	25	32	77	3	3	12	16	38	4	1	13	16	39	–45	25
10 Galway United	36	1	3	32	20	115	0	2	16	10	52	1	1	16	10	63	–95	6

UEFA CHAMPIONS LEAGUE 2011–2012

■ *Denotes player sent off.* * *Winner after extra time.*

FIRST QUALIFYING ROUND FIRST LEG

FC Santa Coloma	(0) 0	F91 Dudelange	(0) 2
Tre Fiori	(0) 0	Valletta	(1) 3

FIRST QUALIFYING ROUND SECOND LEG

F91 Dudelange	(0) 2	FC Santa Coloma	(0) 0
Valletta	(0) 2	Tre Fiori	(1) 1

SECOND QUALIFYING ROUND FIRST LEG

Maribor	(2) 2	F91 Dudelange	(0) 0
Mogren	(1) 1	Litex	(0) 2
Pyunik	(0) 0	Viktoria Plzen	(3) 4
Shamrock R	(1) 1	Flora	(0) 0
Slovan Bratislava	(1) 2	Tobol	(0) 0
Valletta	(1) 2	Ekranas	(3) 3
Bangor C	(0) 0	HJK Helsinki	(1) 3
(Played at Rhyl.)			
Dinamo Zagreb	(1) 3	Neftci	(0) 0
Linfield	(1) 1	BATE Borisov	(1) 1
Maccabi Haifa	(1) 5	Borac	(1) 1
Malmo	(0) 2	HB	(0) 0
Partizan Belgrade	(0) 4	Skendija 79	(0) 0
Rosenborg	(1) 5	Breidablik	(0) 0
Skenderbeu	(0) 0	Apoel	(0) 2
Skonto Riga	(0) 0	Wisla	(1) 1
Sturm Graz	(0) 2	Videoton	(0) 0
Zestafoni	(3) 3	Dacia	(0) 0

Tuesday, 12 July 2011

Shamrock R (1) 1 *(Turner 34)*

Flora (0) 0   5026

Shamrock R: Mannus; O'Donnell (O'Neill 83), Oman, Sullivan, Sives, Stevens, Turner (McCormack 71), Finn, Dennehy, Kelly (McCabe 76), Twigg.
Flora: Pedok; Palatu, Kams, Jurgenson, Baranov, Minkenen, Mosnikov, Luts, Beglarishvili (Herrem 46), Henri Anier (Hannes Anier 88), Alliku (Mashichev 71).

Wednesday, 13 July 2011

Bangor C (0) 0

HJK Helsinki (1) 3 *(Sadik 14, 55, Sorsa 89)*   1189

Bangor C: Idzi; Morley, Roberts, Brewerton, Johnston, Garside, Hoy, Davies, Jones (Wilson 68), Ward (Smyth 67), Bull (Edwards 67).
HJK Helsinki: Wallen; Kansikas, Lindstrom, Sumusalo, Moren, Riihilahti, Bah, Mannstrom (Sorsa 63), Ring, Sadik (Fowler 71), Pukki (Parikka 82).
Played at Rhyl.

Linfield (1) 1 *(Fordyce 5)*

BATE Borisov (1) 1 *(Renan 38 (pen))* 1212

Linfield: Blayney; Casement (Burns BJ 82), Ervin, Watson, Armstrong, Garrett, Lowry, Hanley, Fordyce, Carvill (McCaul 90), Thompson (McAllister 77).

BATE Borisov: Gutor; Filipenko, Yurevich, Bordachev, Simic, Likhtarovich (Olekhnovich 76), Nekhajchik, Renan, Volodko A, Pavlov (Rudik 86), Skavysh (Kontsevoy 70).

SECOND QUALIFYING ROUND SECOND LEG

BATE Borisov	(0) 2	Linfield	(0) 0
Ekranas	(1) 1	Valletta	(0) 0
F91 Dudelange	(0) 1	Maribor	(1) 3
Flora	(0) 0	Shamrock R	(0) 0
HB	(0) 1	Malmo	(0) 1
HJK Helsinki	(2) 10	Bangor C	(0) 0
Litex	(1) 3	Mogren	(0) 0
Neftci	(0) 0	Dinamo Zagreb	(0) 0
Skendija 79	(0) 0	Partizan Belgrade	(0) 1
Tobol	(0) 1	Slovan Bratislava	(1) 1
Viktoria Plzen	(3) 5	Pyunik	(0) 1
Wisla	(0) 2	Skonto Riga	(0) 0
Apoel	(0) 4	Skenderbeu	(0) 0
Borac	(2) 3	Maccabi Haifa	(1) 2
Breidablik	(1) 2	Rosenborg	(0) 0
Dacia	(1) 2	Zestafoni	(0) 0
Videoton	(3) 3	Sturm Graz	(2) 2

Tuesday, 19 July 2011

BATE Borisov (0) 2 *(Nekhajchik 58, Pavlov 61)*

Linfield (0) 0 5200

BATE Borisov: Gutor; Filipenko, Yurevich, Shitov, Simic, Likhtarovich (Olekhnovich 78), Nekhajchik, Renan (Volodko A 64), Pavlov, Patotsky, Kontsevoy (Rodionov 80).
Linfield: Blayney; Casement (Burns BJ 70), Ervin, Watson, Armstrong, Garrett, Lowry, Hanley, Fordyce (McCaul 76), Carvill, McAllister (Burns A 62).

Flora (0) 0

Shamrock R (0) 0 2970

Flora: Pedok; Palatu, Kams, Jurgenson, Baranov, Minkenen, Mosnikov (Beglarishvili 72), Luts, Mashichev (Peitre 84), Henri Anier, Alliku (Dupikov 10).
Shamrock R: Mannus; Oman, Sullivan, Sives, Stevens, Turner (O'Donnell 82), Finn, McCormack, Kelly, Dennehy, Twigg.

HJK Helsinki (2) 10 *(Ring 37, Sadik 44, Zeneli 47, 54, Rafinha 52, Pukki 64, 67, Kastrati 66, 88, Parikka 71)*

Bangor C (0) 0 5944

HJK Helsinki: Wallen; Lindstrom, Sumusalo, Moren, Rafinha, Zeneli, Riihilahti (Fowler 59), Bah, Ring, Sadik (Kastrati 59), Pukki (Parikka 69).
Bangor C: Idzi; Morley, Roberts, Brewerton, Johnston, Hoy (Williams 56), Davies (Garside 73), Jones (Walsh 56), Ward, Wilson, Bull.

THIRD QUALIFYING ROUND FIRST LEG

Apoel	(0) 0	Slovan Bratislava	(0) 0
Dynamo Kiev	(0) 0	Rubin	(1) 2
Ekranas	(0) 0	BATE Borisov	(0) 0
Genk	(0) 2	Partizan Belgrade	(0) 1
Litex	(1) 1	Wisla	(1) 2
Rangers	(0) 0	Malmo	(1) 1
Twente	(1) 2	Vaslui	(0) 0
Zestafoni	(0) 1	Sturm Graz	(0) 1
Benfica	(0) 2	Trabzonspor	(0) 0
FC Copenhagen	(1) 1	Shamrock R	(0) 0
HJK Helsinki	(1) 1	Dinamo Zagreb	(1) 2
Maccabi Haifa	(1) 2	Maribor	(1) 1
Odense	(0) 1	Panathinaikos	(0) 1
Rosenborg	(0) 0	Viktoria Plzen	(1) 1
Standard Liege	(0) 1	Zurich	(0) 1

Tuesday, 26 July 2011

Rangers (0) 0

Malmo (1) 1 *(Larsson 18)* 28,828

Rangers: McGregor; Whittaker, Papac, Bougherra, Weir (Juanma Ortiz 29), Wallace, Davis, McCulloch, Jelavic, Naismith, Edu.

Malmo: Melicharek; Andersson, Halsti, Jansson, Hamad, Pekalski, Durmaz, Wilton Figueiredo (Rexhepi 69), Mutavdzic, Larsson (Yago 81), Mehmeti (Nazari A 54).

Wednesday, 27 July 2011

FC Copenhagen (1) 1 *(Ottesen 4)*

Shamrock R (0) 0 11,571

FC Copenhagen: Wiland; Ottesen, Jorgensen, Thomsen (Sigurdsson 46), Bengtsson, Grindheim, Claudemir, Diouf, Bolanos, Delaney (Absalonsen 61), Cesar Santin (Nordstrand 70).

Shamrock R: Thompson; Rice (Kilduff 90), Oman (Murray 83), Sullivan, Sives, Stevens, Finn, McCormack, Kelly (McCabe 54), Dennehy, Twigg.

THIRD QUALIFYING ROUND SECOND LEG

BATE Borisov	(2) 3	Ekranas	(1) 1
Panathinaikos	(1) 3	Odense	(1) 4
(Behind closed doors.)			
Shamrock R	(0) 0	FC Copenhagen	(1) 2
Dinamo Zagreb	(0) 1	HJK Helsinki	(0) 0
Malmo	(0) 1	Rangers	(1) 1
Maribor	(1) 1	Maccabi Haifa	(1) 1
Partizan Belgrade	(1) 1	Genk	(0) 1
Rubin	(1) 2	Dynamo Kiev	(0) 1
Slovan Bratislava	(0) 0	Apoel	(0) 2
Sturm Graz	(0) 1	Zestafoni	(0) 0
Trabzonspor	(1) 1	Benfica	(1) 1
Vaslui	(0) 0	Twente	(0) 0

Viktoria Plzen	(0) 3	Rosenborg	(1) 2
Wisla	(1) 3	Litex	(0) 1
Zurich	(0) 1	Standard Liege	(0) 0

Tuesday, 2 August 2011

Shamrock R (0) 0

FC Copenhagen (1) 2 *(N'Doye 42, Bolanos 73)*   5901

Shamrock R: Thompson; Murray, Sullivan, Sives, Stevens, Turner, Finn (Rice 75), McCormack, Dennehy, McCabe (Kelly 65), Twigg (Kilduff 75).
FC Copenhagen: Wiland; Ottesen, Sigurdsson, Jorgensen, Bengtsson, Grindheim, Kristensen (Absalonsen 90), Claudemir, Diouf (Cesar Santin 83), Bolanos (Delaney 79), N'Doye.

Wednesday, 3 August 2011

Malmo (0) 1 *(Hamad 80)*

Rangers (1) 1 *(Jelavic 24)*   19,084

Malmo: Melicharek; Andersson, Ricardinho■, Jansson, Hamad, Pekalski, Durmaz, Wilton Figueiredo, Mutavdzic (Rexhepi 46), Larsson, Mehmeti (Stenstrom 33).
Rangers: McGregor; Whittaker■, Wallace, Edu, Bougherra■, McCulloch, Juanma Ortiz (Hemmings 84), Davis, Jelavic, Naismith, Papac.

PLAY-OFF ROUND FIRST LEG

Arsenal	(1) 1	Udinese	(0) 0
BATE Borisov	(0) 1	Sturm Graz	(1) 1
FC Copenhagen	(0) 1	Viktoria Plzen	(0) 3
Lyon	(2) 3	Rubin	(1) 1
Twente	(1) 2	Benfica	(2) 2
Bayern Munich	(1) 2	Zurich	(0) 0
Dinamo Zagreb	(1) 4	Malmo	(1) 1
Maccabi Haifa	(2) 2	Genk	(0) 1
Odense	(0) 1	Villarreal	(0) 0
Wisla	(0) 1	Apoel	(0) 0

Tuesday, 16 August 2011

Arsenal (1) 1 *(Walcott 4)*

Udinese (0) 0   58,159

Arsenal: Szczesny; Sagna, Gibbs (Djourou 46) (Jenkinson 56), Song Billong, Vermaelen, Koscielny, Walcott, Ramsey, Gervinho, Chamakh, Rosicky (Frimpong 73).
Udinese: Handanovic; Danilo, Benatia, Isla, Armero, Ekstrand, Neuton (Pasquale 59), Pinzi (Abdi 87), Asamoah, Agyemang-Badu, Di Natale.

PLAY-OFF ROUND SECOND LEG

Apoel	(1) 3	Wisla	(0) 1
Genk	(2) 2	Maccabi Haifa	(1) 1
(aet; Genk won 4-1 on penalties.)			
Malmo	(0) 2	Dinamo Zagreb	(0) 0
Villarreal	(0) 3	Odense	(0) 0
Zurich	(0) 0	Bayern Munich	(1) 1

Benfica	(0) 3	Twente	(0) 1
Rubin	(0) 1	Lyon	(0) 1
Sturm Graz	(0) 0	BATE Borisov	(1) 2
Udinese	(1) 1	Arsenal	(0) 2
Viktoria Plzen	(0) 2	FC Copenhagen	(1) 1

Wednesday, 24 August 2011

Udinese (1) 1 *(Di Natale 39)*

Arsenal (0) 2 *(Van Persie 55, Walcott 70)*   26,031

Udinese: Handanovic; Danilo, Benatia (Pasquale 87), Isla (Denis 83), Armero, Ekstrand, Neuton, Pinzi (Fabbrini 63), Asamoah, Agyemang-Badu, Di Natale.
Arsenal: Szczesny; Sagna, Jenkinson, Song Billong, Vermaelen, Djourou, Walcott (Arshavin 90), Ramsey, Gervinho (Traore 86), Van Persie, Frimpong (Rosicky 46).

GROUP A

Manchester C	(0) 1	Napoli	(0) 1
Villarreal	(0) 0	Bayern Munich	(1) 2
Bayern Munich	(2) 2	Manchester C	(0) 0
Napoli	(2) 2	Villarreal	(0) 0
Manchester C	(1) 2	Villarreal	(1) 1
Napoli	(1) 1	Bayern Munich	(1) 1
Bayern Munich	(3) 3	Napoli	(1) 2
Villarreal	(0) 0	Manchester C	(2) 3
Bayern Munich	(2) 3	Villarreal	(0) 1
Napoli	(1) 2	Manchester C	(1) 1
Manchester C	(1) 2	Bayern Munich	(0) 0
Villarreal	(0) 0	Napoli	(0) 2

Wednesday, 14 September 2011

Manchester C (0) 1 *(Kolarov 74)*

Napoli (0) 1 *(Cavani 69)*   44,026

Manchester C: Hart; Zabaleta, Kolarov (Clichy 75), Kompany, Lescott, Barry, Nasri (Johnson A 76), Toure Y, Aguero, Dzeko (Tevez 81), Silva.
Napoli: De Sanctis; Aronica, Zuniga, Cannavaro, Campagnaro, Maggio, Gargano, Inler, Hamsik (Santana 89), Cavani (Pandev 84), Lavezzi (Dzemaili 57).

Tuesday, 27 September 2011

Bayern Munich (2) 2 *(Gomez 38, 45)*

Manchester C (0) 0   66,000

Bayern Munich: Neuer; Lahm, Rafinha, Van Buyten, Boateng, Schweinsteiger, Ribery (Robben 90), Luiz Gustavo, Kroos (Tymoschuk 82), Gomez (Petersen 90), Muller.
Manchester C: Hart; Richards, Clichy, Kompany, Toure K, Barry (Kolarov 73), Nasri (Milner 70), Toure Y, Aguero, Dzeko (De Jong 55), Silva.

Tuesday, 18 October 2011

Manchester C (1) 2 *(Marchena 43 (og), Aguero 90)*

Villarreal (1) 1 *(Cani 4)*   43,326

Manchester C: Hart; Zabaleta, Kolarov, De Jong (Aguero 62), Lescott, Kompany, Nasri (Milner 80), Toure Y, Dzeko, Silva, Johnson A (Barry 40).

Villarreal: Diego Lopez; Marchena, Rodriguez, Zapata, Catala, De Guzman (Marcos Gullon 88), Cani (Mario 82), Borja Valero, Soriano, Hernan Perez (Mubarak 80), Rossi.

Wednesday, 2 November 2011

Villarreal (0) 0

Manchester C (2) 3 *(Toure Y 30, 71, Balotelli 45 (pen))*   19,358

Villarreal: Diego Lopez; Marchena, Rodriguez, Musacchio, Catala, Mario, De Guzman (Angel Lopez 78), Borja Valero, Hernan Perez (Joan Oriol 84), Mubarak (Gerard Bordas 77), Joselu.
Manchester C: Hart; Zabaleta, Clichy, Kompany, Savic, De Jong, Milner, Toure Y (Aguero 74), Balotelli (Kolarov 83), Silva (Johnson A 65), Nasri.

Tuesday, 22 November 2011

Napoli (1) 2 *(Cavani 18, 49)*

Manchester C (1) 1 *(Balotelli 33)*   57,575

Napoli: De Sanctis; Dossena (Fernandez 88), Aronica, Cannavaro, Campagnaro, Maggio, Gargano, Inler (Dzemaili 59), Hamsik, Cavani (Pandev 83), Lavezzi.
Manchester C: Hart; Zabaleta (Johnson A 86), Kolarov, Kompany, Lescott, De Jong (Nasri 71), Silva, Toure Y, Balotelli, Dzeko (Aguero 81), Milner.

Wednesday, 7 December 2011

Manchester C (1) 2 *(Silva 37, Toure Y 52)*

Bayern Munich (0) 0   46,002

Manchester C: Hart; Savic, Clichy, Kompany, Lescott, Barry, Silva (Johnson A 84), Toure Y (Balotelli 81), Aguero, Dzeko (De Jong 77), Nasri.
Bayern Munich: Butt; Rafinha, Boateng, Badstuber, Contento, Tymoschuk, Pranjic, Luiz Gustavo, Alaba, Olic, Petersen (Usami 81).

Group A Table	P	W	D	L	F	A	Pts
Bayern Munich	6	4	1	1	11	6	13
Napoli	6	3	2	1	10	6	11
Manchester C	6	3	1	2	9	6	10
Villarreal	6	0	0	6	2	14	0

GROUP B

Internazionale	(0) 0	Trabzonspor	(0) 1
Lille	(1) 2	CSKA Moscow	(0) 2
CSKA Moscow	(1) 2	Internazionale	(2) 3
Trabzonspor	(0) 1	Lille	(1) 1
CSKA Moscow	(1) 3	Trabzonspor	(0) 0
Lille	(0) 0	Internazionale	(1) 1
Internazionale	(1) 2	Lille	(0) 1
Trabzonspor	(0) 0	CSKA Moscow	(0) 0
CSKA Moscow	(0) 0	Lille	(0) 2
Trabzonspor	(1) 1	Internazionale	(1) 1
Internazionale	(0) 1	CSKA Moscow	(0) 2
Lille	(0) 0	Trabzonspor	(0) 0

Group B Table	P	W	D	L	F	A	Pts
Internazionale	6	3	1	2	8	7	10
CSKA Moscow	6	2	2	2	9	8	8
Trabzonspor	6	1	4	1	3	5	7
Lille	6	1	3	2	6	6	6

GROUP C

Basle	(1) 2	Otelul	(0) 1
Benfica	(1) 1	Manchester U	(1) 1
Manchester U	(2) 3	Basle	(0) 3
Otelul	(0) 0	Benfica	(1) 1
Basle	(0) 0	Benfica	(1) 2
Otelul	(0) 0	Manchester U	(0) 2
Benfica	(1) 1	Basle	(0) 1
Manchester U	(1) 2	Otelul	(0) 0
Manchester U	(1) 2	Benfica	(1) 2
Otelul	(0) 2	Basle	(3) 3
Basle	(1) 2	Manchester U	(0) 1
Benfica	(1) 1	Otelul	(0) 0

Wednesday, 14 September 2011

Benfica (1) 1 *(Cardozo 24)*

Manchester U (1) 1 *(Giggs 42)* 63,822

Benfica: Artur Moraes; Luisao, Garay, Emerson, Pereira, Aimar (Matic 75), Javi Garcia, Witsel, Ruben Amorim (Nolito 56), Gaitan (Bruno Cesar 90), Cardozo.
Manchester U: Lindegaard; Smalling, Evra, Carrick, Fabio (Jones 78), Evans, Valencia (Nani 69), Fletcher (Hernandez 68), Giggs, Rooney, Park.

Tuesday, 27 September 2011

Manchester U (2) 3 *(Welbeck 16, 17, Young 90)*

Basle (0) 3 *(Frei F 58, Frei A 60, 76 (pen))* 73,115

Manchester U: De Gea; Fabio (Nani 69), Evra, Carrick, Ferdinand, Jones, Valencia, Anderson (Berbatov 82), Welbeck, Giggs (Park 61), Young.
Basle: Sommer; Steinhofer, Abraham, Park, Dragovic, Cabral, Frei F (Chipperfield 77), Xhaka G, Frei A (Xhaka T 89), Streller (Pak 81), Zoua.

Tuesday, 18 October 2011

Otelul (0) 0

Manchester U (0) 2 *(Rooney 64 (pen), 90 (pen))* 28,047

Otelul: Grahovac; Costin, Salageanu, Rapa, Perendija■, Giurgiu, Frunza (Ilie 83), Antal, Neagu (Pena 72), Filip, Punosevac (Viglianti 87).
Manchester U: Lindegaard; Fabio (Jones 76), Evra, Carrick, Smalling, Vidic■, Valencia (Evans 71), Anderson, Hernandez, Rooney, Nani.

Wednesday, 2 November 2011

Manchester U (1) 2 *(Valencia 8, Sarghi 87 (og))*

Otelul (0) 0 74,847

Manchester U: De Gea; Jones, Fabio, Anderson (Park 80), Ferdinand, Evans (Fryers 89), Valencia, Owen (Hernandez 11), Berbatov, Rooney, Nani.
Otelul: Grahovac; Sarghi, Costin, Salageanu, Rapa, Giurgiu (Paraschiv 81), Ilie (Frunza 53), Antal (Iorga 61), Neagu, Filip, Pena.

Tuesday, 22 November 2011

Manchester U (1) 2 *(Berbatov 30, Fletcher 59)*

Benfica (1) 2 *(Jones 3 (og), Aimar 61)* 74,873

Manchester U: De Gea; Fabio (Smalling 82), Evra, Carrick, Ferdinand, Jones, Valencia (Hernandez 80), Fletcher, Berbatov, Young, Nani.
Benfica: Artur Moraes; Luisao (Miguel Vitor 58), Garay, Emerson, Pereira, Aimar (Ruben Amorim 83), Javi Garcia, Witsel, Gaitan (Matic 67), Bruno Cesar, Rodrigo.

Wednesday, 7 December 2011

Basle (1) 2 *(Streller 9, Frei A 85)*

Manchester U (0) 1 *(Jones 89)* 36,000

Basle: Sommer; Steinhofer, Abraham, Park, Dragovic, Cabral, Frei F, Shiqiri (Stocker 90), Xhaka G (Chipperfield 83), Frei A (Kusunga 87), Streller.
Manchester U: De Gea; Smalling, Evra, Jones, Ferdinand, Vidic (Evans 44), Park (Macheda 82), Giggs, Nani, Rooney, Young (Welbeck 64).

Group C Table	P	W	D	L	F	A	Pts
Benfica	6	3	3	0	8	4	12
Basle	6	3	2	1	11	10	11
Manchester U	6	2	3	1	11	8	9
Otelul	6	0	0	6	3	11	0

GROUP D

Ajax	(0) 0	Lyon	(0) 0
Dinamo Zagreb	(0) 0	Real Madrid	(0) 1
Lyon	(2) 2	Dinamo Zagreb	(0) 0
Real Madrid	(2) 3	Ajax	(0) 0
Dinamo Zagreb	(0) 0	Ajax	(0) 2
Real Madrid	(1) 4	Lyon	(0) 0
Ajax	(2) 4	Dinamo Zagreb	(0) 0
Lyon	(0) 0	Real Madrid	(1) 2
Lyon	(0) 0	Ajax	(0) 0
Real Madrid	(4) 6	Dinamo Zagreb	(0) 2
Ajax	(0) 0	Real Madrid	(2) 3
Dinamo Zagreb	(1) 1	Lyon	(1) 7

Group D Table	P	W	D	L	F	A	Pts
Real Madrid	6	6	0	0	19	2	18
Lyon	6	2	2	2	9	7	8
Ajax	6	2	2	2	6	6	8
Dinamo Zagreb	6	0	0	6	3	22	0

GROUP E

Chelsea	(0) 2	Leverkusen	(0) 0
Genk	(0) 0	Valencia	(0) 0
Leverkusen	(1) 2	Genk	(0) 0
Valencia	(0) 1	Chelsea	(0) 1
Chelsea	(4) 5	Genk	(0) 0

Leverkusen	(0) 2	Valencia	(1) 1
Genk	(0) 1	Chelsea	(1) 1
Valencia	(1) 3	Leverkusen	(1) 1
Leverkusen	(0) 2	Chelsea	(0) 1
Valencia	(4) 7	Genk	(0) 0
Chelsea	(2) 3	Valencia	(0) 0
Genk	(1) 1	Leverkusen	(0) 1

Tuesday, 13 September 2011

Chelsea (0) 2 *(David Luiz 67, Mata 90)*

33,820

Leverkusen (0) 0

Chelsea: Cech; Bosingwa, Cole, Mikel, Ivanovic, David Luiz (Alex 76), Raul Meireles (Lampard 63), Mata, Torres, Sturridge (Anelka 64), Malouda.
Leverkusen: Leno; Kadlec, Reinartz, Toprak, Castro, Ballack (Renato Augusto 66), Rolfes, Sam (Derdiyok 73), Bender (Balitsch 80), Kiessling, Schurrle.

Wednesday, 28 September 2011

Valencia (0) 1 *(Soldado 87 (pen))*

33,791

Chelsea (0) 1 *(Lampard 56)*

Valencia: Diego Alves; Miguel, Mathieu (Piatti 59), Rami, Jordi Alba, Victor Ruiz, Albelda, Banega (Jonas 73), Pablo Hernandez (Feghouli 73), Canales, Soldado.
Chelsea: Cech; Bosingwa, Cole, Mikel, Terry, David Luiz, Ramires (Raul Meireles 66), Lampard (Kalou 83), Torres (Anelka 72), Mata, Malouda.

Wednesday, 19 October 2011

Chelsea (4) 5 *(Raul Meireles 8, Torres 11, 27, Ivanovic 42, Kalou 72)*

38,518

Genk (0) 0

Chelsea: Cech; Bosingwa (Alex 78), Cole (Paulo Ferreira 46), Raul Meireles, Ivanovic, David Luiz, Romeu, Lampard (Kalou 68), Torres, Anelka, Malouda.
Genk: Koteles; Vanden Borre, Masuero (Camus 46), Ngongca, Tozser, Pudil, Hyland, De Bruyne, Buffel, Vossen (Nwanganga 81), Barda (Ndabashinze 71).

Tuesday, 1 November 2011

Genk (0) 1 *(Vossen 61)*

22,584

Chelsea (1) 1 *(Ramires 26)*

Genk: Koteles; Vanden Borre, Ngongca, Tozser, Camus, Jose Nadson, Hyland, Nwanganga (Limbombe 82), De Bruyne, Buffel (Ndabashinze 69), Vossen (Barda 87).
Chelsea: Cech; Bosingwa, Cole, Ramires (Lampard 66), Ivanovic, David Luiz, Raul Meireles, Romeu (Mata 77), Torres, Anelka (Sturridge 66), Malouda.

Wednesday, 23 November 2011

Leverkusen (0) 2 *(Derdiyok 73, Friedrich 90)*

29,285

Chelsea (0) 1 *(Drogba 48)*

Leverkusen: Leno; Friedrich, Kadlec (Derdiyok 71), Schwaab (Schurrle 57), Omer, Castro, Ballack, Rolfes, Sam, Bender, Kiessling (Oczipka 83).
Chelsea: Cech; Ivanovic, Bosingwa, Ramires, Terry, David Luiz (Alex 69), Raul Meireles (Mikel 80), Lampard, Sturridge, Drogba, Mata (Malouda 66).

Tuesday, 6 December 2011

Chelsea (2) 3 *(Drogba 3, 76, Ramires 22)*

Valencia (0) 0   41,109

Chelsea: Cech; Ivanovic, Cole, Ramires (Mikel 65), Terry, David Luiz, Raul Meireles, Romeu, Sturridge, Drogba (Torres 78), Mata (Malouda 83).

Valencia: Diego Alves; Mathieu, Barragan, Rami, Jordi Alba (Aduriz 55), Victor Ruiz, Albelda, Costa (Dani Parejo 77), Feghouli (Pablo Hernandez 65), Soldado, Jonas.

Tuesday, 13 September 2011

Borussia Dortmund (0) 1 *(Perisic 88)*

Arsenal (1) 1 *(Van Persie 42)*   65,590

Borussia Dortmund: Weidenfeller; Hummels, Piszczek, Subotic, Schmelzer, Kehl (Blaszczykowski 68), Bender, Grosskreutz (Perisic 69), Gotze, Kagawa (Mohamed Zidan 85), Lewandowski.

Arsenal: Szczesny; Sagna, Gibbs, Song Billong, Mertesacker, Koscielny, Benayoun, Arteta, Walcott (Frimpong 77), Van Persie (Chamakh 86), Gervinho (Andre Santos 86).

Wednesday, 28 September 2011

Arsenal (2) 2 *(Oxlade-Chamberlain 8, Andre Santos 20)*

Olympiakos (1) 1 *(David Fuster 27)*   59,676

Arsenal: Szczesny; Sagna, Andre Santos, Song Billong, Mertesacker, Frimpong, Arteta, Rosicky, Chamakh (Van Persie 71), Arshavin (Gibbs 83), Oxlade-Chamberlain (Ramsey 67).

Olympiakos: Costanzo; Mellberg, Holebas, Marcano, Torosidis, Ibagaza, David Fuster (Pantelic 79), Orbaiz (Modesto 75), Fejsa, Mirallas (Abdoun 75), Djebbour.

Wednesday, 19 October 2011

Marseille (0) 0

Arsenal (0) 1 *(Ramsey 90)*   33,258

Marseille: Mandanda; Morel, Diawara, Azpilicueta, N'Koulou, Gonzalez (Amalfitano 73), Diarra, Cheyrou (Kabore 87), Valbuena, Remy (Gignac 69), Ayew A.

Arsenal: Szczesny; Jenkinson (Djourou 62), Andre Santos, Song Billong, Mertesacker, Koscielny, Arteta, Walcott (Gervinho 67), Arshavin (Ramsey 78), Van Persie, Rosicky.

Tuesday, 1 November 2011

Arsenal (0) 0

Marseille (0) 0   59,961

Arsenal: Szczesny; Jenkinson, Andre Santos, Song Billong, Mertesacker, Vermaelen, Walcott, Ramsey (Rosicky 66), Gervinho (Arshavin 77), Park (Van Persie 62), Arteta.

Marseille: Mandanda; Morel, Fanni, Diawara, N'Koulou, Diarra, Cheyrou, Valbuena (Gonzalez 74), Remy (Amalfitano 68), Ayew A, Ayew J (Gignac 84).

Wednesday, 23 November 2011

Arsenal (0) 2 *(Van Persie 49, 86)*

Borussia Dortmund (0) 1 *(Kagawa 90)*   59,531

Arsenal: Szczesny; Koscielny (Djourou 83), Andre Santos, Song Billong, Mertesacker, Vermaelen, Walcott (Diaby 85), Ramsey, Gervinho (Benayoun 74), Van Persie, Arteta.
Borussia Dortmund: Weidenfeller; Hummels, Piszczek, Schmelzer, Felipe Santana, Kehl (Barrios 64), Bender (Leitner 25), Grosskreutz, Gotze (Perisic 28), Kagawa, Lewandowski.

Tuesday, 6 December 2011

Olympiakos (2) 3 *(Djebbour 16, David Fuster 36, Modesto 89)*

Arsenal (0) 1 *(Benayoun 57)*   30,816

Olympiakos: Megyeri; Mellberg, Modesto, Holebas (Orbaiz 37), Papadopoulos A, Marcano, Torosidis, Maniatis, David Fuster (Abdoun 64), Mirallas, Djebbour (Papazoglou 90).
Arsenal: Fabianski (Mannone 25); Djourou, Andre Santos (Miquel 51), Coquelin (Rosicky 67), Squillaci, Vermaelen, Benayoun, Frimpong, Chamakh, Arshavin, Oxlade-Chamberlain.

Group E Table	P	W	D	L	F	A	Pts
Chelsea	6	3	2	1	13	4	11
Leverkusen	6	3	1	2	8	8	10
Valencia	6	2	2	2	12	7	8
Genk	6	0	3	3	2	16	3

GROUP F

Borussia Dortmund	(0) 1	Arsenal	(1) 1
Olympiakos	(0) 0	Marseille	(0) 1
Arsenal	(2) 2	Olympiakos	(1) 1
Marseille	(1) 3	Borussia Dortmund	(0) 0
Marseille	(0) 0	Arsenal	(0) 1
Olympiakos	(2) 3	Borussia Dortmund	(1) 1
Arsenal	(0) 0	Marseille	(0) 0
Borussia Dortmund	(1) 1	Olympiakos	(0) 0
Arsenal	(0) 2	Borussia Dortmund	(0) 1
Marseille	(0) 0	Olympiakos	(0) 1
Borussia Dortmund	(2) 2	Marseille	(1) 3
Olympiakos	(2) 3	Arsenal	(0) 1

Group F Table	P	W	D	L	F	A	Pts
Arsenal	6	3	1	2	7	6	11
Marseille	6	3	1	2	7	4	10
Olympiakos	6	3	0	3	8	6	9
Borussia Dortmund	6	1	1	4	6	12	4

GROUP G

Apoel	(0) 2	Zenit	(0) 1
Porto	(1) 2	Shakhtar Donetsk	(1) 1

Shakhtar Donetsk		(0) 1	Apoel						(0) 1
Zenit		(1) 3	Porto						(1) 1
Porto		(1) 1	Apoel						(1) 1
Shakhtar Donetsk		(2) 2	Zenit						(1) 2
Apoel		(1) 2	Porto						(0) 1
Zenit		(1) 1	Shakhtar Donetsk						(0) 0
Shakhtar Donetsk		(0) 0	Porto						(0) 2
Zenit		(0) 0	Apoel						(0) 0
Apoel		(0) 0	Shakhtar Donetsk						(0) 2
Porto		(0) 0	Zenit						(0) 0

Group G Table	P	W	D	L	F	A	Pts
Apoel	6	2	3	1	6	6	9
Zenit	6	2	3	1	7	5	9
Porto	6	2	2	2	7	7	8
Shakhtar Donetsk	6	1	2	3	6	8	5

GROUP H

Barcelona		(1) 2	AC Milan						(1) 2
Viktoria Plzen		(1) 1	BATE Borisov						(0) 1
AC Milan		(0) 2	Viktoria Plzen						(0) 0
BATE Borisov		(0) 0	Barcelona						(3) 5
AC Milan		(1) 2	BATE Borisov						(0) 0
Barcelona		(1) 2	Viktora Plzen						(0) 0
BATE Borisov		(0) 1	AC Milan						(1) 1
Viktoria Plzen		(0) 0	Barcelona						(2) 4
AC Milan		(1) 2	Barcelona						(2) 3
BATE Borisov		(0) 0	Viktoria Plzen						(1) 1
Barcelona		(1) 4	BATE Borisov						(0) 0
Viktoria Plzen		(0) 2	AC Milan						(0) 2

Group H Table	P	W	D	L	F	A	Pts
Barcelona	6	5	1	0	20	4	16
AC Milan	6	2	3	1	11	8	9
Viktoria Plzen	6	1	2	3	4	11	5
BATE Borisov	6	0	2	4	2	14	2

KNOCK OUT ROUND FIRST LEG

Leverkusen		(0) 1	Barcelona						(1) 3
Lyon		(0) 1	Apoel						(0) 0
AC Milan		(2) 4	Arsenal						(0) 0
Zenit		(1) 3	Benfica						(1) 2
CSKA Moscow		(0) 1	Real Madrid						(1) 1
Napoli		(2) 3	Chelsea						(1) 1
Basle		(0) 1	Bayern Munich						(0) 0
Marseille		(0) 1	Internazionale						(0) 0

Wednesday, 15 February 2012

AC Milan (2) 4 *(Boateng 15, Robinho 38, 49, Ibrahimovic 79 (pen))*

Arsenal (0) 0   64,462

AC Milan: Abbiati; Mexes, Antonini, Thiago Silva, Abate, Van Bommel, Boateng (Ambrosini 70), Seedorf (Emanuelson 12), Nocerino, Robinho (Alexandre Pato 84), Ibrahimovic.
Arsenal: Szczesny; Sagna, Gibbs (Oxlade-Chamberlain 66), Song Billong, Vermaelen, Koscielny (Djourou 44), Arteta, Ramsey, Walcott (Henry 46), Van Persie, Rosicky.

Tuesday, 21 February 2012

Napoli (2) 3 *(Lavezzi 39, 65, Cavani 45)*

Chelsea (1) 1 *(Mata 27)*   52,495

Napoli: De Sanctis; Aronica, Zuniga, Cannavaro, Campagnaro, Maggio, Gargano, Inler, Hamsik (Pandev 82), Cavani, Lavezzi (Dzemaili 74).
Chelsea: Cech; Bosingwa (Cole 12), Ivanovic, Ramires, Cahill, David Luiz, Raul Meireles (Essien 70), Sturridge, Drogba, Mata, Malouda (Lampard 70).

KNOCK-OUT ROUND SECOND LEG

Arsenal	(3) 3	AC Milan	(0) 0
Benfica	(1) 2	Zenit	(0) 0
Apoel	(1) 1	Lyon	(0) 0
(aet; Apoel won 4-3 on penalties.)			
Barcelona	(2) 7	Leverkusen	(0) 1
Bayern Munich	(3) 7	Basle	(0) 0
Internazionale	(0) 2	Marseille	(0) 1
Chelsea	(1) 4	Napoli	(0) 1
(aet.)			
Real Madrid	(1) 4	CSKA Moscow	(0) 1

Tuesday, 6 March 2012

Arsenal (3) 3 *(Koscielny 7, Rosicky 26, Van Persie 43 (pen))*

AC Milan (0) 0   59,973

Arsenal: Szczesny; Sagna, Gibbs, Song Billong, Vermaelen, Koscielny, Walcott (Park 84), Rosicky, Gervinho, Van Persie, Oxlade-Chamberlain (Chamakh 75).
AC Milan: Abbiati; Mexes, Thiago Silva, Abate, Van Bommel, Emanuelson, Mesbah (Bonera 90), Nocerino, Robinho, Ibrahimovic, El Shaarawy (Aquilani 70).

Wednesday, 14 March 2012

Chelsea (1) 4 *(Drogba 28, Terry 47, Lampard 75 (pen), Ivanovic 105)*

Napoli (0) 1 *(Inler 55)*   37,784

Chelsea: Cech; Ivanovic, Cole, Essien, Terry (Bosingwa 98), David Luiz, Ramires, Lampard, Sturridge (Torres 63), Drogba, Mata (Malouda 95).
Napoli: De Sanctis; Aronica (Vargas 110), Zuniga, Cannavaro, Campagnaro, Maggio (Dossena 37), Gargano, Inler, Hamsik (Pandev 106), Cavani, Lavezzi.
aet.

QUARTER-FINALS FIRST LEG

Apoel	(0) 0	Real Madrid	(0) 3
Benfica	(0) 0	Chelsea	(0) 1
AC Milan	(0) 0	Barcelona	(0) 0
Marseille	(0) 0	Bayern Munich	(1) 2

Tuesday, 27 March 2012

Benfica (0) 0

Chelsea (0) 1 *(Kalou 75)*

60,830

Benfica: Artur Moraes; Luisao, Emerson, Pereira, Jardel, Aimar (Matic 69), Javi Garcia
(Nolito 81), Witsel, Gaitan, Bruno Cesar (Rodrigo 69), Cardozo.
Chelsea: Cech; Paulo Ferreira (Bosingwa 80), Cole, Mikel, Terry, David Luiz, Raul
Meireles (Lampard 68), Ramires, Torres, Kalou (Sturridge 82), Mata.

QUARTER-FINALS SECOND LEG

Barcelona	(2) 3	AC Milan	(1) 1
Bayern Munich	(2) 2	Marseille	(0) 0
Chelsea	(1) 2	Benfica	(0) 1
Real Madrid	(2) 5	Apoel	(0) 2

Wednesday, 4 April 2012

Chelsea (1) 2 *(Lampard 21 (pen), Raul Meireles 90)*

Benfica (0) 1 *(Javi Garcia 85)*

37,264

Chelsea: Cech; Ivanovic, Cole, Mikel, Terry (Cahill 60), David Luiz, Ramires, Lampard,
Torres (Drogba 88), Kalou, Mata (Raul Meireles 79).
Benfica: Artur Moraes; Emerson, Pereira■, Capdevila, Aimar, Javi Garcia, Witsel, Gaitan (Yannick Djalo 61), Matic, Bruno Cesar (Rodrigo 72), Cardozo (Nelson Oliveira
57).

SEMI-FINALS FIRST LEG

| Bayern Munich | (1) 2 | Real Madrid | (0) 1 |
| Chelsea | (1) 1 | Barcelona | (0) 0 |

Wednesday, 18 April 2012

Chelsea (1) 1 *(Drogba 45)*

Barcelona (0) 0

38,039

Chelsea: Cech; Ivanovic, Cole, Mikel, Terry, Cahill, Ramires (Bosingwa 88), Lampard,
Drogba, Mata (Kalou 74), Raul Meireles.
Barcelona: Valdes; Puyol, Dani Alves, Adriano Correia, Mascherano, Fabregas (Thiago
Alcantara 78), Iniesta, Xavi (Cuenca 87), Busquets, Messi, Sanchez (Pedro 66).

SEMI-FINALS SECOND LEG

| Barcelona | (2) 2 | Chelsea | (1) 2 |
| Real Madrid | (2) 2 | Bayern Munich | (1) 1 |

*(aet; Bayern Munich won 3-1 on penalties: Alaba scored; Ronaldo saved; Gomez scored;
Kaka saved; Kroos saved; Xabi Alonso scored; Lahm saved; Sergio Ramos missed;
Schweinsteiger scored.)*

Tuesday, 24 April 2012

Barcelona (2) 2 *(Busquets 35, Iniesta 43)*

Chelsea (1) 2 *(Ramires 45, Torres 90)* 95,845

Barcelona: Valdes; Puyol, Pique (Dani Alves 26), Mascherano, Fabregas (Keita 74), Iniesta, Xavi, Busquets, Messi, Sanchez, Cuenca (Tello 67).

Chelsea: Cech; Ivanovic, Cole, Mikel, Terry■, Cahill (Bosingwa 12), Ramires, Lampard, Drogba (Torres 80), Mata (Kalou 58), Raul Meireles.

UEFA CHAMPIONS LEAGUE FINAL 2012

Saturday, 19 May 2012

(at Munich, attendance 69,901)

Bayern Munich (0) 1 *(Muller 83)*

Chelsea (0) 1 *(Drogba 88)*

Bayern Munich: Neuer; Lahm, Boateng, Contento, Robben, Schweinsteiger, Ribery (Olic 97), Tymoshchuk, Kroos, Gomez, Muller (Van Buyten 87).

Chelsea: Cech; Bosingwa, Cole, Mikel, Cahill, David Luiz, Mata, Lampard, Drogba, Kalou (Torres 84), Bertrand (Malouda 73).

aet; Chelsea won 4-3 on penalties: Lahm scored; Mata saved; Gomez scored; David Luiz scored; Neuer scored; Lampard scored; Olic saved; Cole scored; Schweinsteiger saved; Drogba scored.

Referee: Proenca (Portugal).

Did You Know?

The 2011–12 Champions League campaign produced another sprinkling of records, not the least of them with winners Chelsea becoming the first London club to win the trophy. Moreover they achieved it the hard way by taking the prize in the final against Bayern Munich, playing on their own ground. On an individual note, Lionel Messi succeeded in equalling the highest number of goals in a season by one player (previously Jose Altafini and Ruud Van Nistelrooy) when he finished the season on fourteen goals. But he also created history with the finest individual feat with five goals for Barcelona against Leverkusen. Another milestone was achieved in the competition when HJK Helsinki defeated Bangor City 10-0 in one of the qualifying rounds. It is also interesting to note that the two favourites for the final Barcelona and Real Madrid were surprisingly knocked out at the semi-final stage.

UEFA CHAMPIONS LEAGUE 2012–2013

PARTICIPATING CLUBS

This list is provisional and subject to final confirmation from UEFA.

UEFA CHAMPIONS LEAGUE GROUP STAGE

Chelsea FC (ENG) – holders
FC Barcelona (ESP)
Manchester United FC (ENG)
FC Bayern München (GER)
Real Madrid CF (ESP)
Arsenal FC (ENG)
FC Porto (POR)
AC Milan (ITA)
Valencia CF (ESP)
SL Benfica (POR)
FC Shakhtar Donetsk (UKR)
FC Zenit St Petersburg (RUS)
FC Schalke 04 (GER)
Manchester City FC (ENG)
Olympiacos FC (GRE)
AFC Ajax (NED)
Juventus (ITA)
Paris Saint-Germain FC (FRA)
Galatasaray AŞ (TUR)
Borussia Dortmund (GER)
Montpellier Hérault SC (FRA)
FC Nordsjælland (DEN)

UEFA CHAMPIONS LEAGUE PLAY-OFF – LEAGUE ROUTE

SC Braga (POR)
FC Spartak Moskva (RUS)
Udinese Calcio (ITA)
LOSC Lille Métropole (FRA)
Málaga CF (ESP
VfL Borussia Mönchengladbach (GER)

UEFA CHAMPIONS LEAGUE THIRD QUALIFYING ROUND – LEAGUE ROUTE

FC Dynamo Kyiv (UKR)
Panathinaikos FC (GRE)
FC København (DEN)
Fenerbahçe SK (TUR)
Club Brugge KV (BEL)
FC Vaslui (ROU)
Feyenoord (NED)
Motherwell (SCO)

UEFA CHAMPIONS LEAGUE THIRD QUALIFYING ROUND – CHAMPIONS ROUTE

RSC Anderlecht (BEL)
Celtic FC (SCO)
CFR 1907 Cluj (ROU)

UEFA CHAMPIONS LEAGUE SECOND QUALIFYING ROUND

FC Basel 1893 (SUI)
FC BATE Borisov (BLR)
FC Salzburg (AUT)
GNK Dinamo Zagreb (CRO)
MŠK Žilina (SVK)
FK Partizan (SRB)
Helsingborgs IF (SWE)
FC Sheriff (MDA)
Debreceni VSC (HUN)
NK Maribor (SVN)
FK Ventspils (LVA)
FC Slovan Liberec (CZE)
WKS Śląsk Wrocław (POL)
HJK Helsinki (FIN)
AEL Limassol FC (CYP)
FK Ekranas (LTU)
FC Zestafoni (GEO)
Shamrock Rovers FC (IRL)
Hapoel Kiryat Shmona FC (ISR)
Molde FK (NOR)
FK Željezničar (BIH)
KR Reykjavík (ISL)
PFC Ludogorets Razgrad (BUL)
The New Saints FC (WAL)
FK Budućnost Podgorica (MNE)
FC Flora Tallinn (EST)
Neftçi PFK (AZE)
FC Shakhter Karagandy (KAZ)
KS Skënderbeu (ALB)
FK Vardar (MKD)
Ulisses FC (ARM)

UEFA CHAMPIONS LEAGUE FIRST QUALIFYING ROUND

Linfield FC (NIR)
F91 Dudelange (LUX)
Valletta FC (MLT)
SP Tre Penne (SMR)
FC Lusitans (AND)
B36 Tórshavn (FRO)

UEFA EUROPA LEAGUE 2011–2012

■ *Denotes player sent off.*

FIRST QUALIFYING ROUND FIRST LEG

Aalesund	(2) 4	Neath Ath	(1) 1
Banants	(0) 0	Metalurgi Rustavi	(0) 1
Banga	(0) 0	Karabakh	(2) 4
Birkirkara	(0) 0	Vllaznia	(1) 1
Buducnost	(0) 1	Flamurtari	(1) 3
Daugava	(0) 0	Tromso	(2) 5
Dinamo Tbilisi	(1) 2	Milsami Orhei	(0) 0
Elfsborg	(3) 4	Fola Esch	(0) 0
Ferencvaros	(2) 3	Ulisses	(0) 0
Fulham	(1) 3	NSI	(0) 0
Honka	(0) 0	Kalju	(0) 0
IBV	(0) 1	St Patrick's Ath	(0) 0
IF	(1) 1	KR	(2) 3
Jagiellonia	(0) 1	Irtysh	(0) 0
Kaerjeng	(0) 1	Hacken	(0) 1
Koper	(0) 1	Shakhtar	(0) 1
Olimpik	(1) 1	Minsk	(1) 1
Rad	(4) 6	Tre Penne	(0) 0
Renova	(1) 2	Glentoran	(1) 1
Siroki	(0) 0	Olimpija	(0) 0
Spartak Trnava	(1) 3	Zeta	(0) 0
The New Saints	(1) 1	Cliftonville	(1) 1
Trans	(1) 1	Rabotnicki	(1) 4
UE Santa Coloma	(0) 0	Paksi	(1) 1
Varazdin	(2) 5	Lusitanos	(0) 1

Thursday, 30 June 2011

Aalesund (2) 4 *(Fuhre 35, Olsen M 37, Ulvestad 48 (pen), Sellin 77)*

Neath Ath (1) 1 *(Trundle 23)*   3847

Aalesund: Sandqvist; Arnefjord, Jaager, Tollas, Fuhre (Phillips 58), Barrantes, Olsen M (Flotre 78), Morrison, Ulvestad, Okoronkwo (Sellin 58), Parr.
Neath Ath: Kendall; Harris, Lewis, Hillier (Cummings 44), O'Leary, Collins, Fowler, Trundle, Jones C (Rees 86), Morgan (Hughes 53), Bowen.

Fulham (1) 3 *(Duff 33, Murphy 61 (pen), Johnson A 70)*

NSI (0) 0   14,910

Fulham: Schwarzer; Baird, Briggs, Murphy, Hughes, Hangeland, Duff, Etuhu (Sidwell 74), Johnson A, Zamora (Dalla Valle 79), Davies (Riise B 69).
NSI: Gango; Joensen, Mikkelsen, Danielsen (Frederiksberg A 78), Lakjuni, Hansen J, Mortensen (Olsen M 86), Jacobsen C, Petersen H, Frederiksberg J, Olsen K (Liknargotu 90).

IBV (0) 1 *(Andri Olafsson 50 (pen))*

St Patrick's Ath (0) 0   555

IBV: Saevarsson; Olafsson F, Christiansen, Garner, Valdimarsson, Sigurbjornsson, Andri Olafsson (Hughes 78), Mellor, Gudmundsson (Borgthorsson 86), Mawejje, Sytnik (Thorarinsson 74).
St Patrick's Ath: Rogers; Pender, Bermingham, Shortall, McMillan, Bradley, Mulcahy (Murphy 84), Doyle, Crowley (McFaul 61), North (Daly 76), Kavanagh.

Renova (1) 2 *(Janchevski 14 (pen), Bajrami 87)*
Glentoran (1) 1 *(Nixon 45)*

1500

Renova: Elezi; Stepanovski M, Stepanovski K (Simovski 47), Bajrami, Emini, Nuhiu F, Ristov, Statovci, Gashi, Trajkovski (Fetai 81), Janchevski (Ismaili 47).
Glentoran: Morris■; Nixon, Hill, Ward, McGovern■, Taylor, Clarke, Cherry (McGuigan 81), O'Hanlon (Murray 57), Boyce, Waterworth (Gibson 85).

The New Saints (1) 1 *(Darlington 26)*
Cliftonville (1) 1 *(Johnston 39)*

927

The New Saints: Harrison; Spender, Evans, Baker, Marriott, Jones, Ruscoe (Hogan 61), Edwards, Williams C (Partridge 71), Darlington, Sharp (Draper 74).
Cliftonville: Brown; Smyth, Seydak (Scannell 57), McVeigh, Catney, Johnston, McMullan (Lynch 75), Donnelly M, Caldwell, Garrett, Donnelly R (Gormley 52).

FIRST QUALIFYING ROUND SECOND LEG

Cliftonville	(0) 0	The New Saints	(1) 1
Flamurtari	(1) 1	Buducnost	(0) 2
Fola Esch	(0) 1	Elfsborg	(1) 1
Glentoran	(1) 2	Renova	(0) 1
(Glentoran won 3-2 on penalties.)			
Hacken	(2) 5	Kaerjeng	(0) 1
Irtysh	(2) 2	Jagiellonia	(0) 0
Kalju	(0) 0	Honka	(0) 2
Karabakh	(2) 3	Banga	(0) 0
KR	(2) 5	IF	(0) 1
Lusitanos	(0) 0	Varazdin	(0) 1
Metalurgi Rustavi	(1) 1	Banants	(0) 1
Milsami Orhei	(0) 1	Dinamo Tbilisi	(0) 3
Minsk	(2) 2	Olimpik	(0) 1
Neath Ath	(0) 0	Aalesund	(0) 2
NSI	(0) 0	Fulham	(0) 0
Olimpija	(2) 3	Siroki	(0) 0
Paksi	(1) 4	UE Santa Coloma	(0) 0
Rabotnicki	(1) 3	Trans	(0) 0
Shakhtar	(1) 2	Koper	(1) 1
St Patrick's Ath	(2) 2	IBV	(0) 0
Tre Penne	(1) 1	Rad	(2) 3
Tromso	(1) 2	Daugava	(1) 1
Ulisses	(0) 0	Ferencvaros	(1) 2
Vllaznia	(1) 1	Birkirkara	(1) 1
Zeta	(0) 2	Spartak Trnava	(0) 1

Thursday, 7 July 2011

Cliftonville (0) 0

The New Saints (1) 1 *(Baker 4)*

1221

Cliftonville: Brown; Symth, Seydak, McVeigh, Catney (Scannell 73), Johnston, McMullan, Donnelly M, Caldwell, Garrett (Steele 85), Donnelly R (Gormley 53).
The New Saints: Harrison; Spender, Evans, Baker (Johnson 38), Marriott, Jones, Hogan, Ruscoe, Partridge (Williams C 64), Draper (Sharp 80), Williams M.

Glentoran (1) 2 *(Clarke 31, Murray 74)*
Renova (0) 1 *(Ismaili 59)*

1424

Glentoran: Hogg; Nixon, Hill, Ward, Johnny Taylor, O'Kane (Carson 62), Clarke, Cherry (Howland 106), O'Hanlon (Murray 71), Boyce, Waterworth.
Renova: Elezi; Stepanovski M, Simovski, Bajrami (Gafuri 90), Emini, Nuhiu F, Ristov, Statovci, Gashi (Janchevski■ 52), Trajkovski, Ismaili.
Glentoran won 3-2 on penalties.

Neath Ath (0) 0 600

Aalesund (0) 2 *(Barrantes 53, Olsen M 79)*

Neath Ath: Kendall; Harris, Rees, Lewis, Hillier, O'Leary, Collins, Fowler (Jones C 63), Trundle, Hughes (Morgan 57), Bowen (Preen 83).
Aalesund: Sandqvist; Arnefjord, Skiri, Jalasto, Skagestad, Barrantes (Ulvestad 85), Larsen, Olsen M (Sandnes 81), Okoronkwo, Parr, Phillips (Flotre 58).

NSI (0) 0 1245

Fulham (0) 0

NSI: Gango; Hansen E, Joensen, Lakjuni, Hansen J, Mortensen (Danielsen 84), Petersen H, Toronjadze (Frederiksberg A 90), Frederiksberg J, Olsen K (Mikkelsen 90), Jacobsen C.
Fulham: Schwarzer; Kelly, Briggs, Sidwell, Senderos, Hangeland, Duff (Dalla Valle 86), Etuhu, Johnson A (Frei 72), Zamora, Greening (Riise B 76).

St Patrick's Ath (2) 2 *(Daly 24, Doyle 36)* 2100

IBV (0) 0

St Patrick's Ath: Rogers; Pender, Bermingham, Shortall (Murphy 84), McMillan E, Bradley, Doyle, McFaul, North (McMillan D 87), Kavanagh, Daly (Crowley 76).
IBV: Dhaira; Olafsson F (Hughes 74), Christiansen, Garner, Valdimarsson (Thorarinsson 81), Sigurbjornsson, Jeffs (Sytnik 62), Andri Olafsson, Mellor, Gudmundsson, Mawejje.

SECOND QUALIFYING ROUND FIRST LEG

Anorthosis	(2) 3	Gagra	(0) 0
Crusaders	(0) 1	Fulham	(1) 3
Differdange	(0) 0	Levadia	(0) 0
Domzale	(0) 1	Split	(1) 2
EB/Streymur	(0) 1	Karabakh	(1) 1
Ferencvaros	(1) 2	Aalesund	(1) 1
FH	(0) 1	Nacional	(1) 1
Flamutari	(0) 0	Jablonec	(0) 2
Floriana	(0) 0	AEK Larnaca	(5) 8
Glentoran	(0) 0	Vorskla	(2) 2
Hacken	(1) 1	Honka	(0) 0
Iskra-Stal	(1) 1	Varazdin	(1) 1
Juvenes/Dogana	(0) 0	Rabotnicki	(0) 1
Kecskemeti	(1) 1	Aktobe	(0) 1
KR	(1) 3	Zilina	(0) 0
KuPS	(1) 1	Gaz Metan	(0) 0
Llanelli	(1) 2	Dinamo Tbilisi	(0) 1
Maccabi Tel Aviv	(3) 3	Xazar	(1) 1
Metalurg Skopje	(0) 0	Lokomotiv Sofia	(0) 0
Metalurgi Rustavi	(0) 1	Irtysh	(0) 1
Metalurgs Liepaya	(0) 1	Salzburg	(3) 4
Minsk	(1) 1	Gaziantep	(0) 1
Olimpija	(1) 2	Bohemians	(0) 0
Orebro	(0) 0	Sarajevo	(0) 0
Paksi	(0) 1	Tromso	(1) 1
Rad	(0) 0	Olympiakos Volos	(0) 1
Rudar	(0) 0	FK Austria	(1) 3
Sant Julia	(0) 0	Bnei Yehuda	(1) 2
Shakhtar	(0) 2	St Patrick's Ath	(0) 1
Shakhtyor	(0) 0	Ventspils	(0) 1
SK Tirana	(0) 0	Spartak Trnava	(0) 0
Slask	(0) 1	Dundee U	(0) 0
Suduva	(0) 1	Elfsborg	(0) 1
Tauras	(0) 2	Den Haag	(0) 3
The New Saints	(0) 1	Midtjylland	(0) 3
TPS Turku	(0) 0	Westerlo	(0) 1

Vaduz	(0) 0	Vojvodina	(0) 2
Valerenga	(0) 1	Mika	(0) 0
Vllaznia	(0) 0	Thun	(0) 0
Zeljeznicar	(0) 1	Serif	(0) 0

Thursday, 14 July 2011

Crusaders (0) 1 *(Adamson 54)*

Fulham (1) 3 *(Briggs 39, Zamora 74, Murphy 77 (pen))*   2477

Crusaders: O'Neill; McCann, Leeman, Magowan, McBride, McKeown, Watson (Faulkner 86), Dallas (Gargan 71), Adamson, Owens (Rainey 83), McMaster.
Fulham: Schwarzer; Baird, Briggs, Murphy, Hughes, Hangeland, Duff (Donegan 86), Etuhu (Sidwell 80), Johnson A (Riise B 79), Zamora, Frei.

Glentoran (0) 0

Vorskla (2) 2 *(Bezus 29, Januzi 38)*   1527

Glentoran: Hogg; Hill, McGovern, Martyn (O'Kane 75), Howland, Carson (O'Hanlon 75), Cherry, Boyce (Burrows 79), Gibson, Waterworth, Murray.
Vorskla: Velichko; Selin, Kurilov, Dallku, Chesnakov, Zakarlyuka (Oberemko 65), Kryvosheenko, Krasnoperov, Januzi, Osipenko (Rebenok 77), Bezus (Chichikov 82).

Llanelli (1) 2 *(Follows 8, 51)*

Dinamo Tbilisi (0) 1 *(Odikadze 81 (pen))*   643

Llanelli: Morris; Jones S, Surman, Grist (Batley 89), Bowen, Corbisiero, Williams, Thomas K (Legg 67), Evans A, Follows (Jones R 72), Bond.
Dinamo Tbilisi: Loria; Homola, Rekhviashvili, Kakubava, Kvekveskiri, Xisco Munoz, Odikadze, Kakhelishvili (Albert Yague 70), Koshkadze, Jighauri (Tekturmanidze 65), Carlos Coto (Lekvtadze 57).

Olimpija (1) 2 *(Vrsic 45 (pen), 76)*

Bohemians (0) 0   6000

Olimpija: Dzafic; Sretenovic, Andelkovic, Vrsic, Lovrecic (Ranic 55), Skerjanc (Omladic 46), Radujko, Bozic, Fink (Cadikovski 78), Jovic, Valencic.
Bohemians: Murphy; Heary, Burns, Price, O'Brien, Brennan, Cahill, Bayly (Traynor 65), Cronin (Rossiter 87), Buckley, Fagan (Flood 63).

Shakhtar (0) 2 *(Vasiljevic 52, 86)*

St Patrick's Ath (0) 1 *(McMillan D 79)*   12,000

Shakhtar: Mokin; Kirov, Vasiljevic, Utabaev, Dzidic, Baizhanov (Dosmanbetov 90), Kukeyev, Vicius, Konysbaev (Borovskiy 90), Khizhnichenko, Finonchenko (Petronije-vic 80).
St Patrick's Ath: Rogers; Pender, Bermingham, Shortall, McMillan E, Bradley (Guthrie 90), Murphy (McMillan D 63), Doyle, McFaul, Crowley (Daly 77), Kavanagh.

Slask (0) 1 *(Voskamp 75)*

Dundee U (0) 0   8300

Slask: Kelemen; Celeban, Pietrasiak, Socha, Mila, Spahic, Elsner, Dudek (Sztylka 87), Gancarczyk (Sobota 61), Cwielong (Voskamp 73), Diaz.
Dundee U: Pernis; Dillon, Dixon, Severin (Allan 88), Watson, Douglas, Flood, Rankin, Goodwillie, Daly, Russell.

The New Saints (0) 1 *(Evans 59)*

Midtjylland (0) 3 *(Hassan 65, Olsen 86 (pen), Albaek 90)*   914

The New Saints: Harrison; Spender, Evans, Baker, Marriott, Jones, Hogan, Ruscoe, Partridge (Williams C 72), Draper (Sharp 67), Williams M (Edwards 59).
Midtjylland: Jensen; Juelsgard Kristensen, Albrechtsen (Nielsen K 30), Ipsa, Pedersen, Poulsen, Olsen, Uzochukwu (Albaek 79), Hassan, Janssen, Igboun (Nworuh 65).

SECOND QUALIFYING ROUND SECOND LEG

Aalesund	(0) 3	Ferencvaros	(1) 1
(aet.)			
AEK Larnaca	(1) 1	Floriana	(0) 0
Aktobe	(0) 0	Kecskemeti	(0) 0
Bnei Yehuda	(1) 2	Sant Julia	(0) 0
Bohemians	(1) 1	Olimpija	(0) 1
Den Haag	(1) 2	Tauras	(0) 0
Dinamo Tbilisi	(3) 5	Llanelli	(0) 0
Dundee U	(3) 3	Slask	(1) 2
Elfsborg	(1) 3	Suduva	(0) 0
FK Austria	(1) 2	Rudar	(0) 0
Fulham	(1) 4	Crusaders	(0) 0
Gagra	(2) 2	Anorthosis	(0) 0
Gaz Metan	(1) 2	KuPS	(0) 0
Gaziantep	(1) 4	Minsk	(0) 1
Honka	(0) 0	Hacken	(1) 2
Irtysh	(0) 0	Metalurgi Rustavi	(1) 2
Jablonec	(2) 5	Flamurtari	(1) 1
Karabakh	(0) 0	EB/Streymur	(0) 0
Levadia	(0) 0	Differdange	(1) 1
Lokomotiv Sofia	(0) 3	Metalurg Skopje	(1) 2
Midtjylland	(3) 5	The New Saints	(0) 2
Mika	(0) 0	Valerenga	(0) 1
Nacional	(0) 2	FH	(0) 0
Olympiakos Volos	(0) 1	Rad	(0) 1
Rabotnicki	(1) 3	Juvenes/Dogana	(0) 0
Salzburg	(0) 0	Metalurgs Liepaya	(0) 0
Sarajevo	(0) 2	Orebro	(0) 0
Serif	(0) 0	Zeljeznicar	(0) 0
Spartak Trnava	(1) 3	SK Tirana	(1) 1
Split	(0) 3	Domzale	(0) 1
St Patrick's Ath	(1) 2	Shakhtar	(0) 0
Thun	(0) 2	Vllaznia	(1) 1
Tromso	(0) 0	Paksi	(0) 3
Varazdin	(2) 3	Iskra-Stal	(1) 1
Ventspils	(0) 3	Shakhtyor	(1) 2
Vojvodina	(0) 1	Vaduz	(1) 3
Vorskla	(2) 3	Glentoran	(0) 0
Westerlo	(0) 0	TPS Turku	(0) 0
Xazar	(0) 0	Maccabi Tel Aviv	(0) 0
Zilina	(1) 2	KR	(0) 0

Thursday, 21 July 2011

Bohemians (1) 1 *(Fagan 34)*

Olimpija (0) 1 *(O'Brien 81 (og))*

1802

Bohemians: Murphy; Heary, Burns (Cahill 61), Price, O'Brien, Rossiter (Downes 81), Brennan, Bayly (Forrester 71), Cronin, Buckley, Fagan.
Olimpija: Dzafic; Sretenovic (Kasnik 86), Salkic, Andelkovic, Vrsic, Lovrecic, Skerjanc, Radujko, Fink (Omladic 46), Jovic, Valencic (Cadikovski 73).

Dinamo Tbilisi (3) 5 *(Xisco Munoz 7, 51, Albert Yague 11, Robertinho 27, Carlos Coto 55)*

Llanelli (0) 0

18,027

Dinamo Tbilisi: Loria; Tomashvili, Rekhviashvili, Kakubava (Homola 25), Kvekveskiri, Xisco Munoz (Jighauri 54), Odikadze, Koshkadze (Tekturmanidze 62), Albert Yague, Carlos Coto, Robertinho.
Llanelli: Morris; Jones S, Surman, Grist, Bowen (Holloway 69), Corbisiero (Venables 46), Williams, Thomas K, Evans A, Follows (Bond 35), Griffiths.

Dundee U (3) 3 *(Watson 2, Goodwillie 5, Daly 44 (pen))*
Slask (1) 2 *(Elsner 15, Dudek 74)*   11,306
Dundee U: Pernis; Dillon, Dixon, Severin (Swanson 77), Kenneth, Watson, Flood, Rankin, Goodwillie, Daly, Russell (Mackay-Steven 81).
Slask: Kelemen; Celeban, Pietrasiak, Socha, Mila, Spahic, Elsner, Dudek (Cetnarski 87), Gancarczyk (Sobota 63), Sztylka, Cwielong (Voskamp 35).

Fulham (1) 4 *(Johnson A 19, Duff 56, Zamora 66, Sidwell 70)*
Crusaders (0) 0   15,676
Fulham: Schwarzer; Senderos, Briggs, Murphy, Hughes, Hangeland, Duff, Sidwell (Etuhu 71), Johnson A (Frei 71), Zamora, Riise J (Riise B 76).
Crusaders: O'Neill; McCann (Faulkner 86), Leeman, Magowan, McBride, McKeown, Watson, Dallas, Adamson (Halliday 84), Owens (Rainey 68), Gargan.

Midtjylland (3) 5 *(Igboun 23, Nworuh 24, 52, Olsen 32 (pen), Hvilsom 90)*
The New Saints (0) 2 *(Darlington 55, 90)*   2650
Midtjylland: Jensen; Juelsgard Kristensen, Ipsa, Sivebaek (Uzochukwu 69), Lauridsen, Poulsen (Hvilsom 46), Olsen, Borring, Albaek, Nworuh, Igboun (Hansen 46).
The New Saints: Harrison; Evans, Baker, Marriott (Giglio 82), Jones, Hogan, Ruscoe (Sharp 46), Seargeant, Partridge (Williams C 62), Edwards, Darlington.

St Patrick's Ath (1) 2 *(McMillan E 14, Doyle 70)*
Shakhtar (0) 0   2250
St Patrick's Ath: Rogers; Pender, Bermingham, Shortall, McMillan E, Bradley, Doyle (Murphy 86), McFaul, North (McMillan D 77), Kavanagh, Daly (Mulcahy 83).
Shakhtar: Mokin; Kirov, Vasiljevic, Utabaev (Borantaev 80), Dzidic, Petronijevic (Dosmanbetov 73), Baizhanov, Kukeyev, Vicius, Konysbaev, Khizhnichenko.

Vorskla (2) 3 *(Januzi 33, 73, Kurilov 36)*
Glentoran (0) 0   8000
Vorskla: Dolganski; Kurilov, Dallku, Chesnakov, Vovkodav, Oberemko (Matveev 46), Kryvosheenko (Osipenko 67), Rebenok, Markoski (Zakarlyuka 46), Januzi, Bezus.
Glentoran: Morris; Hill, McGovern, Johnny Taylor, Howland, Carson, Callacher (McGuigan 29), Cherry, O'Hanlon (Murray 63), Johnston (Beggs 71), Boyce.

THIRD QUALIFYING ROUND FIRST LEG

Bnei Yehuda	(1) 1	Helsingborg	(0) 0
Aalesund	(1) 4	Elfsborg	(0) 0
AEK Larnaca	(0) 3	Mlada Boleslav	(0) 0
Alaniya	(0) 1	Aktobe	(1) 1
Anorthosis	(0) 0	Rabotnicki	(0) 2
Atletico Madrid	(0) 2	Stromsgodset	(0) 1
AZ	(0) 2	Jablonec	(0) 0
Bursa	(0) 2	Gomel	(1) 1
Club Brugge	(1) 4	Karabakh	(0) 1
Differdange	(0) 0	Olympiakos Volos	(0) 3
Dinamo Bucharest	(2) 2	Varazdin	(2) 2
Gaziantep	(0) 0	Legia	(0) 1
Hapoel Tel Aviv	(2) 4	Vaduz	(0) 0
Karpaty	(1) 2	St Patrick's Ath	(0) 0
KR	(1) 1	Dinamo Tbilisi	(1) 4
Levski	(0) 2	Spartak Trnava	(0) 1
Mainz	(1) 1	Gaz Metan	(0) 1
Metalurgi Rustavi	(1) 2	Rennes	(3) 5
Mitdjylland	(0) 0	Guimaraes	(0) 0
Nacional	(3) 3	Hacken	(0) 0
Olimpija	(0) 1	FK Austria	(1) 1
Omonia	(1) 3	Den Haag	(0) 0

Paksi	(1) 1	Hearts	(1) 1
Palermo	(1) 2	Thun	(1) 2
Ried	(1) 2	Brondby	(0) 0
Salzburg	(0) 1	Senica	(0) 0
Slask	(0) 0	Lokomotiv Sofia	(0) 0
Sparta Prague	(2) 5	Sarajevo	(0) 0
Split	(0) 0	Fulham	(0) 0
Stoke C	(1) 1	Hajduk Split	(0) 0
Valerenga	(0) 0	PAOK Salonika	(0) 2
Ventspils	(1) 1	Red Star Belgrade	(1) 2
Vorskla	(0) 0	Sligo R	(0) 0
Young Boys	(2) 3	Westerlo	(1) 1
Zeljeznicar	(0) 0	Maccabi Tel Aviv	(0) 2

Thursday, 28 July 2011

Karpaty (1) 2 *(Fedetskiy 34, Voronkov 90)*

St Patrick's Ath (0) 0   13,000

Karpaty: Bogatinov; Oshchipko, Milosevic, Fedetskiy, Borja Gomez, Khudobyak, Tkachuk, Danilo Avelar (Martynyuk 19), Zenjov, Pacheco (Voronkov 61), Lucas (Cristobal 76).
St Patrick's Ath: Rogers; Pender, Bermingham, Shortall, McMillan E, Murphy (Carroll 72), Mulcahy, Doyle, McFaul, North (McMillan D 46), Daly (Crowley 65).

Paksi (1) 1 *(Sipeki 32)*

Hearts (1) 1 *(Hamill 45 (pen))*   3500

Paksi: Csernyanszki; Heffler, Fiola, Sifter, Balo, Bode, Magasfoldi (Montvai 66), Sipeki, Bartha, Kiss, Vayer.
Hearts: Kello; McGowan, Grainger, Jonsson, Zaliukas, Hamill, Mrowiec, Black, Sutton (Stevenson 79) (Elliott 90), Obua, Templeton (Novikovas 82).

Split (0) 0

Fulham (0) 0   4000

Split: Vukovic; Krizanac, Marcic, Vidic, Budisa, Milovic, Vitaic, Simic (Rebic 57), Erceg, Baraban (Rasic 85), Golubovic (Cop 70).
Fulham: Schwarzer; Baird, Briggs, Murphy, Hughes, Hangeland, Duff, Etuhu (Sidwell 76), Johnson A, Zamora (Kasami 81), Riise J.

Stoke C (1) 1 *(Walters 2)*

Hajduk Split (0) 0   26,322

Stoke C: Begovic; Wilkinson, Wilson, Whelan, Huth, Shawcross, Pennant (Whitehead 75), Delap, Jones, Walters, Etherington (Shotton 88).
Hajduk Split: Subasic; Inoha, Vejic, Maloca, Ruben Lima, Anas Sharbini (Ljubicic 90), Andric, Tomasov (Ahmad Sharbini 85), Brkljaca, Oremus, Vukusic (Vukovic 63).

Vorskla (0) 0

Sligo R (0) 0   8500

Vorskla: Velichko; Selin, Kurilov, Dallku, Chesnakov, Kryvosheenko (Sachko 81), Rebenok, Krasnoperov, Markoski (Zakarlyuka 46), Januzi, Bezus (Oberemko 73).
Sligo R: Clarke; McGuinness, Powell, Keane, Peers, Kirby, Ndo, Ryan, Cretaro (Davoren 77), Blinkhorn (Russell 90), Greene (Doyle 63).

THIRD QUALIFYING ROUND SECOND LEG

Aktobe	(0) 1	Alaniya	(0) 1
(aet; Alaniya won 4-2 on penalties.)			
Brondby	(2) 4	Ried	(0) 2
Den Haag	(0) 1	Omonia	(0) 0
Dinamo Tbilisi	(0) 2	KR	(0) 0

Elfsborg	(0) 1	Aalesund	(0) 1
FK Austria	(1) 3	Olimpija	(0) 2
Fulham	(1) 2	Split	(0) 0
Gaz Metan	(0) 1	Mainz	(1) 1

(aet; Gaz Metan won 4-3 on penalties.)

Gomel	(1) 1	Bursa	(0) 3
Guimaraes	(1) 2	Midtjylland	(1) 1
Hacken	(1) 2	Nacional	(1) 1
Hajduk Split	(0) 0	Stoke C	(0) 1
Hearts	(2) 4	Paksi	(0) 1
Helsingborg	(1) 3	Bnei Yehuda	(0) 0
Jablonec	(0) 1	AZ	(1) 1
Karabakh	(0) 1	Club Brugge	(0) 0
Legia	(0) 0	Gaziantep	(0) 0
Lokomotiv Sofia	(0) 0	Slask	(0) 0

(aet; Slask won 4-3 on penalties.)

Maccabi Tel Aviv	(3) 6	Zeljeznicar	(0) 0
Mlada Boleslav	(0) 2	AEK Larnaca	(1) 2
Olympiakos Volos	(1) 3	Differdange	(0) 0

(Olympiakos Volos demoted from Greek top division and excluded from play-off round.)

PAOK Salonika	(1) 3	Valerenga	(0) 0
Rabotnicki	(0) 1	Anorthosis	(0) 2
Red Star Belgrade	(4) 7	Ventspils	(0) 0
Rennes	(0) 2	Metalurgi Rustavi	(0) 0
Sarajevo	(0) 0	Sparta Prague	(2) 2
Senica	(0) 0	Salzburg	(1) 3
Sligo R	(0) 0	Vorskla	(2) 2
Spartak Trnava	(0) 2	Levski	(1) 1

(aet; Spartak Trnava won 5-4 on penalties.)

St Patrick's Ath	(0) 1	Karpaty	(1) 3
Stromsgodset	(0) 0	Atletico Madrid	(1) 2
Thun	(0) 1	Palermo	(0) 1
Vaduz	(0) 2	Hapoel Tel Aviv	(1) 1
Varazdin	(1) 1	Dinamo Bucharest	(2) 2
Westerlo	(0) 0	Young Boys	(1) 2

Thursday, 4 August 2011

Fulham (1) 2 *(Johnson A 19, Murphy 56 (pen))*

Split (0) 0   17,087

Fulham: Schwarzer; Senderos, Riise J, Murphy, Hughes, Hangeland, Duff (Kasami 89), Etuhu, Johnson A, Zamora (Dembele 76), Dempsey (Briggs 81).
Split: Vukovic; Krizanac, Marcic, Vidic, Budisa, Milovic, Vitaic (Rasic 75), Simic, Erceg, Baraban (Obilinovic 61), Cop (Jordan 83).

Hajduk Split (0) 0

Stoke C (0) 1 *(Milicevic 90 (og))*   33,000

Hajduk Split: Subasic; Milicevic, Maloca, Ruben Lima, Anas Sharbini, Andric, Tomasov (Kukoc 87), Brkljaca, Trebotic (Saric 69), Vukovic (Ahmad Sharbini 56), Vukusic.
Stoke C: Begovic; Huth, Wilson, Whelan, Shawcross, Woodgate, Pennant (Pugh 84), Whitehead, Jones (Diao 77), Walters (Shotton 86), Etherington.

Hearts (2) 4 *(Stevenson 34, 45, Driver 50, Skacel 75)*

Paksi (0) 1 *(Bode 89)*   12,811

Hearts: Kello; McGowan, Grainger, Jonsson, Zaliukas (Hamill 46), Mrowiec, Stevenson, Black, Templeton, Elliott (Sutton 13), Driver (Skacel 63).
Paksi: Csernyanszki; Eger, Heffler, Fiola, Sifter, Balo, Bode, Magasfoldi (Csehi 55), Sipeki, Bartha, Kiss (Montvai 79).

Sligo R (0) 0

Vorskla (2) 2 *(Zakarlyuka 16, Rebenok 17)*   3800

Sligo R: Clarke; McGuinness, Powell, Peers, Ventre, Kirby, Ndo, Ryan, Cretaro (Russell 69), Blinkhorn (Dillon 69), Greene (Doyle 55).
Vorskla: Dolganski; Selin, Kurilov, Dallku, Chesnakov, Zakarlyuka (Oberemko 46), Kryvosheenko, Rebenok, Krasnoperov (Osipenko 80), Markoski, Sachko (Bezus 68).

St Patrick's Ath (0) 1 *(McMillan E 57)*

Karpaty (1) 3 *(Zenjov 22, Khudobyak 64, Oshchipko 83)*   2109

St Patrick's Ath: Rogers; Pender, Bermingham, Shortall, McMillan E (Kenna 69), Bradley (Daly 23), Mulcahy, Doyle (North 61), McFaul, McMillan D, Kavanagh.
Karpaty: Tlumak; Oshchipko, Milosevic, Fedetskiy, Borja Gomez, Khudobyak, Tkachuk, Kopolovets (Voronkov 55), Martynyuk, Zenjov (Pacheco 68), Lucas (Cristobal 76).

PLAY-OFF ROUND FIRST LEG

Aalesund	(1) 2	AZ	(1) 1
AEK Athens	(0) 1	Dinamo Tbilisi	(0) 0
Athletic Bilbao	(0) 0	Trabzonspor	(0) 0
Atletico Madrid	(0) 2	Guimaraes	(0) 0
Besiktas	(1) 3	Alaniya	(0) 0
Braga	(0) 0	Young Boys	(0) 0
Bursa	(1) 1	Anderlecht	(0) 2
Celtic	(0) 0	Sion	(0) 0
(Sion subsequently removed from competition with a 3-0 default.)			
Differdange	(0) 0	Paris St Germain	(1) 4
Ekranas	(0) 1	Hapoel Tel Aviv	(0) 0
FK Austria	(2) 3	Gaz Metan	(1) 1
Fulham	(2) 3	Dnepr	(0) 0
Hannover	(2) 2	Sevilla	(1) 1
Hearts	(0) 0	Tottenham H	(3) 5
HJK Helsinki	(1) 2	Schalke	(0) 0
Lazio	(2) 6	Rabotnicki	(0) 0
Legia	(1) 2	Spartak Moscow	(0) 2
Litex	(1) 1	Dynamo Kiev	(1) 2
Lokomotiv Moscow	(2) 2	Spartak Trnava	(0) 0
Maccabi Tel Aviv	(0) 3	Panathinaikos	(0) 0
Maribor	(0) 2	Rangers	(1) 1
Metalist Kharkiv	(0) 0	Sochaux	(0) 0
Nacional	(0) 0	Birmingham C	(0) 0
Nordsjaelland	(0) 0	Sporting Lisbon	(1) 1
Omonia	(2) 2	Salzburg	(0) 0
PAOK Salonika	(1) 2	Karpaty	(0) 0
Red Star Belgrade	(1) 1	Rennes	(1) 2
Ried	(0) 0	PSV Eindhoven	(0) 0
Rosenborg	(0) 0	AEK Larnaca	(0) 0
Shamrock Rovers	(0) 1	Partizan Belgrade	(1) 1
Slask	(1) 1	Rapid Bucharest	(2) 3
Slovan Bratislava	(0) 1	Roma	(0) 0
Standard Liege	(0) 1	Helsingborg	(0) 0
Steaua	(1) 2	CSKA Sofia	(0) 0
Thun	(0) 0	Stoke C	(1) 1
Vaslui	(2) 2	Sparta Prague	(0) 0
Vorskla	(1) 2	Dinamo Bucharest	(0) 1
Zestafoni	(0) 3	Club Brugge	(2) 3

Thursday, 18 August 2011

Celtic (0) 0

Sion (0) 0
51,795

Celtic: Forster; Wilson M, Mulgrew, Ki, Majstorovic, Cha, Brown, Ledley, Samaras (McCourt 84), Stokes (Maloney 69), Commons (Forrest 56).
Sion: Vanins; Dingsdag, Buhler, Vanczak, Jose Goncalves, Adailton, Feindouno (Rodrigo 90), Obradovic (Gabri 85), Serey Die, Sio, Afonso (Mutsch 51).
Sion subsequently removed from competition with a 3-0 default.

Fulham (2) 3 *(Hughes 38, Dempsey 43, 49)*

Dnepr (0) 0
14,823

Fulham: Schwarzer; Kelly, Briggs, Murphy (Etuhu 67), Hughes, Hangeland, Duff (Dembele 67), Sidwell, Kasami (Johnson 88), Zamora, Dempsey.
Dnepr: Lastuvka; Denisov, Mandzyuk, Cheberyachko, Boateng (Zozulya 56), Rotan, Giuliano (Oliynyk 70), Kulakov, Kravchenko, Kalinic, Konoplyanka.

Hearts (0) 0

Tottenham H (3) 5 *(Van der Vaart 5, Defoe 13, Livermore 28, Bale 63, Lennon 78)*
16,279

Hearts: Kello; Mrowiec (Obua 82), Grainger, Hamill, Webster, Zaliukas, Stevenson, Black, Sutton (Skacel 74), Templeton, Driver (Elliott 65).
Tottenham H: Gomes; Walker, Assou-Ekotto, Van der Vaart (Huddlestone 59), Kaboul, Dawson, Lennon, Kranjcar, Defoe (Pavlyuchenko 79), Livermore, Bale (Townsend 70).

Maribor (0) 2 *(Ibraimi 52, Velikonja 90)*

Rangers (1) 1 *(Juanma Ortiz 31)*
10,900

Maribor: Handanovic; Rajcevic, Arghus, Ibraimi (Milec 86), Viler, Mezga, Mertelj, Beric, Mejac, Volas (Velikonja 79), Filipovic (Cvijanovic 68).
Rangers: McGregor; Goian, Bocanegra, Broadfoot, Wallace, McCulloch, Juanma Ortiz, Davis, Jelavic, Naismith (Lafferty 46), Edu.

Nacional (0) 0

Birmingham C (0) 0
4323

Nacional: Elisson; Felipe Lopes, Danielson, Nuno Pinto, Luis Alberto, Mihelic (Diego Barcellos 46), Skolnik (Elizeu 46), Joao Aurelio, Mateus, Rondon, Edgar Costa (Candeias 69).
Birmingham C: Myhill; Carr, Murphy, Spector, Caldwell, Ridgewell, Burke, Davies, Wood, Redmond, Beausejour.

Shamrock Rovers (0) 1 *(McCabe 81)*

Partizan Belgrade (1) 1 *(Tomic 14)*
4650

Shamrock Rovers: Thompson; Rice (Kilduff 76), Murray, Sullivan, Sives, Stevens, Finn (Turner 46), McCormack, Dennehy (O'Neill 58), McCabe, Twigg.
Partizan Belgrade: Stojkovic; Rankovic, Rnic, Ivanov, Stankovic, Ilic S (Markovic L 85), Kamara, Smiljanic, Tomic, Eduardo (Babovic 66), Jovancic (Markovic S 90).

Thun (0) 0

Stoke C (1) 1 *(Pugh 18)*
7150

Thun: Da Costa■; Luthi, Reinmann, Matic, Schindelholz, Battig, Andrist, Demiri (Sanogo 70), Schneuwly (Wittwer 70), Lustrinelli (Rama 80), Lezcano.
Stoke C: Sorensen; Huth (Wilkinson 50), Tonge, Upson, Shawcross, Whitehead, Pugh, Wilson, Jones (Whelan 66), Walters, Etherington (Arismendi 73).

PLAY-OFF ROUND SECOND LEG

AEK Larnaca	(1) 2	Rosenborg	(0) 1
Alaniya	(0) 2	Besiktas	(0) 0

Anderlecht	(1) 2	Bursa	(1) 2
AZ	(2) 6	Aalesund	(0) 0
Birmingham C	(2) 3	Nacional	(0) 0
Club Brugge	(2) 2	Zestafoni	(0) 0
CSKA Sofia	(0) 1	Steaua	(0) 1
Dinamo Bucharest	(1) 2	Vorskla	(1) 3
Dinamo Tbilisi	(1) 1	AEK Athens	(0) 1
(aet.)			
Dnepr	(1) 1	Fulham	(0) 0
Dynamo Kiev	(0) 1	Litex	(0) 0
Gaz Metan	(1) 1	FK Austria	(0) 0
Guimaraes	(0) 0	Atletico Madrid	(2) 4
Hapoel Tel Aviv	(1) 4	Ekranas	(0) 0
Helsingborg	(0) 1	Standard Liege	(2) 3
Karpaty	(1) 1	PAOK Salonika	(0) 1
Panathinaikos	(0) 2	Maccabi Tel Aviv	(0) 1
Paris St Germain	(0) 2	Differdange	(0) 0
Partizan Belgrade	(1) 1	Shamrock R	(0) 2
(aet.)			
PSV Eindhoven	(0) 5	Ried	(0) 0
Rabotnicki	(1) 1	Lazio	(1) 3
Rangers	(0) 1	Maribor	(0) 1
Rapid Bucharest	(1) 1	Slask	(0) 1
Rennes	(2) 4	Red Star Belgrade	(0) 0
Roma	(1) 1	Slovan Bratislava	(0) 1
Salzburg	(0) 1	Omonia	(0) 0
Schalke	(2) 6	HJK Helsinki	(1) 1
Sevilla	(1) 1	Hannover	(1) 1
Sion	(1) 3	Celtic	(0) 1
Sochaux	(0) 0	Metalist Kharkiv	(3) 4
Sparta Prague	(0) 1	Vaslui	(0) 0
Spartak Moscow	(2) 2	Legia	(2) 3
Spartak Trnava	(1) 1	Lokomotiv Moscow	(0) 1
Sporting Lisbon	(0) 2	Nordsjaelland	(0) 1
Stoke C	(3) 4	Thun	(0) 1
Tottenham H	(0) 0	Hearts	(0) 0
Trabzonspor	(0) 0	Athletic Bilbao	(0) 0

(Trabzonspor replaced Fenerbahce in the Champions League, allowing Athletic Bilbao a walkover.)

Young Boys	(0) 2	Braga	(1) 2

Thursday, 25 August 2011

Birmingham C (2) 3 *(Redmond 15, Murphy 24, Wood 86)*

Nacional (0) 0   27,698

Birmingham C: Myhill; Carr, Murphy, Caldwell, Davies, Spector, Burke (Asante 88), Beausejour, Wood (Jervis 89), Rooney, Redmond.
Nacional: Elisson; Felipe Lopes, Danielson, Claudemir (Edgar Costa 55), Tomasevic, Luis Alberto, Elizeu, Mateus (Oliver 64), Diego Barcellos (Mihelic 55), Candeias, Rondon.

Dnepr (1) 1 *(Shakhov 22)*

Fulham (0) 0   12,750

Dnepr: Lastuvka; Denisov (Strinic 56), Mandzyuk, Cheberyachko (Rotan 57), Inkoom, Boateng, Giuliano (Antonov 72), Kravchenko, Shakhov, Kalinic, Konoplyanka.
Fulham: Schwarzer; Baird, Riise J (Briggs 22), Murphy, Hughes, Hangeland, Duff, Sidwell, Johnson, Dembele (Kasami 71), Dempsey (Etuhu 80).

Partizan Belgrade (1) 1 *(Volkov 35)*

Shamrock R (0) 2 *(Sullivan 58, O'Donnell 113 (pen))*   13,706

Partizan Belgrade: Ilic R; Rankovic, Rnic, Volkov, Ivanov, Ilic S, Vukic (Babovic 58), Kamara■, Tomic, Eduardo (Markovic 85), Jovancic.
Shamrock R: Thompson; Rice, Murray, Sullivan, Sives, Stevens, Turner, Finn, Dennehy (Sheppard 46), McCabe (O'Donnell 68), Twigg (Kilduff 102).
(aet.)

Rangers (0) 1 *(Bocanegra 75)*
Maribor (0) 1 *(Volas 55)* 32,223
Rangers: McGregor; Bocanegra, Wallace (Perry 40), Broadfoot, Goian, Edu, Juanma Ortiz (Healy 67), Davis, Jelavic, Lafferty, Wylde.
Maribor: Handanovic; Rajcevic, Arghus, Ibraimi, Viler, Mezga (Cvijanovic 76), Mertelj, Beric (Marcos Tavares 86), Potokar (Milec 83), Volas, Filipovic.

Sion (1) 3 *(Feindouno 3 (pen), 63, Sio 82)*
Celtic (0) 1 *(Mulgrew 78)* 7100
Sion: Vanins; Dingsdag, Buhler, Vanczak, Adailton, Feindouno, Obradovic (Crettenand 69), Mutsch, Serey Die, Sio, Afonso (Prijovic 6).
Celtic: Forster; Cha, Mulgrew, Ki, Majstorovic■, Wilson K, Kayal (Forrest 72), Brown, Samaras, Hooper, Ledley (Commons 88).

Stoke C (3) 4 *(Upson 24, Jones 31, 72, Whelan 38)*
Thun (0) 1 *(Wittwer 78)* 24,118
Stoke C: Sorensen; Wilkinson, Wilson (Collins 56), Whelan, Shawcross, Upson, Pennant (Soares 55), Whitehead, Jones, Walters (Shotton 63), Pugh.
Thun: Djukic; Luthi, Ghezal, Schneider (Hediger 66), Reinmann, Schindelholz, Battig, Andrist, Demiri (Wittwer 66), Sanogo, Lezcano (Rama 77).

Tottenham H (0) 0
Hearts (0) 0 24,053
Tottenham H: Cudicini; Corluka, Kane, Huddlestone, Dawson (Kaboul 46), Bassong, Carroll, Livermore (Nicholson 76), Pavlyuchenko, Fredericks (Kranjcar 61), Townsend.
Hearts: MacDonald; McGowan, Grainger, Jonsson, Zaliukas, Webster, Templeton, Robinson (Taouil 78), Smith (Suso Santana 82), Novikovas, Skacel (Mrowiec 72).

GROUP STAGE – GROUP A

PAOK Salonika	(0) 0	Tottenham H	(0) 0
Shamrock R	(0) 0	Rubin	(1) 3
Rubin	(0) 2	PAOK Salonika	(1) 2
Tottenham H	(0) 3	Shamrock R	(0) 1
PAOK Salonika	(1) 2	Shamrock R	(0) 1
Tottenham H	(1) 1	Rubin	(0) 0
Rubin	(0) 1	Tottenham H	(0) 0
Shamrock R	(0) 1	PAOK Salonika	(3) 3
Rubin	(2) 4	Shamrock R	(1) 1
Tottenham H	(1) 1	PAOK Salonika	(2) 2
PAOK Salonika	(1) 1	Rubin	(0) 1
Shamrock R	(0) 0	Tottenham H	(3) 4

Thursday, 15 September 2011
PAOK Salonika (0) 0
Tottenham H (0) 0 24,285
PAOK Salonika: Kresic; Contreras, Lino, Malezas, Etto, Fotakis (Ivic 62), Garcia, Arias, Vieirinha, Salpingidis, Athanasiadis.
Tottenham H: Cudicini; Walker, Townsend, Livermore, Corluka, Bassong, Iago Falque (Fredericks 81), Carroll, Pavlyuchenko, Kane, Giovani (Parrett 90).

Shamrock R (0) 0
Rubin (1) 3 *(Martins 2, Noboa 50, Gokdeniz 60)* 6290
Shamrock R: Thompson; O'Donnell, Rice, Murray, Sullivan, Sives, Stevens, Finn (Kilduff 56), McCormack (Dennehy 56), Ricketts (Turner 63), Twigg.
Rubin: Ryzhikov; Bocchetti, Cesar Navas, Kaleshin (Ansaldi 75), Sharonov, Gokdeniz, Ryazantsev, Noboa, Natcho, Haedo Valdez (Dyadyun 64), Martins (Bystrov 46).

Thursday, 29 September 2011

Tottenham H (0) 3 *(Pavlyuchenko 60, Defoe 61, Giovani 65)*

Shamrock R (0) 1 *(Rice 51)*   24,782

Tottenham H: Cudicini; Walker, Carroll, Bassong, Corluka, Livermore, Lennon (Townsend 46), Rose (Kane 80), Pavlyuchenko, Defoe (Iago Falque 73), Giovani.
Shamrock R: Brush; O'Donnell (McCormack 46), Rice, Murray, Sullivan, Sives, Paterson (Stevens 46), Finn (Ricketts 73), Dennehy, McCabe, Twigg.

Thursday, 20 October 2011

PAOK Salonika (1) 2 *(Lazar 12, Vieirinha 63)*

Shamrock R (0) 1 *(Sheppard 48)*   12,776

PAOK Salonika: Chalkias; Cirillo, Lino (Sznaucer 29), Malezas, Etto, Lazar, Ivic, Arias, Vieirinha, Salpingidis (Papazoglou 88), Athanasiadis (Georgiadis 62).
Shamrock R: Thompson; O'Donnell, Rice, Murray, Oman, Sullivan, Stevens, Paterson (Finn 74), Turner (Kilduff 74), Dennehy, Sheppard (McCabe 84).

Tottenham H (1) 1 *(Pavlyuchenko 33)*

Rubin (0) 0   24,058

Tottenham H: Gomes; Walker, Rose, Carroll, Bassong, Livermore, Lennon (Modric 73), Sandro (Kaboul 73), Pavlyuchenko, Defoe, Giovani (Assou-Ekotto 65).
Rubin: Ryzhikov; Bocchetti, Cesar Navas, Kuzmin, Sharonov, Gokdeniz, Ryazantsev (Eremenko 78), Noboa, Natcho, Kasaev (Martins 61), Haedo Valdez.

Thursday, 3 November 2011

Rubin (0) 1 *(Natcho 56)*

Tottenham H (0) 0   21,250

Rubin: Ryzhikov; Bocchetti, Cesar Navas, Kaleshin, Sharonov, Gokdeniz, Ryazantsev (Eremenko 89), Noboa, Natcho, Kasaev (Ansaldi 83), Martins (Haedo Valdez 65).
Tottenham H: Cudicini; Carroll, Fredericks, Bassong, Gallas (Parrett 72), Livermore, Iago Falque, Pienaar, Pavlyuchenko (Kane 75), Defoe, Townsend.

Shamrock R (0) 1 *(Dennehy 51)*

PAOK Salonika (3) 3 *(Salpingidis 7, 38, Fotakis 36)*   6100

Shamrock R: Thompson; O'Donnell, Murray, Sullivan, Sives, Stevens, Turner (Kilduff 46), Dennehy, McCormack (Rice 70), McCabe (Twigg 46), Sheppard.
PAOK Salonika: Chalkias; Cirillo, Lino, Malezas, Sznaucer, Fotakis (Balafas 64), Lazar, Georgiadis (Apostolopoulos 88), Arias, Vieirinha, Salpingidis (Papazoglou 90).

Wednesday, 30 November 2011

Rubin (2) 4 *(Haedo Valdez 10, 51, Natcho 36, Martins 62)*

Shamrock R (1) 1 *(Oman 12)*   15,740

Rubin: Ryzhikov; Bocchetti, Cesar Navas, Kaleshin, Sharonov, Gokdeniz (Ansaldi 69), Ryazantsev (Dyadyun 71), Noboa, Natcho, Haedo Valdez (Kasaev 61), Martins.
Shamrock R: Thompson; Rice, Murray, Oman, Sullivan, Stevens, Paterson (Kilduff 70), Turner (Twigg 81), Finn (O'Donnell 70), Dennehy, Sheppard.

Tottenham H (1) 1 *(Modric 39 (pen))*

PAOK Salonika (2) 2 *(Salpingidis 6, Athanasiadis 14)*   26,229

Tottenham H: Gomes; Corluka, Rose (Bale 63), Modric, Bassong, Gallas, Lennon, Livermore, Kane (Iago Falque 71), Defoe, Pienaar (Walker 67).
PAOK Salonika: Chalkias; Contreras (Cirillo 80), Malezas, Etto, Fotakis, Garcia, Lazar (Arias 83), Georgiadis (Sznaucer 62), Stafylidis■, Salpingidis, Athanasiadis.

Thursday, 15 December 2011

Shamrock R (0) 0

Tottenham H (3) 4 *(Pienaar 29, Townsend 38, Defoe 45, Kane 90)* 7545

Shamrock R: Brush; Rice (O'Donnell 46), Murray, Oman, Sullivan, Stevens, Paterson, Turner, Finn (Twigg 57), Dennehy, Sheppard (Kilduff 74).
Tottenham H: Cudicini; Rose, Assou-Ekotto (Iago Falque 84), Livermore, Kaboul, Townsend, Pienaar, Kranjcar, Defoe (Kane 76), Giovani, Sandro.

Group A Table	P	W	D	L	F	A	Pts
Manchester C	6	3	2	1	11	6	11
Group A Table	P	W	D	L	F	A	Pts
PAOK Salonika	6	3	3	0	10	6	12
Rubin	6	3	2	1	11	5	11
Tottenham H	6	3	1	2	9	4	10
Shamrock R	6	0	0	6	4	19	0

GROUP B

FC Copenhagen	(0) 1	Vorskla	(0) 0
Hannover	(0) 0	Standard Liege	(0) 0
Standard Liege	(0) 3	FC Copenhagen	(0) 0
Vorskla	(0) 1	Hannover	(2) 2
Hannover	(1) 2	FC Copenhagen	(0) 2
Standard Liege	(0) 0	Vorskla	(0) 0
FC Copenhagen	(0) 1	Hannover	(0) 2
Vorskla	(1) 1	Standard Liege	(2) 3
Standard Liege	(1) 2	Hannover	(0) 0
Vorskla	(1) 1	FC Copenhagen	(1) 1
FC Copenhagen	(0) 0	Standard Liege	(1) 1
Hannover	(2) 3	Vorskla	(1) 1

Group B Table	P	W	D	L	F	A	Pts
Standard Liege	6	4	2	0	9	1	14
Hannover	6	3	2	1	9	7	11
FC Copenhagen	6	1	2	3	5	9	5
Vorskla	6	0	2	4	4	10	2

GROUP C

Hapoel Tel Aviv	(0) 0	Rapid Bucharest	(0) 1
PSV Eindhoven	(1) 1	Legia	(0) 0
Legia	(0) 3	Hapoel Tel Aviv	(1) 2
Rapid Bucharest	(1) 1	PSV Eindhoven	(1) 3
Hapoel Tel Aviv	(0) 0	PSV Eindhoven	(0) 1
Rapid Bucharest	(0) 0	Legia	(0) 1
Legia	(0) 3	Rapid Bucharest	(0) 1
PSV Eindhoven	(1) 3	Hapoel Tel Aviv	(2) 3
Legia	(0) 0	PSV Eindhoven	(1) 3
Rapid Bucharest	(1) 1	Hapoel Tel Aviv	(3) 3
Hapoel Tel Aviv	(1) 2	Legia	(0) 0
PSV Eindhoven	(0) 2	Rapid Bucharest	(0) 1

Group C Table	P	W	D	L	F	A	Pts
PSV Eindhoven	6	5	1	0	13	5	16
Legia	6	3	0	3	7	9	9
Hapoel Tel Aviv	6	2	1	3	10	9	7
Rapid Bucharest	6	1	0	5	5	12	3

GROUP D

Lazio	(1) 2	Vaslui	(0) 2
Zurich	(0) 0	Sporting Lisbon	(2) 2
Sporting Lisbon	(2) 2	Lazio	(1) 1
Vaslui	(0) 2	Zurich	(1) 2
Sporting Lisbon	(1) 2	Vaslui	(0) 0
Zurich	(1) 1	Lazio	(1) 1
Lazio	(0) 1	Zurich	(0) 0
Vaslui	(1) 1	Sporting Lisbon	(0) 0
Sporting Lisbon	(1) 2	Zurich	(0) 0
Vaslui	(0) 0	Lazio	(0) 0
Lazio	(1) 2	Sporting Lisbon	(0) 0
Zurich	(0) 2	Vaslui	(0) 0

Group D Table	P	W	D	L	F	A	Pts
Sporting Lisbon	6	4	0	2	8	4	12
Lazio	6	2	3	1	7	5	9
Vaslui	6	1	3	2	5	8	6
Zurich	6	1	2	3	5	8	5

GROUP E

Besiktas	(2) 5	Maccabi Tel Aviv	(0) 1
Dynamo Kiev	(0) 1	Stoke C	(0) 1
Maccabi Tel Aviv	(1) 1	Dynamo Kiev	(1) 1
Stoke C	(1) 2	Besiktas	(1) 1
Dynamo Kiev	(0) 1	Besiktas	(0) 0
Stoke C	(3) 3	Maccabi Tel Aviv	(0) 0
Besiktas	(0) 1	Dynamo Kiev	(0) 0
Maccabi Tel Aviv	(0) 1	Stoke C	(0) 2
Maccabi Tel Aviv	(0) 2	Besiktas	(1) 3
Stoke C	(0) 1	Dynamo Kiev	(1) 1
Besiktas	(0) 3	Stoke C	(1) 1
Dynamo Kiev	(2) 3	Maccabi Tel Aviv	(0) 3

Thursday, 15 September 2011

Dynamo Kiev (0) 1 *(Vukojevic 90)*

Stoke C (0) 1 *(Jerome 55)*   14,550

Dynamo Kiev: Shovkovsky; Betao, Popov, Danilo Silva, Yussuf, Ninkovic (Aliyev 58), Vukojevic, Garmash (Lukman 46) (Brown 75), Milevskiy, Shevchenko, Yarmolenko.
Stoke C: Sorensen; Wilkinson, Shotton (Whitehead 81), Huth, Shawcross, Upson, Diao, Whelan, Jones, Jerome (Pennant 75), Palacios (Walters 87).

Thursday, 29 September 2011

Stoke C (1) 2 *(Crouch 15, Walters 78 (pen))*

Besiktas (1) 1 *(Hilbert 14)*   23,551

Stoke C: Sorensen; Huth, Shotton, Upson, Shawcross, Palacios (Whelan 61), Whitehead, Delap, Crouch, Jerome (Walters 59), Etherington (Pennant 51).
Besiktas: Rustu; Egemen, Sivok, Ismail, Simao, Hilbert, Ricardo Quaresma, Mehmet Aurelio (Holosko 82), Manuel Fernandes, Necip (Ernst 75), Edu.

Thursday, 20 October 2011

Stoke C (3) 3 *(Jones 12, Jerome 24, Shotton 32)*

Maccabi Tel Aviv (0) 0   22,756

Stoke C: Sorensen; Huth (Walters 76), Shotton, Upson, Shawcross, Whitehead, Wilson (Wilkinson 61), Diao, Jones, Jerome■, Etherington (Palacios 79).
Maccabi Tel Aviv: Haimov; Pavicevic (Vered 64), Ziv■, Saban, Medunjanin, Israelevich (Micha 75), Yeini, Puncec, Dahan, Konate, Atar (Colautti 42).

Thursday, 3 November 2011

Maccabi Tel Aviv (0) 1 *(Colautti 90)*

Stoke C (0) 2 *(Whitehead 51, Crouch 64)*   10,368

Maccabi Tel Aviv: Levi; Pavicevic, Saban, Cohen (Vered 46), Lugasi, Medunjanin (Kaat 66), Zizov (Colautti 60), Yeini, Puncec, Konate, Atar.
Stoke C: Sorensen; Wilkinson, Higginbotham, Upson, Huth, Palacios (Arismendi 74), Shotton, Diao (Whelan 65), Jones, Walters (Crouch 61), Whitehead.

Thursday, 1 December 2011

Stoke C (0) 1 *(Jones 81)*

Dynamo Kiev (1) 1 *(Upson 27 (og))*   23,774

Stoke C: Begovic; Huth, Shotton, Upson, Higginbotham, Palacios, Pennant (Whitehead 88), Diao (Fuller 70), Jones (Walters 84), Jerome, Delap.
Dynamo Kiev: Shovkovsky; Betao, Danilo Silva, Khacheridi, Husyev, Yussuf (Ninkovic 85), Aliyev, Vukojevic, Shevchenko (Leandro Almeida 73), Brown, Yarmolenko.

Wednesday, 14 December 2011

Besiktas (0) 3 *(Manuel Fernandes 59 (pen), Mustafa 74, Edu 82)*

Stoke C (1) 1 *(Fuller 29)*   26,118

Besiktas: Rustu; Egemen, Sivok, Ismail, Hilbert, Ernst, Manuel Fernandes, Kavlak, Necip (Julio Alves 77), Hugo Almeida (Edu 75), Holosko (Mustafa 46).
Stoke C: Begovic; Wilkinson (Pennant 27), Higginbotham, Arismendi, Upson■, Palacios, Diao, Delap, Jones, Fuller, Jerome.

Group E Table	P	W	D	L	F	A	Pts
Besiktas	6	4	0	2	13	7	12
Stoke C	6	3	2	1	10	7	11
Dynamo Kiev	6	1	4	1	7	7	7
Maccabi Tel Aviv	6	0	2	4	8	17	2

GROUP F

Paris St Germain	(2) 3	Salzburg	(0) 1
Slovan Bratislava	(1) 1	Athletic Bilbao	(2) 2
Athletic Bilbao	(2) 2	Paris St Germain	(0) 0
Salzburg	(0) 3	Slovan Bratislava	(0) 0
Athletic Bilbao	(0) 2	Salzburg	(2) 2
Slovan Bratislava	(0) 0	Paris St Germain	(0) 0
Paris St Germain	(0) 1	Slovan Bratislava	(0) 0
Salzburg	(0) 0	Athletic Bilbao	(1) 1
Athletic Bilbao	(1) 2	Slovan Bratislava	(1) 1
Salzburg	(1) 2	Paris St Germain	(0) 0
Paris St Germain	(2) 4	Athletic Bilbao	(1) 2
Slovan Bratislava	(2) 2	Salzburg	(2) 3

Group F Table	P	W	D	L	F	A	Pts
Athletic Bilbao	6	4	1	1	11	8	13
Salzburg	6	3	1	2	11	8	10
Paris St Germain	6	3	1	2	8	7	10
Slovan Bratislava	6	0	1	5	4	11	1

GROUP G

AZ	(3) 4	Malmo	(0) 1
FK Austria	(1) 1	Metalist Kharkiv	(0) 2
Malmo	(0) 1	FK Austria	(2) 2
Metalist Kharkiv	(0) 1	AZ	(1) 1
AZ	(0) 2	FK Austria	(2) 2

Malmo	(1) 1	Metalist Kharkiv	(2) 4
FK Austria	(0) 2	AZ	(2) 2
Metalist Kharkiv	(0) 3	Malmo	(0) 1
Malmo	(0) 0	AZ	(0) 0
Metalist Kharkiv	(2) 4	FK Austria	(1) 1
AZ	(1) 1	Metalist Kharkiv	(1) 1
FK Austria	(0) 2	Malmo	(0) 0

Group G Table	P	W	D	L	F	A	Pts
Metalist Kharkiv	6	4	2	0	15	6	14
AZ	6	1	5	0	10	7	8
FK Austria	6	2	2	2	10	11	8
Malmo	6	0	1	5	4	15	1

GROUP H

Birmingham C	(0) 1	Braga	(1) 3
Club Brugge	(2) 2	Maribor	(0) 0
Braga	(0) 1	Club Brugge	(0) 2
Maribor	(1) 1	Birmingham C	(0) 2
Club Brugge	(1) 1	Birmingham C	(1) 2
Maribor	(1) 1	Braga	(1) 1
Birmingham C	(0) 2	Club Brugge	(2) 2
Braga	(3) 5	Maribor	(0) 1
Braga	(0) 1	Birmingham C	(0) 0
Maribor	(1) 3	Club Brugge	(0) 4
Birmingham C	(1) 1	Maribor	(0) 0
Club Brugge	(0) 1	Braga	(0) 1

Thursday, 15 September 2011

Birmingham C (0) 1 *(King 71)*

Braga (1) 3 *(Helder Barbosa 7, 88, Lima 59)*   21,747

Birmingham C: Myhill; Pablo, Murphy, Spector, N'Daw (Burke 60), Ridgewell, Carr, Elliott, King, Rooney (Wood 60), Redmond.
Braga: Quim; Paulo Vinicius, Echiejile, Baiano, Ewerton, Hugo Viana, Djalma, Nuno Gomes (Leandro Salino 73), Alan, Lima (Carlao 82), Helder Barbosa (Paulo Cesar 89).

Thursday, 29 September 2011

Maribor (1) 1 *(Volas 29)*

Birmingham C (0) 2 *(Burke 64, Elliott 79)*   10,000

Maribor: Handanovic; Arghus, Cvijanovic (Ibraimi 71), Lesjak, Viler, Mezga (Crnic 86), Mertelj (Beric 81), Potokar, Milec, Marcos Tavares, Volas.
Birmingham C: Doyle; Pablo, Ridgewell, Spector, Caldwell, Gomis, Burke, Elliott, King (Zigic 65), Beausejour, Fahey.

Thursday, 20 October 2011

Club Brugge (1) 1 *(Akpala 3)*

Birmingham C (1) 2 *(Murphy 26, Wood 90)*   23,936

Club Brugge: Coosemans; Donk, Hogli, Almeback, Vansteenkiste (De Jonghe 60), Zimling, Blondel (Deschilder 82), Dirar, Odjidja-Ofoe, Refaelov (Meunier 63), Akpala.
Birmingham C: Myhill; Spector, Murphy, Caldwell, Pablo (Ridgewell 90), N'Daw, Burke, Elliott, Rooney (King 72), Zigic (Wood 73), Fahey.

Thursday, 3 November 2011

Birmingham C (0) 2 *(Beausejour 55, King 74 (pen))*

Club Brugge (2) 2 *(Meunier 39, Akpala 44)*   26,849

Birmingham C: Doyle; N'Daw, Murphy, Caldwell, Pablo, Spector, Elliott (Burke 66), Fahey, Rooney (Wood 66), Zigic (King 66), Beausejour.
Club Brugge: Kujovic; Donk, Van Gijseghem, Vansteenkiste, Zimling, Dirar, Odjidja-Ofoe, Meunier, Van Acker (Almeback 85), Akpala (Vleminckx 76), Victor Vazquez (Refaelov 81).

Wednesday, 30 November 2011

Braga (0) 1 *(Hugo Viana 51)*

Birmingham C (0) 0   9957

Braga: Quim; Paulo Vinicius, Echiejile (Douglao 68), Ewerton, Hugo Viana, Marcio Mossoro (Fran Merida 84), Djalma, Leandro Salino, Alan, Lima, Helder Barbosa (Paulo Cesar 69).
Birmingham C: Myhill; N'Daw, Murphy, Caldwell, Davies, Spector, Burke, Fahey, Elliott (King 64), Zigic (Wood 76), Beausejour (Redmond 64).

Thursday, 15 December 2011

Birmingham C (1) 1 *(Rooney 24)*

Maribor (0) 0   21,634

Birmingham C: Doyle; Pablo, Murphy, Gomis (N'Daw 73), Davies, Spector, Beausejour, Fahey, Rooney (Mutch 79), Zigic, Redmond (Burke 88).
Maribor: Handanovic; Rajcevic, Arghus (Trajkovski 75), Vidovic, Cvijanovic (Ibraimi 67), Mezga, Mertelj, Potokar, Marcos Tavares (Velikonja 71), Volas, Filipovic.

Group H Table	P	W	D	L	F	A	Pts
Club Brugge	6	3	2	1	12	9	11
Braga	6	3	2	1	12	6	11
Birmingham C	6	3	1	2	8	8	10
Maribor	6	0	1	5	6	15	1

GROUP I

Atletico Madrid	(1) 2	Celtic	(0) 0
Udinese	(1) 2	Rennes	(1) 1
Celtic	(1) 1	Udinese	(0) 1
Rennes	(0) 1	Atletico Madrid	(0) 1
Rennes	(1) 1	Celtic	(0) 1
Udinese	(0) 2	Atletico Madrid	(0) 0
Atletico Madrid	(3) 4	Udinese	(0) 0
Celtic	(2) 3	Rennes	(1) 1
Celtic	(0) 0	Atletico Madrid	(1) 1
Rennes	(0) 0	Udinese	(0) 0
Atletico Madrid	(2) 3	Rennes	(0) 1
Udinese	(1) 1	Celtic	(1) 1

Thursday, 15 September 2011

Atletico Madrid (1) 2 *(Falcao 3, Diego 69)*

Celtic (0) 0   28,960

Atletico Madrid: Courtois; Antonio Lopez, Miranda, Perea, Godin, Diego (Tiago 84), Gabi (Adrian 70), Mario Suarez, Arda, Koke (Reyes 57), Falcao.
Celtic: Forster; Wilson M (Matthews 80), Ki, Mulgrew, Wilson K, Loovens, Ledley (Bangura 78), Kayal, Samaras, Hooper, Forrest (Commons 83).

Thursday, 29 September 2011

Celtic (1) 1 *(Ki 3 (pen))*

Udinese (0) 1 *(Abdi 88 (pen))*   28,476

Celtic: Zaluska; Matthews, Wanyama, Ki, Majstorovic, Mulgrew, Kayal, Ledley (Wilson M 46), Bangura, Hooper, Forrest (Samaras 72).
Udinese: Handanovic; Basta (Benatia 46), Danilo, Ekstrand, Neuton, Abdi, Doubai, Pereyra (Isla 46), Agyemang-Badu, Battocchio, Fabbrini (Armero 67).

Thursday, 20 October 2011

Rennes (1) 1 *(Cha 31 (og))*

Celtic (0) 1 *(Ledley 70)*   21,825

Rennes: Costil; Mangane, Kana Biyik, Mavinga (Theophile Catherine 77), Jebbour, Tettey, Feret, Brahimi (Pitroipa 59), Pajot, Boukari (Kembo-Ekoko 58), Hadji.
Celtic: Forster; Matthews, Mulgrew, Ki (Bangura 90), Loovens, Wanyama, Kayal, Ledley, Stokes, Cha, Forrest.

Thursday, 3 November 2011

Celtic (2) 3 *(Stokes 30, 43, Hooper 82)*

Rennes (1) 1 *(Mangane 2)*   28,578

Celtic: Forster; Matthews, Wanyama, Cha, Majstorovic, Loovens (Fraser 46), Kayal, McCourt (Commons 66), Stokes, Samaras, Forrest (Hooper 79).
Rennes: Costil; Danze, Mangane, Theophile Catherine, Tettey (Doumbia 46), Mandjeck, Feret (Hadji 70), M'Vila■, Pajot, Boukari (Montano 46), Pitroipa.

Wednesday, 30 November 2011

Celtic (0) 0

Atletico Madrid (1) 1 *(Arda 30)*   33,257

Celtic: Forster; Matthews, Ledley (Mulgrew 38), Loovens, Majstorovic, Wanyama (Hooper 46), Kayal, Ki, Samaras, Stokes (Brown 76), Forrest.
Atletico Madrid: Courtois; Miranda, Perea, Filipe Luis, Godin, Diego, Gabi (Paulo Assuncao 90), Mario Suarez, Arda (Juanfran 80), Salvio, Adrian (Falcao 68).

Thursday, 15 December 2011

Udinese (1) 1 *(Di Natale 45)*

Celtic (1) 1 *(Hooper 29)*   15,227

Udinese: Handanovic; Basta, Danilo, Benatia, Armero, Ekstrand, Abdi, Doubai (Isla 46), Asamoah, Agyemang-Badu (Pinzi 29), Di Natale.
Celtic: Forster; Cha, Mulgrew, Ki, Majstorovic, Wanyama, Kayal (Stokes 71), Brown, Samaras (Bangura 83), Hooper, Forrest.

Group I Table	P	W	D	L	F	A	Pts
Atletico Madrid	6	4	1	1	11	4	13
Udinese	6	2	3	1	6	7	9
Celtic	6	1	3	2	6	7	6
Rennes	6	0	3	3	5	10	3

GROUP J

Maccabi Haifa	(0) 1	AEK Larnaca	(0) 0
Steaua	(0) 0	Schalke	(0) 0
AEK Larnaca	(0) 1	Steaua	(0) 1
Schalke	(1) 3	Maccabi Haifa	(1) 1
AEK Larnaca	(0) 0	Schalke	(3) 5
Maccabi Haifa	(3) 5	Steaua	(0) 0
Schalke	(0) 0	AEK Larnaca	(0) 0
Steaua	(2) 4	Maccabi Haifa	(2) 2

AEK Larnaca	(1) 2	Maccabi Haifa	(0) 1
Schalke	(1) 2	Steaua	(1) 1
Maccabi Haifa	(0) 0	Schalke	(1) 3
Steaua	(0) 3	AEK Larnaca	(0) 1

Group J Table	P	W	D	L	F	A	Pts
Schalke	6	4	2	0	13	2	14
Steaua	6	2	2	2	9	11	8
Maccabi Haifa	6	2	0	4	10	12	6
AEK Larnaca	6	1	2	3	4	11	5

GROUP K

Fulham	(1) 1	Twente	(1) 1
Wisla	(0) 1	Odense	(1) 3
Odense	(0) 0	Fulham	(1) 2
Twente	(2) 4	Wisla	(1) 1
Odense	(0) 1	Twente	(2) 4
Wisla	(0) 1	Fulham	(0) 0
Fulham	(2) 4	Wisla	(1) 1
Twente	(2) 3	Odense	(1) 2
Odense	(0) 1	Wisla	(2) 2
Twente	(0) 1	Fulham	(0) 0
Fulham	(2) 2	Odense	(0) 2
Wisla	(1) 2	Twente	(1) 1

Thursday, 15 September 2011

Fulham (1) 1 *(Johnson 19)*

Twente (1) 1 *(Schwarzer 40 (og))*   14,120

Fulham: Schwarzer; Baird, Briggs (Senderos 81), Murphy, Grygera, Hangeland, Sidwell, Kasami (Duff 74), Dembele, Johnson (Zamora 66), Dempsey.
Twente: Mihaylov; Wisgerhof, Cornelisse, Tiendalli, Rosales, Douglas, Brama, Janssen (Landzaat 83), Fer, De Jong, John (Bajrami 68).

Thursday, 29 September 2011

Odense (0) 0

Fulham (1) 2 *(Johnson 36, 88)*   7969

Odense: Wessels; Mendy, Ruud, Reginiussen, Christensen, Johansson, Djemba-Djemba (Skoubo 84), Andreasen, Traore■, Kadrii (Gislason 79), Fall (Utaka 68).
Fulham: Schwarzer; Kelly, Briggs, Murphy (Sidwell 77), Senderos, Hangeland, Duff, Etuhu, Johnson, Kasami (Orlando Sa 84), Dempsey.

Thursday, 20 October 2011

Wisla (0) 1 *(Biton 60)*

Fulham (0) 0   16,377

Wisla: Pareiko; Jaliens, Lamey, Diaz, Chavez■, Wilk, Gargula (Brud 79), Nunez, Kirm (Czekaj 90), Iliev (Boguski 86), Biton.
Fulham: Schwarzer; Kelly, Briggs (Frei 88), Gecov (Sidwell 75), Hughes, Hangeland, Duff, Etuhu, Johnson, Orlando Sa (Kasami 59), Dembele■.

Thursday, 3 November 2011

Fulham (2) 4 *(Duff 5, Johnson 30, 57, Sidwell 79)*

Wisla (1) 1 *(Kirm 9)*   20,319

Fulham: Schwarzer; Kelly, Riise J, Murphy (Sidwell 63), Baird, Hangeland, Duff, Etuhu, Johnson (Kasami 77), Zamora (Frei 72), Dempsey.
Wisla: Pareiko; Jaliens, Lamey, Diaz, Wilk, Gargula (Genkov 61), Nunez, Paljic, Kirm, Brud (Iliev 61), Biton (Jovanovic 88).

Thursday, 1 December 2011

Twente (0) 1 *(Janko 89)*

Fulham (0) 0   25,250

Twente: Mihaylov; Wisgerhof, Tiendalli, Rosales, Douglas, Landzaat, Brama, Bajrami, Fer (John 46), Chadli (Janko 79), De Jong.
Fulham: Schwarzer; Kelly, Riise J, Murphy, Hughes, Hangeland, Duff (Frei 34), Etuhu, Johnson■, Zamora (Orlando Sa 87), Dembele (Kasami 83).

Wednesday, 14 December 2011

Fulham (2) 2 *(Dempsey 27, Frei 31)*

Odense (0) 2 *(Andreasen 64, Fall 90)*   15,757

Fulham: Etheridge; Kelly, Briggs, Baird, Hughes, Hangeland, Dempsey (Duff 72), Gecov, Dembele, Zamora (Orlando Sa 89), Frei.
Odense: Wessels; Mendy (Djemba-Djemba 86), Ruud, Reginiussen, Chris Sorensen, Hoegh, Andreasen, Kadrii (Johansson 69), Gislason, Utaka, Jensen (Fall 78).

Group K Table	P	W	D	L	F	A	Pts
Twente	6	4	1	1	14	7	13
Wisla	6	3	0	3	8	13	9
Fulham	6	2	2	2	9	6	8
Odense	6	1	1	4	9	14	4

GROUP L

Anderlecht	(3) 4	AEK Athens	(1) 1
Sturm Graz	(1) 1	Lokomotiv Moscow	(2) 2
AEK Athens	(0) 1	Sturm Graz	(0) 2
Lokomotiv Moscow	(0) 0	Anderlecht	(1) 2
Lokomotiv Moscow	(0) 3	AEK Athens	(0) 1
Sturm Graz	(0) 0	Anderlecht	(0) 2
AEK Athens	(0) 1	Lokomotiv Moscow	(0) 3
Anderlecht	(1) 3	Sturm Graz	(0) 0
AEK Athens	(1) 1	Anderlecht	(2) 2
Lokomotiv Moscow	(0) 3	Sturm Graz	(0) 1
Anderlecht	(2) 5	Lokomotiv Moscow	(1) 3
Sturm Graz	(0) 1	AEK Athens	(2) 3

Group L Table	P	W	D	L	F	A	Pts
Anderlecht	6	6	0	0	18	5	18
Lokomotiv Moscow	6	4	0	2	14	11	12
AEK Athens	6	1	0	5	8	15	3
Sturm Graz	6	1	0	5	5	14	3

SECOND ROUND FIRST LEG

Braga	(0) 0	Besiktas	(1) 2
Rubin	(0) 0	Olympiakos	(0) 1
Ajax	(0) 0	Manchester U	(0) 2
AZ	(1) 1	Anderlecht	(0) 0
Hannover	(0) 2	Club Brugge	(0) 1
Lazio	(1) 1	Atletico Madrid	(2) 3
Legia	(1) 2	Sporting Lisbon	(0) 2
Lokomotiv Moscow	(0) 2	Athletic Bilbao	(1) 1
Porto	(1) 1	Manchester C	(0) 2
Salzburg	(0) 0	Metalist Kharkiv	(3) 4
Steaua	(0) 0	Twente	(0) 1
Stoke C	(0) 0	Valencia	(1) 1
Trabzonspor	(1) 1	PSV Eindhoven	(2) 2

Udinese	(0) 0	PAOK Salonika	(0) 0
Viktoria Plzen	(1) 1	Schalke	(0) 1
Wisla	(0) 1	Standard Liege	(1) 1

Thursday, 16 February 2012

Ajax (0) 0

Manchester U (0) 2 *(Young 59, Hernandez 85)* 48,966

Ajax: Vermeer; Vertonghen, Anita, Alderweireld, Koppers (Boilesen 63), Aissati, De Jong, Eriksen, Bulykin (Van Rhijn 60), Sulejmani, Ozbiliz (Lukoki 80).
Manchester U: De Gea; Jones, Fabio, Carrick, Ferdinand, Evans, Young (Valencia 76), Cleverley (Scholes 61), Hernandez, Rooney, Nani (Welbeck 86).

Porto (1) 1 *(Silvestre Varela 27)*

Manchester C (0) 2 *(Pereira 55 (og), Aguero 85)* 47,417

Porto: Helton; Rolando, Pereira, Danilo (Mangala 22) (Defour 89), Maicon, Gonzalez, Joao Moutinho, Fernando, Rodriguez J, Silvestre Varela (Kleber 77), Hulk.
Manchester C: Hart; Richards, Clichy, Kompany, Lescott, De Jong, Barry, Silva (Kolarov 83), Balotelli (Aguero 78), Toure Y, Nasri (Zabaleta 88).

Stoke C (0) 0

Valencia (1) 1 *(Mehmet Topal 36)* 24,185

Stoke C: Begovic; Wilkinson, Wilson (Shotton 69), Huth, Shawcross, Palacios (Whitehead 53), Pennant, Delap, Walters, Crouch (Jerome 69), Etherington.
Valencia: Guaita; Mathieu, Rami, Bruno (Miguel 81), Dealbert, Mehmet Topal, Costa, Feghouli, Aduriz (Soldado 79), Jonas, Piatti (Juan Bernat 89).

SECOND ROUND SECOND LEG

Manchester C	(1) 4	Porto	(0) 0
Anderlecht	(0) 0	AZ	(0) 1
Athletic Bilbao	(0) 1	Lokomotiv Moscow	(0) 0
Atletico Madrid	(0) 1	Lazio	(0) 0
Besiktas	(0) 0	Braga	(1) 1
Club Brugge	(0) 0	Hannover	(1) 1
Manchester U	(1) 1	Ajax	(1) 2
Metalist Kharkiv	(1) 4	Salzburg	(0) 1
Olympiakos	(1) 1	Rubin	(0) 0
PAOK Salonika	(0) 0	Udinese	(2) 3
PSV Eindhoven	(3) 4	Trabzonspor	(1) 1
Schalke	(1) 3	Viktoria Plzen	(0) 1
(aet.)			
Sporting Lisbon	(0) 1	Legia	(0) 0
Standard Liege	(0) 0	Wisla	(0) 0
Twente	(1) 1	Steaua	(0) 0
Valencia	(1) 1	Stoke C	(0) 0

Wednesday, 22 February 2012

Manchester C (1) 4 *(Aguero 1, Dzeko 76, Silva 84, Pizarro 86)*

Porto (0) 0 39,538

Manchester C: Hart; Richards, Clichy, Kompany, Lescott, De Jong, Barry (Milner 58), Silva, Aguero (Pizarro 80), Toure Y, Nasri (Dzeko 69).
Porto: Helton; Rolando■, Otamendi (Sapunaru 63), Alex Sandro, Maicon, Gonzalez, Joao Moutinho, Fernando, Rodriguez J (Defour 80), Silvestre Varela (Rodriguez C 63), Hulk.

Thursday, 23 February 2012

Manchester U (1) 1 *(Hernandez 6)*

Ajax (1) 2 *(Ozbiliz 37, Alderweireld 87)*   67,328

Manchester U: De Gea; Rafael, Fabio, Jones, Smalling, Park, Young (Evans 61), Cleverley (Scholes 61), Berbatov (Welbeck 72), Hernandez, Nani.
Ajax: Vermeer; Vertonghen, Anita, Alderweireld, Koppers (Klaassen 46), Van Rhijn, De Jong, Lodeiro (Blind 80), Eriksen (Serero 60), Sulejmani, Ozbiliz.

Valencia (1) 1 *(Jonas 24)*

Stoke C (0) 0   35,000

Valencia: Guaita; Rami, Bruno, Dealbert, Jordi Alba, Mehmet Topal, Dani Parejo, Pablo Hernandez, Aduriz, Jonas (Soldado 63), Piatti (Feghouli 63).
Stoke C: Sorensen; Woodgate, Palacios (Pennant 65), Diao, Huth, Collins, Arismendi (Shotton 65), Delap, Jones, Fuller, Jerome.

THIRD ROUND FIRST LEG

Atletico Madrid	(3) 3	Besiktas	(0) 1
AZ	(0) 2	Udinese	(0) 0
Manchester U	(1) 2	Atheltic Bilbao	(1) 3
Metalist Kharkiv	(0) 0	Olympiakos	(0) 1
Sporting Lisbon	(0) 1	Manchester C	(0) 0
Standard Liege	(2) 2	Hannover	(1) 2
Twente	(0) 1	Schalke	(0) 0
Valencia	(3) 4	PSV Eindhoven	(0) 2

Thursday, 8 March 2012

Manchester U (1) 2 *(Rooney 22, 90 (pen))*

Atheltic Bilbao (1) 3 *(Llorente 44, De Marcos 72, Muniain 89)*   67,000

Manchester U: De Gea; Rafael, Evra, Jones, Smalling (Carrick 55), Evans, Park (Anderson 61), Giggs (Nani 75), Hernandez, Rooney, Young.
Atheltic Bilbao: Iraizoz; Iraola, San Jose, Aurtenetxe, Javi Martinez, Susaeta, Iturraspe, Ander Herrera (Inigo Perez 84), Llorente (Toquero 81), Muniain, De Marcos.

Sporting Lisbon (0) 1 *(Xandao 51)*

Manchester C (0) 0   34,371

Sporting Lisbon: Rui Patricio; Anderson Polga, Insua, Joao Pereira, Daniel Carrico, Xandao, Schaars, Izmailov (Bruno Pereirinha 59), Fernandez (Renato Neto 69), Capel (Carrillo 75), Van Wolfswinkel.
Manchester C: Hart; Kolarov, Clichy, Kompany (Lescott 12), Toure K, Barry (Nasri 59), Milner, De Jong, Aguero, Dzeko (Balotelli 71), Silva.

THIRD ROUND SECOND LEG

Athletic Bilbao	(1) 2	Manchester U	(0) 1
Besiktas	(0) 0	Atletico Madrid	(1) 3
Hannover	(2) 4	Standard Liege	(0) 0
Manchester C	(0) 3	Sporting Lisbon	(2) 2
Olympiakos	(1) 1	Metalist Kharkiv	(0) 2
PSV Eindhoven	(0) 1	Valencia	(0) 1
Schalke	(1) 4	Twente	(1) 1
Udinese	(2) 2	AZ	(1) 1

Thursday, 15 March 2012

Athletic Bilbao (1) 2 *(Llorente 23, De Marcos 65)*

Manchester U (0) 1 *(Rooney 80)*   40,000

Athletic Bilbao: Iraizoz; Iraola, Amorebieta, Aurtenetxe, Javi Martinez, Susaeta, Iturraspe, Ander Herrera (Inigo Perez 82), Llorente (Toquero 40), Muniain (San Jose 88), De Marcos.
Manchester U: De Gea; Rafael, Evra, Carrick (Pogba 63), Ferdinand (Smalling 63), Evans, Park, Giggs (Welbeck 68), Young, Rooney, Cleverley.

Manchester C (0) 3 *(Aguero 60, 82, Balotelli 75 (pen))*

Sporting Lisbon (2) 2 *(Fernandez 33, Van Wolfswinkel 40)*   38,021

Manchester C: Hart; Richards, Kolarov, Savic, Pizarro (Dzeko 55), Silva (Nasri 66), Toure Y, Aguero, Balotelli, Johnson A (De Jong 46).
Sporting Lisbon: Rui Patricio; Anderson Polga, Insua, Daniel Carrico, Xandao, Schaars, Izmailov, Fernandez (Renato Neto 64), Bruno Pereirinha, Capel (Jeffren 63), Van Wolfswinkel (Carrillo 63).

QUARTER-FINALS FIRST LEG

Atletico Madrid	(1) 2	Hannover	(1) 1
AZ	(1) 2	Valencia	(0) 1
Schalke	(1) 2	Athletic Bilbao	(1) 4
Sporting Lisbon	(0) 2	Metalist Kharkiv	(0) 1

QUARTER-FINALS SECOND LEG

Athletic Bilbao	(1) 2	Schalke	(1) 2
Hannover	(0) 1	Atletico Madrid	(0) 2
Metalist Kharkiv	(0) 1	Sporting Lisbon	(1) 1
Valencia	(2) 4	AZ	(0) 0

SEMI-FINALS FIRST LEG

Atletico Madrid	(1) 4	Valencia	(1) 2
Sporting Lisbon	(0) 2	Athletic Bilbao	(0) 1

SEMI-FINALS SECOND LEG

Athletic Bilbao	(2) 3	Sporting Lisbon	(1) 1
Valencia	(0) 0	Atletico Madrid	(0) 1

FINAL

Atletico Madrid	(2) 3	Athletic Bilbao	(0) 0

Did You Know?

Though it is a comparative newcomer to the European club competition scene, UEFA still considers the Europa League to be a continuation of its former UEFA Cup, in the same way that the European Cup of the Champions became the Champions League. There was one other significant change as the Intertoto Cup was discontinued and merged with the new Europa League. However, just as the Champions League has its own anthem, the Europa League has followed in a similar musical fashion. In 2009 composer Yohann Zveig directed the Paris Opera to perform the title tune that is now played before all matches. On the playing side of course Atletico Madrid have now won two of the three tournaments held so far. Initially they defeated Fulham in the final, the London team having gamely battled through from the third qualifying round, a matter of nineteen matches including the final itself.

UEFA EUROPA LEAGUE 2012–2013

The list below is provisional and subject to pending CAS decisions and final confirmation from UEFA.

UEFA EUROPA LEAGUE GROUP STAGE

Club Atlético de Madrid (ESP)
Olympique Lyonnais (FRA)*
Tottenham Hotspur FC (ENG)
Bayer 04 Leverkusen (GER)
FC Rubin Kazan (RUS)*
SSC Napoli (ITA)*
A. Académica de Coimbra (POR)*

UEFA EUROPA LEAGUE PLAY-OFFS

Sporting Clube de Portugal (POR)
PFC CSKA Moskva (RUS)
PSV Eindhoven (NED)*
FC Girondins de Bordeaux (FRA)
VfB Stuttgart (GER)
FC Metalist Kharkiv (UKR)
AZ Alkmaar (NED)
Hapoel Tel-Aviv FC (ISR)*
S.S. Lazio (ITA)
Trabzonspor AŞ (TUR)
Newcastle United FC (ENG)
Levante UD (ESP)
FC Dnipro Dnipropetrovsk (UKR)
FC Dinamo Bucureşti (ROU)*
Atromitos FC (GRE)
Heart of Midlothian FC (SCO)*
FC Midtjylland (DEN)
KSC Lokeren OV (BEL)*
FC Luzern (SUI)

UEFA EUROPA LEAGUE THIRD QUALIFYING ROUND

FC Internazionale Milano (ITA)
Liverpool FC (ENG)
Olympique de Marseille (FRA) [LCW]
Athletic Club (ESP)†
Hannover 96 (GER)
PAOK FC (GRE)
FC Steaua Bucureşti (ROU)
AC Sparta Praha (CZE)
sc Heerenveen (NED)
KRC Genk (BEL)
Bursaspor (TUR)
CS Marítimo (POR)
SK Rapid Wien (AUT)

FC Dinamo Moskva (RUS)
AC Omonia (CYP)*
FC Arsenal Kyiv (UKR)
Dundee United FC (SCO)
AC Horsens (DEN)

UEFA EUROPA LEAGUE SECOND QUALIFYING ROUND

APOEL FC (CYP)
Anorthosis Famagusta FC (CYP)
BSC Young Boys (SUI)
FC Viktoria Plzeň (CZE)
KAA Gent (BEL)
Legia Warszawa (POL)*
PFC Levski Sofia (BUL)
FK Crvena Zvezda (SRB)*
FC Metalurh Donetsk (UKR)*
PFC CSKA Sofia (BUL)
FC Anzhi Makhachkala (RUS)
Vitesse (NED)
FK Mladá Boleslav (CZE)
FC Rapid Bucureşti (ROU)
ŠK Slovan Bratislava (SVK)
HNK Hajduk Split (CRO)
Asteras Tripolis FC (GRE)
Bnei Yehuda Tel-Aviv FC (ISR)
Eskişehirspor (TUR)
SV Ried (AUT)†
AIK Solna (SWE)
AGF Århus (DEN)
Aalesunds FK (NOR)*
Maccabi Netanya FC (ISR)
Servette FC (SUI)
VfB Admira Wacker Mödling (AUT)
Ruch Chorzów (POL)
FC Spartak Trnava (SVK)
Tromsø IL (NOR)
NK Slaven Koprivnica (CRO)
FK Vojvodina (SRB)
Saint Johnstone FC (SCO)
FC Naftan Novopolotsk (BLR)*
FC Shakhtyor Soligorsk (BLR)
FC Inter Turku (FIN)
Videoton FC (HUN)
NK Široki Brijeg (BIH)
Skonto FC (LVA)*
PFC Lokomotiv Plovdiv 1936 (BUL)†

Sligo Rovers FC (IRL)*
FC Dila Gori (GEO)*
FC Milsami Orhei (MDA)*
VMFD Žalgiris (LTU)*

UEFA EUROPA LEAGUE FIRST QUALIFYING ROUND

FC Twente (NED)¶
KKS Lech Poznań (POL)
Rosenborg BK (NOR)
IF Elfsborg (SWE)
Kalmar FF (SWE)†
FC Aktobe (KAZ)
Saint Patrick's Athletic FC (IRL)
Stabæk Fotball (NOR)¶
FC Gomel (BLR)
FC Metalurgi Rustavi (GEO)
FK Sarajevo (BIH)
Bohemian FC (IRL)
FK Senica (SVK)
NK Osijek (CRO)†
FH Hafnarfjördur (ISL)
FC Levadia Tallinn (EST)*
FC Pyunik (ARM)
FC Dacia Chişinău (MDA)
FK Bakı (AZE)*
FK Borac Banja Luka (BIH)
SK Liepājas Metalurgs (LVA)
Bangor City FC (WAL)
FC Differdange 03 (LUX)
Budapest Honvéd FC (HUN)
FK Süduva (LTU)
FK Jagodina (SRB)
Myllykosken Pallo-47 (FIN)¶
KF Tirana (ALB)*
NK Olimpija Ljubljana (SVN)
FK Renova (MKD)*
FC İnter Bakı (AZE)
FK Rudar Pljevlja (MNE)
KuPS Kuopio (FIN)†
FK Skendija 79 (MKD)

Birkirkara FC (MLT)
EB/Streymur (FRO)*
Xäzär Länkäran FK (AZE)
MTK Budapest (HUN)†
FK Metalurg Skopje (MKD)
FC Šiauliai (LTU)
FC Zimbru Chişinău (MDA)
JJK Jyväskylä (FIN)
KS Flamurtari (ALB)
Cliftonville FC (NIR)
FC Torpedo Kutaisi (GEO)
FC Santa Coloma (AND)*
Llanelli AFC (WAL)
Crusaders FC (NIR)†
AS Jeunesse Esch (LUX)
NK Celje (SVN)†
FC Daugava (LVA)
NK Mura (SVN)
FK Zeta (MNE)
ÍBV Vestmannaeyjar (ISL)
JK Trans Narva (EST)
Floriana FC (MLT)
Hibernians FC (MLT)†
FC Ordabasy Shymkent (KAZ)*
Thór Akureyri (ISL)†
FC Zhetysu Taldykorgan (KAZ)
JK Nõmme Kalju (EST)
NSÍ Runavík (FRO)
Portadown FC (NIR)
CS Grevenmacher (LUX)
FC Gandzasar Kapan (ARM)
FK Čelik Nikšić (MNE)*
FC USV Eschen-Mauren (LIE)*
KS Teuta (ALB)
Vikingur (FRO)
UE Santa Coloma (AND)
Cefn Druids AFC (WAL)†
FC Shirak (ARM)*
SP La Fiorita (SMR)*
AC Libertas (SMR)

* – cup winners; † – losing cup finalists; ¶ – Fair Play winners.

PAST EUROPEAN CUP FINALS

Year	Winner	Score	Runner-up	Score
1956	Real Madrid	4	Stade de Rheims	3
1957	Real Madrid	2	Fiorentina	0
1958	Real Madrid*	3	AC Milan	2
1959	Real Madrid	2	Stade de Rheims	0
1960	Real Madrid	7	Eintracht Frankfurt	3
1961	Benfica	3	Barcelona	2
1962	Benfica	5	Real Madrid	3
1963	AC Milan	2	Benfica	1
1964	Internazionale	3	Real Madrid	1
1965	Internazionale	1	SL Benfica	0
1966	Real Madrid	2	Partizan Belgrade	1
1967	Celtic	2	Internazionale	1
1968	Manchester U*	4	Benfica	1
1969	AC Milan	4	Ajax	1
1970	Feyenoord*	2	Celtic	1
1971	Ajax	2	Panathinaikos	0
1972	Ajax	2	Internazionale	0
1973	Ajax	1	Juventus	0
1974	Bayern Munich	1 4	Atletico Madrid	1 0
1975	Bayern Munich	2	Leeds U	0
1976	Bayern Munich	1	St Etienne	0
1977	Liverpool	3	Borussia Moenchengladbach	1
1978	Liverpool	1	FC Brugge	0
1979	Nottingham F	1	Malmö	0
1980	Nottingham F	1	Hamburg	0
1981	Liverpool	1	Real Madrid	0
1982	Aston Villa	1	Bayern Munich	0
1983	Hamburg	1	Juventus	0
1984	Liverpool†	1	Roma	1
1985	Juventus	1	Liverpool	0
1986	Steaua Bucharest†	0	Barcelona	0
1987	Porto	2	Bayern Munich	1
1988	PSV Eindhoven†	0	Benfica	0
1989	AC Milan	4	Steaua Bucharest	0
1990	AC Milan	1	Benfica	0
1991	Red Star Belgrade†	0	Marseille	0
1992	Barcelona	1	Sampdoria	0

PAST UEFA CHAMPIONS LEAGUE FINALS

Year	Winner	Score	Runner-up	Score
1993	Marseille	1	AC Milan	0
(Marseille subsequently stripped of title)				
1994	AC Milan	4	Barcelona	0
1995	Ajax	1	AC Milan	0
1996	Juventus†	1	Ajax	1
1997	Borussia Dortmund	3	Juventus	1
1998	Real Madrid	1	Juventus	0
1999	Manchester U	2	Bayern Munich	1
2000	Real Madrid	3	Valencia	0
2001	Bayern Munich†	1	Valencia	1
2002	Real Madrid	2	Leverkusen	1
2003	AC Milan†	0	Juventus	0
2004	Porto	3	Monaco	0
2005	Liverpool†	3	AC Milan	3
2006	Barcelona	2	Arsenal	1
2007	AC Milan	2	Liverpool	1
2008	Manchester U†	1	Chelsea	1
2009	Barcelona	2	Manchester U	0
2010	Internazionale	2	Bayern Munich	0
2011	Barcelona	3	Manchester U	1
2011	Barcelona	3	Manchester U	1
2012	Chelsea†	1	Bayern Munich	1

† aet; won on penalties.   * aet.

PAST UEFA CUP FINALS

Year	Winner			Runner-up		
1972	Tottenham H	2	1	Wolverhampton W	1	1
1973	Liverpool	3	0	Borussia Moenchengladbach	0	2
1974	Feyenoord	2	2	Tottenham H	2	0
1975	Borussia Moenchengladbach	0	5	Twente Enschede	0	1
1976	Liverpool	3	1	FC Brugge	2	1
1977	Juventus**	1	1	Athletic Bilbao	0	2
1978	PSV Eindhoven	0	3	SEC Bastia	0	0
1979	Borussia Moenchengladbach	1	1	Red Star Belgrade	1	0
1980	Borussia Moenchengladbach	3	0	Eintracht Frankfurt**	2	1
1981	Ipswich T	3	2	AZ 67 Alkmaar	0	4
1982	IFK Gothenburg	1	3	SV Hamburg	0	0
1983	Anderlecht	1	1	Benfica	0	1
1984	Tottenham H†	1	1	RSC Anderlecht	1	1
1985	Real Madrid	3	0	Videoton	0	1
1986	Real Madrid	5	0	Cologne	1	2
1987	IFK Gothenburg	1	1	Dundee U	0	1
1988	Bayer Leverkusen†	0	3	Espanol	0	3
1989	Napoli	2	3	Stuttgart	1	3
1990	Juventus	3	0	Fiorentina	1	0
1991	Internazionale	2	0	AS Roma	0	1
1992	Ajax**	0	2	Torino	0	2
1993	Juventus	3	3	Borussia Dortmund	1	0
1994	Internazionale	1	1	Salzburg	0	0
1995	Parma	1	1	Juventus	0	1
1996	Bayern Munich	2	3	Bordeaux	0	1
1997	Schalke*†	1	0	Internazionale	0	1
1998	Internazionale	3		Lazio	0	
1999	Parma	3		Marseille	0	
2000	Galatasaray†	0		Arsenal	0	
2001	Liverpool§	5		Alaves	4	
2002	Feyenoord	3		Borussia Dortmund	2	
2003	Porto*	3		Celtic	2	
2004	Valencia	2		Marseille	0	
2005	CSKA Moscow	3		Sporting Lisbon	1	
2006	Sevilla	4		Middlesbrough	0	
2007	Sevilla*†	2		Espanyol	2	
2008	Zenit St Petersburg	2		Rangers	0	
2009	Shakhtar Donetsk*	2		Werder Bremen	1	

PAST UEFA EUROPA LEAGUE FINALS

Year	Winner		Runner-up	
2010	Atletico Madrid*	2	Fulham	1
2011	Porto	1	Braga	0
2012	Atletico Madrid	3	Athletic Bilbao	0

*After extra time **Won on away goals †Won on penalties §Won on sudden death.

PAST EUROPEAN CHAMPIONSHIP FINALS

Year	Winners		Runners-up		Venue	Attendance
1960	USSR	2	Yugoslavia	1	Paris	17,966
1964	Spain	2	USSR	1	Madrid	120,000
1968	Italy	2	Yugoslavia	0	Rome	60,000
	(After 1-1 draw)					75,000
1972	West Germany	3	USSR	0	Brussels	43,437
1976	Czechoslovakia	2	West Germany	2	Belgrade	45,000
	(Czechoslovakia won on penalties)					
1980	West Germany	2	Belgium	1	Rome	47,864
1984	France	2	Spain	0	Paris	48,000
1988	Holland	2	USSR	0	Munich	72,308
1992	Denmark	2	Germany	0	Gothenburg	37,800
1996	Germany	2	Czech Republic	1	Wembley	73,611
	(Germany won on sudden death)					
2000	France	2	Italy	1	Rotterdam	50,000
	(France won on sudden death)					
2004	Greece	1	Portugal	0	Lisbon	62,865
2008	Spain	1	Germany	0	Vienna	51,428
2012	Spain	4	Italy	0	Kiev	63,170

PAST WORLD CUP FINALS

Year	Winners		Runners-up		Venue	Att.	Referee
1930	Uruguay	4	Argentina	2	Montevideo	90,000	Langenus (B)
1934	Italy*	2	Czechoslovakia	1	Rome	50,000	Eklind (Se)
1938	Italy	4	Hungary	2	Paris	45,000	Capdeville (F)
1950	Uruguay	2	Brazil	1	Rio de Janeiro	199,854	Reader (E)
1954	West Germany	3	Hungary	2	Berne	60,000	Ling (E)
1958	Brazil	5	Sweden	2	Stockholm	49,737	Guigue (F)
1962	Brazil	3	Czechoslovakia	1	Santiago	68,679	Latychev (USSR)
1966	England*	4	West Germany	2	Wembley	93,802	Dienst (Sw)
1970	Brazil	4	Italy	1	Mexico City	107,412	Glockner (EG)
1974	West Germany	2	Holland	1	Munich	77,833	Taylor (E)
1978	Argentina*	3	Holland	1	Buenos Aires	77,000	Gonella (I)
1982	Italy	3	West Germany	1	Madrid	90,080	Coelho (Br)
1986	Argentina	3	West Germany	2	Mexico City	114,580	Filho (Br)
1990	West Germany	1	Argentina	0	Rome	73,603	Mendez (Mex)
1994	Brazil*	0	Italy	0	Los Angeles	94,194	Puhl (H)
	(Brazil won 3-2 on penalties)						
1998	France	3	Brazil	0	St-Denis	75,000	Belqola (Mor)
2002	Brazil	2	Germany	0	Yokohama	69,029	Collina (I)
2006	Italy*	1	France	1	Berlin	69,000	Elizondo (Arg)
	(Italy won 5-3 on penalties)						
2010	Spain*	1	Holland	0	Johannesburg	84,490	Webb (E)

*After extra time.

EURO 2012 QUALIFYING RESULTS

GROUP A

Belgium	(0) 0	Germany	(0) 1
Kazakhstan	(0) 0	Turkey	(2) 3
Austria	(0) 2	Kazakhstan	(0) 0
Germany	(3) 6	Azerbaijan	(0) 1
Turkey	(0) 3	Belgium	(1) 2
Austria	(1) 3	Azerbaijan	(0) 0
Germany	(1) 3	Turkey	(0) 0
Kazakhstan	(0) 0	Belgium	(0) 2
Azerbaijan	(1) 1	Turkey	(0) 0
Belgium	(1) 4	Austria	(2) 4
Kazakhstan	(0) 0	Germany	(0) 3
Austria	(0) 0	Belgium	(1) 2
Germany	(3) 4	Kazakhstan	(0) 0
Belgium	(3) 4	Azerbaijan	(1) 1
Turkey	(1) 2	Austria	(0) 0
Austria	(0) 1	Germany	(1) 2
Belgium	(1) 1	Turkey	(1) 1
Kazakhstan	(0) 2	Azerbaijan	(0) 1
Azerbaijan	(0) 1	Germany	(2) 3
Azerbaijan	(0) 1	Belgium	(0) 1
Germany	(3) 6	Austria	(1) 2
Turkey	(1) 2	Kazakhstan	(0) 1
Austria	(0) 0	Turkey	(0) 0
Azerbaijan	(0) 3	Kazakhstan	(1) 2
Azerbaijan	(0) 1	Austria	(1) 4
Belgium	(2) 4	Kazakhstan	(0) 1
Turkey	(0) 1	Germany	(1) 3
Germany	(2) 3	Belgium	(0) 1
Kazakhstan	(0) 0	Austria	(0) 0
Turkey	(0) 1	Azerbaijan	(0) 0

Group A Table	P	W	D	L	F	A	Pts
Germany	10	10	0	0	34	7	30
Turkey	10	5	2	3	13	11	17
Belgium	10	4	3	3	21	15	15
Austria	10	3	3	4	16	17	12
Azerbaijan	10	2	1	7	10	26	7
Kazakhstan	10	1	1	8	6	24	4

GROUP B

Andorra	(0) 0	Russia	(1) 2
Armenia	(0) 0	Republic of Ireland	(0) 1
Slovakia	(0) 1	Macedonia	(0) 0
Macedonia	(1) 2	Armenia	(1) 2
Republic of Ireland	(2) 3	Andorra	(1) 1
Russia	(0) 0	Slovakia	(1) 1
Andorra	(0) 0	Macedonia	(1) 2
Armenia	(1) 3	Slovakia	(1) 1
Republic of Ireland	(0) 2	Russia	(2) 3
Armenia	(3) 4	Andorra	(0) 0
Macedonia	(0) 0	Russia	(1) 1
Slovakia	(1) 1	Republic of Ireland	(1) 1
Andorra	(0) 0	Slovakia	(1) 1
Armenia	(0) 0	Russia	(0) 0
Republic of Ireland	(2) 2	Macedonia	(1) 1
Macedonia	(0) 0	Republic of Ireland	(2) 2
Russia	(1) 3	Armenia	(1) 1

Slovakia	(0) 1	Andorra	(0) 0
Andorra	(0) 0	Armenia	(1) 3
Republic of Ireland	(0) 0	Slovakia	(0) 0
Russia	(1) 1	Macedonia	(0) 0
Macedonia	(0) 1	Andorra	(0) 0
Russia	(0) 0	Republic of Ireland	(0) 0
Slovakia	(0) 0	Armenia	(0) 4
Andorra	(0) 0	Republic of Ireland	(2) 2
Armenia	(2) 4	Macedonia	(0) 1
Slovakia	(0) 0	Russia	(0) 1
Macedonia	(0) 1	Slovakia	(0) 1
Republic of Ireland	(1) 2	Armenia	(0) 1
Russia	(4) 6	Andorra	(0) 0

Erevan, 3 September 2010, 8600

Armenia (0) 0

Republic of Ireland (0) 1 *(Fahey 76)*

Armenia: Berezovskiy; Arzumanian, Arakelian, Hovespian, Artur Yedigarian (Manoian 68), Artak Yedigarian (Hambardzumian 71), Pachajian, Mkhitarian, Malakian (Manucharian 78), Mkrtchian K, Movsisian.
Republic of Ireland: Given; Dunne, Kilbane, Whelan, St Ledger-Hall, O'Shea, Lawrence, Green, Keane (Keogh 85), Doyle, McGeady (Fahey 68).
Referee: Szabo (Hungary).

Dublin, 7 September 2010, 40,283

Republic of Ireland (2) 3 *(Kilbane 15, Doyle 41, Keane 54)*

Andorra (1) 1 *(Martinez C 45)*

Republic of Ireland: Given; Dunne, Kilbane, Whelan (Gibson 61), St Ledger-Hall, O'Shea (Kelly 75), Lawrence, Green, Keane, Doyle (Keogh 82), McGeady.
Andorra: Gomes; Lima I, Escura, Marc Bernaus, Martinez C, Josep Ayala (Andorra 71), Vieira, Moreno (Manolo Jimenez 59), Pujol (Oscar Sonejee 86), Silva, Gomez.
Referee: Trattou (Cyprus).

Dublin, 8 October 2010, 50,411

Republic of Ireland (0) 2 *(Keane 72 (pen), Long 78)*

Russia (2) 3 *(Kerzhakov 10, Dzagoev 28, Shirokov 51)*

Republic of Ireland: Given; O'Shea, Kilbane, Whelan (Gibson 66), Dunne, St Ledger-Hall, Lawrence (Long 62), Green, Doyle (Fahey 71), Keane, McGeady.
Russia: Akinfeev; Berezutski V, Ignashevich, Anyukov, Zhirkov, Shirokov, Zyryanov (Semshov 68), Denisov, Dzagoev (Berezutski A 85), Kerzhakov (Pogrebnyak 80), Arshavin.
Referee: Blom (Holland).

Zilina, 12 October 2010, 10,892

Slovakia (1) 1 *(Durica 36)*

Republic of Ireland (1) 1 *(St Ledger-Hall 16)*

Slovakia: Mucha; Zabavnik, Hubocan, Salata, Durica, Karhan, Hamsik, Kucka, Weiss (Holosko 70), Jendrisek (Oravec 84), Sestak (Stoch 70).
Republic of Ireland: Given; O'Shea, Kilbane, Whelan, Dunne, St Ledger-Hall, Green (Gibson 41), Fahey (Keogh 71), Long, Keane, McGeady.
Referee: Mallenco (Spain).

Dublin, 26 March 2011, 33,200

Republic of Ireland (2) 2 *(McGeady 2, Keane 21)*

Macedonia (1) 1 *(Trichkovski 45)*

Republic of Ireland: Westwood; Dunne, O'Dea, Foley, Whelan, McGeady, Kilbane, Gibson (Fahey 77), Doyle (Long 20), Keane (McCarthy 87), Duff.
Macedonia: Nuredinoski; Novevski, Grncharov, Shikov, Popov, Shumulikoski, Demiri (Georgievski 84), Tasevski (Durovski 61), Pandev, Naumoski (Ristic 68), Trichkovski.
Referee: Vad II (Hungary).

Skopje, 4 June 2011, 29,500

Macedonia (0) 0

Republic of Ireland (2) 2 *(Keane 8, 36)*

Macedonia: Bogatinov; Noveski, Grncharov, Shikov, Popov, Shumulikoski, Despotovski (Durovski 57), Demiri (Savic 72), Pandev, Naumoski (Hasani 10), Trichkovski.
Republic of Ireland: Given; O'Dea, O'Shea, Kelly, McGeady, Hunt, Kilbane, Whelan, Andrews, Keane, Cox (Long 64).
Referee: Meyer (Germany).

Dublin, 2 September 2011, 35,480

Republic of Ireland (0) 0

Slovakia (0) 0

Republic of Ireland: Given; Dunne, O'Shea, Ward, St Ledger-Hall, McGeady (Hunt 84), Duff, Whelan, Andrews, Doyle (Cox 64), Keane.
Slovakia: Mucha; Cech, Skrtel, Pekarik, Durica, Karhan, Hamsik, Kucka (Guede 76), Stoch, Weiss (Jendrisek 85), Holosko (Vittek 88).
Referee: Proenca (Portugal).

Moscow, 6 September 2011, 49,515

Russia (0) 0

Republic of Ireland (0) 0

Russia: Malafeev; Berezutski V, Berezutski A, Ignashevich, Anyukov, Zhirkov (Bilyaletdinov 76), Semshov, Shirokov, Zyryanov, Arshavin, Kerzhakov (Pavlyuchenko 54).
Republic of Ireland: Given; Dunne, O'Dea, Ward, Kelly, McGeady, Duff (Hunt 67), Whelan, Andrews, Doyle (Cox 59), Keane.
Referee: Brych (Germany).

Andorra La Vella, 7 October 2011, 860

Andorra (0) 0

Republic of Ireland (2) 2 *(Doyle 8, McGeady 20)*

Andorra: Gomes; Lima I (Oscar Sonejee 80), Marc Bernaus, Garcia E, Martinez C, Martinez A (Lorenzo 78), Josep Ayala, Vieira, Moreno, Pujol (Peppe 59), Silva.
Republic of Ireland: Given; O'Dea, O'Shea, Whelan (Fahey 64), St Ledger-Hall, Andrews, Duff (Hunt 75), McGeady, Doyle (Long 71), Keane, Ward.
Referee: Kovarik (Czech Republic).

Dublin, 11 October 2011, 45,200

Republic of Ireland (1) 2 *(Aleksanyan 43 (og), Dunne 60)*

Armenia (0) 1 *(Mkhitarian 62)*

Republic of Ireland: Given; Kelly, O'Shea, Whelan (Fahey 76), Dunne, St Ledger-Hall, Duff, McGeady (Hunt 67), Doyle■, Cox (Walters 80), Andrews.
Armenia: Berezovskiy■; Hovsepian, Aleksanian, Mkoian, Ghazarian (Sarkisov 63), Mkhitarian, Malakian (Petrosian 28), Mkrtchian K, Hayrapetyin, Pizzelli (Manucharian 53), Movsisian.
Referee: Gonzalez (Spain).

Group B Table	P	W	D	L	F	A	Pts
Russia	10	7	2	1	17	4	23
Republic of Ireland	10	6	3	1	15	7	21
Armenia	10	5	2	3	22	10	17
Slovakia	10	4	3	3	7	10	15
Macedonia	10	2	2	6	8	14	8
Andorra	10	0	0	10	1	25	0

GROUP C

Estonia	(0) 2	Faeroes	(1) 1
Estonia	(1) 1	Italy	(0) 2
Faeroes	(0) 0	Serbia	(2) 3
Slovenia	(0) 0	Northern Ireland	(0) 1
Italy	(3) 5	Faeroes	(0) 0
Serbia	(0) 1	Slovenia	(0) 1
Northern Ireland	(0) 0	Italy	(0) 0
Serbia	(0) 1	Estonia	(0) 3
Slovenia	(2) 5	Faeroes	(0) 1
Estonia	(0) 0	Slovenia	(0) 1
Faeroes	(0) 1	Northern Ireland	(0) 1
Italy	(0) 0	Serbia	(0) 0

(Abandoned 7 minutes; crowd trouble. Italy awarded the match 3-0.)

Serbia	(0) 2	Northern Ireland	(1) 1
Slovenia	(0) 0	Italy	(0) 1
Estonia	(0) 1	Serbia	(1) 1
Northern Ireland	(0) 0	Slovenia	(0) 0
Faeroes	(0) 0	Slovenia	(1) 2
Italy	(2) 3	Estonia	(0) 0
Faeroes	(1) 2	Estonia	(0) 0
Northern Ireland	(1) 4	Faeroes	(0) 0
Faeroes	(0) 0	Italy	(1) 1
Northern Ireland	(0) 0	Serbia	(0) 1
Slovenia	(0) 1	Estonia	(1) 2
Estonia	(2) 4	Northern Ireland	(1) 1
Italy	(0) 1	Slovenia	(0) 0
Serbia	(2) 3	Faeroes	(1) 1
Northern Ireland	(1) 1	Estonia	(0) 2
Serbia	(1) 1	Italy	(1) 1
Italy	(1) 3	Northern Ireland	(0) 0
Slovenia	(1) 1	Serbia	(0) 0

Maribor, 3 September 2010, 12,000

Slovenia (0) 0

Northern Ireland (0) 1 *(Evans C 70)*

Slovenia: Handanovic; Cesar, Jokic, Brecko, Mavric, Koren, Kirm (Dedic 74), Radosavljevic, Birsa, Novakovic (Ilicic 74), Ljubijankic (Matavz 88).
Northern Ireland: Taylor; Baird, McAuley, McCann (Lafferty 67), Hughes, Craigan, Cathcart, Davis, Healy (Evans C 67), Feeney, Brunt (Gorman 89).
Referee: Balaj (Romania).

Belfast, 8 October 2010, 15,200

Northern Ireland (0) 0

Italy (0) 0

Northern Ireland: Taylor; Baird, McAuley, Craigan, Hughes, Evans J, Davis, McCann (Evans C 80), Healy (Lafferty 66), Brunt (McGinn 71), Feeney.
Italy: Viviano; Bonucci, Cassani, Chiellini, Criscito, De Rossi, Pirlo, Mauri (Marchisio 79), Pepe (Rossi 84), Cassano, Borriello (Pazzini 74).
Referee: Chapron (France).

Toftir, 12 October 2010, 1921

Faeroes (0) 1 *(Holst 60)*

Northern Ireland (0) 1 *(Lafferty 76)*

Faeroes: Mikkelsen; Gregersen, Davidsen, Naes, Samuelsen (Hansen A 78), Benjaminsen, Jacobsen, Udsen (Petersen J 68), Holst (Hansen J 85), Edmundsson, Elttor.
Northern Ireland: Taylor; Baird, McAuley, Craigan, Hughes, Evans J, Davis, McGinn (Evans C 83), Lafferty, Feeney (Healy 50), Brunt.
Referee: Zimmermann (Switzerland).

Belgrade, 25 March 2011, 350

Serbia (0) 2 *(Pantelic 65, Tosic 74)*

Northern Ireland (1) 1 *(McAuley 40)*

Serbia: Brkic; Ivanovic, Bisevac, Subotic, Kolarov, Stankovic, Krasic (Petrovic 86), Milijas (Jovanovic 47), Tosic, Ljajic (Ninkovic 47), Pantelic.
Northern Ireland: Camp; Baird, Cathcart, McAuley, Hughes, Evans J (McCourt 86), Evans C, Clingan, Lafferty (Healy 46), Gorman (Feeney 78), Brunt.
Referee: Gumienny (Belgium).

Belfast, 29 March 2011, 14,200

Northern Ireland (0) 0

Slovenia (0) 0

Northern Ireland: Camp; Baird, Cathcart, Craigan, McAuley, Evans J, Evans C (Boyce 90), McCann (McQuoid 72), Brunt, Feeney (McCourt 82), Clingan.
Slovenia: Handanovic; Jokic, Brecko, Mavric, Suler, Koren, Kirm, Bacinovic (Sukalo 90), Ilicic (Ljubijankic 29), Birsa, Novakovic (Dedic 84).
Referee: Kuipers (Holland).

Belfast, 10 August 2011, 15,000

Northern Ireland (1) 4 *(Hughes 5, Davis 66, McCourt 71, 88)*

Faeroes (0) 0

Northern Ireland: Camp; Baird, McAuley (Cathcart 46), Hughes, Evans J, Clingan, Davis, McCann, Evans C (McGinn 59), Healy (Ward 83), McCourt.
Faeroes: Mikkelsen; Naes, Davidsen, Baldvinsson, Gregersen, Benjaminsen, Udsen, Olsen S (Danielsen 75), Holst (Hansen A 68), Edmundsson, Elttor (Mouritsen 75).
Referee: Aleckovic (Bosnia).

Belfast, 2 September 2011, 15,148

Northern Ireland (0) 0

Serbia (0) 1 *(Pantelic 67)*

Northern Ireland: Camp; Baird, Hughes, McAuley, Cathcart, Evans J, Evans C (McGinn 59), Davis, Healy (McQuoid 84), McCann (Feeney 71), Brunt.
Serbia: Jorgacevic; Ivanovic, Subotic, Rajkovic, Kolarov, Stankovic, Kuzmanovic (Fejsa 89), Ninkovic (Petrovic 74), Tosic (Ljajic 79), Pantelic, Jovanovic.
Referee: Einwaller (Austria).

Tallinn, 6 September 2011, 8660

Estonia (2) 4 *(Vunk 28, Kink 32, Zenjov 59, Saag 90)*

Northern Ireland (1) 1 *(Piiroja 40 (og))*

Estonia: Pareiko; Klavan, Piiroja, Jaager, Rahn, Kruglov, Puri (Purje 63), Vunk, Vassiljev, Ahjupera (Zenjov 52), Kink (Saag 88).
Northern Ireland: Camp; Baird, Hughes, McAuley, Cathcart, Clingan, Davis, Brunt, Healy (McQuoid 65), McCann, McGinn (Feeney 65).
Referee: Stalhammar (Sweden).

Belfast, 7 October 2011, 12,604

Northern Ireland (1) 1 *(Davis 22)*

Estonia (0) 2 *(Vassiljev 77 (pen), 84)*

Northern Ireland: Camp; Baird, Hodson, McCann (Healy 83), McAuley, Cathcart, Davis, Clingan (Evans C 32), McCourt, Lafferty (Feeney 69), Brunt.
Estonia: Pareiko; Klavan, Stepanov, Piiroja, Jaager, Kruglov, Dmitrijev, Puri (Purje 57), Vunk, Ahjupera (Zenjov 46), Kink (Vassiljev 65).
Referee: Grafe (Germany).

Pescara, 11 October 2011, 19,480

Italy (1) 3 *(Cassano 22, 53, McAuley 74 (og))*

Northern Ireland (0) 0

Italy: Buffon (De Sanctis 81); Barzagli, Cassani, Chiellini, Balzaretti, De Rossi, Pirlo, Aquilani (Nocerino 69), Montolivo, Giovinco, Cassano (Osvaldo 56).
Northern Ireland: Taylor; Baird, Hodson, Evans C, McAuley, McGivern, Davis, Norwood (McLaughlin C 74), Little, Healy (Feeney 70), Gorman (McGinn 78).
Referee: Lahoz (Spain).

Group C Table	P	W	D	L	F	A	Pts
Italy	10	8	2	0	20	2	26
Estonia	10	5	1	4	15	14	16
Serbia	10	4	3	3	13	12	15
Slovenia	10	4	2	4	11	7	14
Northern Ireland	10	2	3	5	9	13	9
Faeroes	10	1	1	8	6	26	4

GROUP D

France	(0) 0	Belarus	(0) 1
Luxembourg	(0) 0	Bosnia	(3) 3
Romania	(0) 1	Albania	(0) 1
Albania	(1) 1	Luxembourg	(0) 0
Belarus	(0) 0	Romania	(0) 0
Bosnia	(0) 0	France	(0) 2
Albania	(1) 1	Bosnia	(1) 1
Luxembourg	(0) 0	Belarus	(0) 0
France	(0) 2	Romania	(0) 0
Belarus	(1) 2	Albania	(0) 0
France	(1) 2	Luxembourg	(0) 0
Luxembourg	(0) 0	France	(1) 2
Albania	(0) 1	Belarus	(0) 0
Bosnia	(0) 2	Romania	(1) 1
Romania	(1) 3	Luxembourg	(1) 1
Belarus	(1) 1	France	(1) 1
Romania	(2) 3	Bosnia	(0) 0
Belarus	(0) 2	Luxembourg	(0) 0
Bosnia	(0) 2	Albania	(0) 0
Albania	(0) 1	France	(2) 2
Belarus	(0) 0	Bosnia	(2) 2
Luxembourg	(0) 0	Romania	(2) 2
Bosnia	(0) 1	Belarus	(0) 0
Luxembourg	(1) 2	Albania	(0) 1
Romania	(0) 0	France	(0) 0
Bosnia	(4) 5	Luxembourg	(0) 0
France	(2) 3	Albania	(0) 0
Romania	(1) 2	Belarus	(1) 2
Albania	(1) 1	Romania	(0) 1
France	(0) 1	Bosnia	(1) 1

Group D Table	P	W	D	L	F	A	Pts
France	10	6	3	1	15	4	21
Bosnia	10	6	2	2	17	8	20
Romania	10	3	5	2	13	9	14
Belarus	10	3	4	3	8	7	13
Albania	10	2	3	5	7	14	9
Luxembourg	10	1	1	8	3	21	4

GROUP E

Moldova	(0) 2	Finland	(0) 0
San Marino	(0) 0	Holland	(2) 5

Sweden	(0) 2	Hungary	(0) 0
Holland	(2) 2	Finland	(1) 1
Hungary	(0) 2	Moldova	(0) 1
Sweden	(3) 6	San Marino	(0) 0
Hungary	(4) 8	San Marino	(0) 0
Moldova	(0) 0	Holland	(1) 1
Finland	(0) 1	Hungary	(0) 2
Holland	(2) 4	Sweden	(0) 1
San Marino	(0) 0	Moldova	(1) 2
Finland	(1) 8	San Marino	(0) 0
Hungary	(0) 0	Holland	(2) 4
Holland	(1) 5	Hungary	(0) 3
Sweden	(1) 2	Moldova	(0) 1
Moldova	(0) 1	Sweden	(2) 4
San Marino	(0) 0	Finland	(1) 1
San Marino	(0) 0	Hungary	(1) 3
Sweden	(3) 5	Finland	(0) 0
Finland	(2) 4	Moldova	(0) 1
Holland	(3) 11	San Marino	(0) 0
Hungary	(1) 2	Sweden	(0) 1
Finland	(0) 0	Holland	(1) 2
Moldova	(0) 0	Hungary	(1) 2
San Marino	(0) 0	Sweden	(0) 5
Finland	(0) 1	Sweden	(1) 2
Holland	(1) 1	Moldova	(0) 0
Hungary	(0) 0	Finland	(0) 0
Moldova	(1) 4	San Marino	(0) 0
Sweden	(1) 3	Holland	(1) 2

Group E Table	P	W	D	L	F	A	Pts
Holland	10	9	0	1	37	8	27
Sweden	10	8	0	2	31	11	24
Hungary	10	6	1	3	22	14	19
Finland	10	3	1	6	16	16	10
Moldova	10	3	0	7	12	16	9
San Marino	10	0	0	10	0	53	0

GROUP F

Israel	(1) 3	Malta	(1) 1
Greece	(0) 1	Georgia	(1) 1
Latvia	(0) 0	Croatia	(1) 3
Croatia	(0) 0	Greece	(0) 0
Georgia	(0) 0	Israel	(0) 0
Malta	(0) 0	Latvia	(1) 2
Georgia	(0) 1	Malta	(0) 0
Greece	(0) 1	Latvia	(0) 0
Israel	(0) 1	Croatia	(2) 2
Greece	(1) 2	Israel	(0) 1
Latvia	(0) 1	Georgia	(0) 1
Croatia	(2) 3	Malta	(0) 0
Georgia	(0) 1	Croatia	(0) 0
Israel	(1) 2	Latvia	(0) 1
Malta	(0) 0	Greece	(0) 1
Israel	(0) 1	Georgia	(0) 0
Croatia	(0) 2	Georgia	(1) 1
Greece	(2) 3	Malta	(0) 1
Latvia	(0) 1	Israel	(2) 2
Georgia	(0) 0	Latvia	(0) 1
Israel	(0) 0	Greece	(0) 1
Malta	(1) 1	Croatia	(2) 3
Croatia	(0) 3	Israel	(1) 1

Latvia	(1) 1	Greece	(0) 1
Malta	(1) 1	Georgia	(1) 1
Greece	(0) 2	Croatia	(0) 0
Latvia	(1) 2	Malta	(0) 0
Croatia	(0) 2	Latvia	(0) 0
Georgia	(1) 1	Greece	(0) 2
Malta	(0) 0	Israel	(1) 2

Group F Table	P	W	D	L	F	A	Pts
Greece	10	7	3	0	14	5	24
Croatia	10	7	1	2	18	7	22
Israel	10	5	1	4	13	11	16
Latvia	10	3	2	5	9	12	11
Georgia	10	2	4	4	7	9	10
Malta	10	0	1	9	4	21	1

GROUP G

England	(1) 4	Bulgaria	(0) 0
Montenegro	(1) 1	Wales	(0) 0
Bulgaria	(0) 0	Montenegro	(1) 1
Switzerland	(0) 1	England	(1) 3
Montenegro	(0) 1	Switzerland	(0) 0
Wales	(0) 0	Bulgaria	(0) 1
England	(0) 0	Montenegro	(0) 0
Switzerland	(2) 4	Wales	(1) 1
Bulgaria	(0) 0	Switzerland	(0) 0
Wales	(0) 0	England	(2) 2
England	(1) 2	Switzerland	(2) 2
Montenegro	(0) 1	Bulgaria	(0) 1
Bulgaria	(0) 0	England	(3) 3
Wales	(1) 2	Montenegro	(0) 1
England	(1) 1	Wales	(0) 0
Switzerland	(1) 3	Bulgaria	(0) 1
Montenegro	(1) 2	England	(2) 2
Wales	(0) 2	Switzerland	(0) 0
Bulgaria	(0) 0	Wales	(1) 1
Switzerland	(0) 2	Montenegro	(0) 0

Wembley, 3 September 2010, 73,426

England (1) 4 *(Defoe 3, 61, 86, Johnson A 83)*

Bulgaria (0) 0

England: Hart; Johnson G, Cole, Barry, Dawson (Cahill 56) Jagielka, Walcott (Johnson A 74), Gerrard, Defoe (Young A 87), Rooney, Milner.
Bulgaria: Mihaylov; Milanov, Stoyanov, Ivanov, Manolev (Minev 66), Petrov S, Yankov, Petrov M, Angelov, Popov (Peev 79), Bozhinov (Rangelov 63).
Referee: Kassai (Hungary).

Podgorica, 3 September 2010, 7442

Montenegro (1) 1 *(Vucinic 30)*

Wales (0) 0

Montenegro: Bozovic M; Basa, Dzudovic, Jovanovic, Zverotic, Pavicevic, Boskovic B (Bozovic V 74), Pekovic, Vukcevic (Beciraj 87), Vucinic, Dalovic (Novakovic 83).
Wales: Hennessey; Gunter, Bale, Collins J (Morgan C 75), Williams A, Ricketts, Edwards D (Earnshaw 68), Ledley, Morison (Church 78), Bellamy, Vaughan.
Referee: Kakos (Greece).

Basle, 7 September 2010, 37,500

Switzerland (0) 1 *(Shaqiri 71)*

England (1) 3 *(Rooney 10, Johnson A 69, Bent 88)*

Switzerland: Benaglio; Grichting, Lichtsteiner■, Ziegler, Von Bergen, Degen (Streller 64), Schwegler (Costanzo 83), Inler, Margairaz (Shaqiri 46), Frei, Derdiyok.
England: Hart; Johnson G, Cole, Barry, Lescott, Jagielka, Walcott (Johnson A 13), Gerrard, Defoe (Bent 70), Rooney (Wright-Phillips 79), Milner.
Referee: Rizzoli (Italy).

Cardiff, 8 October 2010, 14,061

Wales (0) 0

Bulgaria (0) 1 *(Popov 48)*

Wales: Hennessey; Gunter■, Bale, Collins D, Williams A, Collins J, Ricketts, Edwards D (Church 69), Morison (Robson-Kanu 82), Ledley (King 59), Vaughan.
Bulgaria: Mihaylov; Iliev (Vidanov 37), Ivanov, Bodurov, Zanev, Petrov S, Petrov M, Peev (Rangelov 72), Georgiev, Popov, Makriev (Yankov 87).
Referee: Eriksson (Sweden).

Wembley, 12 October 2010, 73,451

England (0) 0

Montenegro (0) 0

England: Hart; Johnson G, Cole, Barry, Ferdinand, Lescott, Young A (Wright-Phillips 74), Gerrard, Crouch (Davies 70), Rooney, Johnson A.
Montenegro: Bozovic M; Basa, Dzudovic, Jovanovic, Savic, Boskovic B (Beciraj 82), Pekovic, Vukcevic, Zverotic, Novakovic (Kascelan 62), Dalovic (Delibasic 77).
Referee: Grafe (Germany).

Basle, 12 October 2010, 26,000

Switzerland (2) 4 *(Stocker 9, 89, Streller 22, Inler 82 (pen))*

Wales (1) 1 *(Bale 13)*

Switzerland: Benaglio (Wolfli 8); Grichting, Lichtsteiner, Ziegler, Von Bergen, Barnetta, Schwegler (Gelson 90), Inler, Stocker, Frei (Derdiyok 79), Streller.
Wales: Hennessey; Blake (Ribeiro 54), Bale, Collins J, Williams A, Collins D, Edwards D (Morison 77), King, Church, Crofts, Vaughan (MacDonald 89).
Referee: Hamer (Luxembourg).

Cardiff, 26 March 2011, 68,959

Wales (0) 0

England (2) 2 *(Lampard 7 (pen), Bent 15)*

Wales: Hennessey; Gunter, Collins D, King (Vaughan 65), Collins J, Williams A, Crofts, Ramsey, Morison (Evans C 65), Bellamy, Ledley.
England: Hart; Johnson G, Cole, Parker (Jagielka 88), Terry, Dawson, Young A, Lampard, Bent, Rooney (Milner 70), Wilshere (Downing 82).
Referee: Benquerenca (Portugal).

Wembley, 4 June 2011, 84,459

England (1) 2 *(Lampard 37 (pen), Young A 51)*

Switzerland (2) 2 *(Barnetta 32, 35)*

England: Hart; Johnson G, Cole (Baines 30), Parker, Terry, Ferdinand, Walcott (Downing 77), Wilshere, Bent, Lampard (Young A 46), Milner.
Switzerland: Benaglio; Djourou, Senderos, Lichtsteiner, Ziegler, Barnetta (Emeghara 90), Behrami (Dzemaili 58), Inler, Shaqiri, Xhaka, Derdiyok (Mehmedi 74).
Referee: Skomina (Slovenia).

Sofia, 2 September 2011, 27,230

Bulgaria (0) 0

England (3) 3 *(Cahill 13, Rooney 21, 45)*

Bulgaria: Mihaylov; Milanov, Ivanov, Bodurov, Bandalovski (Sarmov 46), Zanev, Petrov S, Petrov M, Georgiev, Popov (Marquinhos 81), Genkov (Bozinhov 61).
England: Hart; Smalling, Cole, Barry (Lampard 80), Terry, Cahill, Young A (Milner 61), Parker, Walcott (Johnson A 83), Rooney, Downing.
Referee: De Bleeckere (Belgium).

Cardiff, 2 September 2011, 8194

Wales (1) 2 *(Morison 29, Ramsey 50)*

Montenegro (0) 1 *(Jovetic 71)*

Wales: Hennessey; Gunter, Bale (Earnshaw 90), Blake, Taylor N, Williams A, Ledley, Ramsey (Crofts 64), Morison (Robson-Kanu 83), Bellamy, Vaughan.
Montenegro: Bozovic M; Batak, Zverotic, Balic (Jovanovic 83), Savic, Pekovic, Drincic, Vukcevic, Vucinic (Delibasic 79), Jovetic, Dalovic (Damjanovic 57).
Referee: Banti (Italy).

Wembley, 6 September 2011, 77,128

England (1) 1 *(Young A 35)*

Wales (0) 0

England: Hart; Smalling, Cole, Lampard (Parker 73), Terry, Cahill, Young A, Barry, Milner, Rooney (Carroll 89), Downing (Johnson A 79).
Wales: Hennessey; Gunter, Bale, Blake, Taylor N, Williams A, Ledley, Crofts, Morison (Earnshaw 68), Collison (King 85), Ramsey.
Referee: Schorgenhofer (Austria).

Podgorica, 7 October 2011, 11,340

Montenegro (1) 2 *(Zverotic 45, Delibasic 90)*

England (2) 2 *(Young A 11, Bent 31)*

Montenegro: Bozovic M; Dzudovic, Zverotic, Savic, Pekovic, Vukcevic, Bozovic V (Delibasic 79), Kascelan (Jovanovic 46), Vucinic, Beciraj (Damjanovic 64), Jovetic.
England: Hart; Jones, Cole, Barry, Terry, Cahill, Walcott (Welbeck 76), Parker, Bent (Lampard 64), Rooney■, Young A (Downing 60).
Referee: Stark (Germany).

Swansea, 7 October 2011, 12,317

Wales (0) 2 *(Ramsey 60 (pen), Bale 71)*

Switzerland (0) 0

Wales: Hennessey; Gunter, Bale, Allen, Blake, Williams A, Crofts (Vaughan 81), Ramsey, Morison (Church 81), Bellamy, Taylor N.
Switzerland: Benaglio; Lichtsteiner, Ziegler■, Von Bergen, Klose, Behrami, Inler, Frei F (Emeghara 71), Shaqiri (Ricardo Rodriguez 62), Xhaka (Mehmedi 81), Derdiyok.
Referee: Kuipers (Holland).

Sofia, 11 October 2011, 1672

Bulgaria (0) 0

Wales (1) 1 *(Bale 45)*

Bulgaria: Mihaylov; Ivanov, Miliev, Manolev (Delev 52), Zanev, Terziev, Petrov S, Gadzhev, Popov (Rangelov 70), Tonev, Domovchiyski (Bozhinov 62).
Wales: Hennessey; Gunter, Bale, Blake (Matthews 41), Taylor N, Williams A, Crofts, Allen, Morison (Church 70), Bellamy, Ramsey.
Referee: Gil (Poland).

Group G Table	P	W	D	L	F	A	Pts
England	8	5	3	0	17	5	18
Montenegro	8	3	3	2	7	7	12
Switzerland	8	3	2	3	12	10	11
Wales	8	3	0	5	6	10	9
Bulgaria	8	1	2	5	3	13	5

GROUP H

Iceland	(1) 1	Norway	(0) 2
Portugal	(2) 4	Cyprus	(2) 4
Denmark	(0) 1	Iceland	(0) 0
Norway	(1) 1	Portugal	(0) 0
Cyprus	(0) 1	Norway	(2) 2
Portugal	(2) 3	Denmark	(0) 1
Denmark	(0) 2	Cyprus	(0) 0
Iceland	(1) 1	Portugal	(2) 3
Cyprus	(0) 0	Iceland	(0) 0
Norway	(0) 1	Denmark	(1) 1
Iceland	(0) 0	Denmark	(0) 2
Portugal	(0) 1	Norway	(0) 0
Cyprus	(0) 0	Portugal	(1) 4
Norway	(0) 1	Iceland	(0) 0
Denmark	(2) 2	Norway	(0) 0
Iceland	(1) 1	Cyprus	(0) 0
Cyprus	(1) 1	Denmark	(4) 4
Portugal	(3) 5	Iceland	(0) 3
Denmark	(1) 2	Portugal	(0) 1
Norway	(2) 3	Cyprus	(1) 1

Group H Table	P	W	D	L	F	A	Pts
Denmark	8	6	1	1	15	6	19
Portugal	8	5	1	2	21	12	16
Norway	8	5	1	2	10	7	16
Iceland	8	1	1	6	6	14	4
Cyprus	8	0	2	6	7	20	2

GROUP I

Liechtenstein	(0) 0	Spain	(2) 4
Lithuania	(0) 0	Scotland	(0) 0
Czech Republic	(0) 0	Lithuania	(1) 1
Scotland	(0) 2	Liechtenstein	(0) 1
Czech Republic	(0) 1	Scotland	(0) 0
Spain	(0) 3	Lithuania	(0) 1
Liechtenstein	(0) 0	Czech Republic	(2) 2
Scotland	(0) 2	Spain	(1) 3
Spain	(0) 2	Czech Republic	(1) 1
Czech Republic	(1) 2	Liechtenstein	(0) 0
Lithuania	(0) 1	Spain	(1) 3
Liechtenstein	(2) 2	Lithuania	(0) 0
Lithuania	(0) 0	Liechtenstein	(0) 0
Scotland	(1) 2	Czech Republic	(0) 2
Scotland	(0) 1	Lithuania	(0) 0
Spain	(3) 6	Liechtenstein	(0) 0
Czech Republic	(0) 0	Spain	(2) 2
Liechtenstein	(0) 0	Scotland	(1) 1
Lithuania	(0) 1	Czech Republic	(3) 4
Spain	(2) 3	Scotland	(0) 1

Kaunas, 3 September 2010, 5248

Lithuania (0) 0

Scotland (0) 0

Lithuania: Karcemarskas; Stankevicius, Skerla, Kijanskas, Mikoliunas (Poskus 71), Semberas, Cesnauskis E, Panka, Sernas (Luksa 80), Radavicius, Danilevicius (Ivaskevicius 90).
Scotland: McGregor; Hutton, Whittaker (Berra 90), McCulloch, Weir, McManus, Robson (McFadden 69), Brown (Morrison 76), Fletcher D, Miller, Naismith.
Referee: Cuneyt (Turkey).

Hampden Park, 7 September 2010, 37,050

Scotland (0) 2 *(Miller 62, McManus 90)*

Liechtenstein (0) 1 *(Frick M 46)*

Scotland: McGregor; Hutton, Wallace L (Robson 54), McCulloch, Weir, McManus, Fletcher D, Brown, Boyd (Naismith 66), Miller, McFadden (Morrison 46).
Liechtenstein: Jehle; Martin Stocklasa, Oehri, Michael Stocklasa, Rechsteiner, Burgmeier, Polverino, Wieser (Buchel R 71), Frick M (D'Elia 79), Erne, Hasler D (Hasler N 90).
Referee: Shvetsov (Ukraine).

Prague, 8 October 2010, 14,922

Czech Republic (0) 1 *(Hubnik 69)*

Scotland (0) 0

Czech Republic: Cech; Hubschman, Hubnik, Suchy, Pospech, Kadlec M, Plasil (Rajnoch 90), Polak, Rosicky, Necid (Holek 84), Magera (Bednar 59).
Scotland: McGregor; Hutton, Whittaker, Morrison (Robson 84), Caldwell G (Iwelumo 76), Weir, McManus, Fletcher D, Mackie (Miller 78), Naismith, Dorrans.
Referee: Bebek (Croatia).

Glasgow, 12 October 2010, 51,322

Scotland (0) 2 *(Naismith 58, Pique 66 (og))*

Spain (1) 3 *(David Villa 44 (pen), Iniesta 56, Llorente 79)*

Scotland: McGregor; Whittaker■, Bardsley, McCulloch (Adam 46), Weir, McManus, Morrison (Maloney 88), Fletcher D, Naismith, Miller, Dorrans (Mackie 80).
Spain: Casillas; Puyol, Sergio Ramos, Pique, Capdevila, Iniesta, Xabi Alonso, David Silva (Llorente 76), Cazorla (Pablo Hernandez 70), Sergio Busquets (Marchena 90), David Villa.
Referee: Busacca (Switzerland).

Glasgow, 3 September 2011, 51,564

Scotland (1) 2 *(Miller 45, Fletcher D 82)*

Czech Republic (0) 2 *(Plasil 78, Kadlec M 90 (pen))*

Scotland: McGregor; Hutton, Bardsley (Wilson D 76), Adam (Cowie 79), Caldwell G, Berra, Brown, Fletcher D, Miller, Naismith (Robson 86), Morrison.
Czech Republic: Lastuvka; Hubschman, Hubnik, Sivok, Rajnoch, Kadlec M, Plasil, Rosicky, Petrzela (Rezek 56), Jiracek (Pekhart 77), Baros (Vacek 90).
Referee: Blom (Holland).

Glasgow, 6 September 2011, 34,071

Scotland (0) 1 *(Naismith 50)*

Lithuania (0) 0

Scotland: McGregor; Whittaker, Bardsley (Crainey 70), Bannan (Snodgrass 84), Caldwell G, Berra, Cowie, Fletcher D, Goodwillie, Naismith, Morrison (Dorrans 79).
Lithuania: Karcemarskas; Zaliukas, Klimavicius, Kijanskas (Danilevicius 61), Cesnauskis E, Mikoliunas (Beniusis 77), Semberas, Pilibaitis, Radavicius, Labukas (Novikovas 46), Sernas.
Referee: Jakobsson (Iceland).

Vaduz, 8 October 2011, 5636

Liechtenstein (0) 0

Scotland (1) 1 *(Mackail-Smith 32)*

Liechtenstein: Jehli; Ritzberger, Martin Stocklasa, Rechsteiner, Kaufmann, Buchel M (Kieber 71), Polverino, Hanselmann (Eberle 75), Hasler N, Frick M, Beck T.
Scotland: McGregor; Hutton, Bardsley, Caldwell G, Berra, Adam (Cowie 76), Morrison, Fletcher D, Naismith, Mackail-Smith, Bannan (Forrest 73).
Referee: Hagen (Norway).

Alicante, 11 October 2011, 27,559

Spain (2) 3 *(David Silva 6, 44, David Villa 54)*

Scotland (0) 1 *(Goodwillie 66 (pen))*

Spain: Valdes; Puyol (Arbeloa 46), Sergio Ramos, Pique, Jordi Alba, Xavi (Llorente 64), David Silva (Thiago Alcantara 55), Cazorla, Sergio Busquets, David Villa, Pedro.
Scotland: McGregor; Hutton, Bardsley, Caldwell G, Berra, Adam (Forrest 63), Morrison, Fletcher D (Cowie 85), Naismith, Mackail-Smith, Bannan (Goodwillie 63).
Referee: Johannesson (Sweden).

Group I Table	P	W	D	L	F	A	Pts
Spain	8	8	0	0	26	6	24
Czech Republic	8	4	1	3	12	8	13
Scotland	8	3	2	3	9	10	11
Lithuania	8	1	2	5	4	13	5
Liechtenstein	8	1	1	6	3	17	4

PLAY-OFFS FIRST LEG

Bosnia	(0) 0	Portugal	(0) 0
Czech Republic	(0) 2	Montenegro	(0) 0
Estonia	(0) 0	Republic of Ireland	(1) 4
Turkey	(0) 0	Croatia	(2) 3

Tallinn, 11 November 2011, 10,500

Estonia (0) 0

Republic of Ireland (1) 4 *(Andrews 13, Walters 67, Keane 71, 88 (pen))*

Estonia: Pareiko; Klavan, Stepanov■, Piiroja■, Jaager, Kruglov, Dmitrijev, Vunk (Lindpere 61), Vassiljev, Ahjupera (Voskoboinikov 55), Kink (Purje 67).
Republic of Ireland: Given; Kelly, Ward, St Ledger-Hall, Dunne, Whelan (Fahey 78), Duff (Hunt 73), McGeady, Walters (Cox 83), Keane, Andrews.
Referee: Kassai (Hungary).

PLAY-OFFS SECOND LEG

Croatia	(0) 0	Turkey	(0) 0
Montenegro	(0) 0	Czech Republic	(0) 1
Portugal	(2) 6	Bosnia	(1) 2
Republic of Ireland	(1) 1	Estonia	(0) 1

Dublin, 15 November 2011, 51,151

Republic of Ireland (1) 1 *(Ward 32)*

Estonia (0) 1 *(Vassiljev 57)*

Republic of Ireland: Given; O'Shea, Ward, St Ledger-Hall, Dunne, Whelan, Duff (Fahey 79), Hunt (McGeady 59), Doyle, Keane (Cox 67), Andrews.
Estonia: Londak; Klavan, Jaager, Teniste, Rahn, Kruglov (Puri 18), Lindpere (Kink 54), Vunk, Vassiljev, Saag, Voskoboinikov (Purje 73).
Referee: Kuipers (Holland).

EURO 2012 FINAL COMPETITION

■ *Denotes player sent off.*

GROUP A

Warsaw, 8 June 2012, 56,070

Poland (1) 1 *(Lewandowski 17)*   **Greece (0) 1** *(Salpingidis 51)*

Poland: Szczesny■; Perquis, Boenisch, Wasilewski, Piszczek, Polanski, Obraniak, Murawski, Blaszczykowski, Rybus (Tyton 70), Lewandowski.
Greece: Chalkias; Holebas, Papadopoulos A (Papadopoulos K 37), Torosidis, Papastathopoulos■, Maniatis, Karagounis, Katsouranis, Ninis (Salpingidis 46), Samaras, Gekas (Fortounis 68).
Referee: Velasco (Spain).

Wroclaw, 8 June 2012, 40,803

Russia (2) 4 *(Dzagoev 15, 79, Shirokov 24, Pavlyuchenko 82)*

Czech Republic (0) 1 *(Pilar 52)*

Russia: Malafeev; Ignashevich, Berezutski A, Anyukov, Zhirkov, Shirokov, Zyryanov, Denisov, Arshavin, Dzagoev (Kokorin 84), Kerzhakov (Pavlyuchenko 73).
Czech Republic: Cech; Hubnik, Sivok, Kadlec, Gebre Selassie, Plasil, Rosicky, Pilar, Jiracek (Petrzela 76), Baros (Lafata 85), Rezek (Hubschman 46).
Referee: Webb (England).

Wroclaw, 12 June 2012, 41,105

Greece (0) 1 *(Gekas 53)*   **Czech Republic (2) 2** *(Jiracek 3, Pilar 6)*

Greece: Chalkias (Sifakis 23); Holebas, Torosidis, Papadopoulos K, Maniatis, Fotakis (Gekas 46), Karagounis, Katsouranis, Samaras, Salpingidis, Fortounis (Mitroglou 71).
Czech Republic: Cech; Sivok, Kadlec, Limbersky, Gebre Selassie, Plasil, Rosicky (Kolar 46), Hubschman, Pilar, Jiracek, Baros (Rajtoral 90).
Referee: Lannoy (France).

Warsaw, 12 June 2012, 55,920

Poland (0) 1 *(Blaszczykowski 57)*   **Russia (1) 1** *(Dzagoev 37)*

Poland: Tyton; Perquis, Boenisch, Wasilewski, Piszczek, Dudka (Mierzejewski 73), Polanski (Matuszczyk 85), Obraniak (Pawel Brozek 90), Murawski, Blaszczykowski, Lewandowski.
Russia: Malafeev; Ignashevich, Berezutski A, Anyukov, Zhirkov, Shirokov, Zyryanov, Denisov, Arshavin, Dzagoev (Izmailov 79), Kerzhakov (Pavlyuchenko 70).
Referee: Stark (Germany).

Wroclaw, 16 June 2012, 41,480

Czech Republic (0) 1 *(Jiracek 72)*   **Poland (0) 0**

Czech Republic: Cech; Sivok, Kadlec, Limbersky, Gabre Selassie, Plasil, Hubschman, Kolar, Pilar (Rezek 88), Jiracek (Rajtoral 84), Baros (Pekhart 90).
Poland: Tyton; Perquis, Boenisch, Wasilewski, Piszczek, Dudka, Polanski (Grosicki 56), Obraniak (Pawel Brozek 73), Murawski (Mierzejewski 73), Blaszczykowski, Lewandowski.
Referee: Thomson (Scotland).

Warsaw, 16 June 2012, 55,614

Greece (1) 1 *(Karagounis 45)*   **Russia (0) 0**

Greece: Sifakis; Torosidis, Papadopoulos K, Papastathopoulos, Maniatis, Tzavelas, Karagounis (Makos 67), Katsouranis, Samaras, Gekas (Holebas 64), Salpingidis (Ninis 83).
Russia: Malafeev; Ignashevich, Berezutski A, Anyukov (Izmailov 81), Zhirkov, Shirokov, Denisov, Arshavin, Glushakov (Pogrebnyak 72), Dzagoev, Kerzhakov (Pavlyuchenko 46).
Referee: Eriksson (Sweden).

Group A Table	P	W	D	L	F	A	Pts
Czech Republic	3	2	0	1	4	5	6
Greece	3	1	1	1	3	3	4
Russia	3	1	1	1	5	3	4
Poland	3	0	2	1	2	3	2

GROUP B

Lvov, 9 June 2012, 32,990

Germany (0) 1 *(Gomez 72)*   **Portugal (0) 0**

Germany: Neuer; Lahm, Boateng, Hummels, Badstuber, Schweinsteiger, Ozil (Kroos 87), Khedira, Gomez (Klose 80), Podolski, Muller (Bender 90).
Portugal: Rui Patricio; Pepe, Bruno Alves, Fabio Coentrao, Joao Pereira, Raul Meireles (Silvestre Varela 80), Nani, Miguel Veloso, Joao Moutinho, Cristiano Ronaldo, Helder Postiga (Nelson Oliveira 70).
Referee: Lannoy (France).

Kharkiv, 9 June 2012, 35,923

Holland (0) 0   Denmark (1) 1 *(Krohn-Dehli 24)*

Holland: Stekelenburg; Heitinga, Vlaar, Van der Wiel (Kuyt 85), Willems, Robben, Sneijder, Van Bommel, De Jong (Van der Vaart 71), Afellay (Huntelaar 71), Van Persie.
Denmark: Andersen; Agger, Kjaer, Poulsen S, Jacobsen, Zemling, Kvist, Eriksen (Schone 74), Krohn-Dehli, Rommedahl (Mikkelsen 84), Bendtner.
Referee: Skomina (Slovenia).

Lvov, 13 June 2012, 31,840

Denmark (1) 2 *(Bendtner 41, 80)*   **Portugal (2) 3** *(Pepe 24, Helder Postiga 36, Silvestre Varela 87)*

Denmark: Andersen; Agger, Kjaer, Poulsen S, Jacobsen, Zimling (Poulsen J 16), Kvist, Eriksen, Krohn-Dehli (Schone 90), Rommedahl (Mikkelsen 60), Bendtner.
Portugal: Rui Patricio; Pepe, Bruno Alves, Fabio Coentrao, Joao Pereira, Raul Meireles (Silvestre Varela 84), Nani (Rolando 89), Miguel Veloso, Joao Moutinho, Cristiano Ronaldo, Helder Postiga (Nelson Oliveira 64).
Referee: Thomson (Scotland).

Kharkiv, 13 June 2012, 37,750

Holland (0) 1 *(Van Persie 73)*   **Germany (2) 2** *(Gomez 24, 38)*

Holland: Stekelenburg; Heitinga, Mathijsen, Van der Wiel, Willems, Robben (Kuyt 83), Sneijder, Van Bommel (Van der Vaart 46), De Jong, Afellay (Huntelaar 46), Van Persie.
Germany: Neuer; Lahm, Boateng, Hummels, Badstuber, Schweinsteiger, Ozil (Kroos 81), Khedira, Gomez (Klose 72), Podolski, Muller (Bender 90).
Referee: Eriksson (Sweden).

Lvov, 17 June 2012, 32,990

Denmark (1) 1 *(Krohn-Dehli 24)*   **Germany (1) 2** *(Podolski 19, Bender 80)*

Denmark: Andersen; Agger, Kjaer, Poulsen S, Jacobsen, Poulsen J (Mikkelsen 82), Zimling (Poulsen C 79), Kvist, Eriksen, Krohn-Dehli, Bendtner.
Germany: Neuer; Lahm, Hummels, Badstuber, Schweinsteiger, Ozil, Khedira, Bender, Gomez (Klose 74), Podolski (Schurrle 64), Muller (Kroos 84).
Referee: Velasco (Spain).

Kharkiv, 17 June 2012, 37,445

Portugal (1) 2 *(Cristiano Ronaldo 28, 74)*   **Holland (1) 1** *(Van der Vaart 11)*

Portugal: Rui Patricio; Pepe, Bruno Alves, Fabio Coentrao, Joao Pereira, Raul Meireles (Custodio 72), Nani (Rolando 87), Miguel Veloso, Joao Moutinho, Cristiano Ronaldo, Helder Postiga (Nelson Oliveira 64).
Holland: Stekelenburg; Mathijsen, Vlaar, Van der Wiel, Willems (Afellay 67), Robben, Sneijder, Van der Vaart, De Jong, Van Persie, Huntelaar.
Referee: Rizzoli (Italy).

Group B Table	P	W	D	L	F	A	Pts
Germany	3	3	0	0	5	2	9
Portugal	3	2	0	1	5	4	6
Denmark	3	1	0	2	4	5	3
Holland	3	0	0	3	2	5	0

GROUP C

Poznan, 10 June 2012, 39,550

Republic of Ireland (1) 1 *(St Ledger-Hall 19)*

Croatia (2) 3 *(Mandzukic 3, 48, Jelavic 43)*

Republic of Ireland: Given; Dunne, O'Shea, Ward, St Ledger-Hall, McGeady (Cox 54), Duff, Whelan, Andrews, Doyle (Walters 53), Keane (Long 75).
Croatia: Pletikosa; Srna, Corluka, Schildenfeld, Strinic, Modric, Rakitic (Dujmovic 90), Perisic (Eduardo da Silva 89), Vukojevic, Jelavic (Kranjcar 72), Mandzukic.
Referee: Kuipers (Holland).

Gdansk, 10 June 2012, 38,869

Spain (0) 1 *(Fabregas 64)*   **Italy (0) 1** *(Di Natale 60)*

Spain: Casillas; Sergio Ramos, Arbeloa, Pique, Jordi Alba, Fabregas (Torres 74), Iniesta, Xabi Alonso, Xavi, David Silva (Jesus Navas 65), Busquets.
Italy: Buffon; Bonucci, Chiellini, De Rossi, Pirlo, Thiago Motta (Nocerino 90), Maggio, Marchisio, Giaccherini, Cassano (Giovinco 65), Balotelli (Di Natale 56).
Referee: Kassai (Hungary).

Poznan, 14 June 2012, 37,096

Italy (1) 1 *(Pirlo 39)*   **Croatia (0) 1** *(Mandzukic 72)*

Italy: Buffon; Bonucci, Chiellini, De Rossi, Pirlo, Thiago Motta (Montolivo 63), Maggio, Marchisio, Giaccherini, Cassano (Giovinco 83), Balotelli (Di Natale 70).
Croatia: Pletikosa; Srna, Corluka, Schildenfeld, Strinic, Modric, Rakitic, Perisic (Pranjic 68), Vukojevic, Jelavic (Eduardo Da Silva 83), Mandzukic (Kranjcar 90).
Referee: Webb (England).

Gdansk, 14 June 2012, 39,150

Spain (1) 4 *(Torres 4, 70, David Silva 49, Fabregas 83)*   **Republic of Ireland (0) 0**

Spain: Casillas; Sergio Ramos, Arbeloa, Pique, Jordi Alba, Iniesta (Cazorla 80), Xabi Alonso (Javi Martinez 65), Xavi, David Silva, Busquets, Torres (Fabregas 74).
Republic of Ireland: Given; Dunne, O'Shea, Ward, St Ledger-Hall, McGeady, Duff (McClean 76), Whelan (Green 80), Andrews, Cox (Walters 46), Keane.
Referee: Proenca (Portugal).

Gdansk, 18 June 2012, 39,076

Croatia (0) 0   **Spain (0) 1** *(Jesus Navas 88)*

Croatia: Pletikosa; Srna, Corluka, Schildenfeld, Vida (Jelavic 66), Strinic, Modric, Pran-jic (Perisic 65), Rakitic, Vukojevic (Eduardo Da Silva 81), Mandzukic.
Spain: Casillas; Sergio Ramos, Arbeloa, Pique, Jordi Alba, Iniesta, Xabi Alonso, Xavi (Negredo 89), David Silva (Fabregas 73), Busquets, Torres (Jesus Navas 61).
Referee: Stark (Germany).

Poznan, 18 June 2012, 38,794

Italy (1) 2 *(Cassano 35, Balotelli 90)*   **Republic of Ireland (0) 0**

Italy: Buffon; Barzagli, Chiellini (Bonucci 57), Balzaretti, Abate, De Rossi, Pirlo, Thi-ago Motta, Marchisio, Cassano (Diamanti 63), Di Natale (Balotelli 75).
Republic of Ireland: Given; Dunne, O'Shea, Ward, St Ledger-Hall, McGeady (Long 65), Duff, Whelan, Andrews■, Doyle (Walters 76), Keane (Cox 86).
Referee: Cuneyt (Turkey).

Group C Table	P	W	D	L	F	A	Pts
Spain	3	2	1	0	6	1	7
Italy	3	1	2	0	4	2	5
Croatia	3	1	1	1	4	3	4
Republic of Ireland	3	0	0	3	1	9	0

GROUP D

Donetsk, 11 June 2012, 47,400

France (1) 1 *(Nasri 39)*   **England (1) 1** *(Lescott 30)*

France: Lloris; Debuchy, Evra, Mexes, Rami, Diarra, Malouda (Martin 85), Ribery, Nasri, Cabaye (Ben Arfa 84), Benzema.

England: Hart; Johnson G, Cole, Gerrard, Terry, Lescott, Milner, Parker (Henderson 78), Welbeck (Walcott 90), Young, Oxlade-Chamberlain (Defoe 77).
Referee: Rizzoli (Italy).

Kiev, 11 June 2012, 64,290

Ukraine (0) 2 *(Schevchenko 55, 61)*   **Sweden (0) 1** *(Ibrahimovic 52)*

Ukraine: Pyatov; Mykhalyk, Selin, Khacheridi, Husyev, Nazarenko, Tymoshchuk, Konoplyanka (Devic 90), Shevchenko (Milevskiy 81), Voronin (Rotan 85), Yarmolenko.
Sweden: Isaksson; Mellberg, Martin Olsson, Granqvist, Lustig, Kallstrom, Elm, Toivonen (Svensson 62), Larsson (Wilhelmsson 68), Ibrahimovic, Rosenberg (Elmander 71).
Referee: Cuneyt (Turkey).

Kiev, 15 June 2012, 64,640

Sweden (0) 2 *(Johnson G 49 (og), Mellberg 59)*

England (1) 3 *(Carroll 23, Walcott 64, Welbeck 78)*

Sweden: Isaksson; Mellberg, Olsson J, Martin Olsson, Granqvist (Lustig 66), Kallstrom, Svensson, Elm (Wilhelmsson 81), Larsson, Ibrahimovic, Elmander (Rosenberg 79).
England: Hart; Johnson G, Cole, Gerrard, Terry, Lescott, Milner (Walcott 61), Parker, Carroll, Welbeck (Oxlade-Chamberlain 90), Young.
Referee: Skomina (Slovenia).

Donetsk, 15 June 2012, 48,000

Ukraine (0) 0   France (0) 2 *(Menez 53, Cayabye 56)*

Ukraine: Pyatov; Mykhalyk, Selin, Khacheridi, Husyev, Nazarenko (Milevskiy 60), Tymoshchuk, Konoplyanka, Shevchenko, Voronin (Devic 46), Yarmolenko (Aliyev 68).
France: Lloris; Debuchy, Clichy, Mexes, Rami, Diarra, Ribery, Menez (Martin 73), Nasri, Cabaye (M'Vila 68), Benzema (Giroud 76).
Referee: Kuipers (Holland).

Donetsk, 19 June 2012, 48,700

England (0) 1 *(Rooney 48)*   **Ukraine (0) 0**

England: Hart; Johnson G, Cole, Gerrard, Terry, Lescott, Milner (Walcott 70), Parker, Welbeck (Carroll 82), Rooney (Oxlade-Chamberlain 87), Milner (Walcott 70).
Ukraine: Pyatov; Selin, Rakitskiy, Khacheridi, Husyev, Tymoshchuk, Konoplyanka, Garmash (Nazarenko 78), Milevskiy (Butko 77), Devic (Shevchenko 70), Yarmolenko.
Referee: Cassai (Hungary).

Kiev, 19 June 2012, 63,010

Sweden (0) 2 *(Ibrahimovic 54, Larsson 90)*   **France (0) 0**

Sweden: Isaksson; Mellberg, Olsson J, Martin Olsson, Granqvist, Kallstrom, Svensson (Holmen 78), Bajrami (Wilhelmsson 46), Toivonen (Wernbloom 78), Larsson, Ibrahimovic.
France: Lloris; Debuchy, Clichy, Mexes, Rami, Diarra, Ribery, Nasri (Menez 77), Ben Arfa (Malouda 59), M'Vila (Giroud 83), Benzema.
Referee: Proenca (Portugal).

Group D Table	P	W	D	L	F	A	Pts
England	3	2	1	0	5	3	7
France	3	1	1	1	3	3	4
Ukraine	3	1	0	2	2	4	3
Sweden	3	1	0	2	5	5	3

QUARTER-FINALS

Warsaw, 21 June 2012, 55,590

Czech Republic (0) 0   Portugal (0) 1 *(Cristiano Ronaldo 79)*

Czech Republic: Cech; Sivok, Kadlec, Limbersky, Gebre Selassie, Plasil, Hubschman (Pekhart 86), Pilar, Jiracek, Darida (Rezek 61), Baros.
Portugal: Rui Patricio; Pepe, Bruno Alves, Fabio Coentrao, Joao Pereira, Raul Meireles (Rolando 88), Nani (Custodio 84), Miguel Veloso, Joao Moutinho, Cristiano Ronaldo, Helder Postiga (Hugo Almeida 40).
Referee: Webb (England).

Gdansk, 22 June 2012, 38,751

Germany (1) 4 *(Lahm 39, Khedira 61, Klose 68, Reus 74)*

Greece (0) 2 *(Samaras 55, Salpingidis 89 (pen))*

Germany: Neuer; Lahm, Boateng, Hummels, Badstuber, Schweinsteiger, Ozil, Khedira, Reus (Gotze 80), Klose (Gomez 80), Schurrle (Muller 67).
Greece: Sifakis; Torosidis, Papadopoulos K, Papastathopoulos, Maniatis, Tzavelas (Fotakis 46), Katsouranis, Makos (Liberopoulos 72), Ninis (Gekas 46), Samaras, Salpingidis.
Referee: Skomina (Slovenia).

Donetsk, 23 June 2012, 47,000

Spain (1) 2 *(Xabi Alonso 19, 90 (pen))*   **France (0) 0**

Spain: Casillas; Sergio Ramos, Arbeloa, Pique, Jordi Alba, Fabregas (Torres 67), Iniesta (Cazorla 84), Xabi Alonso, Xavi, David Silva (Pedro 65), Busquets.
France: Lloris; Reveillere, Debuchy (Menez 64), Clichy, Rami, Koscielny, Malouda (Nasri 65), Ribery, Cabaye, M'Vila (Giroud 79), Benzema.
Referee: Rizzoli (Italy).

Kiev, 24 June 2012, 64,340

England (0) 0   Italy (0) 0

England: Hart; Johnson G, Cole, Gerrard, Terry, Lescott, Milner (Walcott 61), Parker (Henderson 94), Welbeck (Carroll 60), Rooney, Young A.
Italy: Buffon; Barzagli, Bonucci, Balzaretti, Abate (Maggio 90), De Rossi (Nocerino 80), Pirlo, Montolivo, Marchisio, Cassano (Diamanti 78), Balotelli.
Referee: Proenca (Portugal).
aet; Italy won 4-2 on penalties: Balotelli scored; Gerrard scored; Montolivo missed; Rooney scored; Pirlo scored; Young A hit bar; Nocerino scored; Cole saved; Diamanti scored.

SEMI-FINALS

Donetsk, 27 June 2012, 48,000

Portugal (0) 0   Spain (0) 0

Portugal: Rui Patricio; Pepe, Bruno Alves, Fabio Coentrao, Joao Pereira, Raul Meireles (Silvestre Varela 113), Nani, Miguel Veloso (Custodio 106), Joao Moutinho, Cristiano Ronaldo, Hugo Almeida (Nelson Oliveira 81).
Spain: Casillas; Sergio Ramos, Arbeloa, Pique, Jordi Alba, Iniesta, Xabi Alonso, Xavi (Pedro 87), David Silva (Jesus Navas 60), Busquets, Negredo (Fabregas 54).
Referee: Cuneyt (Turkey).
aet; Spain won 4-2 on penalties: Xabi Alonso saved; Joao Moutinho saved; Iniesta scored; Pepe scored; Pique scored; Nani scored; Sergio Ramos scored; Bruno Alves hit bar; Fabregas scored.

Warsaw, 28 June 2012, 55,540

Germany (0) 1 *(Ozil 90 (pen))*   **Italy (2) 2** *(Balotelli 20, 36)*

Germany: Neuer; Lahm, Boateng (Muller 71), Hummels, Badstuber, Schweinsteiger, Ozil, Khedira, Kroos, Gomez (Klose 46), Podolski (Reus 46).
Italy: Buffon; Barzagli, Bonucci, Chiellini, Balzaretti, De Rossi, Pirlo, Montolivo (Thiago Motta 64), Marchisio, Cassano (Diamanti 58), Balotelli (Di Natale 70).
Referee: Lannoy (France).

EURO 2012 FINAL

Sunday, 1 July 2012
(in Kiev, attendance 63,170

Spain (2) 4 *(David Silva 14, Jordi Alba 41, Torres 84, Mata 88)*   **Italy (0) 0**

Spain: Casillas; Sergio Ramos, Arbeloa, Pique, Jordi Alba, Fabregas (Torres 75), Iniesta (Mata 87), Xabi Alonso, Xavi, David Silva (Pedro 59), Busquets.
Italy: Buffon; Barzagli, Bonucci, Chiellini (Balzaretti 21), Abate, De Rossi, Pirlo, Montolivo (Thiago Motta 57), Marchisio, Cassano (Di Natale 46), Balotelli.
Referee: Proenca (Portugal).

WORLD CUP 2014 QUALIFYING RESULTS

■ *Denotes player sent off.*

SOUTH AMERICA

Argentina	(2) 4	Chile	(0) 1
Ecuador	(2) 2	Venezuela	(0) 0
Peru	(0) 2	Paraguay	(0) 0
Uruguay	(3) 4	Bolivia	(1) 2
Bolivia	(0) 1	Colombia	(0) 2
Chile	(2) 4	Peru	(0) 2
Paraguay	(0) 1	Uruguay	(0) 1
Venezuela	(0) 1	Argentina	(0) 0
Argentina	(0) 1	Bolivia	(0) 1
Uruguay	(2) 4	Chile	(0) 0
Colombia	(1) 1	Venezuela	(0) 1
Paraguay	(0) 2	Ecuador	(0) 1
Chile	(1) 2	Paraguay	(0) 0
Colombia	(1) 1	Argentina	(0) 2
Ecuador	(0) 2	Peru	(0) 0
Venezuela	(1) 1	Bolivia	(0) 0
Argentina	(3) 4	Ecuador	(0) 0
Bolivia	(0) 0	Chile	(1) 2
Uruguay	(1) 1	Venezuela	(0) 1
Peru	(0) 0	Colombia	(0) 1
Bolivia	(1) 3	Paraguay	(0) 1
Venezuela	(0) 0	Chile	(0) 2
Ecuador	(0) 1	Colombia	(0) 0
Uruguay	(2) 4	Peru	(1) 2

OCEANIA

Samoa 1, American Samoa 0; Tonga 2, Cook Islands 1; Samoa 1, Tonga 1; American Samoa 1, Cook Islands 1; Cook Islands 2, Samoa 3; American Samoa 2, Tonga 1; American Samoa 2, Tonga 1; Cook Islands 2, Samoa 3; American Samoa 1, Cook Islands 1; Samoa 1, Tonga 1; Tonga 2, Cook Islands 1; Samoa 1, American Samoa 0; Samoa 1, Tahiti 10; Vanuatu 2, New Caledonia 5; Fiji 0, New Zealand 1; Solomon Islands 1, Papua New Guinea 0; Vanuatu 5, Samoa 0; Tahiti 4, New Caledonia 3; Papua New Guinea 1, New Zealand 2; Fiji 0, Solomon Islands 0; New Caledonia 9, Samoa 0; Tahiti 4, Vanuatu 1; Papua New Guinea 1, Fiji 1; New Zealand 1, Solomon Islands 1; Samoa 1, Tahiti 10; Vanuatu 2, New Caledonia 5; Fiji 0, New Zealand 1; Vanuatu 5, Samoa 0; Tahiti 1, Solomon Islands 0; New Zealand 0, New Caledonia 2; Solomon Islands 3, New Zealand 4; Tahiti 1, New Caledonia 0.
The four semi-finalists from Round 2 are: New Caledonia, New Zealand, Solomon Islands and Tahiti.

ASIA

Singapore 0, China 4; Jordan 1, Iraq 3; Kuwait 2, UAE 1; North Korea 1, Japan 0; Lebanon 2, South Korea 1; Tajikistan 0, Japan 4; UAE 0, South Korea 2; Iraq 1, China 0; Kuwait 0, Lebanon 1; Jordan 2, Singapore 0; Uzbekistan 1, North Korea 0; Oman 1, Australia 0; Bahrain 1, Iran 1; Qatar 4, Indonesia 0; Saudi Arabia 3, Thailand 0; Uzbekistan 3, Tajikistan 0; Thailand 0, Australia 1; Qatar 0, Bahrain 0; Indonesia 1, Iran 4; Singapore 0, China 4; Saudi Arabia 0, Oman 0; Tajikistan 1, North Korea 1; Oman 2, Thailand 0; China 3, Jordan 1; UAE 4, Lebanon 2; Bahrain 10, Indonesia 0; Iraq 7, Singapore 1; Iran 2, Qatar 2; Japan 0, Uzbekistan 1; Australia 4, Saudi Arabia 2; South Korea 2, Kuwait 0; Uzbekistan 0, Iran 1; Jordan 1, Iraq 1; Japan 3, Oman 0; Lebanon 0, Qatar 1; Oman 0, Australia 0; Lebanon 1, Uzbekistan 1; Qatar 1, South Korea 4; Japan 6, Jordan 0; Iraq 1, Oman 1; South Korea 3, Lebanon 0; Iran 0, Qatar 0; Australia 1, Japan 1.

CONCACAF

Panama 3, Dominica 0; Curacao 6, US Virgin Islands 1; El Salvador 4, Surinam 0; Canada 4, St Kitts & Nevis 0; Trinidad & Tobago 3, Guyana 0 (match awarded); Grenada 1, Guatemala 4; St Vincent & the Grenadines 0, Belize 2; Haiti 2, Antigua & Barbuda 1; Barbados 1, Bermuda 2; Puerto Rico 3, St Lucia 0; Cayman Islands 1, Dominican Republic 1; Surinam 1, El Salvador 3; Guyana 2, Trinidad & Tobago 1; Dominican Republic 4, Cayman Islands 0; Bermuda 2, Barbados 1; Dominican Republic 4, Cayman Islands 0; Bermuda 2, Barbados 0; Belize 1, St Vincent & the Grenadines 1; US Virgin Islands 0, Curacao 3; Nicaragua 1, Dominica 0; Antigua & Barbuda 1, Haiti 0; Guyana 2, Trinidad & Tobago 1; St Kitts & Nevis 0, Canada 0; St Lucia 0, Puerto Rico 4 (match awarded); Guatemala 3, Grenada 0; Jamaica 2, Guatemala 1; USA 3, Antigua & Barbuda 1; Mexico 3, Guyana 1; Costa Rica 2, El Salvador 2; Cuba 0, Canada 1;

Honduras 0, Panama 2; Guatemala 1, USA 1; Antigua & Barbuda 0, Jamaica 0; El Salvador 1, Mexico 2; Guyana 0, Costa Rica 4; Panama 1, Cuba 0; Canada 0, Honduras 0.

AFRICA

ROUND ONE FIRST LEG
St Thomas & Principe 0, Congo 5; Djibouti 0, Namibia 4; Comoros 0, Mozambique 1; Eritrea 1, Rwanda 1; Swaziland 1, DR Congo 3; Equatorial Guinea 2, Madagascar 0; Chad 1, Tanzania 2; Guinea-Bissau 1, Togo 1; Seychelles 0, Kenya 3; Lesotho 1, Burundi 0; Somalia 0, Ethiopia 0.

ROUND ONE SECOND LEG
Congo 1, St Thomas & Principe 1; Namibia 4, Djibouti 0; Mozambique 4, Comoros 1; Rwanda 3, Eritrea 1; DR Congo 5, Swaziland 1; Madagascar 2, Equatorial Guinea 1; Tanzania 0, Chad 1; Togo 1, Guinea-Bissau 0; Kenya 4, Seychelles 0; Burundi 2, Lesotho 2; Ethiopia 5, Somalia 0.

ROUND TWO

GROUP A	P	W	D	L	F	A	Pts
Ethiopia	2	1	1	0	3	1	4
Central African Rep	2	2	0	1	2	2	3
South Africa	2	0	2	0	2	2	2
Botswana	2	0	1	1	3	1	1

GROUP F	P	W	D	L	F	A	Pts
Nigeria	2	1	1	0	2	1	4
Namibia	2	1	0	1	1	1	3
Malawi	2	0	2	0	1	1	2
Kenya	2	0	1	1	0	1	1

GROUP B	P	W	D	L	F	A	Pts
Tunisia	2	2	0	0	5	2	6
Sierra Leone	2	1	1	0	4	3	4
Equatorial Guinea	2	0	1	1	3	5	1
Cape Verde Islands	2	0	0	2	2	4	0

GROUP G	P	W	D	L	F	A	Pts
Egypt	2	2	0	0	5	2	6
Guinea	2	1	0	1	3	3	3
Zimbabwe	2	0	1	1	0	1	1
Mozambique	2	0	1	1	0	2	1

GROUP C	P	W	D	L	F	A	Pts
Ivory Coast	2	1	1	0	4	2	4
Tanzania	2	1	0	1	2	3	3
Morocco	2	0	2	0	3	3	2
Gambia	2	0	1	1	2	3	1

GROUP H	P	W	D	L	F	A	Pts
Benin	2	1	1	0	2	1	4
Algeria	2	1	0	1	5	2	3
Mali	2	1	0	1	2	2	3
Rwanda	2	0	1	1	1	5	1

GROUP D	P	W	D	L	F	A	Pts
Sudan	2	1	1	0	2	0	4
Ghana	2	1	0	1	7	1	3
Zambia	2	1	0	1	1	2	3
Lesotho	2	0	1	1	0	7	1

GROUP I	P	W	D	L	F	A	Pts
Libya	2	1	1	0	3	2	4
DR Congo	2	1	0	1	2	1	3
Cameroon	2	1	0	1	2	2	3
Togo	2	0	1	1	1	3	1

GROUP E	P	W	D	L	F	A	Pts
Congo	2	1	1	0	1	0	4
Gabon	2	1	1	0	1	0	4
Burkina Faso	2	0	1	1	0	1	1
Niger	2	0	1	1	0	1	1

GROUP J	P	W	D	L	F	A	Pts
Senegal	2	1	1	0	4	2	4
Uganda	2	0	2	0	2	2	2
Angola	2	0	2	0	1	1	2
Liberia	2	0	1	1	3	1	1

WORLD CUP 2014 QUALIFYING FIXTURES

EUROPE

Group A – 7 September 2012 – Wales v Belgium; Croatia v Macedonia **8 September 2012** – Scotland v Serbia. **11 September 2012** – Scotland v Macedonia; Belgium v Croatia; Serbia v Wales. **12 October 2012** – Wales v Scotland; Serbia v Belgium; Macedonia v Croatia. **16 October 2012** – Belgium v Scotland; Macedonia v Serbia; Croatia v Wales. **22 March 2013** – Croatia v Serbia; Scotland v Wales; Macedonia v Belgium. **26 March 2013** – Wales v Croatia; Serbia v Scotland; Belgium v Macedonia. **7 June 2013** – Belgium v Serbia; Croatia v Scotland. **6 September 2013** – Macedonia v Wales; Serbia v Croatia; Scotland v Belgium. **10 September 2013** – Macedonia v Scotland; Wales v Serbia. **11 October 2013** – Wales v Macedonia; Croatia v Belgium. **15 October 2013** – Scotland v Croatia; Belgium v Wales; Serbia v Macedonia.

GROUP B – 7 September 2012 – Malta v Armenia; Bulgaria v Italy. **8 September 2012** –

Denmark v Czech Republic. **11 September 2012** – Italy v Malta; Bulgaria v Armenia. **12 October 2012** – Bulgaria v Denmark; Czech Republic v Malta; Armenia v Italy. **16 October 2012** – Czech Republic v Bulgaria; Italy v Denmark. **22 March 2013** – Czech Republic v Denmark; Bulgaria v Malta. **26 March 2013** – Armenia v Czech Republic; Denmark v Bulgaria; Malta v Italy. **7 June 2013** – Armenia v Malta. **8 June 2013** – Czech Republic v Italy. **11 June 1013** – Denmark v Armenia. **6 September 2013** – Malta v Denmark; Italy v Bulgaria; Czech Republic v Armenia. **10 September 2013** – Malta v Bulgaria; Italy v Czech Republic; Armenia v Denmark. **11 October 2013** – Armenia v Bulgaria; Malta v Czech Republic; Denmark v Italy. **15 October 2013** – Italy v Armenia; Bulgaria v Czech Republic; Denmark v Malta.

GROUP C – 7 September 2012 – Germany v Faeroes; Kazakhstan v Republic of Ireland. **11 September 2012** – Austria v Germany; Sweden v Kazakhstan. **12 October 2012** – Faeroes v Sweden; Kazakhstan v Austria; Republic of Ireland v Germany. **16 October 2012** – Faeroes v Republic of Ireland; Germany v Sweden; Austria v Kazakhstan. **22 March 2013** – Sweden v Republic of Ireland; Austria v Faeroes; Kazakhstan v Germany. **26 March 2013** – Republic of Ireland v Austria; Germany v Kazakhstan. **7 June 2013** – Republic of Ireland v Faeroes; Austria v Sweden. **11 June 2013** – Sweden v Faeroes. **6 September 2013** – Republic of Ireland v Sweden; Germany v Austria; Kazakhstan v Faeroes. **10 September 2013** – Kazakhstan v Sweden; Austria v Republic of Ireland; Faeroes v Germany. **11 October 2013** – Sweden v Austria; Faeroes v Kazakhstan; Germany v Republic of Ireland. **15 October 2013** – Faeroes v Austria; Republic of Ireland v Kazakhstan; Sweden v Germany.

GROUP D – 7 September 2012 – Andorra v Hungary; Holland v Estonia; Estonia v Romania. **11 September 2012** – Turkey v Estonia; Hungary v Holland; Romania v Andorra. **12 October 2012** – Holland v Andorra; Turkey v Romania; Estonia v Hungary. **16 October 2012** – Andorra v Estonia; Hungary v Turkey; Romania v Holland. **22 March 2013** – Andorra v Turkey; Holland v Estonia; Hungary v Romania. **26 March 2013** – Holland v Romania; Estonia v Andorra; Turkey v Hungary. **6 September 2013** – Estonia v Holland; Turkey v Andorra; Romania v Hungary. **10 September 2013** – Romania v Turkey; Hungary v Estonia; Andorra v Holland. **11 October 2013** – Holland v Hungary; Andorra v Romania; Estonia v Turkey. **15 October 2013** – Hungary v Andorra; Romania v Estonia; Turkey v Holland.

GROUP E – 7 September 2012 – Slovenia v Switzerland; Albania v Cyprus; Iceland v Norway. **11 September 2012** – Cyprus v Iceland; Norway v Slovenia; Switzerland v Albania. **12 October 2012** – Albania v Iceland; Switzerland v Norway; Slovenia v Cyprus. **16 October 2012** – Albania v Slovenia; Cyprus v Norway; Iceland v Switzerland. **22 March 2013** – Switzerland v Cyprus; Slovenia v Iceland; Norway v Albania. **7 June 2013** – Iceland v Slovenia; Cyprus v Switzerland; Albania v Norway. **6 September 2013** – Norway v Cyprus; Switzerland v Iceland; Slovenia v Albania. **10 September 2013** – Iceland v Albania; Norway v Switzerland; Cyprus v Slovenia. **11 October 2013** – Slovenia v Norway; Albania v Switzerland; Iceland v Cyprus. **15 October 2013** – Norway v Iceland; Switzerland v Slovenia; Cyprus v Albania.

GROUP F – 7 September 2012 – Luxembourg v Portugal; Russia v Northern Ireland; Azerbaijan v Israel. **11 September 2012** – Northern Ireland v Luxembourg; Israel v Russia; Portugal v Azerbaijan. **12 October 2012** – Luxembourg v Israel; Russia v Portugal. **16 October 2012** – Israel v Luxembourg; Russia v Azerbaijan; Portugal v Northern Ireland. **14 November 2012** – Northern Ireland v Azerbaijan. **22 March 2013** – Luxembourg v Azerbaijan; Northern Ireland v Russia; Israel v Portugal.

26 March 2013 – Northern Ireland v Israel; Azerbaijan v Portugal. **7 June 2013** – Azerbaijan v Luxembourg; Portugal v Russia. **6 September 2013** – Russia v Luxembourg; Northern Ireland v Portugal; Israel v Azerbaijan. **10 September 2013** – Russia v Israel; Luxembourg v Northern Ireland. **11 October 2013** – Portugal v Israel; Azerbaijan v Northern Ireland; Luxembourg v Russia. **15 October 2013** – Portugal v Luxembourg; Azerbaijan v Russia; Israel v Northern Ireland.

GROUP G – 7 September 2012 – Latvia v Greece; Lithuania v Slovakia; Liechtenstein v Bosnia. **11 September 2012** – Greece v Lithuania; Slovakia v Liechtenstein; Bosnia v Latvia. **12 October 2012** – Greece v Bosnia; Liechtenstein v Lithuania; Slovakia v Latvia. **16 October 2012** – Bosnia v Lithuania; Latvia v Liechtenstein; Slovakia v Greece. **22 March 2013** – Bosnia v Greece; Slovakia v Lithuania; Liechteinstein v Latvia. **7 June 2013** – Latvia v Bosnia; Lithuania v Greece; Liechtenstein v Slovakia. **6 September 2013** – Latvia v Lithuania; Liechtenstein v Greece; Bosnia v Slovakia. **10 September 2013** – Greece v Latvia; Slovakia v Bosnia; Lithuania v Liechtenstein. **11 October 2013** – Bosnia v Liechtenstein; Lithuania v Latvia; Greece v Slovakia. **15 October 2013** – Latvia v Slovakia; Greece v Liechtenstein; Lithuania v Bosnia.

GROUP H – 7 September 2012 – Montenegro v Poland; Moldova v England. **11 September 2012** – Poland v Moldova; San Marino v Montenegro; England v Ukraine. **12 October 2012** – England v San Marino; Moldova v Ukraine. **16 October 2012** – Poland v England; Ukraine v Montenegro; San Marino v Moldova. **14 November 2012** – Montenegro v San Marino. **22 March 2013** – San Marino v England; Moldova v Montenegro; Poland v Ukraine. **26 March 2013** – Montenegro v England; Ukraine v Moldova; Poland v San Marino. **7 June 2013** – Moldova v Poland; Montenegro v Ukraine. **6 September 2013** – Poland v Montenegro; Ukraine v San Marino; England v Moldova. **10 September 2013** – San Marino v Poland; Ukraine v England. **11 October 2013** – Ukraine v Poland; England v Montenegro; Moldova v San Marino. **15 October 2013** – England v Poland; San Marino v Ukraine; Montenegro v Moldova.

GROUP I – 7 September 2012 – Georgia v Belarus; Finland v France. **11 September 2012** – Georgia v Spain; France v Belarus. **12 October 2012** – Belarus v Spain; Finland v Georgia. **16 October 2012** – Spain v France; Belarus v Georgia. **22 March 2013** – France v Georgia; Spain v Finland. **26 March 2013** – France v Spain. **7 June 2013** – Finland v Belarus. **11 June 2013** – Belarus v Finland. **6 September 2013** – Georgia v France; Finland v Spain. **10 September 2013** – Belarus v France; Georgia v Finland. **11 October 2013** – Spain v Belarus. **15 October 2013** – France v Finland; Spain v Georgia.

Competition still being played.

EUROPEAN SUPER CUP FINAL 2011

26 August 2011, Monaco (attendance 18,048)

Barcelona (1) 2 *(Messi 39, Fabregas 88)*   **Porto (0) 0**

Barcelona: Valdes; Abidal, Dani Alves, Adriano Correia (Busquets 63), Mascherano, Iniesta, Xavi, Keita, Messi, David Villa (Sanchez 60), Pedro (Fabregas 80).

Porto: Helton; Fucile, Sapunaru, Rolando■, Otamendi, Rodriguez (Silvestre Varela 68), Joao Moutinho, Souza (Fernando 77), Guarin■, Hulk, Kleber (Belluschi 77).

Referee: B. Kuipers (Holland).

FIFA CLUB WORLD CUP FINAL 2011

18 December 2011 (attendance 68,166)

Santos (0) 0   Barcelona (3) 4 *(Messi 17, 81, Xavi 24, Fabregas 45)*

Santos: Rafael Cabral; Edu Dracena, Leo, Danilo (Elano 31), Arouca, Durval, Henrique, Borges (Alan Kardec 79), Ganzo (Ibson 83), Neymar, Bruno Rodrigo.

Barcelona: Valdes; Dani Alves, Pique (Mascherano 56), Fabregas, Puyol (Fontas 85), Xavi, Iniesta, Abidal, Thiago (Pedro 79), Messi, Busquets.

COPA SUDAMERICANA FINAL 2011

First Leg:
LDU Quito 0   Univ de Chile 1

Second Leg:
Univ de Chile 3   LDU Quito 0

COPA AMERICA FINAL 2011

Uruguay (2) 3 *(Suarez 11, Forlan 41, 89)*   **Paraguay (0) 0**

(at River Plate Stadium, Buenos Aires)

Uruguay: Muslera; Maximiliano Pereira, Lugano, Coates, Caceres (Godin 88), Gonzalez, Perez (Eguren 69), Rios, Alvaro Pereira (Cavani 63), Forlan, Suarez.

Paraguay: Villar; Piris, Da Silva, Veron, Marecos, Vera (Estigarribia 64), Ortigoza, Caceres (Perez 64), Riveros, Valdez, Zeballos (Barrios 76).

COPA LIBERTADORES FINAL 2012

First Leg:
Boca Juniors 1   Corinthians 0

Second Leg:
Corinthians 2   Boca Juniors 0

AFRICA CUP OF NATIONS FINAL 2011

Zambia 0   Ivory Coast 0

(in Libreville)

Zambia: Mweene; Himoonde, Musonda (Mulenga 12) (Katongo F 74), Sunzu, Nkausu, Chansa, Kalaba, Sinkala, Katongo C, Mayuka, Lungu.

Ivory Coast: Barry; Toure K, Tiene, Bamba, Zokora (Ya Konan 75), Toure Y (Bony 86), Tiote, Gosso, Drogba, Kalou (Gradel 63), Gervinho.

Referee: B. Diatta (Senegal).

aet; Zambia won 8-7 on penalties.

MLS CUP FINAL 2011

Los Angeles Galaxy 1   Houston Dynamo 0

OTHER BRITISH AND IRISH
INTERNATIONAL MATCHES 2011–2012

Wembley, 12 November 2011, 87,189

England (0) 1 *(Lampard 49)*

Spain (0) 0

England: Hart; Johnson G, Cole, Jones (Rodwell 56), Jagielka, Lescott, Walcott (Downing 46), Parker (Walker 85), Bent (Welbeck 64), Lampard (Barry 57), Milner (Johnson A 76).
Spain: Casillas (Reina 46); Sergio Ramos (Puyol 74), Arbeloa, Jordi Alba, Iniesta (Cazorla 74), Xavi (Mata 46), Busquets (Torres 64), Xabi Alonso, Silva (Fabregas 46), David Villa.
Referee: F. De Bleeckere (Belgium).

Wembley, 15 November 2011, 48,876

England (1) 1 *(Barry 23)*

Sweden (0) 0

England: Hart (Carson 46); Walker, Baines, Jones, Cahill, Terry, Walcott (Milner 58), Rodwell (Sturridge 58), Zamora, Barry, Downing.
Sweden: Isaksson (Wiland 46); Lustig (Wilhelmsson 55), Mellberg (Olsson J 46), Majstorovic, Olsson M, Larsson, Kallstrom (Svensson 70), Ibrahimovic (Toivonen 46), Elmander, Wernbloom, Elm (Bajrami 87).
Referee: P. Kralovec (Czech Republic).

Wembley, 29 February 2012, 76,283

England (0) 2 *(Cahill 85, Young A 89)*

Holland (0) 3 *(Robben 57, 90, Huntelaar 58)*

England: Hart; Richards, Baines, Barry (Milner 46), Smalling (Jones 64), Cahill, Young A, Parker, Welbeck (Campbell 80), Gerrard (Sturridge 33) (Walcott 88), Johnson A (Downing 61).
Holland: Stekelenburg; Boulahrouz (Vlaar 82), Heitinga, Mathijsen, Pieters (Schaars 46), Van Bommel, Kuyt, De Jong N, Van Persie (Huntelaar 46) (De Jong L 62), Sneijder (Emanuelson 76), Robben.
Referee: F. Brych (Germany).

Oslo, 26 May 2012, 21,496

Norway (0) 0

England (1) 1 *(Young 9)*

Norway: Jarstein; Hogli (Ruud 40), Demidov, Hangeland, Riise J, Henriksen, Abdellaoue, Elyounoussi, Pedersen (Grindheim 63), Tettey (Jenssen 89), Braaten.
England: Green; Jones (Kelly 88), Baines, Gerrard (Barry 46) (Oxlade-Chamberlain 73), Jagielka, Lescott, Milner, Parker (Walcott 56), Carroll, Young A (Henderson 73), Downing (Johnson A 85).
Referee: M. Weiner (Germany).

Wembley, 2 June 2012, 85,091

England (1) 1 *(Welbeck 36)*

Belgium (0) 0

England: Hart; Johnson G, Cole, Gerrard (Henderson 83), Cahill (Lescott 19), Terry (Jagielka 70), Milner, Parker, Welbeck (Rooney 53), Young A (Defoe 66), Oxlade-Chamberlain (Walcott 66).
Belgium: Mignolet; Gillet, Vertonghen, Vermaelen, Simons, Mertens (Lukaku 72), Witsel, Mirallas (Chadli 59), Hazard, Fellaini, Dembele.
Referee: P. Rasmussen.

Glasgow, 10 August 2011, 17,582

Scotland (2) 2 *(Kvist Jorgensen 23 (og), Snodgrass 44)*

Denmark (1) 1 *(Eriksen 31)*

Scotland: McGregor; Bardsley, Caldwell G, Wilson D, Crainey, Morrison (Bannan 67), Brown (Cowie 21), Adam (Dorrans 57), Snodgrass (Hanley 88), Naismith (Forrest 74), Miller (Mackail-Smith 57).

Denmark: Sorensen; Poulsen C (Zimling 46), Agger (Jorgensen 58), Boilesen, Kjaer, Kvist, Eriksen, Jacobsen (Silberbauer 73), Rommedahl (Schone 46), Krohn-Delhi (Kadrii 76), Bendtner (Pedersen 46).

Referee: M. Borg (Malta).

Larnaca, 11 November, 2011, 1500

Cyprus (0) 1 *(Christofi 59)*

Scotland (1) 2 *(Miller 23, Mackie 56)*

Cyprus: Georgallides (Kissas 46); Merkis, Alexandrou (Katsis 69), Demetriou (Sielis 46), Parpas (Nicolaou 58), Satsias, Dobrasinovic (Vasilou 74), Solomou, Avraam (Mitidis 46), Christofi, Efrem.

Scotland: McGregor; Whittaker, Bardsley (Crainey 74), Berra, Caldwell G, Cowie, Fletcher D (McArthur 63), Morrison, Miller (Mackail-Smith 63), Mackie (Rhodes 87), Robson (Conway 80).

Referee: M. Levy (Israel).

Koper, 29 February 2012, 4200

Slovenia (1) 1 *(Kirm 33)*

Scotland (1) 1 *(Berra 39)*

Slovenia: Handanovic S; Brecko, Suler, Cesar, Jokic, Birsa (Vuckic 61), Kirm (Pecnik 88), Radosavljevic, Khrin (Matic 84), Dedic (Ljubjankic 82), Ilic.

Scotland: McGregor; Martin, Mulgrew, Caldwell G, Berra, Adam (Bannan 46), Forrest (Robson 86), McArthur, Mackie (Miller 79), Mackail-Smith (Snodgrass 60), Morrison (Dorrans 71).

Referee: A. Stavrev (Macedonia).

Jacksonville, 26 May 2012, 54,894

USA (2) 5 *(Donovan 4, 60, 65, Bradley 11, Jones 70)*

Scotland (1) 1 *(Cameron 15 (og))*

USA: Howard (Guzan 71); Cherundolo, Cameron, Bocanegra (Onyewu 63), Johnson (Castillo 72), Edu (Beckerman 64), Bradley, Jones, Donovan, Boyd (Gomez 64), Torres (Corona 68).

Scotland: McGregor; Bardsley (Martin 59), Mulgrew (Wallace 68), Webster (Berra 82), Caldwell G, McArthur (Whittaker 59), Phillips, Brown, Miller, Bannan (Cowie 51), Maloney (Mackail-Smith 83).

Referee: E. Bonilla (El Salvador).

Cardiff, 10 August 2011, 6378

Wales (0) 1 *(Blake 82)*

Australia (1) 2 *(Cahill 44, Kruse 60)*

Wales: Hennessey; Gunter (Matthews 62), Taylor N, Vaughan (Allen 70), Gabbidon (Blake 46), Williams A, Ramsey (Collison 47), Ledley, Bale, Earnshaw (Morison 62), Bellamy.

Australia: Schwarzer; Wilkshire (Kruse 46), Neill, Spiranovic, Zullo (Sarota 83), Emerton (Williams 48), Kilkenny, Valeri, McKay, Cahill (Troisi 70), McDonald (Jedinak 90).

Referee: K. Tohver (Estonia).

Cardiff, 12 November 2011, 12,637

Wales (2) 4 *(Bale 11, Bellamy 16, Vokes 88, 89)*

Norway (0) 1 *(Huseklepp 61)*

Wales: Hennessey; Gunter, Matthews, Williams A, Blake, Allen (Robson-Kanu 76), Crofts, Ramsey (King 90), Bellamy (Edwards D 90), Morison (Vokes 70), Bale.
Norway: Jarstein (Pettersen 46); Ruud, Waehler (Demidov 46), Hangeland, Riise J, Pedersen, Tettey, Grindheim (Brenne 54), Jenssen (Parr 85), Abdellaoui (Braaten 77), Huseklepp.
Referee: G. Grobelnik (Austria).

Cardiff, 29 February 2012, 23,193

Wales (0) 0

Costa Rica (1) 1 *(Campbell 7)*

Wales: Price; Gunter, Matthews (Ricketts 75), Allen (Collison 63), Blake, Williams A (Gabbidon 70), Robson-Kanu, Crofts, Morison (Vokes 68), Bellamy (Earnshaw 75), Vaughan (Ledley 70).
Costa Rica: Navas; Umana, Salvatierra, Miller, Cunningham (Diaz 88), Barrantes, Azofeifa, Wallace (Gabas 68), Oviedo, Ruiz, Campbell (McDonald 79).
Referee: H. Webb (England).

New Jersey, 27 May 2012, 35,518

Mexico (1) 2 *(De Nigris 43, 89)*

Wales (0) 0

Mexico: Corona; Meza, Salcido, Perez (Torres 71), Rodriguez, Andrade, Barrera (Marquez 76), Moreno, De Nigris, Giovani (Reyna 71), Zavala (Granados 64).
Wales: Brown; Matthews (Ricketts 60), Taylor N (Richards 80), Edwards D (King 71), Gunter, Williams A, Allen, Bellamy, Morison (Vokes 60), Ramsey, Robson-Kanu (Church 60).
Referee: R. Salazar (USA).

Belfast, 29 February 2012, 10,500

Northern Ireland (0) 0

Norway (1) 3 *(Nordtveit 44, Elyounoussi 88, Ruud 90)*

Northern Ireland: Camp; McAuley (Hodson 57), McGivern, Clingan, Hughes (Duff 46), Evans J, Evans C (McCann 46), Davis, Shiels, Paterson (Healy 73), Ferguson (McCourt 69).
Norway: Jarstein; Hogli (Ruud 87), Rogne, Demidov (Reginiussen 60), Riise J, Henriksen (Jenssen 78), Nordtveit, Grindheim (Elyounoussi 60), Pedersen, Abdellaoui (Braaten 46), Huseklepp (Berisha 66).
Referee: H. Jones (Wales).

Amsterdam, 2 June 2012, 50,000

Holland (4) 6 *(Van Persie 11, 29 (pen), Sneijder 15, Afellay 37, 51, Vlaar 78)*

Northern Ireland (0) 0

Holland: Stekelenburg; Van der Wiel, Heitinga, Vlaar, Willems (Schaars 78), Robben (Narsingh 82), Afellay, Van Bommel (Van der Vaart 57), De Jong, Sneijder (Kuyt 70), Van Persie (Huntelaar 57).
Northern Ireland: Camp (Carroll 46); McPake, Hodson, Duff (McArdle 62), Ferguson (Healy 81), Lafferty D (McGivern 46), McCann (Carson 46), Clingan, Norwood, Grigg, Little (McGinn 56).
Referee: R. Schorgenhofer (Austria).

Dublin, 10 August 2011, 20,179

Republic of Ireland (0) 0

Croatia (0) 0

Republic of Ireland: Given (Westwood 64); Kelly, Dunne, St Ledger-Hall, Ward, Duff (Treacy 83), Whelan (O'Dea 74), Gibson, Hunt (Keogh 64), Keane, Long (Cox 83).
Croatia: Pletikosa; Corluka (Vrsaljko 74), Lovren, Simunic, Strinic, Srna, Vekojevic (Dujmovic 87), Modric, Kranjcar (Ilicevic 65), Mandzukic (Kalinic 74), Eduardo (Olic 46).
Referee: T. Hagen (Norway).

Dublin, 29 February 2012, 37,741

Republic of Ireland (0) 1 *(Cox 87)*

Czech Republic (0) 1 *(Baros 50)*

Republic of Ireland: Given; O'Shea, Ward, Whelan (Hunt 63), O'Dea, St Ledger-Hall, Duff (Green 63), Andrews, Long (Cox 71), Keane (Walters 71), McGeady (McClean 79).
Czech Republic: Cech; Gebreselassie (Pilar 66), Limbersky, Sivok, Kadlec M, Petrzela (Rajtoral 66), Resek (Pekhart 88), Stajner (Kolar 59), Plasil, Baros (Lafata 59), Jiracek (Hubschman 46).
Referee: De Sousa (Portugal).

Dublin, 26 May 2012, 37,100

Republic of Ireland (0) 1 *(Long 78)*

Bosnia (0) 0

Republic of Ireland: Westwood; McShane (Kelly 78), Dunne (St Ledger-Hall 70), O'Dea, Ward, Duff (McGeady 46), Whelan (Andrews 46), Gibson, McClean, Keane (Long 62), Doyle (Walters 63).
Bosnia: Begovic; Medunjanin (Stevanovic 46), Pandza, Jahic, Mujdza (Zahirovic 56), Pjanic, Misimovic (Alispahic 81), Rahimic (Vrancic 46), Lulic, Dzeko, Ibisevic (Vranjes 70).
Referee: N. Haenni (Switzerland).

Budapest, 4 June 2012, 17,000

Hungary (0) 0

Republic of Ireland (0) 0

Hungary: Bogdan; Varga, Meszaros, Gyurcso (Koltai 86), Korcsmar, Halmosi (Kadar 69), Pinter (Vanczak 46), Koman, Dsudzsak, Szakaly (Szabics 66), Szalai (Nemeth 79).
Republic of Ireland: Given (Westwood 46); O'Shea, St Ledger-Hall, Dunne, Ward, Duff (Hunt 63), Andrews (Gibson 66), Whelan (Green 85), McGeady, Keane (Cox 60), Doyle (Walters 46).
Referee: K. Hansen (Denmark).

ENGLAND UNDER-21 TEAMS 2011–2012

Watford, 1 September 2011, 7738

England (3) 6 *(Dawson 4, 89, Lansbury 21, 73, Henderson 45, Waghorn 79)*

Azerbaijan (0) 0

England: Butland; Flanagan, Briggs, Rodwell, Caulker, Dawson, Oxlade-Chamberlain (Shelvey 77), Henderson, Wickham (Sordell 67), Lansbury, Delfouneso (Waghorn 67).

Barnsley, 5 September 2011, 9152

England (0) 4 *(Waghorn 58, Sordell 60, Delfouneso 82 (pen), Lansbury 90)*

Israel (1) 1 *(Klibat 25)*

England: Amos; Wisdom (Smith 46), Bennett, Rodwell (Oxlade-Chamberlain 46), Dawson, Baker (Caulker 45), Gosling (Gardner 62), Barkley (Wickham 73), Sordell, Shelvey (Lansbury 46), Waghorn (Delfouneso 62).

Reykjavik, 6 October 2011, 2599

Iceland (0) 0

England (2) 3 *(Oxlade-Chamberlain 12, 14, 49)*

England: Butland; Flanagan, Briggs, Rodwell, Kelly, Dawson, Oxlade-Chamberlain (Barkley 83), Henderson, Sordell, Lansbury, Delfouneso (Waghorn 24) (McEachran 63).

Drammen, 10 October 2011, 2323

Norway (1) 1 *(Berisha 23)*

England (2) 2 *(Dawson 3, Henderson 7)*

England: Butland; Smith, Lowe, Bennett, Dawson, Oxlade-Chamberlain, Henderson, Sordell (Shelvey 81), Lansbury, Barkley (Gardner 55), Baker (Flanagan 71).

Colchester, 10 November 2011, 10,051

England (1) 5 *(Sordell 39, Kelly 57, Dawson 86, Gardner 89, 90)*

Iceland (0) 0

England: Butland; Smith, Clyne, Lowe (Gardner 62), Kelly, Dawson, Oxlade-Chamberlain, Henderson, Sordell, McEachran (Keane W 78), Delfouneso (Sammy Ameobi 11).

Mons, 14 November 2011, 3519

Belgium (0) 2 *(Naessens 72, El Kaddouri 90)*

England (1) 1 *(Kelly 14)*

England: Butland; Kelly, Clyne, Smith, Dawson, Henderson, Oxlade-Chamberlain, McEachran, Lowe (Barkley 90), Sordell (Keane W 78), Sammy Ameobi (Gardner 63).

Middlesbrough, 29 February 2012, 22,647

England (2) 4 *(Lansbury 9, 53, Caulker 36, Oxlade-Chamberlain 90 (pen))*

Belgium (0) 0

England: Butland; Kelly, Rose, McEachran, Caulker, Dawson, Oxlade-Chamberlain, Henderson, Sordell (Keane W 82), Lansbury (Gardner 74), Zaha.

ENGLAND UNDER-16 2011–2012

VICTORY SHIELD

30 September 2011
Wales 0
Scotland 0

12 October 2011 *(at Chesterfield)*
England 3 *(Hunte 17, Bennett 44, 47)*
Northern Ireland 1 *(McDonagh 40)*   4126
(at Chesterfield).
England: Gunn; Aina, Smith-Brown (O'Hanlon 52), Hayden (Birch 41), Ogilvie, Cook, Loftus-Cheek, Bennett, Sonupe (Crowley 58), Hunte (Ojo 46), Marsh (Brown J 41).
Northern Ireland: Mitchell; Gray, Stewart, Harney (Gorman 25), Dummigan, McCawl (Toland 63), McDonagh, Donnelly (Gardner 71), Mullan (Teague 58), Doherty, Hale (Croskry 39).

27 October 2011 *(at Cheltenham)*
England 4 *(Loftus-Cheek 3, Sinclair 14, Kiwomya 67, Alassani 77)*
Wales 0   3477
England: Palmer; Birch (Allassani 41), O'Hanlon, Cullen (Rossiter 66), Morris, Clarke, Crowley (Lyons-Foster 41), Loftus-Cheek, Sinclair (Gilliead 54), Kiwomya, Ojo (Iwobi 54).
Wales: Owen; Jones J (Clarke), Harries, Atyeo, White, Morrell (Walsh 73), Noor (Wilson 78), Francis, Penny, Copp (Charles 59), Smith.

25 November 2011 *(at Inverness)*
Scotland 2 *(McMullan 20, Storie 60 (pen))*
England 4 *(Brown J 7, 31, Iwobi 14, Bennett 59)*   1454
Scotland: Fulton; Hogg (Dykes 76), Sinammon, McGhee, Pascazio, Henderson, McMullan, Walsh (Beaton 76), Stoney, Storie, Waters (McManus 41).
England: Gunn; Aina, Smith-Brown, Morris, Lyons-Foster (Clarke 41), Heaton (Hunte 55), Allassani (Crowley 50), Colkett (Brown R 68), Bennett, Brown J (Kiwomya 41), Iwobi.

FRIENDLY

15 February 2012 *(in Madrid)*
Spain 0
England 1 *(Green 80)*
England: Palmer (Burton 41); Aina (Birch 41), Smith-Brown (Ogilvie 56), Morris, Jones, Clarke, Fewster, Colkett (Ojo 56), Brown J (Brown R 64), Allassani (Green 41), Hunte (Iwobi 64).

THE MONTAIGU TOURNAMENT

3 April 2012 *(in St Laurent)*
Japan 1 *(Sugimoto 79)*
England 1 *(Jones 80)*
England: Atkinson; Birch, Smith-Brown, Morris, Jones, Clarke, Green, Sinclair (Iwobi 61), Brown J (Colkett 48), Hunte, Brown R (Bryan 72).

5 April 2012 *(in St Laurent)*

Morocco 0

England 1 *(Sinclair 8)*

England: Palmer; Morris, Jones (Smith-Brown 61), Clarke, Iwobi (Green 54), Sinclair (Brown J 68), Aina, Crowley, Colkett (Hunte 65), Bryan, Gilliead (Birch 75).

7 April 2012 *(in Montaigu)*

Russia 2

England 2 *(Brown J 49, Bryan 70 (pen))*

Russia won 4-3 on penalties.
England: Atkinson; Smith-Brown, Morris, Clarke, Brown J (Iwobi 66), Hunte, Aina, Colkett (Crowley 57), Brown R (Sinclair 66), Bryan, Gilliead.

9 April 2012 *(in Montaigu)*

France 0

England 1 *(Sinclair 35)*

England: Palmer; Birch, Smith-Brown, Morris, Jones, Iwobi (Gilliead 70), Sinclair (Brown J 73), Hunte, Aina (Clarke 60), Crowley (Brown R 73), Colkett (Bryan 56).

ENGLAND C 2011–2012

FRIENDLY

15 Nov

Gibraltar 3 *(Casciaro 42, Perez 46 (pen), Guilling 54)*

England 1 *(Jennings 80)*   1850

(in Victoria Stadium).
England: Hedge (Edwards 46); Beeley (Killock 46), Newton, Turley, McAuley (Watkins 46), Meikle, Reason, Rose (Davis 46), Willmott (Chambers 46), Boyes (Jennings 46), Kissock (West 46).

INTERNATIONAL CHALLENGE TROPHY

28 Feb

England 1 *(Watkins 90)*

Italy 1 *(Angiulli 48)*   4628

(at Fleetwood).
England: Hedge; Roberts, Brown, Turley, Davis, Oshodi, Coulson, Forbes (Watkins 75), Spencer (Boyes 69), Rose (Chambers 69), Blair (Owens 75).

5 June

Russia Under-23 4 *(Delkin 27, 55, Bibilov 42, Smolov 81 (pen))*

England 0

(in Moscow).
England: Hedge (McDonald 77); Ainge, Garner, McAuley, Brown, Meikle (Owens 77), Forbes (Davis 73), Vincent, Johnson (Coulson 59), Wilson (Brogan 46), Gray.

UEFA UNDER-21 CHAMPIONSHIP 2011–13

QUALIFYING ROUND

GROUP 1
Cyprus 6, San Marino 0
San Marino 0, Bosnia 3
Germany 4, Cyprus 1
Greece 2, Belarus 3
Germany 7, San Marino 0
Belarus 1, Bosnia 1
Cyprus 0, Greece 2
Belarus 0, Germany 1
Greece 2, San Marino 0
Germany 3, Bosnia 0
Cyprus 1, Belarus 3
San Marino 0, Germany 8
Bosnia 5, Cyprus 1
Belarus 1, Greece 3
Cyprus 2, Bosnia 1
Greece 0, Bosnia 1
San Marino 0, Belarus 2
Greece 4, Germany 5
Cyprus 0, Germany 3
Germany 1, Greece 0
San Marino 1, Cyprus 2
Bosnia 3, Belarus 0
San Marino 0, Greece 0
Bosnia 3, San Marino 1

GROUP 2
Lithuania 0, Slovenia 1
Finland 0, Malta 0
Lithuania 1, Malta 2
Finland 1, Slovenia 0
Lithuania 0, Sweden 1
Malta 1, Slovenia 4
Sweden 4, Lithuania 0
Malta 1, Finland 2
Slovenia 2, Ukraine 0
Sweden 1, Slovenia 1
Malta 2, Ukraine 2
Finland 0, Sweden 1
Malta 0, Lithuania 2
Slovenia 2, Lithuania 0
Ukraine 1, Finland 1
Ukraine 2, Lithuania 0
Malta 0, Sweden 1
Ukraine 6, Sweden 0
Slovenia 2, Malta 1
Lithuania 1, Ukraine 0
Slovenia 1, Finland 1
Sweden 4, Malta 0
Finland 1, Ukraine 2
Sweden 3, Finland 0

GROUP 3
Andorra 1, Wales 1
Andorra 0, Montenegro 5
Armenia 4, Montenegro 1
Czech Republic 8, Andorra 0
Andorra 0, Armenia 1
Czech Republic 1, Armenia 1
Montenegro 3, Wales 1
Wales 1, Montenegro 0
Wales 0, Czech Republic 1
Montenegro 4, Andorra 0
Armenia 0, Czech Republic 2
Armenia 0, Wales 0
Wales 4, Andorra 0
Czech Republic 2, Montenegro 1
Andorra 1, Czech Republic 5
Armenia 4, Andorra 1

GROUP 4
Faeroes 0, Northern Ireland 0
Northern Ireland 4, Faeroes 0
Serbia 1, Northern Ireland 0
Northern Ireland 0, Denmark 3
Serbia 5, Faeroes 1
Macedonia 1, Serbia 1
Denmark 4, Faeroes 0
Serbia 0, Denmark 0
Macedonia 1, Faeroes 0
Macedonia 1, Denmark 1
Northern Ireland 0, Serbia 2
Macedonia 1, Northern Ireland 0
Faeroes 1, Macedonia 1
Denmark 6, Macedonia 5
Faeroes 0, Serbia 2

GROUP 5
Croatia 0, Georgia 1
Georgia 2, Spain 7
Switzerland 4, Croatia 0
Spain 2, Georgia 0
Croatia 0, Spain 2
Georgia 0, Switzerland 1
Estonia 0, Croatia 1
Switzerland 5, Georgia 0
Spain 6, Estonia 0
Croatia 4, Estonia 0
Spain 3, Switzerland 0
Estonia 0, Spain 1
Croatia 1, Switzerland 2
Estonia 1, Georgia 2

GROUP 6
Moldova 0, Portugal 2
Albania 0, Poland 3
Poland 0, Russia 2
Albania 4, Moldova 3
Portugal 1, Poland 1
Moldova 0, Russia 6
Poland 4, Albania 3
Russia 2, Portugal 1
Albania 0, Russia 1
Portugal 5, Moldova 0
Poland 0, Moldova 1
Albania 2, Portugal 2
Moldova 2, Poland 4
Portugal 1, Russia 0

Portugal 3, Albania 1
Russia 0, Albania 0

GROUP 7
Turkey 6, Liechtenstein 1
Republic of Ireland 2, Hungary 1
Liechtenstein 0, Turkey 3
Hungary 0, Italy 3
Turkey 1, Republic of Ireland 0
Liechtenstein 2, Italy 7
Turkey 2, Hungary 1
Italy 2, Turkey 0
Liechtenstein 1, Republic of Ireland 4
Turkey 0, Italy 2
Republic of Ireland 2, Liechtenstein 0
Italy 2, Hungary 0
Hungary 1, Turkey 0
Republic of Ireland 2, Italy 2
Liechtenstein 0, Hungary 4

GROUP 8
Iceland 2, Belgium 1
England 6, Azerbaijan 0
Belgium 4, Azerbaijan 1
Iceland 0, Norway 2
Azerbaijan 0, Norway 1
Azerbaijan 0, Norway 2
Iceland 0, England 3
Azerbaijan 2, Belgium 2
Norway 1, England 2
Norway 2, Belgium 2
England 5, Iceland 0
Belgium 2, England 1
Azerbaijan 1, Iceland 0
England 4, Belgium 0
Norway 1, Azerbaijan 0
Iceland 1, Azerbaijan 2
Norway 2, Iceland 1

GROUP 9
Romania 0, Kazakhstan 0
Slovakia 2, Latvia 0
Latvia 0, France 3
Kazakhstan 1, Romania 1
Kazakhstan 0, Slovakia 1
Romania 2, Latvia 0
France 2, Kazakhstan 0
Latvia 0, Slovakia 6
Romania 0, France 2
France 3, Romania 0
France 2, Slovakia 0
Slovakia 0, Romania 2
France 3, Latvia 0
Romania 2, Slovakia 0
Kazakhstan 0, France 3
Kazakhstan 0, Latvia 0

GROUP 10
Luxembourg 1, Austria 4
Bulgaria 0, Holland 1
Scotland 0, Bulgaria 0
Holland 4, Luxembourg 0
Austria 0, Holland 1
Luxembourg 1, Scotland 5
Scotland 2, Austria 2
Bulgaria 3, Luxembourg 2
Austria 0, Bulgaria 2
Holland 1, Scotland 2
Bulgaria 1, Austria 1
Scotland 0, Holland 0
Bulgaria 2, Scotland 2
Luxembourg 0, Holland 5
Austria 4, Luxembourg 1
Holland 5, Bulgaria 0

Competition still being played.

FIFA UNDER-20 WORLD CUP

GROUP A
Mali v South Korea	0-2
Colombia v France	4-1
France v South Korea	3-1
Colombia v Mali	2-0
France v Mali	2-0
Colombia v South Korea	1-0

GROUP B
Cameroon v New Zealand	1-1
Portugal v Uruguay	0-0
Uruguay v New Zealand	1-1
Portugal v Cameroon	1-0
Portugal v New Zealand	1-0
Uruguay v Cameroon	0-1

GROUP C
Costa Rica v Spain	1-4
Australia v Ecuador	1-1
Ecuador v Spain	0-2
Australia v Costa Rica	2-3

Ecuador v Costa Rica	3-0
Australia v Spain	1-5

GROUP D
Nigeria v Guatemala	5-0
Croatia v Saudi Arabia	0-2
Saudi Arabia v Guatemala	6-0
Croatia v Nigeria	2-5
Saudi Arabia v Nigeria	0-2
Croatia v Guatemala	0-1

GROUP E
Brazil v Egypt	1-1
Austria v Panama	0-0
Egypt v Panama	1-0
Brazil v Austria	3-0
Brazil v Panama	4-0
Egypt v Austria	4-0

GROUP F
England v North Korea	0-0
Argentina v Mexico	1-0

Mexico v North Korea	3-0
Argentina v England	0-0
Mexico v England	0-0
Argentina v North Korea	3-0

FIRST ROUND

Portugal v Guatemala	1-0
Argentina v Egypt	2-1
Cameroon v Mexico	1-1
Mexico won 3-0 on penalties.	
Colombia v Costa Rica	3-2
Nigeria v England	1-0
Spain v South Korea	0-0
Spain won 7-6 on penalties.	
Brazil v Saudi Arabia	3-0
France v Ecuador	1-0

QUARTER-FINALS

Portugal v Argentina	0-0
Portugal won 5-4 on penalties.	
Mexico v Colombia	3-1
France v Nigeria	3-2
Brazil v Spain	2-2
Brazil won 4-2 on penalties.	

SEMI-FINALS

France v Portugal	0-2
Brazil v Mexico	2-0

MATCH FOR THIRD PLACE

Mexico v France	3-1

FINAL

Brazil (1) 3 *(Oscar 5, 78, 111)*

Portugal (1) 2 *(Alex 9, Nelson Oliveira 59)* 36,058

(in Bogota)

Brazil: Gabriel; Danilo, Bruno Uvini, Juan Jesus, Fernando, Casemiro, Willian (Allan 46), Philippe Coutinho (Dudu 62), Oscar, Gabriel Silva (Negueba 46), Henrique.

Portugal: Mika; Pele, Nuno Reis, Roderick, Nelson Oliveira, Cedric (Julio Alves 57), Sana (Ricardo Dias 100), Alex (Caetano 82), Danilo, Sergio Oliveira, Mario Rui.

aet.

Referee: M. Geiger (USA).

THE NEXTGEN SERIES TROPHY

Under-19 Teams

GROUP 1	P	W	D	L	F	A	Pts
Barcelona	6	5	0	1	20	9	15
Marseille	6	4	0	2	11	10	12
Celtic	6	3	0	3	11	12	9
Manchester C	6	0	0	6	6	17	0

GROUP 2	P	W	D	L	F	A	Pts
Sporting Lisbon	6	5	1	0	20	6	10
Liverpool	6	2	1	3	9	11	7
Wolfsburg	6	1	3	2	8	9	6
Molde	6	1	1	4	10	21	4

GROUP 3	P	W	D	L	F	A	Pts
Aston Villa	6	4	0	2	15	7	12
Ajax	6	3	1	2	9	7	10
Rosenborg	6	3	0	3	11	11	9
Fenerbahce	6	1	1	4	5	15	4

GROUP 4	P	W	D	L	F	A	Pts
Tottenham H	6	4	2	0	17	6	14
Internazionale	6	3	2	1	8	11	11
Basle	6	1	2	3	4	8	5
PSV Eindhoven	6	1	0	5	9	13	3

QUARTER-FINALS

Aston Villa 1, Marseille 2
Sporting Lisbon 0, Internazionale 1
Tottenham H 1, Liverpool 0
Tottenham H withdrew after breach of rule.
Barcelona 0, Ajax 3

SEMI-FINALS

Liverpool 0, Ajax 6
Internazionale 2, Marseille 0

MATCH FOR THIRD PLACE

Liverpool 2, Marseille 0

FINAL

25 March 2012

(at Leyton Orient)

Ajax (0) 1 *(Denswil 48)*

Internazionale (1) 1 *(Longo 44)* 2500

Ajax: Van Der Hart; Nieuwpoort, Veltman, Denswil, Dijks, Sparkslede, Klassen, Rits (El Hasnaoui 105), De Sa (De Bondt 75), Schoop (Gravenbergh 58), Fischer.

Internazionale: Di Gennaro; Pecorini, Kysela, Spendhofer, M'Baye, Romano, Crisetig, Bessa, Duncan, Longo, Livaja (Alborno 75).

aet; Internazionale won 5-3 on penalties.

Referee: L. Collins (England).

UEFA UNDER-19 CHAMPIONSHIP 2011–2012

Final tournament in Romania

GROUP A

Romania v Czech Republic	1-3
Greece v Republic of Ireland	1-2
Czech Republic v Republic of Ireland	2-1
Romania v Greece	0-1
Republic of Ireland v Romania	0-0
Czech Republic v Greece	1-0

GROUP B

Serbia v Turkey	2-0
Spain v Belgium	4-1
Turkey v Belgium	1-1
Serbia v Spain	0-4
Belgium v Serbia	1-1
Turkey v Spain	3-0

SEMI-FINAL

Czech Republic v Serbia	4-2
Spain v Republic of Ireland	5-0

FINAL

1 August 2011

Czech Republic (0) 2 *(Krejci 52, Lacha 97)*

Spain (0) 3 *(Aurtenetxe 85,*
Paco Alcacer 108, 115) 3700

Czech Republic: Koubek; Brabec, Janos, Kalas, Kaderabek, Skalak (Lacha 79), Jelecek, Krejci, Prikryl (Fantis 102), Hala, Polom (Sladky 36).
Spain: Edgar Badia; Sergi Gomez, Ignasi Miquel, Aurtenetxe, Ruben Pardo, Morata, Alex Fernandez (Campana 55), Sarabia (Juan Muniz 78), Blazquez, Juanmi (Paco Alcacer 54), Deulofeu.
aet.
Referee: S. Attwell (England).

UEFA UNDER-17 CHAMPIONSHIP 2012

ELITE ROUND

GROUP 1
France 1, Italy 0; Sweden 2, Switzerland 0; Italy 0, Sweden 0; France 2, Switzerland 1; Sweden 1, France 3; Switzerland 1, Italy 2

GROUP 2
Czech Republic 0, Poland 2; Belarus 1, Luxembourg 1; Poland 2, Belarus 0; Czech Republic 2, Luxembourg 0; Belarus 0, Czech Republic 0; Luxembourg 1, Poland 3

GROUP 3
Spain 1, Georgia 1; England 1, Ukraine 0; Georgia 1, England 0; Spain 2, Ukraine 2; England 0, Spain 4; Ukraine 0, Georgia 1

GROUP 4
Germany 4, Turkey 0; Portugal 0, Bulgaria 0; Germany 2, Bulgaria 1; Turkey 0; Portugal 3; Portugal 0, Germany 0; Bulgaria 2, Turkey 0

GROUP 5
Serbia 1, Republic of Ireland 0; Holland 4, Albania 0; Serbia 3, Albania 0; Republic of Ireland 1, Holland 2; Holland 1, Serbia 1; Albania 2, Republic of Ireland 1

GROUP 6
Denmark 2, Iceland 2; Scotland 1, Lithuania 0; Denmark 3, Lithuania 1; Iceland 1, Scotland 0; Scotland 2, Denmark 3; Lithuania 0, Iceland 4

GROUP 7
Hungary 2, Belgium 2; Russia 2, Wales 1; Hungary 5, Wales 1; Belgium 3, Russia 0 – *Scoreline was 1-0 before default victory was awarded*; Russia 2, Hungary 3; Wales 0, Belgium 3

Final tournament in Slovenia

GROUP A
Georgia 0, Germany 1; France 2, Iceland 2; France 1, Georgia 1; Iceland 0, Germany 1; Germany 3, France 0; Iceland 0, Georgia 1

GROUP B
Poland 1, Belgium 0; Slovenia 1, Holland 3; Holland 0, Belgium 0; Slovenia 1, Poland 1; Belgium 3, Slovenia 1; Holland 0, Poland 0

SEMI-FINALS
Germany 1, Poland 0
Holland 2, Georgia 0

FINAL

16 May

Germany (0) 1 *(Goretzka 45)*

Holland (0) 1 *(Acolatse 80)*
11,674

Germany: Schnitzler; Dudziak, Sarr, Sule, Itter, Goretzka (Akpoguma 80), Dittgen (Stendera 41), Meyer, Brandenburger, Brandt (Kempf 73), Werner.
Holland: Olij; Ake, Haye, Hendrix, Bazoer, Anderson (Van den Boomen 71), Voest, Trindade de Vilhena, Vloet (Huser 64), Lumu (Acolatse 57), Menig.
aet; Holland won 5-4 on penalties.

POST-WAR INTERNATIONAL APPEARANCES

As at July 2012 *(Season of first cap given)*

Bold type indicates players who have made an international appearance in season 2011–12.

ENGLAND

A'Court, A. (5) 1957/8 Liverpool
Adams, T. A. (66) 1986/7 Arsenal
Agbonlahor, G. (3) 2008/09 Aston Villa
Allen, C. (5) 1983/4 QPR, Tottenham H
Allen, R. (5) 1951/2 WBA
Allen, T. (3) 1959/60 Stoke C
Anderson, S. (2) 1961/2 Sunderland
Anderson, V. (30) 1978/9 Nottingham F,
   Arsenal, Manchester U
Anderton, D. R. (30) 1993/4 Tottenham H
Angus, J. (1) 1960/1 Burnley
Armfield, J. (43) 1958/9 Blackpool
Armstrong, D. (3) 1979/80
   Middlesbrough, Southampton
Armstrong, K. (1) 1954/5 Chelsea
Ashton, D. (1) 2007/08 West Ham U
Astall, G. (2) 1955/6 Birmingham C
Astle, J. (5) 1968/9 WBA
Aston, J. (17) 1948/9 Manchester U
Atyeo, J. (6) 1955/6 Bristol C

Bailey, G. R. (2) 1984/5 Manchester U
Bailey, M. (2) 1963/4 Charlton
Baily, E. (9) 1949/50 Tottenham H
Baines, L. J. (8) 2009/10 Everton
Baker, J. (8) 1959/60 Hibernian, Arsenal
Ball, A. (72) 1964/5 Blackpool, Everton,
   Arsenal
Ball, M. J. (1) 2000/01 Everton
Banks, G. (73) 1962/3 Leicester C,
   Stoke C
Banks, T. (6) 1957/8 Bolton W
Bardsley, D. (2) 1992/3 QPR
Barham, M. (2) 1982/3 Norwich C
Barlow, R. (1) 1954/5 WBA
Barmby, N. J. (23) 1994/5 Tottenham H,
   Middlesbrough, Everton, Liverpool
Barnes, J. (79) 1982/3 Watford, Liverpool
Barnes, P. (22) 1977/8 Manchester C,
   WBA, Leeds U
Barrass, M. (3) 1951/2 Bolton W
Barrett, E. D. (3) 1990/1 Oldham Ath,
   Aston Villa
**Barry, G. (53) 1999/00 Aston Villa,
   Manchester C**

Barton, J. (1) 2006/07 Manchester C
Barton, W. D. (3) 1994/5 Wimbledon,
   Newcastle U
Batty, D. (42) 1990/1 Leeds U, Blackburn
   R, Newcastle U, Leeds U
Baynham, R. (3) 1955/6 Luton T
Beardsley, P. A. (59) 1985/6 Newcastle U,
   Liverpool, Newcastle U
Beasant, D. J. (2) 1989/90 Chelsea
Beattie, J. S. (5) 2002/03 Southampton
Beattie, T. K. (9) 1974/5 Ipswich T
Beckham, D. R. J. (115) 1996/7
   Manchester U, Real Madrid,
   LA Galaxy
Bell, C. (48) 1967/8 Manchester C
**Bent, D. A. (13) 2005/06 Charlton Ath,
   Tottenham H, Sunderland, Aston Villa**
Bentley, D. M. (7) 2007/08 Blackburn R,
   Tottenham H
Bentley, R. (12) 1948/9 Chelsea
Berry, J. (4) 1952/3 Manchester U
Birtles, G. (3) 1979/80 Nottingham F
Blissett, L. (14) 1982/3 Watford,
   AC Milan
Blockley, J. (1) 1972/3 Arsenal
Blunstone, F. (5) 1954/5 Chelsea
Bonetti, P. (7) 1965/6 Chelsea
Bothroyd, J. (1) 2010/11 Cardiff C
Bould, S. A. (2) 1993/4 Arsenal
Bowles, S. (5) 1973/4 QPR
Bowyer, L. D. (1) 2002/03 Leeds U
Boyer, P. (1) 1975/6 Norwich C
Brabrook, P. (3) 1957/8 Chelsea
Bracewell, P. W. (3) 1984/5 Everton
Bradford, G. (1) 1955/6 Bristol R
Bradley, W. (3) 1958/9 Manchester U
Bridge, W. M. (36) 2001/02 Southampton,
   Chelsea, Manchester C
Bridges, B. (4) 1964/5 Chelsea
Broadbent, P. (7) 1957/8
   Wolverhampton W
Broadis, I. (14) 1951/2 Manchester C,
   Newcastle U
Brooking, T. (47) 1973/4 West Ham U
Brooks, J. (3) 1956/7 Tottenham H

Brown, A. (1) 1970/1 WBA
Brown, K. (1) 1959/60 West Ham U
Brown, W. M. (23) 1998/9 Manchester U
Bull, S. G. (13) 1988/9 Wolverhampton W
Butcher, T. (77) 1979/80 Ipswich T,
   Rangers
Butt, N. (39) 1996/7 Manchester U,
   Newcastle U
Byrne, G. (2) 1962/3 Liverpool
Byrne, J. (11) 1961/2 Crystal Palace,
   West Ham U
Byrne, R. (33) 1953/4 Manchester U

Cahill, G. J. (9) 2010/11 Bolton W,
   Chelsea
Callaghan, I. (4) 1965/6 Liverpool
Campbell, F. L. (1) 2011/12 Sunderland
Campbell, S. (73) 1995/6 Tottenham H,
   Arsenal, Portsmouth
Carragher, J. L. (38) 1998/9 Liverpool
Carrick, M. (22) 2000/01 West Ham U,
   Tottenham H, Manchester U
Carroll, A. T. (7) 2010/11 Newcastle U,
   Liverpool
Carson, S. P. (4) 2007/08 Liverpool, WBA
Carter, H. (7) 1946/7 Derby Co
Chamberlain, M. (8) 1982/3 Stoke C
Channon, M. (46) 1972/3 Southampton,
   Manchester C
Charles, G. A. (2) 1990/1 Nottingham F
Charlton, J. (35) 1964/5 Leeds U
Charlton, R. (106) 1957/8 Manchester U
Charnley, R. (1) 1962/3 Blackpool
Cherry, T. (27) 1975/6 Leeds U
Chilton, A. (2) 1950/1 Manchester U
Chivers, M. (24) 1970/1 Tottenham H
Clamp, E. (4) 1957/8 Wolverhampton W
Clapton, D. (1) 1958/9 Arsenal
Clarke, A. (19) 1969/70 Leeds U
Clarke, H. (1) 1953/4 Tottenham H
Clayton, R. (35) 1955/6 Blackburn R
Clemence, R. (61) 1972/3 Liverpool,
   Tottenham H
Clement, D. (5) 1975/6 QPR
Clough, B. (2) 1959/60 Middlesbrough
Clough, N. H. (14) 1988/9 Nottingham F
Coates, R. (4) 1969/70 Burnley,
   Tottenham H
Cockburn, H. (13) 1946/7 Manchester U
Cohen, G. (37) 1963/4 Fulham
Cole, Andy (15) 1994/5 Manchester U
Cole, Ashley (98) 2000/01 Arsenal,
   Chelsea
Cole, C. (7) 2008/09 West Ham U

Cole, J. J. (56) 2000/01 West Ham U,
   Chelsea
Collymore, S. V. (3) 1994/5 Nottingham F,
   Aston Villa
Compton, L. (2) 1950/1 Arsenal
Connelly, J. (20) 1959/60 Burnley,
   Manchester U
Cooper, C. T. (2) 1994/5 Nottingham F
Cooper, T. (20) 1968/9 Leeds U
Coppell, S. (42) 1977/8 Manchester U
Corrigan, J. (9) 1975/6 Manchester C
Cottee, A. R. (7) 1986/7 West Ham U,
   Everton
Cowans, G. (10) 1982/3 Aston Villa, Bari,
   Aston Villa
Crawford, R. (2) 1961/2 Ipswich T
Crouch, P. J. (42) 2004/05 Southampton,
   Liverpool, Portsmouth, Tottenham H
Crowe, C. (1) 1962/3 Wolverhampton W
Cunningham, L. (6) 1978/9 WBA,
   Real Madrid
Curle, K. (3) 1991/2 Manchester C
Currie, A. (17) 1971/2 Sheffield U,
   Leeds U

Daley, A. M. (7) 1991/2 Aston Villa
Davenport, P. (1) 1984/5 Nottingham F
Davies, K. C. (1) 2010/11 Bolton W
Dawson, M. R. (4) 2010/11 Tottenham H
Deane, B. C. (3) 1990/1 Sheffield U
Deeley, N. (2) 1958/9 Wolverhampton W
Defoe, J. C. (48) 2003/04 Tottenham H,
   Portsmouth, Tottenham H
Devonshire, A. (8) 1979/80 West Ham U
Dickinson, J. (48) 1948/9 Portsmouth
Ditchburn, E. (6) 1948/9 Tottenham H
Dixon, K. M. (8) 1984/5 Chelsea
Dixon, L. M. (22) 1989/90 Arsenal
Dobson, M. (5) 1973/4 Burnley, Everton
Dorigo, A. R. (15) 1989/90 Chelsea,
   Leeds U
Douglas, B. (36) 1957/8 Blackburn R
Downing, S. (34) 2004/05 Middlesbrough,
   Aston Villa, Liverpool
Doyle, M. (5) 1975/6 Manchester C
Dublin, D. (4) 1997/8 Coventry C,
   Aston Villa
Dunn, D. J. I. (1) 2002/03 Blackburn R
Duxbury, M. (10) 1983/4 Manchester U
Dyer, K. C. (33) 1999/00 Newcastle U,
   West Ham U

Eastham, G. (19) 1962/3 Arsenal
Eckersley, W. (17) 1949/50 Blackburn R
Edwards, D. (18) 1954/5 Manchester U

Ehiogu, U. (4) 1995/6 Aston Villa,
  Middlesbrough
Ellerington, W. (2) 1948/9 Southampton
Elliott, W. H. (5) 1951/2 Burnley

Fantham, J. (1) 1961/2 Sheffield W
Fashanu, J. (2) 1988/9 Wimbledon
Fenwick, T. (20) 1983/4 QPR,
  Tottenham H
Ferdinand, L. (17) 1992/3 QPR,
  Newcastle U, Tottenham H
Ferdinand, R. G. (81) 1997/8
  West Ham U, Leeds U, Manchester U
Finney, T. (76) 1946/7 Preston NE
Flowers, R. (49) 1954/5
  Wolverhampton W
Flowers, T. (11) 1992/3 Southampton,
  Blackburn R
Foster, B. (5) 2006/07 Manchester U,
  Birmingham C
Foster, S. (3) 1981/2 Brighton
Foulkes, W. (1) 1954/5 Manchester U
Fowler, R. B. (26) 1995/6 Liverpool,
  Leeds U
Francis, G. (12) 1974/5 QPR
Francis, T. (52) 1976/7 Birmingham C,
  Nottingham F, Manchester C,
  Sampdoria
Franklin, N. (27) 1946/7 Stoke C
Froggatt, J. (13) 1949/50 Portsmouth
Froggatt, R. (4) 1952/3 Sheffield W

Gardner, A. (1) 2003/04 Tottenham H
Garrett, T. (3) 1951/2 Blackpool
Gascoigne, P. J. (57) 1988/9 Tottenham H,
  Lazio, Rangers, Middlesbrough
Gates, E. (2) 1980/1 Ipswich T
George, F. C. (1) 1976/7 Derby Co
Gerrard, S. G. (96) 1999/00 Liverpool
Gibbs, K. J. R. (2) 2010/11 Arsenal
Gidman, J. (1) 1976/7 Aston Villa
Gillard, I. (3) 1974/5 QPR
Goddard, P. (1) 1981/2 West Ham U
Grainger, C. (7) 1955/6 Sheffield U,
  Sunderland
Gray, A. A. (1) 1991/2 Crystal Palace
Gray, M. (3) 1998/9 Sunderland
Greaves, J. (57) 1958/9 Chelsea,
  Tottenham H
**Green, R. P. (12) 2004/05 Norwich C,
  West Ham U**
Greenhoff, B. (18) 1975/6 Manchester U,
  Leeds U
Gregory, J. (6) 1982/3 QPR
Guppy, S. (1) 1999/00 Leicester C

Hagan, J. (1) 1948/9 Sheffield U
Haines, J. (1) 1948/9 WBA
Hall, J. (17) 1955/6 Birmingham C
Hancocks, J. (3) 1948/9
  Wolverhampton W
Hardwick, G. (13) 1946/7 Middlesbrough
Harford, M. G. (2) 1987/8 Luton T
Hargreaves, O. (42) 2001/02
  Bayern Munich, Manchester U
Harris, G. (1) 1965/6 Burnley
Harris, P. (2) 1949/50 Portsmouth
Hart, C. (22) 2007/08 Manchester C
Harvey, C. (1) 1970/1 Everton
Hassall, H. (5) 1950/1 Huddersfield T,
  Bolton W
Hateley, M. (32) 1983/4 Portsmouth,
  AC Milan, Monaco, Rangers
Haynes, J. (56) 1954/5 Fulham
Hector, K. (2) 1973/4 Derby Co
Hellawell, M. (2) 1962/3 Birmingham C
**Henderson, J. B. (5) 2010/11 Sunderland,
  Liverpool**
Hendrie, L. A. (1) 1998/9 Aston Villa
Henry, R. (1) 1962/3 Tottenham H
Heskey, E. W. (62) 1998/9 Leicester C,
  Liverpool, Birmingham C, Wigan Ath,
  Aston Villa
Hill, F. (2) 1962/3 Bolton W
Hill, G. (6) 1975/6 Manchester U
Hill, R. (3) 1982/3 Luton T
Hinchcliffe, A. G. (7) 1996/7 Everton,
  Sheffield W
Hinton, A. (3) 1962/3 Wolverhampton W,
  Nottingham F
Hirst, D. E. (3) 1990/1 Sheffield W
Hitchens, G. (7) 1960/1 Aston Villa,
  Internazionale
Hoddle, G. (53) 1979/80 Tottenham H,
  Monaco
Hodge, S. B. (24) 1985/6 Aston Villa,
  Tottenham H, Nottingham F
Hodgkinson, A. (5) 1956/7 Sheffield U
Holden, D. (5) 1958/9 Bolton W
Holliday, E. (3) 1959/60 Middlesbrough
Hollins, J. (1) 1966/7 Chelsea
Hopkinson, E. (14) 1957/8 Bolton W
Howe, D. (23) 1957/8 WBA
Howe, J. (3) 1947/8 Derby Co
Howey, S. N. (4) 1994/5 Newcastle U
Huddlestone, T. A. (3) 2009/10 Tottenham
  H
Hudson, A. (2) 1974/5 Stoke C
Hughes, E. (62) 1969/70 Liverpool,
  Wolverhampton W
Hughes, L. (3) 1949/50 Liverpool

Hunt, R. (34) 1961/2 Liverpool
Hunt, S. (2) 1983/4 WBA
Hunter, N. (28) 1965/6 Leeds U
Hurst, G. (49) 1965/6 West Ham U

Ince, P. (53) 1992/3 Manchester U,
Internazionale, Liverpool,
Middlesbrough

Jagielka, P. N. (12) 2007/08 Everton
James, D. B. (53) 1996/7 Liverpool, Aston
Villa, West Ham U, Manchester C,
Portsmouth
Jarvis, M. T. (1) 2010/11
Wolverhampton W
Jeffers, F. (1) 2002/03 Arsenal
Jenas, J. A. (21) 2002/03 Newcastle U,
Tottenham H
Jezzard, B. (2) 1953/4 Fulham
Johnson, A. (8) 2004/05 Crystal Palace,
Everton
Johnson, A. (11) 2009/10 Manchester C
Johnson, D. (8) 1974/5 Ipswich T,
Liverpool
**Johnson, G. M. C. (40) 2003/04 Chelsea,
Portsmouth, Liverpool**
Johnson, S. A. M. (1) 2000/01 Derby Co
Johnston, H. (10) 1946/7 Blackpool
Jones, M. (3) 1964/5 Sheffield U, Leeds U
Jones, P. A. (5) 2011/12 Manchester U
Jones, R. (8) 1991/2 Liverpool
Jones, W. H. (2) 1949/50 Liverpool

Kay, A. (1) 1962/3 Everton
Keegan, K. (63) 1972/3 Liverpool, SV
Hamburg, Southampton
Kelly, M. R. (1) 2011/12 Liverpool
Kennedy, A. (2) 1983/4 Liverpool
Kennedy, R. (17) 1975/6 Liverpool
Keown, M. R. (43) 1991/2 Everton,
Arsenal
Kevan, D. (14) 1956/7 WBA
Kidd, B. (2) 1969/70 Manchester U
King, L. B. (21) 2001/02 Tottenham H
Kirkland, C. E. (1) 2006/07 Liverpool
Knight, Z. (2) 2004/05 Fulham
Knowles, C. (4) 1967/8 Tottenham H
Konchesky, P. M. (2) 2002/03
Charlton Ath, West Ham U

Labone, B. (26) 1962/3 Everton
**Lampard, F. J. (90) 1999/00 West Ham U,
Chelsea**
Lampard, F. R. G. (2) 1972/3 West Ham U
Langley, J. (3) 1957/8 Fulham

Langton, R. (11) 1946/7 Blackburn R,
Preston NE, Bolton W
Latchford, R. (12) 1977/8 Everton
Lawler, C. (4) 1970/1 Liverpool
Lawton, T. (15) 1946/7 Chelsea, Notts Co
Lee, F. (27) 1968/9 Manchester C
Lee, J. (1) 1950/1 Derby C
Lee, R. M. (21) 1994/5 Newcastle U
Lee, S. (14) 1982/3 Liverpool
Lennon, A. J. (19) 2005/06 Tottenham H
**Lescott, J. P. (20) 2007/08 Everton,
Manchester C**
Le Saux, G. P. (36) 1993/4 Blackburn R,
Chelsea
Le Tissier, M. P. (8) 1993/4 Southampton
Lindsay, A. (4) 1973/4 Liverpool
Lineker, G. (80) 1983/4 Leicester C,
Everton, Barcelona, Tottenham H
Little, B. (1) 1974/5 Aston Villa
Lloyd, L. (4) 1970/1 Liverpool,
Nottingham F
Lofthouse, N. (33) 1950/1 Bolton W
Lowe, E. (3) 1946/7 Aston Villa

Mabbutt, G. (16) 1982/3 Tottenham H
Macdonald, M. (14) 1971/2 Newcastle U
Madeley, P. (24) 1970/1 Leeds U
Mannion, W. (26) 1946/7 Middlesbrough
Mariner, P. (35) 1976/7 Ipswich T, Arsenal
Marsh, R. (9) 1971/2 QPR, Manchester C
Martin, A. (17) 1980/1 West Ham U
Martyn, A. N. (23) 1991/2 Crystal Palace,
Leeds U
Marwood, B. (1) 1988/9 Arsenal
Matthews, R. (5) 1955/6 Coventry C
Matthews, S. (37) 1946/7 Stoke C,
Blackpool
McCann, G. P. (1) 2000/01 Sunderland
McDermott, T. (25) 1977/8 Liverpool
McDonald, C. (8) 1957/8 Burnley
McFarland, R. (28) 1970/1 Derby C
McGarry, W. (4) 1953/4 Huddersfield T
McGuinness, W. (2) 1958/9 Manchester U
McMahon, S. (17) 1987/8 Liverpool
McManaman, S. (37) 1994/5 Liverpool,
Real Madrid
McNab, R. (4) 1968/9 Arsenal
McNeil, M. (9) 1960/1 Middlesbrough
Meadows, J. (1) 1954/5 Manchester C
Medley, L. (6) 1950/1 Tottenham H
Melia, J. (2) 1962/3 Liverpool
Merrick, G. (23) 1951/2 Birmingham C
Merson, P. C. (21) 1991/2 Arsenal,
Middlesbrough, Aston Villa
Metcalfe, V. (2) 1950/1 Huddersfield T

Milburn, J. (13) 1948/9 Newcastle U
Miller, B. (1) 1960/1 Burnley
Mills, D. J. (19) 2000/01 Leeds U
Mills, M. (42) 1972/3 Ipswich T
Milne, G. (14) 1962/3 Liverpool
Milner, J. P. (30) 2009/10 Aston Villa, Manchester C
Milton, C. A. (1) 1951/2 Arsenal
Moore, R. (108) 1961/2 West Ham U
Morley, A. (6) 1981/2 Aston Villa
Morris, J. (3) 1948/9 Derby Co
Mortensen, S. (25) 1946/7 Blackpool
Mozley, B. (3) 1949/50 Derby Co
Mullen, J. (12) 1946/7 Wolverhampton W
Mullery, A. (35) 1964/5 Tottenham H
Murphy, D. B. (9) 2001/02 Liverpool

Neal, P. (50) 1975/6 Liverpool
Neville, G. A. (85) 1994/5 Manchester U
Neville, P. J. (59) 1995/6 Manchester U, Everton
Newton, K. (27) 1965/6 Blackburn R, Everton
Nicholls, J. (2) 1953/4 WBA
Nicholson, W. (1) 1950/1 Tottenham H
Nish, D. (5) 1972/3 Derby Co
Norman, M. (23) 1961/2 Tottenham H
Nugent, D. J. (1) 2006/07 Preston NE

O'Grady, M. (2) 1962/3 Huddersfield T, Leeds U
Osgood, P. (4) 1969/70 Chelsea
Osman, R. (11) 1979/80 Ipswich T
Owen, M. J. (89) 1997/8 Liverpool, Real Madrid, Newcastle U
Owen, S. (3) 1953/4 Luton T
Oxlade-Chamberlain, A. M. D. (5) 2011/12 Arsenal

Paine, T. (19) 1962/3 Southampton
Pallister, G. (22) 1987/8 Middlesbrough, Manchester U
Palmer, C. L. (18) 1991/2 Sheffield W
Parker, P. A. (19) 1988/9 QPR, Manchester U
Parker, S. M. (17) 2003/04 Charlton Ath, Chelsea, Newcastle U, West Ham U, Tottenham H
Parkes, P. (1) 1973/4 QPR
Parlour, R. (10) 1998/9 Arsenal
Parry, R. (2) 1959/60 Bolton W
Peacock, A. (6) 1961/2 Middlesbrough, Leeds U
Pearce, S. (78) 1986/7 Nottingham F, West Ham U

Pearson, Stan (8) 1947/8 Manchester U
Pearson, Stuart (15) 1975/6 Manchester U
Pegg, D. (1) 1956/7 Manchester U
Pejic, M. (4) 1973/4 Stoke C
Perry, W. (3) 1955/6 Blackpool
Perryman, S. (1) 1981/2 Tottenham H
Peters, M. (67) 1965/6 West Ham U, Tottenham H
Phelan, M. C. (1) 1989/90 Manchester U
Phillips, K. (8) 1998/9 Sunderland
Phillips, L. (3) 1951/2 Portsmouth
Pickering, F. (3) 1963/4 Everton
Pickering, N. (1) 1982/3 Sunderland
Pilkington, B. (1) 1954/5 Burnley
Platt, D. (62) 1989/90 Aston Villa, Bari, Juventus, Sampdoria, Arsenal
Pointer, R. (3) 1961/2 Burnley
Powell, C. G. (5) 2000/01 Charlton Ath
Pye, J. (1) 1949/50 Wolverhampton W

Quixall, A. (5) 1953/4 Sheffield W

Radford, J. (2) 1968/9 Arsenal
Ramsey, A. (32) 1948/9 Southampton, Tottenham H
Reaney, P. (3) 1968/9 Leeds U
Redknapp, J. F. (17) 1995/6 Liverpool
Reeves, K. (2) 1979/80 Norwich C, Manchester C
Regis, C. (5) 1981/2 WBA, Coventry C
Reid, P. (13) 1984/5 Everton
Revie, D. (6) 1954/5 Manchester C
Richards, J. (1) 1972/3 Wolverhampton W
Richards, M. (13) 2006/07 Manchester C
Richardson, K. (1) 1993/4 Aston Villa
Richardon, K. E. (8) 2004/05 Manchester C
Rickaby, S. (1) 1953/4 WBA
Ricketts, M. B. (1) 2001/02 Bolton W
Rimmer, J. (1) 1975/6 Arsenal
Ripley, S. E. (2) 1993/4 Blackburn R
Rix, G. (17) 1980/1 Arsenal
Robb, G. (1) 1953/4 Tottenham H
Roberts, G. (6) 1982/3 Tottenham H
Robinson, P. W. (41) 2002/03 Leeds U, Tottenham H
Robson, B. (90) 1979/80 WBA, Manchester U
Robson, R. (20) 1957/8 WBA
Rocastle, D. (14) 1988/9 Arsenal
Rodwell, J. (2) 2011/12 Everton
Rooney, W. (76) 2002/03 Everton, Manchester U
Rowley, J. (6) 1948/9 Manchester U

Royle, J. (6) 1970/1 Everton, Manchester C
Ruddock, N. (1) 1994/5 Liverpool

Sadler, D. (4) 1967/8 Manchester U
Salako, J. A. (5) 1990/1 Crystal Palace
Sansom, K. (86) 1978/9 Crystal Palace, Arsenal
Scales, J. R. (3) 1994/5 Liverpool
Scholes, P. (66) 1996/7 Manchester U
Scott, L. (17) 1946/7 Arsenal
Seaman, D. A. (75) 1988/9 QPR, Arsenal
Sewell, J. (6) 1951/2 Sheffield W
Shackleton, L. (5) 1948/9 Sunderland
Sharpe, L. S. (8) 1990/1 Manchester U
Shaw, G. (5) 1958/9 Sheffield U
Shearer, A. (63) 1991/2 Southampton, Blackburn R, Newcastle U
Shellito, K. (1) 1962/3 Chelsea
Sheringham, E. (51) 1992/3 Tottenham H, Manchester U, Tottenham H
Sherwood, T. A. (3) 1998/9 Tottenham H
Shilton, P. (125) 1970/1 Leicester C, Stoke C, Nottingham F, Southampton, Derby Co
Shimwell, E. (1) 1948/9 Blackpool
Shorey, N, (2) 2006/07 Reading
Sillett, P. (3) 1954/5 Chelsea
Sinclair, T. (12) 2001/02 West Ham U, Manchester C
Sinton, A. (12) 1991/2 QPR, Sheffield W
Slater, W. (12) 1954/5 Wolverhampton W
Smalling, C. (3) 2011/12 Manchester U
Smith, A. (19) 2000/01 Leeds U, Manchester U, Newcastle U
Smith, A. M. (13) 1988/9 Arsenal
Smith, L. (6) 1950/1 Arsenal
Smith, R. (15) 1960/1 Tottenham H
Smith, Tom (1) 1970/1 Liverpool
Smith, Trevor (2) 1959/60 Birmingham C
Southgate, G. (57) 1995/6 Aston Villa, Middlesbrough
Spink, N. (1) 1982/3 Aston Villa
Springett, R. (33) 1959/60 Sheffield W
Staniforth, R. (8) 1953/4 Huddersfield T
Statham, D. (3) 1982/3 WBA
Stein, B. (1) 1983/4 Luton T
Stepney, A. (1) 1967/8 Manchester U
Sterland, M. (1) 1988/9 Sheffield W
Steven, T. M. (36) 1984/5 Everton, Rangers, Marseille
Stevens, G. A. (7) 1984/5 Tottenham H
Stevens, M. G. (46) 1984/5 Everton, Rangers
Stewart, P. A. (3) 1991/2 Tottenham H

Stiles, N. (28) 1964/5 Manchester U
Stone, S. B. (9) 1995/6 Nottingham F
Storey-Moore, I. (1) 1969/70 Nottingham F
Storey, P. (19) 1970/1 Arsenal
Streten, B. (1) 1949/50 Luton T
Sturridge, D. (2) 2011/12 Chelsea
Summerbee, M. (8) 1967/8 Manchester C
Sunderland, A. (1) 1979/80 Arsenal
Sutton, C. R. (1) 1997/8 Blackburn R
Swan, P. (19) 1959/60 Sheffield W
Swift, F. (19) 1946/7 Manchester C

Talbot, B. (6) 1976/7 Ipswich T, Arsenal
Tambling, R. (3) 1962/3 Chelsea
Taylor, E. (1) 1953/4 Blackpool
Taylor, J. (2) 1950/1 Fulham
Taylor, P. H. (3) 1947/8 Liverpool
Taylor, P. J. (4) 1975/6 Crystal Palace
Taylor, T. (19) 1952/3 Manchester U
Temple, D. (1) 1964/5 Everton
Terry, J. G. (77) 2002/03 Chelsea
Thomas, Danny (2) 1982/3 Coventry C
Thomas, Dave (8) 1974/5 QPR
Thomas, G. R. (9) 1990/1 Crystal Palace
Thomas, M. L. (2) 1988/9 Arsenal
Thompson, A. (1) 2003/04 Celtic
Thompson, P. (16) 1963/4 Liverpool
Thompson, P. B. (42) 1975/6 Liverpool
Thompson, T. (2) 1951/2 Aston Villa, Preston NE
Thomson, R. (8) 1963/4 Wolverhampton W
Todd, C. (27) 1971/2 Derby Co
Towers, T. (3) 1975/6 Sunderland
Tueart, D. (6) 1974/5 Manchester C

Ufton, D. (1) 1953/4 Charlton Ath
Unsworth, D. G. (1) 1994/5 Everton
Upson, M. J. (21) 2002/03 Birmingham C, West Ham U

Vassell, D. (22) 2001/02 Aston Villa
Venables, T. (2) 1964/5 Chelsea
Venison, B. (2) 1994/5 Newcastle U
Viljoen, C. (2) 1974/5 Ipswich T
Viollet, D. (2) 1959/60 Manchester U

Waddle, C. R. (62) 1984/5 Newcastle U, Tottenham H, Marseille
Waiters, A. (5) 1963/4 Blackpool
Walcott, T. J. (28) 2005/06 Arsenal
Walker, D. S. (59) 1988/9 Nottingham F, Sampdoria, Sheffield W

Walker, I. M. (4) 1995/6 Tottenham H,
  Leicester C
Walker, K. A. (2) 2011/12 Tottenham H
Wallace, D. L. (1) 1985/6 Southampton
Walsh, P. (5) 1982/3 Luton T
Walters, K. M. (1) 1990/1 Rangers
Ward, P. (1) 1979/80 Brighton
Ward, T. (2) 1947/8 Derby C
Warnock, S. (2) 2007/08 Blackburn R,
  Aston Villa
Watson, D. (12) 1983/4 Norwich C,
  Everton
Watson, D. V. (65) 1973/4 Sunderland,
  Manchester C, Werder Bremen,
  Southampton, Stoke C
Watson, W. (4) 1949/50 Sunderland
Webb, N. (26) 1987/8 Nottingham F,
  Manchester U
Welbeck, D. (9) 2010/11 Manchester U
Weller, K. (4) 1973/4 Leicester C
West, G. (3) 1968/9 Everton
Wheeler, J. (1) 1954/5 Bolton W
White, D. (1) 1992/3 Manchester C
Whitworth, S. (7) 1974/5 Leicester C
Whymark, T. (1) 1977/8 Ipswich T
Wignall, F. (2) 1964/5 Nottingham F
Wilcox, J. M. (3) 1995/6 Blackburn R,
  Leeds U
Wilkins, R. (84) 1975/6 Chelsea,
  Manchester U, AC Milan
Williams, B. (24) 1948/9
  Wolverhampton W
Williams, S. (6) 1982/3 Southampton
Willis, A. (1) 1951/2 Tottenham H

Wilshaw, D. (12) 1953/4 Wolverhampton W
Wilshere, J. A. (5) 2010/11 Arsenal
Wilson, R. (63) 1959/60 Huddersfield T,
  Everton
Winterburn, N. (2) 1989/90 Arsenal
Wise, D. F. (21) 1990/1 Chelsea
Withe, P. (11) 1980/1 Aston Villa
Wood, R. (3) 1954/5 Manchester U
Woodcock, A. (42) 1977/8 Nottingham F,
  FC Cologne, Arsenal
Woodgate, J. S. (8) 1998/9 Leeds U,
  Newcastle U, Real Madrid,
  Tottenham H
Woods, C. C. E. (43) 1984/5 Norwich C,
  Rangers, Sheffield W
Worthington, F. (8) 1973/4 Leicester C
Wright, I. E. (33) 1990/1 Crystal Palace,
  Arsenal, West Ham U
Wright, M. (45) 1983/4 Southampton,
  Derby C, Liverpool
Wright, R. I. (2) 1999/00 Ipswich T,
  Arsenal
Wright, T. (11) 1967/8 Everton
Wright, W. (105) 1946/7
  Wolverhampton W
Wright-Phillips, S. C. (36) 2004/05
  Manchester C, Chelsea, Manchester C

**Young, A. S. (25) 2007/08 Aston Villa,
  Manchester U**
Young, G. (1) 1964/5 Sheffield W
Young, L. P. (7) 2004/05 Charlton Ath

Zamora, R. L. (2) 2010/11 Fulham

NORTHERN IRELAND

Aherne, T. (4) 1946/7 Belfast Celtic,
  Luton T
Anderson, T. (22) 1972/3 Manchester U,
  Swindon T, Peterborough U
Armstrong, G. (63) 1976/7 Tottenham H,
  Watford, Real Mallorca, WBA,
  Chesterfield

**Baird, C. P. (56) 2002/03 Southampton,
  Fulham**
Barr, H. H. (3) 1961/2 Linfield,
  Coventry C
Barton, A. J. (1) 2010/11 Preston NE
Best, G. (37) 1963/4 Manchester U,
  Fulham
Bingham, W. (56) 1950/1 Sunderland,
  Luton T, Everton, Port Vale

Black, K. (30) 1987/8 Luton T,
  Nottingham F
Blair, R. (5) 1974/5 Oldham Ath
Blanchflower, D. (54) 1949/50 Barnsley,
  Aston Villa, Tottenham H
Blanchflower, J. (12) 1953/4
  Manchester U
Blayney, A. (5) 2005/06 Doncaster R,
  Linfield
Bowler, G. C. (3) 1949/50 Hull C
Boyce, L. (4) 2010/11 Werder Bremen
Braithwaite, R. (10) 1961/2 Linfield,
  Middlesbrough
Braniff, K. R. (2) 2009/10 Portadown
Brennan, R. (5) 1948/9 Luton T,
  Birmingham C, Fulham
Briggs, R. (2) 1961/2 Manchester U,
  Swansea

Brotherston, N. (27) 1979/80 Blackburn R

Bruce, W. (2) 1960/1 Glentoran

Brunt, C. (36) 2004/05 Sheffield W, WBA

Bryan, M. A. (2) 2009/10 Watford

Camp, L. M. J. (8) 2010/11 Nottingham F

Campbell, A. (2) 1962/3 Crusaders

Campbell, D. A. (10) 1985/6 Nottingham F, Charlton Ath

Campbell, J. (2) 1950/1 Fulham

Campbell, R. M. (2) 1981/2 Bradford C

Campbell, W. (6) 1967/8 Dundee

Capaldi, A. C. (22) 2003/04 Plymouth Arg, Cardiff C

Carey, J. (7) 1946/7 Manchester U

Carroll, R. E. (20) 1996/7 Wigan Ath, Manchester U, West Ham U, Olympiakos

Carson, J. G. (3) 2010/11 Ipswich T

Carson, S. (1) 2008/09 Coleraine

Casement, C. (1) 2008/09 Ipswich T

Casey, T. (12) 1954/5 Newcastle U, Portsmouth

Caskey, A. (8) 1978/9 Derby C, Tulsa Roughnecks

Cassidy, T. (24) 1970/1 Newcastle U, Burnley

Cathcart, C. G. (9) 2010/11 Blackpool

Caughey, M. (2) 1985/6 Linfield

Clarke, C. J. (38) 1985/6 Bournemouth, Southampton, Portsmouth

Cleary, J. (5) 1981/2 Glentoran

Clements, D. (48) 1964/5 Coventry C, Sheffield W, Everton, New York Cosmos

Clingan, S. G. (33) 2005/06 Nottingham F, Norwich C, Coventry C

Clyde, M.G. (3) 2004/05 Wolverhampon W

Coates, C. (6) 2008/09 Crusaders

Cochrane, D. (10) 1946/7 Leeds U

Cochrane, T. (26) 1975/6 Coleraine, Burnley, Middlesbrough, Gillingham

Connell, T. E. (1) 1977/8 Coleraine

Coote, A. (6) 1998/9 Norwich C

Cowan, J. (1) 1969/70 Newcastle U

Coyle, F. (4) 1955/6 Coleraine, Nottingham F

Coyle, L. (1) 1988/9 Derry C

Coyle, R. (5) 1972/3 Sheffield W

Craig, D. (25) 1966/7 Newcastle U

Craigan, S. J. (54) 2002/03 Partick T, Motherwell

Crossan, E. (3) 1949/50 Blackburn R

Crossan, J. (24) 1959/60 Sparta Rotterdam, Sunderland, Manchester C, Middlesbrough

Cunningham, W. (30) 1950/1 St Mirren, Leicester C, Dunfermline Ath

Cush, W. (26) 1950/1 Glentoran, Leeds U, Portadown

Dallas, S. (1) 2010/11 Crusaders

D'Arcy, S. (5) 1951/2 Chelsea, Brentford

Davis, S. (52) 2004/05 Aston Villa, Fulham, Rangers

Davison, A. J. (3) 1995/6 Bolton W, Bradford C, Grimsby T

Dennison, R. (18) 1987/8 Wolverhampton W

Devine, J. (1) 1989/90 Glentoran

Dickson, D. (4) 1969/70 Coleraine

Dickson, T. (1) 1956/7 Linfield

Dickson, W. (12) 1950/1 Chelsea, Arsenal

Doherty, L. (2) 1984/5 Linfield

Doherty, P. (6) 1946/7 Derby Co, Huddersfield T, Doncaster R

Doherty, T. E. (9) 2002/03 Bristol C

Donaghy, M. (91) 1979/80 Luton T, Manchester U, Chelsea

Donnelly, M. (1) 2008/09 Crusaders

Dougan, D. (43) 1957/8 Portsmouth, Blackburn R, Aston Villa, Leicester C, Wolverhampton W

Douglas, J. P. (1) 1946/7 Belfast Celtic

Dowd, H. (3) 1973/4 Glenavon, Sheffield W

Dowie, I. (59) 1989/90 Luton T, West Ham U, Southampton, Crystal Palace, West Ham U, QPR

Duff, M. J. (24) 2001/02 Cheltenham T, Burnley

Dunlop, G. (4) 1984/5 Linfield

Eglington, T. (6) 1946/7 Everton

Elder, A. (40) 1959/60 Burnley, Stoke C

Elliott, S. (39) 2000/01 Motherwell, Hull C

Evans, C. J. (16) 2008/09 Manchester U, Hull C

Evans, J. G. (29) 2006/07 Manchester U

Farrell, P. (7) 1946/7 Everton

Feeney, J. (2) 1946/7 Linfield, Swansea T

Feeney, W. (1) 1975/6 Glentoran

Feeney, W. J. (46) 2001/02 Bournemouth, Luton T, Cardiff C, Oldham Ath, Plymouth Arg

Ferguson, G. (5) 1998/9 Linfield

Ferguson, S. (3) 2008/09 Newcastle U
Ferguson, W. (2) 1965/6 Linfield
Ferris, R. (3) 1949/50 Birmingham C
Fettis, A. (25) 1991/2 Hull C,
Nottingham F, Blackburn R
Finney, T. (14) 1974/5 Sunderland,
Cambridge U
Fleming, J. G. (31) 1986/7 Nottingham F,
Manchester C, Barnsley
Forde, T. (4) 1958/9 Ards

Gallogly, C. (2) 1950/1 Huddersfield T
Garrett, R. (5) 2008/09 Linfield
Garton, R. (1) 1968/9 Oxford U
Gault, M. (1) 2007/08 Linfield
Gillespie, K. R. (86) 1994/5
Manchester U, Newcastle U, Blackburn
R, Leicester C, Sheffield U
Gorman, R. J. (9) 2009/10
Wolverhampton W
Gorman, W. (4) 1946/7 Brentford
Graham, W. (14) 1950/1 Doncaster R
Gray, P. (26) 1992/3 Luton T, Sunderland,
Nancy, Luton T, Burnley, Oxford U
Gregg, H. (25) 1953/4 Doncaster R,
Manchester U
Grigg, W. D. (1) 2011/12 Walsall
Griffin, D. J. (29) 1995/6 St Johnstone,
Dundee U, Stockport Co

Hamill, R. (1) 1998/9 Glentoran
Hamilton, B. (50) 1968/9 Linfield, Ipswich
T, Everton, Millwall, Swindon T
Hamilton, G. (5) 2002/03 Portadown
Hamilton, W. (41) 1977/8 QPR, Burnley,
Oxford U
Harkin, T. (5) 1967/8 Southport,
Shrewsbury T
Harvey, M. (34) 1960/1 Sunderland
Hatton, S. (2) 1962/3 Linfield
Healy, D. J. (93) 1999/00 Manchester U,
Preston NE, Leeds U, Fulham,
Sunderland, Rangers
Healy, P. J. (4) 1981/2 Coleraine,
Glentoran
Hegan, D. (7) 1969/70 WBA,
Wolverhampton W
Hill, C. F. (27) 1989/90 Sheffield U,
Leicester C, Trelleborg, Northampton T
Hill, J. (7) 1958/9 Norwich C, Everton
Hinton, E. (7) 1946/7 Fulham, Millwall
Hodson, L. J. S. (8) 2010/11 Watford
Holmes, S. P. (1) 2001/02 Wrexham
Horlock, K. (32) 1994/5 Swindon T,
Manchester C

Hughes, A. W. (80) 1997/8 Newcastle U,
Aston Villa, Fulham
Hughes, J. (2) 2005/06 Lincoln C
Hughes, M. A. (2) 2005/06 Oldham Ath
Hughes, M. E. (71) 1991/2 Manchester C,
Strasbourg, West Ham U, Wimbledon,
Crystal Palace
Hughes, P. (3) 1986/7 Bury
Hughes, W. (1) 1950/1 Bolton W
Humphries, W. (14) 1961/2 Ards,
Coventry C, Swansea T
Hunter, A. (53) 1969/70 Blackburn R,
Ipswich T
Hunter, B. V. (15) 1994/5 Wrexham,
Reading
Hunter, V. (2) 1961/2 Coleraine

Ingham, M. G. (3) 2004/05 Sunderland,
Wrexham
Irvine, R. (8) 1961/2 Linfield, Stoke C
Irvine, W. (23) 1962/3 Burnley,
Preston NE, Brighton & HA

Jackson, T. (35) 1968/9 Everton,
Nottingham F, Manchester U
Jamison, A. (1) 1975/6 Glentoran
Jenkins, I. (6) 1996/7 Chester C,
Dundee U
Jennings, P. (119) 1963/4 Watford,
Tottenham H, Arsenal, Tottenham H
Johnson, D. M. (56) 1998/9 Blackburn R,
Birmingham C
Johnston, W. (2) 1961/2 Glenavon,
Oldham Ath
Jones, J. (3) 1955/6 Glenavon
Jones, S. G. (29) 2002/03 Crewe Alex,
Burnley

Keane, T. (1) 1948/9 Swansea T
Kee, P. V. (9) 1989/90 Oxford U, Ards
Keith, R. (23) 1957/8 Newcastle U
Kelly, H. (4) 1949/50 Fulham,
Southampton
Kelly, P. (1) 1949/50 Barnsley
Kennedy, P. H. (20) 1998/9 Watford,
Wigan Ath
Kirk, A. R. (11) 1999/00 Heart of
Midlothian, Boston U, Northampton T,
Dunfermline Ath

Lafferty, D. P. (1) 2011/12 Burnley
Lafferty, K. (30) 2005/06 Burnley,
Rangers
Lawrie, J. (3) 2008/09 Port Vale

Lawther, I. (4) 1959/60 Sunderland, Blackburn R

Lennon, N. F. (40) 1993/4 Crewe Alex, Leicester C, Celtic

Little, A. (8) 2008/09 Rangers

Lockhart, N. (8) 1946/7 Linfield, Coventry C, Aston Villa

Lomas, S. M. (45) 1993/4 Manchester C, West Ham U

Lutton, B. (6) 1969/70 Wolverhampton W, West Ham U

Magennis, J. B. D. (3) 2009/10 Cardiff C, Aberdeen

Magill, E. (26) 1961/2 Arsenal, Brighton & HA

Magilton, J. (52) 1990/1 Oxford U, Southampton, Sheffield W, Ipswich T

Mannus, A. (4) 2003/04 Linfield

Martin, C. (6) 1946/7 Glentoran, Leeds U, Aston Villa

McAdams, W. (15) 1953/4 Manchester C, Bolton W, Leeds U

McAlinden, J. (2) 1946/7 Portsmouth, Southend U

McArdle, R. A. (5) 2009/10 Rochdale, Aberdeen

McAuley, G. (36) 2004/05 Lincoln C, Leicester C, Ipswich T, WBA

McBride, S. (4) 1990/1 Glenavon

McCabe, J. (6) 1948/9 Leeds U

McCann, G. S. (39) 2001/02 West Ham U, Cheltenham T, Barnsley, Scunthorpe U, Peterborough U

McCarthy, J. D. (18) 1995/6 Port Vale, Birmingham C

McCartney, G. (34) 2001/02 Sunderland, West Ham U, Sunderland

McCavana, T. (3) 1954/5 Coleraine

McCleary, J. W. (1) 1954/5 Cliftonville

McClelland, J. (6) 1960/1 Arsenal, Fulham

McClelland, J. (53) 1979/80 Mansfield T, Rangers, Watford, Leeds U

McCourt, F. (6) 1951/2 Manchester C

McCourt, P. J. (10) 2001/02 Rochdale, Celtic

McCoy, R. (1) 1986/7 Coleraine

McCreery, D. (67) 1975/6 Manchester U, QPR, Tulsa Roughnecks, Newcastle U, Heart of Midlothian

McCrory, S. (1) 1957/8 Southend U

McCullough, W. (10) 1960/1 Arsenal, Millwall

McCurdy, C. (1) 1979/80 Linfield

McDonald, A. (52) 1985/6 QPR

McElhinney, G. (6) 1983/4 Bolton W

McEvilly, L. R. (1) 2001/02 Rochdale

McFaul, I. (6) 1966/7 Linfield, Newcastle U

McGarry, J. K. (3) 1950/1 Cliftonville

McGaughey, M. (1) 1984/5 Linfield

McGibbon, P. C. G. (7) 1994/5 Manchester U, Wigan Ath

McGinn, N. (18) 2009/10 Celtic

McGivern, R. (16) 2008/09 Manchester C

McGovern, M. (1) 2009/10 Ross Co

McGrath, R. (21) 1973/4 Tottenham H, Manchester U

McIlroy, J. (55) 1951/2 Burnley, Stoke C

McIlroy, S. B. (88) 1971/2 Manchester U, Stoke C, Manchester C

McKeag, W. (2) 1967/8 Glentoran

McKenna, J. (7) 1949/50 Huddersfield T

McKenzie, R. (1) 1966/7 Airdrieonians

McKinney, W. (1) 1965/6 Falkirk

McKnight, A. (10) 1987/8 Celtic, West Ham U

McLaughlin, C. G. (1) 2011/12 Preston NE

McLaughlin, J. (12) 1961/2 Shrewsbury T, Swansea T

McLean, B. S. (1) 2005/06 Rangers

McMahon, G. J. (17) 1994/5 Tottenham H, Stoke C

McMichael, A. (39) 1949/50 Newcastle U

McMillan, S. (2) 1962/3 Manchester U

McMordie, E. (21) 1968/9 Middlesbrough

McMorran, E. (15) 1946/7 Belfast Celtic, Barnsley, Doncaster R

McNally, B. A. (5) 1985/6 Shrewsbury T

McPake, J. (1) 2011/12 Coventry C

McParland, P. (34) 1953/4 Aston Villa, Wolverhampton W

McQuoid, J. J. B. (5) 2010/11 Millwall

McVeigh, P. (20) 1998/9 Tottenham H, Norwich C

Montgomery, F. J. (1) 1954/5 Coleraine

Moore, C. (1) 1948/9 Glentoran

Moreland, V. (6) 1978/9 Derby Co

Morgan, S. (18) 1971/2 Port Vale, Aston Villa, Brighton & HA, Sparta Rotterdam

Morrow, S. J. (39) 1989/90 Arsenal, QPR

Mulgrew, J. (2) 2009/10 Linfield

Mullan, G. (4) 1982/3 Glentoran

Mulryne, P. P. (27) 1996/7 Manchester U, Norwich C, Cardiff C

Murdock, C. J. (34) 1999/00 Preston NE, Hibernian, Crewe Alex, Rotherham U

Napier, R. (1) 1965/6 Bolton W
Neill, T. (59) 1960/1 Arsenal, Hull C
Nelson, S. (51) 1969/70 Arsenal, Brighton
& HA
Nicholl, C. (51) 1974/5 Aston Villa,
Southampton, Grimsby T
Nicholl, J. M. (73) 1975/6 Manchester U,
Toronto Blizzard, Sunderland, Rangers,
WBA
Nicholson, J. (41) 1960/1 Manchester U,
Huddersfield T
Nolan, I. R. (18) 1996/7 Sheffield W,
Bradford C, Wigan Ath
Norwood, O. J. (6) 2010/11 Manchester U

O'Boyle, G. (13) 1993/4 Dunfermline
Ath, St Johnstone
O'Connor, M. J. (10) 2007/08 Crewe Alex,
Scunthorpe U
O'Doherty, A. (2) 1969/70 Coleraine
O'Driscoll, J. (3) 1948/9 Swansea T
O'Kane, L. (20) 1969/70 Nottingham F
O'Neill, C. (3) 1988/9 Motherwell
O'Neill, H. M. (64) 1971/2 Distillery,
Nottingham F, Norwich C,
Manchester C, Norwich C, Notts Co
O'Neill, J. (1) 1961/2 Sunderland
O'Neill, J. P. (39) 1979/80 Leicester C
O'Neill, M. A. (31) 1987/8 Newcastle U,
Dundee U, Hibernian, Coventry C
Owens, J. (1) 2010/11 Crusaders

Parke, J. (13) 1963/4 Linfield, Hibernian,
Sunderland
Paterson, M. A. (13) 2007/08
Scunthorpe U, Burnley
Patterson, D. J. (17) 1993/4 Crystal
Palace, Luton T, Dundee U
Patterson, R. (5) 2009/10 Coleraine,
Plymouth Arg
Peacock, R. (31) 1951/2 Celtic, Coleraine
Penney, S. (17) 1984/5 Brighton & HA
Platt, J. A. (23) 1975/6 Middlesbrough,
Ballymena U, Coleraine

Quinn, J. M. (46) 1984/5 Blackburn R,
Swindon T, Leicester, Bradford C,
West Ham U, Bournemouth, Reading
Quinn, S. J. (50) 1995/6 Blackpool, WBA,
Willem II, Sheffield W,
Peterborough U, Northampton T

Rafferty, P. (1) 1979/80 Linfield
Ramsey, P. (14) 1983/4 Leicester C
Rice, P. (49) 1968/9 Arsenal

Robinson, S. (7) 1996/7 Bournemouth,
Luton T
Rogan, A. (18) 1987/8 Celtic, Sunderland,
Millwall
Ross, E. (1) 1968/9 Newcastle U
Rowland, K. (19) 1994/5 West Ham U,
QPR
Russell, A. (1) 1946/7 Linfield
Ryan, R. (1) 1949/50 WBA

Sanchez, L. P. (3) 1986/7 Wimbledon
Scott, J. (2) 1957/8 Grimsby T
Scott, P. (10) 1974/5 Everton, York C,
Aldershot
Sharkey, P. (1) 1975/6 Ipswich T
Shields, J. (1) 1956/7 Southampton
Shiels, D. (10) 2005/06 Hibernian,
Doncaster R, Kilmarnock
Simpson, W. (12) 1950/1 Rangers
Sloan, D. (2) 1968/9 Oxford
Sloan, T. (3) 1978/9 Manchester U
Sloan, W. (1) 1946/7 Arsenal
Smith, A. W. (18) 2002/03 Glentoran,
Preston NE
Smyth, S. (9) 1947/8 Wolverhampton W,
Stoke C
Smyth, W. (4) 1948/9 Distillery
Sonner, D. J. (13) 1997/8 Ipswich T,
Sheffield W, Birmingham C,
Nottingham F, Peterborough U
Spence, D. (29) 1974/5 Bury, Blackpool,
Southend U
Sproule, I. (11) 2005/06 Hibernian,
Bristol C
Stevenson, A. (3) 1946/7 Everton
Stewart, A. (7) 1966/7 Glentoran, Derby
Stewart, D. (1) 1977/8 Hull C
Stewart, I. (31) 1981/2 QPR, Newcastle U
Stewart, T. (1) 1960/1 Linfield

Taggart, G. P. (51) 1989/90 Barnsley,
Bolton W, Leicester C
Taylor, M. S. (88) 1998/9 Fulham,
Birmingham C, unattached
Thompson, P. (8) 2005/06 Linfield,
Stockport Co
Thompson, A. L. (2) 2010/11 Watford
Todd, S. (11) 1965/6 Burnley, Sheffield W
Toner, C. (2) 2002/03 Leyton Orient
Trainor, D. (1) 1966/7 Crusaders
Tuffey, J. (8) 2008/09 Partick T,
Inverness CT
Tully, C. (10) 1948/9 Celtic

310

Uprichard, N. (18) 1951/2 Swindon T, Portsmouth

Vernon, J. (17) 1946/7 Belfast Celtic, WBA

Walker, J. (1) 1954/5 Doncaster R
Walsh, D. (9) 1946/7 WBA
Walsh, W. (5) 1947/8 Manchester C
Ward, J. J. (1) 2011/12 Derby Co
Watson, P. (1) 1970/1 Distillery
Webb, S. M. (4) 2005/06 Ross Co
Welsh, S. (4) 1965/6 Carlisle U
Whiteside, N. (38) 1981/2 Manchester U, Everton
Whitley, Jeff (20) 1996/7 Manchester C, Sunderland, Cardiff C

Whitley, Jim (3) 1997/8 Manchester C
Williams, M. S. (36) 1998/9 Chesterfield, Watford, Wimbledon, Stoke C, Wimbledon, Milton Keynes D
Williams, P. (1) 1990/1 WBA
Wilson, D. J. (24) 1986/7 Brighton & HA, Luton, Sheffield W
Wilson, K. J. (42) 1986/7 Ipswich T, Chelsea, Notts C, Walsall
Wilson, S. (12) 1961/2 Glenavon, Falkirk, Dundee
Winchester, C. (1) 2010/11 Oldham Ath
Wood, T. J. (1) 1995/6 Walsall
Worthington, N. (66) 1983/4 Sheffield W, Leeds U, Stoke C
Wright, T. J. (31) 1988/9 Newcastle U, Nottingham F, Manchester C

SCOTLAND

Adam, C. G. (16) 2006/07 Rangers, Blackpool, Liverpool
Aird, J. (4) 1953/4 Burnley
Aitken, G. G. (8) 1948/9 East Fife, Sunderland
Aitken, R. (57) 1979/80 Celtic, Newcastle U, St Mirren
Albiston, A. (14) 1981/2 Manchester U
Alexander, G. (40) 2001/02 Preston NE, Burnley
Alexander, N. (3) 2005/06 Cardiff C
Allan, T. (2) 1973/4 Dundee
Anderson, J. (1) 1953/4 Leicester C
Anderson, R. (11) 2002/03 Aberdeen, Sunderland
Archibald, S. (27) 1979/80 Aberdeen, Tottenham H, Barcelona
Auld, B. (3) 1958/9 Celtic

Baird, H. (1) 1955/6 Airdrieonians
Baird, S. (7) 1956/7 Rangers
Bannan, B. (11) 2010/11 Aston Villa
Bannon, E. (11) 1979/80 Dundee U
Bardsley, P. A. (12) 2010/11 Sunderland
Barr, D. (1) 2008/09 Falkirk
Bauld, W. (3) 1949/50 Heart of Midlothian
Baxter, J. (34) 1960/1 Rangers, Sunderland
Beattie, C. (7) 2005/06 Celtic, WBA
Bell, C. (1) 2010/11 Kilmarnock
Bell, W. (2) 1965/6 Leeds U
Bernard, P. R. (2) 1994/5 Oldham Ath

Berra, C. (20) 2007/08 Heart of Midlothian, Wolverhampton W
Bett, J. (25) 1981/2 Rangers, Lokeren, Aberdeen
Black, E. (2) 1987/8 Metz
Black, I. (1) 1947/8 Southampton
Blacklaw, A. (3) 1962/3 Burnley
Blackley, J. (7) 1973/4 Hibernian
Blair, J. (1) 1946/7 Blackpool
Blyth, J. (2) 1977/8 Coventry C
Bone, J. (2) 1971/2 Norwich C
Booth, S. (21) 1992/3 Aberdeen, Borussia Dortmund, Twente
Bowman, D. (6) 1991/2 Dundee U
Boyd, K. (18) 2005/06 Rangers, Middlesbrough
Boyd, T. (72) 1990/1 Motherwell, Chelsea, Celtic
Brand, R. (8) 1960/1 Rangers
Brazil, A. (13) 1979/80 Ipswich T, Tottenham H
Bremner, D. (1) 1975/6 Hibernian
Bremner, W. (54) 1964/5 Leeds U
Brennan, F. (7) 1946/7 Newcastle U
Broadfoot, K. (4) 2008/09 Rangers
Brogan, J. (4) 1970/1 Celtic
Brown, A. (14) 1949/50 East Fife, Blackpool
Brown, H. (3) 1946/7 Partick Th
Brown, J. (1) 1974/5 Sheffield U
Brown, R. (3) 1946/7 Rangers
Brown, S. (28) 2005/06 Hibernian, Celtic
Brown, W. (28) 1957/8 Dundee, Tottenham H

Brownlie, J. (7) 1970/1 Hibernian

Bryson, C. (1) 2010/11 Kilmarnock

Buchan, M. (34) 1971/2 Aberdeen, Manchester U

Buckley, P. (3) 1953/4 Aberdeen

Burchill, M. J. (6) 1999/00 Celtic

Burke, C. (2) 2005/06 Rangers

Burley, C. W. (46) 1994/5 Chelsea, Celtic, Derby Co

Burley, G. (11) 1978/9 Ipswich T

Burns, F. (1) 1969/70 Manchester U

Burns, K. (20) 1973/4 Birmingham C, Nottingham F

Burns, T. (8) 1980/1 Celtic

Calderwood, C. (36) 1994/5 Tottenham H, Aston Villa

Caldow, E. (40) 1956/7 Rangers

Caldwell, G. (48) 2001/02 Newcastle U, Hibernian, Celtic, Wigan Ath

Caldwell, S. (12) 2000/01 Newcastle U, Sunderland, Burnley, Wigan Ath

Callaghan, W. (2) 1969/70 Dunfermline

Cameron, C. (28) 1998/9 Heart of Midlothian, Wolverhampton W

Campbell, R. (5) 1946/7 Falkirk, Chelsea

Campbell, W. (5) 1946/7 Morton

Canero, P. (1) 2003/04 Leicester C

Carr, W. (6) 1969/70 Coventry C

Chalmers, S. (5) 1964/5 Celtic

Clark, J. (4) 1965/6 Celtic

Clark, R. (17) 1967/8 Aberdeen

Clarke, S. (6) 1987/8 Chelsea

Clarkson, D. (2) 2007/08 Motherwell

Collins, J. (58) 1987/8 Hibernian, Celtic, Monaco, Everton

Collins, R. (31) 1950/1 Celtic, Everton, Leeds U

Colquhoun, E. (9) 1971/2 Sheffield U

Colquhoun, J. (2) 1987/8 Heart of Midlothian

Combe, R. (3) 1947/8 Hibernian

Commons, K. (9) 2008/09 Derby Co, Celtic

Conn, A. (1) 1955/6 Heart of Midlothian

Conn, A. (2) 1974/5 Tottenham H

Connachan, E. (2) 1961/2 Dunfermline Ath

Connelly, G. (2) 1973/4 Celtic

Connolly, J. (1) 1972/3 Everton

Connor, R. (4) 1985/6 Dundee, Aberdeen

Conway, C. (3) 2009/10 Dundee U, Cardiff C

Cooke, C. (16) 1965/6 Dundee, Chelsea

Cooper, D. (22) 1979/80 Rangers, Motherwell

Cormack, P. (9) 1965/6 Hibernian, Nottingham F

Cowan, J. (25) 1947/8 Morton

Cowie, D. (20) 1952/3 Dundee

Cowie, D. M. (10) 2009/10 Watford, Cardiff C

Cox, C. (1) 1947/8 Heart of Midlothian

Cox, S. (24) 1947/8 Rangers

Craig, J. (1) 1976/7 Celtic

Craig, J. P. (1) 1967/8 Celtic

Craig, T. (1) 1975/6 Newcastle U

Crainey, S. D. (12) 2001/02 Celtic, Southampton, Blackpool

Crawford, S. (25) 1994/5 Raith R, Dunfermline Ath, Plymouth Arg

Crerand, P. (16) 1960/1 Celtic, Manchester U

Cropley, A. (2) 1971/2 Hibernian

Cruickshank, J. (6) 1963/4 Heart of Midlothian

Cullen, M. (1) 1955/6 Luton T

Cumming, J. (9) 1954/5 Heart of Midlothian

Cummings. W. (1) 2001/02 Chelsea

Cunningham, W. (8) 1953/4 Preston NE

Curran, H. (5) 1969/70 Wolverhampton W

Dailly, C. (67) 1996/7 Derby Co, Blackburn R, West Ham U, Rangers

Dalglish, K. (102) 1971/2 Celtic, Liverpool

Davidson, C. I. (19) 1998/9 Blackburn R, Leicester C, Preston NE

Davidson, J. (8) 1953/4 Partick Th

Dawson, A. (5) 1979/80 Rangers

Deans, D. (2) 1974/5 Celtic

Delaney, J. (4) 1946/7 Manchester U

Devlin, P. J. (10) 2002/03 Birmingham C

Dick, J. (1) 1958/9 West Ham U

Dickov, P. (10) 2000/01 Manchester C, Leicester C, Blackburn R

Dickson, W. (5) 1969/70 Kilmarnock

Dobie, R. S. (6) 2001/02 WBA

Docherty, T. (25) 1951/2 Preston NE, Arsenal

Dodds, D. (2) 1983/4 Dundee U

Dodds, W. (26) 1996/7 Aberdeen, Dundee U, Rangers

Donachie, W. (35) 1971/2 Manchester C

Donnelly, S. (10) 1996/7 Celtic

Dorrans, G. (8) 2009/10 WBA

Dougall, C. (1) 1946/7 Birmingham C

Dougan, R. (1) 1949/50 Heart of Midlothian
Douglas, R. (19) 2001/02 Celtic, Leicester C
Doyle, J. (1) 1975/6 Ayr U
Duncan, A. (6) 1974/5 Hibernian
Duncan, D. (3) 1947/8 East Fife
Duncanson, J. (1) 1946/7 Rangers
Durie, G. S. (43) 1987/8 Chelsea, Tottenham H, Rangers
Durrant, I. (20) 1987/8 Rangers, Kilmarnock

Elliott, M. S. (18) 1997/8 Leicester C
Evans, A. (4) 1981/2 Aston Villa
Evans, R. (48) 1948/9 Celtic, Chelsea
Ewing, T. (2) 1957/8 Partick Th

Farm, G. (10) 1952/3 Blackpool
Ferguson, B. (45) 1998/9 Rangers, Blackburn R, Rangers
Ferguson, Derek (2) 1987/8 Rangers
Ferguson, Duncan (7) 1991/2 Dundee U, Everton
Ferguson, I. (9) 1988/9 Rangers
Ferguson, R. (7) 1965/6 Kilmarnock
Fernie, W. (12) 1953/4 Celtic
Flavell, R. (2) 1946/7 Airdrieonians
Fleck, R. (4) 1989/90 Norwich C
Fleming, C. (1) 1953/4 East Fife
Fletcher, D. B. (58) 2003/04 Manchester U
Fletcher, S. (8) 2007/08 Hibernian, Burnley, Wolverhampton W
Forbes, A. (14) 1946/7 Sheffield U, Arsenal
Ford, D. (3) 1973/4 Heart of Midlothian
Forrest, J. (1) 1957/8 Motherwell
Forrest, J. (5) 1965/6 Rangers, Aberdeen
Forrest, J. (5) 2010/11 Celtic
Forsyth, A. (10) 1971/2 Partick Th, Manchester U
Forsyth, C. (4) 1963/4 Kilmarnock
Forsyth, T. (22) 1970/1 Motherwell, Rangers
Fox, D. (1) 2009/10 Burnley
Fraser, D. (2) 1967/8 WBA
Fraser, W. (2) 1954/5 Sunderland
Freedman, D. A. (2) 2001/02 Crystal Palace

Gabriel, J. (2) 1960/1 Everton
Gallacher, K. W. (53) 1987/8 Dundee U, Coventry C, Blackburn R, Newcastle U
Gallacher, P. (8) 2001/02 Dundee U

Gallagher, P. (1) 2003/04 Blackburn R
Galloway, M. (1) 1991/2 Celtic
Gardiner, W. (1) 1957/8 Motherwell
Gemmell, T. (2) 1954/5 St Mirren
Gemmell, T. (18) 1965/6 Celtic
Gemmill, A. (43) 1970/1 Derby Co, Nottingham F, Birmingham C
Gemmill, S. (26) 1994/5 Nottingham F, Everton
Gibson, D. (7) 1962/3 Leicester C
Gillespie, G. T. (13) 1987/8 Liverpool
Gilzean, A. (22) 1963/4 Dundee, Tottenham H
Glass, S. (1) 1998/9 Newcastle U
Glavin, R. (1) 1976/7 Celtic
Glen, A. (2) 1955/6 Aberdeen
Goodwillie, D. (3) 2010/11 Dundee U, Blackburn R
Goram, A. L. (43) 1985/6 Oldham Ath, Hibernian, Rangers
Gordon, C. S. (40) 2003/04 Heart of Midlothian, Sunderland
Gough, C. R. (61) 1982/3 Dundee U, Tottenham H, Rangers
Gould, J. (2) 1999/00 Celtic
Govan, J. (6) 1947/8 Hibernian
Graham, A. (11) 1977/8 Leeds U
Graham, G. (12) 1971/2 Arsenal, Manchester U
Grant, J. (2) 1958/9 Hibernian
Grant, P. (2) 1988/9 Celtic
Gray, A. (20) 1975/6 Aston Villa, Wolverhampton W, Everton
Gray, A. D. (2) 2002/03 Bradford C
Gray, E. (12) 1968/9 Leeds U
Gray F. (32) 1975/6 Leeds U, Nottingham F, Leeds U
Green, A. (6) 1970/1 Blackpool, Newcastle U
Greig, J. (44) 1963/4 Rangers
Gunn, B. (6) 1989/90 Norwich C

Haddock, H. (6) 1954/5 Clyde
Haffey, F. (2) 1959/60 Celtic
Hamilton, A. (24) 1961/2 Dundee
Hamilton, G. (5) 1946/7 Aberdeen
Hamilton, W. (1) 1964/5 Hibernian
Hammell, S. (1) 2004/05 Motherwell
Hanley, G. (3) 2010/11 Blackburn R
Hansen, A. (26) 1978/9 Liverpool
Hansen, J. (2) 1971/2 Partick Th
Harper, J. (4) 1972/3 Aberdeen, Hibernian, Aberdeen
Hartford, A. (50) 1971/2 WBA, Manchester C, Everton, Manchester C

Hartley, P. J. (25) 2004/05 Heart of Midlothian, Celtic, Bristol C

Harvey, D. (16) 1972/3 Leeds U

Haughney, M. (1) 1953/4 Celtic

Hay, D. (27) 1969/70 Celtic

Hegarty, P. (8) 1978/9 Dundee U

Henderson, J. (7) 1952/3 Portsmouth, Arsenal

Henderson, W. (29) 1962/3 Rangers

Hendry, E. C. J. (51) 1992/3 Blackburn R, Rangers, Coventry C, Bolton W

Herd, D. (5) 1958/9 Arsenal

Herd, G. (5) 1957/8 Clyde

Herriot, J. (8) 1968/9 Birmingham C

Hewie, J. (19) 1955/6 Charlton Ath

Holt, D. D. (5) 1962/3 Heart of Midlothian

Holt, G. J. (10) 2000/01 Kilmarnock, Norwich C

Holton, J. (15) 1972/3 Manchester U

Hope, R. (2) 1967/8 WBA

Hopkin, D. (7) 1996/7 Crystal Palace, Leeds U

Houliston, W. (3) 1948/9 Queen of the South

Houston, S. (1) 1975/6 Manchester U

Howie, H. (1) 1948/9 Hibernian

Hughes, J. (8) 1964/5 Celtic

Hughes, R. D. (5) 2003/04 Portsmouth

Hughes, S. D. (1) 2009/10 Norwich C

Hughes, W. (1) 1974/5 Sunderland

Humphries, W. (1) 1951/2 Motherwell

Hunter, A. (4) 1971/2 Kilmarnock, Celtic

Hunter, W. (3) 1959/60 Motherwell

Husband, J. (1) 1946/7 Partick Th

Hutchison, D. (26) 1998/9 Everton, Sunderland, West Ham U

Hutchison, T. (17) 1973/4 Coventry C

Hutton, A. (23) 2006/07 Rangers, Tottenham H

Imlach, S. (4) 1957/8 Nottingham F

Irvine, B. (9) 1990/1 Aberdeen

Iwelumo, C. R. (4) 2008/09 Wolverhampton W, Burnley

Jackson, C. (8) 1974/5 Rangers

Jackson, D. (28) 1994/5 Hibernian, Celtic

Jardine, A. (38) 1970/1 Rangers

Jarvie, A. (3) 1970/1 Airdrieonians

Jess, E. (18) 1992/3 Aberdeen, Coventry C, Aberdeen

Johnston, A. (18) 1998/9 Sunderland, Rangers, Middlesbrough

Johnston, M. (38) 1983/4 Watford, Celtic, Nantes, Rangers

Johnston, L. (2) 1947/8 Clyde

Johnston, W. (22) 1965/6 Rangers, WBA

Johnstone, D. (14) 1972/3 Rangers

Johnstone, J. (23) 1964/5 Celtic

Johnstone, R. (17) 1950/1 Hibernian, Manchester C

Jordan, J. (52) 1972/3 Leeds U, Manchester U, AC Milan

Kelly, H. (1) 1951/2 Blackpool

Kelly, J. (2) 1948/9 Barnsley

Kennedy, Jim (6) 1963/4 Celtic

Kennedy, John (1) 2003/04 Celtic

Kennedy, S. (5) 1974/5 Rangers

Kennedy, S. (8) 1977/8 Aberdeen

Kenneth, G. (2) 2010/11 Dundee U

Kerr, A. (2) 1954/5 Partick Th

Kerr, B. (3) 2002/03 Newcastle U

Kyle, K. (10) 2001/02 Sunderland, Kilmarnock

Lambert, P. (40) 1994/5 Motherwell, Borussia Dortmund, Celtic

Law, D. (55) 1958/9 Huddersfield T, Manchester C, Torino, Manchester U, Manchester C

Lawrence, T. (3) 1962/3 Liverpool

Leggat, G. (18) 1955/6 Aberdeen, Fulham

Leighton, J. (91) 1982/3 Aberdeen, Manchester U, Hibernian, Aberdeen

Lennox, R. (10) 1966/7 Celtic

Leslie, L. (5) 1960/1 Airdrieonians

Levein, C. (16) 1989/90 Heart of Midlothian

Liddell, W. (28) 1946/7 Liverpool

Linwood, A. (1) 1949/50 Clyde

Little, R. J. (1) 1952/3 Rangers

Logie, J. (1) 1952/3 Arsenal

Long, H. (1) 1946/7 Clyde

Lorimer, P. (21) 1969/70 Leeds U

Macari, L. (24) 1971/2 Celtic, Manchester U

Macaulay, A. (7) 1946/7 Brentford, Arsenal

MacDougall, E. (7) 1974/5 Norwich C

Mackay, D. (22) 1956/7 Heart of Midlothian, Tottenham H

Mackay, G. (4) 1987/8 Heart of Midlothian

Mackay, M. (5) 2003/04 Norwich C

Maloney, S. R. (20) 2005/06 Celtic, Aston Villa, Celtic, Wigan Ath

Malpas, M. (55) 1983/4 Dundee U
Marshall, D. J. (5) 2004/05 Celtic,
    Cardiff C
Marshall, G. (1) 1991/2 Celtic
Martin, B. (2) 1994/5 Motherwell
Martin, F. (6) 1953/4 Aberdeen
Martin, J. (3) 1964/5 Hibernian,
    Sunderland
Martin, R. K. A. (3) 2010/11 Norwich C
Martis, J. (1) 1960/1 Motherwell
Mason, J. (7) 1948/9 Third Lanark
Masson, D. (17) 1975/6 QPR, Derby C
Mathers, D. (1) 1953/4 Partick Th
Matteo, D. (6) 2000/01 Leeds U
McAllister, B. (3) 1996/7 Wimbledon
McAllister, G. (57) 1989/90 Leicester C,
    Leeds U, Coventry C
McAllister, J. R. (1) 2003/04 Livingston
McArthur, J. (7) 2010/11 Wigan Ath
McAvennie, F. (5) 1985/6 West Ham U,
    Celtic
McBride, J. (2) 1966/7 Celtic
McCall, S. M. (40) 1989/90 Everton,
    Rangers
McCalliog, J. (5) 1966/7 Sheffield W,
    Wolverhampton W
McCann, N. D. (26) 1998/9 Heart of
    Midlothian, Rangers, Southampton
McCann, R. (5) 1958/9 Motherwell
McClair, B. (30) 1986/7 Celtic,
    Manchester U
McCloy, P. (4) 1972/3 Rangers
McCoist, A. (61) 1985/6 Rangers,
    Kilmarnock
McColl, I. (14) 1949/50 Rangers
McCormack, R. (7) 20007/08 Motherwell,
    Cardiff C, Leeds U
McCreadie, E. (23) 1964/5 Chelsea
McCulloch, L. (18) 2004/05 Wigan Ath,
    Rangers
MacDonald, A. (1) 1975/6 Rangers
McDonald, J. (2) 1955/6 Sunderland
McEveley, J. (3) 2007/08 Derby Co
McFadden, J. (48) 2001/02 Motherwell,
    Everton, Birmingham C
McFarlane, W. (1) 1946/7 Heart of
    Midlothian
McGarr, E. (2) 1969/70 Aberdeen
McGarvey, F. (7) 1978/9 Liverpool, Celtic
McGhee, M. (4) 1982/3 Aberdeen
McGinlay, J. (13) 1993/4 Bolton W
McGrain, D. (62) 1972/3 Celtic
McGregor, A. (21) 2006/07 Rangers
McGrory, J. (3) 1964/5 Kilmarnock

McInally, A. (8) 1988/9 Aston Villa,
    Bayern Munich
McInally, J. (10) 1986/7 Dundee U
McInnes, D. (2) 2002/03 WBA
MacKay, D. (14) 1958/9 Celtic
McKean, R. (1) 1975/6 Rangers
MacKenzie, J. (9) 1953/4 Partick Th
McKimmie, S. (40) 1988/9 Aberdeen
McKinlay, T. (22) 1995/6 Celtic
McKinlay, W. (29) 1993/4 Dundee U,
    Blackburn R
McKinnon, Rob (3) 1993/4 Motherwell
McKinnon, Ronnie (28) 1965/6 Rangers
McLaren, Alan (24) 1991/2 Heart of
    Midlothian, Rangers
McLaren, Andy (4) 1946/7 Preston NE
McLaren, Andy (1) 2000/01 Kilmarnock
McLean, G. (1) 1967/8 Dundee
McLean, T. (6) 1968/9 Kilmarnock
McLeish, A. (77) 1979/80 Aberdeen
McLeod, J. (4) 1960/1 Hibernian
MacLeod, M. (20) 1984/5 Celtic, Borussia
    Dortmund, Hibernian
McLintock, F. (9) 1962/3 Leicester C,
    Arsenal
McManus, S. (26) 2006/07 Celtic,
    Middlesbrough
McMillan, I. (6) 1951/2 Airdrieonians,
    Rangers
McNamara, J. (33) 1996/7 Celtic,
    Wolverhampton W
McNamee, D. (4) 2003/04 Livingston
McNaught, W. (5) 1950/1 Raith R
McNaughton, K. (4) 2001/02 Aberdeen,
    Cardiff C
McNeill, W. (29) 1960/1 Celtic
McPhail, J. (5) 1949/50 Celtic
McPherson, D. (27) 1988/9 Heart of
    Midlothian, Rangers
McQueen, G. (30) 1973/4 Leeds U,
    Manchester U
McStay, P. (76) 1983/4 Celtic
McSwegan, G. (2) 1999/00 Heart of
    Midlothian
Mackail-Smith, C. (7) 2010/11
    Peterborough U, Brighton & HA
Mackie, J. C. (5) 2010/11 QPR
Maguire, C. (2) 2010/11 Aberdeen
Millar, J. (2) 1962/3 Rangers
Miller, C. (1) 2000/01 Dundee U
Miller, K. (60) 2000/01 Rangers,
    Wolverhampton W, Celtic, Derby Co,
    Rangers, Bursa, Cardiff C
Miller, L. (3) 2005/06 Dundee U,
    Aberdeen

Miller, W. (6) 1946/7 Celtic
Miller, W. (65) 1974/5 Aberdeen
Mitchell, R. (2) 1950/1 Newcastle U
Mochan, N. (3) 1953/4 Celtic
Moir, W. (1) 1949/50 Bolton W
Moncur, R. (16) 1967/8 Newcastle U
Morgan, W. (21) 1967/8 Burnley,
  Manchester U
Morris, H. (1) 1949/50 East Fife
Morrison, J. C. (20) 2007/08 WBA
Mudie, J. (17) 1956/7 Blackpool
Mulgrew, C. (2) 2011/12 Celtic
Mulhall, G. (3) 1959/60 Aberdeen,
  Sunderland
Munro, F. (9) 1970/1 Wolverhampton W
Munro, I. (7) 1978/9 St Mirren
Murdoch, R. (12) 1965/6 Celtic
Murray, I. (6) 2002/03 Hibernian,
  Rangers
Murray, J. (5) 1957/8 Heart of Midlothian
Murray, S. (1) 1971/2 Aberdeen
Murty, G. S. (4) 2003/04 Reading

**Naismith, S. J. (15) 2006/07 Kilmarnock,
Rangers**
Narey, D. (35) 1976/7 Dundee U
Naysmith, G. A. (46) 1999/00 Heart of
  Midlothian, Everton, Sheffield U
Neilson, R. (1) 2006/07 Heart of
  Midlothian
Nevin, P. K. F. (28) 1985/6 Chelsea,
  Everton, Tranmere R
Nicholas, C. (20) 1982/3 Celtic, Arsenal,
  Aberdeen
Nicholson, B. (3) 2000/01
  Dunfermline Ath
Nicol, S. (27) 1984/5 Liverpool

O'Connor, G. (16) 2001/02 Hibernian,
  Lokomotiv Moscow, Birmingham C
O'Donnell, P. (1) 1993/4 Motherwell
O'Hare, J. (13) 1969/70 Derby Co
O'Neil, B. (7) 1995/6 Celtic, Wolfsburg,
  Derby Co, Preston NE
O'Neil, J. (1) 2000/01 Hibernian
Ormond, W. (6) 1953/4 Hibernian
Orr, T. (2) 1951/2 Morton

Parker, A. (15) 1954/5 Falkirk, Everton
Parlane, D. (12) 1972/3 Rangers
Paton, A. (2) 1951/2 Motherwell
Pearson, S. P. (10) 2003/04 Motherwell,
  Celtic, Derby Co
Pearson, T. (2) 1946/7 Newcastle U
Penman, A. (1) 1965/6 Dundee

Pettigrew, W. (5) 1975/6 Motherwell
Phillips, M. (1) 2011/12 Blackpool
Plenderleith, J. (1) 1960/1 Manchester C
Pressley, S. J. (32) 1999/00 Heart of
  Midlothian
Provan, David (10) 1979/80 Celtic
Provan, Davie (5) 1963/4 Rangers

Quashie, N. F. (14) 2003/04 Portsmouth,
  Southampton, WBA
Quinn, P. (4) 1960/1 Motherwell

Rae, G. P. (14) 2000/01 Dundee, Rangers,
  Cardiff C
Redpath, W. (9) 1948/9 Motherwell
Reilly, L. (38) 1948/9 Hibernian
Rhodes, J. L. (1) 2011/12 Huddersfield T
Ring, T. (12) 1952/3 Clyde
Rioch, B. (24) 1974/5 Derby Co, Everton,
  Derby Co
Riordan, D. G. (3) 2005/06 Hibernian
Ritchie, P. S. (7) 1998/9 Heart of
  Midlothian, Bolton W, Walsall
Ritchie, W. (1) 1961/2 Rangers
Robb, D. (5) 1970/1 Aberdeen
Robertson, A. (5) 1954/5 Clyde
Robertson, D. (3) 1991/2 Rangers
Robertson, H. (1) 1961/2 Dundee
Robertson, J. (16) 1990/1 Heart of
  Midlothian
Robertson, J. G. (1) 1964/5 Tottenham H
Robertson, J. N. (28) 1977/8 Nottingham
  F, Derby Co
Robertson, S. (2) 2008/09 Dundee U
Robinson, B. (4) 1973/4 Dundee
**Robson, B. G. G. (17) 2007/08 Dundee U,
Celtic, Middlesbrough**
Ross, M. (13) 2001/02 Rangers
Rough, A. (53) 1975/6 Partick Th,
  Hibernian
Rougvie, D. (1) 1983/4 Aberdeen
Rutherford, E. (1) 1947/8 Rangers

St John, I. (21) 1958/9 Motherwell,
  Liverpool
Saunders, S. (1) 2010/11 Motherwell
Schaedler, E. (1) 1973/4 Hibernian
Scott, A. (16) 1956/7 Rangers, Everton
Scott, Jimmy (1) 1965/6 Hibernian
Scott, Jocky (2) 1970/1 Dundee
Scoular, J. (9) 1950/1 Portsmouth
Severin, S. D. (15) 2001/02 Heart of
  Midlothian, Aberdeen
Sharp, G. M. (12) 1984/5 Everton
Shaw, D. (8) 1946/7 Hibernian

Shaw, J. (4) 1946/7 Rangers
Shearer, D. (7) 1993/4 Aberdeen
Shearer, R. (4) 1960/1 Rangers
Simpson, N. (4) 1982/3 Aberdeen
Simpson, R. (5) 1966/7 Celtic
Sinclair, J. (1) 1965/6 Leicester C
Smith, D. (2) 1965/6 Aberdeen, Rangers
Smith, E. (2) 1958/9 Celtic
Smith, G. (18) 1946/7 Hibernian
Smith, H. G. (3) 1987/8 Heart of
  Midlothian
Smith, J. (4) 1967/8 Aberdeen,
  Newcastle U
Smith, J. E. (2) 2002/03 Celtic
Snodgrass, R. (5) 2010/11 Leeds U
Souness, G. (54) 1974/5 Middlesbrough,
  Liverpool, Sampdoria
Speedie, D. R. (10) 1984/5 Chelsea,
  Coventry C
Spencer, J. (14) 1994/5 Chelsea, QPR
Stanton, P. (16) 1965/6 Hibernian
Steel, W. (30) 1946/7 Morton, Derby C,
  Dundee
Stein, C. (21) 1968/9 Rangers, Coventry C
Stephen, J. (2) 1946/7 Bradford PA
Stewart, D. (1) 1977/8 Leeds U
Stewart, J. (2) 1976/7 Kilmarnock,
  Middlesbrough
Stewart, M. J. (4) 2001/02 Manchester U,
  Heart of Midlothian
Stewart, R. (10) 1980/1 West Ham U
Stockdale, R. K. (5) 2001/02
  Middlesbrough
Strachan, G. (50) 1979/80 Aberdeen,
  Manchester U, Leeds U
Sturrock, P. (20) 1980/1 Dundee U
Sullivan, N. (28) 1996/7 Wimbledon,
  Tottenham H

Teale, G. (13) 2005/06 Wigan Ath,
  Derby Co
Telfer, P. N. (1) 1999/00 Coventry C
Telfer, W. (1) 1953/4 St Mirren
Thompson, S. (16) 2001/02 Dundee U,
  Rangers
Thomson, K. (3) 2008/09 Rangers,
  Middlesbrough
Thomson, W. (7) 1979/80 St Mirren
Thornton, W. (7) 1946/7 Rangers
Toner, W. (2) 1958/9 Kilmarnock
Turnbull, E. (8) 1947/8 Hibernian

Ure, I. (11) 1961/2 Dundee, Arsenal

Waddell, W. (17) 1946/7 Rangers
Walker, A. (3) 1987/8 Celtic
Walker, J. N. (2) 1992/3 Heart of
  Midlothian, Partick Th
Wallace, I. A. (3) 1977/8 Coventry C
**Wallace, L. (6) 2009/10 Heart of
  Midlothian**
Wallace, R. (1) 2009/10 Preston NE
Wallace, W. S. B. (7) 1964/5 Heart of
  Midlothian, Celtic
Wardhaugh, J. (2) 1954/5 Heart of
  Midlothian
Wark, J. (29) 1978/9 Ipswich T, Liverpool
Watson, J. (2) 1947/8 Motherwell,
  Huddersfield T
Watson, R. (1) 1970/1 Motherwell
**Webster, A. (24) 2002/03 Heart of
  Midlothian, Dundee U**
Weir, A. (6) 1958/9 Motherwell
Weir, D. G. (69) 1996/7 Heart of
  Midlothian, Everton, Rangers
Weir, P. (6) 1979/80 St Mirren, Aberdeen
White, J. (22) 1958/9 Falkirk,
  Tottenham H
Whittaker, S. G. (15) 2009/10 Rangers
Whyte, D. (12) 1987/8 Celtic,
  Middlesbrough, Aberdeen
Wilkie, L. (11) 2001/02 Dundee
Williams, G. (5) 2001/02 Nottingham F
Wilson, A. (1) 1953/4 Portsmouth
Wilson, D. (22) 1960/1 Rangers
Wilson, D. (5) 2010/11 Liverpool
Wilson, I. A. (5) 1986/7 Leicester C,
  Everton
Wilson, M. (1) 2010/11 Celtic
Wilson, P. (1) 1974/5 Celtic
Wilson, R. (2) 1971/2 Arsenal
Winters, R. (1) 1998/9 Aberdeen
Wood, G. (4) 1978/9 Everton, Arsenal
Woodburn, W. (24) 1946/7 Rangers
Wright, K. (1) 1991/2 Hibernian
Wright, S. (2) 1992/3 Aberdeen
Wright, T. (3) 1952/3 Sunderland

Yeats, R. (2) 1964/5 Liverpool
Yorston, H. (1) 1954/5 Aberdeen
Young, A. (8) 1959/60 Heart of
  Midlothian, Everton
Young, G. (53) 1946/7 Rangers
Younger, T. (24) 1954/5 Hibernian,
  Liverpool

WALES

Aizlewood, M. (39) 1985/6 Charlton Ath,
Leeds U, Bradford C, Bristol C,
Cardiff C
Allchurch, I. (68) 1950/1 Swansea T,
Newcastle U, Cardiff C, Swansea T
Allchurch, L. (11) 1954/5 Swansea T,
Sheffield U
Allen, B. (2) 1950/1 Coventry C
Allen, J. M. (8) 2008/09 Swansea C
Allen, M. (14) 1985/6 Watford, Norwich
C, Millwall, Newcastle U

Baker, C. (7) 1957/8 Cardiff C
Baker, W. (1) 1947/8 Cardiff C
**Bale, G. (33) 2005/06 Southampton,
Tottenham H**
Barnard, D. S. (22) 1997/8 Barnsley,
Grimsby T
Barnes, W. (22) 1947/8 Arsenal
**Bellamy, C. D. (69) 1997/8 Norwich C,
Coventry C, Newcastle U,
Blackburn R, Liverpool, West Ham U,
Manchester C, Liverpool**
Berry, G. (5) 1978/9 Wolverhampton W,
Stoke C
Blackmore, C. G. (39) 1984/5
Manchester U, Middlesbrough
Blake, D. J. (9) 2010/11 Cardiff C
Blake, N. A. (29) 1993/4 Sheffield U,
Bolton W, Blackburn R,
Wolverhampton W
Bodin, P. J. (23) 1989/90 Swindon T,
Crystal Palace, Swindon T
Bowen, D. (19) 1954/5 Arsenal
Bowen, J. P. (2) 1993/4 Swansea C,
Birmingham C
Bowen, M. R. (41) 1985/6 Tottenham H,
Norwich C, West Ham U
Boyle, T. (2) 1980/1 Crystal Palace
Bradley, M. S. (1) 2009/10 Walsall
**Brown, J. R. (3) 2005/06 Gillingham,
Blackburn R, Aberdeen**
Browning, M. T. (5) 1995/6 Bristol R,
Huddersfield T
Burgess, R. (32) 1946/7 Tottenham H
Burton, O. (9) 1962/3 Norwich C,
Newcastle U

Cartwright, L. (7) 1973/4 Coventry C,
Wrexham
Charles, J. (38) 1949/50 Leeds U,
Juventus, Leeds U, Cardiff C

Charles, J. M. (19) 1980/1 Swansea C,
QPR, Oxford U
Charles, M. (31) 1954/5 Swansea T,
Arsenal, Cardiff C
Church, S. R. (15) 2008/09 Reading
Clarke, R. (22) 1948/9 Manchester C
Coleman, C. (32) 1991/2 Crystal Palace,
Blackburn R, Fulham
Collins, D. L. (12) 2004/05 Sunderland,
Stoke C
Collins, J. M. (39) 2003/04 Cardiff C,
West Ham U, Aston Villa
Collison, J. D. (11) 2007/08 West Ham U
Cornforth, J. M. (2) 1994/5 Swansea C
Cotterill, D. R. G. B. (19) 2005/06
Bristol C, Wigan Ath, Sheffield U,
Swansea C
Coyne, D. (16) 1995/6 Tranmere R,
Grimsby T, Leicester C, Burnley,
Tranmere R
**Crofts, A. L. (23) 2005/06 Gillingham,
Brighton & HA, Norwich C**
Crossley, M. G. (8) 1996/7 Nottingham F,
Middlesbrough, Fulham
Crowe, V. (16) 1958/9 Aston Villa
Curtis, A. (35) 1975/6 Swansea C,
Leeds U, Swansea C, Southampton,
Cardiff C

Daniel, R. (21) 1950/1 Arsenal,
Sunderland
Davies, A. (13) 1982/3 Manchester U,
Newcastle U, Swansea C, Bradford C
Davies. A. R. (1) 2005/06 Yeovil T
Davies, C. (1) 1971/2 Charlton Ath
Davies, C. M. (5) 2005/06 Oxford U,
Verona, Oldham Ath
Davies, D. (52) 1974/5 Everton,
Wrexham, Swansea C
Davies, G. (16) 1979/80 Fulham,
Manchester C
Davies, R. Wyn (34) 1963/4 Bolton W,
Newcastle U, Manchester C,
Manchester U, Blackpool
Davies, Reg (6) 1952/3 Newcastle U
Davies, Ron (29) 1963/4 Norwich C,
Southampton, Portsmouth
Davies, S. (58) 2000/01 Tottenham H,
Everton, Fulham
Davies, S. I. (1) 1995/6 Manchester U
Davis, G. (3) 1977/8 Wrexham
Deacy, N. (12) 1976/7 PSV Eindhoven,
Beringen

Delaney, M. A. (36) 1999/00 Aston Villa

Derrett, S. (4) 1968/9 Cardiff C

Dibble, A. (3) 1985/6 Luton T, Manchester C

Dorman, A. (3) 2009/10 St Mirren, Crystal Palace

Duffy, R. M. (13) 2005/06 Portsmouth

Durban, A. (27) 1965/6 Derby C

Dwyer, P. (10) 1977/8 Cardiff C

Eardley, N. (16) 2007/08 Oldham Ath, Blackpool

Earnshaw, R. (58) 2001/02 Cardiff C, WBA, Norwich C, Derby Co, Nottingham F, Cardiff C

Easter, J. M. (10) 2006/07 Wycombe W, Plymouth Arg, Milton Keynes D, Crystal Palace

Eastwood, F. (11) 2007/08 Wolverhampton W, Coventry C

Edwards, C. N. H. (1) 1995/6 Swansea C

Edwards, D. (24) 2007/08 Luton T, Wolverhampton W

Edwards, G. (12) 1946/7 Birmingham C, Cardiff C

Edwards, I. (4) 1977/8 Chester, Wrexham

Edwards, R. O. (15) 2002/03 Aston Villa, Wolverhampton W

Edwards, R. W. (4) 1997/8 Bristol C

Edwards, T. (2) 1956/7 Charlton Ath

Emanuel, J. (2) 1972/3 Bristol C

England, M. (44) 1961/2 Blackburn R, Tottenham H

Evans, B. (7) 1971/2 Swansea C, Hereford U

Evans, C. M. (13) 2007/08 Manchester C, Sheffield U

Evans, I. (13) 1975/6 Crystal Palace

Evans, P. S. (2) 2001/02 Brentford, Bradford C

Evans, R. (1) 1963/4 Swansea T

Evans, S. J. (7) 2006/07 Wrexham

Felgate, D. (1) 1983/4 Lincoln C

Fletcher, C. N. (36) 2003/04 Bournemouth, West Ham U, Crystal Palace

Flynn, B. (66) 1974/5 Burnley, Leeds U, Burnley

Ford, T. (38) 1946/7 Swansea T, Aston Villa, Sunderland, Cardiff C

Foulkes, W. (11) 1951/2 Newcastle U

Freestone, R. (1) 1999/00 Swansea C

Gabbidon, D. L. (46) 2001/02 Cardiff C, West Ham U, QPR

Garner, G. (1) 2005/06 Leyton Orient

Giggs, R. J. (64) 1991/2 Manchester U

Giles, D. (12) 1979/80 Swansea C, Crystal Palace

Godfrey, B. (3) 1963/4 Preston NE

Goss, J. (9) 1990/1 Norwich C

Green, C. (15) 1964/5 Birmingham C

Green, R. M. (2) 1997/8 Wolverhampton W

Griffiths, A. (17) 1970/1 Wrexham

Griffiths, H. (1) 1952/3 Swansea T

Griffiths, M. (11) 1946/7 Leicester C

Gunter, C. R. (37) 2006/07 Cardiff C, Tottenham H, Nottingham F

Hall, G. D. (9) 1987/8 Chelsea

Harrington, A. (11) 1955/6 Cardiff C

Harris, C. (24) 1975/6 Leeds U

Harris, W. (6) 1953/4 Middlesbrough

Hartson, J. (51) 1994/5 Arsenal, West Ham U, Wimbledon, Coventry C, Celtic

Haworth, S. O. (5) 1996/7 Cardiff C, Coventry C

Hennessey, T. (39) 1961/2 Birmingham C, Nottingham F, Derby Co

Hennessey, W. R. (38) 2006/07 Wolverhampton W

Hewitt, R. (5) 1957/8 Cardiff C

Hill, M. (2) 1971/2 Ipswich T

Hockey, T. (9) 1971/2 Sheffield U, Norwich C, Aston Villa

Hodges, G. (18) 1983/4 Wimbledon, Newcastle U, Watford, Sheffield U

Holden, A. (1) 1983/4 Chester C

Hole, B. (30) 1962/3 Cardiff C, Blackburn R, Aston Villa, Swansea C

Hollins, D. (11) 1961/2 Newcastle U

Hopkins, J. (16) 1982/3 Fulham, Crystal Palace

Hopkins, M. (34) 1955/6 Tottenham H

Horne, B. (59) 1987/8 Portsmouth, Southampton, Everton, Birmingham C

Howells, R. (2) 1953/4 Cardiff C

Hughes, C. M. (8) 1991/2 Luton T, Wimbledon

Hughes, I. (4) 1950/1 Luton T

Hughes, L. M. (72) 1983/4 Manchester U, Barcelona, Manchester U, Chelsea, Southampton

Hughes, W. (3) 1946/7 Birmingham C

Hughes, W. A. (5) 1948/9 Blackburn R

Humphreys, J. (1) 1946/7 Everton

Jackett, K. (31) 1982/3 Watford
James, G. (9) 1965/6 Blackpool
James, L. (54) 1971/2 Burnley, Derby C,
  QPR, Burnley, Swansea C, Sunderland
James, R. M. (47) 1978/9 Swansea C,
  Stoke C, QPR, Leicester C, Swansea C
Jarvis, A. (3) 1966/7 Hull C
Jenkins, S. R. (16) 1995/6 Swansea C,
  Huddersfield T
Johnson, A. J. (15) 1998/9 Nottingham F,
  WBA
Johnson, M. (1) 1963/4 Swansea T
Jones, A. (6) 1986/7 Port Vale,
  Charlton Ath
Jones, Barrie (15) 1962/3 Swansea T,
  Plymouth Argyle, Cardiff C
Jones, Bryn (4) 1946/7 Arsenal
Jones, C. (59) 1953/4 Swansea T,
  Tottenham H, Fulham
Jones, D. (8) 1975/6 Norwich C
Jones, E. (4) 1947/8 Swansea T,
  Tottenham H
Jones, J. (72) 1975/6 Liverpool, Wrexham,
  Chelsea, Huddersfield T
Jones, K. (1) 1949/50 Aston Villa
Jones, M. A. (2) 2006/07 Wrexham
Jones, M. G. (13) 1999/00 Leeds U,
  Leicester C
Jones, P. L. (2) 1996/7 Liverpool,
  Tranmere R
Jones, P. S. (50) 1996/7 Stockport Co,
  Southampton, Wolverhampton W, QPR
Jones, R. (1) 1993/4 Sheffield W
Jones, T. G. (13) 1946/7 Everton
Jones, V. P. (9) 1994/5 Wimbledon
Jones, W. (1) 1970/1 Bristol R

Kelsey, J. (41) 1953/4 Arsenal
King, A. (12) 2008/09 Leicester C
King, J. (1) 1954/5 Swansea T
Kinsey, N. (7) 1950/1 Norwich C,
  Birmingham C
Knill, A. R. (1) 1988/9 Swansea C
Koumas, J. (34) 2000/01 Tranmere R,
  WBA, Wigan Ath
Krzywicki, R. (8) 1969/70 WBA,
  Huddersfield T

Lambert, R. (5) 1946/7 Liverpool
Law, B. J. (1) 1989/90 QPR
Lea, C. (2) 1964/5 Ipswich T
**Ledley, J. C. (41) 2005/06 Cardiff C,
  Celtic**

Leek, K. (13) 1960/1 Leicester C,
  Newcastle U, Birmingham C,
  Northampton T
Legg, A. (6) 1995/6 Birmingham C,
  Cardiff C
Lever, A. (1) 1952/3 Leicester C
Lewis, D. (1) 1982/3 Swansea C
Llewellyn, C. M. (6) 1997/8 Norwich C,
  Wrexham
Lloyd, B. (3) 1975/6 Wrexham
Lovell, S. (6) 1981/2 Crystal Palace,
  Millwall
Lowndes, S. (10) 1982/3 Newport Co,
  Millwall, Barnsley
Lowrie, G. (4) 1947/8 Coventry C,
  Newcastle U
Lucas, M. (4) 1961/2 Leyton Orient
Lucas, W. (7) 1948/9 Swansea T

MacDonald, S. B. (1) 2010/11 Swansea C
Maguire, G. T. (7) 1989/90 Portsmouth
Mahoney, J. (51) 1967/8 Stoke C,
  Middlesbrough, Swansea C
Mardon, P. J. (1) 1995/6 WBA
Margetson, M. W. (1) 2003/04 Cardiff C
Marriott, A. (5) 1995/6 Wrexham
Marustik, C. (6) 1981/2 Swansea C
**Matthews, A. J. (7) 2010/11 Cardiff C,
  Celtic**
Medwin, T. (30) 1952/3 Swansea T,
  Tottenham H
Melville, A. K. (65) 1989/90 Swansea C,
  Oxford U, Sunderland, Fulham,
  West Ham U
Mielczarek, R. (1) 1970/1 Rotherham U
Millington, A. (21) 1962/3 WBA,
  Crystal P, Peterborough U, Swansea C
Moore, G. (21) 1959/60 Cardiff C,
  Chelsea, Manchester U,
  Northampton T, Charlton Ath
Morgan, C. (23) 2006/07 Milton Keynes
  D, Peterborough U, Preston NE
**Morison, S. W. (15) 2010/11 Millwall,
  Norwich C**
Morris, W. (5) 1946/7 Burnley
Myhill, G. O. (10) 2007/08 Hull C, WBA

Nardiello, D. (2) 1977/8 Coventry C
Nardiello, D. A. (3) 2006/07 Barnsley,
  QPR
Neilson, A. B. (5) 1991/2 Newcastle U,
  Southampton
Nicholas, P. (73) 1978/9 Crystal Palace,
  Arsenal, Crystal Palace, Luton T,
  Aberdeen, Chelsea, Watford

Niedzwiecki, E. A. (2) 1984/5 Chelsea
Nogan, L. M. (2) 1991/2 Watford, Reading
Norman, A. J. (5) 1985/6 Hull C
Nurse, M. T. G. (12) 1959/60 Swansea T, Middlesbrough
Nyatanga, L. J. (34) 2005/06 Derby Co, Bristol C

O'Sullivan, P. (3) 1972/3 Brighton & HA
Oster, J. M. (13) 1997/8 Everton, Sunderland

Page, M. (28) 1970/1 Birmingham C
Page, R. J. (41) 1996/7 Watford, Sheffield U, Cardiff C, Coventry C
Palmer, D. (3) 1956/7 Swansea T
Parry, J. (1) 1950/1 Swansea T
Parry, P. I. (12) 2003/04 Cardiff C
Partridge, D. W. (7) 2004/05 Motherwell, Bristol C
Pascoe, C. (10) 1983/4 Swansea C, Sunderland
Paul, R. (33) 1948/9 Swansea T, Manchester C
Pembridge, M. A. (54) 1991/2 Luton T, Derby C, Sheffield W, Benfica, Everton, Fulham
Perry, J. (1) 1993/4 Cardiff C
Phillips, D. (62) 1983/4 Plymouth Argyle, Manchester C, Coventry C, Norwich C, Nottingham F
Phillips, J. (4) 1972/3 Chelsea
Phillips, L. (58) 1970/1 Cardff C, Aston Villa, Swansea C, Charlton Ath
Pipe, D. R. (1) 2002/03 Coventry C
Pontin, K. (2) 1979/80 Cardiff C
Powell, A. (8) 1946/7 Leeds U, Everton, Birmingham C
Powell, D. (11) 1967/8 Wrexham, Sheffield U
Powell, I. (8) 1946/7 QPR, Aston Villa
Price, L. P. (9) 2005/06 Ipswich T, Derby Co, Crystal Palace
Price, P. (25) 1979/80 Luton T, Tottenham H
Pring, K. (3) 1965/6 Rotherham U
Pritchard, H. K. (1) 1984/5 Bristol C

Ramsey, A. (21) 2008/09 Arsenal
Rankmore, F. (l) 1965/6 Peterborough U
Ratcliffe, K. (59) 1980/1 Everton, Cardiff C
Ready, K. (5) 1996/7 QPR

Reece, G. (29) 1965/6 Sheffield U, Cardiff C
Reed, W. (2) 1954/5 Ipswich T
Rees, A. (1) 1983/4 Birmingham C
Rees, J. M. (1) 1991/2 Luton T
Rees, R. (39) 1964/5 Coventry C, WBA, Nottingham F
Rees, W. (4) 1948/9 Cardiff C, Tottenham H
Ribeiro, C. M. (2) 2009/10 Bristol C
Richards. A. D. J. (1) 2011/12 Swansea C
Richards, S. (1) 1946/7 Cardiff C
Ricketts, S. D. (44) 2004/05 Swansea C, Hull C, Bolton W
Roberts, A. M. (2) 1992/3 QPR
Roberts, D. (17) 1972/3 Oxford U, Hull C
Roberts, G. W. (9) 1999/00 Tranmere R
Roberts, I. W. (15) 1989/90 Watford, Huddersfield T, Leicester C, Norwich C
Roberts, J. G. (22) 1970/1 Arsenal, Birmingham C
Roberts, J. H. (1) 1948/9 Bolton W
Roberts, N. W. (4) 1999/00 Wrexham, Wigan Ath
Roberts, P. (4) 1973/4 Portsmouth
Roberts, S. W. (1) 2004/05 Wrexham
Robinson, C. P. (52) 1999/00 Wolverhampton W, Portsmouth, Sunderland, Norwich C, Toronto Lynx
Robinson, J. R. C. (30) 1995/6 Charlton Ath
Robson-Kanu, T. H. (7) 2009/10 Reading
Rodrigues, P. (40) 1964/5 Cardiff C, Leicester C, Sheffield W
Rouse, V. (1) 1958/9 Crystal Palace
Rowley, T. (1) 1958/9 Tranmere R
Rush, I. (73) 1979/80 Liverpool, Juventus, Liverpool

Saunders, D. (75) 1985/6 Brighton & HA, Oxford U, Derby C, Liverpool, Aston Villa, Galatasaray, Nottingham F, Sheffield U, Benfica, Bradford C
Savage, R. W. (39) 1995/6 Crewe Alexandra, Leicester C, Birmingham C
Sayer, P. (7) 1976/7 Cardiff C
Scrine, F. (2) 1949/50 Swansea T
Sear, C. (1) 1962/3 Manchester C
Sherwood, A. (41) 1946/7 Cardiff C, Newport C
Shortt, W. (12) 1946/7 Plymouth Argyle
Showers, D. (2) 1974/5 Cardiff C
Sidlow, C. (7) 1946/7 Liverpool
Slatter, N. (22) 1982/3 Bristol R, Oxford U

321

Smallman, D. (7) 1973/4 Wrexham,
Everton
Southall, N. (92) 1981/2 Everton
Speed, G. A. (85) 1989/90 Leeds U,
Everton, Newcastle U, Bolton W
Sprake, G. (37) 1963/4 Leeds U,
Birmingham C
Stansfield, F. (1) 1948/9 Cardiff C
Stevenson, B. (15) 1977/8 Leeds U,
Birmingham C
Stevenson, N. (4) 1981/2 Swansea C
Stitfall, R. (2) 1952/3 Cardiff C
Stock, B. B. (3) 2009/10 Doncaster R
Sullivan, D. (17) 1952/3 Cardiff C
Symons, C. J. (37) 1991/2 Portsmouth,
Manchester C, Fulham, Crystal Palace

Tapscott, D. (14) 1953/4 Arsenal,
Cardiff C
Taylor, G. K. (15) 1995/6 Crystal Palace,
Sheffield U, Burnley, Nottingham F
**Taylor, N. J. (9) 2009/10 Wrexham,
Swansea C**
Thatcher, B. D. (7) 2003/04 Leicester C,
Manchester C
Thomas, D. (2) 1956/7 Swansea T
Thomas, M. (51) 1976/7 Wrexham,
Manchester U, Everton,
Brighton & HA, Stoke C, Chelsea,
WBA
Thomas, M. R. (1) 1986/7 Newcastle U
Thomas, R. (50) 1966/7 Swindon T, Derby
C, Cardiff C
Thomas, S. (4) 1947/8 Fulham
Toshack, J. (40) 1968/9 Cardiff C,
Liverpool, Swansea C
Trollope, P. J. (9) 1996/7 Derby Co,
Fulham, Coventry C, Northampton T
Tudur-Jones, O. (6) 2007/08 Swansea C,
Norwich C

Van Den Hauwe, P. W. R. (13) 1984/5
Everton
**Vaughan, D. O. (29) 2002/03 Crewe Alex,
Real Sociedad, Blackpool, Sunderland**

Vaughan, N. (10) 1982/3 Newport Co,
Cardiff C
Vearncombe, G. (2) 1957/8 Cardiff C
Vernon, R. (32) 1956/7 Blackburn R,
Everton, Stoke C
Villars, A. (3) 1973/4 Cardiff C
**Vokes, S. M. (21) 2007/08 Bournemouth,
Wolverhampton W**

Walley, T. (1) 1970/1 Watford
Walsh, I. (18) 1979/80 Crystal Palace,
Swansea C
Ward, D. (2) 1958/9 Bristol R, Cardiff C
Ward, D. (5) 1999/00 Notts Co,
Nottingham F
Webster, C. (4) 1956/7 Manchester U
Weston, R. D. (7) 1999/00 Arsenal,
Cardiff C
Williams, A. (13) 1993/4 Reading,
Wolverhampton W, Reading
**Williams, A. E. (33) 2007/08
Stockport Co, Swansea C**
Williams, A. P. (2) 1997/8 Southampton
Williams, D. G. 1987/8 13, Derby Co,
Ipswich T
Williams, D. M. (5) 1985/6 Norwich C
Williams, G. (1) 1950/1 Cardiff C
Williams, G. E. (26) 1959/60 WBA
Williams, G. G. (5) 1960/1 Swansea T
Williams, G. J. (2) 2005/06 West Ham U,
Ipswich T
Williams, H. (4) 1948/9 Newport Co,
Leeds U
Williams, Herbert (3) 1064/5 Swansea T
Williams, S. (43) 1953/4 WBA,
Southampton
Witcomb, D. (3) 1946/7 WBA,
Sheffield W
Woosnam, P. (17) 1958/9 Leyton Orient,
West Ham U, Aston Villa

Yorath, T. (59) 1969/70 Leeds U,
Coventry C, Tottenham H, Vancouver
Whitecaps
Young, E. (21) 1989/90 Wimbledon,
Crystal Palace, Wolverhampton W

REPUBLIC OF IRELAND

Aherne, T. (16) 1945/6 Belfast Celtic,
  Luton T
Aldridge, J. W. (69) 1985/6 Oxford U,
  Liverpool, Real Sociedad, Tranmere R
Ambrose, P. (5) 1954/5 Shamrock R
Anderson, J. (16) 1979/80 Preston NE,
  Newcastle U
**Andrews, K. J. (32) 2008/09 Blackburn R,
  WBA**

Babb, P. (35) 1993/4 Coventry C,
  Liverpool, Sunderland
Bailham, E. (1) 1963/4 Shamrock R
Barber, E. (2) 1965/6 Shelbourne,
  Birmingham C
Barrett, G. (6) 2002/03 Arsenal,
  Coventry C
Beglin, J. (15) 1983/4 Liverpool
Bennett, A. J. (2) 2006/07 Reading
Best, L. J. B. (7) 2008/09 Coventry C,
  Newcastle U
Bonner, P. (80) 1980/1 Celtic
Braddish, S. (1) 1977/8 Dundalk
Brady, T. R. (6) 1963/4 QPR
Brady, W. L. (72) 1974/5 Arsenal,
  Juventus, Sampdoria, Internazionale,
  Ascoli, West Ham U
Branagan, K. G. (1) 1996/7 Bolton W
Breen, G. (63) 1995/6 Birmingham C,
  Coventry C, West Ham U, Sunderland
Breen, T. (3) 1946/7 Shamrock R
Brennan, F. (1) 1964/5 Drumcondra
Brennan, S. A. (19) 1964/5 Manchester U,
  Waterford
Browne, W. (3) 1963/4 Bohemians
Bruce, A. (2) 2006/07 Ipswich T
Buckley, L. (2) 1983/4 Shamrock R,
  Waregem
Burke, F. (1) 1951/2 Cork Ath
Butler, P. J. (1) 1999/00 Sunderland
Butler, T. (2) 2002/03 Sunderland
Byrne, A. B. (14) 1969/70 Southampton
Byrne, J. (23) 1984/5 QPR, Le Havre,
  Brighton & HA, Sunderland, Millwall
Byrne, J. (2) 2003/04 Shelbourne
Byrne, P. (8) 1983/4 Shamrock R

Campbell, A. (3) 1984/5 Santander
Campbell, N. (11) 1970/1 St Patrick's Ath,
  Fortuna Cologne
Cantwell, N. (36) 1953/4 West Ham U,
  Manchester U
Carey, B. P. (3) 1991/2 Manchester U,
  Leicester C

Carey, J. J. (21) 1945/6 Manchester U
Carolan, J. (2) 1959/60 Manchester U
Carr, S. (44) 1998/9 Tottenham H,
  Newcastle U
Carroll, B. (2) 1948/9 Shelbourne
Carroll, T. R. (17) 1967/8 Ipswich T,
  Birmingham C
Carsley, L. K. (39) 1997/8 Derby Co,
  Blackburn R, Coventry C, Everton
Cascarino, A. G. (88) 1985/6 Gillingham,
  Millwall, Aston Villa, Celtic, Chelsea,
  Marseille, Nancy
Chandler, J. (2) 1979/80 Leeds U
Clark, C. (2) 2010/11 Aston Villa
Clarke, C. R. (2) 2003/04 Stoke C
Clarke, J. (1) 1977/8 Drogheda U
Clarke, K. (2) 1947/8 Drumcondra
Clarke, M. (1) 1949/50 Shamrock R
Clinton, T. J. (3) 1950/1 Everton
Coad, P. (11) 1946/7 Shamrock R
Coffey, T. (1) 1949/50 Drumcondra
Coleman, S. (4) 2010/11 Everton
Colfer, M. D. (2) 1949/50 Shelbourne
Colgan, N. (9) 2001/02 Hibernian,
  Barnsley
Conmy, O. M. (5) 1964/5 Peterborough U
Connolly, D. J. (41) 1995/6 Watford,
  Feyenoord, Wolverhampton W,
  Excelsior, Wimbledon, West Ham U,
  Wigan Ath
Conroy, G. A. (27) 1969/70 Stoke C
Conway, J. P. (20) 1966/7 Fulham,
  Manchester C
Corr, P. J. (4) 1948/9 Everton
Courtney, E. (1) 1945/6 Cork U
Cox, S. R. (15) 2010/11 WBA
Coyle, O. (1) 1993/4 Bolton W
Coyne, T. (22) 1991/2 Celtic, Tranmere R,
  Motherwell
Crowe, G. (2) 2002/03 Bohemians
Cummins, G. P. (19) 1953/4 Luton T
Cuneen, T. (1) 1950/1 Limerick
Cunningham, G. R. (3) 2009/10
  Manchester C
Cunningham, K. (72) 1995/6 Wimbledon,
  Birmingham C
Curtis, D. P. (17) 1956/7 Shelbourne,
  Bristol C, Ipswich T, Exeter C
Cusack, S. (1) 1952/3 Limerick

Daish, L. S. (5) 1991/2 Cambridge U,
  Coventry C
Daly, G. A. (48) 1972/3 Manchester U,
  Derby C, Coventry C, Birmingham C,
  Shrewsbury T

Daly, M. (2) 1977/8 Wolverhampton W
Daly, P. (1) 1949/50 Shamrock R
Deacy, E. (4) 1981/2 Aston Villa
Delaney, D. F. (5) 2007/08 QPR, Ipswich T
Delap, R. J. (11) 1997/8 Derby Co, Southampton
De Mange, K. J. P. P. (2) 1986/7 Liverpool, Hull C
Dempsey, J. T. (19) 1966/7 Fulham, Chelsea
Dennehy, J. (11) 1971/2 Cork Hibernian, Nottingham F, Walsall
Desmond, P. (4) 1949/50 Middlesbrough
Devine, J. (13) 1979/80 Arsenal, Norwich C
Doherty, G. M. T. (34) 1999/00 Luton T, Tottenham H, Norwich C
Donovan, D. C. (5) 1954/5 Everton
Donovan, T. (1) 1979/80 Aston Villa
Douglas, J. (8) 2003/04 Blackburn R, Leeds U
Doyle, C. (1) 1958/9 Shelbourne
Doyle, Colin (1) 2006/07 Birmingham C
Doyle, K. E. (50) 2005/06 Reading, Wolverhampton W
Doyle, M. P. (1) 2003/04 Coventry C
Duff, D. A. (100) 1997/8 Blackburn R, Chelsea, Newcastle U, Fulham
Duffy, B. (1) 1949/50 Shamrock R
Dunne, A. P. (33) 1961/2 Manchester U, Bolton W
Dunne, J. C. (1) 1970/1 Fulham
Dunne, P. A. J. (5) 1964/5 Manchester U
Dunne, R. P. (76) 1999/00 Everton, Manchester C, Aston Villa
Dunne, S. (15) 1952/3 Luton T
Dunne, T. (3) 1955/6 St Patrick's Ath
Dunning, P. (2) 1970/1 Shelbourne
Dunphy, E. M. (23) 1965/6 York C, Millwall
Dwyer, N. M. (14) 1959/60 West Ham U, Swansea T

Eccles, P. (1) 1985/6 Shamrock R
Eglington, T. J. (24) 1945/6 Shamrock R, Everton
Elliott, S. W. (9) 2004/05 Sunderland
Evans, M. J. (1) 1997/8 Southampton

Fagan, E. (1) 1972/3 Shamrock R
Fagan, F. (8) 1954/5 Manchester C, Derby C
Fahey, K. D. (15) 2009/10 Birmingham C
Fairclough, M. (2) 1981/2 Dundalk
Fallon, S. (8) 1950/1 Celtic

Farrell, P. D. (28) 1945/6 Shamrock R, Everton
Farrelly, G. (6) 1995/6 Aston Villa, Everton, Bolton W
Finnan, S. (53) 1999/00 Fulham, Liverpool
Finucane, A. (11) 1966/7 Limerick
Fitzgerald, F. J. (2) 1954/5 Waterford
Fitzgerald, P. J. (5) 1960/1 Leeds U, Chester
Fitzpatrick, K. (1) 1969/70 Limerick
Fitzsimons, A. G. (26) 1949/50 Middlesbrough, Lincoln C
Fleming, C. (10) 1995/6 Middlesbrough
Fogarty, A. (11) 1959/60 Sunderland, Hartlepool U
Folan, C. C. (7) 2008/09 Hull C
Foley, D. J. (6) 1999/00 Watford
Foley, K. P. (8) 2008/09 Wolverhampton W
Foley, T. C. (9) 1963/4 Northampton T
Forde, D. (2) 2010/11 Millwall
Fullam, J. 1960/1 Preston NE, Shamrock R

Gallagher, C. (2) 1966/7 Celtic
Gallagher, M. (1) 1953/4 Hibernian
Galvin, A. (29) 1982/3 Tottenham H, Sheffield W, Swindon T
Gamble, J. (2) 2006/07 Cork C
Gannon, E. (14) 1948/9 Notts Co, Sheffield W, Shelbourne K
Gannon, M. (1) 1971/2 Shelbourne
Gavin, J. T. (7) 1949/50 Norwich C, Tottenham H, Norwich C
Gibbons, A. (4) 1951/2 St Patrick's Ath
Gibson, D. T. D. (19) 2007/08 Manchester U, Everton
Gilbert, R. (1) 1965/6 Shamrock R
Giles, C. (1) 1950/1 Doncaster R
Giles, M. J. (59) 1959/60 Manchester U, Leeds U, WBA, Shamrock R
Given, S. J. J. (125) 1995/6 Blackburn R, Newcastle U, Manchester C, Aston Villa
Givens, D. J. (56) 1968/9 Manchester U, Luton T, QPR, Birmingham C, Neuchatel Xamax
Gleeson, S. M. (2) 2006/07 Wolverhampton W
Glynn, D. (2) 1951/2 Drumcondra
Godwin, T. F. (13) 1948/9 Shamrock R, Leicester C, Bournemouth
Goodman, J. (4) 1996/7 Wimbledon
Goodwin, J. (1) 2002/03 Stockport Co
Gorman, W. C. (2) 1946/7 Brentford

324

Grealish, A. (45) 1975/6 Orient, Luton T, Brighton & HA, WBA

Green, P. J. (12) 2009/10 Derby Co

Gregg, E. (8) 1977/8 Bohemians

Grimes, A. A. (18) 1977/8 Manchester U, Coventry C, Luton T

Hale, A. (13) 1961/2 Aston Villa, Doncaster R, Waterford

Hamilton, T. (2) 1958/9 Shamrock R

Hand, E. K. (20) 1968/9 Portsmouth

Harte, I. P. (64) 1995/6 Leeds U, Levante

Hartnett, J. B. (2) 1948/9 Middlesbrough

Haverty, J. (32) 1955/6 Arsenal, Blackburn R, Millwall, Celtic, Bristol R, Shelbourne

Hayes, A. W. P. (1) 1978/9 Southampton

Hayes, W. E. (2) 1946/7 Huddersfield T

Hayes, W. J. (1) 1948/9 Limerick

Healey, R. (2) 1976/7 Cardiff C

Healy, C. (13) 2001/02 Celtic, Sunderland

Heighway, S. D. (34) 1970/1 Liverpool, Minnesota Kicks

Henderson, B. (2) 1947/8 Drumcondra

Henderson, W. C. P. (6) 2005/06 Brighton & HA, Preston NE

Hennessy, J. (5) 1964/5 Shelbourne, St Patrick's Ath

Herrick, J. (3) 1971/2 Cork Hibernians, Shamrock R

Higgins, J. (1) 1950/1 Birmingham C

Holland, M. R. (49) 1999/00 Ipswich T, Charlton Ath

Holmes, J. (30) 1970/1 Coventry C, Tottenham H, Vancouver Whitecaps

Hoolahan, W. (1) 2007/08 Blackpool

Houghton, R. J. (73) 1985/6 Oxford U, Liverpool, Aston Villa, Crystal Palace, Reading

Howlett, G. (1) 1983/4 Brighton & HA

Hughton, C. (53) 1979/80 Tottenham H, West Ham U

Hunt, N. (3) 2008/09 Reading

Hunt, S. P. (39) 2006/07 Reading, Hull C, Wolverhampton W

Hurley, C. J. (40) 1956/7 Millwall, Sunderland, Bolton W

Ireland, S. J. (6) 2005/06 Manchester C

Irwin, D. J. (56) 1990/1 Manchester U

Kavanagh, G. A. (16) 1997/8 Stoke C, Cardiff C, Wigan Ath

Keane, R. D. (120) 1997/8 Wolverhampton W, Coventry C, Internazionale, Leeds U, Tottenham H, Liverpool, Tottenham H, LA Galaxy

Keane, R. M. (67) 1990/1 Nottingham F, Manchester U

Keane, T. R. (4) 1948/9 Swansea T

Kearin, M. (1) 1971/2 Shamrock R

Kearns, F. T. (1) 1953/4 West Ham U

Kearns, M. (18) 1969/70 Oxford U, Walsall, Wolverhampton W

Kelly, A. T. (34) 1992/3 Sheffield U, Blackburn R

Kelly, D. T. (26) 1987/8 Walsall, West Ham U, Leicester C, Newcastle U, Wolverhampton W, Sunderland, Tranmere R

Kelly, G. (52) 1993/4 Leeds U

Kelly, J. A. (48) 1956/7 Drumcondra, Preston NE

Kelly, J. P. V. (5) 1960/1 Wolverhampton W

Kelly, M. J. (4) 1987/8 Portsmouth

Kelly, N. (1) 1953/4 Nottingham F

Kelly, S. M. (29) 2005/06 Tottenham H, Birmingham C, Fulham

Kenna, J. J. (27) 1994/5 Blackburn R

Kennedy, M. (34) 1995/6 Liverpool, Wimbledon, Manchester C, Wolverhampton W

Kennedy, M. F. (2) 1985/6 Portsmouth

Kenny, P. (7) 2003/04 Sheffield U

Keogh, A. D. (22) 2006/07 Wolverhampton W

Keogh, J. (1) 1965/6 Shamrock R

Keogh, S. (1) 1958/9 Shamrock R

Kernaghan, A. N. (22) 1992/3 Middlesbrough, Manchester C

Kiely, D. L. (11) 1999/00 Charlton Ath, WBA

Kiernan, F. W. (5) 1950/1 Shamrock R, Southampton

Kilbane, K. D. (110) 1997/8 WBA, Sunderland, Everton, Wigan Ath, Hull C

Kinnear, J. P. (26) 1966/7 Tottenham H, Brighton & HA

Kinsella, M. A. (48) 1997/8 Charlton Ath, Aston Villa, WBA

Langan, D. (26) 1977/8 Derby Co, Birmingham C, Oxford U

Lapira, J. (1) 2006/07 Notre Dame

Lawler, J. F. (8) 1952/3 Fulham

Lawlor, J. C. (3) 1948/9 Drumcondra, Doncaster R

Lawlor, M. (5) 1970/1 Shamrock R

Lawrence, L. (15) 2008/09 Stoke C, Portsmouth

Lawrenson, M. (39) 1976/7 Preston NE, Brighton & HA, Liverpool

Lee, A. L. (10) 2002/03 Rotherham U, Cardiff C, Ipswich T
Leech, M. (8) 1968/9 Shamrock R
Long, S. P. (27) 2006/07 Reading, WBA
Lowry, D. (1) 1961/2 St Patrick's Ath

McAlinden, J. (2) 1945/6 Portsmouth
McAteer, J. W. (52) 1993/4 Bolton W, Liverpool, Blackburn R, Sunderland
McCann, J. (1) 1956/7 Shamrock R
McCarthy, J. (3) 2009/10 Wigan Ath
McCarthy, M. (57) 1983/4 Manchester C, Celtic, Lyon, Millwall
McClean, J. (3) 2011/12 Sunderland
McConville, T. (6) 1971/2 Dundalk, Waterford
McDonagh, Jim (25) 1980/1 Everton, Bolton W, Notts C
McDonagh, Jacko (3) 1983/4 Shamrock R
McEvoy, M. A. (17) 1960/1 Blackburn R
McGeady, A. (52) 2003/04 Celtic, Spartak Moscow
McGee, P. (15) 1977/8 QPR, Preston NE
McGoldrick, E. J. (15) 1991/2 Crystal Palace, Arsenal
McGowan, D. (3) 1948/9 West Ham U
McGowan, J. (1) 1946/7 Cork U
McGrath, M. (22) 1957/8 Blackburn R, Bradford Park Avenue
McGrath, P. (83) 1984/5 Manchester U, Aston Villa, Derby C
McLoughlin, A. F. (42) 1989/90 Swindon T, Southampton, Portsmouth
McMillan, W. (2) 1945/6 Belfast Celtic
McNally, J. B. (3) 1958/9 Luton T
McPhail, S. (10) 1999/00 Leeds U
McShane, P. D. (27) 2006/07 WBA, Sunderland, Hull C
Macken, J. (1) 1976/7 Derby Co
Macken, J. P. (1) 2004/05 Manchester C
Mackey, G. (3) 1956/7 Shamrock R
Mahon, A. J. (2) 1999/00 Tranmere R
Malone, G. (1) 1948/9 Shelbourne
Mancini, T. J. (5) 1973/4 QPR, Arsenal
Martin, C. J. (30) 1945/6 Glentoran, Leeds U, Aston Villa
Martin, M. P. (52) 1971/2 Bohemians, Manchester U, WBA, Newcastle U
Maybury, A. (10) 1997/8 Leeds U, Heart of Midlothian, Leicester C
Meagan, M. K. (17) 1960/1 Everton, Huddersfield T, Drogheda
Miller, L. W. P. (21) 2003/04 Celtic, Manchester U, Sunderland, Hibernian
Milligan, M. J. (1) 1991/2 Oldham Ath
Mooney, J. (2) 1964/5 Shamrock R
Moore, A. (8) 1995/6 Middlesbrough

Moran, K. (71) 1979/80 Manchester U, Sporting Gijon, Blackburn R
Moroney, T. (12) 1947/8 West Ham U, Evergreen U
Morris, C. B. (35) 1987/8 Celtic, Middlesbrough
Morrison, C. H. (36) 2001/02 Crystal Palace, Birmingham C, Crystal Palace
Moulson, G. B. (3) 1947/8 Lincoln C
Mucklan, C. (1) 1977/8 Drogheda
Mulligan, P. M. (50) 1968/9 Shamrock R, Chelsea, Crystal Palace, WBA, Shamrock R
Munroe, L. (1) 1953/4 Shamrock R
Murphy, A. (1) 1955/6 Clyde
Murphy, B. (1) 1985/6 Bohemians
Murphy, D. (9) 2006/07 Sunderland
Murphy, Jerry (1) 1979/80 Crystal Palace
Murphy, Joe (2) 2003/04 WBA, Scunthorpe U
Murphy, P. M. (1) 2006/07 Carlisle U
Murray, T. (1) 1949/50 Dundalk

Newman, W. (1) 1968/9 Shelbourne
Nolan, E. W. (3) 2008/09 Preston NE
Nolan, R. (10) 1956/7 Shamrock R

O'Brien, A. (5) 2006/07 Newcastle U
O'Brien, A. J. (26) 2000/01 Newcastle U, Portsmouth
O'Brien, F. (3) 1979/80 Philadelphia Fury
O'Brien, J. M. (3) 2005/06 Bolton W
O'Brien, L. (16) 1985/6 Shamrock R, Manchester U, Newcastle U, Tranmere R
O'Brien, R. (5) 1975/6 Notts Co
O'Byrne, L. B. (1) 1948/9 Shamrock R
O'Callaghan, B. R. (6) 1978/9 Stoke C
O'Callaghan, K. (21) 1980/1 Ipswich T, Portsmouth
O'Cearuill, J. (2) 2006/07 Arsenal
O'Connnell, A. (2) 1966/7 Dundalk, Bohemians
O'Connor, T. (4) 1949/50 Shamrock R
O'Connor, T. (7) 1967/8 Fulham, Dundalk, Bohemians
O'Dea, D. (14) 2009/10 Celtic
O'Driscoll, J. F. (3) 1948/9 Swansea T
O'Driscoll, S. (3) 1981/2 Fulham
O'Farrell, F. (9) 1951/2 West Ham U, Preston NE
O'Flanagan, K. P. (3) 1946/7 Arsenal
O'Flanagan, M. (1) 1946/7 Bohemians
O'Halloran, S. E. (2) 2006/07 Aston Villa
O'Hanlon, K. G. (1) 1987/8 Rotherham U
O'Keefe, E. (5) 1980/1 Everton, Port Vale
O'Leary, D. (68) 1976/7 Arsenal

BRITISH ISLES INTERNATIONAL GOALSCORERS SINCE 1946

Bold type indicates players who have scored an international goal in season 2011–12.

ENGLAND

A'Court, A.	1
Adams, T.A.	5
Allen, R.	2
Anderson, V.	2
Anderton, D.R.	7
Astall, G.	1
Atyeo, P.J.W.	5
Baily, E.F.	5
Baker, J.H.	3
Ball, A.J.	8
Barmby, N.J.	4
Barnes, J.	11
Barnes, P.S.	4
Barry, G.	**3**
Beardsley, P.A.	9
Beattie, J.K.	1
Beckham, D.R.J.	17
Bell, C.	9
Bent, D.A.	**4**
Bentley, R.T.F.	9
Blissett, L.	3
Bowles, S.	1
Bradford, G.R.W.	1
Bradley, W.	2
Bridge, W.M.	1
Bridges, B.J.	1
Broadbent, P.F.	2
Broadis, I.A.	8
Brooking, T.D.	5
Brooks, J.	2
Brown, W.M.	1
Bull, S.G.	4
Butcher, T.	3
Byrne, J.J.	8
Cahill, G.	**2**
Campbell, S.J.	1
Carroll, A.T.	**2**
Carter, H.S.	5
Chamberlain, M.	1
Channon, M.R.	21
Charlton, J.	6
Charlton, R.	49

Chivers, M.	13
Clarke, A.J.	10
Cole, A.	1
Cole, J.J.	10
Connelly, J.M.	7
Coppell, S.J.	7
Cowans, G.	2
Crawford, R.	1
Crouch, P.J.	22
Currie, A.W.	3
Defoe, J.C.	15
Dixon, L.M.	1
Dixon, K.M.	4
Douglas, B.	11
Eastham, G.	2
Edwards, D.	5
Ehiogu, U.	1
Elliott, W.H.	3
Ferdinand, L.	5
Ferdinand, R.G.	3
Finney, T.	30
Flowers, R.	10
Fowler, R.B.	7
Francis, G.C.J.	3
Francis, T.	12
Froggatt, J.	2
Froggatt, R.	2
Gascoigne, P.J.	10
Gerrard, S.G.	19
Goddard, P.	1
Grainger, C.	3
Greaves, J.	44
Haines, J.T.W.	2
Hancocks, J.	2
Hassall, H.W.	4
Hateley, M.	9
Haynes, J.N.	18
Heskey, E.W.	7
Hirst, D.E.	1
Hitchens, G.A.	5
Hoddle, G.	8

Hughes, E.W.	1
Hunt, R.	18
Hunter, N.	2
Hurst, G.C.	24
Ince P.E.C.	2
Jeffers, F.	1
Jenas, J.A.	1
Johnson, A.	2
Johnson, D.E.	6
Johnson, G.M.C.	1
Kay, A.H.	1
Keegan, J.K.	21
Kennedy, R.	3
Keown, M.R.	2
Kevan, D.T.	8
Kidd, B.	1
King, L.B.	2
Lampard, F.J.	**23**
Langton, R.	1
Latchford, R.D.	5
Lawler, C.	1
Lawton, T.	16
Lee, F.	10
Lee, J.	1
Lee, R.M.	2
Lee, S.	2
Lescott, J.	**1**
Le Saux, G.P.	1
Lineker, G.	48
Lofthouse, N.	30
Mabbutt, G.	1
McDermott, T.	3
Macdonald, M.	6
McManaman, S.	3
Mannion, W.J.	11
Mariner, P.	13
Marsh, R.W.	1
Matthews, S.	3
Medley, L.D.	1
Melia, J.	1
Merson, P.C.	3

Milburn, J.E.T. 10
Moore, R.F. 2
Morris, J. 3
Mortensen, S.H. 23
Mullen, J. 6
Mullery, A.P. 1
Murphy, D.B. 1

Neal, P.G. 5
Nicholls, J. 1
Nicholson, W.E. 1
Nugent, D.J. 1

O'Grady, M. 3
Owen, M.J. 40
Own goals 31

Paine, T.L. 7
Palmer, C.L. 1
Parry, R.A. 1
Peacock, A. 3
Pearce, S. 5
Pearson, J.S. 5
Pearson, S.C. 5
Perry, W. 2
Peters, M. 20
Pickering, F. 5
Platt, D. 27
Pointer, R. 2

Ramsay, A.E. 3
Redknapp, J.F. 1
Revie, D.G. 4
Richards, M. 1
Richardson, K.E. 2
Robson, B. 26
Robson, R. 4
Rooney, W. **29**
Rowley, J.F. 6
Royle, J. 2

Sansom, K. 1
Scholes, P. 14
Sewell, J. 3
Shackleton, L.F. 1
Shearer, A. 30
Sheringham, E.P. 11
Smith, A. 1
Smith, A.M. 2
Smith, R. 13
Southgate, G. 2
Steven, T.M. 4

Stiles, N.P. 1
Stone, S.B. 2
Summerbee, M.G. 1

Tambling, R.V. 1
Taylor, P.J. 2
Taylor, T. 16
Terry, J.G. 6
Thompson, P.B. 1
Tueart, D. 2

Upson, M.J. 2

Vassell, D. 6
Viollet, D.S. 1

Waddle, C.R. 6
Walcott, T.J. **4**
Wallace, D.L. 1
Walsh, P. 1
Watson, D.V. 4
Webb, N. 4
Welbeck, D. **2**
Weller, K. 1
Wignall, F. 2
Wilkins, R.G. 3
Wilshaw, D.J. 10
Wise, D.F. 1
Withe, P. 1
Woodcock, T. 16
Worthington, F.S. 2
Wright, I.E. 9
Wright, M. 1
Wright, W.A. 3
Wright-Phillips, S.C. 6

Young, A. S. **6**

SCOTLAND
Aitken, R. 1
Archibald, S. 4

Baird, S. 2
Bannon, E. 1
Bauld, W. 2
Baxter, J.C. 3
Beattie, C. 1
Berra, C. **2**
Bett, J. 1
Bone, J. 1
Booth, S. 6
Boyd, K. 7

Boyd, T. 1
Brand, R. 8
Brazil, A. 1
Bremner, W.J. 3
Broadfoot, K. 1
Brown, A.D. 6
Brown, S. 2
Buckley, P. 1
Burke, C. 2
Burley, C.W. 3
Burns, K. 1

Caldwell, G. 2
Calderwood, C. 1
Caldow, E. 4
Cameron, C. 2
Campbell, R. 1
Chalmers, S. 3
Clarkson, D. 1
Collins, J. 12
Collins, R.V. 10
Combe, J.R. 1
Commons, K. 2
Conn, A. 1
Cooper, D. 6
Craig, J. 1
Crawford, S. 4
Curran, H.P. 1

Dailly, C. 6
Dalglish, K. 30
Davidson, J.A. 1
Dickov, P. 1
Dobie, R.S. 1
Docherty, T.H. 1
Dodds, D. 1
Dodds, W. 7
Duncan, D.M. 1
Durie, G.S. 7

Elliott, M.S. 1

Ferguson, B. 3
Fernie, W. 1
Flavell, R. 2
Fleming, C. 2
Fletcher, D. **5**
Fletcher, S. 1
Freedman, D.A. 1

Gallacher, K.W. 9

Gemmell, T.K (St Mirren) 1
Gemmell, T.K (Celtic) 1
Gemmell, A. 8
Gemmill, S. 1
Gibson, D.W. 3
Gilzean, A.J. 12
Goodwillie, D. **1**
Gough, C.R. 6
Graham, A. 2
Graham, G. 3
Gray, A. 7
Gray, E. 3
Gray, F. 1
Greig, J. 3

Hamilton, G. 4
Harper, J.M. 2
Hartford, R.A. 4
Hartley, P.J. 1
Henderson, J.G. 1
Henderson, W. 5
Hendry, E.C.J. 3
Herd, D.G. 3
Herd, G. 1
Hewie, J.D. 2
Holt, G.J. 1
Holton, J.A. 2
Hopkin, D. 2
Houliston, W. 2
Howie, H. 1
Hughes, J. 1
Hunter, W. 1
Hutchison, D. 6
Hutchison, T. 1

Jackson, C. 1
Jackson, D. 4
Jardine, A. 1
Jess, E. 2
Johnston, A. 2
Johnston, L.H. 1
Johnston, M. 14
Johnstone, D. 2
Johnstone, J. 4
Johnstone, R. 10
Jordan, J. 11

Kyle, K. 1

Lambert, P. 1
Law, D. 30
Leggat, G. 8
Lennox, R. 3
Liddell, W. 6
Linwood, A.B. 1
Lorimer, P. 4

Macari, L. 5
MacDougall, E.J. 3
MacKay, D.C. 4
Mackay, G. 1
MacKenzie, J.A. 1
Mackail-Smith, C. **1**
Mackie, J.C. **2**
MacLeod, M. 1
McAllister, G. 5
McArthur, J. 1
McAvennie, F. 1
McCall, S.M. 1
McCalliog, J. 1
McCann, N. 3
McClair, B. 2
McCoist, A. 19
McCormack, R. 1
McCulloch, L. 1
McFadden, J. 15*
McGhee, M. 2
McGinlay, J. 3
McInally, A. 3
McKimmie, S.I. 1
McKinlay, W. 4
McKinnon, R. 1
McLaren, A. 4
McLean, T. 1
McLintock, F. 1
McManus S. 2
McMillan, I.L. 2
McNeill, W. 3
McPhail, J. 3
McQueen, G. 5
McStay, P. 9
McSwegan, G.J. 1
Maloney, S. 1
Mason, J. 4
Masson, D.S. 5
Miller, K. **16**
Miller, W. 1
Mitchell, R.C. 1

Morgan, W. 1
Morris, H. 3
Morrison, J.C. 1
Mudie, J.K. 9
Mulhall, G. 1
Murdoch, R. 5
Murray, J. 1

Narey, D. 1
Naismith, S. **2**
Naysmith, G.A. 1
Nevin, P.K.F. 5
Nicholas, C. 5

O'Connor, G. 4
O'Hare, J. 5
Ormond, W.E. 2
Orr, T. 1
Own goals **12**

Parlane, D. 1
Pettigrew, W. 2
Provan, D. 1

Quashie, N.F. 1
Quinn, J. 7
Quinn, P. 1

Reilly, L. 22
Ring, T. 2
Rioch, B.D. 6
Ritchie, P.S. 1
Robertson, A. 2
Robertson, J. 3
Robertson, J.N. 8
Robson, B. 1

St John, I. 9
Scott, A.S. 5
Sharp, G. 1
Shearer, D. 2
Smith, G. 4
Snodgrass, R. **1**
Souness, G.J. 4
Steel, W. 12
Stein, C. 10
Stewart, R. 1
Strachan, G. 5
Sturrock, P. 3

The Scottish FA officially changed Robsons's goal against Iceland on 10 September 2008 to McFadden.

Thompson, S.	3
Thornton, W.	1
Waddell, W.	6
Wallace, I.A.	1
Wark, J.	7
Webster, A.	1
Weir, A.	1
Weir, D.	1
White, J.A.	3
Wilkie, L.	1
Wilson, D. (Liverpool)	1
Wilson, D. (Rangers)	9
Young, A.	2

WALES

Allchurch, I.J.	23
Allen, M.	3
Bale, G.	**6**
Barnes, W.	1
Bellamy, C.D.	**19**
Blackmore, C.G.	1
Blake, D.	**1**
Blake, N.A.	4
Bodin, P.J.	3
Bowen, D.I.	3
Bowen, M.	2
Boyle, T.	1
Burgess, W.A.R.	1
Charles, J.	1
Charles, M.	6
Charles, W.J.	15
Church, S.R.	1
Clarke, R.J.	5
Coleman, C.	4
Collins, J.	2
Cotterill, D.	1
Curtis, A.	6
Davies, G.	2
Davies, R.T.	9
Davies, R.W.	6
Davies, Simon	6
Deacy, N.	4
Durban, A.	2
Dwyer, P.	2
Earnshaw, R.	16
Eastwood, F.	4

Edwards, D.	3
Edwards, G.	2
Edwards, R.I.	4
England, H.M.	4
Evans, C.	2
Evans, I.	1
Fletcher, C.	1
Flynn, B.	7
Ford, T.	23
Foulkes, W.J.	1
Giggs, R.J.	12
Giles, D.	2
Godfrey, B.C.	2
Griffiths, A.T.	6
Griffiths, M.W.	2
Harris, C.S.	1
Hartson, J.	14
Hewitt, R.	1
Hockey, T.	1
Hodges, G.	2
Horne, B.	2
Hughes, L.M.	16
James, L.	10
James, R.	7
Jones, A.	1
Jones, B.S.	2
Jones, Cliff	16
Jones, D.E.	1
Jones, J.P.	1
King, A.	1
Koumas, J.	10
Kryzwicki, R.I.	1
Ledley, J.	3
Leek, K.	5
Llewelyn, C.M	1
Lovell, S.	1
Lowrie, G.	2
Mahoney, J.F.	1
Medwin, T.C.	6
Melville, A.K.	3
Moore, G.	1
Morison, S.	**1**
Nicholas, P.	2
O'Sullivan, P.A.	1

Own goals	8
Palmer, D.	1
Parry, P.I.	1
Paul, R.	1
Pembridge, M.A.	6
Phillips, D.	2
Powell, A.	1
Powell, D.	1
Price, P.	1
Ramsay, A.	**5**
Reece, G.I.	2
Rees, R.R.	3
Roberts, P.S.	1
Robinson, C.P.	1
Robinson, J.R.C.	3
Rush, I.	28
Saunders, D.	22
Savage R.W.	2
Slatter, N.	2
Smallman, D.P.	1
Speed, G.A.	7
Symons, C.J.	2
Tapscott, D.R.	4
Taylor, G.J.	1
Thomas, M.	4
Toshack, J.B.	12
Vaughan, D.O.	1
Vernon, T.R.	8
Vokes, S.M.	**4**
Walsh, I.	7
Williams, A.	2
Williams, G.E.	1
Williams, G.G.	1
Woosnam, A.P.	3
Yorath, T.C.	2
Young, E.	1

NORTHERN IRELAND

Anderson, T.	4
Armstrong, G.	12
Barr, H.H.	1
Best, G.	9
Bingham, W.L.	10

REPUBLIC OF IRELAND

BLUE SQUARE PREMIER 2011–2012

(P) *Promoted into division at end of 2010–11 season.*
(R) *Relegated into division at end of 2010–11 season.*

				Total				Home					Away					
	P	W	D	L	F	A	W	D	L	F	A	W	D	L	F	A	GD	Pts
1 Fleetwood T	46	31	10	5	102	48	13	8	2	50	25	18	2	3	52	23	54	103
2 Wrexham	46	30	8	8	85	33	16	3	4	48	17	14	5	4	37	16	52	98
3 Mansfield T	46	25	14	7	87	48	14	6	3	50	25	11	8	4	37	23	39	89
4 York C¶	46	23	14	9	81	45	11	6	6	43	24	12	8	3	38	21	36	83
5 Luton T	46	22	15	9	78	42	15	4	4	48	15	7	11	5	30	27	36	81
6 Kidderminster H	46	22	10	14	82	63	10	7	6	44	32	12	3	8	38	31	19	76
7 Southport	46	21	13	12	72	69	8	8	7	36	39	13	5	5	36	30	3	76
8 Gateshead	46	21	11	14	69	62	11	8	4	39	26	10	3	10	30	36	7	74
9 Cambridge U	46	19	14	13	57	41	11	6	6	31	16	8	8	7	26	25	16	71
10 Forest Green R	46	19	13	14	66	45	11	5	7	37	25	8	8	7	29	20	21	70
11 Grimsby T	46	19	13	14	79	60	12	4	7	51	28	7	9	7	28	32	19	70
12 Braintree T (P)	46	17	11	18	76	80	11	5	7	39	34	6	6	11	37	46	–4	62
13 Barrow	46	17	9	20	62	76	12	6	5	39	25	5	3	15	23	51	–14	60
14 Ebbsfleet U (P)	46	14	12	20	69	84	7	6	10	34	39	7	6	10	35	45	–15	54
15 Alfreton T (P)	46	15	9	22	62	86	8	6	9	39	48	7	3	13	23	38	–24	54
16 Stockport Co (R)	46	12	15	19	58	74	8	7	8	35	28	4	8	11	23	46	–16	51
17 Lincoln C (R)	46	13	10	23	56	66	8	6	9	32	24	5	4	14	24	42	–10	49
18 Tamworth	46	11	15	20	47	70	7	9	7	30	30	4	6	13	17	40	–23	48
19 Newport County AFC	46	11	14	21	53	65	8	6	9	22	22	3	8	12	31	43	–12	47
20 AFC Telford U (P)	46	10	16	20	45	65	9	6	8	24	26	1	10	12	21	39	–20	46
21 Hayes & Yeading U	46	11	8	27	58	90	5	5	13	26	41	6	3	14	32	49	–32	41
22 Darlington	46	11	13	22	47	73	8	7	8	24	24	3	6	14	23	49	–26	36
23 Bath C	46	7	10	29	43	89	5	4	14	27	41	2	6	15	16	48	–46	31
24 Kettering T	46	8	9	29	40	100	5	5	13	25	47	3	4	16	15	53	–60	30

Darlington deducted 10 points. Kettering T deducted 3 points. ¶York C promoted via play-offs.

Leading Goalscorers 2010–2011

	Club	League	Play-Offs	FA Cup	Total
Jamie Vardy	(Fleetwood T)	31	0	3	34
Matt Green	(Mansfield T)	29	0	0	29
Jon Shaw	(Gateshead)	27	0	3	30
Liam Hearn	(Grimsby T)	26	0	2	28
Tony Gray	(Southport)	24	0	0	24
Jake Speight	(Wrexham)	21	0	0	21
Andrew Mangan	(Fleetwood T)	19	0	2	21
Calum Willock	(Ebbsfleet U)	19	0	0	19
Yan Klukowski	(Forest Green R)	18	0	0	18
Jason Walker	(York C)	18	0	0	18
Ben Wright	(Braintree T)	17	0	1	18
Andy Cook	(Barrow)	17	0	0	17

BLUE SQUARE PREMIER RESULTS 2011–2012

	AFC Telford U	Alfreton T	Barrow	Bath C	Braintree T	Cambridge U	Darlington	Ebbsfleet U	Fleetwood T	Forest Green R	Gateshead	Grimsby T	Hayes & Yeading U	Kettering T	Kidderminster H	Lincoln C	Luton T	Mansfield T	Newport Co	Southport	Stockport Co	Tamworth	Wrexham	York C
AFC Telford U	—	1-0	2-1	2-1	1-0	1-2	3-3	0-2	1-4	2-0	1-2	0-0	1-1	3-1	2-1	1-2	0-2	0-0	2-1	0-1	1-1	1-0	0-2	0-0
Alfreton T	0-0	—	1-0	0-1	0-1	2-1	3-1	2-2	1-4	1-6	1-1	2-5	3-1	1-1	3-1	1-3	0-0	3-6	3-2	0-0	6-1	5-2	1-4	0-2
Barrow	2-1	1-0	—	0-1	0-4	1-3	3-0	3-1	4-0	0-2	1-2	2-2	1-1	3-0	3-1	1-0	0-0	2-3	3-1	2-2	1-0	1-1	3-1	0-0
Bath C	3-1	0-3	0-1	—	1-1	3-4	2-0	2-3	1-4	0-2	4-2	2-2	0-1	0-1	4-1	1-0	1-1	1-1	3-2	1-2	0-2	1-0	0-1	0-1
Braintree T	2-1	1-0	0-4	1-1	—	3-2	3-1	2-3	1-2	1-5	3-1	5-0	0-3	2-1	3-3	2-0	3-1	1-1	1-0	0-0	2-2	3-1	0-0	0-1
Cambridge U	1-0	1-2	1-3	3-4	2-0	—	2-1	0-2	2-0	3-1	0-1	0-1	2-1	2-0	2-0	2-3	1-1	1-2	2-0	3-0	2-2	0-1	1-1	0-1
Darlington	1-0	0-1	3-0	0-0	1-0	2-0	—	0-2	0-1	0-1	0-1	0-1	1-1	1-1	2-0	2-2	1-1	0-2	1-1	0-3	0-1	3-0	1-0	2-2
Ebbsfleet U	3-2	1-1	3-1	2-2	1-1	0-0	1-3	—	1-3	1-1	3-1	3-1	3-1	1-0	2-2	2-2	2-2	0-3	1-4	1-2	2-1	2-2	2-4	0-0
Fleetwood T	2-2	1-2	1-2	3-0	3-1	1-0	2-0	6-2	—	0-0	3-1	2-1	1-3	3-0	1-3	3-3	0-2	2-0	2-3	2-2	2-1	3-1	0-5	1-1
Forest Green R	2-1	4-1	3-0	4-1	0-2	0-1	2-1	3-1	1-2	—	2-1	1-0	1-0	1-1	0-0	3-1	3-0	1-0	2-2	2-3	2-1	1-1	1-1	1-1
Gateshead	3-0	2-0	5-2	1-0	1-1	2-1	3-2	1-2	1-0	1-0	—	1-0	3-0	2-1	2-3	1-2	0-1	3-0	3-0	2-3	2-0	0-0	1-1	3-2
Grimsby T	2-0	5-2	3-1	6-0	1-2	2-1	0-0	2-3	2-3	2-1	2-0	—	2-0	1-2	1-2	1-1	2-2	0-0	3-2	2-0	7-0	1-0	1-4	2-3
Hayes & Yeading U	0-0	3-1	1-1	1-1	2-1	0-0	3-1	4-3	1-1	1-1	2-3	3-0	—	6-1	3-1	1-0	0-5	1-3	3-2	2-0	1-2	0-2	1-3	2-4
Kettering T	2-1	0-2	0-2	1-1	5-4	3-1	5-0	2-2	0-2	1-0	2-1	1-2	6-1	—	0-1	2-1	1-2	0-3	2-0	5-1	1-1	2-0	0-2	1-5
Kidderminster H	2-2	3-1	3-1	4-1	3-3	2-0	2-0	2-2	1-3	0-0	2-3	1-2	3-1	0-1	—	1-0	1-1	0-3	5-0	1-3	1-0	4-0	0-1	1-1
Lincoln C	1-1	1-0	1-2	2-0	3-1	5-0	3-4	3-0	1-0	0-1	1-0	2-1	2-0	2-1	1-0	—	1-1	1-0	1-1	0-3	1-0	3-0	0-1	0-2
Luton T	1-1	1-0	1-0	1-1	4-1	2-0	1-0	1-0	3-1	0-1	5-1	0-0	4-2	1-2	1-1	1-1	—	1-0	2-1	0-1	2-1	2-1	1-2	1-2
Mansfield T	0-0	3-2	7-0	4-1	3-4	3-4	3-4	3-3	1-2	5-1	1-1	1-2	3-2	0-3	0-3	1-0	1-1	—	2-1	2-2	1-1	1-2	0-0	1-1
Newport Co	3-2	1-0	1-0	1-0	1-1	1-0	2-0	1-1	1-1	1-1	1-0	2-0	4-0	2-0	5-0	1-1	0-1	1-0	—	2-0	5-0	2-1	2-0	2-0
Southport	2-2	2-1	2-1	3-4	1-0	0-1	3-3	0-6	0-1	1-0	1-0	1-3	3-3	5-1	1-3	0-3	3-3	3-1	5-0	—	1-1	2-0	0-1	1-1
Stockport Co	2-2	0-0	3-2	4-0	5-1	2-2	2-1	3-2	0-6	1-0	0-1	2-2	2-1	1-1	1-0	1-0	1-3	0-1	1-1	1-3	—	3-1	0-0	1-1
Tamworth	4-0	2-2	2-3	0-1	6-2	1-1	2-1	2-4	2-4	1-2	1-1	4-1	4-1	2-0	4-0	3-0	2-0	1-3	2-1	0-1	1-1	—	1-2	2-1
Wrexham	0-1	0-1	3-1	2-0	0-0	2-2	2-2	0-3	0-3	1-0	2-1	2-0	2-0	0-2	0-1	0-1	1-2	2-2	0-0	2-2	4-0	3-0	—	0-3
York C	0-1	3-1	0-1	1-0	0-1	1-1	2-2	2-2	0-1	1-0	1-2	2-1	2-4	1-5	1-1	0-2	1-1	1-1	2-0	1-2	1-1	0-0	0-0	—

BLUE SQUARE PREMIER PLAY-OFFS 2011–2012

SEMI-FINALS FIRST LEG

York C	(1) 1	Mansfield T	(1) 1
Luton T	(2) 2	Wrexham	(0) 0

SEMI-FINALS SECOND LEG

Mansfield T	(0) 0	York C	(0) 1
Wrexham	(0) 2	Luton T	(1) 1

FINAL (at Wembley)

Sunday, 20 May 2012

Luton T (1) 1 *(Gray 2)*

York C (1) 2 *(Chambers 26, Blair 47)* 39,265

Luton T: Tyler; Osano, Howells, Keane, Kovacs, Pilkington G, Lawless, Watkins (McAllister) (O'Connor), Fleetwood (Kissock), Gray, Willmott.
York C: Ingham; Challinor (Brown), Gibson, Smith C, Doig, Parslow, Oyebanjo, Blair, Walker (McLaughlin), Chambers (Reed), Meredith.
Referee: J. Simpson (Lancs).

ATTENDANCES BY CLUB 2011–2012

	Aggregate 2011–12	Average 2011–12	Highest Attendance 2011–12
Luton Town	140,560	6,111	8,415 v Kidderminster H
Wrexham	87,549	3,806	5,812 v. AFC Telford U
Stockport County	84,567	3,676	6,393 v. Tamworth
Grimsby Town	76,085	3,308	6,672 v. Lincoln C
York City	71,700	3,117	4,295 v. Wrexham
Mansfield Town	61,685	2,681	4,830 v. Lincoln C
Cambridge United	55,956	2,432	4,796 v. Luton T
Lincoln City	53,990	2,347	5,506 v. Grimsby T
Fleetwood Town	52,079	2,264	4,994 v. Wrexham
AFC Telford United	52,066	2,263	4,591 v. Wrexham
Darlington	50,658	2,202	6,413 v. York C
Kidderminster Harriers	48,191	2,095	3,565 v. Mansfield T
Kettering Town	32,187	1,399	3,247 v. Luton T
Newport County	31,042	1,349	1,675 v. Grimsby T
Southport	29,669	1,289	2,589 v. Fleetwood T
Barrow	29,015	1,261	2,190 v. York C
Tamworth	25,237	1,097	1,923 v. Wrexham
Alfreton Town	24,454	1,063	3,354 v. Mansfield T
Forest Green Rovers	23,796	1,034	1,848 v. Stockport Co
Ebbsfleet United	23,396	1,017	1,651 v. Luton T
Braintree Town	20,603	895	2,029 v. Cambridge U
Gateshead	19,381	842	1,604 v. York C
Bath City	18,942	823	1,158 v. Luton T
Hayes & Yeading	8,671	377	1,015 v. Luton T

APPEARANCES AND GOALSCORERS 2011–2012

AFC TELFORD U

League Appearances: Adams, 14(6); Blackburn, 19; Brooke, 6(5); Brown, 29(5); Cain, 15(8); Chamberlain, 1(1); Davies, 29(5); Farrell, 7(9); Futcher, 3; Jackson, 8; Jones, 9(6); Killock, 32(3); King, 2(2); Kinniburgh, 1; Meechan, 2(3); Mills, 7(9); Newton, 33; Perry, 13(6); Pitt, 4; Platt, 2(1); Preston, 25(3); Proudlock, 6(12); Reid, 4(1); Rodgers, 8(3); Rooney, 7(9); Salmon, 38; Samuels, 7(10); Sharp, 32(5); Smith, 15(2); Trainer, 34(2); Valentine, 35(2); Weir-Daley, (2); Whitehead, 13(1); Young, 46.

Goals – League (45): Sharp 11, Newton 4 (2 pens), Trainer 4, Brown 3, Davies 3, Jones 3, Brooke 2, Farrell 2, Mills 2, Proudlock 2, Adams 1, Blackburn 1, Jackson 1, Killock 1, Meechan 1, Perry 1, Preston 1, Rooney 1, Smith 1.

FA Cup (5): Pitt 2, Sharp 2, Killock 1.

ALFRETON T

League Appearances: Arnold, 27(1); Brogan, (2); Broughton, 2; Brown, 38(2); Church, 6; Clay, 2(2); Clayton, 30(10); Conneely, 8(1); Cunnington, 7(4); Day, 15; Deverdics, 3(3); Eagle, 2(1); Ellison, 1(7); Franklin, 37(2); Franks, 21(2); Hall, 5(7); Hawes, 2(2); Holdsworth, 2(2); Jarman, 25(14); Kempson, 13; Law, 30(8); Lowson, 20; Mackin, 11; Meadows, 3(1); Moult, J. 33(4); Moult, L. 1; Mullan, 16(18); Potter, 2; Quinn, 17; Senior, 7(12); Stevenson, 3; Stewart, 11; Streete, 40(3); Wilson, A. 26(7); Wilson, M. 12(2); Young, G. 28(2).

Goals – League (62): Jarman 12 (6 pens), Brown 8, Clayton 7, Arnold 6, Moult 6, Wilson, A. 6, Cunnington 2, Streete 2, Broughton 1 (1 pen), Church 1, Clay 1, Ellison 1, Kempson 1, Law 1, Mackin 1 (1 pen), Meadows 1, Mullan 1, Quinn 1, Wilson, M. 1, own goals 2.

FA Cup (3): Jarman 2 (2 pens), Brown 1.

BARROW

League Appearances: Almond, 10(13); Baker, 31(8); Bolland, 28(1); Boyes, 39(3); Brooke, 1(5); Cook, 34(3); Cudworth, 1; Dixon, (1); Edwards, 4; Ferrell, 13(2); Harvey, 10(3); Hollis, 2(1); Hone, 25(1); Hulbert, 7(1); Hurst, 31; Jackson, 4; Lomax, 22(4); Mackreth, 36(7); Moyo, 4(5); Nicholas, 11(9); Owen, 31(2); Pearson, M. 9(1); Pearson, S. 14; Quinn, 18; Rowe, 6(4); Rutherford, 32(8); Sheridan, 1(1); Skelton, 43; Smith, 36(4); Turner, 5.

Goals – League (62): Cook 17, Boyes 16 (1 pen), Baker 9 (5 pens), Mackreth 5, Jackson 3, Smith 3, Bolland 2, Almond 1, Harvey 1, Hollis 1, Pearson, M. 1, Rowe 1, Rutherford 1, own goal 1.

FA Cup (5): Boyes 4, Rutherford 1.

BATH C

League Appearances: Agdestein, 3; Amadi-Holloway, 3(2); Bryan, 1(3); Burnell, 32(1); Canham, M. 36(2); Canham, S. 22(2); Carvalho-Landell, 1; Clough, 10(2); Connolly, 41(2); Cook, 13(11); Doherty, 1; Egan, (8); Gallinagh, 32; Garner, 36; Hogg, 34(8); Jones, 39(1); Matthews, 10; Murray, 15(19); Phillips, 24(7); Preece, 25(4); Rollo, 7(9); Russell, 17(14); Shephard, 1(4); Simpson, 34(2); Smith, (3); Stonehouse, 32(6); Swallow, 7(2); Watkins, 28(9).

Goals – League (43): Canham, S. 9, Murray 7 (1 pen), Canham, M. 6 (6 pens), Watkins 5, Connolly 4, Phillips 3, Jones 2, Bryan 1, Clough 1, Cook 1, Gallinagh 1, Hogg 1, Russell 1, Stonehouse 1.

FA Cup (3): Canham, S. 1, Connolly 1, Gallinagh 1.

BRAINTREE T

League Appearances: Appoil-Kupi, (2); Assombalonga, 5; Bailey-Dennis, 34(3); Bentley, (1); Chilaka, 6(19); Constantine, (1); Davis, 39; Gibson, 8; Guy, 1(7); James-Lewis, 2(2); Johnson, 5(10); Kiernan, 3(1); Marks, 41(1); McCammon, 1(4); McDonald, 46; McLeod, (1); O'Connor, 23(5); Paine, 40(1); Peters, 23(3); Pooley, (2); Quinton, 12(30); Reason, 44; Stevens, 5(4); Symons, 36(6); Thomas, 43; Vose, 1(4); Wells, 25(1); Wright, 40(1); Yiadom, A. 24(4).

Goals – League (76): Wright 17 (4 pens), Marks 14, Reason 11 (3 pens), Yiadom 7, Assombalonga 5, Thomas 5, Davis 3, Bailey-Dennis 2, Chilaka 2, Gibson 2 (1 pen), Paine 2, Quinton 2, Guy 1, McCammon 1, Stevens 1, Symons 1.

FA Cup (3): Davis 1, Wright 1, Yiadom 1.

CAMBRIDGE U

League Appearances: Ambrusics, 1; Berry, 40(3); Brighton, (2); Carew, 29; Charles, 6(13); Corker, (1); Coulson, 32; Dawkin, 2(3); Dunk, 18(5); Eades, 8(2); Gash, 32(8); Hudson, 13(5); Hughes, 9(12); Hurst, (1); Jackson, 3(2); Jarvis, 36(5); Jennings, 41; Johnson, 2; Kinniburgh, 2(1); Marriott, 10(1); McAuley, 28(3); Murtagh, (7); Naisbitt, 45; Patrick, 1(18); Pell, 7; Platt, 2(3); Pugh, 10(3); Roberts, 40; Shaw, 41(1); Thorpe, 13(13); Tiryaki, 5(1); Winn, 10(3); Wylde, 20(2).

Goals – League (57): Gash 7, Shaw 7, Berry 6, Dunk 6, Carew 5 (1 pen), Marriott 3, Pugh 3 (1 pen), Roberts 3, Hughes 2, Jennings 2, McAuley 2, Pell 2, Platt 2, Charles 1, Dawkin 1, Eades 1, Patrick 1, Tiryaki 1, Winn 1, Wylde 1.
FA Cup (9): Berry 2, Carew 2, Coulson 2, Charles 1, Patrick 1, Wylde 1.

DARLINGTON
League Appearances: Arnison, 31(3); Atkinson, 10(5); Bagnall, 2; Barton, (4); Bowman, 28(12); Bridge-Wilkinson, 23(5); Brough, 2(4); Broughton, 11; Brown, 30; Campbell, 4(8); Chandler, 23(1); Ferguson, 2(4); Geohaghon, 5; Gray, J. 3(8); Gray, P. 1(1); Harrison, 7(3); Hatch, 17(5); Hollis, 9; Hopson, 14(1); Johnson, 9; Keltie, 14(1); Lambert, (13); Lee, 24; McReady, 30(7); Miller, 16; Nixon, 1; Pickford, 17; Purcell, 5; Purkiss, 12; Ramshaw, 4(7); Reach, 2(3); Rodney, 1; Rundle, 36(2); Russell, 22; Sanchez-Munoz, 5(3); Smith, (1); Soderberg, 6; Taylor, G. 19; Taylor, K. 35(1); Wainwright, 11(1); Walshaw, 15(3).
Goals – League (47): Bowman 10 (1 pen), Bridge-Wilkinson 6 (5 pens), Rundle 5, Hatch 3, Walshaw 3, Chandler 2, Hopson 2, McReady 2, Taylor, G. 2, Arnison 1, Barton 1, Broughton 1, Campbell 1, Hollis 1, Lambert 1, Lee 1, Purcell 1, Reach 1, Sanchez-Munoz 1, own goals 2.
FA Cup (1): Bowman 1.

EBBSFLEET U
League Appearances: Adams, (1); Azeez, 2(13); Barrett, 19(7); Bellamy, 7(4); Cronin, 10; Darvill, 4(5); Easton, 6; Edwards, 31; Enver-Marum, 34(4); Fakinos, 7(5); Ginty, (13); Herd, 18(4); Howe, 37(4); Lorraine, 30(1); Mambo, 24; Marwa, 39(2); McNeil, 3(1); Phipp, 32(8); Pinney, 17(8); Shakes, 25(16); Simpemba, 17(3); Smith, 12(1); Stavrinou, 5(7); Stone, 44(1); Ugwu, 8(1); Welch, 2; West, 35(1); Willock, 38(5).
Goals – League (69): Willock 19 (4 pens), Enver-Marum 13, West 8, Pinney 7, Shakes 7, Ugwu 4 (1 pen), Phipp 3 (1 pen), Darvill 2, Barrett 1, Bellamy 1, Ginty 1 (1 pen), Herd 1, Lorraine 1, Mambo 1.

FA Cup (0).

FLEETWOOD T
League Appearances: Allen, (2); Atkinson, 15(2); Barry, 2; Beeley, 32(1); Briggs, 8(8); Brodie, 16(18); Brown, J. 18(3); Brown, S. 3(1); Cavanagh, 23; Charnock, 4; Clancy, 7(4); Cox, 3(3); Crowther, (3); Davies, 46; Donnelly, 2(3); Edwards, 7; Flynn, 3; Fowler, 17(2); Goodall, 29(2); Harvey, 3(2); Holmes, 3; Hughes, 1; Jackson, 4; Linwood, 3; Mangan, 39(2); McGuire, 34(4); McNulty, 39; Milligan, 19(6); Pond, 29(5); Rose, 8(2); Rowe, (2); Seddon, 22(16); Till, 9(9); Vardy, 34(2); Vieira, 16(8); Wassmer, 3; Wilson, 5.
Goals – League (102): Vardy 31, Mangan 19 (5 pens), Brodie 9 (1 pen), Vieira 9 (1 pen), Seddon 8, Milligan 4 (3 pens), Cavanagh 3, Clancy 3, Jackson 2, Rose 2, Atkinson 1, Beeley 1, Briggs 1, Charnock 1, Cox 1, Donnelly 1, McGuire 1, Pond 1, Till 1, own goals 3.
FA Cup (13): Milligan 3 (1 pen), Vardy 3, Mangan 2, Brodie 1, Charnock 1, Clancy 1, McGuire 1, Seddon 1.

FOREST GREEN R
League Appearances: Allen, 10(6); Bangura, 11(1); Bittner, 19(1); Bond, 4; Bulman, 5; Collins, 12; Forbes, 40(1); Graham, 21(7); Griffin, 19(9); Henderson, 14(8); Henry, (1); Hodgkiss, 46; Imudia, 1(1); Klukowski, 38(8); Matthews, (3); McDonald, 6(5); Norwood, 34(4); Oshodi, 30; Paterson, (1); Pook, (7); Rowe, 22(6); Russell, 18; Sandell, 3; Stokes, 45; Styche, 9(7); Taylor, 27(2); Thomson, 19(9); Todd, 2; Turk, 2(10); Turley, 38(1); Uwezu, 8(17); Wright, 3(4).
Goals – League (66): Klukowski 18 (4 pens), Taylor 10, Styche 8, Griffin 7, Forbes 3, Norwood 3, Collins 2, Henderson 2, Stokes 2, Turley 2, Uwezu 2, Wright 2, McDonald 1, Thomson 1, own goals 3.
FA Cup (1): Hodgkiss 1.

GATESHEAD
League Appearances: Airey, 1(1); Alnwick, 6; Baxter, 24(3); Brittain, 10(10); Carruthers, 19(2); Chandler, 13; Clark, 40; Cummins, 41(2); Curtis, 38; Deasy, 15; Dummett, 10; Farman, 25; Fisher, 7(13); Gate, 36(3); Gilles, 19(8); Hatch, 8(3); Henderson, 5(1); Magnay, 3(1); Marwood, 5(16); Moore, 13(11); Moyes, 1; Mulligan, 2(12); Nix, 2(6); O'Brien, 11(1); Odhiambo, 20(5); Odubade, 27(2); Rents, 24(5); Shaw, 43; Turnbull, 38(3).
Goals – League (69): Shaw 27 (5 pens), Cummins 9, Gate 7, Odubade 7, Hatch 4, Brittain 3, Gilles 3, Moore 3, Curtis 2, Chandler 1, Henderson 1, Turnbull 1, own goal 1.
FA Cup (6): Shaw 3, Fisher 2, Cummins 1.

GRIMSBY T
League Appearances: Antwi, 4; Artus, 23(6); Church, 15(6); Coulson, 38(5); Disley, 44; Duffy, 17(18); Eagle, 3(8); Elding, 27(16); Garner, 13(1); Green, 5(1); Hearn, 42; Hughes-Mason, 2(9);

Kempson, 18(1); L'Anson, 12(1); Makofo, 15(3); McCarthy, 4(1); McKeown, 46; Miller, 20; Panther, 7; Pearson, 27(3); Ridley, 12; Silk, 21(3); Soares, 8(3); Southwell, (1); Spencer, 1(6); Thanoj, 14(9); Thompson, 3; Townsend, 27; Winn, 6(4); Wood, 28(4); Wright, 4.
Goals – League (79): Hearn 26, Elding 12 (2 pens), Coulson 8, Duffy 6, Makofo 4, Garner 3, Pearson 3, Hughes-Mason 2, Miller 2, Antwi 1, Artus 1, Church 1, Disley 1, Green 1, L'Anson 1, Thanoj 1, Thompson 1, Townsend 1, Wood 1, Wright 1, own goals 2.
FA Cup (8): Duffy 3, Hearn 2, Eagle 1, Makofo 1, Southwell 1.

HAYES & Y

League Appearances: Ajala, 3(7); Argent, 16(1); Arnold, 31; Bassele, 1(3); Bayley, 5(4); Beasant, 3; Bell-Baggie, (1); Bentley, 32(2); Berry, (1); Bettamer, (7); Cadmore, 46; Collins, 18(17); Crockford, 10(9); Elder, 2(4); Evans, (4); Federico, (1); Folkes, 7(1); Franks, 7; Gameiao, 1(4); Gladwin, 1(1); Hand, 26; John, 12; Joseph-Dubois, 20(2); Koo-Boothe, 1; Lee, 13(6); Legg, (1); Mackie, 7(4); Marsaud, (3); McClure, 1; Mingoia, 7(1); Monteiro, 1; Morris, 2(1); Moutaouakil, 15(1); Mulley, 1; Noble, (2); O'Brien, 6(1); Owusu, 13(8); Pacquette, 13(5); Pele, 16(2); Pentney, 9; Preddie, 3(4); Rose, 3(1); Saville, 2(2); Sinclair, 2; Soares, 31; Spence, 19(1); Thalassitis, 5; Ujah, 16; Walsh, 16(1); Warren, (7); Wickham, 1(1); Williams, 38(1); Wishart, 22(14); Wynters, 2.
Goals – League (58): Soares 15 (5 pens), Collins 8, Wishart 5, Pacquette 4, Williams 4, Owusu 3, Thalassitis 3, Cadmore 2, Hand 2 (2 pens), Joseph-Dubois 2, Mingoia 2, Bentley 1, Crockford 1, Mackie 1, McClure 1, Pele 1, Sinclair 1, own goals 2.
FA Cup (2): Crockford 1, Soares 1 (pen).

KETTERING T

League Appearances: Ashikodi, 16(1); Bridges, 33(2); Challinor, 2(2); Clapham, 2(1); Cross, (2); Cunnington, A. 9(3); Dance, 1(2); Davis, 36; Dawkin, 9(3); Deeney, 3; Dempster, 5; Dobson, (1); Dossou, (1); Ford, 7(3); Gray, 8(1); Haxhia, 3(1); Hornby, 3(1); Hughes-Mason, 9(3); Ifil, J. 28; Ifil, P. 22(1); Jack, 3; Jones, 2(8); Joyce, 8(1); Kelly, 26(1); Koo-Boothe, 10(3); Marna, 15(2); McKenzie, 6(3); Meechan, 17(4); Mills, 17(1); Navarro, 13(3); Noubissie, 26(6); O'Leary, 11; Palmer, 1; Parry, 1; Petranyuk, (3); Pryor, 3(6); Ralph, 13(1); Roper, 1; Sangare, 27(2); Sekajia, 1(1); Smith, 3; Swaibu, 5(1); Taft, 10(4); Thomson, (4); Van Engel, 1(4); Verma, 22; Walker, 40; Warren, 1; Westwood, 9; Williams, 1; Wyke, 12; York, 5(3).
Goals – League (40): Marna 8 (1 pen), Ashikodi 6 (1 pen), Cunnington 5 (1 pen), Bridges 3, Sangare 3, Verma 3 (1 pen), McKenzie 2, Mills 2, Wyke 2 (1 pen), Dawkin 1, Ford 1, Hughes-Mason 1, Jones 1, Joyce 1, Westwood 1.
FA Cup (3): Marna 2, McKenzie 1.

KIDDERMINSTER H

League Appearances: Bird, 4; Bradley, 7(8); Breeden, 28; Briscoe, 11(2); Byrne, 20(6); Cresswell, (3); Demetriou, 23(3); Gittings, 25(5); Guinan, 25(13); Hankin, 23(4); Hendrie, 13(2); Jamile, 1; Johnson, 11(1); Jones, 38(1); Lewis, 12; Lyness, 6; Malbon, 14(3); Marshall, 23; Matt, 23(8); McQuilkin, (2); Medley, 7(6); Phelan, 8(7); Rowe, 3(12); Sharpe, 21(1); Storer, 38(1); Thompson-Brown, (3); Vaughan, 40; Vincent, 21(7); Williams, Marc 10(12); Williams, Mike 28; Wright, N. 23(20); Wright, T. (2).
Goals – League (82): Wright, N. 15 (4 pens), Byrne 9, Matt 9, Malbon 8, Guinan 7, Gittings 5, Jones 4, Vaughan 4 (4 pens), Rowe 3, Vincent 3, Hankin 2, Storer 2, Williams, Marc 2, Bradley 1, Jamile 1, Marshall 1, McQuilkin 1, Phelan 1, Sharpe 1, Williams, Mike 1, own goals 2.
FA Cup (1): Guinan 1.

LINCOLN C

League Appearances: Almond, 3(2); Anderson, J. 1; Anyon, J. 38; Arnaud, (1); Barraclough, 4(8); Beardsley, (1); Bore, 11; Broughton, D. 1; Christophe, 22(5); Cobb, (1); Cunningham, 2; Farman, 8; Fuseini, A. 15(2); Gowling, 36(1); Hinds, 8; Hone, D. 9; Laurent, 5(9); Lloyd, 3(9); Louis, 14; McCallum, G. 17(1); McCammon, 2(4); Medley, (6); Miller, 8; Nelson, 9(1); Nicolau, 14(5); Nutter, 46; O'Keefe, J. 4(6); Pacquette, 9(4); Perry, 14(9); Platt, 14; Power, 42; Robinson, (1); Robson, 15; Rodney, 2(4); Russell, 17(9); Sheridan, 12(7); Sinclair, 23(1); Smith, 18(7); Taylor, 10(14); Thomas, (1); Thompson, 26(1); Watson, 3(2); Watts, A. 11; Williams, 10(1).
Goals – League (56): Smith 7, Louis 6, Power 4 (2 pens), Taylor 4, Lloyd 3, McCallum 3, Pacquette 3, Perry 3, Bore 2, Christophe 2, McCammon 2, Nutter 2, Platt 2, Almond 1, Fuseini 1, Hinds 1, Hone 1, Laurent 1, Miller 1, O'Keefe 1, Russell 1, Thompson 1, own goals 4.
FA Cup (2): Smith 2.

LUTON T

League Appearances: Antwi, 12; Asafu-Adjaye, 7(2); Barnes-Homer, 1; Beckwith, 8; Blackett, 5(4); Boucaud, 4(3); Brunt, (5); Carden, 1; Crow, 23(6); Dance, 21(5); Fleetwood, 22(15); Gleeson, 8(2); Gray, 9; Hand, 11(2); Henry, (2); Howells, 42; Keane, 33; Kissock, 7(14); Kovacs, 37;

Lawless, 38; McAllister, 4(10); Morgan-Smith, 15(2); O'Connor, 21(13); Osano, 28; Pilkington, G. 33; Pilkington, K. 12; Poku, 5(5); Samuel, (1); Taylor, 15(2); Tyler, 34; Walker, D. (1); Watkins, 20(14); Willmott, 29(10); Woolley, (1); Wright, 1(3).

Goals – League (78): Fleetwood 11, Crow 9, Morgan-Smith 9, Willmott 8, Gray 5, Howells 5, O'Connor 5 (1 pen), Watkins 5, Kovacs 4, Dance 3, Antwi 2, Hand 2, Lawless 2, Beckwith 1, Keane 1, McAllister 1, Pilkington, G. 1 (1 pen), Taylor 1, Wright 1, own goals 2.

FA Cup (8): O'Connor 4 (1 pen), Dance 1, Fleetwood 1, Watkins 1, Wright 1.

Play-Offs (4): Gray 2, Fleetwood 1, Pilkington, G. 1 (pen).

MANSFIELD T

League Appearances: Andrew, 1(4); Bell, 1; Bolland, 4(6); Briscoe, 25(13); Connor, 4(11); Dempster, 11(1); Dyer, 42(3); Edwards, 2(1); Freeman, 9; Futcher, 13; Geohaghon, 13; Green, 44(1); Hegarty, 2; Howell, 28(5); Hutchinson, 5(7); Kelly, (1); Kendrick, 15; Marriott, 45; Meikle, 33(9); Moult, (1); Murray, 39; Naylor, 5; O'Neill, 43; Redmond, 1; Rhead, 2(13); Riley, 26(2); Roberts, 16(1); Rodney, (2); Smith, 8(4); Stevenson, 6(1); Sutton, 39(2); Thompson, 6(1); Todd, 6(2); Verma, 4(1); Wood, (1); Worthington, 8(9).

Goals – League (87): Green 29 (3 pens), Briscoe 12, Dyer 8, Meikle 7, Howell 5, Connor 4, Dempster 3, O'Neill 3, Roberts 3, Geohaghon 2, Rhead 2, Smith 2, Futcher 1, Hutchinson 1 (1 pen), Marriott 1, Stevenson 1, Todd 1, Verma 1, own goal 1.

FA Cup (1): Dyer 1.

Play-Offs (1): Dyer 1.

NEWPORT CO

League Appearances: Baker, 17(3); Buchanan, 26(10); Chapman, 4(1); Charles, 13; Darlow, 8; Doherty, 18(1); Evans, 3; Foley, 32(9); Franks, 1; Gilligan, 3(1); Greening, (1); Harris, 1(8); Hatswell, 9(3); Hughes, 36(2); Jardim, 3(4); Jarvis, 20(11); Knights, 12(10); Matthews, 6(3); McAllister, 19(6); Miller, 20(4); Minshull, 17; Pipe, 33(1); Porter, 13; Potter, 16; Reid, 5(7); Robson, 7; Rodgers, 31(5); Rogers, 7(7); Rose, D. 24; Rose, R. 5(7); Sandell, 10; Selino, 1; Thompson, 22(1); Velez, 3(1); Warren, 35; Yakubu, 26.

Goals – League (53): Rose, D. 11 (2 pens), Foley 10 (1 pen), Jarvis 6, Buchanan 5, Yakubu 5, Rose, R. 3, Warren 3, Harris 2, Sandell 2 (1 pen), Charles 1, Hatswell 1, Knights 1, Minshull 1, Reid 1, Rogers 1.

FA Cup (4): Foley 1, Jarvis 1, McAllister 1, Rodgers 1.

SOUTHPORT

League Appearances: Akrigg, 40(3); Aley, 2(1); Benjamin, 7(18); Brown, 11(9); Carden, 2(19); Daly, (6); Davis, 14(4); Ellison, 6(9); Grand, 42; Gray, 44; Guthrie, 2(3); Kissock, 4; Ledsham, 37(2); Lee, 17; Lever, 23(8); McMillan, 43; Moogan, 26(11); Mukendi, 11(2); Nemes, 3; O'Keefe, 5(2); Ordish, (2); Osborne, 1(3); Owens, 37(2); Parry, 20(4); Poku, 21(1); Putterill, (2); Sheridan, 2(1); Smith, 37; Stephenson, 1(5); Walker, 7(5); Whalley, 41.

Goals – League (72): Gray 24 (8 pens), Whalley 10, Grand 4, Ledsham 4, Owens 4, Lee 3, Mukendi 3, Brown 2, Ellison 2, Lever 2 (1 pen), Stephenson 2, Walker 2, Akrigg 1, Davis 1, Guthrie 1, Kissock 1, Moogan 1, Sheridan 1, own goals 4.

FA Cup (2): Akrigg 1, Owens 1.

STOCKPORT CO

League Appearances: Blackburn, 12(3); Bounab, 10(1); Brownhill, (2); Chadwick, 17(2); Chamberlain, (5); Cole, 7(9); Connor, 19(2); Darkwah, C. (7); Edwards, 11; Elliott, 33(9); Fraughan, 6(3); German, 10(6); Glennon, M. 24; Gritton, 6(5); Hall, 1; Halls, A. 29(1); Halstead, 4; Hattersley, 8; Hirmer, (1); Holden, 29(4); King, 5; Lynch, M. 5(1); Mainwaring, M. 15; McCann, 11(8); McConville, 21(2); Miles, 11(3); Newton, 7; Nolan, 18(13); O'Donnell, D. 32(2); Ormson, 13; Parker, (1); Paton, 15; Piergianni, 39(2); Rose, J. 6(4); Routledge, 12(2); Rowe, D. 11(4); Rowe, D. 17(9); Say, (1); Sheridan, 24(3); Turnbull, 14; Whitehead, 4(13).

Goals – League (58): Chadwick 7 (1 pen), Elliott 7, Hattersley 6, Rowe 6 (1 pen), McConville 4 (1 pen), Paton 4, Piergianni 4, Connor 3, German 3, Darkwah 2, O'Donnell 2, Rose 2, Rowe 2, Sheridan 2 (1 pen), Holden 1, Newton 1, Whitehead 1, own goal 1.

FA Cup (0).

TAMWORTH

League Appearances: Baldock, 3; Barrow, 26(4); Bradley, 15(2); Cain, 12(4); Christie, 22(11); Collins, 6; Collister, 3; Courtney, 18(1); Farah, 1(2); Francis, 35(1); Grayson, 1(3); Green, 40; Gudger, 6(5); Habergham, 28(2); Headley, (1); Healy, (1); Hedge, 43; Hubbins, 1; Isaac, 8(1); Kanyuka, 11; Lake-Gaskin, 1; Marna, 10(1); McDonald, 21(9); McKoy, 14; Mills, 9(11); Nix, 9(2); Oji, 12; Patterson, 26(14); Reece, 4(3); Reynolds, 2(1); Shariff, 13(11); Smith, 15(1); St Aimie, 18(12); Tait, 40(1); Taylor, 6(2); Thomas, 24(13); Valentim, (1); Wilson, 3.

Goals – League (47): Christie 11 (6 pens), St Aimie 7 (1 pen), Patterson 5 (1 pen), Marna 4 (1 pen), McDonald 3, Mills 3, Thomas 3, Barrow 2, Shariff 2, Bradley 1, Courtney 1, Francis 1, Gudger 1, Tait 1, Taylor 1, Wilson 1.

FA Cup (7): Patterson 3, St Aimie 2, Christie 1 (pen), Francis 1.

WREXHAM

League Appearances: Alfei, 5; Anoruo, (3); Ashton, 43; Cieslewicz, 18(26); Clarke, 19(8); Clowes, 1; Colbeck, 1(3); Creighton, 38(1); Evans, (1); Fowler, 14(3); Harris, 38; Hunt, 4(9); Keates, 23(5); Knight-Percival, 43; Leslie, 10(3); Little, 3(14); Maxwell, 10; Mayebi, 36; Morrell, 31(10); Moss, (1); Obeng, C. 29; Ogleby, 2(4); Pogba, 27(10); Speight, 33(5); Taylor, (1); Tolley, 29(5); Tomassen, (2); Walker, 1; Westwood, 12(2); Wright, D. 26(6); Wright, S. 10(1).

Goals – League (85): Speight 21 (7 pens), Pogba 11 (1 pen), Morrell 10, Cieslewicz 6, Wright, D. 6, Tolley 5, Knight-Percival 4, Creighton 3, Harris 3, Clarke 2, Colbeck 2, Fowler 2, Keates 2 (1 pen), Ashton 1 (1 pen), Leslie 1, Obeng 1, Ogleby 1, Westwood 1, own goals 3.

FA Cup (9): Morrell 3, Cieslewicz 1, Knight-Percival 1, Pogba 1, Tolley 1, Wright, D. 1, own goal 1.

Play-Offs (2): Cieslewicz 1, Morrell 1.

YORK C

League Appearances: Ashikodi, 2(6); Blair, 37(4); Blinkhorn, 3(12); Bopp, 1(1); Boucaud, 23; Brown, 6(1); Challinor, 35(4); Chambers, 34(8); Doig, 10; Fyfield, 25(8); Gibson, 8; Henderson, 2(4); Ingham, 43; Kelly, (1); Kerr, 33(1); McGurk, 18(1); McLaughlin, 42(2); Meredith, 43; Moke, 11(15); Musselwhite, 3; Oyebanjo, 19(2); Parslow, 17(10); Pilkington, 10(8); Potts, 2(8); Reed, 17(18); Smith, 31; Swallow, (2); Tonne, 2(1); Walker, 29(1).

Goals – League (81): Walker 18 (3 pens), Blair 10, McLaughlin 10, Reed 10 (1 pen), Chambers 9, Fyfield 3, Moke 3, Smith 3, Challinor 2, Meredith 2, Oyebanjo 2, Pilkington 2, Ashikodi 1, Blinkhorn 1, Boucaud 1, Henderson 1, McGurk 1, Tonne 1, own goal 1.

FA Cup (1): McLaughlin 1.

Play-Offs (4): Blair 2, Chambers 1, own goal 1.

BLUE SQUARE NORTH AND SOUTH PLAY-OFFS 2011–2012

BLUE SQUARE NORTH		BLUE SQUARE SOUTH	
SEMI-FINALS FIRST LEG		**SEMI-FINALS FIRST LEG**	
Gainsborough Trinity 2 *(Connor 6, 13)*		**Sutton U 1** *(Holloway 67 og)*	
FC Halifax T 2 *(Gregory 44, 85)*	2380	**Welling U 2** *(Clarke 25, Healy 71)*	1255
Nuneaton T 1 *(Glover 2)*		**Basingstoke T 0**	
Guiseley 1 *(Wilson 90)*	1476	**Dartford 1** *(Noble 46)*	1691
SEMI-FINALS SECOND LEG		**SEMI-FINALS SECOND LEG**	
FC Halifax T 0		**Welling U 0**	
Gainsborough Trinity 1 *(Clarke 65)*	3468	**Sutton U 0**	1408
Guiseley 0		**Dartford 2** *(Bradbrook 57, Wilkinson 73)*	
Nuneaton T 1 *(Brown 2)*	1676	**Basingstoke T 1** *(McAuley 68)*	2210
FINAL		**FINAL**	
Gainsborough Trinity 0		**Dartford 1** *(Noble 4)*	
Nuneaton T 1 *(Brown 17)*	3280	**Welling 0**	4088

BLUE SQUARE NORTH 2011–2012

(P) *Promoted into division at end of 2010–11 season.*
(R) *Relegated into division at end of 2010–11 season.*

			Total				Home				Away					
	P	W	D	L	F	A	W	D	L	F	A	W	D	L	F	A	GD	Pts
1 Hyde U	42	27	9	6	90	36	15	5	1	55	17	12	4	5	35	19	54	90
2 Guiseley	42	25	10	7	87	50	15	3	3	52	24	10	7	4	35	26	37	85
3 FC Halifax T (P)	42	21	11	10	80	59	10	5	6	41	33	11	6	4	39	26	21	74
4 Gainsborough Trinity	42	23	5	14	74	60	14	2	5	38	22	9	3	9	36	38	14	74
5 Nuneaton T¶	42	22	12	8	73	41	13	4	4	36	19	9	8	4	37	22	32	72
6 Stalybridge Celtic	42	20	11	11	83	64	13	2	6	48	33	7	9	5	35	31	19	71
7 Worcester C	42	18	11	13	63	58	10	7	4	31	20	8	4	9	32	38	5	65
8 Altrincham (R)	42	17	10	15	90	71	10	6	5	49	31	7	4	10	41	40	19	61
9 Droylsden	42	16	11	15	83	86	10	6	5	46	35	6	5	10	37	51	–3	59
10 Bishop's Stortford	42	17	7	18	70	75	8	4	9	35	30	9	3	9	35	45	–5	58
11 Boston U	42	15	9	18	60	67	6	8	7	28	29	9	1	11	32	38	–7	54
12 Harrogate T	42	14	11	17	59	68	7	8	6	25	25	7	3	11	34	43	–9	53
13 Colwyn Bay (P)	42	15	8	19	55	70	9	3	9	31	39	6	5	10	24	31	–15	53
14 Gloucester C	42	15	7	20	53	60	8	3	10	25	27	7	4	10	28	33	–7	52
15 Histon (R)	42	12	15	15	67	72	5	9	7	41	41	7	6	8	26	31	–5	51
16 Corby T	42	14	8	20	65	71	6	1	14	33	43	8	7	6	32	28	–6	50
17 Workington	42	13	11	18	55	61	8	6	7	31	28	5	5	11	24	33	–6	50
18 Vauxhall Motors	42	14	8	20	63	78	8	4	9	27	33	6	4	11	36	45	–15	50
19 Solihull Moors	42	13	10	19	44	54	9	4	8	29	25	4	6	11	15	29	–10	49
20 Hinckley U	42	13	9	20	75	90	5	5	11	36	43	8	4	9	39	47	–15	48
21 Blyth Spartans	42	7	13	22	51	81	5	5	11	30	38	2	8	11	21	43	–30	34
22 Eastwood T	42	4	8	30	37	105	1	7	13	22	53	3	1	17	15	52	–68	20

Nuneaton Town deducted 6 points. ¶Nuneaton T promoted via play-offs.

BLUE SQUARE SOUTH 2011–2012

			Total				Home				Away					
	P	W	D	L	F	A	W	D	L	F	A	W	D	L	F	A	GD	Pts
1 Woking	42	30	7	5	92	41	15	4	2	43	18	15	3	3	49	23	51	97
2 Dartford¶	42	26	10	6	89	40	15	4	2	52	19	11	6	4	37	21	49	88
3 Welling U	42	24	9	9	79	47	14	6	1	42	18	10	3	8	37	29	32	81
4 Sutton U (P)	42	20	14	8	68	53	12	6	3	39	24	8	8	5	29	29	15	74
5 Basingstoke T	42	20	11	11	65	50	10	6	5	35	29	10	5	6	30	21	15	71
6 Chelmsford C	42	18	13	11	67	44	8	5	8	33	25	10	8	3	34	19	23	67
7 Dover Ath	42	17	15	10	62	49	7	8	6	26	24	10	7	4	36	25	13	66
8 Boreham Wood	42	17	10	15	66	58	11	5	5	43	26	6	5	10	23	32	8	61
9 Tonbridge Angels (P)	42	15	12	15	70	67	10	4	7	41	34	5	8	8	29	33	3	57
10 Salisbury C (P)	42	15	12	15	55	54	9	4	8	27	21	6	8	7	28	33	1	57
11 Dorchester T	42	16	8	18	58	65	7	4	10	30	37	9	4	8	28	28	–7	56
12 Eastleigh	42	15	9	18	57	63	10	5	6	36	25	5	4	12	21	38	–6	54
13 Weston Super Mare	42	14	9	19	58	71	8	6	7	34	35	6	3	12	24	36	–13	51
14 Truro C (P)	42	13	9	20	65	80	7	3	11	33	37	6	6	9	32	43	–15	48
15 Staines T	42	12	10	20	53	63	4	6	11	25	39	8	4	9	28	24	–10	46
16 Farnborough	42	15	6	21	52	79	9	0	12	21	32	6	6	9	31	47	–27	46
17 Bromley	42	10	15	17	52	66	4	10	7	23	24	6	5	10	29	42	–14	45
18 Eastbourne Borough (R)	42	12	9	21	54	69	7	4	10	29	33	5	5	11	25	36	–15	45
19 Havant & Waterlooville	42	11	11	20	64	75	7	6	8	39	34	4	5	12	25	41	–11	44
20 Maidenhead U	42	11	10	21	49	74	4	6	11	25	41	7	4	10	24	33	–25	43
21 Hampton & Richmond	42	10	12	20	53	69	3	7	11	22	39	7	5	9	31	30	–16	42
22 Thurrock	42	5	11	26	33	84	2	7	12	13	36	3	4	14	20	48	–51	26

Farnborough deducted 5 points. ¶Dartford promoted via play-offs.

EVO-STIK NORTHERN PREMIER 2011–2012

			Total				Home					Away					
	P	W	D	L	F	A	W	D	L	F	A	W	D	L	F	A	GD	Pts
1 Chester	42	31	7	4	102	29	16	4	1	55	12	15	3	3	47	17	73	100
2 Northwich Victoria	42	26	8	8	73	43	13	4	4	35	19	13	4	4	38	24	30	83
3 Chorley	42	24	7	11	76	48	13	5	3	41	19	11	2	8	35	29	28	79
4 Bradford Park Avenue¶	42	24	6	12	77	49	15	1	5	43	20	9	5	7	34	29	28	78
5 Hednesford T	42	21	10	11	67	49	9	8	4	36	21	12	2	7	31	28	18	73
6 FC United	42	21	9	12	83	51	11	5	5	45	25	10	4	7	38	26	32	72
7 Marine	42	19	9	14	56	50	6	4	11	22	30	13	5	3	34	20	6	66
8 Rushall Olympic	42	17	10	15	52	51	11	5	5	27	21	6	5	10	25	30	1	61
9 North Ferriby U	42	16	10	16	56	70	10	5	6	35	28	6	5	10	21	42	–14	58
10 Nantwich T	42	15	13	14	65	61	10	7	4	33	21	5	6	10	32	40	4	57
11 Kendal T	42	15	8	19	78	83	8	5	8	41	39	7	3	11	37	44	–5	53
12 Ashton U	42	15	8	19	61	67	10	1	10	34	32	5	7	9	27	35	–6	53
13 Buxton	42	15	8	19	64	77	7	3	11	33	45	8	5	8	31	32	–13	53
14 Matlock T	42	12	14	16	52	54	10	5	6	33	21	2	9	10	19	33	–2	50
15 Worksop T	42	13	10	19	56	76	8	4	9	34	39	5	6	10	22	37	–20	49
16 Stafford Rangers (R)	42	12	12	18	60	65	5	9	7	30	29	7	3	11	30	36	–5	48
17 Whitby T	42	12	11	19	57	80	4	8	9	32	43	8	3	10	25	37	–23	46
18 Stocksbridge PS	42	10	12	20	57	75	6	7	8	34	31	4	5	12	23	44	–18	42
19 Frickley Ath	42	10	12	20	48	69	7	4	10	23	27	3	8	10	25	42	–21	42
20 Chasetown	42	10	11	21	50	75	4	6	11	23	36	6	5	10	27	39	–25	41
21 Mickleover Sports	42	11	10	21	67	85	6	4	11	37	42	5	6	10	30	43	–18	40
22 Burscough	42	5	11	26	54	104	1	4	16	27	58	4	7	10	27	46	–50	23

Northwich Victoria deducted 3 points and relegated to Division 1 South. Nantwich T deducted 1 point. Mickleover Sports deducted 3 points. Whitby T deducted 1 point. ¶Bradford Park Avenue promoted via play-offs.

EVO-STIK SOUTHERN PREMIER 2011–2012

			Total				Home					Away					
	P	W	D	L	F	A	W	D	L	F	A	W	D	L	F	A	GD	Pts
1 Brackley T	42	25	10	7	92	48	16	3	2	59	20	9	7	5	33	28	44	85
2 Oxford C¶	42	22	11	9	68	41	12	7	2	37	12	10	4	7	31	29	27	77
3 AFC Totton	42	21	11	10	81	43	13	6	2	46	13	8	5	8	35	30	38	74
4 Chesham U	42	21	10	11	76	53	15	3	3	42	22	6	7	8	34	31	23	73
5 Cambridge C	42	21	9	12	78	52	13	5	3	51	19	8	4	9	27	33	26	72
6 Stourbridge	42	20	12	10	67	45	14	6	1	43	13	6	6	9	24	32	22	72
7 Leamington	42	18	15	9	60	47	13	6	2	38	21	5	9	7	22	26	13	69
8 St Albans C (R)	42	17	11	14	72	77	11	6	4	45	36	6	5	10	27	41	–5	62
9 Barwell	42	17	10	15	70	61	10	6	5	40	31	7	4	10	30	30	9	61
10 Bedford T	42	15	10	17	60	69	7	4	10	30	33	8	6	7	30	36	–9	55
11 Chippenham T	42	14	11	17	55	53	8	4	9	28	23	6	7	8	27	30	2	53
12 Frome T	42	12	16	14	44	49	4	10	7	16	22	8	6	7	28	27	–5	52
13 Bashley	42	13	13	16	58	74	6	9	6	32	33	7	4	10	26	41	–16	52
14 Hitchin T	42	13	12	17	54	57	8	5	8	31	29	5	7	9	23	28	–3	51
15 Redditch U (R)	42	14	9	19	45	50	8	5	8	25	26	6	4	11	20	24	–5	51
16 Banbury U	42	13	10	19	54	61	7	7	7	30	25	6	3	12	24	36	–7	49
17 Weymouth	42	13	9	20	54	75	9	5	7	31	29	4	4	13	23	46	–21	48
18 Arlesey T	42	12	11	19	43	60	6	5	10	20	28	6	6	9	23	32	–17	47
19 Hemel Hempstead T	42	10	14	18	46	66	6	8	7	29	30	4	6	11	17	36	–20	44
20 Evesham U	42	12	8	22	49	71	6	3	12	25	35	6	5	10	24	36	–22	44
21 Swindon Supermarine	42	12	8	22	50	86	6	4	11	25	42	5	7	9	25	44	–36	44
22 Cirencester T	42	7	9	26	40	78	2	4	15	15	36	5	5	11	25	42	–38	30

¶Oxford C promoted via play-offs.

RYMAN PREMIER LEAGUE 2011–2012

	Total						Home					Away						
	P	W	D	L	F	A	W	D	L	F	A	W	D	L	F	A	GD	Pts
1 Billericay T	42	24	13	5	82	38	13	6	2	44	21	11	7	3	38	17	44	85
2 AFC Hornchurch¶	42	26	4	12	68	35	11	4	6	29	13	15	0	6	39	22	33	82
3 Lowestoft T	42	25	7	10	80	53	14	5	2	41	23	11	2	8	39	30	27	82
4 Wealdstone	42	20	15	7	76	39	12	6	3	40	21	8	9	4	36	18	37	75
5 Bury T	42	22	9	11	85	55	12	6	3	42	21	10	3	8	43	34	30	75
6 Lewes (R)	42	21	10	11	55	47	12	6	3	34	23	9	4	8	21	24	8	73
7 Hendon	42	21	9	12	69	44	9	7	5	32	26	12	2	7	37	18	25	72
8 Canvey Island	42	22	5	15	66	55	10	1	10	34	29	12	4	5	32	26	11	71
9 Cray Wanderers	42	20	8	14	74	55	9	4	8	33	31	11	4	6	41	24	19	68
10 East Thurrock U	42	18	8	16	70	65	10	3	8	33	26	8	5	8	37	39	5	62
11 Kingstonian	42	18	7	17	58	64	9	3	9	29	34	9	4	8	29	30	–6	61
12 Metropolitan Police	42	18	6	18	63	46	11	2	8	33	18	7	4	10	30	28	17	60
13 Wingate & Finchley	42	16	11	15	63	79	9	4	8	35	44	7	7	7	28	35	–16	59
14 Concord Rangers	42	16	9	17	72	66	7	6	8	39	34	9	3	9	33	32	6	57
15 Margate	42	15	9	18	66	65	9	3	9	37	29	6	6	9	29	36	1	54
16 Carshalton Ath	42	14	10	18	48	55	7	3	11	22	26	7	7	7	26	29	–7	52
17 Harrow Borough	42	13	8	21	53	70	7	5	9	28	35	6	3	12	25	35	–17	47
18 Hastings U	42	13	8	21	43	61	6	5	10	21	24	7	3	11	22	37	–18	47
19 Leatherhead	42	11	8	23	46	62	6	3	12	21	33	5	5	11	25	29	–16	41
20 Aveley	42	5	12	25	41	88	2	6	13	20	49	3	6	12	21	39	–47	27
21 Tooting & Mitcham	42	7	6	29	47	116	3	4	14	23	58	4	2	15	24	58	–69	27
22 Horsham	42	3	6	33	38	105	1	2	18	18	57	2	4	15	20	48	–67	14

Horsham deducted 1 point. ¶AFC Hornchurch promoted via play-offs.

MACWHIRTER WELSH LEAGUE 2011–2012

	P	W	D	L	F	A	GD	Pts
1 Cambrian & Clydach	30	16	10	4	78	25	53	58
2 Taffs Well	30	16	4	10	60	42	18	52
3 Haverfordwest Co	30	15	7	8	58	43	15	52
4 Bryntirion Ath	30	16	3	11	52	43	9	51
5 AFC Porth	30	13	9	8	54	36	18	48
6 Barry T	30	12	10	8	48	37	11	46
7 Goytre U	30	12	8	10	71	55	16	44
8 Bridgend T	30	13	5	12	50	41	9	44
9 Ton Pentre	30	9	16	5	48	40	8	43
10 Pontardawe T	30	11	9	10	48	53	–5	42
11 West End	30	11	5	14	53	62	–9	38
12 Cwmbran Celtic	30	12	2	16	32	54	–22	38
13 Aberaman Ath	30	8	9	13	46	55	–9	33
14 Cwmaman Institute	30	7	8	15	36	59	–23	29
15 Cardiff Corinthians	30	6	10	14	50	67	–17	28
16 Caerau (Ely)	30	4	3	23	37	109	–72	15

FA PREMIER RESERVE LEAGUE 2011–12

BARCLAYS PREMIER RESERVE LEAGUE NORTH

		P	W	D	L	F	A	GD	Pts
1	Manchester U	22	15	4	3	58	23	35	49
2	Liverpool	22	9	8	5	44	30	14	35
3	Everton	22	9	8	5	38	29	9	35
4	Sunderland	22	9	5	8	38	36	2	32
5	Newcastle U	22	7	4	11	38	58	–20	25
6	Wigan Ath	22	5	9	8	27	37	–10	24
7	Blackburn R	22	4	10	8	18	22	–4	22
8	Bolton W	22	3	8	11	23	40	–17	17

BARCLAYS PREMIER RESERVE LEAGUE SOUTH

		P	W	D	L	F	A	GD	Pts
1	Aston Villa	22	13	4	5	45	22	23	43
2	Fulham	22	12	4	6	46	25	21	40
3	Arsenal	22	11	5	6	36	25	11	38
4	WBA	22	11	2	9	36	31	5	35
5	Chelsea	22	7	7	8	42	43	–1	28
6	Wolverhampton W	22	6	5	11	26	41	–15	23
7	Swansea C	22	4	8	10	21	38	–17	20
8	Norwich C	22	2	7	13	26	62	–36	13

MANCHESTER UNITED – APPEARANCES AND GOALS

Amos 10, Blackett 1+3, Brady 0+1, Brown 6, Cleverley 2, Cofie 0+5, Cole 15, Daehli 0+1, Da Silva F. 3, Da Silva R. 1, De Laet 10, Diouf 6, Drinkwater 1, Fletcher 2, Fornasier 8+6, Fryers 19, Gibson 3, Giverin 0+3, James 5+1, Johnstone 9, Jones 1, Keane M. 21+1, Keane W. 18+3, Kuszczak 2, Leao 0+1, Lindegaard 1, Lingard 15+4, McGinty 6+1, Macheda 4, Massacci 0+3, Morrison 1+2, Norwood 2, Petrucci 18+3, Pogba 16, Smalling 1, Thorpe 6+7, Tunnicliffe 8+2, van Velzen 0+3, Vermijl 17+3, Veseli 1+2, Wilson 0+1, Wootton 3+1.

Goals: Keane W. 15, Diouf 7, Petrucci 7, Lingard 6, Keane M. 4, Cole 3, Pogba 3, De Laet 2, Morrison 2, Brown 1, Fryers 1, Macheda 1, Massacci 1, Smalling 1, Tunnicliffe 1, Vermijl 1, own goals 2.

ASTON VILLA – APPEARANCES AND GOALS

Albrighton 4, Baker 8, Bannan 6, Barrett 4+2, Barton 1+3, Bryan 1, Burke 15, Caira 2+6, Cameron 17+4, Carruthers 15+2, Clark 5, Coleman +1, Cuellar 2, Darkin 1+2, Delfouneso 3, Devine +1, Donacien 10+1, Drennan 6+5, Gardner 9, Graham 2+5, Grealish 4+5, Guzan 2, Herd 5, Hogg 1, Johnson 21, Kinsella 2+2, Lichaj 7, Lowry 7, Melvin 1, Nelson-Addy 6+4, Robinson 8+5, Siegrist B 16, Stevens 10, Taylor 6+4, Ward C +1, Watkins M 1, Webb 10+1, Weimann 6, Williams 19.

Goals: Weimann 9, Drennan 5, Gardner 5, Johnson 5, Robinson 5, Burke 4, Carruthers 4, Bannan 3, Albrighton 1, Delfouneso 1, Lichaj 1, Taylor 1, own goal 1.

PREMIER RESERVE LEAGUE FINAL

Manchester United 0   Aston Villa 0

(at Old Trafford, 10 May 2012, attendance 5130).

Manchester U: Johnstone; Fornasier (Vermijl), Fryers, Thorpe (Brady), Keane M, Wootton, Cole, Tunnicliffe, Keane W, Petrucci (King), Lingard.

Aston Villa: Siegrist; Webb, Stevens, Gardner, Williams, Baker, Carruthers, Grealish (Cameron), Drennan (Graham), Bannan, Johnson.

Manchester U won 3-1 on penalties: Bannan scored; King scored; Carruthers saved; Lingard scored; Johnson saved; Keane W scored; Cameron saved.

FA ACADEMY UNDER-18 LEAGUE 2011–2012

GROUP A	P	W	D	L	F	A	GD	Pts
Fulham	28	18	0	10	73	48	25	54
Southampton	28	15	8	5	59	30	29	53
Arsenal	28	16	4	8	56	37	19	52
Charlton Ath	28	15	5	8	58	32	26	50
West Ham U	28	14	4	10	55	45	10	46
Crystal Palace	28	13	5	10	47	46	1	44
Chelsea	28	11	6	11	52	51	1	39
Norwich C	28	10	3	15	47	53	–6	33
Ipswich T	28	6	7	15	40	58	–18	25
Portsmouth	28	6	6	16	33	60	–27	24

GROUP B	P	W	D	L	F	A	GD	Pts
Leicester C	28	17	6	5	75	50	25	57
Coventry C	28	17	5	6	57	38	19	56
Reading	28	15	9	4	63	36	27	54
Tottenham H	28	13	8	7	71	53	18	47
Aston Villa	28	11	7	10	64	52	12	40
Cardiff C	28	7	6	15	37	52	–15	27
Watford	28	6	8	14	34	56	–22	26
Birmingham C	28	7	4	17	28	55	–27	25
Milton Keynes D	28	4	6	18	49	107	–58	18
Bristol C	28	4	5	19	28	55	–27	17

GROUP C	P	W	D	L	F	A	GD	Pts
Blackburn R	28	17	5	6	57	39	18	56
Manchester C	28	17	3	8	60	41	19	54
Liverpool	28	15	6	7	53	37	16	51
Wolverhampton W	28	15	3	10	60	50	10	48
Everton	28	13	4	11	60	45	15	43
Stoke C	28	12	7	9	45	41	4	43
Bolton W	28	9	5	14	41	48	–7	32
Manchester U	28	8	7	13	48	56	–8	31
Crewe Alex	28	8	5	15	40	60	–20	29
WBA	28	7	4	17	39	63	–24	25

GROUP D	P	W	D	L	F	A	GD	Pts
Newcastle U	28	17	4	7	59	39	20	55
Leeds U	28	16	5	7	60	31	29	53
Derby Co	28	12	6	10	54	45	9	42
Barnsley	28	12	5	11	44	36	8	41
Sheffield U	28	11	6	11	41	45	–4	39
Sunderland	28	11	5	12	50	51	–1	38
Middlesbrough	28	11	4	13	41	54	–13	37
Sheffield W	28	7	5	16	34	59	–25	26
Huddersfield T	28	5	8	15	35	65	–30	23
Nottingham F	28	5	5	18	36	64	–28	20

Academy Play-Off Semi-Finals
Fulham 2, Leicester C 1
Blackburn R 2, Newcastle U 0

Academy Final
Fulham 2, Blackburn 0

THE CENTRAL LEAGUE 2011–12

CENTRAL DIVISION	P	W	D	L	F	A	GD	Pts
Sheffield U	12	6	4	2	25	9	16	22
Derby Co	12	6	3	3	26	16	10	21
Nottingham F	12	5	3	4	24	20	4	18
Port Vale	12	4	3	5	12	21	–9	15
Walsall	12	4	3	5	17	27	–10	15
Burton Alb	12	4	1	7	24	27	–3	13
Stoke C	12	3	3	6	15	23	–8	12

WEST DIVISION	P	W	D	L	F	A	GD	Pts
Preston NE	12	8	1	3	25	12	13	25
Burnley	12	7	2	3	33	19	14	23
Tranmere R	12	6	1	5	27	17	10	19
Morecambe	12	5	2	5	21	26	–5	17
Wrexham	12	3	6	3	23	24	–1	15
Macclesfield T	12	3	1	8	20	40	–20	10
Oldham Ath	12	2	3	7	16	27	–11	9

EAST DIVISION	P	W	D	L	F	A	GD	Pts
Middlesbrough	12	9	1	2	32	15	17	28
Bradford C	12	7	2	3	24	20	4	23
Hull C	12	5	2	5	25	16	9	17
Hartlepool U	12	5	1	6	20	18	2	16
Rotherham U	12	4	2	6	13	20	–7	14
Gateshead	12	4	1	7	14	24	–10	13
Scunthorpe U	12	3	1	8	16	31	–15	10

THE CENTRAL LEAGUE CUP GROUPS

GROUP A	P	W	D	L	F	A	GD	Pts
Manchester C	3	2	0	1	12	4	8	6
Preston NE	3	2	0	1	7	5	2	6
Tranmere R	3	1	0	2	6	8	–2	3
Morecambe	3	1	0	2	5	13	–8	3

GROUP B	P	W	D	L	F	A	GD	Pts
Derby Co	4	3	1	0	10	3	7	10
Stoke C	4	2	2	0	11	4	7	8
Rotherham U	4	2	0	2	7	10	–3	6
Chesterfield	4	1	1	2	5	5	0	4
Port Vale	4	0	0	4	4	15	–11	0

GROUP C	P	W	D	L	F	A	GD	Pts
Sunderland	4	3	1	0	16	3	13	10
Hull C	4	2	1	1	15	9	6	7
Gateshead	4	2	0	2	5	7	–2	6
Hartlepool U	4	1	1	2	10	11	–1	4
Scunthorpe U	4	0	1	3	3	19	–16	1

SEMI-FINALS
Stoke C 1, Manchester C 4
Derby Co 3, Sunderland 2

FINAL
Manchester C v Derby Co
To be played in August.

THE FOOTBALL COMBINATION 2011–12

Northern Section	P	W	D	L	GD	Pts	Southern Section	P	W	D	L	GD	Pts
Colchester U	8	5	0	3	8	15	Forest Green R	10	5	3	2	5	18
Southend U	8	5	0	3	7	15	Brighton & HA	10	5	2	3	2	17
Luton T	8	4	2	2	6	14	Cheltenham T	10	5	0	5	4	15
Stevenage	8	2	2	4	–13	8	AFC Bournemouth	10	4	2	4	1	14
Oxford U	8	1	2	5	–8	5	Crawley T	10	4	1	5	2	13
							Torquay U	10	3	0	7	–14	9

TOTESPORT CUP FINAL 2010–11
Sunderland 3, Walsall 0

WOMEN'S FOOTBALL 2011–12

WOMEN'S LEAGUE TABLES 2011–12

WOMEN'S SUPER LEAGUE 2011

	P	W	D	L	GD	Pts
Arsenal	14	10	2	2	20	32
Birmingham C	14	8	5	1	16	29
Everton	14	7	4	3	6	25
Lincoln	14	6	3	5	2	21
Bristol Academy	14	4	4	6	–6	16
Chelsea	14	4	3	7	–5	15
Doncaster R Belles	14	2	3	9	–17	9
Liverpool	14	1	4	9	–16	7

FA WOMEN'S PREMIER LEAGUE 2011–2012

NATIONAL DIVISION

	P	W	D	L	GD	Pts
Sunderland	18	13	3	2	31	42
Leeds U	18	13	2	3	26	41
Aston Villa	18	7	6	5	3	27
Barnet	18	7	5	6	9	26
Charlton Ath	18	7	5	6	1	26
Coventry C	18	7	5	6	0	26
Watford	18	5	2	11	–23	17
Cardiff C	18	4	4	10	–8	16
Reading	18	5	1	12	–18	16
Nottingham F	18	4	3	11	–21	15

NORTHERN DIVISION

	P	W	D	L	GD	Pts
Manchester C	18	13	1	4	39	40
Sheffield	18	11	2	5	18	35
Leicester C	18	10	4	4	22	34
Blackburn R	18	9	5	4	20	32
Derby Co	18	9	5	4	14	32
Sporting Club Alb	18	8	5	5	13	29
Preston NE	18	7	3	8	0	24
Rochdale AFC	18	4	3	11	–14	15
Rotherham U	18	3	4	11	–19	13
Leeds C Vixens	18	0	0	18	–93	0

SOUTHERN DIVISION

	P	W	D	L	GD	Pts
Portsmouth	18	12	3	3	27	39
Colchester U	18	10	5	3	16	35
West Ham U	18	10	4	4	14	34
Brighton & HA	18	8	3	7	0	27
Gillingham	18	6	5	7	–7	23
Tottenham H	18	6	4	8	–1	22
QPR	18	5	5	8	–9	20
Millwall Lionesses	18	4	5	9	–13	17
Plymouth Arg	18	5	2	11	–19	17
Keynsham T	18	3	6	9	–8	15

WOMEN'S LEAGUE CUP FINAL 2011–2012

Sunday, 6 May 2012

(at Northampton, attendance 641)

Leeds U (0) 1   Sunderland (1) 2

Leeds U: Draycott; Emmonds (Johnson), Sharp, Birkby (Lipman), Sykes, Huegett, Rich (Danby), Galton, Holmes, Turner, Holbrook.
Scorer: Huegett 90 (pen)
Sunderland: Laws; Holmes (Salicki), Greenwell, Furness, Wilson, McDougall, Mead (Ramshaw), Gutteridge, Williams, Devine, Lee.
Scorer: Gutteridge 9, 66
Referee: P. Forrester.

WOMEN'S FA CUP FINAL 2011–2012

Saturday, 26 May 2012

(at Ashton Gate, attendance 8723)

Birmingham C (0) 2   Chelsea (0) 2

Birmingham C: Spencer; Weston, Harrop (Aluko), Bassett, Williams R, Carney, Potter, Moore, Taylor, Unitt, Westwood.
Scorers: Williams R 90, Carney 111.
Chelsea: Telford; Fay (Perry), Bonner, Sherwood, Buet, Lander (Longhurst), Rafferty, Bleazard, Ingle, Susi, Coombs (Spence).
Scorers: Lander 70, Longhurst 101.
aet; Birmingham C won 3-2 on penalties.
Referee: N. Walker.

UEFA WOMEN'S CHAMPIONS LEAGUE 2011–2012

QUALIFYING ROUND

GROUP 1
PAOK 3, CS Goliador 0; Young Boys 3, ZFK Nase 1; PAOK 0, ZFK Nase 1; CS Goliador 0, Young Boys 7; Young Boys 1, PAOK 1; ZFK Nase 6, CS Goliador 0

GROUP 2
MTK 12, Liepajas 0; 1st Dezembro 1, ASA Tel Aviv 1; ASA Tel Aviv 1, MTK 0; 1st Dezembro 4, Liepajas 0; MTK 0, 1 Dezembro 0; Liepajas 1, ASA Tel Aviv 4

GROUP 3
Rayo Vallecano 1, Peamount 0; Krka 1, Parnu 2; Rayo Vallecano 4, Parnu 1; Peamount 7, Krka 0; Krka 0, Rayo Vallecano 4; Parnu 1, Peamount 5

GROUP 4
Gintra 4, Atasehir 1; Sarajevo 1, Olimpia Cluj 3; Olimpia Cluj 5, Gintra 0; Sarajevo 4, Atasehir 1; Gintra 1, Sarajevo 2; Atasehir 1, Olimpia Cluj 4

GROUP 5
Klaksvik 1, Mosta 0; Glasgow City 4, Spartak 0; Glasgow City 8, Mosta 0; Spartak 4, Klaksvik 2; Klaksvik 0, Glasgow City 5; Mosta 0, Spartak 11

GROUP 6
Unia Raciborz 0, Slovan Bratislava 1; PK-35 10, Ada 0; Slovan Bratislava 0, PK-35 1; Unia Raciborz 8, Ada 0; PK-35 1, Unia Raciborz 1; Ada 0, Slovan Bratislava 16

GROUP 7
Legenda Chernigiv 2, Swansea 0; Apollon 14, Progres 0; Legenda Chernigiv 8, Progres 0; Swansea 0, Apollon 8; Apollon 1, Legenda Chernigiv 1; Progres 0, Swansea 4

GROUP 8
Bobruichanka 7, Crusaders 0; NSA Sofia 1, Osijek 1; NSA Sofia 1, Crusaders 0; Osijek 1, Bobruichanka 0; Bobruichanka 3, NSA Sofia 0; Crusaders 1, Osijek 5

FIRST ROUND FIRST LEG
Standard 0, Brondby 2; ASA Tel Aviv 0, Torres 2; CSHVSM 2, Neulengbach 1; Olimpia Cluj 0, Lyon 9; Apollon 2, Sparta Prague 1; PK-35 1, Rayo Vallecano 4; Osijek 0, Gothenburg 4; Thor 0, Potsdam 6; Twente 0, Rossiyanka 2; Stabaek 1, Frankfurt 0; Young Boys 0, Fortuna 3; Peamount 0, Paris St Germain 2; Bobruichanka 0, Arsenal 4; Bristol Academy 1, Voronezh 1; Glasgow City 1, Valur 1; Tavagnacco 2, Malmo 1

FIRST ROUND SECOND LEG
Torres 3, ASA Tel Aviv 2; Frankfurt 4, Stabaek 1; Sparta Prague 2, Apollon 1; Paris St Germain 3, Peamount 0; Voronezh 4, Bristol Academy 2; Arsenal 6, Bobruichanka 0; Lyon 3, Olimpia Cluj 0; Fortuna 2, Young Boys 1; Potsdam 8, Thor 2; Neulengbach 5, CSHVSM 0; Rossiyanka 1, Twente 0; Valur 0, Glasgow City 3; Brondby 3, Standard 4; Rayo Vallecano 3, PK-35 0; Malmo 5, Tavagnacco 0; Gothenburg 7, Osijek 0

SECOND ROUND FIRST LEG
Frankfurt 3, Paris St Germain 0; Potsdam 10, Glasgow City 0; Brondby 2, Torres 1; Neulengbach 1, Malmo 3; Fortuna 0, Gothenburg 1; Sparta Prague 0, Lyon 6; Voronezh 0, Rossiyanka 4; Rayo Vallecano 1, Arsenal 1

SECOND ROUND SECOND LEG
Malmo 1, Neulengbach 0; Gothenburg 3, Fortuna 2; Glasgow City 0, Potsdam 7; Arsenal 5, Rayo Vallecano 1; Rossiyanka 3, Voronezh 3; Lyon 6, Sparta Prague 0; Torres 1, Brondby 3; Paris St Germain 2, Frankfurt 1

QUARTER-FINALS FIRST LEG
Arsenal 3, Gothenburg 1; Potsdam 2, Rossiyanka 0; Lyon 4, Brondby 0; Malmo 1, Frankfurt 0

QUARTER-FINALS SECOND LEG
Gothenburg 1, Arsenal 0; Rossiyanka 0, Potsdam 3; Brondby 0, Lyon 4; Frankurt 3, Malmo 0

SEMI-FINALS FIRST LEG
Arsenal 1, Frankfurt 2
Lyon 5, Potsdam 1

SEMI-FINALS SECOND LEG
Frankfurt 2, Arsenal 0
Potsdam 0, Lyon 0

FINAL

17 May (in Munich).

Lyon (2) 2 *(Le Sommer 15 (pen), Abily 28)*

Frankfurt (0) 0　　　　　　　　50,212

Lyon: Bouhaddi; Renard, Henry, Schelin (Ötaki 88), Le Sommer (Rosana 65), Necib (Dickenmann 49), Cruz Trana, Franco, Bompastor, Viguier, Abily.
Frankfurt: Schumann; Lewandowski, Kumagai, Thunebro, Behringer, Marozsan, Weber (Percival 61), Huth (Crnogorcevic 64), Garefrekas, Bartusiak, Simsek (Landstrom 83).
Referee: Palmqvist (Sweden).

ENGLAND WOMEN'S INTERNATIONAL MATCHES 2011–2012

EUROPEAN CHAMPIONSHIP

17 Sept *(in Omladinski).*
Serbia 2 *(Podovac 55, Smiljkovic 90)*   **England 2** *(Yankey 6, Slovic 19 (og))*
England: Brown; Susi, Unitt, Scott J, Bradley, Stoney, White E, Bassett, Dowie (Williams R 46), Carney, Yankey.

22 Sept *(at Swindon).*
England 4 *(Yankey 1, White E 5, Houghton 56, Williams R 87)*   **Slovenia 0**   3878
England: Bardsley; Scott A, Unitt, Houghton, Bradley (Whelan 76), Stoney, Clarke (Buet 90), Williams F, White E, Carney, Yankey (Williams R 81).

27 Oct *(in Zwolle).*
Holland 0   England 0   8850
England: Bardsley; Scott A, Unitt, Scott J, Bradley, Stoney, Clarke (Houghton 46), Williams F, White E, Carney, Yankey.

23 Nov*(at Doncaster).*
England 2 *(Clarke 41, White E 51)*   **Serbia 0**   4112
England: Bardsley; Scott A, Unitt, Scott J, Bradley, Stoney, Clarke, Williams F (Houghton 77), White E (Williams R 87), Carney, Yankey (Smith K 70).

31 Mar *(in Vrbovec).*
England 6 *(Williams R 4, Clarke 15, Unitt 18, White E 35, Houghton 45, 68)*   **Croatia 0**
England: Bardsley; Scott A, Unitt, Scott J, Bassett, Houghton, White E (Aluko 62), Williams F (Moore 46), Williams R, Carney (Asante 46), Clarke.

17 June *(at Salford City Stadium).*
England 1 *(Yankey 67)*   **Holland 0**   5505
England: Brown; Scott A, Houghton, Scott J, Bradley, Stoney, Aluko, Williams F, Williams R (White E 46), Carney (Asante 72).

21 June *(at Velenje).*
Slovenia 0
England 4 *(Scott J 29, 43, Carney 54, Williams R 85)*   200
England: Brown; Scott A, Bradley, Stoney, Houghton (Rafferty 61), Scott J, Asante, Aluko, Williams F (Williams R 70), Yankey, White E (Carney 46).

CYPRUS CUP

28 Feb*(in Larnaca).*
England 2 *(Smith K 35 (pen), 88 (pen), Carney 50)*   **Finland 1** *(Kukkonen 7)*
England: Chamberlain; Scott A, Stoney, Carney, Williams F, White E (Williams R 71), Smith K, Bassett, Houghton, Moore, Smith S (Clarke 83).

1 Mar *(in Larnaca).*
England 1 *(Williams F 75)*   **Switzerland 0**
England: Brown (Chamberlain 64); Unitt, Scott J, Bradley (Houghton 32), Carney (White E 64), Williams F, Clarke, Williams R, Susi, Smith S (Moore 64), Whelan (Stoney 16).

4 Mar *(in Larnaca).*
France 3 *Necib 11, Delie 49, Thiney 80)*   **England 0**
England: Bardsley; Scott A, Scott J, Stoney, Carney, White E, Smith K (Williams R 57), Clarke (Telford 72), Bassett, Houghton, Asante (Williams F 46).

6 Mar
Italy 3 *(Panico 59, Conti 64, Gabbiadini 86)*   **England 1** *(Moore 25)*
(in Larnaca).
England: Brown (Chamberlain 60); Scott A, Unitt, Stoney, Williams F, Williams R (White E 59), Susi (Carney 69), Bassett, Houghton (Scott J 46), Moore, Smith S.

FIFA 2011 WOMEN'S WORLD CUP

FINALS IN GERMANY
Competition completed from last year.

QUARTER-FINALS
England 1, France 1 – *France won 4-3 on penalties;* Germany 0, Japan 1; Sweden 3, Australia 1; Brazil 2, USA 2 – *USA won 5-3 on penalties.*

SEMI-FINALS
France 1, USA 3; Japan 3, Sweden 1

MATCH FOR THIRD PLACE
Sweden 2, France 1

FINAL
Japan 2, USA 2
Japan won 3-1 on penalties.

WOMEN'S EURO 2011–2013

PRELIMINARY ROUND

GROUP 1
Lithuania 1, Macedonia 1; Luxembourg 2, Latvia 0; Luxembourg 1, Macedonia 5; Latvia 1, Lithuania 0; Lithuania 4, Luxembourg 1; Macedonia 1, Latvia 0

GROUP 2
Georgia 0, Malta 1; Faeroes 2, Armenia 1; Armenia 0, Georgia 0; Faeroes 2, Malta 0; Malta 1, Armenia 1; Georgia 1, Faeroes 0

GROUP STAGE

GROUP 1
Bosnia 0, Italy 1; Poland 0, Russia 2 – *Russia awarded 3-0 victory by default;* Russia 4, Bosnia 1; Macedonia 0, Italy 9; Poland 2, Greece 0; Macedonia 1, Greece 1; Italy 2, Russia 0; Poland 4, Bosnia 0; Macedonia 2, Bosnia 6; Greece 0, Russia 4; Poland 0, Italy 5; Macedonia 0, Poland 3; Italy 2, Greece 0; Greece 2, Bosnia 3; Russia 8, Macedonia 0; Greece 1, Poland 1; Italy 4, Bosnia 0; Russia 0, Italy 2; Greece 2, Macedonia 2; Italy 9, Macedonia 0; Russia 4, Greece 0; Bosnia 0, Poland 2; Poland 4, Macedonia 0; Bosnia 0, Russia 1

GROUP 2
Kazakhstan 0, Romania 3; Germany 4, Switzerland 1; Turkey 1, Spain 10; Switzerland 4, Romania 1; Kazakhstan 2, Turkey 0; Turkey 0, Kazakhstan 0; Romania 0, Germany 3; Spain 3, Switzerland 2; Kazakhstan 0, Spain 4; Romania 7, Turkey 1; Germany 17, Kazakhstan 0; Romania 0, Spain 4; Turkey 1, Romania 2; Switzerland 8, Kazakhstan 0; Spain 2, Germany 2; Turkey 0, Germany 5; Romania 3, Kazakhstan 0; Germany 5, Spain 0; Switzerland 5, Turkey 0; Spain 13, Kazakhstan 0; Switzerland 0, Germany 6; Germany 5, Romania 0; Switzerland 4, Spain 3; Spain 4, Turkey 0; Romania 4, Switzerland 2

GROUP 3
Iceland 6, Bulgaria 0; Belgium 2, Hungary 1; Iceland 3, Norway 1; Norway 6, Hungary 0; Iceland 0, Belgium 0; Hungary 0, Iceland 1; Bulgaria 0, Northern Ireland 1; Belgium 1, Norway 1; Northern Ireland 0, Iceland 2; Bulgaria 0, Hungary 4; Belgium 5, Bulgaria 0; Northern Ireland 3, Norway 1; Bulgaria 0, Belgium 1; Hungary 2, Northern Ireland 2; Belgium 2, Northern Ireland 2; Bulgaria 0, Norway 3; Hungary 0, Norway 5; Belgium 1, Iceland 0; Northern Ireland 0, Hungary 1; Northern Ireland 4, Bulgaria 1; Norway 11, Bulgaria 0; Iceland 3, Hungary 0; Hungary 1, Belgium 3; Norway 2, Northern Ireland 0; Bulgaria 0, Iceland 10

GROUP 4
Israel 0, France 5; Wales 0, Republic of Ireland 2; Republic of Ireland 1, France 3; Israel 1, Scotland 6; Republic of Ireland 2, Israel 0; Wales 1, France 4; France 5, Israel 0; Scotland 2, Wales 2; Israel 0, Wales 2; France 2, Scotland 0; France 4, Wales 0; Scotland 2, Republic of Ireland 1; Scotland 8, Israel 0; Republic of Ireland 0, Wales 1; Wales 5, Israel 0; Republic of Ireland 0, Scotland 1

GROUP 5
Belarus 2, Estonia 1; Estonia 1, Ukraine 4; Ukraine 0, Slovakia 0; Finland 6, Estonia 0; Slovakia 3, Estonia 1; Belarus 2, Finland 2; Slovakia 3, Belarus 0; Ukraine 0, Belarus 1; Slovakia 0, Finland 1; Ukraine 5, Estonia 0; Finland 2, Slovakia 0; Estonia 2, Belarus 4; Ukraine 1, Finland 2; Finland 4, Belarus 0; Slovakia 0, Ukraine 2

GROUP 6
Serbia 2, England 2; Holland 6, Serbia 0; England 4, Slovenia 0; Croatia 0, Holland 3; Slovenia 1, Serbia 2; Croatia 3, Slovenia 3; Holland 0, England 0; Serbia 4, Croatia 2; Slovenia 0, Holland 2; England 2, Serbia 0; Holland 2, Croatia 0; Croatia 0, England 6; Holland 3, Slovenia 1; Croatia 1, Serbia 4; England 1, Holland 0; Serbia 0, Holland 4; Slovenia 0, England 4

GROUP 7
Armenia 0, Portugal 8; Austria 1, Czech Republic 1; Armenia 0, Denmark 5; Czech Republic 1, Portugal 0; Denmark 3, Austria 0; Austria 3, Armenia 0; Portugal 0, Denmark 3; Portugal 0, Austria 1; Czech Republic 5, Armenia 0; Denmark 11, Armenia 0; Portugal 6, Armenia 0; Portugal 2, Czech Republic 5; Armenia 2, Austria 4; Czech Republic 0, Denmark 2; Austria 1, Portugal 0; Czech Republic 2, Austria 3; Denmark 1, Czech Republic 0
Competition still being played.

351

THE FA TROPHY 2011–2012

FINAL (at Wembley) – Saturday, 12 May 2012
Newport Co (0) 0
York C (0) 2 *(Blair 65, Oyebanjo 72)*   19,844
Newport Co: Thompson; Hughes, Pipe, Minshull, Warren, Yakubu, Foley, Jarvis (Harris), Evans, Porter (Knights), Rose R (Buchanan).
York C: Ingham; Oyebanjo, Meredith, Smith C, Parslow, McLaughlin (Fyfield), Walker (Reed), Gibson, Blair, Chambers (Moke), Challinor.
Referee: G. Mills.

THE FA VASE 2011–2012

FINAL (at Wembley) – Sunday, 13 May 2012
Dunston UTS (0) 2 *(Bulford 33, 79)*
West Auckland T (0) 0   5126
Dunston UTS: Connell; Cattanach, Galbraith, Robson, Swailes, Young, Shaw, Dixon, Goddard (Preen), Bulford (Craggs), McAndrew.
West Auckland T: Bell; Pattinson, Green, Gibson, Parker, Stephenson (Hindmarsh), Banks, Hudson, Moffat, Rae, Nicholls (Young).
Referee: P. Dixon.

THE FA YOUTH CUP 2011–2012

FINAL FIRST LEG – Friday, 20 April 2012
Chelsea (2) 4 *(Chalobah 20, Baker 28, Feruz 60, 69)*
Blackburn R (0) 0   3142
Chelsea: Blackman; Kane, Davey, Ake, Nditi, Chalobah, Affane (Kiwomya 53), Swift, Feruz (Mitchell 78), Baker, Piazon.
Blackburn R: Unwin; Wylie (Lenihan 61), Beesley, Hands (Cotton 61), Edwards, O'Connell, Osaye, Hanley R, Haley (Payne 82), O'Sullivan, Fernandez.

FINAL SECOND LEG – Wednesday, 9 May 2012
Blackburn R (1) 1 *(Payne 25)*
Chelsea (0) 0   1490
Blackburn R: Urwin; Daly, Edwards, O'Connell, Wylie, Mason (Laverty), Cotton (Boland), Hanley R, Hernandez, Payne (Haley), O'Sullivan.
Chelsea: Blackman; Kane, Davey, Nkumu (Loftus-Cheek), Gordon (Nditi), Swift, Chalobah, Baker, Affane (Kiwomya), Feruz, Piazon.

THE FA SUNDAY CUP 2011–2012

FINAL (at Sunderland) – Sunday, 29 April 2012
Hetton Lyons CC (2) 5 *(Byrne 4, 19, Moore 52, Capper 60, Craggs 90)*
Canada (0) 1 *(Fargan 70)*
Hetton Lyons CC: Finch; Griffiths, Hunter, Price, Moore, Capper, Graydon (Ellison), Walton, Davison, Byrne (Davis), Watson (Craggs).
Canada: Brookfield; Wardle, O'Rourke, McNabb, Fargan, Downey (Hanley), O'Brien, Riley, Tames, Furlong (Williams A), Williams G (Davies).

THE FA COUNTY YOUTH CUP 2011–2012

FINAL (at Colchester) – Sunday, 22 April 2012
Essex (2) 4 *(Sartain 3, Walshe 5, Ibe 93, 119)*
West Riding (1) 2 *(Eastwood 9, Jackson 61)*   586
Essex: Pitman; Shepherd, Hall, Bertram-Cooper, Vickers, Levett, Sartain (Miller 108), Richardson (Ibe 63), Jones, Walshe, Norris.
West Riding: Hagreen; Swales, Bolton, Eastwood (McGurk 98), Webster, Hall (McPhee 87), Robson, Robinson, Harris, Brownlee (Feather 63), Jackson.
(aet.)
Referee: T. Robinson (Sussex).

FOOTBALL TITLES FOR YOUR LIBRARY

THE MEN WHO NEVER WERE by Jack Rollin & Tony Brown
The expunged Football League season of 1939–40.
ISBN 978-1-905891-11-5. £12.

THE FORGOTTEN CUP by Jack Rollin & Tony Brown
The FA Cup competition of 1945–46.
ISBN 978-1-899468-86-7. £10.

SUNK WITHOUT TRACE: THE CHINGFORD TOWN STORY
by Jack Rollin. An account of the brief rise and fall of the club
in the Southern League from 1947 to 1950.
ISBN 978-1-905891-46-7. £8.

THE ARMY GAME by Jack Rollin
A history of the Army FA, to be published during 2012–13.
ISBN 978-1-905891-65-8.
Also by Jack, a definitive account of football in the 1930s, to
complement his 1940s "Soccer at War".
Please see www.soccerdata.com for publication dates.

WIGAN BOROUGH IN THE FOOTBALL LEAGUE
by Garth Dykes. Full match details and a comprehensive who's
who of the club's players during their time in the League.
ISBN 978-1-905891-53-5. £12.

THE FA SOURCE BOOK 1863–1883 by Tony Brown
A year-by-year account of changes to the laws of the game and
lists of the clubs in membership.
ISBN 978-1-905891-52-8. £14.

FOOTBALL LEAGUE PLAYERS' RECORDS 1888–1939
by Michael Joyce. Career details of all Football League players
during this period.
Third edition ISBN 978-1-905891-61-0.
Also published in 2012, a new edition of Barry Hugman's post-
war players' records, now in two volumes 1946–1992 and 1993–
2012.
Details on www.soccerdata.com.

THE FOOTBALL LEAGUE MATCH BY MATCH 1888–1970
A set of 55 volumes giving detailed results, scorers and line-up
grids for all Football League seasons from 1888/89 to 1969/70.
£12 per volume, £500 for the set.

THE NATIONAL FOOTBALL ARCHIVE
2012 sees the launch of a new website with every match line-up
of Football League and Premier League clubs, in league and
cups, from 1888 to date. Every player is fully indexed so that his
complete career details can be seen. The database contains
more than 40,000 players, 400,000 team line-ups and 600,000
goal scorers. www.enfa.co.uk.

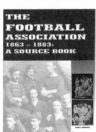

Please send orders for books to Tony Brown, 4 Adrian Close,
Toton, Nottingham NG9 6FL.
10% of the value of your order (to a maximum of £4) will be a
welcome contribution to postage costs. Please make cheques
payable to Tony Brown or use Paypal.

NATIONAL LIST OF REFEREES FOR SEASON 2012–2013

ADCOCK, JG (James) Nottinghamshire
ATKINSON, M (Martin) West Yorkshire
ATTWELL, SB (Stuart) Warwickshire
BATES, A (Tony) Staffordshire
BERRY, CJ (Carl) Surrey
BOND, DS (Darren) Lancashire
BOOTH, R (Russell) Nottinghamshire
BOYESON, C (Carl) East Yorkshire
BRATT, SJ (Steve) West Midlands
BROWN, M (Mark) East Yorkshire
CLATTENBURG, M (Mark) County Durham
CLARK, RM (Richard) Northumberland
COLLINS, LM (Lee) Surrey
COOTE, D (David) Nottinghamshire
DAVIES, A (Andy) Hampshire
DEADMAN, D (Darren) Cambridgeshire
DEAN, ML (Mike) Wirral
DOWD, P (Phil) Staffordshire
DRYSDALE, D (Darren) Lincolnshire
DUNCAN, SAJ (Scott) Newcastle-upon-Tyne
D'URSO, AP (Andy) Essex
EAST, R (Roger) Wiltshire
ELTRINGHAM, G (Geoff) Tyne & Wear
FOY, CJ (Chris) Merseyside
FRIEND, KA (Kevin) Leicestershire
GIBBS, PN (Phil) West Midlands
GRAHAM F (Fred) Essex
HAINES, A (Andy) Tyne & Wear
HALSEY, MR (Mark) Lancashire
HARRINGTON, T (Tony) Cleveland
HAYWOOD, M (Mark) West Yorkshire
HEYWOOD, M (Mark) Cheshire
HOOPER, SA (Simon) Wiltshire
ILDERTON, EL (Eddie) Tyne & Wear
JONES, MJ (Michael) Cheshire
KETTLE, TM (Trevor) Rutland
LANGFORD, O (Oliver) West Midlands
LEWIS, RL (Rob) Shropshire
LININGTON, JJ (James) Isle of Wight
MADLEY, AJ (Andy) West Yorkshire

MADLEY, RJ (Bobby) West Yorkshire
MALONE, BJ (Brendan) Wiltshire
MARRINER, AM (André) West Midlands
MARTIN, SJ (Stephen) Staffordshire
MASON, LS (Lee) Lancashire
MATHIESON, SW (Scott) Cheshire
MILLER, NS (Nigel) County Durham
MILLER, P (Pat) Bedfordshire
MOHAREB, D (Dean) Cheshire
MOSS, J (Jon) West Yorkshire
NAYLOR, MA (Michael) South Yorkshire
OLIVER, M (Michael) Northumberland
PAWSON, CL (Craig) South Yorkshire
PHILLIPS, DJ (David) West Sussex
PROBERT, LW (Lee) Wiltshire
ROBINSON, TJ (Tim) West Sussex
RUSHTON, SJ (Steve) Staffordshire
RUSSELL, MP (Mick) Hertfordshire
SALISBURY, G (Graham) Lancashire
SARGINSON, CD (Chris) Staffordshire
SCOTT, GD (Graham) Oxfordshire
SHELDRAKE, D (Darren) Surrey
SHOEBRIDGE, RL (Rob) Derbyshire
SIMPSON, J (Jeremy) Lancashire
STROUD, KP (Keith) Hampshire
SUTTON, GJ (Gary) Lincolnshire
SWARBRICK, ND (Neil) Lancashire
TANNER, SJ, (Steve) Somerset
TAYLOR, A (Anthony) Cheshire
TIERNEY, P Paul) Lancashire
WARD, GL (Gavin) Surrey
WAUGH, J (Jock) South Yorkshire
WEBB, D (David) County Durham
WEBB, HM (Howard) South Yorkshire
WHITESTONE, D (Dean) Northamptonshire
WILLIAMSON, IG, (Iain) Berkshire
WOOLMER, KA (Andy) Northamptonshire
WRIGHT, KK (Kevin) Cambridgeshire

ENGLISH LEAGUE FIXTURES 2012–2013

Sky Sports   †ESPN   All fixtures subject to change.

Friday, 17 August 2012
npower Football League Championship
Cardiff C v Huddersfield T* (7.45)

Saturday, 18 August 2012
Barclays Premier League
Arsenal v Sunderland
Fulham v Norwich C
Newcastle U v Tottenham H† (5.30)
QPR v Swansea C
Reading v Stoke C
WBA v Liverpool
West Ham U v Aston Villa

npower Football League Championship
Barnsley v Middlesbrough
Birmingham C v Charlton Ath
Burnley v Bolton W
Crystal Palace v Watford
Derby Co v Sheffield W
Hull C v Brighton & HA
Ipswich T v Blackburn R
Leeds U v Wolverhampton W* (12.45)
Leicester C v Peterborough U
Millwall v Blackpool
Nottingham F v Bristol C

npower Football League One
Bury v Brentford
Crawley T v Scunthorpe U
Crewe Alex v Notts Co
Hartlepool U v Swindon T
Milton Keynes D v Oldham Ath
Portsmouth v Bournemouth
Preston NE v Colchester U
Sheffield U v Shrewsbury T
Stevenage v Carlisle U
Tranmere v Leyton Orient
Walsall v Doncaster R
Yeovil T v Coventry C

npower Football League Two
AFC Wimbledon v Chesterfield
Bristol R v Oxford U
Cheltenham T v Dagenham & R
Exeter C v Morecambe
Fleetwood T v Torquay U

Gillingham v Bradford C
Plymouth Arg v Aldershot T
Port Vale v Barnet
Rochdale v Northampton T
Rotherham U v Burton Alb
Southend U v Accrington S
York C v Wycombe W

Sunday, 19 August 2012
Barclays Premier League
Wigan Ath v Chelsea* (1.30)
Manchester C v Southampton* (4.00)

Monday, 20 August 2012
Barclays Premier League
Everton v Manchester U* (8.00)

Tuesday, 21 August 2012
npower Football League Championship
Blackpool v Leeds U
Bolton W v Derby Co
Brighton & HA v Cardiff C
Bristol C v Crystal Palace
Charlton Ath v Leicester C
Huddersfield T v Nottingham F
Middlesbrough v Burnley
Peterborough U v Millwall
Sheffield W v Birmingham C
Watford v Ipswich T
Wolverhampton W v Barnsley

npower Football League One
Bournemouth v Milton Keynes D
Brentford v Yeovil T
Carlisle U v Tranmere
Colchester U v Portsmouth
Coventry C v Sheffield U
Doncaster R v Bury
Leyton Orient v Stevenage
Notts Co v Hartlepool U
Oldham Ath v Walsall
Scunthorpe U v Crewe Alex
Shrewsbury T v Preston NE
Swindon T v Crawley T

npower Football League Two
Accrington S v Port Vale
Aldershot T v Exeter C

Barnet v Bristol R
Bradford C v Fleetwood T
Burton Alb v AFC Wimbledon
Chesterfield v Rochdale
Dagenham & R v Plymouth Arg
Morecambe v York C
Northampton T v Rotherham U
Oxford U v Southend U
Torquay U v Cheltenham T
Wycombe W v Gillingham

Wednesday, 22 August 2012
npower Football League Championship
Blackburn R v Hull C

Friday, 24 August 2012
npower Football League Championship
Bolton W v Nottingham F* (7.45)

Saturday, 25 August 2012
Barclays Premier League
Aston Villa v Everton
Chelsea v Newcastle U† (5.30)
Manchester U v Fulham
Norwich C v QPR
Southampton v Wigan Ath
Sunderland v Reading
Swansea C v West Ham U* (12.45)
Tottenham H v WBA

npower Football League Championship
Blackburn R v Leicester C
Blackpool v Ipswich T
Brighton & HA v Barnsley
Bristol C v Cardiff C
Charlton Ath v Hull C
Huddersfield T v Burnley
Middlesbrough v Crystal Palace
Peterborough U v Leeds U
Sheffield W v Millwall
Watford v Birmingham C
Wolverhampton W v Derby Co

npower Football League One
Bournemouth v Preston NE
Brentford v Crewe Alex
Carlisle U v Portsmouth
Colchester U v Sheffield U
Coventry C v Bury
Doncaster R v Crawley T
Leyton Orient v Hartlepool U
Notts Co v Walsall
Oldham Ath v Stevenage
Scunthorpe U v Yeovil T
Shrewsbury T v Tranmere
Swindon T v Milton Keynes D

npower Football League Two
Accrington S v Exeter C
Aldershot T v Cheltenham T
Barnet v York C
Bradford C v AFC Wimbledon
Burton Alb v Fleetwood T
Chesterfield v Rotherham U
Dagenham & R v Gillingham

Morecambe v Port Vale
Northampton T v Southend U
Oxford U v Plymouth Arg
Torquay U v Rochdale
Wycombe W v Bristol R

Sunday, 26 August 2012
Barclays Premier League
Stoke C v Arsenal* (1.30)
Liverpool v Manchester C* (4.00)

Saturday, 1 September 2012
Barclays Premier League
Chelsea v Reading
Manchester C v QPR† (5.30)
Newcastle U v Aston Villa
Swansea C v Sunderland
Tottenham H v Norwich C
WBA v Everton
West Ham U v Fulham* (12.45)
Wigan Ath v Stoke C

npower Football League Championship
Barnsley v Bristol C
Birmingham C v Peterborough U
Burnley v Brighton & HA
Cardiff C v Wolverhampton W
Crystal Palace v Sheffield W
Derby Co v Watford
Hull C v Bolton W
Ipswich T v Huddersfield T
Leeds U v Blackburn R
Leicester C v Blackpool
Millwall v Middlesbrough
Nottingham F v Charlton Ath

npower Football League One
Bury v Notts Co
Crawley T v Leyton Orient
Crewe Alex v Coventry C
Hartlepool U v Scunthorpe U
Milton Keynes D v Carlisle U
Portsmouth v Oldham Ath
Preston NE v Swindon T
Sheffield U v Bournemouth
Stevenage v Shrewsbury T
Tranmere v Colchester U
Walsall v Brentford
Yeovil T v Doncaster R

npower Football League Two
AFC Wimbledon v Dagenham & R
Bristol R v Morecambe
Cheltenham T v Accrington S
Exeter C v Burton Alb
Fleetwood T v Aldershot T
Gillingham v Chesterfield
Plymouth Arg v Northampton T
Port Vale v Torquay U
Rochdale v Barnet
Rotherham U v Bradford C
Southend U v Wycombe W
York C v Oxford U

Sunday, 2 September 2012
Barclays Premier League
Liverpool v Arsenal* (1.30)
Southampton v Manchester U* (4.00)

Saturday, 8 September 2012
npower Football League One
Brentford v Colchester U
Bury v Preston NE
Crewe Alex v Tranmere
Doncaster R v Oldham Ath
Hartlepool U v Carlisle U
Notts Co v Shrewsbury T
Scunthorpe U v Sheffield U
Swindon T v Leyton Orient
Walsall v Milton Keynes D
Yeovil T v Bournemouth

npower Football League Two
Accrington S v Bradford C
Barnet v Gillingham
Bristol R v Aldershot T
Morecambe v Fleetwood T
Northampton T v AFC Wimbledon
Oxford U v Exeter C
Port Vale v Rotherham U
Rochdale v Burton Alb
Southend U v Dagenham & R
Torquay U v Plymouth Arg
Wycombe W v Cheltenham T
York C v Chesterfield

Sunday, 9 September 2012
Barclays Premier League
Coventry C v Stevenage* (1.15)
Crawley T v Portsmouth* (3.30)

Friday, 14 September 2012
npower Football League Championship
Charlton Ath v Crystal Palace* (7.45)

Saturday, 15 September 2012
Barclays Premier League
Arsenal v Southampton
Aston Villa v Swansea C
Fulham v WBA
Manchester U v Wigan Ath
Norwich C v West Ham U* (12.45)
QPR v Chelsea
Stoke C v Manchester C
Sunderland v Liverpool† (5.30)

npower Football League Championship
Barnsley v Blackpool
Bolton W v Watford
Brighton & HA v Sheffield W
Bristol C v Blackburn R
Burnley v Peterborough U
Cardiff C v Leeds U
Huddersfield T v Derby Co
Hull C v Millwall
Middlesbrough v Ipswich T
Nottingham F v Birmingham C
Wolverhampton W v Leicester C

npower Football League One
Bournemouth v Hartlepool U
Carlisle U v Swindon T
Colchester U v Doncaster R
Leyton Orient v Brentford
Milton Keynes D v Yeovil T
Oldham Ath v Notts Co
Portsmouth v Walsall
Preston NE v Crawley T
Sheffield U v Bury
Shrewsbury T v Scunthorpe U
Stevenage v Crewe Alex
Tranmere v Coventry C

npower Football League Two
AFC Wimbledon v Rochdale
Aldershot T v Morecambe
Bradford C v Barnet
Burton Alb v Oxford U
Cheltenham T v Southend U
Chesterfield v Wycombe W
Dagenham & R v Accrington S
Exeter C v York C
Fleetwood T v Northampton T
Gillingham v Bristol R
Plymouth Arg v Port Vale
Rotherham U v Torquay U

Sunday, 16 September 2012
Barclays Premier League
Reading v Tottenham H* (4.00)

Monday, 17 September 2012
Barclays Premier League
Everton v Newcastle U* (8.00)

Tuesday, 18 September 2012
npower Football League Championship
Birmingham C v Bolton W
Blackpool v Middlesbrough
Crystal Palace v Nottingham F
Derby Co v Charlton Ath
Ipswich T v Wolverhampton W
Leeds U v Hull C
Leicester C v Burnley
Millwall v Cardiff C
Peterborough U v Bristol C
Sheffield W v Huddersfield T
Watford v Brighton & HA

npower Football League One
Bournemouth v Brentford
Carlisle U v Crewe Alex
Colchester U v Crawley T
Leyton Orient v Yeovil T
Milton Keynes D v Notts Co
Oldham Ath v Scunthorpe U
Portsmouth v Swindon T
Preston NE v Hartlepool U
Sheffield U v Doncaster R
Shrewsbury T v Coventry C
Stevenage v Walsall
Tranmere v Bury

npower Football League Two
AFC Wimbledon v Torquay U
Aldershot T v Barnet
Bradford C v Morecambe
Burton Alb v York C
Cheltenham T v Oxford U
Chesterfield v Accrington S
Dagenham & R v Northampton T
Exeter C v Wycombe W
Fleetwood T v Port Vale
Gillingham v Southend U
Plymouth Arg v Bristol R
Rotherham U v Rochdale

Wednesday, 19 September 2012
npower Football League Championship
Blackburn R v Barnsley

Friday, 21 September 2012
npower Football League Championship
Blackburn R v Middlesbrough* (7.45)

Saturday, 22 September 2012
Barclays Premier League
Chelsea v Stoke C
Newcastle U v Norwich C
Southampton v Aston Villa
Swansea C v Everton* (12.45)
Tottenham H v QPR
WBA v Reading
West Ham U v Sunderland
Wigan Ath v Fulham

npower Football League Championship
Birmingham C v Barnsley
Blackpool v Huddersfield T
Crystal Palace v Cardiff C
Derby Co v Burnley
Ipswich T v Charlton Ath
Leeds U v Nottingham F
Leicester C v Hull C
Millwall v Brighton & HA
Peterborough U v Wolverhampton W
Sheffield W v Bolton W
Watford v Bristol C

npower Football League One
Brentford v Oldham Ath
Bury v Milton Keynes D
Coventry C v Carlisle U
Crawley T v Tranmere
Crewe Alex v Leyton Orient
Doncaster R v Stevenage
Hartlepool U v Shrewsbury T
Notts Co v Portsmouth
Scunthorpe U v Colchester U
Swindon T v Bournemouth
Walsall v Preston NE
Yeovil T v Sheffield U

npower Football League Two
Accrington S v Aldershot T
Barnet v Rotherham U
Bristol R v Fleetwood T
Morecambe v Plymouth Arg

Northampton T v Chesterfield
Oxford U v Bradford C
Port Vale v Gillingham
Rochdale v Dagenham & R
Southend U v Exeter C
Torquay U v Burton Alb
Wycombe W v AFC Wimbledon
York C v Cheltenham T

Sunday, 23 September 2012
Barclays Premier League
Liverpool v Manchester U* (1.30)
Manchester C v Arsenal* (4.00)

Saturday, 29 September 2012
Barclays Premier League
Arsenal v Chelsea* (12.45)
Everton v Southampton
Fulham v Manchester C
Manchester U v Tottenham H† (5.30)
Norwich C v Liverpool
Reading v Newcastle U
Stoke C v Swansea C
Sunderland v Wigan Ath

npower Football League Championship
Barnsley v Ipswich T
Bolton W v Crystal Palace
Brighton & HA v Birmingham C
Bristol C v Leeds U
Burnley v Millwall
Cardiff C v Blackpool
Charlton Ath v Blackburn R
Huddersfield T v Watford
Hull C v Peterborough U
Middlesbrough v Leicester C
Nottingham F v Derby Co
Wolverhampton W v Sheffield W

npower Football League One
Bournemouth v Walsall
Carlisle U v Crawley T
Colchester U v Hartlepool U
Leyton Orient v Doncaster R
Milton Keynes D v Crewe Alex
Oldham Ath v Coventry C
Portsmouth v Scunthorpe U
Preston NE v Yeovil T
Sheffield U v Notts Co
Shrewsbury T v Swindon T
Stevenage v Bury
Tranmere v Brentford

npower Football League Two
AFC Wimbledon v Accrington S
Aldershot T v York C
Bradford C v Port Vale
Burton Alb v Northampton T
Cheltenham T v Morecambe
Chesterfield v Torquay U
Dagenham & R v Wycombe W
Exeter C v Bristol R
Fleetwood T v Barnet
Gillingham v Rochdale

Plymouth Arg v Southend U
Rotherham U v Oxford U

Sunday, 30 September 2012
Barclays Premier League
Aston Villa v WBA* (4.00)

Monday, 1 October 2012
Barclays Premier League
QPR v West Ham U* (8.00)

Tuesday, 2 October 2012
npower Football League Championship
Barnsley v Peterborough U
Bolton W v Leeds U
Brighton & HA v Ipswich T
Bristol C v Millwall
Burnley v Sheffield W
Cardiff C v Birmingham C
Charlton Ath v Watford
Huddersfield T v Leicester C
Hull C v Blackpool
Middlesbrough v Derby Co
Nottingham F v Blackburn R
Wolverhampton W v Crystal Palace

npower Football League One
Brentford v Shrewsbury T
Bury v Carlisle U
Coventry C v Milton Keynes D
Crawley T v Bournemouth
Crewe Alex v Oldham Ath
Doncaster R v Preston NE
Hartlepool U v Sheffield U
Notts Co v Stevenage
Scunthorpe U v Tranmere
Swindon T v Colchester U
Walsall v Leyton Orient
Yeovil T v Portsmouth

npower Football League Two
Accrington S v Rotherham U
Barnet v Exeter C
Bristol R v Cheltenham T
Morecambe v Chesterfield
Northampton T v Gillingham
Oxford U v AFC Wimbledon
Port Vale v Dagenham & R
Rochdale v Bradford C
Southend U v Burton Alb
Torquay U v Aldershot T
Wycombe W v Plymouth Arg
York C v Fleetwood T

Saturday, 6 October 2012
Barclays Premier League
Chelsea v Norwich C
Liverpool v Stoke C
Manchester C v Sunderland* (12.45)
Swansea C v Reading
Tottenham H v Aston Villa
WBA v QPR
West Ham U v Arsenal† (5.30)
Wigan Ath v Everton

npower Football League Championship
Birmingham C v Huddersfield T
Blackburn R v Wolverhampton W
Blackpool v Charlton Ath
Crystal Palace v Burnley
Derby Co v Brighton & HA
Ipswich T v Cardiff C
Leeds U v Barnsley
Leicester C v Bristol C
Millwall v Bolton W
Peterborough U v Nottingham F
Sheffield W v Hull C
Watford v Middlesbrough

npower Football League One
Brentford v Crawley T
Bury v Swindon T
Coventry C v Bournemouth
Crewe Alex v Hartlepool U
Doncaster R v Shrewsbury T
Leyton Orient v Sheffield U
Milton Keynes D v Portsmouth
Notts Co v Tranmere
Oldham Ath v Preston NE
Stevenage v Scunthorpe U
Walsall v Carlisle U
Yeovil T v Colchester U

npower Football League Two
Accrington S v Rochdale
Aldershot T v Chesterfield
Bristol R v Northampton T
Cheltenham T v Fleetwood T
Dagenham & R v Bradford C
Exeter C v Port Vale
Morecambe v Burton Alb
Oxford U v Gillingham
Plymouth Arg v AFC Wimbledon
Southend U v Barnet
Wycombe W v Torquay U
York C v Rotherham U

Sunday, 7 October 2012
Barclays Premier League
Southampton v Fulham* (1.30)
Newcastle U v Manchester U* (4.00)

Saturday, 13 October 2012
npower Football League One
Bournemouth v Leyton Orient
Carlisle U v Notts Co
Colchester U v Stevenage
Crawley T v Bury
Hartlepool U v Doncaster R
Portsmouth v Crewe Alex
Preston NE v Milton Keynes D
Scunthorpe U v Brentford
Sheffield U v Oldham Ath
Shrewsbury T v Walsall
Swindon T v Coventry C
Tranmere v Yeovil T

npower Football League Two
AFC Wimbledon v Cheltenham T

Barnet v Plymouth Arg
Bradford C v York C
Burton Alb v Bristol R
Chesterfield v Dagenham & R
Fleetwood T v Wycombe W
Gillingham v Aldershot T
Northampton T v Exeter C
Port Vale v Oxford U
Rochdale v Morecambe
Rotherham U v Southend U
Torquay U v Accrington S

Saturday, 20 October 2012
Barclays Premier League
Fulham v Aston Villa
Liverpool v Reading
Manchester U v Stoke C
Norwich C v Arsenal† (5.30)
Swansea C v Wigan Ath
Tottenham H v Chelsea* (12.45)
WBA v Manchester C
West Ham U v Southampton

npower Football League Championship
Birmingham C v Leicester C
Bolton W v Bristol C
Brighton & HA v Middlesbrough
Burnley v Blackpool
Charlton Ath v Barnsley
Crystal Palace v Millwall
Derby Co v Blackburn R
Huddersfield T v Wolverhampton W
Hull C v Ipswich T
Nottingham F v Cardiff C
Sheffield W v Leeds U
Watford v Peterborough U

npower Football League One
Bournemouth v Tranmere
Colchester U v Carlisle U
Coventry C v Notts Co
Doncaster R v Brentford
Hartlepool U v Crawley T
Milton Keynes D v Stevenage
Oldham Ath v Leyton Orient
Portsmouth v Shrewsbury T
Preston NE v Sheffield U
Swindon T v Scunthorpe U
Walsall v Crewe Alex
Yeovil T v Bury

npower Football League Two
Aldershot T v Rotherham U
Barnet v Northampton T
Bradford C v Cheltenham T
Bristol R v Torquay U
Exeter C v Chesterfield
Fleetwood T v AFC Wimbledon
Gillingham v Burton Alb
Morecambe v Southend U
Oxford U v Accrington S
Plymouth Arg v Rochdale
Port Vale v Wycombe W
York C v Dagenham & R

Sunday, 21 October 2012
Barclays Premier League
Sunderland v Newcastle U* (1.30)
QPR v Everton* (4.00)

Tuesday, 23 October 2012
npower Football League Championship
Barnsley v Crystal Palace
Blackpool v Nottingham F
Bristol C v Burnley
Cardiff C v Watford
Ipswich T v Derby Co
Leeds U v Charlton Ath
Leicester C v Brighton & HA
Middlesbrough v Hull C
Millwall v Birmingham C
Peterborough U v Huddersfield T
Wolverhampton W v Bolton W

npower Football League One
Brentford v Coventry C
Bury v Hartlepool U
Carlisle U v Oldham Ath
Crawley T v Milton Keynes D
Crewe Alex v Swindon T
Leyton Orient v Colchester U
Notts Co v Bournemouth
Scunthorpe U v Preston NE
Sheffield U v Walsall
Shrewsbury T v Yeovil T
Stevenage v Portsmouth
Tranmere v Doncaster R

npower Football League Two
AFC Wimbledon v Bristol R
Accrington S v York C
Burton Alb v Port Vale
Cheltenham T v Plymouth Arg
Chesterfield v Fleetwood T
Dagenham & R v Exeter C
Northampton T v Bradford C
Rochdale v Oxford U
Rotherham U v Morecambe
Southend U v Aldershot T
Torquay U v Gillingham
Wycombe W v Barnet

Wednesday, 24 October 2012
npower Football League Championship
Blackburn R v Sheffield W

Saturday, 27 October 2012
Barclays Premier League
Arsenal v QPR
Everton v Liverpool* (12.45)
Manchester C v Swansea C† (5.30)
Newcastle U v WBA
Reading v Fulham
Southampton v Tottenham H
Stoke C v Sunderland
Wigan Ath v West Ham U

npower Football League Championship
Barnsley v Nottingham F
Blackburn R v Watford

Blackpool v Brighton & HA
Bristol C v Hull C
Cardiff C v Burnley
Ipswich T v Sheffield W
Leeds U v Birmingham C
Leicester C v Crystal Palace
Middlesbrough v Bolton W
Millwall v Huddersfield T
Peterborough U v Derby Co
Wolverhampton W v Charlton Ath

npower Football League One
Brentford v Hartlepool U
Bury v Walsall
Carlisle U v Bournemouth
Crawley T v Oldham Ath
Crewe Alex v Yeovil T
Leyton Orient v Coventry C
Notts Co v Doncaster R
Scunthorpe U v Milton Keynes D
Sheffield U v Portsmouth
Shrewsbury T v Colchester U
Stevenage v Swindon T
Tranmere v Preston NE

npower Football League Two
AFC Wimbledon v Gillingham
Accrington S v Bristol R
Burton Alb v Bradford C
Cheltenham T v Exeter C
Chesterfield v Barnet
Dagenham & R v Aldershot T
Northampton T v Port Vale
Rochdale v Fleetwood T
Rotherham U v Plymouth Arg
Southend U v York C
Torquay U v Morecambe
Wycombe W v Oxford U

Sunday, 28 October 2012
Barclays Premier League
Aston Villa v Norwich C* (1.30)
Chelsea v Manchester U* (4.00)

Saturday, 3 November 2012
Barclays Premier League
Fulham v Everton
Manchester U v Arsenal* (12.45)
Norwich C v Stoke C
Sunderland v Aston Villa
Swansea C v Chelsea
Tottenham H v Wigan Ath
West Ham v Manchester C† (5.30)

npower Football League Championship
Birmingham C v Ipswich T
Bolton W v Cardiff C
Brighton & HA v Leeds U
Burnley v Wolverhampton W
Charlton Ath v Middlesbrough
Crystal Palace v Blackburn R
Derby Co v Blackpool
Huddersfield T v Bristol C
Hull C v Barnsley

Nottingham F v Millwall
Sheffield W v Peterborough U
Watford v Leicester C

Sunday, 4 November 2012
Barclays Premier League
QPR v Reading* (1.30)
Liverpool v Newcastle U* (4.00)

Monday, 5 November 2012
Barclays Premier League
WBA v Southampton* (8.00)

Tuesday, 6 November 2012
npower Football League Championship
Birmingham C v Bristol C
Bolton W v Leicester C
Brighton & HA v Peterborough U
Burnley v Leeds U
Charlton Ath v Cardiff C
Crystal Palace v Ipswich T
Derby Co v Barnsley
Huddersfield T v Blackburn R
Hull C v Wolverhampton W
Nottingham F v Middlesbrough
Sheffield W v Blackpool
Watford v Millwall

npower Football League One
Bournemouth v Shrewsbury T
Colchester U v Notts Co
Coventry C v Crawley T
Doncaster R v Crewe Alex
Hartlepool U v Tranmere
Milton Keynes D v Leyton Orient
Oldham Ath v Bury
Portsmouth v Brentford
Preston NE v Carlisle U
Swindon T v Sheffield U
Walsall v Scunthorpe U
Yeovil T v Stevenage

npower Football League Two
Aldershot T v Wycombe W
Barnet v Torquay U
Bradford C v Chesterfield
Bristol R v Southend U
Exeter C v AFC Wimbledon
Fleetwood T v Rotherham U
Gillingham v Cheltenham T
Morecambe v Accrington S
Oxford U v Dagenham & R
Plymouth Arg v Burton Alb
Port Vale v Rochdale
York C v Northampton T

Saturday, 10 November 2012
Barclays Premier League
Arsenal v Fulham
Aston Villa v Manchester U* (5.30)
Everton v Sunderland
Newcastle U v West Ham U
Reading v Norwich C
Southampton v Swansea C

Stoke C v QPR
Wigan Ath v WBA

npower Football League Championship
Barnsley v Huddersfield T
Blackburn R v Birmingham C
Blackpool v Bolton W
Bristol C v Charlton Ath
Cardiff C v Hull C
Ipswich T v Burnley
Leeds U v Watford
Leicester C v Nottingham F
Middlesbrough v Sheffield W
Millwall v Derby Co
Peterborough U v Crystal Palace
Wolverhampton W v Brighton & HA

npower Football League One
Brentford v Carlisle U
Bury v Portsmouth
Coventry C v Scunthorpe U
Crewe Alex v Colchester U
Doncaster R v Bournemouth
Leyton Orient v Shrewsbury T
Milton Keynes D v Sheffield U
Notts Co v Crawley T
Oldham Ath v Tranmere
Stevenage v Preston NE
Walsall v Swindon T
Yeovil T v Hartlepool U

npower Football League Two
Accrington S v Northampton T
Aldershot T v Bradford C
Bristol R v Chesterfield
Cheltenham T v Burton Alb
Dagenham & R v Rotherham U
Exeter C v Fleetwood T
Morecambe v Barnet
Oxford U v Torquay U
Plymouth Arg v Gillingham
Southend U v Port Vale
Wycombe W v Rochdale
York C v AFC Wimbledon

Sunday, 11 November 2012
Barclays Premier League
Manchester C v Tottenham H* (1.30)
Chelsea v Liverpool* (4.00)

Saturday, 17 November 2012
Barclays Premier League
Arsenal v Tottenham H* (12.45)
Liverpool v Wigan Ath
Manchester C v Aston Villa
Newcastle U v Swansea C
Norwich C v Manchester U† (5.30)
QPR v Southampton
Reading v Everton
WBA v Chelsea

npower Football League Championship
Birmingham C v Hull C
Bolton W v Barnsley
Bristol C v Blackpool

Burnley v Charlton Ath
Cardiff C v Middlesbrough
Crystal Palace v Derby Co
Huddersfield T v Brighton & HA
Leicester C v Ipswich T
Millwall v Leeds U
Nottingham F v Sheffield W
Peterborough U v Blackburn R
Watford v Wolverhampton W

npower Football League One
Bournemouth v Oldham Ath
Carlisle U v Leyton Orient
Colchester U v Bury
Crawley T v Walsall
Hartlepool U v Coventry C
Portsmouth v Doncaster R
Preston NE v Brentford
Scunthorpe U v Notts Co
Sheffield U v Stevenage
Shrewsbury T v Crewe Alex
Swindon T v Yeovil T
Tranmere v Milton Keynes D

npower Football League Two
AFC Wimbledon v Aldershot T
Barnet v Accrington S
Bradford C v Exeter C
Burton Alb v Dagenham & R
Chesterfield v Oxford U
Fleetwood T v Plymouth Arg
Gillingham v Morecambe
Northampton T v Wycombe W
Port Vale v York C
Rochdale v Bristol R
Rotherham U v Cheltenham T
Torquay U v Southend U

Sunday, 18 November 2012
Barclays Premier League
Fulham v Sunderland* (4.00)

Monday, 19 November 2012
Barclays Premier League
West Ham U v Stoke C* (8.00)

Tuesday, 20 November 2012
npower Football League One
Bournemouth v Stevenage
Carlisle U v Doncaster R
Colchester U v Coventry C
Crawley T v Yeovil T
Hartlepool U v Oldham Ath
Portsmouth v Leyton Orient
Preston NE v Notts Co
Scunthorpe U v Bury
Sheffield U v Crewe Alex
Shrewsbury T v Milton Keynes D
Swindon T v Brentford
Tranmere v Walsall

npower Football League Two
AFC Wimbledon v Southend U
Barnet v Oxford U
Bradford C v Plymouth Arg

Burton Alb v Aldershot T
Chesterfield v Cheltenham T
Fleetwood T v Accrington S
Gillingham v Exeter C
Northampton T v Morecambe
Port Vale v Bristol R
Rochdale v York C
Rotherham U v Wycombe W
Torquay U v Dagenham & R

Saturday, 24 November 2012
Barclays Premier League
Aston Villa v Arsenal† (5.30)
Everton v Norwich C
Manchester U v QPR
Southampton v Newcastle U
Stoke C v Fulham
Swansea C v Liverpool* (12.45)
Tottenham H v West Ham U
Wigan Ath v Reading

npower Football League Championship
Barnsley v Cardiff C
Blackburn R v Millwall
Blackpool v Watford
Brighton & HA v Bolton W
Charlton Ath v Huddersfield T
Derby Co v Birmingham C
Hull C v Burnley
Ipswich T v Peterborough U
Leeds U v Crystal Palace
Middlesbrough v Bristol C
Sheffield W v Leicester C
Wolverhampton W v Nottingham F

npower Football League One
Brentford v Sheffield U
Bury v Bournemouth
Coventry C v Portsmouth
Crewe Alex v Crawley T
Doncaster R v Scunthorpe U
Leyton Orient v Preston NE
Milton Keynes D v Colchester U
Notts Co v Swindon T
Oldham Ath v Shrewsbury T
Stevenage v Tranmere
Walsall v Hartlepool U
Yeovil T v Carlisle U

npower Football League Two
Accrington S v Gillingham
Aldershot T v Port Vale
Bristol R v Bradford C
Cheltenham T v Barnet
Dagenham & R v Fleetwood T
Exeter C v Rotherham U
Morecambe v AFC Wimbledon
Oxford U v Northampton T
Plymouth Arg v Chesterfield
Southend U v Rochdale
Wycombe W v Burton Alb
York C v Torquay U

Sunday, 25 November 2012
Barclays Premier League
Sunderland v WBA* (1.30)
Chelsea v Manchester C* (4.00)

Tuesday, 27 November 2012
Barclays Premier League
Aston Villa v Reading* (8.00)
Manchester U v West Ham U
Southampton v Norwich C
Stoke C v Newcastle U
Sunderland v QPR
Swansea C v WBA
Tottenham H v Liverpool

npower Football League Championship
Barnsley v Burnley
Blackpool v Birmingham C
Brighton & HA v Bristol C
Charlton Ath v Peterborough U
Derby Co v Cardiff C
Hull C v Crystal Palace
Ipswich T v Nottingham F
Leeds U v Leicester C
Middlesbrough v Huddersfield T
Sheffield W v Watford
Wolverhampton W v Millwall

Wednesday, 28 November 2012
Barclays Premier League
Chelsea v Fulham
Everton v Arsenal
Wigan Ath v Manchester C* (8.00)

npower Football League Championship
Blackburn R v Bolton W

Saturday, 1 December 2012
Barclays Premier League
Arsenal v Swansea C
Fulham v Tottenham H
Liverpool v Southampton
Manchester C v Everton
Newcastle U v Wigan Ath
Norwich C v Sunderland
QPR v Aston Villa
Reading v Manchester U
WBA v Stoke C
West Ham U v Chelsea

npower Football League Championship
Birmingham C v Middlesbrough
Bolton W v Ipswich T
Bristol C v Wolverhampton W
Burnley v Blackburn R
Cardiff C v Sheffield W
Crystal Palace v Brighton & HA
Huddersfield T v Leeds U
Leicester C v Derby Co
Millwall v Charlton Ath
Nottingham F v Hull C
Peterborough U v Blackpool
Watford v Barnsley

Saturday, 8 December 2012
Barclays Premier League
Arsenal v WBA
Aston Villa v Stoke C
Everton v Tottenham H
Fulham v Newcastle U
Manchester C v Manchester U
Southampton v Reading
Sunderland v Chelsea
Swansea C v Norwich C
West Ham U v Liverpool
Wigan Ath v QPR

npower Football League Championship
Blackburn R v Cardiff C
Charlton Ath v Brighton & HA
Crystal Palace v Blackpool
Derby Co v Leeds U
Huddersfield T v Bolton W
Ipswich T v Millwall
Leicester C v Barnsley
Nottingham F v Burnley
Peterborough U v Middlesbrough
Sheffield W v Bristol C
Watford v Hull C
Wolverhampton W v Birmingham C

npower Football League One
Brentford v Milton Keynes D
Bury v Leyton Orient
Carlisle U v Sheffield U
Colchester U v Oldham Ath
Coventry C v Walsall
Crawley T v Shrewsbury T
Hartlepool U v Stevenage
Preston NE v Crewe Alex
Scunthorpe U v Bournemouth
Swindon T v Doncaster R
Tranmere v Portsmouth
Yeovil T v Notts Co

npower Football League Two
Barnet v AFC Wimbledon
Bradford C v Torquay U
Bristol R v Dagenham & R
Burton Alb v Accrington S
Fleetwood T v Southend U
Northampton T v Cheltenham T
Oxford U v Aldershot T
Plymouth Arg v York C
Port Vale v Chesterfield
Rochdale v Exeter C
Rotherham U v Gillingham
Wycombe W v Morecambe

Saturday, 15 December 2012
Barclays Premier League
Chelsea v Southampton
Liverpool v Aston Villa
Manchester U v Sunderland
Newcastle U v Manchester C
Norwich C v Wigan Ath
QPR v Fulham
Reading v Arsenal

Stoke C v Everton
Tottenham H v Swansea C
WBA v West Ham U

npower Football League Championship
Barnsley v Sheffield W
Birmingham C v Crystal Palace
Blackpool v Blackburn R
Bolton W v Charlton Ath
Brighton & HA v Nottingham F
Bristol C v Derby Co
Burnley v Watford
Cardiff C v Peterborough U
Hull C v Huddersfield T
Leeds U v Ipswich T
Middlesbrough v Wolverhampton W
Millwall v Leicester C

npower Football League One
Bournemouth v Colchester U
Crewe Alex v Bury
Doncaster R v Coventry C
Leyton Orient v Scunthorpe U
Milton Keynes D v Hartlepool U
Notts Co v Brentford
Oldham Ath v Swindon T
Portsmouth v Preston NE
Sheffield U v Tranmere
Shrewsbury T v Carlisle U
Stevenage v Crawley T
Walsall v Yeovil T

npower Football League Two
AFC Wimbledon v Rotherham U
Accrington S v Wycombe W
Aldershot T v Rochdale
Cheltenham T v Port Vale
Chesterfield v Burton Alb
Dagenham & R v Barnet
Exeter C v Plymouth Arg
Gillingham v Fleetwood T
Morecambe v Oxford U
Southend U v Bradford C
Torquay U v Northampton T
York C v Bristol R

Saturday, 22 December 2012
Barclays Premier League
Chelsea v Aston Villa
Liverpool v Fulham
Manchester C v Reading
Newcastle U v QPR
Southampton v Sunderland
Swansea C v Manchester U
Tottenham H v Stoke C
WBA v Norwich C
West Ham U v Everton
Wigan Ath v Arsenal

npower Football League Championship
Birmingham C v Burnley
Blackburn R v Brighton & HA
Blackpool v Wolverhampton W
Crystal Palace v Huddersfield T

Derby Co v Hull C
Ipswich T v Bristol C
Leeds U v Middlesbrough
Leicester C v Cardiff C
Millwall v Barnsley
Peterborough U v Bolton W
Sheffield W v Charlton Ath
Watford v Nottingham F

npower Football League One
Brentford v Stevenage
Bury v Shrewsbury T
Coventry C v Preston NE
Crawley T v Sheffield U
Crewe Alex v Bournemouth
Doncaster R v Milton Keynes D
Hartlepool U v Portsmouth
Notts Co v Leyton Orient
Scunthorpe U v Carlisle U
Swindon T v Tranmere
Walsall v Colchester U
Yeovil T v Oldham Ath

npower Football League Two
Accrington S v Plymouth Arg
Barnet v Burton Alb
Bristol R v Rotherham U
Morecambe v Dagenham & R
Northampton T v Aldershot T
Oxford U v Fleetwood T
Port Vale v AFC Wimbledon
Rochdale v Cheltenham T
Southend U v Chesterfield
Torquay U v Exeter C
Wycombe W v Bradford C
York C v Gillingham

Wednesday, 26 December 2012
Barclays Premier League
Arsenal v West Ham U
Aston Villa v Tottenham H
Everton v Wigan Ath
Fulham v Southampton
Manchester U v Newcastle U
Norwich C v Chelsea
QPR v WBA
Reading v Swansea C
Stoke C v Liverpool
Sunderland v Manchester C

npower Football League Championship
Barnsley v Birmingham C
Bolton W v Sheffield W
Brighton & HA v Millwall
Bristol C v Watford
Burnley v Derby Co
Cardiff C v Crystal Palace
Charlton Ath v Ipswich T
Huddersfield T v Blackpool
Hull C v Leicester C
Middlesbrough v Blackburn R
Nottingham F v Leeds U
Wolverhampton W v Peterborough U

npower Football League One
Bournemouth v Yeovil T
Carlisle U v Hartlepool U
Colchester U v Brentford
Leyton Orient v Swindon T
Milton Keynes D v Walsall
Oldham Ath v Doncaster R
Portsmouth v Crawley T
Preston NE v Bury
Sheffield U v Scunthorpe U
Shrewsbury T v Notts Co
Stevenage v Coventry C
Tranmere v Crewe Alex

npower Football League Two
AFC Wimbledon v Northampton T
Aldershot T v Bristol R
Bradford C v Accrington S
Burton Alb v Rochdale
Cheltenham T v Wycombe W
Chesterfield v York C
Dagenham & R v Southend U
Exeter C v Oxford U
Fleetwood T v Morecambe
Gillingham v Barnet
Plymouth Arg v Torquay U
Rotherham U v Port Vale

Saturday, 29 December 2012
Barclays Premier League
Arsenal v Newcastle U
Aston Villa v Wigan Ath
Everton v Chelsea
Fulham v Swansea C
Manchester U v WBA
Norwich C v Manchester C
QPR v Liverpool
Reading v West Ham U
Stoke C v Southampton
Sunderland v Tottenham H

npower Football League Championship
Barnsley v Blackburn R
Bolton W v Birmingham C
Brighton & HA v Watford
Bristol C v Peterborough U
Burnley v Leicester C
Cardiff C v Millwall
Charlton Ath v Derby Co
Huddersfield T v Sheffield W
Hull C v Leeds U
Middlesbrough v Blackpool
Nottingham F v Crystal Palace
Wolverhampton W v Ipswich T

npower Football League One
Bournemouth v Crawley T
Carlisle U v Bury
Colchester U v Swindon T
Leyton Orient v Walsall
Milton Keynes D v Coventry C
Oldham Ath v Crewe Alex
Portsmouth v Yeovil T
Preston NE v Doncaster R

Sheffield U v Hartlepool U
Shrewsbury T v Brentford
Stevenage v Notts Co
Tranmere v Scunthorpe U

npower Football League Two
AFC Wimbledon v Oxford U
Aldershot T v Torquay U
Bradford C v Rochdale
Burton Alb v Southend U
Cheltenham T v Bristol R
Chesterfield v Morecambe
Dagenham & R v Port Vale
Exeter C v Barnet
Fleetwood T v York C
Gillingham v Northampton T
Plymouth Arg v Wycombe W
Rotherham U v Accrington S

Tuesday, 1 January 2013
Barclays Premier League
Chelsea v QPR
Liverpool v Sunderland
Manchester C v Stoke C
Newcastle U v Everton
Southampton v Arsenal
Swansea C v Aston Villa
Tottenham H v Reading
WBA v Fulham
West Ham U v Norwich C
Wigan Ath v Manchester U

npower Football League Championship
Birmingham C v Cardiff C
Blackburn R v Nottingham F
Blackpool v Hull C
Crystal Palace v Wolverhampton W
Derby Co v Middlesbrough
Ipswich T v Brighton & HA
Leeds U v Bolton W
Leicester C v Huddersfield T
Millwall v Bristol C
Peterborough U v Barnsley
Sheffield W v Burnley
Watford v Charlton Ath

npower Football League One
Brentford v Bournemouth
Bury v Tranmere
Coventry C v Shrewsbury T
Crawley T v Colchester U
Crewe Alex v Carlisle U
Doncaster R v Sheffield U
Hartlepool U v Preston NE
Notts Co v Milton Keynes D
Scunthorpe U v Oldham Ath
Swindon T v Portsmouth
Walsall v Stevenage
Yeovil T v Leyton Orient

npower Football League Two
Accrington S v Chesterfield
Barnet v Aldershot T
Bristol R v Plymouth Arg

Morecambe v Bradford C
Northampton T v Dagenham & R
Oxford U v Cheltenham T
Port Vale v Fleetwood T
Rochdale v Rotherham U
Southend U v Gillingham
Torquay U v AFC Wimbledon
Wycombe W v Exeter C
York C v Burton Alb

Saturday, 5 January 2013
npower Football League One
Brentford v Leyton Orient
Bury v Sheffield U
Coventry C v Tranmere
Crawley T v Preston NE
Crewe Alex v Stevenage
Doncaster R v Colchester U
Hartlepool U v Bournemouth
Notts Co v Oldham Ath
Scunthorpe U v Shrewsbury T
Swindon T v Carlisle U
Walsall v Portsmouth
Yeovil T v Milton Keynes D

npower Football League Two
Accrington S v Dagenham & R
Barnet v Bradford C
Bristol R v Gillingham
Morecambe v Aldershot T
Northampton T v Fleetwood T
Oxford U v Burton Alb
Port Vale v Plymouth Arg
Rochdale v AFC Wimbledon
Southend U v Cheltenham T
Torquay U v Rotherham U
Wycombe W v Chesterfield
York C v Exeter C

Saturday, 12 January 2013
Barclays Premier League
Arsenal v Manchester C
Aston Villa v Southampton
Everton v Swansea C
Fulham v Wigan Ath
Manchester U v Liverpool
Norwich C v Newcastle U
QPR v Tottenham H
Reading v WBA
Stoke C v Chelsea
Sunderland v West Ham U

npower Football League Championship
Barnsley v Leeds U
Bolton W v Millwall
Brighton & HA v Derby Co
Bristol C v Leicester C
Burnley v Crystal Palace
Cardiff C v Ipswich T
Charlton Ath v Blackpool
Huddersfield T v Birmingham C
Hull C v Sheffield W
Middlesbrough v Watford

Nottingham F v Peterborough U
Wolverhampton W v Blackburn R

npower Football League One
Bournemouth v Swindon T
Carlisle U v Coventry C
Colchester U v Scunthorpe U
Leyton Orient v Crewe Alex
Milton Keynes D v Bury
Oldham Ath v Brentford
Portsmouth v Notts Co
Preston NE v Walsall
Sheffield U v Yeovil T
Shrewsbury T v Hartlepool U
Stevenage v Doncaster R
Tranmere v Crawley T

npower Football League Two
AFC Wimbledon v Wycombe W
Aldershot T v Accrington S
Bradford C v Oxford U
Burton Alb v Torquay U
Cheltenham T v York C
Chesterfield v Northampton T
Dagenham & R v Rochdale
Exeter C v Southend U
Fleetwood T v Bristol R
Gillingham v Port Vale
Plymouth Arg v Morecambe
Rotherham U v Barnet

Saturday, 19 January 2013
Barclays Premier League
Chelsea v Arsenal
Liverpool v Norwich C
Manchester C v Fulham
Newcastle U v Reading
Southampton v Everton
Swansea C v Stoke C
Tottenham H v Manchester U
WBA v Aston Villa
West Ham U v QPR
Wigan Ath v Sunderland

npower Football League Championship
Birmingham C v Brighton & HA
Blackburn R v Charlton Ath
Blackpool v Cardiff C
Crystal Palace v Bolton W
Derby Co v Nottingham F
Ipswich T v Barnsley
Leeds U v Bristol C
Leicester C v Middlesbrough
Millwall v Burnley
Peterborough U v Hull C
Sheffield W v Wolverhampton W
Watford v Huddersfield T

npower Football League One
Brentford v Tranmere
Bury v Stevenage
Coventry C v Oldham Ath
Crawley T v Carlisle U
Crewe Alex v Milton Keynes D

Doncaster R v Leyton Orient
Hartlepool U v Colchester U
Notts Co v Sheffield U
Scunthorpe U v Portsmouth
Swindon T v Shrewsbury T
Walsall v Bournemouth
Yeovil T v Preston NE

npower Football League Two
Accrington S v AFC Wimbledon
Barnet v Fleetwood T
Bristol R v Exeter C
Morecambe v Cheltenham T
Northampton T v Burton Alb
Oxford U v Rotherham U
Port Vale v Bradford C
Rochdale v Gillingham
Southend U v Plymouth Arg
Torquay U v Chesterfield
Wycombe W v Dagenham & R
York C v Aldershot T

Saturday, 26 January 2013
npower Football League Championship
Barnsley v Millwall
Bolton W v Peterborough U
Brighton & HA v Blackburn R
Bristol C v Ipswich T
Burnley v Birmingham C
Cardiff C v Leicester C
Charlton Ath v Sheffield W
Huddersfield T v Crystal Palace
Hull C v Derby Co
Middlesbrough v Leeds U
Nottingham F v Watford
Wolverhampton W v Blackpool

npower Football League One
Bournemouth v Crewe Alex
Carlisle U v Scunthorpe U
Colchester U v Walsall
Leyton Orient v Notts Co
Milton Keynes D v Doncaster R
Oldham Ath v Yeovil T
Portsmouth v Hartlepool U
Preston NE v Coventry C
Sheffield U v Crawley T
Shrewsbury T v Bury
Stevenage v Brentford
Tranmere v Swindon T

npower Football League Two
AFC Wimbledon v Port Vale
Aldershot T v Northampton T
Bradford C v Wycombe W
Burton Alb v Barnet
Cheltenham T v Rochdale
Chesterfield v Southend U
Dagenham & R v Morecambe
Exeter C v Torquay U
Fleetwood T v Oxford U
Gillingham v York C
Plymouth Arg v Accrington S
Rotherham U v Bristol R

Tuesday, 29 January 2013
Barclays Premier League
Arsenal v Liverpool
Aston Villa v Newcastle U
Manchester U v Southampton
Norwich C v Tottenham H
QPR v Manchester C
Reading v Chelsea
Stoke C v Wigan Ath
Sunderland v Swansea C

Wednesday, 30 January 2013
Barclays Premier League
Everton v WBA
Fulham v West Ham U

Saturday, 2 February 2013
Barclays Premier League
Arsenal v Stoke C
Everton v Aston Villa
Fulham v Manchester U
Manchester C v Liverpool
Newcastle U v Chelsea
QPR v Norwich C
Reading v Sunderland
WBA v Tottenham H
West Ham U v Swansea C
Wigan Ath v Southampton

npower Football League Championship
Birmingham C v Nottingham F
Blackburn R v Bristol C
Blackpool v Barnsley
Crystal Palace v Charlton Ath
Derby Co v Huddersfield T
Ipswich T v Middlesbrough
Leeds U v Cardiff C
Leicester C v Wolverhampton W
Millwall v Hull C
Peterborough U v Burnley
Sheffield W v Brighton & HA
Watford v Bolton W

npower Football League One
Bury v Doncaster R
Crawley T v Swindon T
Crewe Alex v Scunthorpe U
Hartlepool U v Notts Co
Milton Keynes D v Bournemouth
Portsmouth v Colchester U
Preston NE v Shrewsbury T
Sheffield U v Coventry C
Stevenage v Leyton Orient
Tranmere v Carlisle U
Walsall v Oldham Ath
Yeovil T v Brentford

npower Football League Two
AFC Wimbledon v Burton Alb
Bristol R v Barnet
Cheltenham T v Torquay U
Exeter C v Aldershot T
Fleetwood T v Bradford C
Gillingham v Wycombe W

Plymouth Arg v Dagenham & R
Port Vale v Accrington S
Rochdale v Chesterfield
Rotherham U v Northampton T
Southend U v Oxford U
York C v Morecambe

Saturday, 9 February 2013
Barclays Premier League
Aston Villa v West Ham U
Chelsea v Wigan Ath
Liverpool v WBA
Manchester U v Everton
Norwich C v Fulham
Southampton v Manchester C
Stoke C v Reading
Sunderland v Arsenal
Swansea C v QPR
Tottenham H v Newcastle U

npower Football League Championship
Blackburn R v Ipswich T
Blackpool v Millwall
Bolton W v Burnley
Brighton & HA v Hull C
Bristol C v Nottingham F
Charlton Ath v Birmingham C
Huddersfield T v Cardiff C
Middlesbrough v Barnsley
Peterborough U v Leicester C
Sheffield W v Derby Co
Watford v Crystal Palace
Wolverhampton W v Leeds U

npower Football League One
Bournemouth v Portsmouth
Brentford v Bury
Carlisle U v Stevenage
Colchester U v Preston NE
Coventry C v Yeovil T
Doncaster R v Walsall
Leyton Orient v Tranmere
Notts Co v Crewe Alex
Oldham Ath v Milton Keynes D
Scunthorpe U v Crawley T
Shrewsbury T v Sheffield U
Swindon T v Hartlepool U

npower Football League Two
Accrington S v Southend U
Aldershot T v Plymouth Arg
Barnet v Port Vale
Bradford C v Gillingham
Burton Alb v Rotherham U
Chesterfield v AFC Wimbledon
Dagenham & R v Cheltenham T
Morecambe v Exeter C
Northampton T v Rochdale
Oxford U v Bristol R
Torquay U v Fleetwood T
Wycombe W v York C

Saturday, 16 February 2013
npower Football League Championship
Barnsley v Brighton & HA
Birmingham C v Watford
Burnley v Huddersfield T
Cardiff C v Bristol C
Crystal Palace v Middlesbrough
Derby Co v Wolverhampton W
Hull C v Charlton Ath
Ipswich T v Blackpool
Leeds U v Peterborough U
Leicester C v Blackburn R
Millwall v Sheffield W
Nottingham F v Bolton W

npower Football League One
Bury v Coventry C
Crawley T v Doncaster R
Crewe Alex v Brentford
Hartlepool U v Leyton Orient
Milton Keynes D v Swindon T
Portsmouth v Carlisle U
Preston NE v Bournemouth
Sheffield U v Colchester U
Stevenage v Oldham Ath
Tranmere v Shrewsbury T
Walsall v Notts Co
Yeovil T v Scunthorpe U

npower Football League Two
AFC Wimbledon v Bradford C
Bristol R v Wycombe W
Cheltenham T v Aldershot T
Exeter C v Accrington S
Fleetwood T v Burton Alb
Gillingham v Dagenham & R
Plymouth Arg v Oxford U
Port Vale v Morecambe
Rochdale v Torquay U
Rotherham U v Chesterfield
Southend U v Northampton T
York C v Barnet

Tuesday, 19 February 2013
npower Football League Championship
Barnsley v Wolverhampton W
Birmingham C v Sheffield W
Burnley v Middlesbrough
Cardiff C v Brighton & HA
Crystal Palace v Bristol C
Derby Co v Bolton W
Hull C v Blackburn R
Ipswich T v Watford
Leeds U v Blackpool
Leicester C v Charlton Ath
Millwall v Peterborough U
Nottingham F v Huddersfield T

Saturday, 23 February 2013
Barclays Premier League
Arsenal v Aston Villa
Fulham v Stoke C
Liverpool v Swansea C
Manchester C v Chelsea

Newcastle U v Southampton
Norwich C v Everton
QPR v Manchester U
Reading v Wigan Ath
WBA v Sunderland
West Ham U v Tottenham H

npower Football League Championship
Blackburn R v Leeds U
Blackpool v Leicester C
Bolton W v Hull C
Brighton & HA v Burnley
Bristol C v Barnsley
Charlton Ath v Nottingham F
Huddersfield T v Ipswich T
Middlesbrough v Millwall
Peterborough U v Birmingham C
Sheffield W v Crystal Palace
Watford v Derby Co
Wolverhampton W v Cardiff C

npower Football League One
Bournemouth v Sheffield U
Brentford v Walsall
Carlisle U v Milton Keynes D
Colchester U v Tranmere
Coventry C v Crewe Alex
Doncaster R v Yeovil T
Leyton Orient v Crawley T
Notts Co v Bury
Oldham Ath v Portsmouth
Scunthorpe U v Hartlepool U
Shrewsbury T v Stevenage
Swindon T v Preston NE

npower Football League Two
Accrington S v Cheltenham T
Aldershot T v Fleetwood T
Barnet v Rochdale
Bradford C v Rotherham U
Burton Alb v Exeter C
Chesterfield v Gillingham
Dagenham & R v AFC Wimbledon
Morecambe v Bristol R
Northampton T v Plymouth Arg
Oxford U v York C
Torquay U v Port Vale
Wycombe W v Southend U

Tuesday, 26 February 2013
npower Football League One
Bournemouth v Coventry C
Carlisle U v Walsall
Colchester U v Yeovil T
Crawley T v Brentford
Hartlepool U v Crewe Alex
Portsmouth v Milton Keynes D
Preston NE v Oldham Ath
Scunthorpe U v Stevenage
Sheffield U v Leyton Orient
Shrewsbury T v Doncaster R
Swindon T v Bury
Tranmere v Notts Co

npower Football League Two
AFC Wimbledon v Plymouth Arg
Barnet v Southend U
Bradford C v Dagenham & R
Burton Alb v Morecambe
Chesterfield v Aldershot T
Fleetwood T v Cheltenham T
Gillingham v Oxford U
Northampton T v Bristol R
Port Vale v Exeter C
Rochdale v Accrington S
Rotherham U v York C
Torquay U v Wycombe W

Saturday, 2 March 2013
Barclays Premier League
Aston Villa v Manchester C
Chelsea v WBA
Everton v Reading
Manchester U v Norwich C
Southampton v QPR
Stoke C v West Ham U
Sunderland v Fulham
Swansea C v Newcastle U
Tottenham H v Arsenal
Wigan Ath v Liverpool

npower Football League Championship
Barnsley v Bolton W
Blackburn R v Peterborough U
Blackpool v Bristol C
Brighton & HA v Huddersfield T
Charlton Ath v Burnley
Derby Co v Crystal Palace
Hull C v Birmingham C
Ipswich T v Leicester C
Leeds U v Millwall
Middlesbrough v Cardiff C
Sheffield W v Nottingham F
Wolverhampton W v Watford

npower Football League One
Brentford v Scunthorpe U
Bury v Crawley T
Coventry C v Swindon T
Crewe Alex v Portsmouth
Doncaster R v Hartlepool U
Leyton Orient v Bournemouth
Milton Keynes D v Preston NE
Notts Co v Carlisle U
Oldham Ath v Sheffield U
Stevenage v Colchester U
Walsall v Shrewsbury T
Yeovil T v Tranmere

npower Football League Two
Accrington S v Torquay U
Aldershot T v Gillingham
Bristol R v Burton Alb
Cheltenham T v AFC Wimbledon
Dagenham & R v Chesterfield
Exeter C v Northampton T
Morecambe v Rochdale
Oxford U v Port Vale

Plymouth Arg v Barnet
Southend U v Rotherham U
Wycombe W v Fleetwood T
York C v Bradford C

Tuesday, 5 March 2013
npower Football League Championship
Birmingham C v Blackpool
Bolton W v Blackburn R
Bristol C v Brighton & HA
Burnley v Barnsley
Cardiff C v Derby Co
Crystal Palace v Hull C
Huddersfield T v Middlesbrough
Leicester C v Leeds U
Millwall v Wolverhampton W
Nottingham F v Ipswich T
Peterborough U v Charlton Ath
Watford v Sheffield W

Saturday, 9 March 2013
Barclays Premier League
Arsenal v Everton
Fulham v Chelsea
Liverpool v Tottenham H
Manchester C v Wigan Ath
Newcastle U v Stoke C
Norwich C v Southampton
QPR v Sunderland
Reading v Aston Villa
WBA v Swansea C
West Ham U v Manchester U

npower Football League Championship
Birmingham C v Derby Co
Bolton W v Brighton & HA
Bristol C v Middlesbrough
Burnley v Hull C
Cardiff C v Barnsley
Crystal Palace v Leeds U
Huddersfield T v Charlton Ath
Leicester C v Sheffield W
Millwall v Blackburn R
Nottingham F v Wolverhampton W
Peterborough U v Ipswich T
Watford v Blackpool

npower Football League One
Bournemouth v Doncaster R
Carlisle U v Brentford
Colchester U v Crewe Alex
Crawley T v Notts Co
Hartlepool U v Yeovil T
Portsmouth v Bury
Preston NE v Stevenage
Scunthorpe U v Coventry C
Sheffield U v Milton Keynes D
Shrewsbury T v Leyton Orient
Swindon T v Walsall
Tranmere v Oldham Ath

npower Football League Two
AFC Wimbledon v York C
Barnet v Morecambe

Bradford C v Aldershot T
Burton Alb v Cheltenham T
Chesterfield v Bristol R
Fleetwood T v Exeter C
Gillingham v Plymouth Arg
Northampton T v Accrington S
Port Vale v Southend U
Rochdale v Wycombe W
Rotherham U v Dagenham & R
Torquay U v Oxford U

Tuesday, 12 March 2013
npower Football League One
Brentford v Swindon T
Bury v Scunthorpe U
Coventry C v Colchester U
Crewe Alex v Sheffield U
Doncaster R v Carlisle U
Leyton Orient v Portsmouth
Milton Keynes D v Shrewsbury T
Notts Co v Preston NE
Oldham Ath v Hartlepool U
Stevenage v Bournemouth
Walsall v Tranmere
Yeovil T v Crawley T

npower Football League Two
Accrington S v Fleetwood T
Aldershot T v Burton Alb
Bristol R v Port Vale
Cheltenham T v Chesterfield
Dagenham & R v Torquay U
Exeter C v Gillingham
Morecambe v Northampton T
Oxford U v Barnet
Plymouth Arg v Bradford C
Southend U v AFC Wimbledon
Wycombe W v Rotherham U
York C v Rochdale

Saturday, 16 March 2013
Barclays Premier League
Aston Villa v QPR
Chelsea v West Ham U
Everton v Manchester C
Manchester U v Reading
Southampton v Liverpool
Stoke C v WBA
Sunderland v Norwich C
Swansea C v Arsenal
Tottenham H v Fulham
Wigan Ath v Newcastle U

npower Football League Championship
Barnsley v Watford
Blackburn R v Burnley
Blackpool v Peterborough U
Brighton & HA v Crystal Palace
Charlton Ath v Millwall
Derby Co v Leicester C
Hull C v Nottingham F
Ipswich T v Bolton W
Leeds U v Huddersfield T
Middlesbrough v Birmingham C

Sheffield W v Cardiff C
Wolverhampton W v Bristol C

npower Football League One
Brentford v Preston NE
Bury v Colchester U
Coventry C v Hartlepool U
Crewe Alex v Shrewsbury T
Doncaster R v Portsmouth
Leyton Orient v Carlisle U
Milton Keynes D v Tranmere
Notts Co v Scunthorpe U
Oldham Ath v Bournemouth
Stevenage v Sheffield U
Walsall v Crawley T
Yeovil T v Swindon T

npower Football League Two
Accrington S v Barnet
Aldershot T v AFC Wimbledon
Bristol R v Rochdale
Cheltenham T v Rotherham U
Dagenham & R v Burton Alb
Exeter C v Bradford C
Morecambe v Gillingham
Oxford U v Chesterfield
Plymouth Arg v Fleetwood T
Southend U v Torquay U
Wycombe W v Northampton T
York C v Port Vale

Saturday, 23 March 2013
npower Football League One
Bournemouth v Bury
Carlisle U v Yeovil T
Colchester U v Milton Keynes D
Crawley T v Crewe Alex
Hartlepool U v Walsall
Portsmouth v Coventry C
Preston NE v Leyton Orient
Scunthorpe U v Doncaster R
Sheffield U v Brentford
Shrewsbury T v Oldham Ath
Swindon T v Notts Co
Tranmere v Stevenage

npower Football League Two
AFC Wimbledon v Morecambe
Barnet v Cheltenham T
Bradford C v Bristol R
Burton Alb v Wycombe W
Chesterfield v Plymouth Arg
Fleetwood T v Dagenham & R
Gillingham v Accrington S
Northampton T v Oxford U
Port Vale v Aldershot T
Rochdale v Southend U
Rotherham U v Exeter C
Torquay U v York C

Saturday, 30 March 2013
Barclays Premier League
Arsenal v Reading
Aston Villa v Liverpool

Everton v Stoke C
Fulham v QPR
Manchester C v Newcastle U
Southampton v Chelsea
Sunderland v Manchester U
Swansea C v Tottenham H
West Ham U v WBA
Wigan Ath v Norwich C

npower Football League Championship
Blackburn R v Blackpool
Charlton Ath v Bolton W
Crystal Palace v Birmingham C
Derby Co v Bristol C
Huddersfield T v Hull C
Ipswich T v Leeds U
Leicester C v Millwall
Nottingham F v Brighton & HA
Peterborough U v Cardiff C
Sheffield W v Barnsley
Watford v Burnley
Wolverhampton W v Middlesbrough

npower Football League One
Brentford v Notts Co
Bury v Crewe Alex
Carlisle U v Shrewsbury T
Colchester U v Bournemouth
Coventry C v Doncaster R
Crawley T v Stevenage
Hartlepool U v Milton Keynes D
Preston NE v Portsmouth
Scunthorpe U v Leyton Orient
Swindon T v Oldham Ath
Tranmere v Sheffield U
Yeovil T v Walsall

npower Football League Two
Barnet v Dagenham & R
Bradford C v Southend U
Bristol R v York C
Burton Alb v Chesterfield
Fleetwood T v Gillingham
Northampton T v Torquay U
Oxford U v Morecambe
Plymouth Arg v Exeter C
Port Vale v Cheltenham T
Rochdale v Aldershot T
Rotherham U v AFC Wimbledon
Wycombe W v Accrington S

Monday, 1 April 2013
npower Football League Championship
Barnsley v Leicester C
Birmingham C v Wolverhampton W
Blackpool v Crystal Palace
Bolton W v Huddersfield T
Brighton & HA v Charlton Ath
Bristol C v Sheffield W
Burnley v Nottingham F
Cardiff C v Blackburn R
Hull C v Watford
Leeds U v Derby Co

Middlesbrough v Peterborough U
Millwall v Ipswich T

npower Football League One
Bournemouth v Scunthorpe U
Crewe Alex v Preston NE
Doncaster R v Swindon T
Leyton Orient v Bury
Milton Keynes D v Brentford
Notts Co v Yeovil T
Oldham Ath v Colchester U
Portsmouth v Tranmere
Sheffield U v Carlisle U
Shrewsbury T v Crawley T
Stevenage v Hartlepool U
Walsall v Coventry C

npower Football League Two
AFC Wimbledon v Barnet
Accrington S v Burton Alb
Aldershot T v Oxford U
Cheltenham T v Northampton T
Chesterfield v Port Vale
Dagenham & R v Bristol R
Exeter C v Rochdale
Gillingham v Rotherham U
Morecambe v Wycombe W
Southend U v Fleetwood T
Torquay U v Bradford C
York C v Plymouth Arg

Saturday, 6 April 2013
Barclays Premier League
Chelsea v Sunderland
Liverpool v West Ham U
Manchester U v Manchester C
Newcastle U v Fulham
Norwich C v Swansea C
QPR v Wigan Ath
Reading v Southampton
Stoke C v Aston Villa
Tottenham H v Everton
WBA v Arsenal

npower Football League Championship
Birmingham C v Millwall
Bolton W v Wolverhampton W
Brighton & HA v Leicester C
Burnley v Bristol C
Charlton Ath v Leeds U
Crystal Palace v Barnsley
Derby Co v Ipswich T
Huddersfield T v Peterborough U
Hull C v Middlesbrough
Nottingham F v Blackpool
Sheffield W v Blackburn R
Watford v Cardiff C

npower Football League One
Bournemouth v Notts Co
Colchester U v Leyton Orient
Coventry C v Brentford
Doncaster R v Tranmere
Hartlepool U v Bury

Milton Keynes D v Crawley T
Oldham Ath v Carlisle U
Portsmouth v Stevenage
Preston NE v Scunthorpe U
Swindon T v Crewe Alex
Walsall v Sheffield U
Yeovil T v Shrewsbury T

npower Football League Two
Aldershot T v Southend U
Barnet v Chesterfield
Bradford C v Northampton T
Bristol R v AFC Wimbledon
Exeter C v Dagenham & R
Fleetwood T v Rochdale
Gillingham v Torquay U
Morecambe v Rotherham U
Oxford U v Wycombe W
Plymouth Arg v Cheltenham T
Port Vale v Burton Alb
York C v Accrington S

Saturday, 13 April 2013
Barclays Premier League
Arsenal v Norwich C
Aston Villa v Fulham
Chelsea v Tottenham H
Everton v QPR
Manchester C v WBA
Newcastle U v Sunderland
Reading v Liverpool
Southampton v West Ham U
Stoke C v Manchester U
Wigan Ath v Swansea C

npower Football League Championship
Barnsley v Charlton Ath
Blackburn R v Derby Co
Blackpool v Burnley
Bristol C v Bolton W
Cardiff C v Nottingham F
Ipswich T v Hull C
Leeds U v Sheffield W
Leicester C v Birmingham C
Middlesbrough v Brighton & HA
Millwall v Crystal Palace
Peterborough U v Watford
Wolverhampton W v Huddersfield T

npower Football League One
Brentford v Portsmouth
Bury v Oldham Ath
Carlisle U v Preston NE
Crawley T v Coventry C
Crewe Alex v Doncaster R
Leyton Orient v Milton Keynes D
Notts Co v Colchester U
Scunthorpe U v Walsall
Sheffield U v Swindon T
Shrewsbury T v Bournemouth
Stevenage v Yeovil T
Tranmere v Hartlepool U

npower Football League Two
AFC Wimbledon v Exeter C
Accrington S v Morecambe
Burton Alb v Plymouth Arg
Cheltenham T v Gillingham
Chesterfield v Bradford C
Dagenham & R v Oxford U
Northampton T v York C
Rochdale v Port Vale
Rotherham U v Fleetwood T
Southend U v Bristol R
Torquay U v Barnet
Wycombe W v Aldershot T

Tuesday, 16 April 2013
npower Football League Championship
Barnsley v Derby Co
Blackpool v Sheffield W
Bristol C v Birmingham C
Cardiff C v Charlton Ath
Ipswich T v Crystal Palace
Leeds U v Burnley
Leicester C v Bolton W
Middlesbrough v Nottingham F
Millwall v Watford
Peterborough U v Brighton & HA
Wolverhampton W v Hull C

Wednesday, 17 April 2013
npower Football League Championship
Blackburn R v Huddersfield T

Saturday, 20 April 2013
Barclays Premier League
Fulham v Arsenal
Liverpool v Chelsea
Manchester U v Aston Villa
Norwich C v Reading
QPR v Stoke C
Sunderland v Everton
Swansea C v Southampton
Tottenham H v Manchester C
WBA v Newcastle U
West Ham U v Wigan Ath

npower Football League Championship
Birmingham C v Leeds U
Bolton W v Middlesbrough
Brighton & HA v Blackpool
Burnley v Cardiff C
Charlton Ath v Wolverhampton W
Crystal Palace v Leicester C
Derby Co v Peterborough U
Huddersfield T v Millwall
Hull C v Bristol C
Nottingham F v Barnsley
Sheffield W v Ipswich T
Watford v Blackburn R

npower Football League One
Bournemouth v Carlisle U
Colchester U v Shrewsbury T
Coventry C v Leyton Orient
Doncaster R v Notts Co

Hartlepool U v Brentford
Milton Keynes D v Scunthorpe U
Oldham Ath v Crawley T
Portsmouth v Sheffield U
Preston NE v Tranmere
Swindon T v Stevenage
Walsall v Bury
Yeovil T v Crewe Alex

npower Football League Two
Aldershot T v Dagenham & R
Barnet v Wycombe W
Bradford C v Burton Alb
Bristol R v Accrington S
Exeter C v Cheltenham T
Fleetwood T v Chesterfield
Gillingham v AFC Wimbledon
Morecambe v Torquay U
Oxford U v Rochdale
Plymouth Arg v Rotherham U
Port Vale v Northampton T
York C v Southend U

Saturday, 27 April 2013
Barclays Premier League
Arsenal v Manchester U
Aston Villa v Sunderland
Chelsea v Swansea C
Everton v Fulham
Manchester C v West Ham U
Newcastle U v Liverpool
Reading v QPR
Southampton v WBA
Stoke C v Norwich C
Wigan Ath v Tottenham H

npower Football League Championship
Barnsley v Hull C
Blackburn R v Crystal Palace
Blackpool v Derby Co
Bristol C v Huddersfield T
Cardiff C v Bolton W
Ipswich T v Birmingham C
Leeds U v Brighton & HA
Leicester C v Watford
Middlesbrough v Charlton Ath
Millwall v Nottingham F
Peterborough U v Sheffield W
Wolverhampton W v Burnley

npower Football League One
Brentford v Doncaster R
Bury v Yeovil T
Carlisle U v Colchester U
Crawley T v Hartlepool U
Crewe Alex v Walsall
Leyton Orient v Oldham Ath
Notts Co v Coventry C
Scunthorpe U v Swindon T
Sheffield U v Preston NE
Shrewsbury T v Portsmouth
Stevenage v Milton Keynes D
Tranmere v Bournemouth

npower Football League Two
AFC Wimbledon v Fleetwood T

Accrington S v Oxford U
Burton Alb v Gillingham
Cheltenham T v Bradford C
Chesterfield v Exeter C
Dagenham & R v York C
Northampton T v Barnet
Rochdale v Plymouth Arg
Rotherham U v Aldershot T
Southend U v Morecambe
Torquay U v Bristol R
Wycombe W v Port Vale

Saturday, 4 May 2013
Barclays Premier League
Fulham v Reading
Liverpool v Everton
Manchester U v Chelsea
Norwich C v Aston Villa
QPR v Arsenal
Sunderland v Stoke C
Swansea C v Manchester C
Tottenham H v Southampton
WBA v Wigan Ath
West Ham U v Newcastle U

npower Football League Championship
Birmingham C v Blackburn R
Bolton W v Blackpool
Brighton & HA v Wolverhampton W
Burnley v Ipswich T
Charlton Ath v Bristol C
Crystal Palace v Peterborough U
Derby Co v Millwall
Huddersfield T v Barnsley
Hull C v Cardiff C
Nottingham F v Leicester C
Sheffield W v Middlesbrough
Watford v Leeds U

Sunday, 12 May 2013
Barclays Premier League
Arsenal v Wigan Ath
Aston Villa v Chelsea
Everton v West Ham U
Fulham v Liverpool
Manchester U v Swansea C
Norwich C v WBA
QPR v Newcastle U
Reading v Manchester C
Stoke C v Tottenham H
Sunderland v Southampton

Sunday, 19 May 2013
Barclays Premier League
Chelsea v Everton
Liverpool v QPR
Manchester C v Norwich C
Newcastle U v Arsenal
Southampton v Stoke C
Swansea C v Fulham
Tottenham H v Sunderland
WBA v Manchester U
West Ham U v Reading
Wigan Ath v Aston Villa

BLUE SQUARE PREMIER FIXTURES 2012–2013

Saturday, 11 August 2012
Barrow v AFC Telford
Braintree T v Hyde U
Dartford v Tamworth
Forest Green R v Cambridge U
Hereford U v Macclesfield T
Lincoln C v Kidderminster
Luton T v Gateshead
Mansfield T v Newport Co
Nuneaton T v Ebbsfleet U
Southport v Grimsby T
Stockport Co v Alfreton T
Wrexham v Woking

Tuesday, 14 August 2012
AFC Telford v Forest Green R
Alfreton T v Southport
Cambridge U v Lincoln C
Ebbsfleet U v Braintree T
Gateshead v Mansfield T
Grimsby T v Stockport Co
Hyde U v Barrow
Kidderminster v Luton T
Macclesfield T v Wrexham
Newport Co v Nuneaton T
Tamworth v Hereford U
Woking v Dartford

Saturday, 18 August 2012
AFC Telford v Braintree T
Alfreton T v Hereford U
Cambridge U v Southport
Ebbsfleet U v Wrexham
Gateshead v Forest Green R
Grimsby T v Nuneaton T
Hyde U v Luton T
Kidderminster v Mansfield T
Macclesfield T v Dartford
Newport Co v Lincoln C
Tamworth v Stockport Co
Woking v Barrow

Saturday, 25 August 2012
Barrow v Alfreton T
Braintree T v Newport Co
Dartford v Kidderminster
Forest Green R v Woking
Hereford U v Ebbsfleet U
Lincoln C v Macclesfield T
Luton T v AFC Telford
Mansfield T v Hyde U
Nuneaton T v Cambridge U
Southport v Tamworth
Stockport Co v Gateshead
Wrexham v Grimsby T

Monday, 27 August 2012
AFC Telford v Stockport Co
Alfreton T v Nuneaton T
Cambridge U v Dartford
Ebbsfleet U v Luton T
Gateshead v Lincoln C

Grimsby T v Mansfield T
Hyde U v Southport
Kidderminster v Forest Green R
Macclesfield T v Barrow
Newport Co v Hereford U
Tamworth v Wrexham

Tuesday, 28 August 2012
Woking v Braintree T
September Fixtures

Saturday, 1 September 2012
Barrow v Kidderminster
Braintree T v Tamworth
Dartford v Alfreton T
Forest Green R v Hyde U
Hereford U v Grimsby T
Lincoln C v Ebbsfleet U
Luton T v Macclesfield T
Mansfield T v Woking
Nuneaton T v Gateshead
Southport v AFC Telford
Stockport Co v Cambridge U
Wrexham v Newport Co

Tuesday, 4 September 2012
Barrow v Grimsby T
Braintree T v Kidderminster
Dartford v Newport Co
Forest Green R v Ebbsfleet U
Hereford U v Woking
Lincoln C v Alfreton T
Luton T v Cambridge U
Mansfield T v Tamworth
Nuneaton T v AFC Telford
Southport v Gateshead
Stockport Co v Macclesfield T
Wrexham v Hyde U

Saturday, 8 September 2012
AFC Telford v Lincoln C
Alfreton T v Luton T
Cambridge U v Wrexham
Ebbsfleet U v Mansfield T
Gateshead v Dartford
Grimsby T v Forest Green R
Hyde U v Hereford U
Kidderminster v Southport
Macclesfield T v Braintree T
Newport Co v Stockport Co
Tamworth v Barrow
Woking v Nuneaton T

Saturday, 15 September 2012
Barrow v Newport Co
Cambridge U v AFC Telford
Dartford v Hereford U
Forest Green R v Alfreton T
Gateshead v Tamworth
Kidderminster v Grimsby T
Lincoln C v Hyde U
Luton T v Wrexham

375

Mansfield T v Braintree T
Nuneaton T v Macclesfield T
Southport v Ebbsfleet U
Stockport Co v Woking

Saturday, 22 September 2012
AFC Telford v Mansfield T
Alfreton T v Kidderminster
Braintree T v Stockport Co
Ebbsfleet U v Barrow
Grimsby T v Luton T
Hereford U v Cambridge U
Hyde U v Nuneaton T
Macclesfield T v Forest Green R
Newport Co v Southport
Tamworth v Lincoln C
Woking v Gateshead
Wrexham v Dartford

Tuesday, 25 September 2012
AFC Telford v Newport Co
Braintree T v Dartford
Cambridge U v Kidderminster
Ebbsfleet U v Woking
Grimsby T v Gateshead
Hereford U v Forest Green R
Hyde U v Alfreton T
Lincoln C v Nuneaton T
Macclesfield T v Mansfield T
Southport v Stockport Co
Tamworth v Luton T
Wrexham v Barrow

Saturday, 29 September 2012
Alfreton T v Braintree T
Barrow v Cambridge U
Dartford v Hyde U
Forest Green R v Lincoln C
Gateshead v AFC Telford
Kidderminster v Macclesfield T
Luton T v Southport
Mansfield T v Hereford U
Newport Co v Grimsby T
Nuneaton T v Wrexham
Stockport Co v Ebbsfleet U
Woking v Tamworth
October Fixtures

Saturday, 6 October 2012
AFC Telford v Woking
Braintree T v Barrow
Cambridge U v Mansfield T
Ebbsfleet U v Kidderminster
Grimsby T v Dartford
Hereford U v Stockport Co
Hyde U v Gateshead
Lincoln C v Luton T
Macclesfield T v Alfreton T
Southport v Nuneaton T
Tamworth v Newport Co
Wrexham v Forest Green R

Tuesday, 9 October 2012
Alfreton T v Grimsby T
Barrow v Southport
Dartford v AFC Telford
Forest Green R v Tamworth
Gateshead v Macclesfield T

Kidderminster v Hyde U
Luton T v Braintree T
Mansfield T v Lincoln C
Newport Co v Ebbsfleet U
Nuneaton T v Hereford U
Stockport Co v Wrexham
Woking v Cambridge U

Saturday, 13 October 2012
AFC Telford v Grimsby T
Barrow v Dartford
Ebbsfleet U v Alfreton T
Gateshead v Cambridge U
Hereford U v Braintree T
Hyde U v Tamworth
Luton T v Nuneaton T
Macclesfield T v Newport Co
Mansfield T v Forest Green R
Stockport Co v Kidderminster
Woking v Southport
Wrexham v Lincoln C

Saturday, 27 October 2012
Alfreton T v AFC Telford
Braintree T v Wrexham
Cambridge U v Hyde U
Dartford v Mansfield T
Forest Green R v Luton T
Grimsby T v Macclesfield T
Kidderminster v Gateshead
Lincoln C v Stockport Co
Newport Co v Woking
Nuneaton T v Barrow
Southport v Hereford U
Tamworth v Ebbsfleet U
November Fixtures

Tuesday, 6 November 2012
AFC Telford v Ebbsfleet U
Dartford v Forest Green R
Gateshead v Alfreton T
Hereford U v Luton T
Hyde U v Grimsby T
Lincoln C v Braintree T
Macclesfield T v Tamworth
Newport Co v Cambridge U
Nuneaton T v Mansfield T
Southport v Wrexham
Stockport Co v Barrow
Woking v Kidderminster

Saturday, 10 November 2012
Alfreton T v Newport Co
Barrow v Lincoln C
Braintree T v Gateshead
Cambridge U v Macclesfield T
Ebbsfleet U v Hyde U
Forest Green R v Stockport Co
Grimsby T v Woking
Kidderminster v Nuneaton T
Luton T v Dartford
Mansfield T v Southport
Tamworth v AFC Telford
Wrexham v Hereford U

Saturday, 17 November 2012
AFC Telford v Kidderminster
Barrow v Forest Green R

Cambridge U v Tamworth
Dartford v Southport
Grimsby T v Braintree T
Lincoln C v Hereford U
Macclesfield T v Ebbsfleet U
Mansfield T v Luton T
Newport Co v Hyde U
Nuneaton T v Stockport Co
Woking v Alfreton T
Wrexham v Gateshead
December Fixtures

Saturday, 1 December 2012
Alfreton T v Cambridge U
Braintree T v Macclesfield T
Ebbsfleet U v Grimsby T
Forest Green R v Nuneaton T
Gateshead v Newport Co
Hereford U v AFC Telford
Hyde U v Woking
Kidderminster v Wrexham
Luton T v Barrow
Southport v Lincoln C
Stockport Co v Mansfield T
Tamworth v Dartford

Tuesday, 4 December 2012
AFC Telford v Barrow
Alfreton T v Wrexham
Braintree T v Forest Green R
Ebbsfleet U v Cambridge U
Gateshead v Grimsby T
Hereford U v Mansfield T
Lincoln C v Woking
Macclesfield T v Hyde U
Newport Co v Luton T
Nuneaton T v Dartford
Stockport Co v Southport
Tamworth v Kidderminster

Saturday, 8 December 2012
Barrow v Hereford U
Cambridge U v Gateshead
Dartford v Lincoln C
Forest Green R v Macclesfield T
Grimsby T v Tamworth
Hyde U v AFC Telford
Kidderminster v Newport Co
Luton T v Alfreton T
Mansfield T v Ebbsfleet U
Southport v Braintree T
Woking v Stockport Co
Wrexham v Nuneaton T

Saturday, 22 December 2012
AFC Telford v Luton T
Alfreton T v Barrow
Cambridge U v Nuneaton T
Ebbsfleet U v Hereford U
Gateshead v Stockport Co
Grimsby T v Wrexham
Hyde U v Mansfield T
Kidderminster v Dartford
Macclesfield T v Lincoln C
Newport Co v Braintree T
Tamworth v Southport
Woking v Forest Green R

Wednesday, 26 December 2012
Barrow v Gateshead
Braintree T v Cambridge U
Dartford v Ebbsfleet U
Forest Green R v Newport Co
Hereford U v Kidderminster
Lincoln C v Grimsby T
Luton T v Woking
Mansfield T v Alfreton T
Nuneaton T v Tamworth
Southport v Macclesfield T
Stockport Co v Hyde U
Wrexham v AFC Telford

Saturday, 29 December 2012
Barrow v Macclesfield T
Braintree T v Woking
Dartford v Cambridge U
Forest Green R v Kidderminster
Hereford U v Newport Co
Lincoln C v Gateshead
Luton T v Ebbsfleet U
Mansfield T v Grimsby T
Nuneaton T v Alfreton T
Southport v Hyde U
Stockport Co v AFC Telford
Wrexham v Tamworth
January Fixtures

Tuesday, 1 January 2013
AFC Telford v Wrexham
Alfreton T v Mansfield T
Cambridge U v Braintree T
Ebbsfleet U v Dartford
Gateshead v Barrow
Grimsby T v Lincoln C
Hyde U v Stockport Co
Kidderminster v Hereford U
Macclesfield T v Southport
Newport Co v Forest Green R
Woking v Luton T

Wednesday, 2 January 2013
Tamworth v Nuneaton T

Saturday, 5 January 2013
AFC Telford v Southport
Alfreton T v Dartford
Cambridge U v Stockport Co
Ebbsfleet U v Lincoln C
Gateshead v Nuneaton T
Grimsby T v Hereford U
Hyde U v Forest Green R
Kidderminster v Barrow
Macclesfield T v Luton T
Newport Co v Wrexham
Tamworth v Braintree T
Woking v Mansfield T

Saturday, 12 January 2013
Barrow v Woking
Braintree T v AFC Telford
Dartford v Macclesfield T
Forest Green R v Gateshead
Hereford U v Alfreton T
Lincoln C v Newport Co
Luton T v Hyde U
Mansfield T v Kidderminster

377

Nuneaton T v Grimsby T
Southport v Cambridge U
Stockport Co v Tamworth
Wrexham v Ebbsfleet U

Saturday, 19 January 2013
AFC Telford v Alfreton T
Braintree T v Grimsby T
Ebbsfleet U v Tamworth
Gateshead v Woking
Hereford U v Dartford
Hyde U v Cambridge U
Lincoln C v Wrexham
Macclesfield T v Kidderminster
Newport Co v Barrow
Nuneaton T v Luton T
Southport v Mansfield T
Stockport Co v Forest Green R

Tuesday, 22 January 2013
AFC Telford v Gateshead
Barrow v Stockport Co
Cambridge U v Ebbsfleet U
Dartford v Braintree T
Forest Green R v Hereford U
Grimsby T v Hyde U
Luton T v Lincoln C
Mansfield T v Nuneaton T
Tamworth v Macclesfield T
Woking v Newport Co
Wrexham v Southport

Saturday, 26 January 2013
Alfreton T v Tamworth
Cambridge U v Grimsby T
Dartford v Barrow
Gateshead v Hereford U
Hyde U v Ebbsfleet U
Kidderminster v Woking
Lincoln C v Forest Green R
Luton T v Stockport Co
Macclesfield T v AFC Telford
Nuneaton T v Braintree T
Southport v Newport Co
Wrexham v Mansfield T

Tuesday, 29 January 2013
Kidderminster v AFC Telford
February Fixtures

Saturday, 2 February 2013
AFC Telford v Cambridge U
Barrow v Luton T
Braintree T v Lincoln C
Ebbsfleet U v Macclesfield T
Forest Green R v Wrexham
Grimsby T v Alfreton T
Hereford U v Southport
Mansfield T v Dartford
Newport Co v Kidderminster
Stockport Co v Nuneaton T
Tamworth v Gateshead
Woking v Hyde U

Saturday, 9 February 2013
Alfreton T v Woking
Braintree T v Hereford U
Ebbsfleet U v Gateshead

Grimsby T v AFC Telford
Hyde U v Macclesfield T
Kidderminster v Cambridge U
Lincoln C v Dartford
Luton T v Forest Green R
Mansfield T v Barrow
Newport Co v Tamworth
Nuneaton T v Southport
Wrexham v Stockport Co

Tuesday, 12 February 2013
AFC Telford v Hyde U
Cambridge U v Alfreton T
Dartford v Luton T
Forest Green R v Braintree T
Gateshead v Kidderminster
Hereford U v Wrexham
Macclesfield T v Nuneaton T
Newport Co v Mansfield T
Southport v Barrow
Stockport Co v Lincoln C
Tamworth v Grimsby T
Woking v Ebbsfleet U

Saturday, 16 February 2013
AFC Telford v Tamworth
Alfreton T v Macclesfield T
Barrow v Nuneaton T
Braintree T v Southport
Ebbsfleet U v Stockport Co
Forest Green R v Dartford
Gateshead v Wrexham
Hereford U v Lincoln C
Hyde U v Kidderminster
Luton T v Newport Co
Mansfield T v Cambridge U
Woking v Grimsby T

Saturday, 23 February 2013
Cambridge U v Hereford U
Dartford v Stockport Co
Grimsby T v Ebbsfleet U
Kidderminster v Alfreton T
Lincoln C v Barrow
Luton T v Mansfield T
Macclesfield T v Gateshead
Newport Co v AFC Telford
Nuneaton T v Forest Green R
Southport v Woking
Tamworth v Hyde U
Wrexham v Braintree T

Tuesday, 26 February 2013
Alfreton T v Hyde U
Barrow v Wrexham
Braintree T v Luton T
Dartford v Grimsby T
Lincoln C v Mansfield T
Newport Co v Gateshead
Nuneaton T v Kidderminster
Stockport Co v Hereford U
Tamworth v Cambridge U
March Fixtures

Saturday, 2 March 2013
Barrow v Tamworth
Cambridge U v Forest Green R
Gateshead v Braintree T

378

Hereford U v Nuneaton T
Hyde U v Newport Co
Kidderminster v Ebbsfleet U
Macclesfield T v Grimsby T
Mansfield T v AFC Telford
Southport v Dartford
Stockport Co v Luton T
Woking v Lincoln C
Wrexham v Alfreton T

Saturday, 9 March 2013
AFC Telford v Macclesfield T
Braintree T v Nuneaton T
Cambridge U v Woking
Dartford v Wrexham
Ebbsfleet U v Newport Co
Forest Green R v Barrow
Gateshead v Hyde U
Grimsby T v Kidderminster
Lincoln C v Southport
Luton T v Hereford U
Mansfield T v Stockport Co
Tamworth v Alfreton T

Tuesday, 12 March 2013
Alfreton T v Ebbsfleet U
Macclesfield T v Woking
Southport v Forest Green R

Saturday, 16 March 2013
Alfreton T v Gateshead
Ebbsfleet U v Southport
Forest Green R v Mansfield T
Grimsby T v Cambridge U
Hereford U v Barrow
Hyde U v Dartford
Kidderminster v Tamworth
Newport Co v Macclesfield T
Nuneaton T v Lincoln C
Stockport Co v Braintree T
Woking v AFC Telford
Wrexham v Luton T

Saturday, 23 March 2013
Barrow v Ebbsfleet U
Braintree T v Alfreton T
Dartford v Gateshead
Forest Green R v Grimsby T
Hereford U v Hyde U
Lincoln C v AFC Telford
Luton T v Tamworth
Mansfield T v Macclesfield T
Nuneaton T v Woking
Southport v Kidderminster
Stockport Co v Newport Co
Wrexham v Cambridge U

Saturday, 30 March 2013
AFC Telford v Nuneaton T
Alfreton T v Lincoln C
Cambridge U v Luton T
Ebbsfleet U v Forest Green R
Gateshead v Southport
Grimsby T v Barrow

Hyde U v Wrexham
Kidderminster v Braintree T
Macclesfield T v Stockport Co
Newport Co v Dartford
Tamworth v Mansfield T
Woking v Hereford U
April Fixtures

Monday, 1 April 2013
Barrow v Hyde U
Braintree T v Ebbsfleet U
Dartford v Woking
Forest Green R v AFC Telford
Hereford U v Tamworth
Lincoln C v Cambridge U
Luton T v Kidderminster
Mansfield T v Gateshead
Nuneaton T v Newport Co
Southport v Alfreton T
Stockport Co v Grimsby T
Wrexham v Macclesfield T

Saturday, 6 April 2013
AFC Telford v Dartford
Alfreton T v Stockport Co
Barrow v Mansfield T
Cambridge U v Newport Co
Ebbsfleet U v Nuneaton T
Gateshead v Luton T
Grimsby T v Southport
Hyde U v Braintree T
Kidderminster v Lincoln C
Macclesfield T v Hereford U
Tamworth v Forest Green R
Woking v Wrexham

Saturday, 13 April 2013
Braintree T v Mansfield T
Cambridge U v Barrow
Ebbsfleet U v AFC Telford
Forest Green R v Southport
Hereford U v Gateshead
Lincoln C v Tamworth
Luton T v Grimsby T
Newport Co v Alfreton T
Nuneaton T v Hyde U
Stockport Co v Dartford
Woking v Macclesfield T
Wrexham v Kidderminster

Saturday, 20 April 2013
AFC Telford v Hereford U
Alfreton T v Forest Green R
Barrow v Braintree T
Dartford v Nuneaton T
Gateshead v Ebbsfleet U
Grimsby T v Newport Co
Hyde U v Lincoln C
Kidderminster v Stockport Co
Macclesfield T v Cambridge U
Mansfield T v Wrexham
Southport v Luton T
Tamworth v Woking

OTHER FIXTURES 2012–2013

July 2012

05 Thur	UEFA EL Q1 (1)
12 Thur	UEFA EL Q1 (2)
17 Tue	UEFA CL 2Q (1)
18 Wed	UEFA CL 2Q (1)
19 Thur	UEFA EL Q2 (1)
24 Tue	UEFA CL 2Q (2)
25 Wed	UEFA CL 2Q (2)
26 Thur	UEFA EL Q2 (2)
31 Tue	UEFA CL 3Q (1)

August 2012

01 Wed	UEFA CL 3Q (1)
02 Thur	UEFA EL Q3 (1)
07 Tue	UEFA CL 3Q (2)
08 Wed	UEFA CL 3Q (2)
09 Thur	UEFA EL Q3 (2)
11 Sat	Olympic Football Final (Wembley Stadium)
	FA Cup with Budweiser EP
12 Sun	FA Community Shield
15 Wed	International (Friendly)
	Football League Cup 1
18 Sat	Premier and Football Leagues – Season Starts
21 Tue	UEFA CL PO (1)
22 Wed	UEFA CL PO (1)
23 Thurs	UEFA EL PO (1)
25 Sat	FA Cup with Budweiser P
28 Tue	UEFA CL PO (2)
29 Wed	UEFA CL PO (2)
	Football League Cup 2
30 Thurs	UEFA EL PO (2)
31 Fri	UEFA Super Cup

September 2012

01 Sat	FA Vase 1Q
03 Mon	FA Youth Cup P+
05 Wed	Football League Trophy 1
07 Fri	Moldova v England – FIFA World Cup Qualifier
08 Sat	FA Cup with Budweiser 1Q
11 Tue	England v Ukraine – FIFA World Cup Qualifier
15 Sat	FA Vase 2Q
17 Mon	FA Youth Cup 1Q+
18 Tue	UEFA CL MD1
19 Wed	UEFA CL MD1
20 Thurs	UEFA EL MD1
22 Sat	FA Cup with Budweiser 2Q
26 Wed	Football League Cup 3
29 Sat	FA Trophy P

October 2012

01 Mon	FA Youth Cup 2Q+
02 Tue	UEFA CL MD2
03 Wed	UEFA CL MD2
04 Thurs	UEFA EL MD2
06 Sat	FA Cup with Budweiser 3Q
10 Wed	Football League Trophy 2
12 Fri	England v San Marino – FIFA World Cup Qualifier
13 Sat	FA Vase 1P
	FA County Youth Cup 1*
15 Mon	FA Youth Cup 3Q+
16 Tue	Poland v England – FIFA World Cup Qualifier
20 Sat	FA Cup with Budweiser 4Q
23 Tue	UEFA CL MD3
24 Wed	UEFA CL MD3
25 Thurs	UEFA EL MD3
27 Sat	FA Trophy 1Q
31 Wed	Football League Cup 4

November 2012

03 Sat	FA Cup with Budweiser 1P
	FA Youth Cup 1P*
06 Tue	UEFA CL MD4
07 Wed	UEFA CL MD4
08 Thurs	UEFA EL MD4
10 Sat	FA Trophy 2Q
	FA County Youth Cup 2*
14 Wed	Sweden v England – FIFA World Cup Qualifier
	FA Cup with Budweiser 1PR
17 Sat	FA Vase 2P
	FA Youth Cup 2P*
20 Tue	UEFA CL MD5
21 Wed	UEFA CL MD5
22 Thurs	UEFA EL MD5
24 Sat	FA Trophy 3Q

December 2012

01 Sat	FA Cup with Budweiser 2P
04 Tue	UEFA CL MD6
05 Wed	UEFA CL MD6
	Football League Trophy AQF
06 Thurs	UEFA EL MD6
08 Sat	FA Vase 3P
12 Wed	FA Cup with Budweiser 2PR
	Football League Cup 5
15 Sat	FA Trophy 1P
	FA Youth Cup 3P*
	FA County Youth Cup 3*

January 2013

05 Sat	FA Cup with Budweiser 3P
09 Wed	Football League Cup SF1
	Football League Trophy ASF
12 Sat	FA Trophy 2P
16 Wed	FA Cup with Budweiser 3PR

19 Sat	FA Vase 4P
	FA Youth Cup 4P*
23 Wed	Football League Cup SF2
26 Sat	FA Cup with Budweiser 4P
	FA County Youth Cup 4*

February 2013

02 Sat	FA Trophy 3P
06 Wed	International (Friendly)
	FA Cup with Budweiser 4PR
	Football League Trophy AF1
09 Sat	FA Vase 5P / FA Youth Cup 5P*
12 Tue	UEFA CL 16 (1)
13 Wed	UEFA CL 16 (1)
14 Thurs	UEFA EL 32 (1)
16 Sat	FA Cup with Budweiser 5P
19 Tue	UEFA CL 16 (1)
20 Wed	UEFA CL 16 (1)
21 Thurs	UEFA EL 32 (2)
23 Sat	FA Trophy 4P
	FA Youth Cup 6P*
	FA County Youth Cup SF*
24 Sun	Football League Cup Final
27 Wed	FA Cup with Budweiser 5PR
	Football League Trophy AF2

March 2013

02 Sat	FA Vase 6P
05 Tue	UEFA CL 16 (2)
06 Wed	UEFA CL 16 (2)
07 Thurs	UEFA EL 16 (1)
09 Sat	FA Cup with Budweiser 6P
	FA Trophy SF1
12 Tue	UEFA CL 16 (2)
13 Wed	UEFA CL 16 (2)
14 Thurs	UEFA EL 16 (2)
16 Sat	FA Trophy SF2 / FA Youth Cup SF1*
20 Wed	FA Cup with Budweiser 6PR
22 Fri	San Marino v England – FIFA World Cup Qualifier
23 Sat	FA Vase SF1
26 Tue	Montenegro v England – FIFA World Cup Qualifier
30 Sat	FA Vase SF2
	FA Youth Cup SF2*

April 2013

03 Wed	UEFA CL QF (1)
04 Thurs	UEFA EL QF (1)
07 Sun	Football League Trophy Final
09 Tue	UEFA CL QF (1)
10 Wed	UEFA CL QF (2)
11 Thurs	UEFA EL QF (2)
13 Sat	FA Cup with Budweiser SF
14 Sun	FA Cup with Budweiser SF
20 Sat	FA County Youth Cup Final (prov)
23 Tue	UEFA CL SF (1)
24 Wed	UEFA CL SF (1)
25 Thurs	UEFA EL SF (1)
27 Sat	Football League 1 and 2 – Season Ends
30 Tue	UEFA CL SF (2)

May 2013

01 Wed	UEFA CL SF (2)
02 Thurs	UEFA EL SF (2)
04 Sat	FA Trophy Final
	Football League Championship – Season Ends
	Football League 1 and 2 Play-off SF1
05 Sun	FA Vase Final
08 Wed	Football League 1 and 2 Play-off SF2
11 Sat	FA Cup with Budweiser Final
	Football League Championship Play-off SF1
15 Wed	UEFA EL Final (at ArenaA, Amsterdam)
	Football League Championship Play-off SF2
18 Sat	Football League 2 Play-off Final
19 Sun	Football League 1 Play-off Final
	Premier League Season Ends
25 Sat	UEFA CL Final (at Wembley)
27 Mon	Football League Championship Play-off Final

June 2013

| 08 Sat | International (Qualifier) |
| 12 Wed | International (Qualifier) |

Friday 6 September 2013 – England v Moldova – FIFA World Cup Qualifier
Tuesday 10 September 2013 – Ukraine v England – FIFA World Cup Qualifier
Friday 11 October 2013 – England v Mon   tenegro – FIFA World Cup Qualifier
Tuesday 15 October 2013 – England v Poland – FIFA World Cup Qualifier

* closing date of round
\+ week commencing

STOP PRESS

SUMMER TRANSFER DIARY 2012

With Newco Rangers relegated to Scottish League Division 3, Stranraer are promoted to Division 2, Airdrie United to Division 1 and Dundee to the Scottish Premier League. The fixtures published in this edition do not reflect the changes caused by this situation.

Portsmouth deducted ten points ... Terry cleared in Court ... England Under-19s lose to Greece ... Capello for Russia ... Capital One League Cup.

April 30 Lukas Podolski, Cologne to Arsenal £11,900,000.

May 15 Ritchie De Laet, Manchester U to Leicester C; Matty James, Manchester U to Leicester C. **May 16** Garath McCleary, Nottingham F to Reading. **May 17** Jonathan Franks, Middlesbrough to Hartlepool U; James Severn, Derby Co to Scunthorpe U. **May 18** Jamie Vardy, Fleetwood T to Leicester C £1,000,000. **May 21** Harlee Dean, Southampton to Brentford; Adam Forshaw, Everton to Brentford; Stephen Henderson, Portsmouth to West Ham U. **May 22** Trevor Carson, Sunderland to Bury. **May 23** Romain Amalfitano, Reims to Newcastle U. **May 24** David Amoo, Liverpool to Preston NE; Fabio Aurelio, Liverpool to Gremio; Andrew Davies, Stoke C to Bradford C; Chris Kirkland, Wigan Ath to Sheffield W; Lomana LuaLua, Blackpool to Karabuk. **May 25** Joe Lewis, Peterborough U to Cardiff C. **May 26** Richard Wright, Ipswich T to Preston NE. **May 28** Paul Jones, Peterborough U to Crawley T; Kieran Lee, Oldham Ath to Sheffield W. **May 29** Lee Holmes, Southampton to Preston NE; Grant Leadbitter, Ipswich T to Middlesbrough; Jeffrey Monakana, Arsenal to Preston NE; Joel Ward, Portsmouth to Crystal Palace £400,000; Aaron Wildig, Cardiff C to Shrewsbury T. **May 30** Elliott Hewitt, Macclesfield T to Ipswich T; Scott Malone, Bournemouth to Millwall £750,000 + part exchange; Josh McQuoid, Millwall to Bournemouth part exchange.

June 3 Dirk Kuyt, Liverpool to Fenerbahce £1,000,000. **June 4** Eden Hazard, Lille to Chelsea £32,000,000. **June 6** Danny Swanson, Dundee U to Peterborough U. **June 7** Niko Kranjcar, Tottenham H to Dynamo Kiev £5,750,000; Ben Glasgow, Arsenal to Stoke C; Aaron Martin, Southampton to Crystal Palace (loan). **June 8** Kelvin Etuhu, Portsmouth to Barnsley; Joe Mattock, WBA to Sheffield W. **June 10** Jay Rodriguez, Burnley to Southampton £7,000,000. **June 11** Rhys Bennett, Bolton W to Rochdale; Louis Harris, Wolverhampton W to AFC Wimbledon. **June 12** Jody Morris, St Johnstone to Bristol C; Nick Powell, Crewe Alex to Manchester U. **June 13** Jussi Jaaskelainen, Bolton W to West Ham U; Jon Parkin, Cardiff C to Fleetwood T. **June 14** Sam Cowler, West Ham U to Barnet; George Williams, Milton Keynes D to Fulham; Dave Syers, Bradford C to Doncaster R. **June 15** Bartosz Bialkowski, Southampton to Notts Co; Luke O'Neill, Mansfield T to Burnley. **June 18** Sol Bamba, Leicester C to Trabzonspor; Andrew Johnson, Fulham to QPR; Ryan Nelsen, Tottenham H to QPR; Robert Olejnik, Torquay U to Peterborough U; Gary Roberts, Huddersfield T to Swindon T. **June 19** Adam Drury, Norwich C to Leeds U; Jacob Mellis, Chelsea to Barnsley; Bjorn Sigurdarson, Lillestrom to Wolverhampton W. **June 20** Mohamed Diame, Wigan Ath to West Ham U; Ryan Doble, Southampton to Shrewsbury T; Didier Drogba, Chelsea to Shanghai Shenhua; Paul Green, Derby Co to Leeds U; Tomasz Kuszczak, Manchester U to Brighton & HA. **June 21** Anthony Gardner, Crystal Palace to Sheffield W; Robert Green, West Ham U to QPR; Chris Maguire, Derby Co to Sheffield W; Jay McEveley, Barnsley to Swindon T; Mido, Zamalek to Barnsley; Tommy Miller, Huddersfield T to Swindon T; Alan Navarro, Brighton & HA to Swindon T. **June 22** Shinji Kagawa, Borussia Dortmund to Manchester U £17,000,000; Jordon Mutch, Birmingham C to Cardiff C; Frank Nouble, West Ham U to Wolverhampton W; Jamie Tank, Walsall to Wolverhampton W £20,000. **June 23** Sean Scannell, Crystal Palace to Huddersfield T. **June 25** Danny Murphy, Fulham to Blackburn R; Bruno Saltor, Valencia to Brighton & HA. **June 26** Olivier Giroud, Montpellier to Arsenal £13,000,000; Michael Jacobs, Northampton T to Derby Co; James Wallace, Everton to Tranmere R. **June 27** Robbie Blake, Bolton W to Doncaster R; Alban Bunjaku, Arsenal to Sevilla; Vedran Corluka, Tottenham H to Lokomotiv Moscow; Samba Diakite, Nancy to QPR; Paul Dixon, Dundee U to Huddersfield T; Joan Angel Roman, Manchester C to Barcelona. **June 28** Jordan Brown, West Ham U to Barnet; Thomas Cruise, Arsenal to Torquay U; Jamie McAllister, Bristol C to Yeovil T; Mladen Petric, Hamburg to Fulham; Michael Poke, Brighton & HA to Torquay U; Ayegbeni Yakubu, Blackburn R to Guangzhou. **June 29** Keith Andrews, WBA to Bolton W; Ben Foster, Birmingham C to WBA; Danny Guthrie, Newcastle U to Reading; Oliver Norwood, Manchester U to Huddersfield T. **June 30** Pavel Pogrebnyak, Fulham to Reading; Steven Whittaker, Rangers to Norwich C.

July 1 George McCartney, Sunderland to West Ham U. **July 2** Leon Best, Newcastle U to Blackburn R £3,000,000; Carlos Cuellar, Aston Villa to Sunderland; Fabio da Silva, Manchester U to QPR (loan); Ryan Edwards, Blackburn R to Rochdale (loan); Karim El Ahmadi, Feyenoord to Aston Villa; Jonathan Grounds, Middlesbrough to Oldham Ath; Brett Ormerod, Blackpool to Wrexham; Stuart Parnaby, unattached to Middlesbrough; Joe

Rafferty, Liverpool to Rochdale; Nathan Ralph, Peterborough U to Yeovil T. **July 3** Lee Angol, Tottenham H to Wycombe W; Will Atkinson, Hull C to Bradford C; Jacob Butterfield, Barnsley to Norwich C; Jamal Campbell-Ryce, Bristol C to Notts Co; Gary Doherty, Charlton Ath to Wycombe W; Nuno Gomes, Braga to Blackburn R; Chris Hackett, Millwall to Northampton T; Paul Pogba, Manchester U to Juventus; George Porter, Leyton Orient to Burnley; Daniel Waller, Fulham to Arsenal. **July 4** Christian Burgess, Arsenal to Middlesbrough; Lee Croft, Derby Co to Oldham Ath (loan); Lateef Elford-Alliyu, WBA to Bury; Rene Gilmartin, Watford to Plymouth Arg; Ashley Hemmings, Wolverhampton W to Walsall; Matt Mills, Leicester C to Bolton W; Steven Naismith, Rangers to Everton; Freddie Sears, West Ham U to Colchester U; Gylfi Sigurdsson, Hoffenheim to Tottenham H £8,000,000; Oliver Norburn, Leicester C to Bristol R; Aaron Wilbraham, Norwich C to Crystal Palace; Anthony Flood, Southend U to St Patrick's Ath. **July 5** Ben Alnwick, Tottenham H to Barnsley; Greg Cunningham, Manchester C to Bristol C; Stephen Darby, Liverpool to Bradford C; Fraser Forster, Newcastle U to Celtic £2,000,000; Kevin Kilbane, Hull C to Coventry C; Fabio Nunes, Portimonense to Blackburn R; Jon Otsemobor, Sheffield W to Milton Keynes D; Jason Shackell, Derby Co to Burnley £1,100,000; Joe McKee, Burnley to Bolton W; Sean Goss, Exeter C to Manchester U £100,000. **July 6** Gael Bigirimana, Coventry C to Newcastle U £1,000,000; Wayne Bridge, Manchester C to Brighton & HA (loan); Adam Clayton, Leeds U to Huddersfield T; Steven Davis, Rangers to Southampton; Denilson, Arsenal to Sao Paulo (loan); Jake Forster-Caskey, Brighton & HA to Oxford U (loan); Asamoah Gyan, Sunderland to Al Ain; Matthew Lowton, Sheffield U to Aston Villa £3,000,000; Nathaniel Mendez-Laing, Wolverhampton W to Peterborough U; Sascha Riether, Cologne to Fulham (loan); Pierce Sweeney, Bray W to Reading; Chris Weale, Leicester C to Shrewsbury T; Jonathan Woodgate, Stoke C to Middlesbrough. **July 7** Salomon Kalou, Chelsea to Lille. **July 9** Michael Bostwick, Stevenage to Peterborough U; Jake Caprice, Crystal Palace to Blackpool; Luke Chambers, Nottingham F to Ipswich T; Mark Connolly, Bolton W to Crawley T; Jordan Cook, Sunderland to Charlton Ath; Eldin Jakupovic, Aris to Hull C; Peter Lovenkrands, Newcastle U to Birmingham C; Park, Manchester U to QPR £2,000,000; Christian Ribeiro, Bristol C to Scunthorpe U; Lawrie Wilson, Stevenage to Charlton Ath. **July 10** Diogo Amado, Leiria to Sheffield W; Chico, Genoa to Swansea C £2,000,000; Jonathan de Guzman, Villarreal to Swansea C (loan); Gavin Hoyte, Arsenal to Dagenham & R; Emmanuel Ledesma, Walsall to Middlesbrough; David Lucas, Rochdale to Birmingham C; Nicky Shorey, WBA to Reading; Joao Silva, Everton to Levski; Alan Smith, Newcastle U to Milton Keynes D; Aaron Mokoena, Portsmouth to Bidvest Wits. **July 11** Yassine El Ghanassy, Gent to WBA (loan); Paddy Kenny, QPR to Leeds U; Joel Lynch, Nottingham F to Huddersfield T. **July 12** Miles Addison, Derby Co to Bournemouth; Yaser Kasim, Brighton & HA to Luton T (loan); Hayden Mullins, Portsmouth to Birmingham C; Etien Velikonja, Maribor to Cardiff C; Jan Vertonghen, Ajax to Tottenham H; Hugo Rodallega, Wigan Ath to Fulham. **July 13** Darren Ambrose, Crystal Palace to Birmingham C; Fabio Borini, Roma to Liverpool £10,500,000; John Cofie, Manchester U to Sheffield U (loan); Karleigh Osborne, Brentford to Millwall; Maxi Rodriguez, Liverpool to Newell's Old Boys. **July 14** Paul Coutts, Preston NE to Derby Co. **July 16** Florent Cuvelier, Stoke C to Walsall (loan); Fraser Fyvie, Aberdeen to Wigan Ath; Kenny Miller, Cardiff C to Vancouver Whitecaps; Clinton Morrison, Sheffield W to Colchester U; Nejc Pecnik, Nacional to Sheffield W. **July 17** Ryan Brunt, Stoke C to Leyton Orient (loan); Andrew Lonergan, Leeds U to Bolton W; Adrian Mariappa, Watford to Reading; Chris Gunter, Nottingham F to Reading; Bongani Khumalo, Tottenham H to PAOK Salonika (loan); Liam Palmer, Sheffield W to Tranmere R; Joe Mills, Reading to Burnley (loan). **July 18** Marko Futacs, Portsmouth to Leicester C; Nathan Clarke, Huddersfield T to Leyton Orient; Michael Liddle, Sunderland to Accrington S; Ryan Allsop, Millwall to Leyton Orient; Lee Hills, Crystal Palace to Stevenage; Modibo Maiga, Sochaux to West Ham U £4,700,000; Joseph Mills, Reading to Burnley (loan). **July 19** Nathaniel Clyne, Crystal Palace to Southampton; Callum Ball, Derby Co to Coventry C (loan); Richard Keogh, Coventry C to Derby Co; Scott Loach, Watford to Ipswich T; Nick Proschwitz, Paderborn to Hull C £2,600,000.

Johnstone's Paint Trophy

6 Sept 2011 Accrington amended goalscorer from Dunbavin to Amond.

FA Cup

28 Jan 2012 Swindon T substitute was Louis Thompson not Nathan Thompson.

Blackpool

Ground capacity is 16,220.

Crawley T

Director of Football: Steve Coppell.

Nottingham F

Manager: Sean O'Driscoll.

Watford

Additional appointments: Assistant Manager: Giancarlo Corradini; First Team Coach: Adolfo Sormani; Head of Medical: Marco Cesarini.

Now you can buy any of these other bestselling sports titles from your bookshop or *direct from the publisher.*

Sky Sports Football Yearbook 2012–2013	Glenda Rollin and Jack Rollin	£25.00
Jonny: My Autobiography	Jonny Wilkinson	£7.99
Manchester United Ruined My Life	Colin Shindler	£7.99
Playfair Cricket Annual 2012	Ian Marshall	£7.99
My Manchester United Years	Sir Bobby Charlton	£8.99
My England Years	Sir Bobby Charlton	£7.99
Gazza: My Story	Paul Gascoigne	£9.99
Being Gazza	Paul Gascoigne	£6.99
The Doc	Tommy Docherty	£8.99

TO ORDER SIMPLY CALL THIS NUMBER

01235 400 414

or visit our website:
www.headline.co.uk
Prices and availability subject to change without notice.